# ISSUES IN CULTURAL ANTHROPOLOGY

NATIVE AMERICAN STUDENT ASSOCIATION
FORT STEILACOOM COMMUNITY COLLEGE
9401 FARWEST DRIVE S.W.
TACOMA, WA 98498
PHONE: (206) 964-6626

# ISSUES IN CULTURAL ANTHROPOLOGY
# SELECTED READINGS

David W. McCurdy

*Macalester College*

James P. Spradley

*Macalester College*

Little, Brown and Company

*Boston • Toronto*

Library of Congress Catalog Card No. 78-71868

ISBN 0-316-555266
9   8   7   6   5   4   3
MV

Published simultaneously in Canada
by Little, Brown & Company (Canada) Limited

Printed in the United States of America

*Acknowledgments*
1. Robin Fox, "The Cultural Animal." Reprinted by permission of the Smithsonian Institution Press from "The Cultural Animal" by Robin Fox, in *Man and Beast: Comparative Social Behavior,* edited by J. F. Eisenberg and Wilton S. Dillon: pages 275–96. Washington, D.C.: Smithsonian Institution Press, 1971.
2. Marshall Sahlins, "The Uses and Abuses of Biology." From the chapter "Critique of the Vulgar Sociobiology" by Marshall Sahlins from *The Use and Abuse of Biology: An Anthropological Critique of Sociobiology* by Marshall Sahlins. Copyright © 1976 by The University of Michigan. Reprinted by permission of The University of Michigan Press and the author.
3. Clifford Geertz, "The Impact of the Concept of Culture on the Concept of Man." In *New Views of Man,* edited by John R. Platt. Copyright © 1965 by the University of Chicago. Reprinted by permission of The University of Chicago Press.
4. Benjamin Lee Whorf, "The Relation of Habitual Thought and Behavior to Language." From Leslie Spier, A. Irving Hallowell, and Stanley S. Newman, editors, *Language, Culture, and Personality: Essays in Memory of Edward Sapir.* Published 1941 by Sapir Memorial Publication Fund, Menasha, Wisconsin; 1960 by University of Utah Press. Reprinted by permission of University of Utah Press.
5. Dorothy Lee, "Lineal and Nonlineal Codifications of Reality." From *Psychosomatic Medicine* 12:89–97, 1950. Reprinted by permission of Elsevier North-Holland Publishing Co., Inc.
6. Michael Cole and Sylvia Scribner, "Culture and Language." From M. Cole and S. Scribner, *Culture and Thought,* copyright © 1974 by John Wiley & Sons, Inc. Reprinted by permission of John Wiley & Sons, Inc.
7. Leslie A. White, "The Definition and Prohibition of Incest." From *The Science of Culture*

by Leslie A. White. Copyright 1949 by Leslie A. White. Copyright renewed © 1976 by Crocker National Bank as Executor of the Estate of Leslie A. White. Reprinted with the permission of Farrar, Straus & Giroux, Inc.

8. David F. Aberle, Urie Bronfenbrenner, Eckhard H. Hess, Daniel R. Miller, David M. Schneider, and James N. Spuhler, "The Incest Taboo and the Mating Patterns of Animals." Reproduced by permission of the American Anthropological Association from the *American Anthropologist* 65:253–65, 1963.

9. Arthur P. Wolf, "Childhood Association and Sexual Attraction: A Further Test of the Westermarck Hypothesis." Reproduced by permission of the American Anthropological Association from the *American Anthropologist* 72:503–15, 1970.

10. George Peter Murdock, "The Nuclear Family." Reprinted with permission of Macmillan Publishing Co., Inc., from *Social Structure* by George Peter Murdock. Copyright © 1949 by Macmillan Publishing Co., Inc.; renewed 1977 by George Peter Murdock.

11. M. J. Levy, Jr., and L. A. Fallers, "The Family: Some Comparative Considerations." Reproduced by permission of the American Anthropological Association from the *American Anthropologist* 61:647–51, 1959.

12. Richard N. Adams, "An Inquiry into the Nature of the Family." From *Essays in the Science of Culture in Honor of Leslie A. White,* edited by Gertrude E. Dole and Robert L. Carniero. Copyright © 1960 by Harper & Row, Publishers, Inc. By permission of Thomas Y. Crowell.

13. Robert McC. Netting, "Women's Weapons: The Politics of Domesticity among the Kofyar." Reproduced by permission of the American Anthropological Association from the *American Anthropologist* 71:1037–46, 1969.

14. Peggy R. Sanday, "Female Status in the Public Domain." Reprinted from *Woman, Culture, and Society,* edited by Michelle Zimbalist Rosaldo and Louise Lamphere, with the permission of the publishers, Stanford University Press. © 1974 by the Board of Trustees of the Leland Stanford Junior University.

15. Karen Sacks, "Engels Revisited: Women, The Organization of Production, and Private Property." Reprinted from *Woman, Culture, and Society,* edited by Michelle Zimbalist Rosaldo and Louise Lamphere, with the permission of the publishers, Stanford University Press. © 1974 by the Board of Trustees of the Leland Stanford Junior University.

16. Marvin Harris, "The Cultural Ecology of India's Sacred Cattle." From *Current Anthropology* 7:51–56, 1966. © 1966 by The Wenner-Gren Foundation for Anthropological Research. Reprinted by permission of The University of Chicago Press. This article was discussed by several authors in an accompanying section entitled "CA Comment" (pp. 60–64): Nirmal K. Bose, Morton Klass, Kalervo Oberg, Marvin Opler, Wayne Suttles, and Andrew P. Vayda, with reply by Marvin Harris.

17. Alan Heston, "An Approach to the Sacred Cow of India." From *Current Anthropology* 12:191–97, 1971. © 1971 by The Wenner-Gren Foundation for Anthropological Research. Reprinted by permission of The University of Chicago Press. This article was discussed by several authors in an accompanying section entitled "CA Comment" (pp. 197–208): John W. Bennett, James W. Hamilton, Marvin Harris, Michael M. Horowitz, Joan Mencher, Moni Nag, Manning Nash, and H. K. Schneider, with reply by Alan Heston.

18. Stanley A. Freed and Ruth S. Freed, "Cattle in a North Indian Village." From *Ethnology* 11:399–408 (1972). Reprinted by permission.

19. Wayne Suttles, "Affinal Ties, Subsistence, and Prestige Among the Coast Salish." Reproduced by permission of the American Anthropological Association from the *American Anthropologist* 62:296–305, 1960.

20. Stuart Piddocke, "The Potlatch System of the Southern Kwakiutl: A New Perspective." From the *Southwestern Journal of Anthropology* 21(3):244–64, 1965. Reprinted by permission of the *Journal of Anthropological Research.*

21. Philip Drucker and Robert F. Heizer, "To Make My Name Good: A Reexamination of the Southern Kwakiutl Potlatch." From Philip Drucker and Robert F. Heizer, *To Make My Name Good: A Reexamination of the Southern Kwakiutl Potlatch.* Copyright © 1967 by The Regents of the University of California; reprinted by permission of the University of California Press.

22. Andrew P. Vayda, "Phases of the Process of War and Peace Among the Marings of New Guinea." From *Oceania* XLII:1–23, 1971. Reprinted by permission.

23. Robert McC. Netting, "Kofyar Armed Conflict: Social Causes and Consequences." From *Journal of Anthropological Research* 30(3):139–53, 1974. Reprinted by permission.

24. William Tulio Divale and Marvin Harris, "Population, Warfare, and the Male Supremacist Complex." Reproduced by permission of the American Anthropological Association from the *American Anthropologist* 78:521–38, 1976.

25. Morris E. Opler, "Spirit Possession in a Rural Area of Northern India." From *Reader in Comparative Religion* by William A. Lessa and Evon Z. Vogt. Copyright © 1958 by Harper & Row, Publishers, Inc. By permission of Harper & Row, Publishers, Inc.

26. Stanley A. Freed and Ruth S. Freed, "Spirit Possession as Illness in a North Indian Village." From *Ethnology* 3:152–71, 1964. Reprinted by permission.

27. R. L. Stirrat, "Demonic Possession in Roman Catholic Sri Lanka." From *Journal of Anthropological Research* 33(2):133–57, 1977. Reprinted by permission.

# PREFACE

This book looks at cultural anthropology through articles about the major issues that have concerned and sometimes divided anthropologists. Because anthropology is a comparative discipline, drawing on data from human societies all over the world, its questions are broad and fundamental, significant to an understanding of human existence. The questions—such as why is there religion and what accounts for war—are also familiar, even to people unacquainted with anthropology. As a result, they provide an excellent entry to learning about the discipline.

Although the articles in this book focus on basic issues in the field, we have maintained the traditional divisions associated with courses in cultural anthropology: culture, language, social organization, kinship, rank, ecology, economic systems, politics, and religion. But although these nine divisions form the overall outline, each is associated with a particular issue, and each issue is developed by three interrelated articles. For example, Chapter II, "Culture," includes an introduction that discusses the concept of culture and ends by introducing an issue related to culture: Which is more important in determining behavior, culture or biology? The three articles in this section (by Fox, Sahlins, and Geertz) take different viewpoints on the question, allowing the reader to see the issue from several different perspectives.

Focusing on issues and some of the controversy surrounding them shows more clearly the ferment that marks the process of anthropology as a science. Many textbooks by a single author are hampered by the need to survey agreed-upon information in cultural anthropology, so they tend to present the data, concepts, and explanations of anthropology as static, well accepted facts. But a series of articles about a particular issue can demonstrate disagreement yet still develop ideas fully. The articles give a more realistic picture of what the process of science is like, they reveal the debate that surrounds ideas, and they show the development and refinement that take place when scientists challenge one another.

Using issues as the main point of focus has another important advantage: it provides much greater context for understanding. All three articles in each chapter are about the same problem. Usually they are arranged historically to demonstrate the unfolding of particular debates and lines of argument. Often later articles cite earlier ones, contributing to a sense of integration. Each restates the problem, adding to the general context of the topic. Individual articles that might normally require additional explanation become comprehensible in this larger context.

Another advantage of a book of readings designed around issues, each with a cluster of related articles, is that it demonstrates different styles of debate. For example, consider Chapter VI, "Rank and Inequality." In an attempt to account for the sources of female power, Netting draws his conclusions from a single case, that of the Kofyar. A second article, by Sanday, employs formally drawn cross-cultural samples of societies as the basis for the test of various hypotheses. The final article, by Sacks, also uses a broad cross-cultural reference, but in a selective and more specifically comparative way.

Related articles also take different explanatory or theoretical positions. In Chapter IV, "Kinship and Social Organization," White takes a social and a cultural evolutionary approach to the explanation of the incest taboo. Aberle and his associates look at the taboo as a cultural entity based on a clear biological need. Wolf sees the taboo as an outgrowth of a psychological process rooted in childhood experience.

The approach taken in this reader also reveals something about the nature of anthropological problems themselves. Some involve disagreement over the explanation of a particular issue. For example, the authors discussing the incest taboo agree more or less on the nature of what is to be explained, but they disagree over the way to account for it. Issues may also surround a particular theoretical assertion, such as the Sapir-Whorf hypothesis presented in Chapter III, "Language and Communication." There the debate is over whether or not a particular explanation fits the data. Some issues revolve around basic concepts and their definitions, as illustrated in Chapter V, "Kinship Groups." There the argument involves the definition of the nuclear family and its position as the fundamental building block of kinship systems. And some disagreements arise over the anthropological data themselves. The discussion of the potlatch in Chapter VIII," Economic Systems," reveals not only a difference in theoretical interpretation, but also a difference over the nature of the potlatch and the ecological conditions under which Northwest Coast Indians lived several decades ago.

Finally, we believe this reader is especially valuable as a basis for class discussion. When discussion sections and their leaders must deal with several unrelated articles, continuity and associated understanding often suffer. An integrated set of articles surrounding a clearly defined issue intensifies interest and facilitates discussion. Only one context is required for the discussion instead of one for each article, and progress toward an understanding of one article helps comprehension of the others.

We would like to thank several colleagues for their careful reviews of the manuscript: Robert L. Bee, University of Connecticut; Karl G. Heider, University of South Carolina; John T. Omohundro, State University of New York at Potsdam; Frederick A. Peterson, West Virginia Wesleyan College; and Alex Stepick, University of Texas at Dallas.

# CONTENTS

## LANGUAGE AND COMMUNICATION   49

### ISSUE   The Sapir-Whorf hypothesis: Does language shape perception?

## KINSHIP AND SOCIAL ORGANIZATION  93

### ISSUE   The incest taboo: Why is it found in every society?

# KINSHIP GROUPS                                    136

### ISSUE   The foundation of kinship: Is the nuclear family the universal building block of kinship systems?

## THE ECONOMIC SYSTEM      241

### ISSUE   The potlatch: Why do Northwest Coast Indians give away their wealth?

 ## SYSTEMS OF POLITICS AND LAW      280

### ISSUE   Human warfare: Why do people fight?

# RELIGIOUS SYSTEMS                                                     341

## ISSUE   Demonic possession: What explains possession by evil spirits?

# ISSUES IN CULTURAL ANTHROPOLOGY

# ETHNOLOGY
# AND EXPLANATION

In 1806 the British government sent James Tod, an army colonel, to join a newly established embassy in the Indian principality of Sindia. His arrival there began a remarkable career in exploration. Tod traveled often with army detachments and special surveying parties in order to survey and map what is now largely the modern state of Rajasthan. But more than this, Tod grew to know his Indian hosts. He visited communities throughout the countryside, learned local languages, and noted down customs. When he was assigned as a political officer to the Maharana of Udaipur in 1818, he carried out an exhaustive review of the state's archives and records in an attempt to understand its history and form of government. Tod returned to England in 1822, the victim of ill health, and lived out his final years writing about the land he had come to know so well. His book, the *Annals and Antiquities of Rajasthan,* runs to several volumes and thousands of pages. It stands as a monument to human inquisitiveness and the desire to know and understand. It also represents the spirit of scientific inquiry that was overtaking Europeans in the nineteenth century and announces a new kind of awareness: the recognition of human variation.

This awareness accompanied European colonial expansion. Like Tod, thousands of Europeans traveled overseas to virtually every part of the earth as

1

their countries vied for lucrative trade routes, the control of natural resources, and ready-made markets. Some of the travelers were civil servants and army personnel, sent to administrate and pacify new territories. Others were the missionaries, settlers, and traders who followed in the wake of colonial expansion. These people maintained ties with their homelands. They wrote letters, reports, and books. They occasionally came home on leave or to retire. As a result, information about far-flung colonialized peoples grew substantially, and it often proved sensational. People were told that there were cannibals, headhunters, and fire walkers; they heard of people who never wore clothes, who spoke in unintelligible grunts, and who worshipped idols, spirits, and devils. Although some descriptions, such as the writings of Colonel Tod, were relatively accurate, much of the information that reached Europe was unreliable. The civil servants and missionaries who reported it often failed to learn local languages or customs. Instead, they tended to interpret what they saw according to their own feelings of Western superiority and the needs associated with their administrative and ministerial duties.

But the intellectual impact remained; it was clear from the new information that human behavior varied much more profoundly than insulated Europeans had ever imagined. And there was enough material to map out some of the differences in detail. For example, it was evident that the size and membership of families varied and that kinsmen were classified in different ways from one society to the next. Values, beliefs, customs, and arts all varied significantly.

The realization that humans behaved differently from one society to another came at a time of scientific ferment in Europe. Physicists, chemists, geologists, and other natural scientists had begun to unlock the secrets of the physical world. Naturalists set the stage for biology by roaming the earth in search of new animal and plant species. And it was social philosophers and others interested in human nature who began to speculate on the causes of human variation and eventually to call themselves anthropologists.

People like Colonel Tod were not anthropologists; they were simply individuals who happened to be in other parts of the world where different peoples lived and who enjoyed describing their encounters with foreign customs and life ways. Instead, the first anthropologists were theoreticians. They worked and read about the people of the world from the comfort of their homes and studies. They puzzled over the human differences they encountered in books without seeing customs for themselves. Occasionally, they would write to colonial outposts for more information, and a few had limited encounters with non-Western peoples, but by and large, they lived up to a critical label that was later applied to them: "armchair anthropologists."

Yet the founders of anthropology set the course that the discipline continues on today. They established a science of cross-cultural (between or among cultures) human behavior. Although much of what they did seems highly speculative now, their aim was the explanation of human custom and action.

To be sure, anthropological theory is much more complex and varied today, but the discipline continues the explanatory emphasis of its founders. It deals with the problems raised by cross-cultural variation; its ultimate goal is the theoretical explanation of human behavior, custom, and belief in the cross-cultural context. The process of accounting for human behavior, which includes classification, comparison, and explanation, is called *ethnology.*

The purpose of this book is to introduce you to anthropology through the task of ethnology. The volume includes a series of articles that deal with some of the interesting and important questions asked by anthropologists. It reveals that there are disagreements over assumptions, definitions, and explanations. Like all scientists, anthropologists uncover new data, invent new categories, and make new assertions about the nature of their subject, human behavior. In order to understand the ethnological enterprise more clearly, it is necessary to say something more about the steps anthropologists follow to arrive at explanation: ethnography, classification, comparison, and explanation.

## ETHNOGRAPHY

When Colonel Tod toured the Indian countryside, he occasionally stopped in villages to rest, make geographic surveys, and work on maps. Inevitably, he also took time out to talk with people living nearby, to observe their activities, and to participate in their events. Over the years, he learned a wealth of information about Indian customs and beliefs. He discovered something about the structure of families, kinds of work, house building, ways to treat illness, problems of marrying off daughters, effects of gods and goddesses, and countless other things that defined the local ways of life. By today's standards, his observations and questions were inadequate and unsystematic (partly because he was more interested in history than customs). Nevertheless, although he did not know it, he was conducting ethnographic research.

*Ethnography* is the task of discovering and describing a society's culture. Culture, in turn, consists of the beliefs and behavior people learn and share as members of a society. (For a much fuller discussion of culture, see Chapter II.) Ethnographic field work does not fit the usual stereotype of scientific inquiry. There are no laboratories in ethnographic research, except, perhaps, for the "natural laboratories" in which people live. Cultural anthropologists rarely conduct controlled experiments in which they test the relationship between two variables. Nor can they achieve a scientific detachment from the people who are the objects of their study. They cannot even regularly use survey techniques such as structured questionnaires, although such research is becoming more possible as more is known about particular cultures.

Instead, like Tod, they go to the field, establish residence, and settle down among the people they wish to understand. They don't experiment, they listen.

They don't manipulate controlled variables, they observe people acting in the enormously complex context of daily life. They aren't detached, they take an active role in a busy community of human beings. Anthropological field work is a uniquely human adventure; it involves ethnographers intimately with those they wish to learn about.

Strangely enough, the intimate involvement of field work is an advantage. Ethnographers use their relationship with people and their place in the community to unlock the secrets of cultural behavior and knowledge. They attempt to develop a relationship of trust so that their "informants" will teach them about the meaning of their rituals, the shape of their disputes, the ways to become important, and a host of other things that are significant to them.

Because ethnography aims at the discovery of detailed life ways, a personal immersion in culture pays off. Some anthropologists liken ethnography to the experience a child has while growing up. As he or she gets older, the child learns the language, categories, and behaviors of his or her parents and other adults. Although decidedly not children, ethnographers attempt to do the same thing; they try to learn about a way of life that is foreign to them in such detail that they could eventually become part of it.

We have already noted that most of the early anthropologists were theoreticians, not ethnographers; they depended on other people to do their field work for them. But this changed by the turn of the century. Colonial governments required more accurate data about the peoples they were trying to administrate and, perhaps more important, people with scientific training in which careful data-gathering techniques were stressed applied their knowledge to ethnographic field work.

Perhaps the best example of such a person is Franz Boas. Boas, a German by birth, was trained as a physicist. As part of the research for his thesis on the color of sea water, he spent time in the Aleutians and visited native peoples living on nearby islands and the mainland. Eventually, interested by people rather than sea water, he began a long series of field trips to the Northwest Coast of British Columbia, where he studied the Kwakiutl Indians. (See Chapter V for a discussion of Northwest Coast culture.) His new interests led to a position at Columbia University, where he founded the first department of anthropology in the United States.

Boas became exceptionally critical of the theoretical speculations of the first anthropologists; these theories simply did not fit or explain the first-hand data he collected in the field. More than ever, he became convinced that anthropologists must do field work first, that ethnography should precede the creation of theory. Since Boas trained nearly all the cultural anthropologists in the United States for several decades, his views of field work found a permanent place in the discipline, and field research is a basic requirement of graduate training in anthropology today. The same emphasis took hold in Britain under the guidance of Rivers, Radcliffe-Brown, and Malinowski. Today, this emphasis on first-hand field research has resulted in the publication of thousands of ethnographies (ethnographic monographs) on hundreds of different cultures, providing a broad bank of data from which to generate and test explanations.

Many anthropologists are attracted to the discipline by the adventure and challenge of ethnographic field work. But ethnographic discovery and description is just the first step in the process of cross-cultural explanation. The next task in the ethnological process is classification.

## CLASSIFICATION

Classification is the process of treating a number of different things as though they are the same. The tendency to classify things is human; everyone everywhere creates and uses categories. The main reason for classification is our need to make the world simple and manageable. We are surrounded by an infinite variety of things we can discriminate among with our senses. Although we don't really think about it this way because we do class things together; everything that we sense with our eyes, ears, nose, and hands is unique, a little different from previous experience. Linguists can prove that no one ever says the same word exactly the same way twice. The moon never looks exactly the same. No two automobiles are quite alike; each has its own scratches, dents, weathered areas, streaks of dirt, and other attributes.

If people attempted to deal with life as a continuous set of unique experiences and things, it would be impossible to communicate with one another about it. There would be no way to teach children about their environment, warn others of impending danger, or exchange information about needed tasks at work. Our remedy is to employ a cultural classification for things, discriminating as much detail about them as we feel is necessary. Thus we speak in linguistic categories called "words" that we hear the same, although they are never quite spoken the same way. We identify vehicles called "cars," even though no two of them are exactly alike. We see the moon in the sky no matter when, where, or how it appears to us. Classification enables us to order and deal with our world, to predict what it will do and relate its parts.

Classification in the context of the ethnological task does exactly the same thing. As anthropologists accumulate more and more ethnographic data, they discover what seems to be an endless variety of behavior, custom, and belief. To talk about it, to predict how it will work and what its internal relationships might be, anthropologists must classify these data. They must find ways of putting different things together on the basis of common attributes. And, of course, they do. A review of any anthropological textbook will reveal an enormous number of terms that categorize ethnographic data: *economic sys-*

*tem, supernatural being, patrilineal descent, brother-sister avoidance,* and *cross-cousin marriage* are but a few examples. As you read the articles reprinted in this book you will encounter many terms that label anthropological categories. Indeed, one of the main tasks of any anthropology student is to learn this language of classification associated with the discipline.

But the task of classifying things is not easy. Even in everyday life we may find it difficult to distinguish the classes of things we sense. A white speck in the daytime sky, for example, may be the moon or a small cloud. Lights in the night sky are variously interpreted as meteors, planets, stars, swamp gas, aircraft, secret weapons, and flying saucers. We also argue about what things should be classed together. What size price rise should be labeled "inflationary"? What are the indicators of poverty? Are mopeds motor vehicles?

Anthropologists face the same problem when they attempt to create categories of ethnographic data. (A good example of a definitional problem is found below in Chapter V, where articles by Murdock, Levy and Fallers, and Adams attempt to define the category "family.") In actuality, there are always a number of ways to classify things; the final decision hangs on what is most useful to people. An interesting example of this comes from the everyday life of the restaurant world. Recently a new food chain opened restaurants in which customers buy their food by weight, rather than item. Patrons move along food displays, taking what they want and paying according to the weight, using a flat rate per quarter pound, of their choices. Because weight is important to food for the first time and because some foods are cheap to buy but heavy, the managers and employees of this chain have invented food categories such as "water weight food" and "heavy slice bread." Their classes reflect what is significant to them.

Solutions to problems of classification in anthropology follow the same path. Arguments for particular classifications usually depend on utility; new information, just like the new attribute of weight for food, may cause a change in definition. Because anthropology is a relatively new science, and because its data are so complex, there is still a great deal of disagreement over formal categories and classes. Almost every article in this volume discusses key definitions, at least to some extent, as a prelude to explanation. This is important, for classification is essential to the next task of ethnology, comparison.

## COMPARISON

Comparison is the process of relating a set of things to see how they are alike and different. When we wish to buy a new car we are apt to compare dealerships, looking at such factors as price, guarantees, and service reputation before we decide where to make the purchase. We may also compare different car models and brands on the basis of cost, size, drive train, power, room, and so forth. We do so in order to make a choice that fits our values, not to discover differences and to ask how these occur.

But this second question is precisely what concerns anthropologists when they conduct comparisons within or between societies. We have already seen how an emerging recognition of cross-cultural differences stimulated the birth of anthropology. It should come as no surprise that comparison continues to generate problems, theories, and explanations in the process of anthropological inquiry. Just a quick review of the topics in this volume—incest, family, women's status, sacred cows, potlatches, war, spirit possession—hint at the range of problems that cross-cultural comparison can yield.

One of the unique strengths of anthropology is the contribution to social and behavioral explanation that cross-cultural comparative studies can make. Because most other social scientists concentrate their research efforts on Western society and culture, their generalizations and theories may be "culture bound." Anthropologists can test such theories to see if they work for people everywhere, and if they don't, they can try to modify them for more general application.

The explanation of the rising divorce rate in the United States provides a good example. Some have argued that the rate of divorce correlates with the degree of industrialization. Industrialization, they assert, creates independent salaried individuals who occasionally must move to keep working. Local communities, families, and interpersonal obligations suffer disorganization; and, dependent on these factors, social pressure against divorce fails to prevent the practice as well as it once did. Testing this assertion for Japan, one anthropologist discovered that divorce rates fell markedly following industrialization in the last century and remained low until after the Second World War. The reason was not the hypothesized effect of industrialization as a disruption on family and community life. This seems to be the same for both societies. Instead the difference stemmed from the circumstances under which divorce occurred. American couples end marriage because of incompatibility and interpersonal conflict; in Japan it is the husband's family that dissolves the marriage. Consequently, when the Japanese family was weakened by the onset of industrialization, its power to divorce also diminished and the divorce rate fell. It is in ways like this that cross-cultural comparison can lead to the refinement and reordering of theory.

It also seems useful to point out different cross-cultural comparative strategies, for these are reflected in the articles that follow. Anthropologists may use the *case study method,* in which they compare a detailed analysis of a single culture with apparently similar or at least related material from other societies.

Netting focuses on Kofyar society in his articles on women's status in Chapter VI and on war in Chapter IX. Stanley and Ruth Freed discuss material from a single Indian village in their articles on the usefulness of the sacred cow and the nature of spirit possession found in Chapters VII and X, respectively.

Anthropologists may also use the technique of *limited comparisons,* analyzing just a few societies that differ in some crucial respect but which appear similar in many other ways. The advantage of such an approach is the control it provides over many aspects of culture that might otherwise be considered possible variables. None of the articles reprinted in this volume displays these ideal features, but a few represent loosely structured limited comparisons. Whorf compares the linguistic structure of Hopi and Standard European to show their effects on culture and perception in Chapter II. In the same chapter, Lee takes a similar approach for English and Trobriand.

Finally, there is the *cross-cultural correlational approach,* which involves the testing of theory against a broad sample of cultures drawn from around the world. The advantage of cross-cultural correlational studies is their ability to test theories with broad applicability to people everywhere. At least two of the articles reprinted in this text represent cross-cultural correlational studies. In Chapter VI, Peggy Sanday uses a large sample of societies to test several theories on the differential power of women. Divale and Harris follow the same pattern in their discussion of the causes of war in Chapter IX. With these comparative strategies in mind, let us now turn to the final ethnological step, explanation.

## EXPLANATION

The word "theory" frightens many people. They associate it with unintelligible scientific treatises, personal brilliance, and the challenging world of numbers and formulas. Without trying to diminish the remarkable achievements of the many scientists who have contributed to theory, it is still important to see theory for what it is: explanation. All of us spend a lifetime explaining things. We regularly account for the happenings of daily life: A friend is late for a party "because he always takes too long to get dressed." Someone is tired this morning "because she stayed up too late last night." Taxes have gone up "because those Washington bureaucrats spend too much money."

These explanations, as well all others, share some general characteristics. All state the things to be explained, the so-called *problems.* In the above examples, a problem was implied for each explanation. Why was someone late? Why was someone tired? Why have taxes gone up? Explanations also all achieve understanding by linking the things to be explained to other things called *variables.* Variables, to put it simply, are things that vary. Imagine, for example, that you have a dog who is normally friendly and composed. Occasionally, however, he becomes agitated, pants, and retreats to a spot behind the furnace in the basement. This change in his behavior presents you with a problem, Why does the dog hide behind the furnace? In your attempt to answer this question, you soon observe that this hiding behavior is related to thunderstorms; one always occurs with the other. Such storms represent variations in the weather; they are a variable. Similarly, the fact that someone takes a long time to dress is a variable that relates to his lateness. Staying up too late at night is a variable related to an individual's tiredness. Washington bureaucrats who spend too much money represent a variable related to higher taxes.

Anthropological explanations follow the same pattern; they contain the things to be explained, or problems, and the related variables that account for them. Some years ago, for example, anthropologist Bronislaw Malinowski was puzzled by the problem of magic as it was practiced by people living in the Trobriand Islands near New Guinea. Magic, he discovered, was an important part of daily activity, but, strangely, its appearance was selective. It occurred in association with some activities, such as canoe building and deep sea fishing, but was absent from others, such as lagoon fishing. Further observation convinced Malinowski that the explanation for this difference lay with the variable, anxiety. Deep sea fishing and sea-going canoes were both associated with uncertainty and danger. Men were lost in storms at sea; fish were often absent from fishing grounds for days at a time. Despite a first-rate knowledge of canoe building, sailing, navigation, and fishing, such dangers and uncertainties remained, and the inability to control them directly led Trobrianders to use a supernatural method, magic. Magic, argued Malinowski, had no actual effect on Trobrianders' safety or success at finding fish, but it did give them confidence, a confidence that helped to reduce the anxiety caused by technological impotence. Thus, he concluded, magic occurs because it is a successful way of reducing anxiety when normal techniques fail.

The fundamental structure of explanations, but especially the notion of variables, is useful for the classification of anthropological theories including those reprinted in this volume. Anthropological explanations are often complex and involved. Each has many unique features and a separate identity. Without classification, explanations prove hard to understand and remember. But classification has been difficult in anthropology. The science is young, and there is as yet no generally accepted paradigm for organizing theory. A number of ways exist, and each of them focuses on important aspects of theory and is useful for an understanding of the explanatory enterprise. Unfortunately, we lack the space to review most of these approachs to classification here. Instead, we will use a system of classification based on the kinds of variables often employed in anthropological explanations, in the hope that its simplicity will provide at least a rudimentary framework for organizing the explanations found in the articles that follow. In particular, we will discuss biological, environmental, sociocultural, and psychological variables.

Some of the articles reprinted in this volume stress *biological variables,* those inherited through the genetic material passed on from one generation to the next. Fox's article in Chapter II, for example, argues that many of our basic behavior patterns, such as sex, male dominance, and rank, are inherited characteristics, bequeathed to us by our primate ancestors. In the same section, Geertz asserts that culture has resulted from and played a part in the inheritance process. Aberle et al. explain the incest taboo in Chapter IV by noting the detrimental genetic effects of inbreeding. Wolf, in the same section, implies that the incest taboo results from a lack of mutual sexual interest afflicting males and females who are brought up together. The inherited tendency toward male dominance is an implied condition underlying the discussion of women's status in Chapter VI.

Other articles stress the imperatives of humankind's *physical environment* as variables that explain many problems. This approach is particularly evident in arguments that relate problems to human population pressures and the need for people to meet their physical requirements. All three articles in Chapter VII on the cultural ecology of India's sacred cattle have arguments that fall into this approach, as do those of Piddocke and Suttles in their discussion of the potlatch in Chapter VIII. The importance of population pressure also surfaces in the articles on war in Chapter IX.

Still other articles emphasize *sociocultural variables* that relate to social life and the needs humans derive from living together in groups. (See the introduction to Chapter IV for a fuller discussion of human social needs.) Explanations of this sort often emphasize the basic needs for the maintenance of society, such as well-defined roles, social goals, groups, and means of social control. White makes such an argument in Chapter IV when he argues that the incest taboo ties families together through the exchange of spouses. So do Drucker and Heizer when they account for the Kwakiutl potlatch as a way for men to validate their social status and for kingroups to cement ties to each other. In Chapter IV, Sanday argues that the status of women is linked to their economic role in society. Sacks asserts that low female status is associated with social classes and stratification.

Finally, some of the articles emphasize *psychological variables,* such as anxiety, fear, and personality type. We have already seen this kind of argument in our discussion of Malinowski and magic above. The clearest use of psychological variables occurs in Chapter X, where Opler and Freed and Freed account for demonic spirit possession as a way to reduce both internal and external anxiety.

## ISSUES IN ANTHROPOLOGY

Just as one's neighbors and friends may not all agree on the causes of inflation or the reasons for an acquaintance's tired condition, so do anthropologists regularly disagree on the explanation for different human behaviors and beliefs. This disagreement takes at least two forms. It may occur over the facts involved in a particular explanation. In Chapter VII, for example, there is disagreement over the ecological effects of India's cattle. Chapter VIII contains an argument over the degree to which Northwest Coast Indians faced privation at certain times of year. Anthropologists may also disagree about theoretical interpretation. In Chapter III, the main argument has to do with whether the incest taboo can be accounted for with biological, sociocultural, or psychological explanations. Many articles contain differences over both facts and theory.

The articles in this book are organized around some of the major disagreements or issues that have involved professional anthropologists. In Chapter II, we look at the controversy over the importance of inheritance versus culture in the generation of human behavior. The relative importance of language as a shaper of human reality forms the issue in Chapter II. Chapter IV deals with the different explanations of the universal incest taboo. Chapter V looks at the issue of how to define the family. The causes of differential female status form the topic of Chapter VI, while Chapter VII deals with the controversy over the relative ecological importance of cattle in India. Chapter VIII looks at differing interpretations of the Northwest Coast Indian potlatch; Chapter IX deals with the causes of war. Finally, Chapter X presents different views explaining demonic possession.

# CULTURE

**ISSUE** Sociobiology: Is human behavior inherited or learned?

It may come as a surprise to learn that anthropologists disagree about the definition of culture. After all, culture defines the subject matter of cultural anthropology; ethnography is the task of discovering and describing culture. The concept is central to the discipline. Yet despite its importance, culture is defined in numerous ways. For most anthropologists, this variation is manageable; they understand the different emphases that underlie particular definitions and they choose a view of culture that fits the direction of their own research and interests. But for people who are less well acquainted with cultural anthropology, definitional variety is confusing and blocks a basic understanding of what culture is about.

One way to facilitate a clearer feeling for what culture means is to think of the term as a name for something. Naming things is a regular feature of our existence. As something, or a class of things we experience, takes on importance, we are apt to give it a label. Thus waitresses, for example, learned long ago that customers crowd into restaurants at certain times of the day, causing a work overload for employees. They labeled these crowded times "rushes." Musicians in dixieland jazz bands discovered that they could hold the interest of crowds better and also give themselves a rest if they varied the tempo of the tunes they played. Not surprisingly, they now classify tunes according to tempo, using such labels as "blues," "stompers," "medium bounce tunes," and "barn burners."

Like waitresses and dixieland jazz musicians, anthropologists also encountered something that became important to them: the description of the ways people lived in other parts of the world. One of the first things that emerged from these descriptions was the realization that the world contained hundreds of named groups, such as the Sioux, Masai, Laos, Berbers, and so on. These groups appeared to be organized, and they often seemed to operate as independent political entities. The term "society" was used to label them.

But there was a second important feature of these reports that attracted attention: Each society seemed to have its own unique way of life, its own special configuration of beliefs, customs, and behaviors. Pygmies, for example, moved about in the Ituri rain forest of Africa, hunting and gathering for a living. They were egalitarian by most standards and permitted their children great freedom. Bantu-speaking villagers lived nearby in permanent communities. They gardened in the forest and demonstrated signs of social stratification. In these and other ways, the Pygmies and Bantus displayed basic differences from each other. And the same thing was true for the other societies found in the world.

It was these different configurations of custom, belief, and behavior, each associated with a particular society, to which anthropologists gave the name "culture." Culture labeled the total way of life for each group. It is what made one society different from another. The British anthropologist E. B. Tylor was the first person to capture this idea of culture in a complete way. In 1871 he wrote, "Culture . . . is that complex whole which includes knowledge, belief, art, law, morals, customs, and any other capabilities and habits acquired by man as a member of society." We largely follow Tylor's definition in this book when we define culture as the beliefs and behavior that people learn and share as members of a society.

An important attribute of culture, really an article of faith for many anthropologists, is *learning*. Culture, they assert, is learned, not inherited biologically. Proof for this view seems to abound. A child born to Chinese parents, but raised in the United States, will probably behave like other Americans. People change their culture within a single lifetime, not in the many generations required by genetic mutation and selection. Cultural variety is far too great to be explained by inheritance mechanisms. In short, learning is the key to human adaptation, and culture labels what is learned. Recently, however, this preeminent place for learning has been challenged. Several anthropologists, ethologists, and biologists suggest that inherited behavioral tendencies play a much more important role in determining human behavior than we like to admit. Most recently, Edward Wilson has argued that genes will try to perpetuate themselves so that humans, like any animals, will have inherited behavior patterns that reflect genetic success. His position, labeled *sociobiology*, has stirred up a serious controversy in anthropology that is still building today.

The articles in this chapter reflect on the issue of inheritance versus cultural meaning. In the first article, Fox argues that culture is the means by which we express a variety of biologically programmed behavioral tendencies. In the second, Sahlins argues that there is no obvious one to one relationship between certain human behaviors and biological needs, that the cultural meaning of behavior must be considered. Finally, Geertz asserts that biological and cultural heritage cannot be treated separately. Both affect each other to construct a single, synthesized definition of humankind.

# 1

## THE CULTURAL ANIMAL
### Robin Fox

*Few anthropologists would argue that particular aspects of culture, such as marriage, family structure, courtship, and religion, are involuntary behaviors based on instinct. But some, like Robin Fox in this work, take the position that there are inherited predispositions, often shared with other primates, that underlie such culturally defined activities and social arrangements. People, he asserts, cannot be viewed apart from their biological heritage. Instead, they should be seen as animals, like other beings, but animals whose biological directions can be overlaid and expressed through culture.*

Primitive mythologies testify to the enduring fascination of man with the problem of his own relationship to the natural world. For *Homo* is burdened with being *sapiens,* and one thing this *sapientia* drives him to is a ceaseless and almost passionate inquiry about his status—what T. H. Huxley aptly called *An Enquiry into Man's Place in Nature.* And like Darwin and Huxley, the primitive seeks an answer to the eternal paradox: We are obviously part of nature, and in particular we are part of the animal world, and yet we are set apart from nature by the very fact of knowing that we are part of it. Not only does no other animal know it is going to die, but no other animal knows it is alive—in any sense in which we would normally use the word "know." And no other animal concerns itself with the problem of its own uniqueness. But man is obsessed with it. He is forever seeking to define himself—a task as yet uncompleted—and to do so he has to establish the boundaries between himself and the animal world.

In their mythologies the primitives solve the problem in various ways, most usually by having man descend from an animal ancestor, or rather, various groups of men descend from various animal ancestors. We might like to think that this represents an anticipation of Darwin, but unfor-

tunately most primitives believe in acts of special creation, so we have to disqualify them. One of these acts of creation, however, is usually the clue to the essential difference: be it language, fire, the art of cooking, rules about incest, and so on, that are the diacritics of humanity. We do not communicate, convert energy, eat, or breed quite like the animals, and hence we make that crucial breakthrough from nature to culture, and become the cultural animal.

Not only do we become cultural, we become divine. In many of our ego-boosting mythologies we do not differ simply in degree from the animals, we differ in kind. It is not some simple attribute—like the ability to make fire—but the possession of a divine spark that renders us *in essence* different, that carves out a gulf between us and "brute creation." Here again we cannot seem to settle the matter, and much argument, as we know, ensues about where brute creation stops and the divine human starts. Any human group is ever ready to consign another recognizably different human group to the other side of the boundary. It is not enough to possess culture to be fully human, one must possess *our* culture. Even universalistic religions, which were happy to define man as an animal with a soul, were often not too sure by what criterion one recognized the possession of the *anima,* and categories of *Homo sylvestris* and *Homo feralis* were invented to take care of marginal cases. But at least in the western world this definition sufficed (and for many still suffices) until the eighteenth century savants began to look down on such arguments as perhaps too emotional, and substituted reason as the defining characteristic of man. Linnaeus, to whom we owe our pretentious zoological title, was very much a child of the eighteenth century. Souls were not to be trusted, it seems, since one never knew quite what they were up to, and animals may very well have them. But brute creation did not have reason and that was obvious enough. Soulful our furry friends may be, but rational they are not. They could probably adore God, but they could not understand Pythagoras.

Darwin undermined this stance as much as the position of the religiously orthodox. He noted what in fact many predecessors, including Linnaeus himself, and even Immanuel Kant, had noted—the striking anatomical similarity between ourselves and the rest of the order *Primates* and ultimately between ourselves and the rest of the vertebrates. What Darwin added was theory that could explain how this striking relationship came about, other than by some whim of the Almighty or by Lamarckian effort of will. Now this caused many people other than Bishop Wilberforce to feel that human dignity and uniqueness were in danger. That great anticleric, Samuel Butler, castigated Darwin for "banishing mind from the universe." He had blurred the distinctions that we had assumed were inviolable. We had emerged gradually from the animal world by a natural process, not suddenly by a supernatural one. The moral was plain to the soul merchants and the reason merchants alike: We in fact differed only in degree and not in kind from our cousins. The reaction was interesting. The anatomical argument was quickly adopted and became its own kind of orthodoxy. Despite a few skirmishes the battle was over before it was fought.

The anatomist W. E. LeGros Clark (1957) said recently that it is astonishing to think people ever doubted the anatomical continuity between ourselves and the other primates. And indeed it does seem absurd today, to the extent that when I am faced with an unrepentant fundamentalist I confess I am unable to cope with him. I have no ready-made arguments for defending the self-evident, and so fare badly, thus confirming his worst fears about the conspiracy of the ungodly.

In the hundred years between the appearance of *The Origin of Species* and today, a large (although still too limited) amount of fossil evidence has come to light documenting the gradual transition that what Darwin saw *must* have happened, even in the absence of direct evidence. As far as anatomy was concerned then, the case rested. But human behavior was somehow exempted from the same rubric.

Darwin published in 1873 his most remarkable work, *The Expression of the Emotions in Man and Animals.* Whatever we may think of his specific conclusions, his message was clear enough: In many areas of behavior we show great similarities to our cousins; their behavior, like their anatomy, has evolved through the process of natural selection, ergo, so has ours. Anatomy and behavior, structure and function, were of course intimately linked, and what was true for one was true for the other.

Even in the biological sciences, the impact of this line of thinking was not immediate, and it is only comparatively recently that biologists have been investigating in a serious way the evolution of animal-behavior systems. The reasons for this are not our concern here, although the historians of science should be working on them. But one reason we should note: Investigations of animal behavior really got going under the aegis of Pavlovian-style behaviorism, which is not evolutionary in orientation and has scant respect for anything that is claimed to be innate. A similar reaction (or was it even a reaction?) happened in the social sciences. Darwin had blurred the distinctions all right, and even reason did not appear to be so firmly enthroned now, so anthropology took on the role of "Defender of the Faith" in human uniqueness and weighed in with culture as the defining characteristic. Of course, as with their predecessors, they were never able to define very clearly what this was.

So, as in the older myths of those other primitives, the nature of our uniqueness remains something of a mystery. Very roughly, "culture," in anthropological parlance, refers to traditional modes of behaving and thinking that are passed on from one generation to another by social learning of one kind or another. We get a little uneasy when told that animal communities also have "traditions" that get passed on, so we retreat into symbols. Culture is couched in symbols and it is by means of these that it is passed on. Preeminent among the symbol systems is language, and when all else fails we can cling to language. "By their speech ye shall know them" —and to this we will return later.

The social and behavioral sciences thus sidestepped Darwin's challenge. This maneuver was aided by a number of developments. Behaviorism dominated psychology, and "instinct theory" fell into disrepute. Behaviorism was rigorous and "scientific" while instinct theory— primarily under McDougal—seemed nothing more than a kind of thesaurus of human attributes. The eugenics movement which put such store in biological aspects of behavior became more and more entangled with racism, and any attempt to show that there were important biological components in behavior was regarded as incipient racism, and still is in many quarters. In sociology, the "social Darwinists" also fell into disrepute. They were not really Darwinians in the sense in which I am using the term; they simply used analogies from Darwinian biological theory and applied them, usually wrongly, to social processes. Their wrongheaded use of evolutionary doctrines to support the excesses of laissez-faire capitalism eventually sent them into oblivion. With them,

the proverbial baby went out with the proverbial bath water. Henceforth, any explanation of a social phenomenon that was "Darwinian" or "biological" was ipso facto erroneous in the social sciences, and that was that. Marx and Durkheim dominated sociology, and while the latter had problems with the autonomy of the subject, his doctrine that the social must be explained in terms of the social and not reduced to any lower level (like the biological, of course) held almost complete sway.

Anthropologists continued to pronounce. Sir Arthur Keith (1948) even set a limit below which culture was impossible. The brain, he said, had to reach a size of 750 cubic centimeters before any fossil primate could be considered a "man." This gave substance to the anthropological belief that culture was, in the words of Malinowski, "all of a piece." One never found people with religion but no language, or law but no religion, and so on. If they had one they had all, and it must have happened at that point when the brain reached the size necessary for culture to "occur."

One can immediately see the similarities between this and the Catholic doctrine as ennunciated in the encyclical *Humani generis* where it is allowed that man may have evolved in body à la Darwin, but insisted that at some point an immortal soul was injected into the painfully evolving body. God would have had to wait, it seems, until his chosen primate had crossed Keith's "cerebral rubicon" before doing anything so presumptuous. Anthropologists, also, were almost maniacally preoccupied with explaining cultural differences. They were really not very interested in what made men man, but in what made one lot of men different from another lot.

As a student I had the litany chanted at me: Biological universals cannot explain cultural differentials. And of course at one level they cannot. Muslims, I was told, take off their shoes to go into church while Christians take off their hats. Now find me a biological explanation for that! I was never sure I wanted to find any kind of explanation for it. It seemed to me a pretty arbitrary thing. And anyway, what explanation was I offered? I will not bore you with the answer since I do not want to shake your faith in anthropology too much. But I will confess that even in those salad days I was plaguing my teachers with the question: If we do not really know what biological universals there are, then how can we study the cultural differentials in the first place? How to study the variables without the constants? In response, I was told that biological universals were simply primitive drives like hunger and sex. The fact that sex was universal did not explain why some cultures were polygynous and others monogamous. Maybe not, I thought, but it might explain why they were all adulterous. After all, sex is a very complex business, and might it not be that behavior resulting from it was more than just these rather gray and amorphous urges that I was presented with. Look at the courtship of birds and animals, for example. Ah, came back the answer, but that is *genetic,* whereas human courtship is *cultural.*

When all this was going on—some fifteen years ago in London—I had no ready answer. Anyway, I wanted to pass my exams. It all depends, I thought to myself and in secret, upon what you want to explain. All human cultures have some kind of courtship ceremonies, and when you look at them they look very much alike despite the different cultural trappings. If all you want to explain is why in America girls wear their dates' fraternity pins while in Fiji they put hibiscus flowers behind their ears, that is fine. But (a) it does not seem worth explaining, and (b) there probably is no explanation in any scientific sense—it is just what they do. These are simply ways of getting the same courtship job done, and the interesting thing to me is the universality of various similar symbolic devices. Has each culture independently invented the idea that the girl should declare her allegiance in this kind of way, or is there perhaps something more subtle about courtship than we imagined, something uncultural, something unlearned?

To be fair to anthropology, it was fighting on several fronts and often shot at the wrong targets. The "no links between biology and culture" argument was partly an attack on the racists who wanted to explain seeming inequalities between cultures as a result of biological differences. Again the baby went out with the soapsuds when anthropology strenuously set its face against *any* connection between culture and biology, even at the universal level. At best—as for example in the work of Malinowski—culture could be seen as a response to a rather drab set of "biological imperatives," but then this kind of Malinowskian functionalism soon fell into disrepute as well, since it did nothing to explain cultural differences. While I am on with my catalog of complaints, let me add that as far as I could see, for all its obsession with cultural differences, anthropology in fact did nothing to explain them. What it did was to take cultural differences as given and use them to explain other things—largely other cultural differences. All the things that might have explained cultural differences, such as racial variation, environment, history, and diffusion, were at one time or another ruled out of court.

All in all, for a variety of ideological reasons, the anthropological profession, along with psychology and sociology, kept the world safe for humanity by refusing to allow that anything about culture could be "reduced" to biology, and hence kept the gap between us and the brutes nicely wide. We were the "cultural animal" all right, but stress was entirely on the cultural while the animal was relegated to a few odd things like blinking, sucking, feeling hungry, and copulating. Ninety-nine percent of our behavior, it was held, was "learned" and hence cultural. And what was more there was no limit to what could be learned. The human infant was a *tabula rasa* on which culture imprinted itself, and the subsequent behavior of the infant was therefore wholly a matter of which particular culture had been imprinted on it. The differences between cultures in their beliefs, behaviors, and institutions was so great that any considerations of common biological traits were totally irrelevant.

We get to the crux of what I want to say by raising the question: Were not anthropologists suffering from ethnographic dazzle? I borrow the term from linguistics where "orthographic dazzle" refers to the difficulty some people have of sorting out pronunciation from spelling. In some respects and at some levels—the levels of beliefs, of formal institutions—cultures are dazzlingly different. Why are the Japanese the way they are, as opposed to the Americans, the Russians, the Hottentots, and so on? This is a fascinating question. But as I have said, the anthropological answer is rather lame "they are different because they do things differently." Mostly anthropology tells us about the *consequences* of doing things differently, and tells it very well indeed. But are societies and cultures really very different at the level of forms and processes? Or are they not in some ways depressingly the same? Do we not time after time in society after society come up with the same processes carried out under a variety of symbolic disguises? I think we do, and if we can get past the cultural or ethnographic dazzle we can see that this is so. Thus, if you look at the behavior of what my colleague Lionel Tiger (1969) has called *Men in Groups,* you find that whatever the overt cultural differences in male-group behavior at the level of symbolism, actual practices and beliefs, and even emotional and other expressive features, in society after society one thing stands out: Men form themselves into associations from which they exclude women. These associations vary in their expressed purposes but in many of their processes they are remarkably uniform. A seemingly bewildering variety of male behavior can be reduced in effect to a few principles once this is grasped.

Similarly I have tried to show that the seemingly endless variety of kinship and marriage arrangements known to man are in fact variations on a few simple themes. The same can be said of political arrangements, which, despite their cultural variety, are reducible to a few

structural forms. Once one gets behind the surface manifestation, the uniformity of human behavior and of human social arrangements is remarkable. None of this should surprise a behavioral zoologist; we are, after all, dealing with a uniform species divided into a number of populations. This being a species of rather highly developed mammals one would expect a lot of local differences in traditions between the various populations, but one would expect these differences to reflect species-specific units of behavior. Thus, every species has a complex of social behavior made up of recognizable units—a complex which distinguishes it from other species—but these units may well be put together in different ways by different populations adapting to different environments. But one does not find a baboon troop, for all its ingenuity, adapting like a herd of horses and vice versa. The baboons can only adapt with the material at hand in their stock of behavior units, and the same is true of man.

The degree of flexibility in human populations is obviously greater, but a great deal of it is at the symbolic level. We can tell the story in many different ways, but it is the same old story we are telling. And if we depart too far from the plot—which we have the capacity to do—the result may well be a truly dramatic chaos. For this is man's hang-up. Unlike the baboon or the horse, we can imagine things that are different from the plot laid down for us, and we can put our dreams into practice. The question then is, will the dream work? If you accept that all behavior is culturally learned and that man can learn anything, then the answer is yes. The only limit is human ingenuity. We can invent any kind of society and culture for ourselves. If you believe, as by now it should be obvious I do, that we have a species-specific repertoire of behavior that can be combined successfully only in certain ways, then the answer is no. There are definite limits to what this animal can do, to the kinds of societies it can operate, to the kinds of culture it can live with. But there is no end to its dreams and its fantasies. While its social behavior may have strict limits, its imagination has none.

I have jumped here to my conclusion without detailing the whole route. Let me postpone the latter for a little longer to press home this point. We mentioned earlier that language was the chief characteristic of our species, the crucial distinguishing feature. This is true and can be used to illustrate the point. It is now well established that the capacity for language acquisition and use lies in the brain on the one hand and in the speech organs on the other, and overall in the complex relations between the two. Linguists like Chomsky (1957, 1964, 1965) and psychologists like Lenneberg (1967) argue that the capacity for grammatical speech is somehow "in" the brain, and matures as the child matures. Thus every human child has the capacity for grammatical speech, and is ready, as it were, to be programmed with whatever actual grammar its culture provides. Now we know that the latter are many and astonishing in their variety, and that their variation is arbitrary.

There is no "explanation" why the English say "horse," the French "cheval," and the Germans "pferd." There is no explanation why any particular pattern of sounds signifies an object or action (with the possible exception of onomatopoeia). This is quite arbitrary. Nevertheless, the speech patterns of all languages are known to operate on a few basic principles which linguists have worked out, and the semantic patterns may well also be reducible in this way, once what Chomsky calls the "deep structures" of all languages are known. Once these are discovered, we can write the "universal grammar" which will tell us the few principles upon which all actual grammars rest. We can do this because despite the enormous variety of "surface grammars" they all are doing the same job and are constrained to do it in a limited number of ways. Thus no language exists that a linguist cannot record with the universal phonetic alphabet in the first place, and analyze with universally applicable techniques of semantic analysis in the second. We can invent artificial languages based

on binary signals, or other codes, which require different "grammars," but "natural languages" all can be broken down, first into phones, then phonemes, then morphemes, then lexemes, and so on up to the higher levels of grammaticality.

The rest of culture is probably like this. The potential for it lies in the biology of the species. We have the kinds of cultures and societies we have because we are the kind of species we are. They are built out of our behavioral repertoire and are analyzable into its elements and their combinations. Like language, the capacity for specific kinds of behavior is in us, but exactly how this will be manifested will depend on the information fed into the system. The system here is the behavior potential of the individual; the information is the culture he is socialized in. But in the same way as he can only learn a language that follows the normal rules of grammaticality for human languages, so he can only learn a grammar of behavior that follows the parallel rules in the behavioral sphere. Of course in either case he can try departing from normal grammaticality, but in either case he will then get gibberish, linguistic or behavioral.

We generally do not try to manipulate language because the matter is out of our hands, but with behavior we are continually producing gibbering illiterates, and until we understand the deep structure of the behavioral grammar within which we weave our cultural variations, we will continue to do so. No one wants to produce linguistic gibberish since verbal communication breaks down; but we constantly produce behavioral gibberish and then wonder why social communication breaks down. The answer of those who believe that anything is possible since everything is cultural is: Try to invent yet more and more different languages with any kind of grammaticality you can think of. My answer is: Find out how the universal grammar works and then bring changes within that framework; invent new behavioral languages that do not violate the principles of basic grammaticality.

At least two monarchs in history are said to have tried the experiment of isolating children at

birth and keeping them isolated through childhood, to see if they would spontaneously produce a language when they matured. The
Egyptian Psammetichos, in the seventh century
B.C., and later James IV of Scotland, in the
fifteenth century A.D. Both, it seemed did not
doubt that untutored children would speak, although King James' hope that they would speak
Hebrew was perhaps a little optimistic.

I do not doubt that they *could* speak and
that, theoretically, given time, they or their offspring would invent and develop a language despite their never having been taught one.
Furthermore, this language, although totally
different from any known to us, would be analyzable by linguists on the same basis as other
languages and translatable into all known languages. But I would push this further. If our new
Adam and Eve could survive and breed—still in
total isolation from any cultural influences—
then eventually they would produce a society
which would have laws about property, rules
about incest and marriage, customs of taboo and
avoidance, methods of settling disputes with a
minimum of bloodshed, beliefs about the supernatural and practices relating to it, a system of
social status and methods of indicating it, initiation ceremonies for young men, courtship practices including the adornment of females,
systems of symbolic body adornment generally,
certain activities and associations set aside for
men from which women were excluded, gam-
bling of some kind, a tool- and weapon-making
industry, myths and legends, dancing, adultery,
and various doses of homicide, suicide, homo-
sexuality, schizophrenia, psychosis and neuro-
ses, and various practitioners to take advantage
of or cure these, depending on how they are
viewed. I could extend the list but this will
suffice.

In short, the new Adam and Eve would not
only produce, as our monarchs suspected, a recognizable human language, but a recognizable
human culture and society. It might not be in
content quite like any we have come across: Its
religious beliefs might be different, but it would

have some; its marriage rules might be unique (I
doubt it), but it would have them and their type
would be recognized; its status structure might
be based on an odd criterion, but there would be
one; its initiation ceremonies might be unbeliev-
ably grotesque but they would exist; its use or
treatment of schizophrenia might be bizarre, but
there it would be. All these things would be there
because we are the kind of animal that does these
kinds of things.

In the same way, in a zoo one can rear infant
baboons who know nothing of the state in which
their ancestors and wild cousins lived, and yet
when they reach maturity they produce a social
structure with all the elements found in the wilds
and of which they have no experience. Their
capacity to produce a unique "language" is of
course much more limited than that of our hypothetical naive group of humans, but in both cases
the basic grammaticality of behavior will be operative. In the same way that a linguist could
take our Garden of Eden tribe and analyze its
totally unique language, so an anthropologist
would be able to analyze its totally unique kinship system or mythology or whatever, because
the basic rules of the universal grammar would
be operating.

(Actually in the interests of accuracy I
should add a rider here to the effect that the
experiment might be impossible to perform. It is
one of the ground rules of the universal behavioral grammar of all primates—not just humans
—that if you take young infants away from maternal care at a critical period they will grow up
to be very disturbed indeed and may well perpetuate this error by maltreating their own children
in turn. Thus our experiment may well produce
a group of very maladjusted adults and the
whole thing founders rather quickly. But at least
this gives us one element of the universal system:
Some method has to be found of associating
mother and child closely and safely during certain critical periods. If isolated during critical
periods, not only can the animal not learn *anything* at all, it loses the potential to learn at any
other time. It has to learn certain things at cer-

tain times—true of language and of many other areas of behavior.)

To return to our human tribe developed *de novo* in our experimental Eden: What I am saying may not seem very remarkable but it goes against the grain of the anthropological orthodoxy. Without any exposure to cultural traditions our tribe would develop *very specific* and highly complex patterns of behavior, and probably very quickly—within a matter of a few generations, once they had developed a language. They would do so for the same reason that the baboons produce a baboon social system in captivity—because it is in the beast. And it is not just a very general capacity that is in the beast —not just the capacity to learn, and to learn easily—which is all the culturalists need to assume, it is the capacity to learn some things rather than others, and to learn some things easily rather than others, and to learn some rather specific things into the bargain.

This is a very important point. I am not positing that initiation ceremonies or male rituals are instinctive, in any old sense of that term. I am positing that they are an outcome of the biology of the animal because it is programmed to behave in certain ways that will produce these phenomena, given a certain input of information. If this input does not occur then the behavior will not occur or will occur only in a modified or distorted form. (This is, in fact, more like the modern theory of instinct, but to go into the ramifications of this would take too long.) The human organism is like a computer which is set up or "wired" in a particular way. It is thus in a state of readiness—at various points in the life cycle—to process certain kinds of information. The information has to be of a certain type, but the actual "message" can vary considerably. If the information is received, then the computer stores it and uses it to go on to the next task. If you confuse the system, the machine very easily breaks down and might even blow the fuses if you really mix up the program. Of course to push this analogy to its logical conclusion we would have to have computers feeding each

other information to simulate the human situation. Only when they were synchronized would the total system run properly.

This is—although very crude—a different model from that of the old "instinctivists" or of the "behaviorists." To the instinctivists, behavior resulted simply from the manifestation of innate tendencies which in interaction produced such things as territorialism, maternal behavior, or acquisitiveness. To the behaviorists the infant was, as we have seen, a *tabula rasa* and behavior ultimately was the result of learning via conditioning. (Psychoanalysis leans to the instinctivist end, but is a special case in some ways.) Culturalists in anthropology and the social sciences share the *tabula rasa* view and see all behavior above the primitive-drive level as a result of the learning of a particular culture. My view sees the human organism as wired in a certain way so that it can process information about certain things like language and rules about sex, and not other things, and that it can only process this information at certain times and in certain ways. This wiring is geared to the life cycle so that at any one moment in a population of *Homo sapiens* there will be individuals with a certain "store" of behavior at one stage of the cycle giving out information to others at another stage, the latter being wired to treat the information in a certain way. As an outcome of the interaction of these individuals at various stages, certain "typical" relationships will emerge. This may seem either tortuous or obvious, but I can assure you it *is* a different way of viewing human behavior and social structure than the orthodox one. The orthodox view says: When in trouble, change the program because we can write any program we want to. What we should say is: When in trouble, find out what is in the wiring, because only then will we know what programs we can safely write.

The culturalists only acknowledge a very general "capacity for culture," if they acknowledge anything at all about the general characteristics of the species. To them, all culture is pure human invention and is passed on from generation to generation by symbolic learning. Thus, logically, it follows that if ever this store of culture should be lost, it is improbable that it would be invented again in the same forms. Thus something as specific as totemism and exogamy—that old anthropological chestnut—has to be seen in this view as a pure intellectual invention, and it would be unlikely that it would be invented again. I do not think so. I think my tribe with no experience of any other human culture and no knowledge of totemism and exogamy would produce both very quickly, and what is more these phenomena would be immediately recognizable and analyzable by anthropologists. In fact those anthropologists like Tylor who argued for the "psychic unity of mankind" were acknowledging a similar position. They argued that such customs had not been invented in one area and diffused throughout the world, but were stock responses of the human psyche to external pressures. They were somehow reflections of "human nature," a phrase that we have been discouraged from using. The argument for psychic unity also had to face the "constants can explain variables" charge, but we have dealt with that one already.

The psychic unity argument, however, was never pushed as far as I am pushing it. The universal psyche for these anthropologists had no specific content; it was a capacity to do human things, but most of its proponents would have maintained it was a general learning capacity and that culture was invented. As I have said, at one level this is true—at the level of specific content—but we must not be dazzled by this into ignoring those basic processes and forms that crop up with regular monotony. (Here we must not slip into the error of thinking that *universal processes* necessarily produce *uniform results*. Far from it. This is not true even in the plant kingdom and is even less true in the animal.)

I can now return to the problem of the route by which I reached this conclusion. The question that had been plaguing me throughout my undergraduate career was really, "How do we

know what's in the wiring and how did it get there?" For we can find out really what it is all about only if we know how it was constructed and to what end it was produced. It is no good trying to use an analog computer as if it were a digital computer since they were designed for different uses. The answer to this should have been obvious, and soon became so. What is in the wiring of the human animal got there by the same route as it got into any other animal—by mutation and natural selection. These "great constructors" as Konrad Lorenz calls them, had produced remarkable end products in the social behavior of all kinds of animals, reptiles, birds, fishes, and insects. And it is here that the message of Lorenz and his associates becomes important: Behavior evolves just as structure evolves and the evolution of the two is intimately linked.

Now we are back to Darwin's principle from which this paper started and from which anthropology so disastrously departed at the turn of the century. What the behavioral zoologists (in Europe usually known as ethologists) showed us was that units of behavior evolve on the same principle as units of anatomy and physiology—that a head movement that was part of a bird's innate repertoire of actions has an adaptive significance as great as the evolution of the wing itself. The head movement may be precisely the thing that inhibits the attack of another bird, for example, and over the millennia has become "fixed" as a signal recognized by the species as an inhibitor. Even if one does not accept that humans have "instincts" of this kind (I think they have a few but not many), the point is well taken that one should look at behavior as the end product of evolution and analyze it in terms of the selection pressures that produced it. If we have this marvelous flexibility in our learning patterns then this is a feature of the biology of our species and we should ask *why* we have this flexibility. What selection pressures operated to bring about this particular biological feature? Our enormous dependence on culture as a mode of adaptation itself stands in need of explanation, for this too is a species-specific characteristic, and its gets us into trouble as much as it raises us to glory. It is a two-edged weapon in the fight for survival, and the simple brutes with their instinctive headwagging may well live to have the last laugh.

But the brutes, it has transpired, are not so simple. When one looks at our cousins, the other primates, the complexity of their social behavior is amazing. One thing the ethologists taught us to do was to compare the behavior of closely related species in order to get at the "proto-behavior" of the group of animals concerned. The continuing flow of excellent material on nonhuman primates in the wild shows us how many and subtle are the resemblances between ourselves and our simian relatives. Wider afield, the growing science of animal behavior shows that many mammals, and vertebrates generally, have social systems which duplicate features of our own society, and in which similar processes occur, and even similar social pathologies. Lorenz (1966) showed how aggression was the basis of social bonding; Wynne-Edwards (1962) postulated that the "conventionalized competition" which controlled aggression was itself rooted in the control of numbers; Chance (1962) demonstrated that among primates the elementary social bond was that between males rather than that between males and females, and so on. The politics of macaque monkeys suggests that Aristotle was right: Insofar as he is a primate, man is by nature a political animal. (It is significant that quoting this, the phrase *by nature* is often omitted.) Ants can have societies, but ants cannot have politics. Politics only occurs when members can change places in a hierarchy as a result of competition. So man is more than social; he is political, and he is political because he is that kind of primate—terrestrial and gregarious.

As a consequence it becomes more and more obvious that we have a considerable animal heritage and hence a great store of comparative data to draw on in making generalizations about our own species. It forces upon us this observation:

If we find our own species displaying certain patterns of social behavior that duplicate those of other similar species—depending, of course, on the level of similarity—we will often need to say only that these patterns are what we would expect from a terrestrial primate, a land-dwelling mammal, a gregarious vertebrate, or whatever. Of course some aspects of these patterns and a great deal of their content will be unique, but this is only to say that they will be species-specific. Every species is unique since it is the end product of a particular path of evolution.

The real question—What is the nature of the uniqueness?—brings us back to where we started. And we cannot answer that question until we know what we have in common with all other species, and with some other species, and with only closely related species. Thus the argument that we differ from all other species as a result of the triumph of culture over biology I find false, because culture is an aspect of our biological difference from other species. It is the name for a kind of behavior found in our species which ultimately depends on an organ, the brain, in which we happen to have specialized. Thus differences between ourselves and other primates for example do not stem from the fact that we have in some way *overcome* our primate natures, but stem from the fact that we are a different kind of primate with a different kind of nature. At the level of forms and processes we behave culturally because it is in our nature to behave culturally, because mutation and natural selection have produced this animal which must behave culturally, must invent rules, make myths, speak languages, and form men's clubs in the same way as the hamadryas baboon has to form harems, adopt infants, and bite his wives on the neck.

But why culture? Why did our simian ancestors not content themselves with a much less flexible, and perhaps at the time less vulnerable, way of coping with nature's exigencies? This is where another strand of evidence comes in—the material on human evolution. In Darwin's day this was practically nonexistent and even now it is relatively meager. But we now can trace with some confidence the general picture of man's evolution over at least four million years, and we have evidence that the hominoid line may well go back over thirty million. This is not the place for a detailed exposition of what we know, and all I can do is to point out some of the implications of our new knowledge.

You will remember that Sir Arthur Keith set the limit of brain size below which was mere animal at 750 cc. The modern human brain averages about 1400 cc, roughly twice that of Keith's minimum. The brain of the chimpanzee is roughly 400 cc, that of the gorilla 500 cc. Now to cut a long story short, the modern discoveries have shown that hominids have existed for at least two million years and probably longer, and that at that early date in their evolution they were indulging in activities that imply the existence of cultural traditions, even if of a rudimentary form. The most striking evidence of this is the existence of tool-making industries first in bone and horn and then in stone (wood does not survive but was undoubtedly used) in small-brained hominids in East and South Africa. Two million years ago, our ancestors with brain sizes ranging from 435 cc to 680 cc—little better, you see, than the gorilla—were doing very human things, cultural things, before having reached the Rubicon. They were hunting, building shelters, making tools, treating skins, living in base camps and possibly many other things (speaking languages perhaps?) that we cannot know directly, while their morphology was still predominantly ape-like and their brains in some cases smaller than the modern apes. What was not ape-like about them was their dentition and their bipedal stance. In these features they were well launched on the road to humanity since both reflect the adaptation to a hunting way of life which differentiates these animals from their primate cousins.

You will note that I say these "animals"—I might just as easily have said these "men"—and this is the moral of the story. What the record of evolution shows is no sharp break between man and animal that can be pinpointed at a certain brain size or anything else. What it shows is a very gradual transition in which changes in locomotion led the way and in which the brain was something of a sluggard. The pelvis of the Australopithecinae—those man-apes of South and East Africa—is strikingly human and totally unlike anything in an ape, because these were bipedal creatures; but the brain was, if anything, smaller than that of a gorilla—an animal not noted for its cultural achievements.

The moral goes deeper. Once launched on the way to humanity through bipedalism, hunting, and the use of tools, our ancestors became more dependent on their brains than their predecessors had been. If they were going to survive largely by skill and cunning and rapid adaptation to the changing circumstances of the Pleistocene epoch, then a premium was put on the capacity for cultural behavior about which we have been speaking. Man took the cultural way before he was clearly distinguishable from the animals, and in consequence found himself stuck with this mode of adaptation. It turned out to be very successful, although for a while it must have been touch and go. But because he became dependent on culture, mutation and natural selection operated to improve on the organ most necessary to cultural behavior, namely the brain and in particular the neocortex with its important functions of association and control. Those animals, therefore, that were best able to be cultural were favored in the struggle for existence. Man's anatomy, physiology, and behavior therefore are in large part the *result* of culture. His large and efficient brain is a consequence of culture as much as its cause. He does not have a culture because he has a large brain; he has a large brain because several million years ago his little-brained ancestors tried the cultural way to survival. Of course, the correct way to view this is as a "feedback" process. As cultural pressures grew, so did selection pressures for better brains, and as better brains emerged, culture could take new leaps forward thus in turn exerting more pressures, and so on.

Again this is an over-simplified account, and the actual picture of the evolution of the brain is much more complex. But in essence it is true, and for our immediate purposes enough to make the point that our uniqueness is a biological uniqueness and that culture does not in some mysterious sense represent a break with biology. Our present biological makeup is a consequence among other things of cultural selection pressures. We are, therefore, biologically constituted to produce culture, not simply because by some accident we got a brain that could do cultural things, but because the cultural things themselves propelled us into getting a larger brain. We are not simply the *producers* of institutions like the family, science, language, religion, warfare, kinship systems, and exogamy; we are the *product* of them. Hence, it is scarcely surprising that we continually reproduce that which produced us. We were selected to do precisely this, and in the absence of tuition our mythical tribe would do it all over again in the same way. It is not only the *capacity* for culture then that lies in the brain, it is the *forms* of culture, the universal grammar of language and behavior.

This then is how it all got into the wiring of the human computer. Once we know these facts about human evolution there is no great mystery in principle about the production of culture by human beings and the relative uniformity of its processes. There are many mysteries of fact which will never be solved since we can only infer the behavior of fossil man and never observe it. But in principle, once we accept that culture is the major selection pressure operating on the evolution of human form and behavior, and that it has produced an animal wired for the processing of various cultural programs, then the problem of the uniqueness of man becomes a problem on the same level as the problem of the uniqueness of any other animal species.

Putting together the insights of the ethologists and the students of human evolution, we can scan the behavior of related species for aspects of behavior that are common to all primates, and beyond that we can look to mammals and vertebrates for clues. For in the process of evolution we did not cease to be primates or mammals. In fact, as Weston LaBarre (1955) has said, part of our success lies in exaggerating certain mammalian tendencies rather than in losing them—length of suckling, for example. Much of our behavior and in particular our social arrangements can be seen as a variation on common primate and gregarious mammalian themes. Certain "unique" aspects—such as the use of true language—can be investigated for what they are, biological specializations produced by the unique evolutionary history of the species.

This perspective enables us to look at human society and behavior comparatively without any necessity to propound theories of the total and essential difference between ourselves and other animals. It puts the obvious uniqueness into perspective and does not allow us to lose sight of our commonality with the animal kingdom. We are the cultural animal all right, but both terms should be given equal weight, and one does not contradict the other. For the last time then, let me say that culture does not represent a triumph over nature, for such a thing is impossible; it represents an end product of a natural process. It is both the producer and the product of our human nature, and in behaving culturally we are behaving naturally.

To bury this issue once and for all, at least to my own satisfaction, let me add a word about the nature of culture as opposed to the nature of instinct. It is often said that man has "lost" all his instincts. I think this is a bit too extreme. If we might paraphrase Oscar Wilde: To lose some of one's instincts is unfortunate, to lose all of them smacks of carelessness. No species could afford to be that careless. But it is true that in terms of innate mechanisms which produce items of behavior complete at their first performance and relatively unmodifiable by experience, man has very few. Instead, it is often claimed, he has intelligence, foresight, wisdom and the like, and the enormous capacity to learn. Now in ditching instinct and opting for intelligence man took something of a risk, since instinct does provide a surety of response that has been evolved from trial and error over millions of years. Ant societies are much better organized and more efficient than any human societies and are driven wholly on instinctive mechanisms. But again instinct has its costs. It is too rigid. Changed circumstances cannot be met by a rapid adjustment in behavior, and insects and animals heavily dependent on instinct have to wait for processes of genetic change to effect changes in the instincts themselves before they can adjust. The higher we go up the phyletic scale the less true this is of course and with man least true of all. Thus there is a cost-benefit analysis involved in the shedding of innate instincts in favor of more complex modes of behaving.

The crux of the matter is this: Even if a species sheds its dependence on instincts, it still has to do the same things that instincts were designed to do. To put it into our earlier language, culture has to do the same job that instinct had been doing. This is another paradox, I suppose, but an intriguing one, because to get culture to do the same jobs as instinct had been doing, one had to make cultural behavior in many ways like instinctive behavior. It had to be unconscious so that it did not require thought for its operation, it had to be "automatic" so that certain stimuli would automatically produce it, and it had to be common to all members of the population.

If we look at our cultural behavior, how much of it is in fact intelligent and conscious, and how much is at that unthinking automatic response level? The answer, of course, is that the vast majority of our behavior is the latter, absorbed during our socialization and built into our patterns of habitual thought, belief, and response. Habit indeed is, as William James said, the great flywheel of society. Anthropologists speak of covert or unconscious culture to refer to this iceberg of assumptions, values, and habitual responses. And sitting over all of them, of course, is the great evolutionary invention of conscience, superego, moral sense, or whatever you want to call it. The sense of guilt, of having

broken the taboos, the rules, the laws of the tribe, keeps most of us in line most of the time. Conscience is an empty cannister that culture fills, but once filled, it becomes a dynamic controller of behavior. Most of our behavior, however, never even rises to the point where conscience and the sense of guilt need to step in. We do what we do from habit, even down to tiny little details of gestures and twitches of the facial muscles. Most of this we never think about, but we rapidly recognize when other people are not behaving "normally" and we lock them up in asylums as lunatics. Think only of the example of the man walking down the road in the rain without a raincoat, smiling, shoulders back, head facing the sky. Clearly a madman. He should be hunched, hurrying, and looking miserable, with his jacket collar up at least.

The genius of nature here stands revealed and the paradox is resolved. Of course most of our learned cultural behavior in fact operates almost exactly like instinct and, as we have seen, this has to be the case. The customs and usages of the tribe, although not instinctive themselves, had to do the same job as instincts and hence had to be built into the automatic habit patterns of the tribal members, with guilt as a safeguard. (This was not foolproof, but neither is instinct itself.) So the same effect is achieved, and those habits which have proved useful in survival become part of the behavioral repertoire of the people. But—and here is the genius bit—these habits can be changed within a generation. One does not have to wait for the long process of natural selection to operate before these quasi-instinctual behaviors can be modified. They can be modified very rapidly to meet changing circumstances. Thus one has all the benefits of instinctive behavior without waiting for instincts to evolve. At any one time the rigidity of cultural habits will be just as invulnerable to change as any instinct—as we well know if we reflect on the persistence of traditions—and habits are very conservative. Since most of them are passed on by means other than direct tuition, they tend to persist over generations despite changes in overt education. But they can be changed relatively rapidly compared with the time span needed for changes in genetic material. Thus man can make rapid adjustments without anarchy (which does not mean that he always does so).

Here again we see learned, cultural behavior as yet another kind of biological adaptation. At this level, other species also display behavior of the same kind, and the higher in the scale they are, the more dependent they become on habits transferred over the generations by learning rather than instincts transferred in the genetic code. But always we must keep in mind that this is not a sharp distinction. The code is not silent about learning and habits. If the position taken here is anywhere near correct, then instructions about habitual behavior are as much in the code as instructions about instinctive behavior.

The model of behavior sees the human actor as a bundle of potentialities rather than a *tabula rasa:* potentialities for action, for instinct, for learning, for the development of unconscious habits. These potentials or predispositions or biases are the end product of a process of natural selection peculiar to our species. One consequence of this view is that much of the quasi-instinctive cultural behavior of man can be studied in much the same way and by much the same methods as ethologists study the truly instinctive behavior of other animals. Many strands of investigation seem to be leading in this direction at the moment.

The kind of overall investigation that emerges from this theoretical position would utilize primarily three kinds of data: Data from human behavior both contemporary and known in history; data on animal behavior, particularly that on wild primates; data on hominid evolution with special attention to the evolution of the brain. Eventually data from genetics—molecular genetics, behavior genetics, and population genetics—will have to be included. But this is perhaps jumping ahead too far. At the moment the best we can say is that we should be prepared to use genetic data when we become sophisticated enough to incorporate it.

We began with the theme of human uniqueness and should end with my point that our uniqueness has to be interpreted in the same way as the uniqueness of any other species. We have to ask "How come?" How did culture get into the wiring? How did the great constructors operate to produce this feature, which, like everything else about us is not antinature, or superorganic, or extrabiological, or any of the other demagogic fantasy-states that science and religion imagine for us? Darwin did not banish mind from the universe as Butler feared; indeed, he gave us a basis for explaining how mind got into the universe in the first place. And it got there—as did every other natural and biological feature—by natural selection. The tool-making animal needed mind to survive; that is, he needed language and culture and the reorganization of experience that goes with these. And having got the rudiments and become dependent on them, there was no turning back. There was no retreat to the perilous certainty of instinct. It was mind or nothing. It was classification and verbalization, rules and laws, mnemonics and knowledge, ritual and art, that piled up their pressures on the precarious species, demanding better and better brains to cope with this new organ—culture—now essential to survival. Two related processes, thought and self-control, evolved hand in hand, and their end product is the cultural animal, which speaks and rules itself because that is the kind of animal it is; because speaking and self-discipline have made it what it is; because it is what it produces and was produced by what it is.

## REFERENCES

CHANCE, M. R. A.
    1962    "The Nature and Special Features of
            the Instinctive Social Bond of
            Primates." In *Social Life of Early Man,*
            S. L. Washburn, editor. London:
            Methuen.

CHOMSKY, N.
    1957    *Syntactic Structures.* The Hague:
            Mouton & Co.

1964  *Current Issues in Linguistic Theory.* The Hague: Mouton & Co.

1965  *Aspects of the Theory of Syntax.* Cambridge: MIT Press.

KEITH, SIR A.

1948  *A New Theory of Human Evolution.* London: Watts & Co.

LABARRE, W.

1955  *The Human Animal.* Chicago: University of Chicago Press.

LE GROS CLARK, W. E.

1957  *History of the Primates.* Chicago: University of Chicago Press.

LENNEBERG, E. H.

1967  *Biological Foundations of Language.* New York: John Wiley and Sons.

LORENZ, K.

1966  *On Aggression.* London: Methuen.

TIGER, L.

1969  *Men in Groups.* New York: Random House.

WYNNE-EDWARDS, V. C.

1962  *Animal Dispersion in Relation to Social Behavior.* London: Oliver and Boyd.

# 2

# THE USES AND ABUSES OF BIOLOGY

*Marshall Sahlins*

*In the previous article, Fox argues that human behavior, although it varies in detail from one society to the next, everywhere acts out a system of basic inherited dispositions, such as sexuality, aggressiveness, and male bonding. More recently, Edward Wilson and others have refined this position by the addition of a genetic rationale for the inheritance of social behavior patterns. In this article, Marshall Sahlins criticizes positions such as Fox's, which he calls "vulgar sociobiology," and those of Wilson, which he terms "scientific sociobiology," by arguing for the separation of biological urges from meaningful cultural behavior. Basically, he claims, there is no necessarily obvious relationship between a biological urge and the behavior that stimulates and expresses it. War, for example, is often cited as an example of human aggression. But fighting of this sort, argues Sahlins, can start over almost anything, and those who participate in it often fail to feel aggressive. In the end, it is culture that gives meaning to human behavior and defines its relationship to human needs.*

> *"They're trying to kill me," Yossarian told him calmly.*
> *"No one's trying to kill you," Clevinger cried.*
> *"Then why are they shooting at me?" Yossarian asked.*
> *"They're shooting at everyone," Clevinger answered. "They're trying to kill everyone."*
> *"And what difference does that make?" . . .*
> *"Who's they?" he wanted to know. "Who, specifically, do you think is trying to murder you?"*
> *"Every one of them," Yossarian told him.*

Taken generally, the vulgar sociobiology consists in the explication of human social behavior as the expression of the needs and drives of the human organism, such propensities having been constructed in human nature by biological evolution.

Anthropologists will recognize the close parallel to the "functionalism" of Malinowski, who likewise tried to account for cultural phenomena by the biological needs they satisfied. It has been said that for Malinowski culture was a gigantic metaphorical extension of the physiological processes of digestion.

It would take more effort, however, to recognize the thesis of vulgar sociobiology in the works of scientific biologists such as E. O. Wilson, R. L. Trivers, W. D. Hamilton, R. Alexander, or M. West-Everhard. These scholars have not been concerned as such to make the case that human social organization represents natural human dispositions. That thesis has been the preoccupation of authors of the recent past, proponents of a less rigorous biological determinism, such as Ardrey, Lorenz, Morris, Tiger, and Fox. Scientific sociobiology is distinguished by a more rigorous and comprehensive attempt to place social behavior on sound evolutionary principles, notably the principle of the self-maximization of the individual genotype, taken as the fundamental logic of natural selection. Yet by the nature of that attempt, the main proposition of the vulgar sociobiology becomes also the necessary premise of a scientific sociobiology. The latter merely anchors the former in genetic-evolutionary processes. The chain of biological causation is accordingly lengthened: from genes through phenotypical dispositions to characteristic social interactions. But the idea of a necessary correspondence between the last two, between human emotions or needs and human social relations, remains indispensable to the scientific analysis.

The position of the vulgar sociobiology is that innate human drives and dispositions, such as aggressiveness or altruism, male "bonding," sexuality of a certain kind or a parental interest in one's offspring, are realized in social institutions of a corresponding character. The interaction of organisms will inscribe these organic tendencies in their social relations. Accordingly, there is a one-to-one parallel between the character of human biological propensities and the properties of human social systems. Corresponding to human aggressiveness we find among all men a taste for violence and warfare, as well as territoriality and systems of social ranking or dominance. Marriage, adultery, harlotry, and (male) promiscuity may be understood as expressions of a bisexual and highly sexual species. A long period of infant dependency finds its cultural analogue in universal norms of motherhood and fatherhood. Note that this kind of reasoning is also implicitly, explicitly, and extensively adopted by Wilson and his coworkers. *Sociobiology* opens with a discussion of the critical relevance of the hypothalmic and limbic centers of the human brain, as evolved by natural selection, to the formulation of any ethical or moral philosophy. These centers are said to "flood our consciousness with emotions" and to "orchestrate our behavioral responses" in such a way as to maximally proliferate the responsible genes. But most generally the thesis of the vulgar sociobiology is built into the scientific sociobiologist's idea of social organization. For him, any Durkheimian notion of the independent existence and persistence of the social fact is a lapse into mysticism. Social organization is rather, and nothing more than, the behavioral outcome of the interaction of organisms having biologically fixed inclinations. There is nothing in society that was not first in the organisms. The ensuing system of statuses and structures is a function of demography and disposition, of the distribution in the group of animals of different age, sex, or other classes, each with its characteristic behavioral propensities. Therefore, we can always resolve the empirical social forms into the behavioral inclinations of the organisms in question, and that resolution will be exhaustive and comprehensive. The idea I want to convey is one of isomorphism between the biological properties and the social properties.

Related to this premise of isomorphism is a mode of discourse characteristic of vulgar sociobiology, which amounts to a nomenclature or classification of social behavior. I refer to the famous temptations of anthropomorphism. Observing animal social relations and statuses, we recognize in them certain similarities to human institutions: as between territorial competition and human warfare, animal dominance and human rank or class, mating and marriage, and so forth. The analogy, the argument runs, is often indeed a functional homology; that is, it is based on common genetic capacities and phylogenetic continuities, an evolutionary identity of the dispositional underpinning. It follows that the social behaviors in question, human and nonhuman alike, deserve the same designation, which is to say that they belong in the same class of social relations. Usually the English name for the animal activity is taken as the general (or unmarked) label of the class, such that war is subsumed in "territoriality" or chieftainship in "dominance." Sometimes, however, the marked or anthropological term is adopted as the general name for the class and applied also to the animal counterparts. This, of course, smuggles in certain important propositions about the "culture" of animals. Again the anthropomorphic inclination is not confined to the vulgar sociobiology. To take a random and limited sample from Wilson's *Sociobiology: The New Synthesis*, we read of animal societies that have "polygyny," "castes," "slaves," "despots," "matrilineal social organization," "aunts," "queens," "family chauvinism," "culture," "cultural innovation," "agriculture," "taxes," and "investments," as well as "costs" and "benefits."

I shall not be concerned with this an-thropomorphic taxonomy, which has been justly and effectively criticized by many others, so much as with the essential anthropological problem in the thesis of vulgar sociobiology. It is a problem that has often recurred in the history of anthropological thought, not only with Malinowski but principally in the "personality and culture" school of the 1940s and 1950s. The inability to resolve the problem in favor of psychological explanations of culture accounts for the more modest aims of that school at present, as well as for the change of name to "psychological anthropology." The problem is that there is no necessary relation between the phenomenal form of a human social institution and the individual motivations that may be realized or satisfied therein. The idea of a fixed correspondence between innate human dispositions and human social forms constitutes a weak link, a rupture in fact, in the chain of sociobiological reasoning.

Let me explain first by a very simple example, a matter of commonplace observation. Consider the relation between warfare and human aggression—what Wilson at one point calls "the true, biological joy of warfare." It is evident that the people engaged in fighting wars—or for that matter, any kind of fighting—are by no means necessarily aggressive, either in the course of action or beforehand. Many are plainly terrified. People engaged in wars may have any number of motivations to do so, and typically these stand in some contrast to a simple behaviorist characterization of the event as "violence." Men may be moved to fight out of love (as of country) or humaneness (in light of the brutality attributed to the enemy), for honor or some sort of self-esteem, from feelings of guilt or to save the world for democracy. It is a priori difficult to conceive—and a fortiori even more difficult for an anthropologist to conceive—of any human disposition that cannot be satisfied by war, or more correctly, that cannot be socially mobilized for its prosecution. Compassion, hate, generosity, shame, prestige, emulation, fear, contempt, envy, greed— ethnographically the energies that move men to fight are practically coterminous with the range of human motivations. And that by virtue of another common-place of anthropological and ordinary experience: that the reasons people fight are not the reasons wars take place.

If the reasons why millions of Americans fought in World War II were laid end to end, they would not account for the occurrence or the nature of that war. No more than from the mere fact of their fighting could one understand their reasons. For war is not a relation between individuals but between states (or other socially constituted polities), and people participate in them not in their capacities as individuals or as human beings but as social beings—and indeed not exactly that, but only in a specifically contextualized social capacity. "They're trying to kill me," Yossarian told him calmly. "No one's trying to kill you." "Then why are they shooting at me?" Yossarian might have had some relief from the answer of a Rousseau rather than a Clevinger. In a stunning passage of the *Social Contract,* Rousseau justifies the title some would give him as the true ancestor of anthropology by arguing the status of war as a phenomenon of *cultural* nature—precisely against the Hobbesian view of a war of every man against every man grounded in human nature. "War," Rousseau wrote, "is not a relation between man and man, but between State and State, and *individuals are enemies accidentally, not as men, nor even as citizens, but as soldiers;* not as members of their country but as its defenders. Finally, each State can have for enemies only other States, and not men; for between things disparate in nature there can be no real relation" (italics added).

The general point is that human needs and dispositions are not just realized, fulfilled, or expressed in war; they are mobilized. It is certain that a capacity for aggression can be, and often is, symbolically trained and unleashed. But aggression need not be present at all in a man bombing an unseen target in the jungle from a height of 25,000 feet, even as it is always so contingent on the cultural context that, as in the case of the ancient Hawaiians, an army of thousands, upon seeing one of their members suc-cessfully dragged off as a sacrifice to the enemy's gods, will suddenly drop its weapons and fly to the mountains. Aggression does not regulate social conflict, but social conflict does regulate aggression. Moreover, any number of different needs may be thus engaged, exactly because satisfaction does not depend on the formal character of the institution but on the meaning attributed to it. For men, emotions are symbolically orchestrated and fulfilled in social actions. As for the actions themselves, as social facts their appropriateness does not lie in their correspondence to human dispositions but in their relations to the cultural context: as an act of war is related to an international power structure, godless Communism, insolent nationalism, diminishing capital funds, and the national distribution of oil.

Is violence an act of aggression, generosity a sign of "altruism"? Ethnographers of Melanesia as well as psychoanalysts of America will readily testify that aggression is often satisfied by making large and unrequited gifts. For as the Eskimo also say, "Gifts make slaves, as whips make dogs." On the other hand, a person may well hit another out of a true concern for the latter's welfare. One man's altruism becomes some child's sore behind; and, "Believe me, I'm doing this for your own good. It hurts me more than it hurts you." There is, in human affairs, a motivational arbitrariness of the social sign that runs parallel to, in fact is due to, Saussure's famous referential arbitrariness of the linguistic sign. Any given psychological disposition is able to take on an indefinite set of institutional realizations. We war on the playing fields of Ann Arbor, express sexuality by painting a picture, even indulge our aggressions and commit mayhem by writing books and giving lectures. Conversely, it is impossible to say in advance what needs may be realized by any given social activity. That is why Ruth Benedict, upon examining diverse patterns of culture, came to the conclusion that one cannot define a given social domain by a characteristic human motive, such as economics by the drive to accumulate wealth or politics by the quest for power. The act of exchange? It may well find inspiration in a hedonistic greed, but just as well in pity, aggression, dominance, love, honor, or duty.

"Pleasure" (or "satisfaction," or "utility") is not a natural phenomenon like the "five senses" of the physical organism. For every man it is determined by the social medium in which he lives; and consequently when it is adopted as a tool of analysis or a term of explanation of that social order, its adoption means the assumption in advance of all that social fabric of which an explanation is being sought. We hold this truth to be self-evident, that men who live by democracy, or by capital, will find in it their happiness, and that is all that is self-evident (Ayres 1944, p. 75).

In sum, the sociobiological reasoning from evolutionary phylogeny to social morphology is interrupted by culture. One could be persuaded to accept the more dubious or unproved assertions at the base of this logical chain; for example, that human emotional dispositions are genetically controlled and that the genetic controls were sedimented by adaptive processes at a time beyond memory. It still would not follow that the constraints of the biological base "orchestrate our behavioral responses" and account thereby for the present social arrangements of men. For between the basic drives that may be attributed to human nature and the social structures of human culture there enters a critical indeterminacy. The same human motives appear in different cultural forms, and different motives appear in the same forms. A fixed correspondence being lacking between the character of society and the human character, there can be no biological determinism.

Culture is the essential condition of this freedom of the human order from emotional or motivational necessity. Men interact in the terms of a system of meanings, attributed to persons and the objects of their existence, but precisely as these attributes are symbolic they cannot be dis-

covered in the intrinsic properties of the things to which they refer. The process rather is one of valuation of certain "objective" properties. An animal stands as an ancestor, and even so the son of a man's brother may be one of the clan of the ancestor's descendants while the son of his sister is an outsider, and perhaps, an enemy. Yet if matrilineal descent were deemed salient, all this would be reversed and the sister's son not a stranger but one's own proper heir. For the inhabitants of a Polynesian island, the sea is a "higher" social element than the land and the trade winds blowing from east to west likewise are conceived to proceed from "above" to "below." Accordingly, a house is oriented with its sacred sides toward the east and toward the sea, and only men who are of the appropriate chiefly descent should build these sides, which once finished will be the domestic domain of a man and his senior sons, who relative to the women of the family are "chiefly." By the same token, only the men will fish on the deep sea or cultivate in the higher land; whereas, their women work exclusively in the village and inside the reef, that is, the land side of the sea. The social arrangements are constructed on a meaningful logic, which in fact constitutes a human world out of an "objective" one which can offer to the former a variety of possible distinctions but no necessary significations. Thus, while the human world depends on the senses, and the whole panoply of organic characteristics supplied by biological evolution, its freedom from biology consists in just the capacity to give these their own sense.

In the symbolic event, a radical discontinuity is introduced between culture and nature. The isomorphism between the two required by the sociobiological thesis does not exist. The symbolic system of culture is not just an expression of human nature, but has a form and dynamic consistent with its properties as meaningful, which make it rather an intervention in nature. Culture is not ordered by the primitive emotions of the hypothalmus; it is the emotions which are organized by culture. We have not to deal, therefore, with a biological sequence of events proceeding from the genotype to the social type by way of a phenotype already programmed for social behavior by natural selection. The structure of determinations is a hierarchical one set the other way round: a meaningful system of the world and human experience that was already in existence before any of the current human participants were born, and that from birth engages their natural dispositions as the instruments of a symbolic project. If thus necessary to the symbolic function, these dispositions are in the same measure insufficient to an anthropological explanation since they cannot specify the cultural content of any human social order.

(The proposition that human emotions are culturally constituted, although here stated synchronically, as a recurrent fact of social life could also be extended phylogenetically. As Clifford Geertz [1973] has so effectively argued, to say that a given human disposition is "innate" is not to deny that it was also culturally produced. The biology of mankind has been shaped by culture, which is itself considerably older than the human species as we know it. Culture was developed in the hominid line about three million years ago. The modern species of man, *Homo sapiens,* originated and gained ascendancy about one hundred thousand years ago. It is reasonable to suppose that the dispositions we observe in modern man, and notably the capacity—indeed, the necessity—to organize and define these dispositions symbolically, are effects of a prolonged cultural selection. "Not only ideas," Geertz writes, "but emotions too, are cultural artifacts in man" [ibid., p. 81]. When the full implications of this simple but powerful argument are finally drawn, a great deal of what passes today for the biological "basis" of human behavior will be better understood as the cultural mediation of the organism.)

We can see now that the theoretical demand of sociobiology for an isomorphism of behavioral traits and social relations requires an empirical procedure that is equally erroneous. Sociobiology is compelled to take a naive behaviorist view of human social acts. Observing war-

fare, the sociobiologist concludes he is in the presence of an underlying aggression. Seeing an act of food sharing, he knows it as a disposition toward altruism. For him, the appearance of a social fact is the same thing as its motivation; he immediately places the first within a category of the second. Yet the understanding must remain as superficial as the method, since for people, these are not simply acts but meaningful acts. As for the acts, their cultural reasons for being lie elsewhere, even as the participants' reasons for doing may betray all the appearances.

By a roundabout way we thus return to the true issue in anthropomorphic terminology, for the error in metaphorically assimilating cultural forms to animal behaviors is the same as is involved in translating the contents of social relations in terms of their motivations. Both are procedures of what Sartre (1963) calls "the terror." Sartre applies the phrase to "vulgar Marxist" reductions of superstructural facts to infrastructural determinations, art for example to economics, such that Valéry's poetry becomes "a species of bourgeois idealism"; but it will do as well for the analogous reductions to the human species favored by the vulgar sociobiology. To speak of World War II, the sporadic combats between Australian bands or New Guinea headhunting as acts of aggression or territoriality is likewise an "inflexible refusal to differentiate," a program of elimination whose aim is "total assimilation at the least possible cost." In a similar way, it dissolves the autonomous and variable cultural contents beyond all hope of recovering them. The method consists of taking the concrete properties of an act, such as war, the actual character of World War II or Vietnam, as merely an ostensible appearance. The real truth of such events lies elsewhere; essentially, they are "aggression." But note that in so doing, one provides causes—"aggression," "sexuality," "egotism," etc.—which themselves have the appearance of being basic and fundamental but are in reality abstract and indeterminate. Meanwhile, in this resolution of the concrete instance to an abstract reason, everything distinctively cultural about the act has been allowed to escape. We can never get back to its empirical specifications—who actually fights whom, where, when, how, and why—because all these properties have been dissolved in the biological characterization. It is, as Sartre says, "a bath of sulphuric acid." To attribute any or all human wars, dominance hierarchies, or the like to human aggressiveness is a kind of bargain made with reality in which an understanding of the phenomenon is gained at the cost of everything we know about it. We have to suspend our comprehension of what it is. But a theory ought to be judged as much by the ignorance it demands as by the knowledge it purports to afford. Between "aggression" and Vietnam, "sexuality" and cross-cousin marriage, "reciprocal altruism" and the exchange rate of red shell neck-laces, biology offers us merely an enormous intellectual void. Its place can be filled only by a theory of the nature and dynamics of culture as a meaningful system. Within the void left by biology lies the whole of anthropology.

## REFERENCES CITED

AYRES, CLARENCE.
  1944.  *The theory of economic progress.* Chapel Hill: University of North Carolina Press.
GEERTZ, CLIFFORD.
  1973.  *The interpretation of cultures.* New York: Basic Books.
SARTRE, JEAN-PAUL.
  1963.  *Search for a method.* New York: Vintage Books.

# 3

# THE IMPACT OF THE CONCEPT OF CULTURE ON THE CONCEPT OF MAN

*Clifford Geertz*

*In this article, cultural anthropologist Clifford Geertz argues that humans cannot be defined by a concept of stratified layers, with biology at the bottom overlaid by culture at the top. Culture is not, according to Geertz, a veneer covering people's biological nature. Instead, human beings can be understood only if biology and culture are looked on as part of a single human system. Biology makes culture possible, but culture affected the course of human biological evolution. Synthesized into a single system, both serve to define humanity.*

## I

Toward the end of his recent study of the ideas used by tribal peoples, *La Pensée Sauvage,* the French anthropologist, Lévi-Strauss, remarks that scientific explanation does not consist, as we have been led to imagine, in the reduction of the complex to the simple. Rather, it consists, he says, in a substitution of a complexity more intelligible for one which is less. So far as the study of man is concerned, one may go even farther, I think, and argue that explanation often consists of substituting complex pictures for simple ones while striving somehow to retain the persuasive clarity that went with the simple ones.

Elegance remains, I suppose, a general scientific ideal; but in the social sciences, it is very often in departures from that ideal that truly creative developments occur. Scientific advancement commonly consists in a progressive complication of what once seemed a beautifully simple set of notions but now seems an unbearably simplistic one. It is after this sort of disenchantment occurs that intelligibility, and thus explanatory power, comes to rest on the possibility of substituting the involved but comprehensible for the involved but incomprehensible to which Lévi-Strauss refers. Whitehead once offered to the natural sciences the maxim: "Seek simplicity and distrust it"; to the social sciences he might well have offered "Seek complexity and order it."

Certainly, the study of culture has developed as though this maxim were being followed. The rise of a scientific concept of culture amounted to, or at least was connected with, the overthrow of the view of human nature dominant in the Enlightenment—a view that, whatever else may be said for or against it, was both clear and simple—and its replacement by a view not only more complicated but enormously less clear. The attempt to clarify it, to reconstruct an intelligible account of what man is, has underlain scientific thinking about culture ever since. Having sought complexity and, on a scale grander than they ever imagined, found it, anthropologists became entangled in a tortuous effort to order it. And the end is not yet in sight.

The Enlightenment view of man was, of course, that he was wholly of a piece with nature and shared in the general uniformity of composition which natural science, under Bacon's urging and Newton's guidance, had discovered there. There is, in brief, a human nature as regularly organized, as thoroughly invariant, and as marvelously simple as Newton's universe. Perhaps some of its laws are different, but there *are* laws; perhaps some of its immutability is ob-

scured by the trappings of local fashion, but it *is* immutable.

A quotation that Lovejoy (whose magisterial analysis I am following here) gives from an Enlightenment historian, Mascou, presents the position with the useful bluntness one often finds in a minor writer:

> The stage setting [in different times and places] is, indeed, altered, the actors change their garb and their appearance; but their inward motions arise from the same desires and passions of men, and produce their effects in the vicissitudes of kingdoms and peoples.[1]

Now, this view is hardly one to be despised; nor, despite my easy references a moment ago to "overthrow," can it be said to have disappeared from contemporary anthropological thought. The notion that men are men under whatever guise and against whatever backdrop has not been replaced by "other mores, other beasts."

Yet, cast as it was, the Enlightenment concept of the nature of human nature had some much less acceptable implications, the main one being that, to quote Lovejoy himself this time, "anything of which the intelligibility, verifiability, or actual affirmation is limited to men of a special age, race, temperament, tradition or condition is [in and of itself] without truth or value, or at all events without importance to a reasonable man."[2] The great, vast variety of differences among men, in beliefs and values, in customs and institutions, both over time and from place to place, is essentially without significance in defining his nature. It consists of mere accretions, distortions even, overlaying and obscuring what is truly human—the constant, the general, the universal—in man.

---

[1] Arthur O. Lovejoy, *Essays in the History of Ideas* (New York: G. P. Putnam's Sons, Capricorn Books, 1960), p. 173. © 1948 by The Johns Hopkins Press.

[2] *Ibid.*, p. 80.

Thus, in a passage now notorious, Dr. Johnson saw Shakespeare's genius to lie in the fact that "his characters are not modified by the customs of particular places, unpractised by the rest of the world; by the peculiarities of studies or professions, which can operate upon but small numbers; or by the accidents of transient fashions or temporary opinions."[3] And Racine regarded the success of his plays on classical themes as proof that "the taste of Paris . . . conforms to that of Athens; my spectators have been moved by the same things which, in other times, brought tears to the eyes of the most cultivated classes of Greece."[4]

The trouble with this kind of view, aside from the fact that it sounds comic coming from someone as profoundly English as Johnson or as French as Racine, is that the image of a constant human nature independent of time, place, and circumstance, of studies and professions, transient fashions and temporary opinions, may be an illusion, that what man is may be so entangled with where he is, who he is, and what he believes that it is inseparable from them. It is precisely the consideration of such a possibility that led to the rise of the concept of culture and the decline of the uniformitarian view of man. Whatever else modern anthropology asserts—and it seems to have asserted almost everything at one time or another—it is firm in the conviction that men unmodified by the customs of particular places do not in fact exist, have never existed, and most important, could not in the very nature of the case exist. There is, there can be, no backstage where we can go to catch a glimpse of Mascou's actors as "real persons" lounging about in street clothes, disengaged from their profession, displaying with artless candor their spontaneous desires and unprompted passions. They may change their roles, their styles of acting, the dramas in which

they play; but—as Shakespeare himself of course remarked—they are always performing.

This circumstance makes the drawing of a line between what is natural, universal, and constant in man and what is conventional, local, and variable extraordinarily difficult. In fact, it suggests that to draw such a line is to falsify the human situation, or at least to misrender it seriously.

Consider Balinese trance. The Balinese fall into extreme dissociated states in which they perform all sorts of spectacular activities—biting off the heads of living chickens, stabbing themselves with daggers, throwing themselves wildly about, speaking with tongues, performing miraculous feats of equilibration, mimicking sexual intercourse, eating feces, and so on—rather more easily and much more suddenly than most of us fall asleep. Trance states are a crucial part of every ceremony. In some, fifty or sixty people may fall, one after the other ("like a string of firecrackers going off," as one observer puts it), emerging anywhere from five minutes to several hours later, totally unaware of what they have been doing and convinced, despite the amnesia, that they have had the most extraordinary and deeply satisfying experience a man can have. What does one learn about human nature from this sort of thing and from the thousand similarly peculiar things anthropologists discover, investigate, and describe? That the Balinese are peculiar sorts of beings, South Sea Martians? That they are just the same as we at base, but with some peculiar, but really incidental, customs we do not happen to have gone in for? That they are innately gifted or even instinctively driven in certain directions rather than others? Or that human nature does not exist and men are pure and simply what their culture makes them?

It is among such interpretations as these, all unsatisfactory, that anthropology has attempted to find its way to a more viable concept of man, one in which culture, and the variability of culture, would be taken into account rather than written off as caprice and prejudice and yet, at

---

[3] "Preface to Shakespeare," *Johnson on Shakespeare* (London: Oxford University Press, 1931), pp. 11–12.

[4] From the Preface to *Iphigénie.*

the same time, one in which the governing principle of the field, "the basic unity of mankind," would not be turned into an empty phrase. To take the giant step away from the uniformitarian view of human nature is, so far as the study of man is concerned, to leave the Garden. To entertain the idea that the diversity of custom across time and over space is not a mere matter of garb and appearance, of stage settings and comedic masques, is to entertain also the idea that humanity is as various in its essence as it is in its expression. And with that reflection some well-fastened philosophical moorings are loosed and an uneasy drifting into perilous waters begins.

Perilous, because if one discards the notion that Man, with a capital "M," is to be looked for "behind," "under," or "beyond" his customs and replaces it with the notion that he, uncapitalized, is to be looked for "in" them, one is in some danger of losing sight of him altogether. Either he dissolves, without residue, into his time and place, a child and perfect captive of his age, or he becomes a conscripted soldier in a vast Tolstoian army, engulfed in one or another of the terrible historical determinisms with which we have been plagued from Hegel forward. We have had, and to some extent still have, both of these aberrations in the social sciences—one marching under the banner of cultural relativism, the other under that of cultural evolution. But we also have had, and more commonly, attempts to avoid them by seeking in culture patterns themselves the defining elements of a human existence which, although not constant in expression, are yet distinctive in character.


II

Attempts to locate man amid the body of his customs have taken several directions, adopted diverse tactics; but they have all, or virtually all, proceeded in terms of a single overall intellectual strategy: what I will call, so as to have a stick to beat it with, the "stratigraphic" conception of the relations between biological, psychological, social, and cultural factors in human life. In this conception, man is a composite of "levels," each superimposed upon those beneath it and underpinning those above it. As one analyzes man, one peels off layer after layer, each such layer being complete and irreducible in itself, revealing another, quite different sort of layer underneath. Strip off the motley forms of culture and one finds the structural and functional regularities of social organization. Peel off these in turn and one finds the underlying psychological factors— "basic needs" or what-have-you—that support and make them possible. Peel off psychological factors and one is left with the biological foundations—anatomical, physiological, neurological —of the whole edifice of human life.

The attraction of this sort of conceptualization, aside from the fact that it guaranteed the established academic disciplines their independence and sovereignty, was that it seemed to make it possible to have one's cake and eat it. One did not have to assert that man's culture was all there was to him in order to claim that it was, nonetheless, an essential and irreducible, even a paramount ingredient in his nature. Cultural facts could be interpreted against the background of noncultural facts without either dissolving them into that background or dissolving that background into them. Man was a hierarchically stratified animal, a sort of evolutionary deposit, in whose definition each level—organic, psychological, social, and cultural—had an assigned and incontestable place. To see what he really was, we had to superimpose findings from the various relevant sciences —anthropology, sociology, psychology, biology —upon one another like so many patterns in a *moiré;* and when that was done, the cardinal importance of the cultural level, the only one distinctive to man, would naturally appear, as would what it had to tell us, in its own right, about what he really was. For the eighteenth-century image of man as the naked reasoner that appeared when he took his cultural costumes off, the anthropology of the late nineteenth and early twentieth centuries substituted the image of man as the transfigured animal that appeared when he put them on.

At the level of concrete research and specific analysis, this grand strategy came down, first, to a hunt for universals in culture, for empirical uniformities that, in the face of the diversity of customs around the world and over time, could be found everywhere in about the same form, and, second, to an effort to relate such universals, once found, to the established constants of human biology, psychology, and social organization. If some customs could be ferreted out of the cluttered catalogue of world culture as common to all local variants of it, and if these could then be connected in a determinate manner with certain invariant points of reference on the subcultural levels, then at least some progress might be made toward specifying which cultural traits are essential to human existence and which merely adventitious, peripheral, or ornamental. In such a way, anthropology could determine cultural dimensions of a concept of man commensurate with the dimensions provided, in a similar way, by biology, psychology, or sociology.

In essence, this is not altogether a new idea. The notion of a *consensus gentium* (a consensus of all mankind)—the notion that there are some things that all men will be found to agree upon as right, real, just, or attractive and that these things are, therefore, in fact right, real, just, or attractive—was present in the Enlightenment and probably has been present in some form or another in all ages and climes. It is one of those ideas that occur to almost anyone sooner or later. Its development in modern anthropology, however—beginning with Clark Wissler's elaboration in the nineteen-twenties of what he called "the universal cultural pattern," through Bronislaw Malinowski's presentation of a list of "universal institutional types" in the early forties, up to G. P. Murdock's elaboration of a set of "common-denominators of culture" during and since World War II—added something new. It added the notion that, to quote Clyde Kluck-

hohn, perhaps the most persuasive of the *consensus gentium* theorists, "some aspects of culture take their specific forms solely as a result of historical accidents; others are tailored by forces which can properly be designated as universal."[5] With this, man's cultural life is split in two: part of it is, like Mascou's actors' garb, independent of men's Newtonian "inward motions"; part is an emanation of those motions themselves. The question that then arises is, Can this halfway house between the eighteenth and twentieth centuries really stand?

Whether it can or not depends on whether the dualism between empirically universal aspects of culture rooted in subcultural realities and empirically variable aspects not so rooted can be established and sustained. And this, in turn, demands (1) that the universals proposed be substantial ones and not empty categories; (2) that they be specifically grounded in particular biological, psychological, or sociological processes, not just vaguely associated with "underlying realities"; and (3) that they can convincingly be defended as core elements in a definition of humanity in comparison with which the much more numerous cultural particularities are of clearly secondary importance. On all three of these counts it seems to me that the *consensus gentium* approach fails; rather than moving toward the essentials of the human situation, it moves away from it.

The reason the first of these requirements—that the proposed universals be substantial ones and not empty or near empty categories—has not been met is that it cannot. There is a logical conflict between asserting that, say, "religion," "marriage," or "property" are empirical universals and giving them very much in the way of specific content, for to say that they are empirical universals is to say that they have the same content, and to say they have the same content is to fly in the face of the undeniable fact that they do not. If one defines religion generally and

[5]A. L. Kroeber (ed.), *Anthropology Today* (Chicago: University of Chicago Press, 1953), p. 516.

indeterminately—as man's most fundamental orientation to reality, for example—then one cannot at the same time assign to that orientation a highly circumstantial content, for clearly what composes the most fundamental orientation to reality among the transported Aztecs, lifting pulsing hearts torn live from the chests of human sacrifices toward the heavens, is not what comprises it among the stolid Zuni, dancing their great mass supplications to the benevolent gods of rain. The obsessive ritualism and unbuttoned polytheism of the Hindus expresses a rather different view of what the really real is really like from the uncompromising monotheism and austere legalism of Sunni Islam. Even if one does try to get down to less abstract levels and assert, as Kluckhohn did, that a concept of the afterlife is universal or, as Malinowski did, that a sense of Providence is universal, the same contradiction haunts one. To make the generalization about an afterlife stand up alike for the Confucians and the Calvinists, the Zen Buddhists and the Tibetan Buddhists, one has to define it in most general terms, indeed—so general, in fact, that whatever force it seems to have virtually evaporates. So, too, with any notion of a "sense of Providence," which can include under its wing both Navaho notions about the relations of gods to men and Trobriand ones. And as with religion, so with "marriage," "trade," and all the rest of what A. L. Kroeber aptly called "fake universals," down to so seemingly tangible a matter as "shelter." That everywhere people mate and produce children, have some sense of mine and thine, and protect themselves in one fashion or another from rain and sun are neither false nor, from some points of view, unimportant; but they are hardly very much help in drawing a portrait of man that will be a true and honest likeness and not an untenanted "John Q. Public" sort of cartoon.

My point, which should be clear and I hope will become even clearer in a moment, is not that there are no generalizations that can be made about man as man, save that he is a most various animal, or that the study of culture has nothing

to contribute toward the uncovering of such generalizations. My point is that such generalizations are not to be discovered through a Baconian search for cultural universals, a kind of public-opinion polling of the world's peoples in search of a *consensus gentium* that does not in fact exist, and, further, that the attempt to do so leads to precisely the sort of relativism the whole approach was expressly designed to avoid. "Zuñi culture prizes restraint," Kluckhohn writes; "Kwakiutl culture encourages exhibitionism on the part of the individual These are contrasting values, but in adhering to them the Zuñi and Kwakiutl show their allegiance to a universal value; the prizing of the distinctive norms of one's culture."[6] This is sheer evasion, but it is only more apparent, not more evasive, than discussions of cultural universals in general. What, after all, does it avail us to say, with Herskovits, that "morality is a universal, and so is enjoyment of beauty, and some standard for truth," if we are forced in the very next sentence, as he is, to add that "the many forms these concepts take are but products of the particular historical experience of the societies that manifest them"?[7] Once one abandons uniformitarianism, even if, like the *consensus gentium* theorists, only partially and uncertainly, relativism is a genuine danger; but it can be warded off only by facing directly and fully the diversities of human culture, the Zuñi's restraint and the Kwakiutl's exhibitionism, and embracing them within the body of one's concept of man, not by gliding past them with vague tautologies and forceless banalities.

Of course, the difficulty of stating cultural universals which are at the same time substantial also hinders fulfilment of the second requirement facing the *consensus gentium* approach, that of grounding such universals in particular

---

[6]Clyde Kluckhohn, *Culture and Behavior* (New York: Free Press of Glencoe, a division of The Macmillan Co., 1962), p. 280.

[7]Melville J. Herskovits, *Cultural Anthropology* (New York: Alfred A. Knopf, Inc., 1955), p. 364.

biological, psychological, or sociological processes. But there is more to it than that: the "stratigraphic" conceptualization of the relationships between cultural and non-cultural factors hinders such a grounding even more effectively. Once culture, psyche, society, and organism have been converted into separate scientific "levels," complete and autonomous in themselves, it is very hard to bring them back together again.

The most common way of trying to do so is through the utilization of what are called "invariant points of reference." These points are to be found, to quote one of the most famous statements of this strategy—the "Toward a Common Language for the Areas of the Social Sciences" memorandum produced by Talcott Parsons, Kluckhohn, O. H. Taylor, and others in the early forties—

in the nature of social systems, in the biological and psychological nature of the component individuals, in the external situations in which they live and act, in the necessity of coordination in social systems. In [culture] ... these "foci" of structure are never ignored. They must in some way be "adapted to" or "taken account of."

Cultural universals are conceived to be crystallized responses to these unevadable realities, institutionalized ways of coming to terms with them.

Analysis consists, then, of matching assumed universals to postulated underlying necessities, attempting to show there is some goodness of fit between the two. On the social level, reference is made to such irrefragable facts as that all societies, in order to persist, must reproduce their membership or allocate goods and services, hence the universality of some form of family or some form of trade. On the psychological level, recourse is had to basic needs like personal growth—hence the ubiquity of educational institutions—or to panhuman problems, like the Oedipal predicament—hence the ubiquity of

punishing gods and nurturant goddesses. Biologically, there is metabolism and health; culturally, dining customs and curing procedures. And so on. The tack is to look at underlying human requirements of some sort or other and then to try to show that those aspects of culture that are universal are, to use Kluckhohn's figure again, "tailored" by these requirements.

The problem here is, again, not so much whether in a general way this sort of congruence exists but whether it is more than a loose and indeterminate one. It is not difficult to relate some human institutions to what science (or common sense) tells us are requirements for human existence, but it is very much more difficult to state this relationship in an unequivocal form. Not only does almost any institution serve a multiplicity of social, psychological, and organic needs (so that to say that marriage is a mere reflex of the social need to reproduce, or that dining customs are a reflex of metabolic necessities, is to court parody), but there is no way to state in any precise and testable way the interlevel relationships that are conceived to hold. Despite first appearances, there is no serious attempt here to apply the concepts and theories of biology, psychology, or even sociology to the analysis of culture (and, of course, not even a suggestion of the reverse exchange) but merely a placing of supposed facts from the cultural and subcultural levels side by side so as to induce a vague sense that some kind of relationship between them—an obscure sort of "tailoring"—obtains. There is no theoretical integration here at all but a mere correlation, and that intuitive, of separate findings. With the levels approach, we can never, even by invoking "invariant points of reference," construct genuine functional interconnections between cultural and non-cultural factors, only more or less persuasive analogies, parallelisms, suggestions, and affinities.

However, even if I am wrong (as, admittedly, many anthropologists would hold) in claiming that the *consensus gentium* approach can produce neither substantial universals nor specific connections between cultural and non-cultural phenomena to explain them, the question still remains whether such universals should be taken as the central elements in the definition of man, whether a lowest common denominator view of humanity is what we want anyway. This is, of course, now a philosophical question, not as such a scientific one; but the notion that the essence of what it means to be human is most clearly revealed in those features of human culture that are universal rather than in those that are distinctive to this people or that is a prejudice we are not necessarily obliged to share. Is it in grasping such general facts—that man has everywhere some sort of "religion"—or in grasping the richness of this religious phenomenon or that—Balinese trance or Indian ritualism, Aztec human sacrifice or Zuni rain dancing —that we grasp him? Is the fact that "marriage" is universal (if it is) as penetrating a comment on what we are as the facts concerning Himalayan polyandry, or those fantastic Australian marriage rules, or the elaborate bride-price systems of Bantu Africa? The comment that Cromwell was the most typical Englishman of his time precisely in that he was the oddest may be relevant in this connection, too: it may be in the cultural particularities of people—in their oddities—that some of the most instructive revelations of what it is to be generically human are to be found; and the main contribution of the science of anthropology to the construction—or reconstruction—of a concept of man may then lie in showing us how to find them.


## III

The major reason why anthropologists have shied away from cultural particularities when it came to a question of defining man and have taken refuge instead in bloodless universals is that, faced as they are with the enormous variation in human behavior, they are haunted by a fear of historicism, of becoming lost in a whirl of cultural relativism so convulsive as to deprive them of any fixed bearings at all. Nor has there not been some occasion for such a fear: Ruth Benedict's *Patterns of Culture,* probably the most popular book in anthropology ever published in this country, with its strange conclusion that anything one group of people is inclined toward doing is worthy of respect by another, is perhaps only the most outstanding example of the awkward positions one can get into by giving oneself over rather too completely to what Marc Bloch called "the thrill of learning singular things." Yet the fear is a bogy. The notion that unless a cultural phenomenon is empirically universal it cannot reflect anything about the nature of man is about as logical as the notion that because sickle-cell anemia is, fortunately, not universal it cannot tell us anything about human genetic processes. It is not whether phenomena are empirically common that is critical in science—else why should Becquerel have been so interested in the peculiar behavior of uranium?—but whether they can be made to reveal the enduring natural processes that underly them. Seeing heaven in a grain of sand is not a trick only poets can accomplish.

In short, we need to look for systematic relationships among diverse phenomena, not for substantive identities among similar ones. And to do that with any effectiveness, we need to replace the "stratigraphic" conception of the relations between the various aspects of human existence with a synthetic one; that is, one in which biological, psychological, sociological, and cultural factors can be treated as variables within unitary systems of analysis. The establishment of a common language in the social sciences is not a matter of mere co-ordination of terminologies or, worse yet, of coining artificial new ones; nor is it a matter of imposing a single set of categories upon the area as a whole. It is a matter of integrating different types of theories and concepts in such a way that one can formulate meaningful propositions embodying findings now sequestered in separate fields of study.

In attempting to launch such an integration from the anthropological side and to reach, thereby, an exacter image of man, I want to propose two ideas. The first of these is that culture is best seen not as complexes of concrete behavior patterns—customs, usages, traditions, habit clusters—as has, by and large been the case up to now, but as a set of control mechanisms—plans, recipes, rules, instructions (what computer engineers call "programs")—for the governing of behavior. The second is that man is precisely the animal most desperately dependent upon such extragenetic, outside-the-skin control mechanisms, such cultural programs, for ordering his behavior.

Neither of these ideas is entirely new, but a number of recent developments, both within anthropology and in other sciences (cybernetics, information theory, neurology, molecular genetics) have made them susceptible of more precise statement as well as lending them a degree of empirical support they did not previously have. And out of such reformulations of the concept of culture and of the role of culture in human life comes, in turn, a definition of man stressing not so much the empirical commonalities in his behavior, from place to place and time to time, but rather the mechanisms by whose agency the breadth and indeterminateness of his inherent capacities are reduced to the narrowness and specificity of his actual accomplishments. One of the most significant facts about us may finally be that we all begin with the natural equipment to live a thousand kinds of life but end in the end having lived only one.

The "control mechanism" view of culture begins with the assumption that human thought is basically both social and public—that its natural habitat is the house yard, the market place, and the town square. Thinking consists not of "happenings in the head" (though happenings there and elsewhere are necessary for it to occur) but of a traffic in what have been called, by G. H. Mead and others, significant symbols—words for the most part but also gestures, drawings, musical sounds, mechanical devices like clocks, or natural objects like jewels—anything, in fact, that is disengaged from its mere actuality and used to impose meaning upon experience. From the point of view of any particular individual, such symbols are largely given. He finds them already current in the community when he is born, and they remain, with some additions, subtractions, and partial alterations he may or may not have had a hand in, in circulation there after he dies. While he lives he uses them, or some of them, sometimes deliberately and with care, most often spontaneously and with ease, but always with the same end in view: to put a construction upon the events through which he lives, to orient himself within "the ongoing course of experienced things," to adopt a vivid phrase of John Dewey's.

Man is so in need of such symbolic sources of illumination to find his bearings in the world because the non-symbolic sort that are constitutionally ingrained in his body cast so diffused a light. The behavior patterns of lower animals are, at least to a much greater extent, given to them with their physical structure; genetic sources of information order their actions within much narrower ranges of variation, the narrower and more thoroughgoing the lower the animal. For man, what are innately given are extremely general response capacities, which, although they make possible far greater plasticity, complexity, and on the scattered occasions when everything works as it should, effectiveness of behavior, leave it much less precisely regulated. This, then, is the second face of our argument: Undirected by culture patterns—organized systems of significant symbols—man's behavior would be virtually ungovernable, a mere chaos of pointless acts and exploding emotions, his experience virtually shapeless. Culture, the accumulated totality of such patterns, is not just an ornament of human existence but—the principal basis of its specificity—an essential condition for it.

Within anthropology some of the most telling evidence in support of such a position comes from recent advances in our understanding of what used to be called the descent of man: the emergence of *Homo sapiens* out of his general primate background. Of these advances three are of critical importance: (1) the discarding of a sequential view of the relations between the physical evolution and the cultural development of man in favor of an overlap or interactive view; (2) the discovery that the bulk of the biological changes that produced modern man out of his most immediate progenitors took place in the central nervous system and most especially in the brain; (3) the realization that man is, in physical terms, an incomplete, an unfinished, animal; that what sets him off most graphically from non-men is less his sheer ability to learn (great as that is) than how much and what particular sorts of things he *has* to learn before he is able to function at all. Let me take each of these points in turn.

The traditional view of the relations between the biological and the cultural advance of man was that the former, the biological, was for all intents and purposes completed before the latter, the cultural, began. That is to say, it was again stratigraphic: Man's physical being evolved, through the usual mechanisms of genetic variation and natural selection, up to the point where his anatomical structure had arrived at more or less the status at which we find it today; then cultural development got underway. At some particular stage in his phylogenetic history, a marginal genetic change of some sort rendered him capable of producing and carrying culture, and thenceforth his form of adaptive response to environmental pressures was almost exclusively cultural rather than genetic. As he spread over the globe he wore furs in cold climates and loin cloths (or nothing at all) in warm ones; he didn't alter his innate mode of response to environmental temperature. He made weapons to extend his inherited predatory powers and cooked foods to render a wider range of them digestible. Man became man, the story continues, when, having crossed some mental Rubicon, he became able to transmit "knowledge, belief, law, morals, custom" (to quote the items of Sir Edward Tylor's classical definition of culture) to his descendents and his neighbors through teaching and to acquire them from his ancestors and his neighbors through learning. After that magical moment, the advance of the hominids depended almost entirely on cultural accumulation, on the slow growth of conventional practices, rather than, as it had for ages past, on physical organic change.

The only trouble is that such a moment does not seem to have existed. By the most recent estimates the transition to the cultural mode of life took the genus *Homo* over a million years to accomplish; and stretched out in such a manner, it involved not one or a handful of marginal genetic changes but a long, complex, and closely ordered sequence of them.

In the current view, the evolution of *Homo sapiens*—modern man—out of his immediate pre-*sapiens* background got definitively underway nearly two million years ago with the appearance of the now famous Australopithecines —the so-called ape men of southern and eastern Africa—and culminated with the emergence of *sapiens* himself only some one to two hundred thousand years ago. Thus, as at least elemental forms of cultural, or if you wish protocultural, activity (simple toolmaking, hunting, and so on) seem to have been present among some of the Australopithecines, there was an overlap of, as I say, well over a million years between the beginning of culture and the appearance of man as we know him today. The precise dates—which are tentative and which further research may alter in one direction or another—are not critical; what is critical is that there was an overlap and that it was a very extended one. The final phases (final to date, at any rate) of the phylogenetic history of man took place in the same grand geological era—the so-called Ice Age—as the initial phases of his cultural history. Men have birthdays, but man does not.

What this means is that culture, rather than being added on, so to speak, to a finished or virtually finished animal, was ingredient, and centrally ingredient, in the production of that animal itself. The slow, steady, almost glacial growth of culture through the Ice Age altered the balance of selection pressures for the evolving *Homo* in such a way as to play a major directive role in his evolution. The perfection of tools, the adoption of organized hunting and gathering practices, the beginnings of true family organization, the discovery of fire, and most critically, though it is as yet extremely difficult to trace it out in any detail, the increasing reliance upon systems of significant symbols (language, art, myth, ritual) for orientation, communication, and self-control all created for man a new environment to which he was then obliged to adapt. As culture, step by infinitesimal step, accumulated and developed, a selective advantage was given to those individuals in the population most able to take advantage of it—the effective hunter, the persistent gatherer, the adept toolmaker, the resourceful leader—until what had been a small-brained, protohuman *Homo australopithecus* became the large-brained fully human *Homo sapiens.* Between the cultural pattern, the body, and the brain, a positive feedback system was created in which each shaped the progress of the other, a system in which the interaction among increasing tool use, the changing anatomy of the hand, and the expanding representation of the thumb on the cortex is only one of the more graphic examples. By submitting himself to governance by symbolically mediated programs for producing artifacts, organizing social life, or expressing emotions, man determined, if unwittingly, the culminating stages of his own biological destiny. Quite literally, though quite inadvertently, he created himself.

Though, as I mentioned, there were a number of important changes in the gross anatomy of genus *Homo* during this period of his crystallization—in skull shape, dentition, thumb size, and so on—by far the most important and dramatic were those that evidently took place in the central nervous system; for this was the period when the human brain, and most particularly the forebrain, ballooned into its present top-heavy proportions. The technical problems are complicated and controversial here; but the main point is that though the Australopithecines had a torso and arm configuration not drasti-

cally different from our own, and a pelvis and leg formation at least well launched toward our own, they had cranial capacities hardly larger than those of the living apes—that is to say, about a third to a half of our own. What sets true men off most distinctly from protomen is apparently not over-all bodily form but complexity of nervous organization. The overlap period of cultural and biological change seems to have consisted in an intense concentration on neural development and perhaps associated refinements of various behaviors—of the hands, bipedal locomotion, and so on—for which the basic anatomical foundations—mobile shoulders and wrists, a broadened ilium, and so on—had already been securely laid. In itself, this is perhaps not altogether startling; but, combined with what I have already said, it suggests some conclusions about what sort of animal man is that are, I think, rather far not only from those of the eighteenth century but from those of the anthropology of only ten or fifteen years ago.

Most bluntly, it suggests that there is no such thing as a human nature independent of culture. Men without culture would not be the clever savages of Golding's *Lord of the Flies* thrown back upon the cruel wisdom of their animal instincts; nor would they be the nature's noblemen of Enlightenment primitivism or even, as classical anthropological theory would imply, intrinsically talented apes who had somehow failed to find themselves. They would be unworkable monstrosities with very few useful instincts, fewer recognizable sentiments, and no intellect: mental basket cases. As our central nervous system—and most particularly its crowning curse and glory, the neocortex—grew up in great part in interaction with culture, it is incapable of directing our behavior or organizing our experience without the guidance provided by systems of significant symbols. What happened to us in the Ice Age is that we were obliged to abandon the regularity and precision of detailed genetic control over our conduct for the flexibility and adaptability of a more generalized, though of course no less real, genetic control over it. To supply the additional information necessary to be able to act, we were forced, in turn, to rely more and more heavily on cultural sources—the accumulated fund of significant symbols. Such symbols are thus not mere expressions, instrumentalities, or correlates of our biological, psychological, and social existence; they are prerequisites of it. Without men, no culture, certainly; but equally, and more significantly, without culture, no men.

We are, in sum, incomplete or unfinished animals who complete or finish ourselves through culture—and not through culture in general but through highly particular forms of it: Dobuan and Javanese, Hopi and Italian, upper-class and lower-class, academic and commercial. Man's great capacity for learning, his plasticity, has often been remarked, but what is even more critical is his extreme dependence upon a certain sort of learning: the attainment of concepts, the apprehension and application of specific systems of symbolic meaning. Beavers build dams, birds build nests, bees locate food, baboons organize social groups, and mice mate on the basis of forms of learning that rest predominantly on the instructions encoded in their genes and evoked by appropriate patterns of external stimuli: physical keys inserted into organic locks. But men build dams or shelters, locate food, organize their social groups, or find sexual partners under the guidance of instructions encoded in flow charts and blueprints, hunting lore, moral systems, and aesthetic judgments: conceptual structures molding formless talents.

We live, as one writer has neatly put it, in an "information gap." Between what our body tells us and what we have to know in order to function, there is a vacuum we must fill ourselves, and we fill it with information (or misinformation) provided by our culture. The boundary between what is innately controlled and what is culturally controlled in human behavior is an ill-defined and wavering one. Some things are, for all intents and purposes, entirely controlled intrinsically: we need no more cultural guidance to learn how to breathe than a fish needs to learn how to swim. Others are almost certainly largely

cultural: we do not attempt to explain on a genetic basis why some men put their trust in centralized planning and others in the free market, though it might be an amusing exercise. Almost all complex human behavior is, of course, the vector outcome of the two. Our capacity to speak is surely innate; our capacity to speak English is surely cultural. Smiling at pleasing stimuli and frowning at unpleasing ones are surely in some degree genetically determined (even apes screw up their faces at noxious odors); but sardonic smiling and burlesque frowning are equally surely predominantly cultural, as is perhaps demonstrated by the Balinese definition of a madman as someone who, like an American, smiles when there is nothing to laugh at. Between the basic ground plans for our life that our genes lay down—the capacity to speak or to smile—and the precise behavior we in fact execute—speaking English in a certain tone of voice, smiling enigmatically in a delicate social situation—lies a complex set of significant symbols under whose direction we transform the first into the second, the ground plans into the activity.

Our ideas, our values, our acts, even our emotions, are, like our nervous system itself, cultural products—products manufactured, indeed, out of tendencies, capacities, and dispositions with which we were born, but manufactured none the less. Chartres is made of stone and glass. But it is not just stone and glass; it is a cathedral, and not only a cathedral, but a particular cathedral built at a particular time by certain members of a particular society. To understand what it means, to perceive it for what it is, you need to know rather more than the generic properties of stone and glass and rather more than what is common to all cathedrals. You need to understand also—and, in my opinion, most critically—the specific concepts of the relations between God, man, and architecture that, having governed its creation, it consequently embodies. It is no different with men: they, too, every last one of them, are cultural artifacts.

## IV

Whatever differences they may show, the approaches to the definition of human nature adopted by the Enlightenment and by classical anthropoloy have one thing in common: they are both basically typological. They endeavor to construct an image of man as a model, an archetype, a Platonic idea or an Aristotelian form, with respect to which actual men—you, me, Churchill, Hitler, and the Bornean headhunter —are but reflections, distortions, approximations. In the Enlightenment case, the elements of this essential type were to be uncovered by stripping the trappings of culture away from actual men and seeing what then was left—natural man. In classical anthropology, it was to be uncovered by factoring out the commonalities in culture and seeing what then appeared—consensual man. In either case, the result is the same as tends to emerge in all typological approaches to scientific problems generally: the differences among individuals and among groups of individuals are rendered secondary. Individuality comes to be seen as eccentricity, distinctiveness as accidental deviation from the only legitimate object of study for the true scientist: the underlying, unchanging, normative type. In such an approach, however elaborately formulated and resourcefully defended, living detail is drowned in dead stereotype: we are in quest of a metaphysical entity, Man with a capital "M," in the interests of which we sacrifice the empirical entity we in fact encounter, man with a small "m."

The sacrifice is, however, as unnecessary as it is unavailing. There is no opposition between general theoretical understanding and circumstantial understanding, between synoptic vision and a fine eye for detail. It is, in fact, by its power to draw general propositions out of particular phenomena that a scientific theory—indeed, science itself—is to be judged. If we want to discover what man amounts to, we can only find it in what men are: and what men are, above all other things, is various. It is in understanding that variousness—its range, its nature, its basis,

and its implications—that we shall come to construct a concept of human nature that, more than a statistical shadow and less than a primitivist dream, has both substance and truth.

It is here, to come round finally to my title, that the concept of culture has its impact on the concept of man. When seen as a set of symbolic devices for controlling behavior, extrasomatic sources of information, culture provides the link between what men are intrinsically capable of becoming and what they actually, one by one, in fact become. Becoming human is becoming individual, and we become individual under the guidance of cultural patterns, historically created systems of meaning in terms of which we give form, order, point, and direction to our lives. And the cultural patterns involved are not general but specific—not just "marriage" but a particular set of notions about what men and women are like, how spouses should treat one another, or who should properly marry whom; not just "religion" but belief in the wheel of karma, the observance of a month of fasting, or the practice of cattle sacrifice. Man is to be defined neither by his innate capacities alone, as the Enlightenment sought to do, nor by his actual behaviors alone, as much of contemporary social science seeks to do, but rather by the link between them, by the way in which the first is transformed into the second, his generic potentialities focused into his specific performances. It is in man's *career,* in its characteristic course, that we can discern, however dimly, his nature, and though culture is but one element in determining that course, it is hardly the least important. As culture shaped us as a single species— and is no doubt still shaping us—so too it shapes us as separate individuals. This, neither an unchanging subcultural self nor an established cross-cultural consensus, is what we really have in common.

Oddly enough—though on second thought, perhaps not so oddly—many of our subjects seem to realize this more clearly than we anthropologists ourselves. In Java, for example, where I have done much of my work, the people quite flatly say, "To be human is to be Javanese." Small children, boors, simpletons, the insane, the flagrantly immoral, are said to be *ndurung djawa,* "not yet Javanese." A "normal" adult capable of acting in terms of the highly elaborate system of etiquette, possessed of the delicate aesthetic perceptions associated with music, dance, drama, and textile design, responsive to the subtle promptings of the divine residing in the stillnesses of each individual's inward-turning consciousness, is *sampun djawa,* "already Javanese," that is, already human. To be human is not just to breathe; it is to control one's breathing, by yoga-like techniques, so as to hear in inhalation and exhalation the literal voice of God pronouncing His own name—*hu Allah.* It is not just to talk; it is to utter the appropriate words and phrases in the appropriate social situations in the appropriate tone of voice and with the appropriate evasive indirection. It is not just to eat; it is to prefer certain foods cooked in certain ways and to follow a rigid table etiquette in consuming them. It is not even just to feel but to feel certain quite distinctively Javanese (and essentially untranslatable) emotions— "patience," "detachment," "resignation," "respect."

To be human here is thus not to be Everyman; it is to be a particular kind of man, and of course men differ: "Other fields," the Javanese say, "other grasshoppers." Within the society, differences are recognized, too—the way a rice peasant becomes human and Javanese differs from the way a civil servant does. This is not a matter of tolerance and ethical relativism, for not all ways of being human are regarded as equally admirable by far; the way the local Chinese go about it is, for example, intensely dispraised. The point is that there are different ways; and to shift to the anthropologist's perspective now, it is in a systematic review and analysis of these—of the Plains Indian's bravura, the Hindu's obsessiveness, the Frenchman's rationalism, the Berber's anarchism, the American's optimism (to list a series of tags I should not like to have to defend as such)—that we will find out what it is, or can be, to be a man.

We must, in short, descend into detail, past the misleading tags, past the metaphysical types, past the empty similarities to grasp firmly the essential character of not only the various cultures but the various sorts of individuals within each culture if we wish to encounter humanity face to face. In this area, the road to the general, to the revelatory, simplicities of science lies through a concern with the particular, the circumstantial, the concrete, but a concern organized and directed in terms of the sort of theoretical analyses that I have touched upon— analyses of physical evolution, of the functioning of the nervous system, of social organization, of psychological process, of cultural patterning, and so on—and, most especially, in terms of the interplay among them. That is to say, the road lies, like any genuine quest, through a terrifying complexity.

"Leave him alone for a moment or two," Robert Lowell writes, not as one might suspect of the anthropologist but of that other eccentric inquirer into the nature of man, Nathaniel Hawthorne.

> Leave him alone for a moment or two,
> and you'll see him with his head
> bent down, brooding, brooding,
> eyes fixed on some chip,
> some stone, some common plant,
> the commonest thing,
> as if it were the clue.
> The disturbed eyes rise,
> furtive, foiled, dissatisfied
> from meditation on the true
> and insignificant.[8]

Bent over his own chips, stones, and common plants, the anthropologist broods, too, upon the true and insignificant, glimpsing in it, or so he thinks, fleetingly and insecurely, the disturbing, changeful image of himself.

---

[8]Reprinted from "Hawthorne," in *For the Union Dead,* by permission of Farrar, Straus, & Giroux, Inc., and Faber & Faber, Ltd., p. 39. Copyright © 1964 by Robert Lowell.

# LANGUAGE
# AND COMMUNICATION

ISSUE   The Sapir-Whorf hypothesis: Does language shape perception?

Communication is essential to social life. Group dwellers from insects to humans must exchange information about needs, dangers, and required activities if they are to work together effectively. Without this ability to coordinate their activities, members of groups would lose the adaptive advantages of social life in a confusion of disjointed acts.

Some systems of communication are inherited; individual organisms are born with the ability to send and receive a limited number of messages. African termites, for example, exchange information by emitting secretions that they lick from one another's bodies. Using this means, they can communicate information about threats to the colony or the need for the queen to lay more eggs, destined to become soldiers needed because of those lost to the predations of an anteater. Inherited systems of communication may be complex, but they are relatively inflexible. They can change only through the slow process of mutation and natural selection.

Learning has been the evolutionary answer to the problem of inflexible communication systems. If animals can learn new messages while they are alive, they can respond immediately to needs and threats without the loss of members. It is not surprising to discover that learning plays an important part in the communications systems of many animals, although for most, inheritance is still critical as well. Wolves, for example, inherit the tendency to mark pack territory with their urine. But they also learn the different urine scents of individual wolves so that the presence and identity of any number of animals can be signaled by this single medium.

Learning plays a central part in human communication. In the United States we learn that a car horn signals for our attention, that after shave lotion indicates attractiveness and cleanliness, that a smile means support, and that a Mercedes-Benz 450 SL means wealth. Even more important, we learn to produce and interpret a range of vocal sounds that permit us to exchange an almost endless variety of messages.

Language is the system of knowledge people use to generate and interpret speech, this system of vocal sounds. Language is the code by which all humans produce standardized speech sounds, arrange them in sequence, and assign meaning to them. Although we inherit the ability to acquire language, we do not inherit the particular sounds, arrangements, and meanings that it defines. These are learned.

Is language, however, as flexible as we make it out to be? Most people think of their language as a tool. They have thoughts they wish to express, and language is the handy medium by which to do so. Language is simply a way to classify natural reality, they feel, and to put it into a form that can be communicated. Yet once a language is learned, might not the way it represents experience affect how people perceive the things around them?

This is the thesis of two anthropologists, Edward Sapir and Benjamin Lee Whorf. Sapir and especially his student, Whorf, argued that there is a remarkable correlation between the way people speak and the way they perceive their worlds. And beyond this, Whorf argued that language actually shaped the way people could think about new experience. The orderliness of Newtonian physics arose in part, he argued, from the lineal nature of the English language. A Hopi Indian, whose language lacks this lineality, would be more at home with Einstein's relativity, a view of the world that still defies understanding by most lineal language speakers in the West.

The Sapir-Whorf hypothesis caused a great deal of interest in anthropology, linguistics, and psychology. A statement of the hypothesis appears in an article by Whorf included in this chapter. An application of the hypothesis is manifested by the work of Lee. There have been a number of critics of the hypothesis, however, and several anthropologists and psychologists have sought to test its implications cross-culturally. The article by Cole and Scribner at the end of this chapter reviews and assesses some of this work.

# 4

## THE RELATION OF HABITUAL THOUGHT AND BEHAVIOR TO LANGUAGE

*Benjamin Lee Whorf*

*Benjamin Lee Whorf was a student of Edward Sapir and became an authority on the Hopi Indian language among others. He was also a fire inspector and drew heavily on his work with fire victims for illustrative material. In this article, originally written in 1939 but published in 1941, Whorf argues that language correlates with perception and that it may actually determine the way people perceive reality. He notes, for example, that words often affect the way people decide to act. Employees at one factory, he discovered, would treat "full" gasoline drums with great care, but lacked respect for "empty" ones, despite the fact that the gasoline fumes in empty drums are much more volatile. The careless actions are precipitated by the lack of danger associated with the word "empty." Most of the article deals with the different way in which words and grammar relate to perception in Hopi and Standard European. Whorf also argues that the grammatical structure of these languages may promote or inhibit certain ways of thinking about the world.*

*Human beings do not live in the objective world alone, nor alone in the world of social activity as ordinarily understood, but are very much at the mercy of the particular language which has become the medium of expression for their society. It is quite an illusion to imagine that one adjusts to reality essentially without the use of language and that language is merely an incidental means of solving specific problems of communication or reflection. The fact of the matter is that the "real world" is to a large extent unconsciously built up on the language habits of the group. . . . We see and hear and otherwise experience very largely as we do because the language habits of our community predispose certain choices of interpretation.*

EDWARD SAPIR

There will probably be general assent to the proposition that an accepted pattern of using words is often prior to certain lines of thinking and forms of behavior, but he who assents often sees in such a statement nothing more than a platitudinous recognition of the hypnotic power of philosophical and learned terminology on the one hand or of catchwords, slogans, and rallying cries on the other. To see only thus far is to miss the point of one of the important interconnections which Sapir saw between language, culture, and psychology, and succinctly expressed in the introductory quotation. It is not so much in these special uses of language as in its constant ways of arranging data and its most ordinary everyday analysis of phenomena that we need to recognize the influence it has on other activities, cultural and personal.

## THE NAME OF THE SITUATION AS AFFECTING BEHAVIOR

I came in touch with an aspect of this problem before I had studied under Dr. Sapir, and in a field usually considered remote from linguistics. It was in the course of my professional work for a fire insurance company, in which I undertook the task of analyzing many hundreds of reports of circumstances surrounding the start of fires, and in some cases, of explosions. My analysis was directed toward purely physical conditions, such as defective wiring, presence or lack of air spaces between metal flues and woodwork, etc., and the results were presented in these terms. Indeed it was undertaken with no thought that any other significances would or could be revealed. But in due course it became evident that not only a physical situation *qua* physics, but the meaning of that situation to people, was sometimes a factor, through the behavior of the people, in the start of the fire. And this factor of meaning was clearest when it was a LINGUISTIC MEANING, residing in the name or the linguistic description commonly applied to the situation. Thus, around a storage of what are called "gasoline drums," behavior will tend to a certain type, that is, great care will be exercised; while around a storage of what are called "empty gasoline drums," it will tend to be different—careless, with little repression of smoking or of tossing cigarette stubs about. Yet the "empty" drums are perhaps the more dangerous, since they contain explosive vapor. Physically the situation is hazardous, but the linguistic analysis according to regular analogy must employ the word 'empty,' which inevitably

suggests lack of hazard. The word 'empty' is used in two linguistic patterns: (1) as a virtual synonym for 'null and void, negative, inert,' (2) applied in analysis of physical situations without regard to, e.g., vapor, liquid vestiges, or stray rubbish, in the container. The situation is named in one pattern (2) and the name is then "acted out" or "lived up to" in another (1), this being a general formula for the linguistic conditioning of behavior into hazardous forms.

In a wood distillation plant the metal stills were insulated with a composition prepared from limestone and called at the plant "spun limestone." No attempt was made to protect this covering from excessive heat or the contact of flame. After a period of use, the fire below one of the stills spread to the "limestone," which to everyone's great surprise burned vigorously. Exposure to acetic acid fumes from the stills had converted part of the limestone (calcium carbonate) to calcium acetate. This when heated in a fire decomposes, forming inflammable acetone. Behavior that tolerated fire close to the covering was induced by use of the name "limestone," which because it ends in "-stone" implies noncombustibility.

A huge iron kettle of boiling varnish was observed to be overheated, nearing the temperature at which it would ignite. The operator moved it off the fire and ran it on its wheels to a distance, but did not cover it. In a minute or so the varnish ignited. Here the linguistic influence is more complex; it is due to the metaphorical objectifying (of which more later) of "cause" as contact or the spatial juxtaposition of "things"—to analyzing the situation as 'on' versus 'off' the fire. In reality, the stage when the external fire was the main factor had passed; the overheating was now an internal process of convection in the varnish from the intensely heated kettle, and still continued when 'off' the fire.

An electric glow heater on the wall was little used, and for one workman had the meaning of a convenient coathanger. At night a watchman entered and snapped a switch, which action he verbalized as 'turning on the light.' No light appeared, and this result he verbalized as 'light is burned out.' He could not see the glow of the heater because of the old coat hung on it. Soon the heater ignited the coat, which set fire to the building.

A tannery discharged waste water containing animal matter into an outdoor settling basin partly roofed with wood and partly open. This situation is one that ordinarily would be verbalized as "pool of water." A workman had occasion to light a blowtorch near by, and threw his match into the water. But the decomposing waste matter was evolving gas under the wood cover, so that the setup was the reverse of "watery." An instant flare of flame ignited the woodwork, and the fire quickly spread into the adjoining building.

A drying room for hides was arranged with a blower at one end to make a current of air along the room and thence outdoors through a vent at the other end. Fire started at a hot bearing on the blower, which blew the flames directly into the hides and fanned them along the room, destroying the entire stock. This hazardous setup followed naturally from the term 'blower' with its linguistic equivalence to 'that which blows,' implying that its function necessarily is to 'blow.' Also its function is verbalized as 'blowing air for drying,' overlooking that it can blow other things, e.g., flames and sparks. In reality, a blower simply makes a current of air and can exhaust as well as blow. It should have been installed at the vent end to DRAW the air over the hides, then through the hazard (its own casing and bearings), and thence outdoors.

Beside a coal-fired melting pot for lead reclaiming was dumped a pile of "scrap lead"—a misleading verbalization, for it consisted of the lead sheets of old radio condensers, which still had paraffin paper between them. Soon the paraffin blazed up and fired the roof, half of which was burned off.

Such examples, which could be greatly multiplied, will suffice to show how the cue to a certain line of behavior is often given by the analogies of the linguistic formula in which the situation is spoken of, and by which to some degree it is analyzed, classified, and allotted its place in that world which is "to a large extent unconsciously built up on the language habits of the group." And we always assume that the linguistic analysis made by our group reflects reality better than it does.

## GRAMMATICAL PATTERNS AS INTERPRETATIONS OF EXPERIENCE

The linguistic material in the above examples is limited to single words, phrases, and patterns of limited range. One cannot study the behavioral compulsiveness of such material without suspecting a much more far-reaching compulsion from large-scale patterning of grammatical categories, such as plurality, gender and similar classifications (animate, inanimate, etc.), tenses, voices, and other verb forms, classifications of the type of "parts of speech," and the matter of whether a given experience is denoted by a unit morpheme, an inflected word, or a syntactical combination. A category such as number (singular vs. plural) is an attempted interpretation of a whole large order of experience, virtually of the world or of nature; it attempts to say how experience is to be segmented, what experience is to be called "one" and what "several." But the difficulty of appraising such a far-reaching influence is great because of its background character, because of the difficulty of standing aside from our own language, which is a habit and a cultural *non est disputandum,* and scrutinizing it objectively. And if we take a very dissimilar language, this language becomes a part of nature, and we even do to it what we have already done to nature. We tend to think in our own language in order to examine the exotic language. Or we find the task of unraveling the purely morphological intricacies so gigantic that it seems to absorb all else. Yet the problem, though difficult, is feasible; and the best approach is through an exotic language, for in its study we are at long last pushed willy-nilly out of our ruts. Then we find that the exotic language is a mirror held up to our own.

In my study of the Hopi language, what I now see as an opportunity to work on this problem was first thrust upon me before I was clearly aware of the problem. The seemingly endless task of describing the morphology did finally end. Yet it was evident, especially in the light of Sapir's lectures on Navaho, that the description of the LANGUAGE was far from complete. I knew for example the morphological formation of plurals, but not how to use plurals. It was evident that the category of plural in Hopi was not the same thing as in English, French, or German. Certain things that were plural in these languages were singular in Hopi. The phase of investigation which now began consumed nearly two more years.

The work began to assume the character of a comparison between Hopi and western European languages. It also became evident that even the grammar of Hopi bore a relation to Hopi culture, and the grammar of European tongues to our own "Western" or "European" culture. And it appeared that the interrelation brought in those large subsummations of experience by language, such as our own terms 'time,' 'space,' 'substance,' and 'matter.' Since, with respect to the traits compared, there is little difference between English, French, German, or other European languages with the POSSIBLE (but doubtful) exception of Balto-Slavic and non-Indo-European, I have lumped these languages into one group called SAE, or "Standard Average European."

That portion of the whole investigation here to be reported may be summed up in two questions: (1) Are our own concepts of 'time,' 'space,' and 'matter' given in substantially the same form by experience to all men, or are they in part conditioned by the structure of particular languages? (2) Are there traceable affinities between (a) cultural and behavioral norms and (b) large-scale linguistic patterns? (I should be the last to pretend that there is anything so definite as "a

correlation" between culture and language, and especially between ethnological rubrics such as 'agricultural, hunting,' etc., and linguistic ones like 'inflected,' 'synthetic,' or 'isolating.'[1] When I began the study, the problem was by no means so clearly formulated, and I had little notion that the answers would turn out as they did.

## PLURALITY AND NUMERATION IN SAE AND HOPI

In our language, that is SAE, plurality and cardinal numbers are applied in two ways: to real plurals and imaginary plurals. Or more exactly if less tersely: perceptible spatial aggregates and metaphorical aggregates. We say 'ten men' and also 'ten days.' Ten men either are or could be objectively perceived as ten, ten in one group perception[2] —ten men on a street corner, for instance. But 'ten days' cannot be objectively experienced. We experience only one day, today; the other nine (or even all ten) are something conjured up from memory or imagination. If 'ten days' be regarded as a group it must be as an "imaginary," mentally constructed group. Whence comes this mental pattern? Just as in the case of the fire-causing errors, from the fact that our language confuses the two different situations, has but one pattern for both. When we speak of 'ten steps forward, ten strokes on a bell,' or any similarly described cyclic sequence,

---

[1] We have plenty of evidence that this is not the case. Consider only the Hopi and the Ute, with languages that on the overt morphological and lexical level are as similar as, say, English and German. The idea of "correlation" between language and culture, in the generally accepted sense of correlation, is certainly a mistaken one.

[2] As we say, 'ten at the SAME TIME,' showing that in our language and thought we restate the fact of group perception in terms of a concept 'time,' the large linguistic component of which will appear in the course of this paper.

"times" of any sort, we are doing the same thing as with 'days.' CYCLICITY brings the response of imaginary plurals. But a likeness of cyclicity to aggregates is not unmistakably given by experience prior to language, or it would be found in all languages, and it is not.

Our AWARENESS of time and cyclicity does contain something immediate and subjective— the basic sense of "becoming later and later." But, in the habitual thought of us SAE people, this is covered under something quite different, which though mental should not be called subjective. I call it OBJECTIFIED, or imaginary, because it is patterned on the OUTER world. It is this that reflects our linguistic usage. Our tongue makes no distinction between numbers counted on discrete entities and numbers that are simply "counting itself." Habitual thought then assumes that in the latter the numbers are just as much counted on "something" as in the former. This is objectification. Concepts of time lose contact with the subjective experience of "becoming later" and are objectified as counted QUANTITIES, especially as lengths, made up of units as a length can be visibly marked off into inches. A 'length of time' is envisioned as a row of similar units, like a row of bottles.

In Hopi there is a different linguistic situation. Plurals and cardinals are used only for entities that form or can form an objective group. There are no imaginary plurals, but instead ordinals used with singulars. Such an expression as 'ten days' is not used. The equivalent statement is an operational one that reaches one day by a suitable count. 'They stayed ten days' becomes 'they stayed until the eleventh day' or 'they left after the tenth day.' 'Ten days is greater than nine days' becomes 'the tenth day is later than the ninth.' Our "length of time" is not regarded as a length but as a relation between two events in lateness. Instead of our linguistically promoted objectification of that datum of consciousness we call 'time,' the Hopi language has not laid down any pattern that would cloak the subjective "becoming later" that is the essence of time.

## NOUNS OF PHYSICAL QUANTITY IN SAE AND HOPI

We have two kinds of nouns denoting physical things: individual nouns, and mass nouns, e.g., 'water, milk, wood, granite, sand, flour, meat.' Individual nouns denote bodies with definite outlines: 'a tree, a stick, a man, a hill.' Mass nouns denote homogeneous continua without implied boundaries. The distinction is marked by linguistic form; e.g., mass nouns lack plurals,[3] in English drop articles, and in French take the partitive article *du, de la, des*. The distinction is more widespread in language than in the observable appearance of things. Rather few natural occurrences present themselves as unbounded extents; 'air' of course, and often 'water, rain, snow, sand, rock, dirt, grass.' We do not encounter 'butter, meat, cloth, iron, glass,' or most "materials" in such kind of manifestation, but in bodies small or large with definite outlines. The distinction is somewhat forced upon our description of events by an unavoidable pattern in language. It is so inconvenient in a great many cases that we need some way of individualizing the mass noun by further linguistic devices. This is partly done by names of body-types: 'stick of wood, piece of cloth, pane of glass, cake of soap'; also, and even more, by introducing names of containers though their contents be the real issue: 'glass of water, cup of coffee, dish of food, bag of flour, bottle of beer.' These very common container formulas, in which 'of' has an obvious, visually perceptible meaning ("contents"), influence our feeling about the less obvious type-body formulas: 'stick

---

[3]It is no exception to this rule of lacking a plural that a mass noun may sometimes coincide in lexeme with an individual noun that of course has a plural; e.g., 'stone' (no pl.) with 'a stone' (pl. 'stones'). The plural form denoting varieties, e.g., 'wines' is of course a different sort of thing from the true plural; it is a curious outgrowth from the SAE mass nouns, leading to still another sort of imaginary aggregates, which will have to be omitted from this paper.

of wood, lump of dough,' etc. The formulas are very similar: individual noun plus a similar relator (English 'of'). In the obvious case this relator denotes contents. In the inobvious one it "suggests" contents. Hence the 'lumps, chunks, blocks, pieces,' etc., seem to contain something, a "stuff," "substance," or "matter" that answers to the 'water,' 'coffee,' or 'flour' in the container formulas. So with SAE people the philosophic "substance" and "matter" are also the naïve idea; they are instantly acceptable, "common sense." It is so through linguistic habit. Our language patterns often require us to name a physical thing by a binomial that splits the reference into a formless item plus a form.

Hopi is again different. It has a formally distinguished class of nouns. But this class contains no formal subclass of mass nouns. All nouns have an individual sense and both singular and plural forms. Nouns translating most nearly our mass nouns still refer to vague bodies or vaguely bounded extents. They imply indefiniteness, but not lack, of outline and size. In specific statements, 'water' means one certain mass or quantity of water, not what we call "the substance water." Generality of statement is conveyed through the verb or predicator, not the noun. Since nouns are individual already, they are not individualized by either type-bodies or names of containers, if there is no special need to emphasize shape or container. The noun itself implies a suitable type-body or container. One says, not 'a glass of water' but *kəᐧyi* 'a water,' not 'a pool of water' but *paᐧhə*, [4] not 'a dish of cornflour' but *ŋəmni* 'a (quantity of) cornflour,' not 'a piece of meat' but *sikʷi* 'a meat.' The language has neither need for nor analogies on which to build the

concept of existence as a duality of formless item and form. It deals with formlessness through other symbols than nouns.

## PHASES OF CYCLES IN SAE AND HOPI

Such terms as 'summer, winter, September, morning, noon, sunset' are with us nouns, and have little formal linguistic difference from other nouns. They can be subjects or objects, and we say 'at sunset' or 'in winter' just as we say 'at a corner' or 'in an orchard.'[5] They are pluralized and numerated like nouns of physical objects, as we have seen. Our thought about the referents of such words hence becomes objectified. Without objectification, it would be a subjective experience of real time, i.e. of the consciousness of "becoming later and later"—simply a cyclic phase similar to an earlier phase in that ever-later-becoming duration. Only by imagination can such a cyclic phase be set beside another and another in the manner of a spatial (i.e. visually perceived) configuration. But such is the power of linguistic analogy that we do so objectify cyclic phasing. We do it even by saying 'a phase' and 'phases' instead of, e.g., 'phasing.' And the pattern of individual and mass nouns, with the resulting binomial formula of formless item plus form, is so general that it is implicit for all nouns, and hence our very generalized formless items like 'substance, matter,' by which we can fill out the binomial for an enormously wide range of nouns. But even these are not quite generalized enough to take in our phase nouns. So for the phase nouns we have made a formless item, 'time.' We have made it by using 'a time,' i.e. an occasion or a phase, in the pattern of a mass noun, just as from 'a summer' we make 'summer' in the pattern of a mass noun. Thus with our binomial formula we can say and think

---

[4]Hopi has two words for water quantities; *kəᐧyi* and *paᐧhə*. The difference is something like that between 'stone' and 'rock' in English, *paᐧhə* implying greater size and "wildness"; flowing water, whether or not outdoors or in nature, is *paᐧhə;* so is 'moisture.' But, unlike 'stone' and 'rock,' the difference is essential, not pertaining to a connotative margin, and the two can hardly ever be interchanged.

[5]To be sure, there are a few minor differences from other nouns, in English for instance in the use of the articles.

'a moment of time, a second of time, a year of time.' Let me again point out that the pattern is simply that of 'a bottle of milk' or 'a piece of cheese.' Thus we are assisted to imagine that 'a summer' actually contains or consists of such-and-such a quantity of 'time.'

In Hopi however all phase terms, like 'summer, morning,' etc., are not nouns but a kind of adverb, to use the nearest SAE analogy. They are a formal part of speech by themselves, distinct from nouns, verbs, and even other Hopi "adverbs." Such a word is not a case form or a locative pattern, like 'des Abends' or 'in the morning.' It contains no morpheme like one of 'in the house' or 'at the tree.'[6] It means 'when it is morning' or 'while morning-phase is occurring.' These "temporals" are not used as subjects or objects, or at all like nouns. One does not say 'it's a hot summer' or 'summer is hot'; summer is not hot, summer is only WHEN conditions are hot, WHEN heat occurs. One does not say 'THIS summer,' but 'summer now' or 'summer recently.' There is no objectification, as a region, an extent, a quantity, of the subjective duration feeling. Nothing is suggested about time except the perpetual "getting later" of it. And so there is no basis here for a formless item answering to our 'time.'

## TEMPORAL FORMS OF VERBS IN SAE AND HOPI

The three-tense system of SAE verbs colors all our thinking about time. This system is amalgamated with that larger scheme of objectification of the subjective experience of duration

already noted in other patterns—in the binomial formula applicable to nouns in general, in temporal nouns, in plurality and numeration. This objectification enables us in imagination to "stand time units in a row." Imagination of time as like a row harmonizes with a system of THREE tenses; whereas a system of TWO, an earlier and a later, would seem to correspond better to the feeling of duration as it is experienced. For if we inspect consciousness we find no past, present, future, but a unity embracing complexity. EVERYTHING is in consciousness, and everything in consciousness IS, and is together. There is in it a sensuous and a nonsensuous. We may call the sensuous—what we are seeing, hearing, touching—the 'present' while in the nonsensuous the vast image-world of memory is being labeled 'the past' and another realm of belief, intuition, and uncertainty 'the future'; yet sensation, memory, foresight, all are in consciousness together—one is not "yet to be" nor another "once but no more." Where real time comes in is that all this in consciousness is "getting later," changing certain relations in an irreversible manner. In this "latering" or "durating" there seems to me to be a paramount contrast between the newest, latest instant at the focus of attention and the rest—the earlier. Languages by the score get along well with two tenselike forms answering to this paramount relation of "later" to "earlier." We can of course CONSTRUCT AND CONTEMPLATE IN THOUGHT a system of past, present, future, in the objectified configuration of points on a line. This is what our general objectification tendency leads us to do and our tense system confirms.

In English the present tense seems the one least in harmony with the paramount temporal relation. It is as if pressed into various and not wholly congruous duties. One duty is to stand as objectified middle term between objectified past and objectified future, in narration, discussion, argument, logic, philosophy. Another is to denote inclusion in the sensuous field: 'I SEE him.' Another is for nomic, i.e. customarily or generally valid, statements: 'We SEE with our eyes.' These varied uses introduce confusions of

---

[6]'Year' and certain combinations of 'year' with name of season, rarely season names alone, can occur with a locative morpheme 'at,' but this is exceptional. It appears like historical detritus of an earlier different patterning, or the effect of English analogy, or both.

thought, of which for the most part we are unaware.

Hopi, as we might expect, is different here too. Verbs have no "tenses" like ours, but have validity-forms ("assertions"), aspects, and clause-linkage forms (modes), that yield even greater precision of speech. The validity-forms denote that the speaker (not the subject) reports the situation (answering to our past and present) or that he expects it (answering to our future)[7] or that he makes a nomic statement (answering to our nomic present). The aspects denote different degrees of duration and different kinds of tendency "during duration." As yet we have noted nothing to indicate whether an event is sooner or later than another when both are REPORTED. But need for this does not arise until we have two verbs: i.e. two clauses. In that case the "modes" denote relations between the clauses, including relations of later to earlier and of simultaneity. Then there are many detached words that express similar relations, supplementing the modes and aspects. The duties of our three-tense system and its tripartite linear objectified "time" are distributed among various verb categories, all different from our tenses; and there is no more basis for an objectified time in Hopi verbs than in other Hopi patterns; although this does not in the least hinder the verb forms and other patterns from being closely adjusted to the pertinent realities of actual situations.

---

[7]The expective and reportive assertions contrast according to the "paramount relation." The expective expresses anticipation existing EARLIER than objective fact, and coinciding with objective fact LATER than the status quo of the speaker, this status quo, including all the subsummation of the past therein, being expressed by the reportive. Our notion "future" seems to represent at once the earlier (anticipation) and the later (afterwards, what will be), as Hopi shows. This paradox may hint of how elusive the mystery of real time is, and how artificially it is expressed by a linear relation of past-present-future.

## DURATION, INTENSITY, AND TENDENCY IN SAE AND HOPI

To fit discourse to manifold actual situations, all languages need to express durations, intensities, and tendencies. It is characteristic of SAE and perhaps of many other language types to express them metaphorically. The metaphors are those of spatial extension, i.e. of size, number (plurality), position, shape, and motion. We express duration by 'long, short, great, much, quick, slow,' etc.; intensity by 'large, great, much, heavy, light, high, low, sharp, faint,' etc.; tendency by 'more, increase, grow, turn, get, approach, go, come, rise, fall, stop, smooth, even, rapid, slow;' and so on through an almost inexhaustible list of metaphors that we hardly recognize as such, since they are virtually the only linguistic media available. The nonmetaphorical terms in this field, like 'early, late, soon, lasting, intense, very, tending,' are a mere handful, quite inadequate to the needs.

It is clear how this condition "fits in." It is part of our whole scheme of OBJECTIFYING—imaginatively spatializing qualities and potentials that are quite nonspatial (so far as any spatially perceptive senses can tell us). Noun-meaning (with us) proceeds from physical bodies to referents of far other sort. Since physical bodies and their outlines in PERCEIVED SPACE are denoted by size and shape terms and reckoned by cardinal numbers and plurals, these patterns of denotation and reckoning extend to the symbols of nonspatial meanings, and so suggest an IMAGINARY SPACE. Physical shapes 'move, stop, rise, sink, approach,' etc., in perceived space; why not these other referents in their imaginary space? This has gone so far that we can hardly refer to the simplest nonspatial situation without constant resort to physical metaphors. I "grasp" the "thread" of another's arguments, but if its "level" is "over my head" my attention may "wander" and "lose touch" with the "drift" of it, so that when he "comes" to his "point" we differ "widely," our "views" being indeed so "far apart" that the "things" he says "appear" "much" too arbitrary, or even "a lot" of nonsense!

The absence of such metaphor from Hopi speech is striking. Use of space terms when there is no space involved is NOT THERE—as if on it had been laid the taboo teetotal! The reason is clear when we know that Hopi has abundant conjugational and lexical means of expressing duration, intensity, and tendency directly as such, and that major grammatical patterns do not, as with us, provide analogies for an imaginary space. The many verb "aspects" express duration and tendency of manifestations, while some of the "voices" express intensity, tendency, and duration of causes or forces producing manifestations. Then a special part of speech, the "tensors," a huge class of words, denotes only intensity, tendency, duration, and sequence. The function of the tensors is to express intensities, "strengths," and how they continue or vary, their rate of change; so that the broad concept of intensity, when considered as necessarily always varying and/or continuing, includes also tendency and duration. Tensors convey distinctions of degree, rate, constancy, repetition, increase and decrease of intensity, immediate sequence, interruption or sequence after an interval, etc., also QUALITIES of strengths, such as we should express metaphorically as smooth, even, hard, rough. A striking feature is their lack of resemblance to the terms of real space and movement that to us "mean the same." There is not even more than a trace of apparent derivation from space terms.[8] So, while Hopi in its

nouns seems highly concrete, here in the tensors it becomes abstract almost beyond our power to follow.

## HABITUAL THOUGHT IN SAE AND HOPI

The comparison now to be made between the habitual thought worlds of SAE and Hopi speakers if of course incomplete. It is possible only to touch upon certain dominant contrasts that appear to stem from the linguistic differences already noted. By "habitual thought" and "thought world" I mean more than simply language, i.e. than the linguistic patterns themselves. I include all the analogical and suggestive value of the patterns (e.g., our "imaginary space" and its distant implications), and all the give-and-take between language and the culture as a whole, wherein is a vast amount that is not linguistic but yet shows the shaping influence of language. In brief, this "thought world" is the microcosm that each man carries about within himself, by which he measures and understands what he can of the macrocosm.

The SAE microcosm has analyzed reality largely in terms of what it calls "things" (bodies and quasibodies) plus modes of extensional but formless existence that it calls "substances" or "matter." It tends to see existence through a binomial formula that expresses any existent as a spatial form plus a spatial formless continuum related to the form, as contents is related to the outlines of its container. Nonspatial existents are imaginatively spatialized and charged with similar implications of form and continuum.

---

[8]One such trace is that the tensor 'long in duration,' while quite different from the adjective 'long' of space, seems to contain the same root as the adjective 'large' of space. Another is that 'somewhere' of space used with certain tensors means 'at some indefinite time.' Possibly however this is not the case and it is only the tensor that gives the time element, so that 'somewhere' still refers to space and that under these conditions indefinite space means simply general ap-

plicability, regardless of either time or space. Another trace is that in the temporal (cycle word) 'afternoon' the element meaning 'after' is derived from the verb 'to separate.' There are other such traces, but they are few and exceptional, and obviously not like our own spatial metaphorizing.

The Hopi microcosm seems to have analyzed reality largely in terms of EVENTS (or better "eventing"), referred to in two ways, objective and subjective. Objectively, and only if perceptible physical experience, events are expressed mainly as outlines, colors, movements, and other perceptive reports. Subjectively, for both the physical and nonphysical, events are considered the expression of invisible intensity factors, on which depend their stability and persistence, or their fugitiveness and proclivities. It implies that existents do not "become later and later" all in the same way; but some do so by growing like plants, some by diffusing and vanishing, some by a procession of metamorphoses, some by enduring in one shape till affected by violent forces. In the nature of each existent able to manifest as a definite whole is the power of its own mode of duration: its growth, decline, stability, cyclicity, or creativeness. Everything is thus already "prepared" for the way it now manifests by earlier phases, and what it will be later, partly has been, and partly is in act of being so "prepared." An emphasis and importance rests on this preparing or being prepared aspect of the world that may to the Hopi correspond to that "quality of reality" that 'matter' or 'stuff' has for us.

## HABITUAL BEHAVIOR FEATURES OF HOPI CULTURE

Our behavior, and that of Hopi, can be seen to be coordinated in many ways to the linguistically conditioned microcosm. As in my fire casebook, people act about situations in ways which are like the ways they talk about them. A characteristic of Hopi behavior is the emphasis on preparation. This includes announcing and getting ready for events well beforehand, elaborate precautions to insure persistence of desired conditions, and stress on good will as the preparer of right results. Consider the analogies of the day-counting pattern alone. Time is mainly reckoned "by day" *(taLk, -tala)* or "by night" *(tok),* which words are not nouns but tensors,

the first formed on a root "light, day," the second on a root "sleep." The count is by ORDINALS. This is not the pattern of counting a number of different men or things, even though they appear successively, for, even then, they COULD gather into an assemblage. It is the pattern of counting successive reappearances of the SAME man or thing, incapable of forming an assemblage. The analogy is not to behave about day-cyclicity as to several men ("several days"), which is what WE tend to do, but to behave as to the successive visits of the SAME MAN. One does not alter several men by working upon just one, but one can prepare and so alter the later visits of the same man by working to affect the visit he is making now. This is the way the Hopi deal with the future—by working within a present situation which is expected to carry impresses, both obvious and occult, forward into the future event of interest. One might say that Hopi society understands our proverb 'Well begun is half done,' but not our 'Tomorrow is another day.' This may explain much in Hopi character.

This Hopi preparing behavior may be roughly divided into announcing, outer preparing, inner preparing, covert participation, and persistence. Announcing, or preparative publicity, is an important function in the hands of a special official, the Crier Chief. Outer preparing is preparation involving much visible activity, not all necessarily directly useful within our understanding. It includes ordinary practicing, rehearsing, getting ready, introductory formalities, preparing of special food, etc. (all of these to a degree that may seem overelaborate to us), intensive sustained muscular activity like running, racing, dancing, which is thought to increase the intensity of development of events (such as growth of crops), mimetic and other magic, preparations based on esoteric theory involving perhaps occult instruments like prayer sticks, prayer feathers, and prayer meal, and finally the great cyclic ceremonies and dances, which have the significance of preparing rain and crops. From one of the verbs meaning "prepare" is derived the noun for "harvest" or "crop": *na'twani* 'the prepared' or the 'in preparation.'[9]

Inner preparing is use of prayer and meditation, and at lesser intensity good wishes and good will, to further desired results. Hopi attitudes stress the power of desire and thought. With their "microcosm" it is utterly natural that they should. Desire and thought are the earliest, and therefore the most important, most critical and crucial, stage of preparing. Moreover, to the Hopi, one's desires and thoughts influence not only his own actions, but all nature as well. This too is wholly natural. Consciousness itself is aware of work, of the feel of effort and energy, in desire and thinking. Experience more basic than language tells us that, if energy is expended, effects are produced. WE tend to believe that our bodies can stop up this energy, prevent it from affecting other things until we will our BODIES to overt action. But this may be so only because we have our own linguistic basis for a theory that formless items like "matter" are things in themselves, malleable only by similar things, by more matter, and hence insulated from the powers of life and thought. It is no more unnatural to think that thought contacts everything and pervades the universe than to think, as we all do, that light kindled outdoors does this. And it is not unnatural to suppose that thought, like any other force, leaves everywhere traces of effect. Now, when WE think of a certain actual rosebush, we do not suppose that our thought goes to that actual bush, and engages with it, like a searchlight turned upon it. What then do we suppose our consciousness is dealing with when we are thinking of that rosebush? Probably we think it is dealing with a "mental image" which is not the rosebush but a mental surrogate of it. But why should it be NATURAL to think that our thought deals with a surrogate and not with the real

rosebush? Quite possibly because we are dimly aware that we carry about with us a whole imaginary space, full of mental surrogates. To us, mental surrogates are old familiar fare. Along with the images of imaginary space, which we perhaps secretly know to be only imaginary, we tuck the thought-of actually existing rosebush, which may be quite another story, perhaps just because we have that very convenient "place" for it. The Hopi thought-world has no imaginary space. The corollary to this is that it may not locate thought dealing with real space anywhere but in real space, nor insulate real space from the effects of thought. A Hopi would naturally suppose that his thought (or he himself) traffics with the actual rosebush—or more likely, corn plant —that he is thinking about. The thought then should leave some trace of itself with the plant in the field. If it is a good thought, one about health and growth, it is good for the plant; if a bad thought, the reverse.

The Hopi emphasize the intensity-factor of thought. Thought to be most effective should be vivid in consciousness, definite, steady, sustained, charged with strongly felt good intentions. They render the idea in English as 'concentrating, holding it in your heart, putting your mind on it, earnestly hoping.' Thought power is the force behind ceremonies, prayer sticks, ritual smoking, etc. The prayer pipe is regarded as an aid to "concentrating" (so said my informant). Its name, *na'twanpi,* means 'instrument of preparing.'

Covert participation is mental collaboration from people who do not take part in the actual affair, be it a job of work, hunt, race, or ceremony, but direct their thought and good will toward the affair's success. Announcements often seek to enlist the support of such mental helpers as well as of overt participants, and contain exhortations to the people to aid with their active good will.[10] A similarity to our concepts

---

[9]The Hopi verbs of preparing naturally do not correspond neatly to our "prepare"; so that *na'twani* could also be rendered 'the practiced-upon, the tried-for,' and otherwise.

[10]See, e.g., Ernest Beaglehole, *Notes on Hopi economic life* (Yale University Publications in Anthropology, no. 15, 1937), especially the reference to

of a sympathetic audience or the cheering section at a football game should not obscure the fact that it is primarily the power of directed thought, and not merely sympathy or encouragement, that is expected of covert participants. In fact these latter get in their deadliest work before, not during, the game! A corollary to the power of thought is the power of wrong thought for evil; hence one purpose of covert participation is to obtain the mass force of many good wishers to offset the harmful thought of ill wishers. Such attitudes greatly favor cooperation and community spirit. Not that the Hopi community is not full of rivalries and colliding interests. Against the tendency to social disintegration in such a small, isolated group, the theory of "preparing" by the power of thought, logically leading to the great power of the combined, intensified, and harmonized thought of the whole community, must help vastly toward the rather remarkable degree of cooperation that, in spite of much private bickering, the Hopi village displays in all the important cultural activities.

Hopi "preparing" activities again show a result of their linguistic thought background in an emphasis on persistence and constant insistent repetition. A sense of the cumulative value of innumerable small momenta is dulled by an objectified, spatialized view of time like ours, enhanced by a way of thinking close to the subjective awareness of duration, of the ceaseless "latering" of events. To us, for whom time is a motion on a space, unvarying repetition seems to scatter its force along a row of units of that space, and be wasted. To the Hopi, for whom time is not a motion but a "getting later" of everything that has ever been done, unvarying repetition is not wasted but accumulated. It is storing up an invisible change that holds over

into later events.[11] As we have seen, it is as if the return of the day were felt as the return of the same person, a little older but with all the impresses of yesterday, not as "another day," i.e. like an entirely different person. This principle joined with that of thought-power and with traits of general Pueblo culture is expressed in the theory of the Hopi ceremonial dance for furthering rain and crops, as well as in its short, piston-like tread, repeated thousands of times, hour after hour.

## SOME IMPRESSES OF LINGUISTIC HABIT IN WESTERN CIVILIZATION

It is harder to do justice in few words to the linguistically conditioned features of our own culture than in the case of the Hopi, because of both vast scope and difficulty of objectivity—because of our deeply ingrained familiarity with the attitudes to be analyzed. I wish merely to sketch certain characteristics adjusted to our linguistic binomialism of form plus formless item or "substance," to our metaphoricalness, our imaginary space, and our objectified time. These, as we have seen, are linguistic.

From the form-plus-substance dichotomy the philosophical views most traditionally char-

---

the announcement of a rabbit hunt, and on p. 30, description of the activities in connection with the cleaning of Toreva Spring—announcing, various preparing activities, and finally, preparing the continuity of the good results already obtained and the continued flow of the spring.

[11] This notion of storing up power, which seems implied by much Hopi behavior, has an analog in physics: acceleration. It might be said that the linguistic background of Hopi thought equips it to recognize naturally that force manifests not as motion or velocity, but as cumulation or acceleration. Our linguistic background tends to hinder in us this same recognition, for having legitimately conceived force to be that which produces change, we then think of change by our linguistic metaphorical analog, motion, instead of by a pure motionless changingness concept, i.e. accumulation or acceleration. Hence it comes to our naïve feeling as a shock to find from physical experiments that it is not possible to define force by motion, that motion and speed, as also "being at rest," are wholly relative, and that force can be measured only by acceleration.

acteristic of the "Western world" have derived huge support. Here belong materialism, psychophysical parallelism, physics—at least in its traditional Newtonian form—and dualistic views of the universe in general. Indeed here belongs almost everything that is "hard, practical common sense." Monistic, holistic, and relativistic views of reality appeal to philosophers and some scientists, but they are badly handicapped in appealing to the "common sense" of the Western average man—not because nature herself refutes them (if she did, philosophers could have discovered this much), but because they must be talked about in what amounts to a new language. "Common sense," as its name shows, and "practicality" as its name does not show, are largely matters of talking so that one is readily understood. It is sometimes stated that Newtonian space, time, and matter are sensed by everyone intuitively, whereupon relativity is cited as showing how mathematical analysis can prove intuition wrong. This, besides being unfair to intuition, is an attempt to answer offhand question (1) put at the outset of this paper, to answer which this research was undertaken. Presentation of the findings now nears its end, and I think the answer is clear. The offhand answer, laying the blame upon intuition for our slowness in discovering mysteries of the Cosmos, such as relativity, is the wrong one. The right answer is: Newtonian space, time, and matter are no intuitions. They are recepts from culture and language. That is where Newton got them.

Our objectified view of time is, however, favorable to historicity and to everything connected with the keeping of records, while the Hopi view is unfavorable thereto. The latter is too subtle, complex, and ever-developing, supplying no ready-made answer to the question of when "one" event ends and "another" begins. When it is implicit that everything that ever happened still is, but is in a necessarily different form from what memory or record reports, there is less incentive to study the past. As for the present, the incentive would be not to record it but to treat it as "preparing." But OUR objectified time puts before imagination something

like a ribbon or scroll marked off into equal blank spaces, suggesting that each be filled with an entry. Writing has no doubt helped toward our linguistic treatment of time, even as the linguistic treatment has guided the uses of writing. Through this give-and-take between language and the whole culture we get, for instance:

1. Records, diaries, bookkeeping, accounting, mathematics stimulated by accounting.
2. Interest in exact sequence, dating, calendars, chronology, clocks, time wages, time graphs, time as used in physics.
3. Annals, histories, the historical attitude, interest in the past, archaeology, attitudes of introjection toward past periods, e.g., classicism, romanticism.

Just as we conceive our objectified time as extending in the future in the same way that it extends in the past, so we set down our estimates of the future in the same shape as our records of the past, producing programs, schedules, budgets. The formal equality of the spacelike units by which we measure and conceive time leads us to consider the "formless item" or "substance" of time to be homogeneous and in ratio to the number of units. Hence our prorata allocation of value to time, lending itself to the building up of a commercial structure based on time-prorata values: time wages (time work constantly supersedes piece work), rent, credit, interest, depreciation charges, and insurance premiums. No doubt this vast system, once built, would continue to run under any sort of linguistic treatment of time; but that it should have been built at all, reaching the magnitude and particular form it has in the Western world, is a fact decidedly in consonance with the patterns of the SAE languages. Whether such a civilization as ours would be possible with widely different linguistic handling of time is a large question—in our civilization, our linguistic patterns and the fitting of our behavior to the temporal order are what they are, and they are in accord. We are of course stimulated to use calendars, clocks, and watches, and to try to measure time ever more precisely;

this aids science, and science in turn, following these well-worn cultural grooves, gives back to culture an ever-growing store of applications, habits, and values, with which culture again directs science. But what lies outside this spiral? Science is beginning to find that there is something in the Cosmos that is not in accord with the concepts we have formed in mounting the spiral. It is trying to frame a NEW LANGUAGE by which to adjust itself to a wider universe.

It is clear how the emphasis on "saving time" which goes with all the above and is very obvious objectification of time, leads to a high valuation of "speed," which shows itself a great deal in our behavior.

Still another behavioral effect is that the character of monotony and regularity possessed by our image of time as an evenly scaled limitless tape measure persuades us to behave as if that monotony were more true of events than it really is. That is, it helps to routinize us. We tend to select and favor whatever bears out this view, to "play up to" the routine aspects of existence. One phase of this is behavior evincing a false sense of security or an assumption that all will always go smoothly, and a lack in foreseeing and protecting ourselves against hazards. Our technique of harnessing energy does well in routine performance, and it is along routine lines that we chiefly strive to improve it—we are, for example, relatively uninterested in stopping the energy from causing accidents, fires, and explosions, which it is doing constantly and on a wide scale. Such indifference to the unexpectedness of life would be disastrous to a society as small, isolated, and precariously poised as the Hopi society is, or rather once was.

Thus our linguistically determined thought world not only collaborates with our cultural idols and ideals, but engages even our unconscious personal reactions in its patterns and gives them certain typical characters. One such character, as we have seen, is CARELESSNESS, as in reckless driving or throwing cigarette stubs into waste paper. Another of different sort is GESTURING when we talk. Very many of the gestures made by English-speaking people at least, and probably by all SAE speakers, serve to illustrate, by a movement in space, not a real spatial reference but one of the nonspatial references that our language handles by metaphors of imaginary space. That is, we are more apt to make a grasping gesture when we speak of grasping an elusive idea than when we speak of grasping a doorknob. The gesture seeks to make a metaphorical and hence somewhat unclear reference more clear. But, if a language refers to nonspatials without implying a spatial analogy, the reference is not made any clearer by gesture. The Hopi gesture very little, perhaps not at all in the sense we understand as gesture.

It would seem as if kinesthesia, or the sensing of muscular movement, though arising before language, should be made more highly conscious by linguistic use of imaginary space and metaphorical images of motion. Kinesthesia is marked in two facets of European culture: art and sport. European sculpture, an art in which Europe excels, is strongly kinesthetic, conveying great sense of the body's motions; European painting likewise. The dance in our culture expresses delight in motion rather than symbolism or ceremonial, and our music is greatly influenced by our dance forms. Our sports are strongly imbued with this element of the "poetry of motion." Hopi races and games seem to emphasize rather the virtues of endurance and sustained intensity. Hopi dancing is highly symbolic and is performed with great intensity and earnestness, but has not much movement or swing.

Synesthesia, or suggestion by certain sense receptions of characters belonging to another sense, as of light and color by sounds and vice versa, should be made more conscious by a linguistic metaphorical system that refers to nonspatial experiences by terms for spatial ones, though undoubtedly it arises from a deeper source. Probably in the first instance metaphor arises from synesthesia and not the reverse; yet metaphor need not become firmly rooted in linguistic pattern, as Hopi shows. Nonspatial experience has one well-organized sense, HEARING—for smell and taste are but little organized. Nonspatial consciousness is a realm chiefly of thought, feeling, and SOUND. Spatial consciousness is a realm of light, color, sight, and touch, and presents shapes and dimensions. Our metaphorical system, by naming nonspatial experiences after spatial ones, imputes to sounds, smells, tastes, emotions, and thoughts qualities like the colors, luminosities, shapes, angles, textures, and motions of spatial experience. And to some extent the reverse transference occurs; for, after much talking about tones as high, low, sharp, dull, heavy, brilliant, slow, the talker finds it easy to think of some factors in spatial experience as like factors of tone. Thus we speak of "tones" of color, a gray "monotone," a "loud" necktie, a "taste" in dress: all spatial metaphor in reverse. Now European art is distinctive in the way it seeks deliberately to play with synesthesia. Music tries to suggest scenes, color, movement, geometric design; painting and sculpture are often consciously guided by the analogies of music's rhythm; colors are conjoined with feeling for the analogy to concords and discords. The European theater and opera seek a synthesis of many arts. It may be that in this way our metaphorical language that is in some sense a confusion of thought is producing, through art, a result of far-reaching value—a deeper esthetic sense leading toward a more direct apprehension of underlying unity behind the phenomena so variously reported by our sense channels.

## HISTORICAL IMPLICATIONS

How does such a network of language, culture, and behavior come about historically? Which was first: the language patterns or the cultural norms? In main they have grown up together, constantly influencing each other. But in this partnership the nature of the language is the factor that limits free plasticity and rigidifies channels of development in the more autocratic way. This is so because a language is a system, not just an assemblage of norms. Large systematic outlines can change to something really new only very slowly, while many other cultural innovations are made with comparative quickness. Language thus represents the mass mind; it is affected by inventions and innovations, but affected little and slowly, whereas TO inventors and innovators it legislates with the decree immediate.

The growth of the SAE language-culture complex dates from ancient times. Much of its metaphorical reference to the nonspatial by the spatial was already fixed in the ancient tongues, and more especially in Latin. It is indeed a marked trait of Latin. If we compare, say Hebrew, we find that, while Hebrew has some allusion to not-space as space, Latin has more. Latin terms for nonspatials, like *educo, religio, principia, comprehendo,* are usually metaphorized physical references: lead out, tying back, etc. This is not true of all languages—it is quite untrue of Hopi. The fact that in Latin the direction of development happened to be from spatial to nonspatial (partly because of secondary stimulation to abstract thinking when the intellectually crude Romans encountered Greek culture) and that later tongues were strongly stimulated to mimic Latin, seems a likely reason for a belief, which still lingers on among linguists, that this is the natural direction of semantic change in all languages, and for the persistent notion in Western learned circles (in strong contrast to Eastern ones) that objective experience is prior to subjective. Philosophies make out a weighty case for the reverse, and certainly the direction of development is sometimes the reverse. Thus the Hopi word for "heart" can be shown to be a late formation within Hopi from a root meaning think or remember. Or consider what has happened to the word "radio" in such a sentence as "he bought a new radio," as compared to its prior meaning "science of wireless telephony."

In the Middle Ages the patterns already formed in Latin began to interweave with the increased mechanical invention, industry, trade, and scholastic and scientific thought. The need for measurement in industry and trade, the stores and bulks of "stuffs" in various containers, the type-bodies in which various goods were handled, standardizing of measure and weight units, invention of clocks and measurement of "time," keeping of records, accounts, chronicles, histories, growth of mathematics and the partnership of mathematics and science, all cooperated to bring our thought and language world into its present form.

In Hopi history, could we read it, we should find a different type of language and a different set of cultural and environmental influences working together. A peaceful agricultural society isolated by geographic features and nomad enemies in a land of scanty rainfall, arid agriculture that could be made successful only by the utmost perseverance (hence the value of persistence and repetition), necessity for collaboration (hence emphasis on the psychology of teamwork and on mental factors in general), corn and rain as primary criteria of value, need of extensive PREPARATIONS and precautions to assure crops in the poor soil and precarious climate, keen realization of dependence upon nature favoring prayer and a religious attitude toward the forces of nature, especially prayer and religion directed toward the ever-needed blessing, rain—these things interacted with Hopi linguistic patterns to mold them, to be molded again by them, and so little by little to shape the Hopi world outlook.

To sum up the matter, our first question asked in the beginning [of this article] is answered thus: Concepts of "time" and "matter" are not given in substantially the same form by experience to all men but depend upon the nature of the language or languages through the use of which they have been developed. They do not depend so much upon ANY ONE SYSTEM (e.g., tense, or nouns) within the grammar as upon the ways of analyzing and reporting experience which have become fixed in the language as integrated "fashions of speaking" and which cut across the typical grammatical classifica-

tions, so that such a "fashion" may include lexical, morphological, syntactic, and otherwise systemically diverse means coordinated in a certain frame of consistency. Our own "time" differs markedly form Hopi "duration." It is conceived as like a space of strictly limited dimensions, or sometimes as like a motion upon such a space, and employed as an intellectual tool accordingly. Hopi "duration" seems to be inconceivable in terms of space or motion, being the mode in which life differs from form, and consciousness *in toto* from the spatial elements of consciousness. Certain ideas born of our own time-concept, such as that of absolute simultaneity, would be either very difficult to express or impossible and devoid of meaning under the Hopi conception, and would be replaced by operational concepts. Our "matter" is the physical subtype of "substance" or "stuff," which is conceived as the formless extensional item that must be joined with form before there can be real existence. In Hopi there seems to be nothing corresponding to it; there are no formless extensional items; existence may or may not have form, but what it also has, with or without form, is intensity and duration, these being nonextensional and at bottom the same.

But what about our concept of "space," which was also included in our first question? There is no such striking difference between Hopi and SAE about space as about time, and probably the apprehension of space is given in substantially the same form by experience irrespective of language. The experiments of the Gestalt psychologists with visual perception appear to establish this as a fact. But the CONCEPT OF SPACE will vary somewhat with language, because, as an intellectual tool,[12] it is so closely linked with the concomitant employment of other intellectual tools, of the order of "time" and "matter," which are linguistically conditioned. We see things with our eyes in the same space forms as the Hopi, but our idea of space

---

[12]Here belong "Newtonian" and "Euclidean" space, etc.

has also the property of acting as a surrogate of nonspatial relationships like time, intensity, tendency, and as a void to be filled with imagined formless items, one of which may even be called 'space.' Space as sensed by the Hopi would not be connected mentally with such surrogates, but would be comparatively "pure," unmixed with extraneous notions.

As for our second question: There are connections but not correlations or diagnostic correspondences between cultural norms and linguistic patterns. Although it would be impossible to infer the existence of Crier Chiefs from the lack of tenses in Hopi, or vice versa, there is a relation between a language and the rest of the culture of the society which uses it. There are cases where the "fashions of speaking" are closely integrated with the whole general culture, whether or not this be universally true, and

there are connections within this integration, between the kind of linguistic analyses employed and various behavioral reactions and also the shapes taken by various cultural developments. Thus the importance of Crier Chiefs does have a connection, not with tenselessness itself, but with a system of thought in which categories different from our tenses are natural. These connections are to be found not so much by focusing attention on the typical rubrics of linguistic, ethnographic, or sociological description as by examining the culture and the language (always and only when the two have been together historically for a considerable time) as a whole in which concatenations that run across these departmental lines may be expected to exist, and, if they do exist, eventually to be discoverable by study.

# 5

## LINEAL AND NONLINEAL CODIFICATIONS OF REALITY
*Dorothy Lee*

*As Whorf argued it, different languages punctuate, categorize, and call attention to various aspects of reality. As a result, individuals from distinct societies learn different codes for representing reality and are constrained to think about reality in different ways. In this article, Dorothy Lee strives to show how the language of the people living in the Trobriand Islands (off New Guinea) emphasizes a lack of lineality, while English calls attention to lineal order. There are no tenses, for example, in Trobriand language, nor are there comparisons or step-by-step ordering of words. Even Trobriand descriptions of events do not follow what we would consider a "natural" historical progression. Lee's article represents a fine illustration of how Whorf's hypothesis can be applied. It also signals some of its difficulties, as a critical look at Lee's examples of lineal and nonlineal language forms may indicate.*

The people of the Trobriand Islands codify, and probably apprehend, reality nonlineally in contrast to our own lineal phrasing. Basic to my

investigation of the codification of reality on these two societies, is the assumption that a member of a given society not only codifies experienced reality through the use of the specific language and other patterned behavior characteristics of his culture, but that he actually grasps reality only as it is presented to him in this code. The assumption is not that reality itself is relative; rather, that it is differently punctuated and categorized, or that different aspects of it are noticed by, or presented to the participants of different cultures. If reality itself were not absolute, then true communication of course would be impossible. My own position is that there is an absolute reality, and that communication is possible. If, then, that which the different codes refer to is ultimately the same, a careful study and analysis of a different code and of the culture to which it belongs, should lead us to concepts which are ultimately comprehensible, when translated into our own code. It may even, eventually, lead us to aspects of reality from which our own code excludes us.

It is a corollary of this assumption that the specific phrasing of reality can be discovered through intensive and detailed analysis of any aspect of culture. My own study was begun with an analysis of linguistic formulation, only because it is in language that I happen to be best able to discover my clues. To show how these clues can be discovered and used as guides to the apprehension of reality, as well as to show what I mean by codification, I shall present at first concrete material from the field of language.

That a word is not the reality, not the thing which it represents, has long been a commonplace to all of us. The thing which I hold in my hand as I write, *is* not a pencil; I *call* it a pencil. And it remains the same whether I call it *pencil, molyvi, Bleistift,* or *siwiqoq.* These words are different sound-complexes applied to the same reality; but is the difference merely one of sound-complex? Do they refer to the same *perceived* reality? *Pencil* originally meant little tail; it delimited and named the reality according to form. *Molyvi* means lead and refers to the writing element. *Bleistift* refers both to the form and to the writing-element. *Siwiqoq* means painting-stick

and refers to observed function and form. Each culture has phrased the reality differently. To say that *pencil,* for example, applies primarily to form is no idle etymologic statement. When we use this word metaphorically, we refer neither to writing element nor to function, but to form alone; we speak of a pencil of light, or a styptic pencil.

When I used the four words for this object, we all knew what reality was referred to; we knew the meaning of the word. We could visualize the object in my hand, and the words all delimited it in the same way; for example, none of them implied that it was a continuation of my fist. But the student of ethnography often has to deal with words which punctuate reality into different phrasings from the ones with which he is familiar. Let us take, for instance, the words for "brother" and "sister." We go to the islands of Ontong Java to study the kinship system. We ask our informant what he calls his sister and he says *ave;* he calls his brother *kainga.* So we equate *ave* with "sister" and *kainga* with "brother." By way of checking our information we ask the sister what she calls her brother; it turns out that for her, *ave* is "brother," not "sister" as we were led to expect; and that it is her sister whom she calls *kainga.*

The same reality, the same actual kinship is present there as with us; but we have chosen a different aspect for naming. We are prepared to account for this; we say that both cultures name according to what we would call a certain type of blood relationship; but whereas we make reference to absolute sex, they refer to relative sex. Further inquiry, however, discloses that in this, also, we are wrong. Because in our own culture we name relatives according to formal definition and biologic relationship, we have thought that this formulation represents reality; and we have tried to understand the Ontong Javanese relationship terms according to these distinctions which, we believe, are given in nature. But the Ontong Javanese classifies relatives according to a different aspect of reality, differently punctuated. And because of this, he applies *kainga* as well to a wife's sister and a husband's brother; to a man's brother's wife and a woman's sister's husband, as well as to a number of other individuals.

Neither sex nor blood relationship, then, can be basic to this term. The Ontong Javanese name according to their everyday behavior and experience, not according to formal definition. A man shares the ordinary details of his living with his brothers and their wives for a large part of the year; he sleeps in the same large room, he eats with them, he jokes and works around the house with them; the rest of the year he spends with his wife's sisters and their husbands, in the same easy companionship. All these individuals are *kainga* to one another. The *ave,* on the other hand, names a behavior of great strain and propriety; it is based originally upon the relative sex of siblings, yes, but it does not signify biologic fact alone. It names a social relationship, a behavior, an emotional tone. *Ave* can never spend their adult life together, except on rare and temporary occasions. They can never be under the same roof alone together, cannot chat at ease together, cannot refer even distantly to sex in the presence of each other, not even to one's sweetheart or spouse; more than that, everyone else must be circumspect when the *ave* of someone of the group is present. The *ave* relationship also carries special obligations toward a female *ave* and her children. *Kainga* means a relationship of ease, full of shared living, of informality, gaiety; *ave* names one of formality, prohibition, strain.

These two cultures, theirs and our own, have phrased and formulated social reality in completely different ways, and have given their formulation different names. The word is merely the name of this specific cultural phrasing. From this one instance we might formulate the hypothesis—a very tentative one—that among the Ontong Javanese names describe emotive experiences, not observed forms or functions. But we cannot accept this as fact, unless further investigation shows it to be implicit in the rest of their patterned behavior, in their vocabulary and the morphology of their language, in their ritual and their other organized activity.

One more instance, this time from the language of the Wintu Indians of California, will deal with the varying aspect or segmentation of experience which is used as a basis of classification. To begin with, we take the stem *muk.* On the basis of this stem we form the word *mukeda,* which means: "I turned the basket bottom up"; we form *mukuhara,* which means: "The turtle is moving along"; and we form *mukurumas,* which means: "automobile." Upon what conceivable principle can an automobile be put in the same category as a turtle and a basket? There is such a principle, however, and it operates also when the Wintu calls the activity of laundering, *to make foam continuously.* According to this principle, he uses only one stem, (puq or poq) to form words for all of the following:

puqeda: I just pushed a peg into the
    ground.
olpuqal: He is sitting on one haunch.
poqorahara: Birds are hopping along.
olpoqoyabe: There are mushrooms
    growing.
tunpoqoypoqoya: You walk shortskirted,
                stifflegged ahead of me.

It is difficult for us to discover the common denominator in the different formations from this one stem, or even to believe that there can be one. Yet, when we discover the principle underlying the classification, the categories themselves are understandable. Basic to the classification is the Wintu view of himself as observer; he stays outside the event. He passes no judgment on essence, and where we would have used kinesthetic or participatory experience as the basis of naming, he names as an observer only, for the shape of the activity or the object. The turtle and the automobile can thus naturally be grouped together with the inverted baskets. The mushroom standing on its stem, the fist grasping a peg against the ground, the stiff leg topped by a short skirt or by the body of a bird or of a man resting on a haunch, obviously all belong together in one category. But the progress of a grasshopper cannot be categorized with that of a hopping bird. We, who classify on a different basis, apprehend the hop of the two kinesthetically and see it as basically the same in both cases; but the Wintu see the difference in recurrent shape, which is all-important to them, and so name the two by means of completely different stems. Again, when we discover this principle, it is easy to see that from the observer's point of view laundering is the making of a lot of foam; and to see why, when beer was introduced to the Wintu, it was named *laundry*.

I have discussed at length the diversity of codification of reality in general, because it is the foundation of the specific study which I am about to present. I shall speak of the formulation of experienced reality among the Trobriand Islanders in comparison to our own; I shall speak of the nature of expectancy, of motivation, of satisfaction, as based upon a reality which is differently apprehended and experienced in two different societies; which is, in fact, for each, a different reality. The Trobriand Islanders were studied by the late Bronislaw Malinowski, who has given us the rich and circumstantial material about them which has made this study possible. I have given a detailed presentation of some implications of their language elsewhere; but since it was in their language that I first noticed the absence of lineality, which led me to this study, I shall give here a summary of the implications of the language.

A Trobriand word refers to a self-contained concept. What we consider an attribute of a predicate, is to the Trobriander an ingredient. Where I would say, for example, "A good gardener," or "The gardener is good," the Trobriand word would include both "gardener" and "goodness"; if the gardener loses the goodness, he has lost a defining ingredient, he is

something else, and he is named by means of a completely different word. A taytu (a species of yam) contains a certain degree of ripeness, bigness, roundedness, etc.; without one of these defining ingredients, it is something else, perhaps a *bwanawa* or a *yowana*. There are no adjectives in the language; the rare words dealings with qualities are substantivized. The term *to be* does not occur; it is used neither attributively nor existentially, since existence itself is contained; it is an ingredient of being.

Events and objects are self-contained points in another respect; there is a series of beings, but no becoming. There is no temporal connection between objects. The taytu always remains itself; it does not *become* overripe; over-ripeness is an ingredient of another, a different being. At some point, the taytu *turns into a yowana,* which contains over-ripeness. And the yowana, over-ripe as it is, does not put forth shoots, does not *become* a sprouting yowana. When sprouts appear, it ceases to be itself; in its place appears a *silasata.* Neither is there a temporal connection made—or, according to our own premises, perceived—between events; in fact, temporality is meaningless. There are no tenses, no linguistic distinction between past or present. There is no arrangement of activities or events into means and ends, no causal or teleologic relationships. What we consider a causal relationship in a sequence of connected events, is to the Trobriander an ingredient of a patterned whole. He names this ingredient *u'ula.*

There is no automatic relating of any kind in the language. Except for the rarely used verbal it-differents and it-sames, there are no terms of comparison whatever. And we find in an analysis of behavior that the standard for behavior and of evaluation is non-comparative.

These implications of the linguistic material suggest to my mind an absence of axiomatic lineal connection between events or objects in the Trobriand apprehension of reality, and this implication. as I shall attempt to show below, is reinforced in their definition of activity. In our own culture, the line is so basic, that we take it for granted, as given in reality. We see it in visible nature, between material points, and we see it between metaphorical points such as days or acts. It underlies not only our thinking, but also our aesthetic apprehension of the given; it is basic to the emotional climax which has so much value for us, and, in fact, to the meaning of life itself. In our thinking about personality and character, we have taken for granted the presence of the line.

In our academic work, we are constantly acting in terms of an implied line. When we speak of *ap*plying an *at*tribute, for example, we visualize the process as lineal, coming from the outside. If I make a picture of an apple on the board, and want to show that one side is green and the other red I connect these attributes with the pictured apple by means of lines, as a matter of course; how else would I do it? When I organize my data, I *draw* conclusions *from* them. I *trace* a relationship between my facts. I describe a pattern as a *web* of relationships. Look at a lecturer who makes use of gestures; he is constantly making lineal connections in the air. And a teacher with chalk in hand will be drawing lines on the board whether he be a psychologist, a historian, or a paleontologist.

Preoccupation with social facts merely as self-contained facts is mere antiquarianism. In my field, a student of this sort would be an amateur or a dilettante, not an anthropologist. To be an anthropologist, he can arrange his facts in an upward slanting line, in a *unilinear* or *multilinear course* of development; or in *parallel lines* or *converging lines.* Or he may arrange them geographically, with *lines* of diffusion connecting them; or schematically, using *concentric circles.* Or at least, he must indicate what his study *leads to,* what new insights we can *draw from* it. To be accorded status, he must use the guiding line as basic.

The line is found or presupposed in most of our scientific work. It is present in the *induction* and the *deduction* of science and logic. It is present in the philosopher's phrasing of means and ends as lineally connected. Our statistical facts are presented lineally as a *graph* or reduced to a normal *curve.* And all of us, I think, would be lost without our *diagrams.* We *trace* a historical development; we *follow the course* of history and evolution *down* to the present and *up from* the ape; and it is interesting to note, in passing, that whereas both evolution and history are lineal, the first goes up the blackboard, the second goes down.

Our psychologists picture motivation as external, connected with the act through a line, or, more recently, entering the organism through a lineal channel and emerging transformed, again lineally, as response. I have seen lineal pictures of nervous impulses and heartbeats, and with them I have seen pictured lineally a second of time. These were photographs, you will say, of existing fact, of reality; a proof that the line is present in reality. But I am not convinced, perhaps due to my ignorance of mechanics, that we have not created our recording instruments in such a way that they have to picture time and motion, light and sound, heartbeats and nerve impulses lineally, on the unquestioned assumption of the line as axiomatic. The line is omnipresent and inescapable, and so we are incapable of questioning the reality of its presence.

When we see a *line* of trees, or a *circle* of stones, we assume the presence of a connecting line which is not actually visible. And we assume it metaphorically when we follow a *line* of thought, a *course* of action or the *direction* of an argument; when we *bridge* a gap in the conversation, or speak of the *span* of life or of teaching a *course,* or lament our *interrupted career.* We make children's embroidery cards and puzzle cards on this assumption; our performance tests and even our tests for sanity often assume that the line is present in nature and, at most, to be discovered or given visual existence.

But is the line present in reality? Malinowski, writing for members of our culture and using idiom which would be comprehensible to them, described the Trobriand village as follows: "Concentrically with the circular row of yam houses there runs a ring of dwelling huts." He saw, or at any rate, he represented the village as two circles. But in the texts which he recorded, we find that the Trobrianders at no time mention circles or rings or even rows when they refer to their villages. Any word which they use to refer to a village, such as *a* or *this,* is prefixed by the substantival element *kway* which means *bump* or *aggregate of bumps.* This is the element which they use when they refer to a pimple or a bulky rash; or to canoes loaded with yams. In their terms, a village is an aggregate of bumps; are they blind to the circles? Or did Malinowski create the circles himself, out of his cultural axiom?

Again, for us as well as in Malinowski's description of the Trobrianders, which was written necessarily in terms meaningful to us, all effective activity is certainly not a haphazard aggregate of acts, but a lineally planned series of acts leading to an envisioned end. Their gardening with all its specialized activities, both technical and magical, leading to a rich harvest; their *kula* involving the cutting down of trees, the communal dragging of the tree to the beach, the rebuilding or building of large sea-worthy canoes, the provisioning, the magical and ceremonial activities involved—surely all these can be carried through only if they are lineally conceived.

But the Trobrianders do not describe their activity lineally; they do no dynamic relating of acts; they do not use even so innocuous a connective as *and.* Here is part of a description of the planting of coconut: "Thou-approach-there coconut thou-bring-here-we-plant-coconut thou-go thou-plant our coconut. This-here it-emerge sprout. We-push-away this we-push-away this-other coconut-husk-fiber together sprout it-sit together root." We who are accustomed to seek lineal continuity, cannot help supplying it as we read this; but the continuity is not given in the Trobriand text, and all Trobriand speech, according to Malinowski, is "jerky," given in points, not in connecting lines. The only connective I know of in Trobriand is the *pela* which I mentioned above; a kind of preposition which also means "to jump."

I am not maintaining here that the Trobrianders cannot see continuity; rather that lineal connection is not automatically made by them, as a matter of course. At Malinowski's persistent questioning, for example, they did attempt to explain their activities in terms of cause or motivation, by stating possible "results" of uncooperative action. But Malinowski found their answers confused, self-contradictory, inconsistent; their preferred answer was, "It was ordained of old"—pointing to an ingredient value of the act instead of giving an explanation based on lineal connection.

And when they were not trying to find answers to leading questions, the Trobrianders made no such connection in their speech. They assumed, for example, that the validity of a magical spell lay, not in its results, not in proof, but in its very being; in the appropriateness of its inheritance, in its place within the patterned activity, in its being performed by the appropriate person, in its realization of its mythical basis. To seek validity through proof was foreign to their thinking, yet they attempted to do so at the ethnographer's request. I should add here that their names for constellations imply that here they do see lineal figures; I cannot investigate the significance of this, as I have no contextual material. At any rate, I would like to emphasize that, even if the Trobriander does occasionally supply connecting lines between points, his perception and experience do not automatically fall into a lineal framework.

The fact remains that Trobrianders embark on, what is certainly for us, a series of acts which "must require" planning and purposiveness. They engage in acts of gift-giving and gift-receiving which we can certainly see as an exchange of gifts if we want to. When we plot their journeys, we find that they do go from point to point, they do navigate a course, whether they say so or not. Do they merely refrain from giving linguistic expression to something which they actually recognize in nature? On the nonlinguistic level, do they act on an assumption of a lineality which is given no place in their linguistic formulation?

I believe that, where valued activity is concerned, the Trobrianders do not act on an assumption of lineality at any level. There is organization or rather coherence in their acts because Trobriand activity is patterned activity. One act within this pattern brings into existence a pre-ordained cluster of acts. Perhaps one might find a parallel in our culture in the making of a sweater. When I embark on knitting one, the ribbing at the bottom does not *cause* the making of the neckline, nor of the sleeves or the armholes; and it is not part of a lineal series of acts. Rather it is an indispensable part of a patterned activity which includes all these other acts. Again, when I choose a dress pattern, the acts involved in the making of the dress are already present for me. They are embedded in the pattern which I have chosen.

In this same way, I believe, can be seen the Trobriand insistence that though intercourse is a necessary preliminary to conception, it is not the cause of conception. There are a number of acts in the pattern of procreating; one is intercourse, another the entrance of the spirit of a dead Trobriander into the womb. However, there is a further point here. The Trobrianders, when pressed by the ethnographer or teased by the neighboring Dobuans, showed signs of intense embarrassment, giving the impression that they were trying to maintain unquestioningly a stand in which they had to believe. This, I think, is because pattern is truth and value for them; in fact, acts and being derive value from the embedding pattern.

So the question of the perception of a line remains. It is because they find value in pattern that the Trobrianders act according to nonlineal pattern; not because they cannot perceive lineality.

But all Trobriand activity does not contain value; and when it does not, it assumes lineality, and is utterly despicable. For example, the pattern of sexual intercourse includes the giving of a gift from the boy to the girl; but if a boy gives a gift so as to win the girl's favor, he is despised. Again, the kula pattern includes the eventual reception of a gift from the original recipient; the pattern is such that it keeps the acts physically and temporally completely disparate. In spite of this, however, some men are accused of giving gifts as an inducement to their kula partner to give them a specially good kula gift. Such men are labeled with the vile phrase: he barters. But this means that, unvalued and despised, lineal behavior does exist. In fact, there are villages in the interior whose inhabitants live mainly by bartering manufactured articles for yams. The inhabitants of Omarakana, about whom Malinowski's work and this study are mainly concerned, will barter with them, but consider them pariahs.

This is to say that it is probable that the Trobrianders experience reality in nonlineal pattern because this is the valued reality; and that they are capable of experiencing lineally, when value is absent or destroyed. It is not to say, however, that this in itself means that lineality is given, is present in nature, and that pattern is not. Our own insistence on the line, such as lineal causality, for example, is also often based on unquestioned belief or value. To return to the subject of procreation, the husband in our culture, who has long hoped, and tried in vain, to beget children, will nevertheless maintain that intercourse causes conception; perhaps with the same stubbornness and embarrassment which the Trobrianders exhibited when maintaining the opposite.

The line in our culture not only connects, but it moves. And as we think of a line as moving from point to point, connecting one to the other, so we conceive of roads as *running from* locality *to* locality. A Trobriander does not speak of roads either as connecting two points, or as *running from* point *to* point. His paths are self-contained, named as independent units; they are not *to* and *from,* that are *at.* And he himself is *at;* he has no equivalent for our *to* or *from.* There is, for instance, the myth of Tudava, who goes—in our view—from village to village and from island to island planting and offering yams.

The Trobriand text puts it this way: "Kitava it-shine village already (i.e. completed) he-is-over. 'I-sail I-go Iwa'; Iwa he-anchor he-go ashore . . . He-sail Digumenu . . . They-drive (him off) . . . he-go Kwaywata." Point after point is enumerated, but his sailing from and to is given as a discrete event. In our view, he is actually following a southeasterly course, more or less; but this is not given as course or line, and no directions are even mentioned. In fact, in the several texts referring to journeyings in the Archipelago, no words occur for the cardinal directions. In sailing, the "following" winds are named according to where they are *at,* the place where they strike the canoe, such as wind-striking-the-outrigger-beam; not according to where they *come from.* Otherwise, we find names for the southwest wind (youyo), and the northwest wind (bombatu), but these are merely substantival names which have nothing to do with direction; names for kinds of wind.

When a member of our society gives an unemotional description of a person, he follows an imaginary line, usually downward: from head to foot, from tip to toe, from hair to chin. The Navaho do the opposite, following a line upward. The Trobriander follows no line, at least none that I can see. "My head boils," says a kula spell; and it goes on to enumerate the parts of the head as follows: nose, occiput, tongue, larynx, speech, mouth. Another spell casting a protective fog, runs as follows: "I befog the hand, I befog the foot, I befog the head, I befog the shoulders . . ." There is a magic formula where we do recognize a line, but it is one which Malinowski did not record verbatim at the time, but which he put down later from memory; and it is not improbable that his memory edited the formula according to the lineality of his culture.

When the Trobriander enumerates the parts of a canoe, he does not follow any recognizable lineal order: "Mist . . . surround me my mast . . . the nose of my canoe . . . my sail . . . my steering oar . . . my canoe-gunwale . . . my canoe-bottom . . . my prow . . . my rib . . . my threading-stick . . . my prow-board . . . my transverse stick . . . my canoe-side."

Malinowski diagrams the garden site as a square piece of land subdivided into squares; the Trobrianders refer to it in the same terms as those which they use in referring to a village—a bulky object or an aggregate of bumps. When the plots in the garden site are apportioned to the gardeners, the named plots are assigned by name, the others by location along each named side of the garden. After this, the inner plots, the "belly" of the garden, are apportioned. Following along a physical rim is a procedure which we find elsewhere also. In a spell naming villages on the main island, there is a long list of villages which lie along the coast northward, then westward around the island, then south. To us, of course, this is lineal order. But we have no indication that the Trobrianders see other than geographical location, point after point, as they move over a physically continuous area; the line as a guide to procedure is not necessarily implied. No terms are used here which might be taken as an implication of continuity; no "along the coast" or "around" or "northward."

When we in our culture deal with events or experiences of the self, we use the line as guide for various reasons, two of which I shall take up here. First, we feel we must arrange events chronologically in a lineal order; how else could our historians discover the causes of a war or a revolution or a defeat? Among the Trobrianders, what corresponds to our history is an aggregate of anecdotes, that is, unconnected points, told without respect to chronological sequence, or development, or causal relationship; with no grammatical distinction made between words referring to past events, or to present or contemplated ones. And in telling an anecdote, they take no care that a temporal sequence should be followed. For instance, they said to Malinowski, "They-eat-taro, they-spew-taro, they-disgusted-taro"; but if time, as we believe, is a moving line, then the revulsion came first in time, the vomiting was the result, coming afterward. Again, they say, "This-here . . . ripes . . . falls-down truly gives-birth . . . sits seed in belly-his"; but certainly the seed is there first, and the birth follows in time, if time is lineal.

Secondly, we arrange events and objects in a sequence which is climactic, in size and intensity, in emotional meaning, or according to some other principle. We often arrange events from earlier to later, not because we are interested in historical causation, but because the present is the climax of our history. But when the Trobriander relates happenings, there is no developmental arrangement, no building up of emotional tone. His stories have no plot, no lineal development, no climax. And when he repeats his garden spell, his list is neither climactic, nor anticlimactic; it sounds merely untidy to us:

The belly of my garden lifts
The belly of my garden rises
The belly of my garden reclines
The belly of my garden
    is-a-bushhen's-nest-in-lifting
The belly of my garden is-an-anthill
The belly of my garden lifts-bends
The belly of my garden
    is-an-ironwood-tree-in-lifting
The belly of my garden lies-down
The belly of my garden burgeons.

When the Trobrianders set out on their great ceremonial kula expedition, they follow a pre-established order. First comes the canoe of the Tolab wage, an obscure subclan. Next come the canoes of the great chiefs. But this is not climactic; after the great chiefs come the commoners. The order derives meaning not from lineal sequence, but from correspondence with a present, experienced, meaningful pattern, which is the recreation or realization of the mythical pattern; that which has been ordained of old and is forever. Its meaning does not lie in an item-to-item relationship, but in fitness, in the repetition of an established unit.

An ordering of this sort gives members of our society a certain esthetic dysphoria except when, through deliberate training, we learn to go beyond our cultural expectation; or, when we are too young to have taken on the phrasings of our culture. When we manipulate objects naively, we arrange them on some climactic lineal principle. Think of a college commencement, with the faculty arranged in order of rank or length of tenure or other mark of importance; with the students arranged according to increasing physical height, from shortest to tallest, actually the one absolutely irrelevant principle as regards the completion of their college education, which is the occasion for the celebration. Even when the sophisticated avoid this principle, they are not unconscious of it, they are deliberately avoiding something which is there.

And our arrangement of history, when we ourselves are personally involved, is mainly climactic. My great grandmother sewed by candle light, my grandmother used a kerosene lamp, my mother did her studying by gaslight, I did it by a naked electric ceiling light, and my children have diffused fluorescent lighting. This is progress; this is the meaningful sequence. To the Trobriander, climax in history is abominable, a denial of all good, since it would imply not only the presence of change, but also that change increases the good; but to him value lies in sameness, in repeated pattern, in the incorporation of all time within the same point. What is good in life is exact identity with all past Trobriand experience, and all mythical experience.

There is no boundary between past Trobriand existence and the present; he can indicate that an action is completed, but this does not mean that the action is past; it may be completed and present or timeless. Where we would say "Many years ago" and use the past tense, the Trobriander will say, "In my father's childhood" and use non-temporal verbs; he places the event situationally, not temporally. Past, present, and future are presented linguistically as the same, are present in his existence, and sameness with what we call the past and with myth, represents value to the Trobriander. Where we see a developmental line, the Trobriander sees a point, at most a swelling in value. Where we find pleasure and satisfaction in moving away from the point, in change as variety or progress, the Trobriander finds it in the repetition of the known, in maintaining the point; that is, in what we call monotony.

Esthetic validity, dignity, and value come to the Trobriander not through arrangement into a climactic line, but rather in the undisturbed incorporation of the events within their original, nonlineal order. The only history which has meaning for him is that which evokes the value of the point, or which, in the repetition, swells the value of the point. For example, every occasion in which a kula object participates becomes an ingredient of its being and swells its value; all these occasions are enumerated with great satisfaction, but the lineal course of the traveling kula object is not important.

As we see our history climactically, so do we plan future experiences climactically, leading up to future satisfaction or meaning. Who but a very young child would think of starting a meal with strawberry shortcake and ending it with spinach? We have come to identify the end of the meal with the height of satisfaction, and we identify semantically the words dessert and reward, only because of the similarity of their position in a climactic line. The Trobriand meal has no dessert, no line, no climax. The special bit, the relish, is eaten *with* the staple food; it is not something to "look *forward to,*" while disposing of a meaningless staple.

None of the Trobriand activities is fitted into a climactic line. There is no job, no labor, no drudgery which finds its reward outside the act. All work contains its own satisfaction. We cannot speak of S–R here, as all action contains its own immanent "stimulus." The present is not a means to future satisfaction, but good in itself, as the future is also good in itself; neither better nor worse, neither climactic nor anticlimactic, in fact, not lineally connected nor removed.

It follows that the present is not evaluated in terms of its place within a course of action leading upward to a worthy end. In our culture, we can rarely evaluate the present in itself. I tell you that Sally is selling notions at Woolworth's, but this in itself means nothing. It acquires some

meaning when I add that she has recently graduated from Vassar. However, I go on to tell you that she has been assistant editor of *Vogue,* next a nursemaid, a charwoman, a public school teacher. But this is a mere jumble; it makes no sense and has no meaning, because the series leads to nothing. You cannot relate one job to another, and you are unable to see them discretely simply as part of her being. However, I now add that she is gathering material for a book on the working mother. Now all this falls in line, it makes sense in terms of a career. Now her job is good and it makes her happy, because it is part of a planned climactic line leading to more pay, increased recognition, higher rank. There was a story in a magazine about the college girl who fell in love with the milkman one summer; the reader felt tense until it was discovered that this was just a summer job, that it was only a means for the continuation of the man's education in the Columbia Law School. Our evaluation of happiness and unhappiness is bound with this motion along an envisioned line leading to a desired end. In the fulfillment of this course or career—not in the fulfillment of the self as point —do we find value. Our conception of freedom rests on the principle of non-interference with this moving line, non-interruption of the intended course of action.

It is difficult to tell whether climax is given in experience at all, or whether it is always imposed on the given. At a time when progress and evolution were assumed to be implicit in nature, our musicians and writers gave us climactic works. Nowadays, our more reflective art does not present experience climactically. Then, is emotion itself climactic? Climax, for us, evokes "thrill" or "drama." But we have cultures, like the Tikopia, where life is lived, to our perception, on an even emotive plane without thrill or climax. Experiences which "we know to be" climactic, are described without climax by them. For example, they, as well as the Trobrianders, described intercourse as an aggregate of pleasurable experiences. But Malinowski is disturbed by this; he cannot place the erotic kiss in Trobriand experience, since it has no climactic function.

In our culture, childbearing is climactic. Pregnancy is represented by the usual obstetrician as an uncomfortable means to a dramatic end. For most women, all intensity of natural physical experience is nowadays removed from the actual birth itself; but the approach of birth nevertheless is a period of mounting tension, and drama is supplied by the intensive social recognition of the event, the dramatic accumulation of gifts, flowers, telegrams. A pregnancy is not formally announced since, if it does not eventuate in birth, it has failed to achieve its end; and failure to reach the climax brings shame. In its later stages it may be marked with a shower; but the shower looks forward to the birth, it does not celebrate the pregnancy itself. Among the Trobrianders, pregnancy has meaning in itself, as a state of being. At a first pregnancy, there is a long ceremonial involving "preparatory" work on the part of many people, which merely celebrates the pregnancy. It does not anchor the baby, it does not *have as its purpose* a more comfortable time during the pregnancy, it *does not lead to* an easier birth or a healthy baby. It makes the woman's skin white, and makes her be at her most beautiful; yet this *leads to* nothing, since she must not attract men, not even her own husband.

Are we then right in accepting without question the presence of a line in reality? Are we in a position to say with assurance that the Trobrianders are wrong and we are right? Much of our present-day thinking, and much of our evaluation, are based on the premise of the line and of the line as good. Students have been refused admittance to college because the autobiographic sketch accompanying their application showed absence of the line; they lacked purposefulness and ability to plan; they were inadequate as to character as well as intellectually. Our conception of personality formation, our stress on the significance of success and failure and of

frustration in general, is based on the axiomatically postulated line. Yet can there be blocking without presupposed lineal motion or effort? If I walk along a path because I like the country, or if it is not important to get to a particular point at a particular time, then the insuperable puddle from the morning's shower is not frustrating; I throw stones into it and watch the ripples, and then choose another path. If the undertaking is of value in itself, a point good in itself, and not because it leads to something, then failure has no symbolic meaning; it merely results in no cake for supper, or less money in the family budget; it is not personally destructive. But failure is devastating in our culture, because it is not failure of the undertaking alone; it is the moving, becoming, lineally conceived self which has failed.

Ethnographers have occasionally remarked that the people whom they studied showed no annoyance when interrupted. Is this an indication of mild temper, or might it be the case that they were not interrupted at all, as there was no expectation of lineal continuity? Such questions are new in anthropology and most ethnographers therefore never thought of recording material which would answer them. However, we do have enough material to make us question the line as basic to all experience; whether it is actually present in given reality or not, it is not always present in experienced reality. We cannot even take it for granted as existing among those members of our society who are not completely or naively steeped in their culture, such as many of our artists, for example. And we should be very careful, in studying other cultures, to avoid the unexamined assumption that their actions are based on the predication of a lineal reality.

**REFERENCE**

*Being and Value in a Primitive Culture.* Journal of Philosophy 46:401–415 (1949). See references under *Being and Value in a Primitive Culture.*

# 6

## CULTURE AND LANGUAGE

### Michael Cole and Sylvia Scribner

*The Sapir-Whorf hypothesis has stimulated a large number of studies by anthropologists, sociolinguists, and psycholinguists interested in the relationship between language and perception. For the most part, these studies attempt in a controlled way, to test simple relationships between aspects of language and perception cross-culturally. In this chapter from a larger work, Cole and Scribner review some of the cross-cultural testing of the Sapir-Whorf hypothesis. They look at studies testing the relationship between perception and linguistically coded color categories, and grammatical emphasis on shape and size relationship. They find that in these cases reality may actually affect language. They conclude, however, that most tests have been run on the linguistic coding of things that can actually be perceived. A study of the linguistic treatment of ideas might well show the operation of Whorf's assertions so that the book on this interesting hypothesis is by no means closed.*

Any attempt to understand the relation between culture and cognition must consider the question of language at an early stage in the inquiry. Language is both the medium through which we obtain a great deal of our data concerning culture and cognition and, according to some theories, the major determinant of our thought processes.

The first point is obvious: almost all of our data concerning cultural differences in cognitive processes are obtained via verbal reports or other linguistic responses. Each of the examples given in the introduction makes use of linguistic evidence, although the particular nature of the evidence differs from case to case. This condition imposes on the investigator an obligation to disentangle those differences in performance that may be the result solely of linguistic differences from those caused by differences in the cognitive operations under investigation. We will deal with some of these difficulties and how they have been handled when we discuss the various problem areas that have been the subject of cross cultural research.

The second point requires extensive consideration. It is not only *not* obvious, it is counter to most of our intuitions. To say that language is a cause of the way we perceive or think seems to put the cart before the horse; most of us conceive of language as the vehicle through which we give expression to our perceptions and thoughts and look upon the particular language used for the purpose of expression as an unimportant accident of birth. Nevertheless, it can be argued that just the opposite relation holds true.

## LINGUISTIC RELATIVITY: THE WHORFIAN HYPOTHESIS

Benjamin Whorf, an American authority on Indian languages, maintained that language is not a way of expressing or packaging thought but rather is a mold that shapes our thoughts. The world can be perceived and structured in many ways, and the language we learn as children directs the particular way we see and structure it. This view, which for many years was influential in the social sciences, is forcefully stated in the following passage by Whorf:

It was found that the background linguistic system (in other words, the grammar) of each language is not merely a reproducing instrument for voicing ideas but rather is itself the shaper of ideas, the program and guide for the individual's mental activity, for his analysis of impressions, for his synthesis of his mental stock in trade. . . . We dissect nature along lines laid down by our native languages. The categories and types that we isolate from the world of phenomena we do not find there because they stare every observer in the face; on the contrary, the world is presented in a kaleidoscopic flux of impressions which has to be organized by our minds—and this means largely by the linguistic systems in our minds. We cut nature up, organize it into concepts, and ascribe significances as we do, largely because we are parties to an agreement to organize it in this way—an agreement that holds throughout our speech community and is codified in the patterns of our language. The agreement is, of course, an implicit and unstated one. *BUT ITS TERMS ARE ABSOLUTELY OBLIGATORY;* we cannot talk at all except by subscribing to the organization and classification of data which the agreement decrees. . . . We are thus introduced to a new principle of relatively, which holds that all observers are not led by the same physical evidence to the same picture of the universe unless their linguistic backgrounds are similar, or can in some way be calibrated (Whorf, 1956, pp. 212–214).

The Whorfian hypothesis of the language-cognition relationship actually contains two propositions, which are best analyzed separately. The first maintains that the world is differently experienced and conceived in different language communities. This proposition has come to be known as *linguistic relativity.* The second proposition goes beyond the simple statement that there are differences in cognition associated with differences in language to claim that language actually *causes* these differences. This doctrine of *linguistic determinism* is essentially a conception of a one-way causal sequence among cognitive processes with language playing the directing role.

This conception clearly transcends the issue of cultural differences in thought, which first intrigued Whorf, and zeroes in on a kernel problem in psychology. The question—Which is primary, language or conceptual thought?—has historically been, and to this day remains, one of the most controversial issues in psychology and one that has involved the world's leading developmental psychologists in theoretical combat. The language-thought problem provides a vivid illustration of how concern with cultural variation inevitably draws the social scientist into consideration of basic developmental processes that are presumed to occur in all human beings in all cultures.

Extreme forms of linguistic relativity and determinism would have serious implications, not only for mankind's study of himself, but for his study of nature as well, because it would close the door to objective knowledge once and for all. If the properties of the environment are known only through the infinitely varying selective and organizing mechanisms of language, what we perceive and experience is in some sense arbitrary. It is not necessarily related to what is "out there" but only to how our particular language community has agreed to *talk about* what is "out there." Our exploration of the universe would be restricted to the features coded by our language, and exchange of knowledge across cultures would be limited, if not impossible.

Perhaps it is fortunate that evidence related to the Whorfian hypothesis indicates that language is a less powerful factor in its constraints on perception and thought than Whorf believed it to be. It is most convenient to review the evidence in terms of the different aspects of language that Whorf thought might influence cognition. The first is the way in which individual units of meaning slice up the nonlinguistic world (the vocabulary or lexicon of a language). The second is "fashions of speaking," or rules for combining basic units of meaning (the grammar of a language). Whorf also suggested that these aspects of language were related both to other *cultural* characteristics (such as cultural attitudes toward time, toward quantification, and the like) and to *individual* characteristics (the single person's perception and thought).

The cultural phenomena that might be related to language characteristics are most commonly investigated by anthropologists, whereas individual behavior is primarily the province of psychologists. Because our aim in this book is to acquaint the reader with cross-cultural research in psychology, we will be reviewing only the data relating to the level of individual behavior. It is important that the reader keep in mind the fact that any generalizations suggested by this evidence do not necessarily apply to Whorf's insights about the integrated nature of various aspects of *culture,* nor do we mean to depreciate the importance of cultural analysis in its own right.

Our discussion will also be limited to the question of linguistic *relativity*—that is, that the world is differently experienced in different language communities—and will ignore the claim that language causes these differences. We think that propositions about causal relations among language, perception, and thought, such as those asserted by the doctrine of linguistic *determinism,* require study in a developmental perspective. To determine whether language or thought is the prior or more basic cognitive capacity, we would want to investigate how *changes* in either class of operations (linguistic or conceptual) affect the other. The cross-cultural data thus far collected on the Whorfian hypothesis are not of this kind. They are correlational in nature—that is, they show the association of one behavior with another, but they do not show whether either behavior causes or determines the other.

## The Lexicon

Whorf's writings, supplemented by much anthropological data, contain numerous examples of how languages differ in the way their vocabularies segment the perceptual world. A classic illustration is the fact that languages vary widely in the number of color terms they possess and the parts of the color spectrum to which the terms refer. Some early observers of this phenomenon attributed the unfamiliar color categories to conceptual confusion on the part of their informants. When it was discovered that Homeric Greek, was deficient (by our standards) in color names, a debate ensued as to whether the early Greeks were color-blind. And, as we have seen, psychologists such as Werner have drawn conclusions about the "primitive" and "syncretic" level of perception among tribal peoples from an analysis of their color terms.

Here are some additional examples given by Whorf: The Hopi use a single word to name all flying things except birds (airplanes, insects, aviators), whereas our language has a separate word for each of these things. On the other hand, the Eskimo have many different words for snow —flying snow, slushy snow, dry snow—while we get along with one.

What is the significance of such lexical differences? Does the fact that a language does not have separate terms for certain phenomena mean that the users of this language are unable to distinguish these phenomena from others? Are Americans unable to see the differences that Eskimo see in snow? Or, to take an example that seems absurd on the face of it, is the Hopi unable to make a visual distinction between an aviator and an insect?

Certain aspects of language behavior challenge Whorf's thesis that the absence or presence of a lexical distinction can be taken as an indicator of a corresponding perceptual or conceptual distinction. His own linguistic behavior—his ability to translate the Eskimo terms for snow into English phrases—is evidence to the contrary. While it may not be possible to translate one language into another with term-for-term correspondence, while much may be lost in the process, the preservation and expression of at least some part of the original meaning argues against any hard-and-fast identification of word categories with thought categories. Nor is language interchangeability a skill confined to trained linguists; there are bilinguals among the general populace in most language communities. The importation of words from one language into another is a further example of the flexibility of languages in respect to vocabulary and a demonstration that the existing lexicon does not exhaust the discriminations of which the language users are capable. Rivers, in one of the earliest cross cultural studies in perception (Rivers, 1901) cites the example of Murray Islanders who had no indigenous term for the color blue but borrowed the English term and modified it to resemble the other members of their color vocabulary (*bulubulu*). On the basis of these facts and comparative language studies, the linguist Charles Hockett (1954, p. 122) has concluded that the question of lexical diversity can best be expressed as follows: Languages differ among themselves not so much as to what *can* be said in them but rather as to what it is relatively *easy to say.*

This formulation disposes of sweeping conclusions relating *all* lexical differences to differences in the way people perceive and think about the world, but it does not help us determine whether any *particular* set of distinctions encoded in a language lexicon are apprehended by individuals whose language lacks this set. To test this question requires some means of measuring perceptual and conceptual discriminations independently of language discriminations. If individuals give differential nonlinguistic responses to specifically different stimulus dimensions, we can infer that they are discriminating these dimensions even though they may lack terms in which to express them. An example would be accurate performance by a Zuni Indian in judg-

ing whether two colors in the orange-yellow range of the color spectrum are the same or different according to their measurable physical attributes in spite of the fact that his language does not contain separate terms for colors in this range. Since we know also that sometimes under a particular set of circumstances, individuals may not make distinctions they actually are capable of making, a further test would be a training experiment to determine whether individuals can learn to apply different lexical terms to classifications not expressed in their natural language. (See Heider, 1972, for the report of a successful learning experiment of this kind conducted among the Dani, a New Guinean population still living in a stone age culture.)

Most of the studies conducted by psychologists to test the impact of lexical distinctions on cognition have proceeded from the weaker version of the influence of vocabulary differences stated by Hockett (that it is *easier* to say something in one language than in another). Brown and Lenneberg (1954), who carried out one of the first experimental studies in this area, reasoned that the ease with which a distinction is expressed in a language is related to the frequency with which its referent perceptual discrimination is required in everyday life. For example, Eskimos are constantly required to make such judgments about snows, whereas Americans may need to make such judgments only under rare and special circumstances. There should be a relation, then, between the more nameable perceptual categories and their availability for various cognitive operations, or as these authors put it, "The more nameable categories are nearer the top of the cognitive 'deck' " (p. 456).

For their perceptual domain they chose categories in the color space. Besides the classical interest in this domain, color space commended itself for investigation because it has been exhaustively mapped and measured and offers a set of physical dimensions against which varying color terminologies can be matched. The three dimensions of physical variation—hue, brightness, and saturation—are treated in the color space as continuous gradations that can be segmented more or less arbitrarily by language—a seemingly ideal representation of Whorf's general conception of the relation between language and reality.

Brown and Lenneberg chose memory as the cognitive process to relate to the linguistic variable of nameability or *codability*. Part of the way we remember an experience such as a color, they thought, is by remembering a word or name for it. Therefore, those color experiences that can be easily and adequately described in words should be more available in a memory test than others less easily verbalized.

Their first experiment was performed with English-speaking subjects on the assumption that a relation between codability and memory demonstrated within one language should also hold within other languages, and between languages as well. The subjects were presented with 24 color chips one at a time and instructed to name the color as quickly as possible. Several measures of the subjects' responses were found to be systematically related: the longer the name, the longer it took the subject to begin to say it and the less agreement there was among subjects in the terms used to name that particular color. The amount of naming agreement among subjects was selected as the most useful measure of codability.

The relation between codability and memory availability was then studied in a recognition experiment with a new group of subjects. Four of the 24 color chips were presented to a subject for a 5-second inspection period; then the chips were removed and the subject was asked to pick them out from an array of 120 colors. The number of correct identifications made by the subject was expressed as a recognition score. Under these circumstances there was a small correlation between codability (agreement on the name for a color) and recognition. When the memory task was made more difficult by introducing a delay period, filled with distracters, be-

tween the presentation of the color chips and their later identification, the correlation was much stronger. When the memory task was simplified by presenting one color for later identification and by having an immediate recognition test, the correlation almost vanished. Under these latter conditions a measure of *visual discriminability* correlated significantly with recognition, emphasizing the close relation between the physical event and memory instead of the relation between language and memory.

The relation between codability and recognition under difficult memory conditions was confirmed in a second study (Lenneberg and Roberts, 1956) conducted among the Zuni Indians of the southwestern United States. The authors hypothesized that the Zuni would have trouble remembering colors in the yellow-orange section of the color spectrum, since their language does not distinguish between these two colors. In this carefully conducted experiment, they found that monolingual Zuni did indeed make the most errors in recognition of these colors followed by subjects who spoke both Zuni and English, with monolingual English-speakers making the fewest errors.

These experiments were widely quoted as evidence for a weak version of linguistic relativity. But further investigation showed that the demonstrated relation between codability and recognition did not hold up for all colors. Burnham and Clark (1955) secured recognition data for another array of colors that did not differ as distinctively in hue as the array in the original study. Lenneberg (1961) took these recognition data and correlated them with codability data he had secured independently for this color array. He found that correlation was a negative one— the better the naming agreement, the lower the recognition score! Evidently, a short distinctive lexical term like *blue* is useful for remembering a color blue when it is surrounded by colors of distinctive hues (red, yellow, green, etc.), but it does not help in the selection of a particular blue from an array of blues of different brightnesses and saturations. Here a phrase—"the cloudy blue with a gray tinge"—may be more useful.

In an attempt to resolve this contradiction, Lantz and Stefflre (1964) developed a new method of measuring codability which they called *communication accuracy*. Viewing memory as a situation in which an individual communicates to himself through time, they argued that items communicated accurately *inter*personally (that is, to another person) would also be more accurately communicated *intra*personally (to oneself). They presented test colors to a group of subjects who were asked to describe them in such a way as to enable others to pick them out of an array. The descriptions were then read to a second group who tried to find the colors from among the recognition array. This procedure yielded very high and statistically significant correlations between communication accuracy and recognition scores for *both* the Brown-Lenneberg and Burnham-Clark color arrays. On the other hand, communication accuracy and naming agreement (the original measure of codability) were not highly correlated.

These results were replicated and extended for non-English-speakers in a study by Stefflre, Vales, and Morely (1966) conducted in Yucatan, Mexico. They worked with two different language groups—Mayan Indians, whose native language, Yucatec, contains relatively few color terms, and students at the University of Yucatan, whose native language, Spanish, has a color vocabulary similar to English.

For each language group a clear correlation was established between communication accuracy for particular colors and the errors that subjects *within that language* made when trying to recognize colors a short time later. The speakers of the two languages found different colors easy to communicate, so that the recognition errors of Yucatec-speakers were not the same as those of Spanish-speakers. Here is clear evidence that errors in recognition are associated with the linguistic, or communication, code more strongly than with the physical attributes of the colors being recognized.

The same general results were obtained by Wang (1972) using the Lantz and Stefflre technique with American college students. Wang first obtained communication accuracy scores for a large set of colors. Then for each color he picked two color names that produced low accuracy; one of the two names biased selection to one side of the test color, the other to the opposite side. When a new group of subjects was presented the colors using the biasing color names, recognition scores were found to err in the direction predictable from the name.

Lantz and Stefflre explained the superiority of the communication measure in predicting recognition scores by the facct that it allows flexibility in the particular verbal expression (single- or multi-word name, phrase, etc.) used to characterize the target stimulus.

The kind of formulation presented here of relation between language and behavior emphasizes the productivity of language—*new descriptions may be formed spontaneously* [italics added] and function to encode stimuli effectively. . . . Any description of the relation between language and behavior or language and thought that does not take this into account and emphasizes only the role of dictionary words and/or the grammatical categories will find it difficult to deal with the facts found in a particular experimental context (Lantz and Stefflre, 1964, p. 481).

In addition to their contribution to the language-cognition problem, the Lantz-Stefflre study shows the limitations of any attempt to relate cognitive behavior to *static* characteristics of language without taking into account the dynamic functions that language can serve within various problem-solving situations. Their communication measure points to a whole new set of language variables connected with language *use* that might be expected to influence cognition. If *intra*personal communication is related to *inter*personal communication, then the social processes of communication within various cultures need to be studied: What form do they take and what aspects of experience are most commonly verbalized and communicated? Looking back at the original Brown-Lenneberg study, we note that their hypothesis of the relationship between codability and memory rested on the assumption their subjects actively applied and stored verbal labels for the test colors. This, too, is an instance of language *use* in a particular situation and an additional demonstration of the fact that the activities of the subject are a crucial intervening variable in attempts to test language-cognition relationships.

In the last few years, the linguistic relativity thesis has been challenged even within the color domain. As we have indicated, the color space was long considered a source of uniform, physical variation, which languages partition arbitrarily into color-name categories. Research conducted by two anthropologists (Berlin and Kay, 1969) suggests that this is not the case. They asked speakers of 20 different languages to choose the best examples of their languages' basic color terms from an array of color chips, and to indicate, in addition, all the chips that could be called by that name. As expected, the boundaries of the color terms varied widely, but the best examples (Berlin and Kay called them the *focal colors*) were stable; instead of being randomly distributed throughout the array they were tightly clustered around 11 basic colors—8 chromatic colors, whose English names are *red, yellow, green, blue, brown, orange, pink,* and *purple*—and 3 achromatic colors, *black, white,* and *gray.* Berlin and Kay argue that the emphasis on cross-cultural differences in linguistic encoding of colors has stemmed from investigators' preoccupation with variable color *boundaries* to the neglect of common *focal color referents.*

In a series of studies, Heider (1972), explored the psychological implications of these reputedly universal focal colors. After refining the location of each of the focal colors in the color space, she tested to see whether these colors were the most codable *across language families.*

Subjects spoke languages belonging to the Indo-European, Austronesian, Sino-Tibetan, and Afro-Asiatic families, plus Hungarian, and Japanese. The results were quite clear: focal colors were given shorter names and were named more quickly than nonfocal colors (the two measures of codability used in this study). A third study, modeled after the Brown-Lenneberg experiments demonstrated that focal colors could be remembered more accurately than nonfocal colors *even by speakers of a language that lacks basic hue terms.* The Dani of New Guinea, whose color lexicon is restricted to two basic terms meaning, roughly, dark and light, showed memory superiority for focal colors over nonfocal colors similar to that shown by the comparison group of American subjects whose language has a term for each member of the entire set of focal colors. What does this imply about the role of language in this task? Data from another series of experiments (Heider and Olivier, 1972) has led Heider to conclude that there may be a *visual* rehearsal process in the recognition task which is separable from a *verbal* rehearsal process. Visual memory images may be isomorphic to visual images of colors that are physically present, and thus more responsive to perceptually salient characteristics of the stimuli and more resistant to language-related distortion. In Brown and Lenneberg's easy memory task, recognition could be accounted for, as we have seen, by the perceptual property of discriminability. Just which memory tasks call out visual rather than verbal memory processes in which populations, what the nature of the interaction may be between these two processes and what kind of "verbal encoding" is employed in a given situation are all important questions which studies of this kind must answer.

It is interesting to observe how a line of research originally inspired by notions of linguistic relativity has now led to the claim that there are certain universals or invariants in the relation between one area of perceptual experience and language lexicons. In spite of the great variety of terms for colors and the unstable boundaries separating one color class from another, certain colors seem to be universally salient and easier to remember. On the strength of this evidence Heider (1972) suggests that the customary understanding of the relationship between language terms and concepts may be the reverse of what it is customarily understood to be. "In short, far from being a domain well suited to the study of the effects of language on thought, the color space would seem to be a prime example of the influence of underlying perceptual-cognitive factors on the formation and reference of linguistic categories" (p. 20).

## Grammar

Not only do languages differ with respect to the way in which their vocabularies cut up the world, they also differ with respect to the way in which individual units of meaning get combined. Whorf was especially fascinated by these structural features of language, which he called "fashions of speaking," and he emphasized their importance in molding, unconsciously, the language community's view of reality. He pointed out, for example, that English verbs take different forms in accordance with the temporal distinctions, past, present, and future. These obligatory temporal references fit in with our culture's concept of time as a never-ending line and our preoccupation with its measurement (as witness our calendars and clocks in almost infinite variety). However, Hopi words that function as verbs—including words that we clearly treat as nouns, such as lightning and puff-of-smoke—emphasize duration rather than time of occurrence. Another example of a structural fashion of speaking is supplied by Lee (1938), who describes verbs in the Wintu (California Indian) language as being classified by "validity modes." If the event being spoken of is a matter of hearsay, one word is used; if it is an event actually observed by the *speaker* (not the subject of the sentence), another verb is used. Hence, different words for *to hear* might be used by a witness to a crime who "heard" the gun go off

and by the policeman relating the witness's claim of having "heard" the gun go off.

As in the case of the linguistic evidence relating to lexical differences, we are not sure what to make of these instances. Whorf and others would have us believe that they reflect inescapable constraints on our thinking, but the evidence relevant to thought is all via language; no independent indicator of cognition is offered. We have to infer thought processes from general cultural indices (whose meaning we find it difficult to agree upon) or from other linguistic evidence, which we also believe to be related to cognition. In either event we are treading on very thin ice.

We know of only two experiments that present nonlinguistic evidence relevant to the influence of grammar on cognitive activities. The first was conducted by Carroll and Casagrande (1958) on a Navaho Indian reservation. In the Navaho language certain verbs that refer to manipulation of things require special forms, depending on what kind of thing is being handled: there is one verb form if the object is round and thin, another for a long flexible object, still another for a long rigid object, and so on. Since the Navaho grammar forces attention to the shape, form, and material of things, it is reasonable to assume that the behavior of Navahos toward things might be guided by these particular attributes to a greater extent than is the behavior of non-Navaho speakers. So Carroll and Casagrande reasoned.

They chose to investigate the saliency of these attributes in the object-sorting behavior of matched age groups of Navaho children, one speaking only Navaho, the other speaking only English. The children's actual task was to match an object with one of a pair of objects shown by the experimenter. A presentation pair might be a yellow rope and a blue stick, as shown in Figure 1. The child would then be shown a yellow stick and asked which one of the presentation pair it belonged with. Results confirmed expectations about attribute saliency: Navaho-speaking children tended to match the items on the basis of form rather than color at younger ages

Show the child:

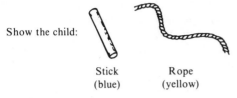

Stick        Rope
(blue)      (yellow)

**FIGURE 1**
**Objects used to study the influence of grammar on cognition (fashioned after Carroll and Casagrande, 1958).**

than the English-speaking children did. Unhappily for the theory, when the same matching task was given to middle-class English-speaking children in metropolitan Boston, they too showed a preference for form over color—a preference that Carroll and Casagrande accounted for by the abundant experience with shapes and forms which these children had acquired in the course of playing with toys. They concluded that in this particular task, form choices could be mediated by *either* language or nonlanguage experience and that, overall, the results show that grammatical categories do influence matching. Note, however, that this is a very benign form of linguistic relativity, much more consistent with the idea that concepts are differentially available in different cultures rather than with the idea that they are exclusive to some one particular culture.

A recent experiment by Cole and his associates (1969) reinforces this interpretation. Their experiment took advantage of the fact that in the Kpelle language of Liberia, comparisons of size are not symmetric as they are in English. Thus, in comparing a large and small person, a Kpelle would always refer to the larger, his remark translating as "John, he is big past Joe." Although it is possible for him to say the equivalent of "Joe is smaller than John," the Kpelle expression translates as "Joe, in smallness surpasses John," and it is rarely if ever used.

This observation was combined with a standard experiment, known as a *transposition experiment,* which has been used extensively to study

the development of conceptual behavior in children. The experiment is most easily understood when we consider a particular example, such as that shown in Figure 2. In this example, the child is first taught always to choose the larger of two blocks presented to him by the experimenter. In successive trials the physical placement of the two blocks is randomized so that size is the only reliable cue for determining which block is correct. After the subject reliably picks the correct block, he is presented with two other blocks also different in size. The question is: Will the subject choose the block that is the same size (or closest to the same size) as the block that was correct during training, or will he pick the block that bears the same size *relation* to its paired mate as the correct block did to its mate during training? For example, if, as shown in Figure 2, block 6, the larger block, is correct during training, then, when the subject is presented with the pair of blocks 6 and 7 (condition A) will he choose 6 (the same) or 7 (the larger)? When the block bearing the correct size relation is chosen, the subject is said to show transposition.

1. Train the child that the large block is correct.

2. Then test on one of the following pairs.

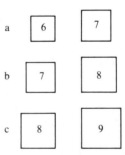

**FIGURE 2**
**Design for a transposition experiment.**

Three groups of Kpelle children participated in the experiment: monolingual Kpelle-speaking children aged 4 to 6, nonliterate children aged 6 to 8 who spoke a little English in addition to Kpelle, and 6 to 8-year-old first-graders who could speak a good deal of English and who were beginning to read and write. The same blocks and the same testing procedures were used also with a group of 4- to 5-year-old American nursery school children.

When the experiment was actually run, some groups were trained to choose the smaller block and others to choose the larger, and they were tested on different combinations of smaller or larger blocks. If the Kpelle are used to making size comparisons by singling out the larger member first, we might expect monolingual Kpelle speakers to learn the larger-than relationship faster and to transpose it to test trials more readily than any of the other comparison groups. But this was not the case. Virtually all of the children showed transposition, regardless of their language and school background, and regardless of whether they were being tested on the larger-than or the smaller-than relationship. Moreover, learning to choose the larger block during training was no more rapid than learning to choose the smaller block.

These findings imply that the Kpelle preference for comparing the larger of two things to the smaller has no influence on discrimination learning. Here, as in the work reported earlier on perception of focal colors, we seem to be dealing with stimulus properties and relationships that exert a strong control over behavior. Two aspects of the Kpelle children's behavior in this task did seem affected, however. On the very first trial of training, before the subject had any information about the problem, all the Kpelle children showed a significant preference for the larger block, while the American children did not. Second, when the test phase was over and subjects were asked why they had made the choices they did, Kpelle subjects were better able to justify their responses if they were trained to

choose the larger block, but American subjects showed no difference in the adequacy of their justifications as a function of which training block was correct.

Like the result of Carroll and Casagrande's research, and in fact like virtually all of the experimentally derived results relating to language and cognition in a cross-cultural context, these data point to limitations on the generality of the linguistic relativity hypothesis. We will defer any attempt to summarize the present status of the hypothesis until we look briefly at some proposals that all languages, in spite of their heterogeneity, share certain *common* ways of coding experience. These propositions constitute a hypothesis about *linguistic universality.*

## LINGUISTIC UNIVERSALITY

The Whorfian hypothesis is primarily concerned with the referential aspect of language: how it maps experience, what it points to (denotative meaning). But there is another aspect of language, which expresses the qualities of experience—the feelings, images, and relationships that words arouse (sometimes referred to as connotative meaning). One of the largest, most systematic, and sustained cross-cultural investigations of language and thought in the last decade has been concerned with testing the generality of this aspect of meaning. With the help of cooperating social scientists in twelve countries (Japan, Hong Kong, India, Afghanistan, Iran, Lebanon, Yugoslavia, Poland, Finland, Holland, Belgium, and France), Charles Osgood (1964), a leading American psycholinguist, has been studying affective meaning systems through the use of a special measuring instrument he devised, called the *semantic differential.*

The basic procedure of the semantic differential is this: a subject is presented with a list of verbal concepts: *mother, bread, communism, teacher,* for example. Then he is given a list of antonym qualifiers (represented by adjectives in English) such as *good-bad, honest-dishonest, hot-cold*. The subject has to rate each concept against each qualifier pair using a number from 1 to 7, with the 1 standing for an extreme quality of the left-hand member of the pair (*good* in the first example given), the 7 for an extreme quality of the right-hand member of the pair *(bad)*, and the other numbers for intermediate qualities. In a dozen or more factorial studies conducted with American English-speaking subjects, Osgood and his associates kept finding that the rating results could be described in terms of three dominant factors or dimensions of meaning: an *evaluative* factor (represented by scales like *good-bad*); a *potency* factor (represented by scales like *strong-weak*); and an *activity* factor (represented by scales like *fast-slow*). The problem then arose: Is this semantic framework limited to Americans speaking the English language or is it "shared by all humans regardless of their language or culture?" To find out, Osgood and his associates prepared a list of 100 familiar concepts that had been selected by linguists and anthropologists as "culture fair." This list was translated into the indigenous language, and from then on the work was conducted entirely in the various native tongues. Qualifiers and their opposites were elicited from groups of high school boys in each country. Scales were constructed, based on their responses, and then new groups of subjects were asked to rate the original 100 concepts against these scales.

The results to date indicate that the same three dimensions of meaning (evaluation, potency, and activity) describe the rating judgments in all the languages studied, although individual concepts are rated differently from culture to culture on these semantic factors. Stated a little differently, the structure of connotative meaning is the same from culture to culture, while the connotative meanings of particular concepts are culture specific. Osgood attributes this aspect of linguistic universality to the fact that his scales tap emotional feelings mediated by the affective nervous system which

is "panhuman biologically" (Osgood, 1963, p. 320). A limitation in respect to "universality" to which we might draw attention is that his subject populations were all *educated* groups. In view of the strong homogenizing influence of education on the performance of cognitive tasks, to be described in later chapters, this restriction may be quite important.

Osgood goes on to suggest that universality of affective meaning systems may also account for the phenomena of metaphor and *verbal-visual synesthesia*. A classic study on metaphor conducted by Asch (1961) investigated how terms referring to physical properties of things *(hard, straight, hot)* are used to characterize psychological attributes of persons ("John is a very cold person"). He found strikingly similar metaphoric applications in such dissimilar languages as Hebrew, Greek, Chinese, Thai, Hausa, and Burmese.

Verbal-visual synethesia is a phenomenon in which words are regularly paired with certain pictorial representations rather than with others, as in the pairing of *happy* with an arrow pointing upward instead of downward. This was one of the fascinating results found by Osgood in a cross-cultural study demonstrating the generality of visual-verbal synesthetic tendencies among Navaho, Mexican-Spanish, Anglo, and Japanese subjects (1960).

Somewhat more research has been devoted to another related phenomenon known as *phonetic symbolism*—the appropriateness of the relation between the sound of a word and its meaning. The *tinkle* of an icecube in a glass or the *boom* of the drum in the Salvation Army band might be considered to have appropriate verbal expression in the sense that the word sounds help to communicate some attributes of their referents.

Edward Sapir initiated research in phonetic symbolism in the 1920s by using a vocabulary of artificial words. (His and other early work are reviewed in Brown, 1958, Chap. 4). Brown, Black, and Horowitz (1955) carried out a well-controlled, specifically cross-language study which begat a series of investigations still under way. Twenty-one pairs of English antonyms *(warm-cold, heavy-light)* were translated into Chinese, Czech, and Hindi and were given to American college students unfamiliar with these languages. Told only the dimensions along which the words varied, the students were able to make better-than-chance discriminations concerning the meanings of the individual words in all three languages. To illustrate: given the pair of Chinese words *ch'ing* and *ch'ung* and the information that one means light and the other heavy, subjects tended to correctly guess *ch'ing* as light.

In many variations of this task using different languages and different methods of word presentation, investigators have repeatedly demonstrated above-chance matching of word meaning to word form. Correct matchings have been made even when each of the two members of a word pair was presented in a different language —*light* in Czech and *heavy* in Japanese, for example (Klank, Huang, and Johnson, 1971). A start has been made in identifying *which* sounds give cues to *which* meanings. Some evidence links vowel sound to meanings of magnitude: it has been found that high and front vowels occur proportionately more often in words denoting smallness, and low back vowels in words denoting largeness in *both* Chinese and English.

The first indication that the correspondence between the sound of a word and its meaning may influence cognitive processes comes from a recently reported Russian study on verbal memory (Baihdurashvili, 1972). Two groups of subjects were required to memorize lists of word pairs composed of a Japanese word and a word in the subject's native language. For the first group, the Japanese word was paired with a native word of the same meaning; the second group had a list in which the same Japanese words were paired with native words of different meanings. The first group learned more rapidly and showed greater retention of the material, evidencing, in the investigator's words, "the lawful character of naming in a natural language" (p. 411).

Taken together, work in the semantic differential, synesthesia, metaphor, and phonetic symbolism seem to offer impressive support for the argument that certain qualities of experience are given common expression in many languages and cultures, differ as they may among themselves in other characteristics.

At this point we might stop to consider for a moment the implications of work in *language universals*.

Joseph Greenberg (1966), G. A. Miller (1970), and others have singled out for attention various features of phonology (sound systems), grammar, and lexicon that all languages seem to share. Miller refers to these as "general design features" of language and suggests that their existence points to common physiological and psychological processes or capacities shared by all men. Chomsky (1968) maintains that these commonly shared features are themselves derived from base structures, which are built-in components of the human mind. These base structures make possible, and at the same time constrain, all language development. The task of psychology, he contends, is to search out the nature of these mental mechanisms underlying linguistic competence. But while it may be relatively simple to identify the basic mechanisms accounting for universal features in phonology (the limited variety of articulates possible to human speech apparatus, for example), it is another matter entirely to identify the psychological processes that might account for universals in grammar and lexicon. To add to the difficulty, the question of the relation between underlying psychological processes and linguistic competence has become the subject of a nonproductive debate pitting genetic innate mechanisms against learning mechanisms. On the other hand, developmental psycholinguists, studying the acquisition of language in the first few years of the child's life, are contributing information suggesting that there may be certain sequences in language mastery that are independent of features of particular languages (Smith and Miller, 1966) and that might at some future time help to elucidate the question of language universals. Fundamentally important as these issues are, we will not explore them further in this discussion because they revolve around a somewhat different question from that concerning us. Chomsky, Miller, and others are asking the question: What are the cognitive operations underlying the acquisition and use of language? In other words, what capacities do we need in order to speak? The problem tackled in this chapter has been that of specifying the interrelations *between* language processes and other cognitive operations: How are speech and thinking related to each other?

## SUMMARY

Our review of the research evidence bearing on the Whorfian hypothesis certainly makes untenable any strong version of linguistic relativity. It is probable that the majority of scholars would agree in rejecting those of Whorf's formulations that stress the *arbitrary* character of the language-experience relationship and the inescapable and rigid constraints imposed on cognitive processes by language. Yet in spite of the patchiness of the evidence, few would be likely to allow linguistic relativity no role whatsoever. Here are some of the reasons we would give for keeping the question open.

1. First we would want to stress the limited nature of the experimental operations that have been brought to bear on the hypothesis. While there were good reasons for choosing to investigate linguistic relativity through color terminology, the superior intelligence of hindsight suggests this may have been something short of an ideal strategy. It is very likely that the expression of perceptual experience is most constrained by certain salient and stable stimulus attributes and is less responsive to the variability introduced by language. It may very well be that

the "filtering effect" of language is greatest in respect to domains of phenomena that are definable, not in terms of physical properties, but in terms of attributes that are culturally specified. One thinks of such domains as social roles, for example; attributes defining categories of people (unlike those defining colors) are assigned by culture not nature. Or consider the area of ideology or theoretical work in general, where concepts largely acquire their meanings through their being embedded in explanatory verbal networks. It is here that language may play the greatest role in shaping the person's view of reality, in influencing his memory and thinking processes, and in contributing to his understanding or misunderstanding of other cultures. But such a proposition brings us around full circle to the difficulty with which we started: Can this hypothesis be tested empirically, and how?

2. A second point that should be made is that the demonstration of universal relations between aspects of language and cognition does not automatically make moot the question of culturally relative differences. Nor is it necessarily paradoxical that there should be both universals and differences in any domain of human experience. By now it is clear that the relations between language and cognition are not likely to be exhausted in a few general propositions. The growing body of research dealing with language and thought is uncovering multiple and complex interrelations between them. Our understanding will grow as theoretical work and cross-cultural research succeed in elaborating these multiple relations in both their universal *and* their particular aspects.

3. Finally, while Whorf's view of the particular characteristics of language important for cognition has not been disproved, there appear to be more fruitful ways today of investigating the classic questions. In our analysis of the Brown-Lenneberg experiments on color codability and memory we pointed out that the hypothesized effects of language operated only through some assumed *verbal activity* on the part of the subject. None of the experimenters

suggested that the vocabulary item as a static piece of information was responsible for the accuracy of recognition; all stressed what the subject did with it. These observations led us to point out the possible important implications of different *uses* of language for cognition. This indeed has been a subject of intensive research in the last few years, although not in the area traditionally designated as cross-cultural; this research has been stimulated by social class and subcultural comparisons within one society (principally the United States and England). A new field of *sociolinguistics* is showing rapid growth, its credo being that language cannot be understood except in its use functions—as human communication sensitive to the social contexts in which it is carried out. One of the seminal thinkers in this field, Basil Bernstein, has delineated different forms of speech codes that he considers characteristic of the English working class and English middle class, respectively, and that he feels significantly affect their learning experiences (1972). Bernstein has been concerned with how members of certain social strata develop characteristic ways of using speech to communicate with one another. This is seemingly a far cry from the characteristics of language that interested Whorf, but Bernstein specifically acknowledges his debt to Whorf for alerting him to the "selective effect of culture (acting through its patterning of social relationships) upon the *patterning* of grammar together with the pattern's semantic and thus cognitive significance" (1972, p. 224). In this young and potentially rich field of investigation of how individuals use their language not only for social communication but as a tool for thought, Whorf still lives.

# REFERENCES

Asch, S. E. The metaphor: a psychological inquiry. In M. Henle, *Documents of Gestalt psychology.* Berkeley: University of California Press, 1961, 324–333.

Baihdurashvili, A. G. Summarized in report of the Fourth Congress of the Psychological Society of the USSR. *Soviet Psychology,* 1972, *X,* 359–423.

Berlin, B., & Kay, P. *Basic color terms.* Berkeley: University of California Press, 1969.

Bernstein, B. Social class, language, and socialization. In S. Moscovici (Ed.), *The psychosociology of language.* Chicago: Markham Publishing Co., 1972, 222–242.

Brown, R. *Words and things.* New York: The Free Press, 1958.

Brown, R., Black, A. H., & Horowits, A. E. Phonetic symbolism in natural language. *Journal of Abnormal and Social Psychology,* 1955, *50,* 388–393.

Brown, R., & Lenneberg, E. H. A study of language and cognition. *Journal of Abnormal and Social Psychology,* 1954, *49,* 454–462.

Burnham, R. W., & Clark, J. R. A test of hue memory. *Journal of Applied Psychology,* 1955, *39,* 164–172.

Carroll, J. B., & Casagrande, J. B. The function of language classifications in behavior. In E. E. Macoby, T., M. Newcomb, & E. L. Hartley (Eds.), *Readings in social psychology.* New York: Holt, Rinehart and Winston, 1958.

Cole, M., Gay, J., & Glick, J. Communication skills among the Kpelle of Liberia. Paper presented at the Society for Research in Child Development Meeting, Santa Monica, Calif., March 1969.

Cole, M., Gay, J., Glick, J., & Sharp, D. W. Linguistic structure and transposition. *Science,* 1969, *164,* 90–91.

Heider, E. R. Universals in color naming and memory. *Journal of Experimental Psychology,* 1972, *93,* 10–20.

Heider, E. R., & Olivier, D. C. The structure of the color space in naming and memory for two languages. *Cognitive Psychology,* 1972, *3,* 337–355.

Hockett, C. Chinese versus English: an exploration of the Whorfian theses. In H. Hoijer (Ed.), *Language in culture.* Chicago: University of Chicago Press, 1954.

Klank, L. J. K., Huang, Y. H., & Johnson, R. C. Determinants of success in matching word pairs in tests of phonetic symbolism. *Journal of Verbal Learning and Verbal Behavior,* 1971, *10,* 140–148.

Lantz, D., & Stefflre, V. Language and cognition revisited. *Journal of Abnormal and Social Psychology,* 1964, *69,* 472–481.

Lee, D. Conceptual implications of an Indian language. *Philosophy of Science,* 1938, *5,* 89–102.

Lenneberg, E. H., & Roberts, J. The language of experience, a study in methodology. Memoir 13. *International Journal of American Linguistics,* 1956, 22.

Miller, G. A. Linguistic communication as a biological process. Herbert Spencer Lecture, Oxford University, Nov. 13, 1970.

Osgood, C. E. Language universals and psycholinguistics. In J. H. Greenberg, *Universals of language.* Cambridge: The M.I.T. Press, 1963, 299–322.

Osgood, C. E. Semantic differential technique in the comparative study of cultures. *American Anthropologist,* 1964, *66,* 171–200.

Osgood, C. E. The cross-cultural generality of visual-verbal synesthetic tendencies. *Behavioral Science,* 1960, *5,* 146–169.

Rivers, W. H. R. Introduction and vision. In A. C. Haddon (Ed.), *Reports of the Cambridge anthropological expedition to the Torres Straits.* Vol. II, Pt. 1 Cambridge, England: The University Press, 1901.

Smith, J., & Miller, G. A. *The genesis of language.* Cambridge, Mass.: M.I.T. Press, 1966.

Stefflre, V., Vales, V., & Morley, L. Language and cognition in Yucatan: A cross-cultural replication. *Journal of Personality and Social Psychology,* 1966, *4,* 112–115.

Wang, H. S. Y. Codability and recognition memory for colors. Presented at Eastern Psychological Association Convention, Boston, 1972.

Whorf, B. L. *Language, thought and reality.* Boston: M.I.T. Press; New York: Wiley, 1956.

# KINSHIP AND SOCIAL ORGANIZATION

**ISSUE**  The incest taboo: Why is it found in every society?

We Americans value our independence. We buy books by the thousands on how to look out for ourselves, or "number one," as we call it. We worry about our "personal development"; we complain about being "stifled" by other people; we cling to our automobiles, drawn by the lure of personal freedom and the chance to be alone with our thoughts. Above all we hate to admit that others influence our actions. We don't like to be affected by "social pressure."

Yet, like people everywhere we do live with other human beings in the context of organized social groups. From the time we are born until we die, we are surrounded by people—parents, friends, fellow workers, neighbors, classmates, and countless others. We depend on them for our physical and emotional needs. Our self-esteem rests on what they think of us. In fact, our desire for personal independence is really a *social* value, held and supported by the many people we interact with every day.

Social living may be universal, but it is also a struggle to maintain. Humans have their own personal needs and wants, which conflict with requirements of the group. Subgroup interests may impede mutual activity within the larger society. The need to compete for scarce resources divides rather than unites. To overcome these divisive tendencies, we employ several strategies. Culture itself tends to unite people. It provides them with common language, a system of classification, and rules for action that make for predictability and a sense of belonging together. Common social values bring people together, providing them with mutual goals. Regular association with the same people promotes a sense of social familiarity and cohesion. So does organization built around such factors as common territory, age, rank, interests, and especially kinship.

Kinship systems are the cultural rules for organizing interaction among kin. They appear to be based on the biological realities of mating and reproduction. Mothers, and perhaps fathers, feel a special sense of obligation and emotional attachment toward their helpless and dependent young. Mates also may develop a strong emotional link to one another. Kinship systems elaborate on these emotions, developing them into such culturally defined units as the family (see Chapter V) and larger groups, such as lineages, clans, kindreds, and moieties. They define relationships between fathers and sons, nieces and uncles, brides and fathers-in-law. They regulate and legitimize mating through the institution of marriage.

But the ways kinship systems organize people are highly varied. There are a variety of ways to identify kin, leading to as many differences in kinship behavior. Yet, amidst the enormous variety of kinship rules, one stands out because it is universal, the incest taboo. In every society sexual relations between primary relatives—children and their parents, brothers and sisters— are prohibited. In every society as well, this prohibition is extended to some other relatives, although the human targets of the extensions vary. For most people, the notion of incest also engenders a feeling of horror, disbelief, or acute embarrassment.

Because it represents a universal pattern in a sea of diversity, anthropologists have long been puzzled by the incest taboo. Why, they have asked, is the taboo universal among primary relatives? Why is it variously extended? What causes the emotional climate that surrounds it?

The articles presented in this section attempt to answer some of these questions. White suggests that the incest taboo is a culturally generated rule that promotes the organization of larger groups through marriage alliances. Aberle and his associates feel that the taboo evolved as a cultural answer to the problem of inbreeding and sexual competition. Wolf suggests that the taboo simply reflects lack of sexual interest among primary relatives. As we examine these three attempts to explain the universality of the incest taboo, we will also gain an understanding of other aspects of kinship systems.

# 7

## THE DEFINITION AND PROHIBITION OF INCEST
*Leslie A. White*

*The late anthropologist Leslie White headed the resurgence of interest in cultural evolution in the United States. He was convinced that societies evolved by means of their cultural symbolic systems toward larger, more internally complex groups, stimulated by an inevitable progress in technology and the need to adapt. In this article, he applies this approach to the problem of the incest taboo. He rejects explanations that label the incest taboo as instinctual and argues strongly for the existence of sexual attraction among close family members. Such attraction, he asserts, must be culturally overcome so that families will marry out (practice exogamy), thereby allying themselves with other families to form larger groups. These larger groups will, in turn, facilitate defense and eliminate the endogamous families that failed to practice the taboo. Extensions of the taboo to other relatives vary, White argues, because alliances through marriage will fit particular kinship arrangements, adding support to his claims about the social function of the prohibition.*

> *Again and again in the world's history, savage tribes must have had plainly before their minds the simple practical alternative between marrying-out and being killed out.*
>
> E. B. Tylor*

The subject of incest has a strange fascination for man. He was preoccupied with it long before he developed the art of writing. We find incestuous episodes in the mythologies of countless peoples. And in advanced cultures, from Sophocles to Eugene O'Neill, incest has been one of the most popular of all literary themes. Men seem never to tire of it but continue to find it ever fresh and absorbing. Incest must indeed be reckoned as one of man's major interests in life.

Yet, despite this intense and perennial concern, it is a fact that incest is but little understood even today. Men of science have been obliged all too often to admit that they are baffled and to declare that it is too mysterious, too obscure, to yield to rational interpretation, at least for the present.

One of the more common explanations of the universal prohibition of incest is that it is instinctive. Thus Robert H. Lowie, a distinguished anthropologist, once accepted "Hobhouse's view that the sentiment is instinctive."[1] To "explain" an element of behavior by saying that it is "instinctive" contributes little to our understanding of it as a rule. Sometimes it merely conceals our ignorance with a verbal curtain of pseudo-knowledge. To say that prohibitions against incest are "instinctive" is of course to declare that there is a natural, inborn and innate feeling of

---

*Tylor, 1888, p. 267.

[1]Lowie, 1920, p. 15.

revulsion toward unions with close relatives. But if this were the case, why should societies enact strict laws to prevent them? Why should they legislate against something that everyone already wishes passionately to avoid? Do not, as a matter of fact, the stringent and worldwide prohibitions indicate a universal and powerful desire for sexual unions with one's relatives?[2] There are further objections to the instinct theory. Some societies regard marriage with a first cousin as incestuous while others do not. Are we to assume that the instinct varies from tribe to tribe? Certainly when we consider our own legal definitions of incest, which vary from state to state, to claim that a biological instinct can recognize state boundary lines is somewhat grotesque. In some societies it is incestuous to marry a parallel cousin (a child of your father's brother or of your mother's sister) but it is permissible, and may even be mandatory, to marry a cross cousin (a child of your father's sister or of your mother's brother). We cannot see how "instinct" can account for this, either; in fact, we cannot see how instinct can distinguish a cross cousin from a parallel cousin. It is usually incestuous to marry a clansman even though no genealogical connection whatever can be discovered with him, whereas marriage with a close relative in *another* clan may be permissible. Plainly, the instinct theory does not help us at all, and it is not easy to find a scientist to defend it today.[3]

---

[2]"Freud has shown all but conclusively that incestuous tendencies represent one of the most deeply rooted impulses of the individual." (Goldenweiser, 1937, p. 303, fn. 11.)

[3]In 1932, Professor Lowie abandoned the instinct theory of incest prohibitions. But he comes no closer to an explanation than to observe that "the aversion to incest is, therefore, best regarded as a primeval cultural adaptation" (Lowie, 1933, p. 67). In one of his recent works (Lowie, 1940, p. 232), he again discusses incest but goes no further than to suggest that "the horror of incest is not inborn, though it is doubtless a very ancient cultural feature."

Another theory, championed generations ago by Lewis H. Morgan and others, and not without defenders today, is that incest was defined and prohibited because inbreeding causes biological degeneration.[4] This theory is so plausible as to seem self-evident, but it is wrong for all that. In the first place, inbreeding as such does not cause degeneration; the testimony of biologists is conclusive on this point. To be sure, inbreeding intensifies the inheritance of traits, good or bad. If the offspring of a union of brother and sister are inferior it is because the parents were of inferior stock, not because they were brother and sister. But superior traits as well as inferior ones can be intensified by inbreeding, the plant and animal breeders frequently resort to this device to improve their strains. If the children of brother-sister or father-daughter unions in our own society are frequently feeble-minded or otherwise inferior it is because feeble-minded individuals are more likely to break the powerful incest tabu than are normal men and women and hence more likely to beget degenerate offspring. But in societies where brother-sister marriages are permitted or required, at least within the ruling family, as in ancient Egypt, aboriginal Hawaii and Incaic Peru, we may find excellence. Cleopatra was the offspring of brother-sister marriages continued through several generations and she was "not only handsome, vigorous, intellectual, but also prolific ... as perfect a specimen of the human race as could be found in any age or class of society."[5]

But there is still another objection to the degeneration theory as a means of accounting for the origin of prohibitions against incest. A number of competent ethnographers have claimed that certain tribes are quite ignorant of the nature of the biological process of reproduction, specifically, that they are unaware of the relationship between sexual intercourse and pregnancy. Or, they may believe that coitus is

---

[4]*See* Morgan, 1877, pp. 69, 378, 424.
[5]Mahaffy, 1915, p. 1.

prerequisite to pregnancy but not the cause of it.[6] B. Malinowski, for example, claims that the Trobriand Islanders denied that copulation has anything to do with pregnancy, not only among human beings but among the lower animals as well.[7] This thesis of ignorance of the facts of life among primitive peoples has been challenged by other enthnologists, and I am not prepared to adjudicate the dispute. But it may be pointed out that such ignorance should not be very surprising. Once a fact becomes well known there is a tendency to regard it as self-evident. But the relationship between coitus and pregnancy, a condition that would not be discovered until weeks or even a few months later, is anything but obvious. Furthermore, pregnancy does not always follow intercourse. And knowing primitive man's penchant for explaining so many things, the phenomena of life and death especially, in terms of supernatural forces or agents, we should not be surprised to find some tribes even today who do not understand the physiology of paternity.

At any rate, there must have been a time at which such understanding was not possessed by any members of the human race. We have no reason to believe that apes have *any* appreciation of these facts, and it must have taken man a long time to acquire it. There are reasons, however, as we shall show later on, for believing that incest tabus appeared in the very earliest stage of human social evolution, in all probability prior to an understanding of paternity. The reason for the prohibition of inbreeding could not therefore have been a desire to prevent deterioration of stock if the connection between copulation and the birth of children was not understood.

This thesis receives additional support from a consideration of the kinship systems of many

primitive peoples. In these systems a person calls many of his collateral relatives "brother" and "sister," namely, his parallel cousins of several degrees for example, and the children of his mother's and father's parallel cousins, also of several degrees. Marriage between individuals who call each other "brother" and "sister" is strictly prohibited by the incest tabu, even though they be cousins of the third or fourth degree. But marriage with a *first cross cousin* may be permitted and often is required. Now these people may not understand the biology of conception and pregnancy, but they know which woman bore each child. Thus we see that the marriage rules disregard the degree of biological relationship so far as preventing inbreeding is concerned; they may prohibit marriage with a fourth parallel cousin who is called "brother" or "sister," but permit or require marriage with a first cross cousin who is called "cousin." Obviously, the kinship terms express sociological rather than biological relationships. Obvious also is the fact that the incest tabus follow the pattern of social ties rather than those of blood.

But suppose that inbreeding did produce inferior offspring; are we to suppose that ignorant, magic-ridden savages could have established this correlation without rather refined statistical techniques? How could they have isolated the factor of inbreeding from numerous others such as genetics, nutrition, illnesses of mother and infant, etc., without some sort of medical criteria and measurements—even though crude—and without even the rudiments of statistics?

Finally, if we should grant that inbreeding does produce degeneracy, and that primitive peoples were able to recognize this fact, why did they prohibit marriage with a parallel cousin while allowing or even requiring union with a cross cousin? Both are equally close biologically. Or, why was marriage with a clansman prohibited even though the blood tie was so remote that it could not be established genealogically with the data available to memory, while marriage with a non-clansman was permitted even though he was a close blood relative? Obviously the de-

---

[6] *See* Montagu, 1937, both for a discussion of this subject and for bibliographic references to other articles.

[7] *See* Malinowski, 1929b, especially pp. 153 ff., 3, 171.

generacy theory is as weak as the instinct hypothesis, although it may be more engaging intellectually.

Sigmund Freud's theory is ingenious and appealing—in a dramatic sort of way at least. Proceeding from Darwin's conjectures concerning the primal social state of man, based upon what was then known about anthropoid apes, and utilizing W. Robertson Smith's studies of totemism and sacrifice, Freud developed the following thesis: in the earliest stage of human society, people lived in small groups each of which was dominated by a powerful male, the Father. This individual monopolized all females in the group, daughters as well as mothers. As the young males grew up and became sexually mature, the Father drove them away to keep them from sharing his females with him.

"One day," says Freud, "the expelled brothers joined forces, slew and ate the father, and thus put an end to the father horde. Together they dared and accomplished what would have remained impossible for them singly."[8] But they did not divide their Father's women among themselves as they had planned. Now that he was dead their hatred and aggressiveness disappeared, and their love and respect for him came to the fore. As a consequence, they determined to give him in death the submission and obedience they had refused in life. They made therefore a solemn pact to touch none of their Father's women and to seek mates elsewhere. This pledge was passed on from one generation to the next:[9] you must have nothing to do with the women of your father's household, i.e., of your own group, but must seek other mates. In this way the incest tabu and the institution of exogamy came into being.

This part of *Totem and Taboo* is great drama and not without value as an interpretation of powerful psychological forces, just as *Hamlet* is great drama in the same sense. But as ethnology, Freud's theory would still be inadequate even if this much were verifiable. It does not even attempt to account for the many and varied forms of incest prohibition.

It is not our purpose here to survey and criticize all of the many theories that have been advanced in the past to account for the definition and prohibition of incest. We may however briefly notice two others before we leave the subject, namely, those of E. Westermarck and Emile Durkheim.

Westermarck's thesis that "the fundamental cause of the exogamous prohibitions seems to be the remarkable absence of erotic feelings between persons living very closely together from childhood, leading to a positive feeling of aversion when the act is thought of,"[10] is not in accord with the facts in the first place and would still be inadequate if it were. Propinquity does not annihilate sexual desire, and if it did there would be no need for stringent prohibitions. Secondly, incest tabus are frequently in force between persons not living in close association.

Durkheim attempts to explain the prohibition of incest as a part of his general theory of totemism. The savage knew intuitively, Durkheim reasoned, that blood is a vital fluid or principle. To shed the blood of one's own totemic group would be a great sin or crime. Since blood would be shed in the initial act of intercourse, a man must eschew all women of his own totem. Thus the tabu against incest and rules of exogamy came into being.[11] This theory is wholly inadequate ethnologically. Tabus against incest

---

[8]Freud, 1931, p. 247.

[9]In another work (1938, p. 617, fn. 1), Freud suggests, if he does not say so outright, that the incest tabu became incorporated into the germ plasm and was consequently transmitted by means of biological heredity: "The incest barrier probably belongs to the historical acquisitions of humanity and, like other moral taboos, it must be fixed in many individuals through organic heredity."

[10]Westermarck, 1921, Table of Contents for Ch. 20.

[11]Durkheim, 1898, pp. 50 ff.

are much more widespread than totemism; the former are virtually universal, the latter is far from being so. And the theory does not even attempt to explain the many diverse forms of the definition and prohibition of incest.

In view of repeated attempts and as many failures to account for the origin of definitions of incest and of rules regulating its prohibition, is it any wonder that many scholars, surveying decades of fruitless theories, have become discouraged and have come to feel that the problem is still too difficult to yield to scientific interpretation?

In the same work in which he presented his theory, but some pages earlier, Freud said: "Still, in the end, one is compelled to subscribe to Frazer's resigned statement, namely, that we do not know the origin of incest dread and do not even know how to guess at it."[12]

Ralph Linton treats of the subject as follows:[13]

The causes which underlie such limitations on marriage, technically known as incest regulations, are very imperfectly understood. Since these regulations are of universal occurrence, it seems safe to assume that their causes are everywhere present, but biological factors can be ruled out at once. Close inbreeding is not necessarily injurious. . . . Neither are purely social explanations of incest regulations altogether satisfactory, since the forms which these regulations assume are extremely varied. . . . It seems possible that there are certain psychological factors involved, but these can hardly be strong enough or constant enough to account for the institutionalization of incest regulations. . . .

They have probably originated from a combination of all these factors. . . .

In other words, *somewhere* in the man-culture situation lie the causes of incest regulations, but where they are and why and how they are exercised are matters too obscure for description or explanation.

The late Alexander Goldenweiser, a prominent disciple of Franz Boas, never discovered the secret of the prohibition of incest. In *Early Civilization* he spoke of certain tabus that "are everywhere reinforced by the so-called 'horror of incest,' an emotional reaction of somewhat mysterious origin."[14] Fifteen years later, in *Anthropology,* his last major work, he could go no further than to repeat these identical words.[15]

The sociologists have little to offer. Kimball Young, for example, disavows instinct as the source of incest prohibitions, but he advances no further explanation than to assert that "the taboo is a rather constant and expected result arising from the very nature of the social interaction between parents and children and among the children themselves"[16] —which is virtually equivalent to no explanation at all.

The late Clark Wissler, one of the foremost anthropologists of our day, observes.[17]

. . . so far as we can see, the only facts sufficiently well established to serve as a starting point are that anti-incest responses of some kind are universal among mankind. As to why these are universal, we are no nearer a solution than before.

These are discouraging words indeed. "Anti-incest responses" help us no more than "an instinctive horror" of incest. But in the phrase "we are no nearer a solution [now] than before," we

---

[12]Freud, 1931, p. 217. Frazer's statement was: "Thus the ultimate origin of exogamy and with it the law of incest—since exogamy was devised to prevent incest—remains a problem nearly as dark as ever." (*Totemism and Exogamy,* Vol. I, p. 165.)

[13]Linton, 1936, pp. 125–126.

[14]Goldenweiser, 1922, p. 242.

[15]*Idem.,* 1937, p. 303.

[16]Young, 1942, p. 406.

[17]Wissler, 1929, p. 145.

may find a clue to a way out of the dilemma. Perhaps these theorists have been on the wrong track. Science has found itself on the wrong track countless times during its relatively brief career so far. So many [times], in fact, that many of the important achievements of science consist, not in the discovery of some new fact or principle, but in erecting signs which read "Blind alley. Do not enter!" Phrenology was one of these blind alleys. But until it has been explored, how can one know whether a passage is a blind alley or a corridor leading to a new world? Once it has been found to be a blind alley, however, other scientists need not and should not waste their time exploring it again. Perhaps we are confronted by blind alleys in the various theories of incest and exogamy that we have just surveyed. Wissler's admission that "we are no nearer a solution [now] than before" would lead us to think so.

Fortunately we are not in the situation of a mariner who has lost his bearings and who must try to recover his true course. We do not need to seek a new path in the hope of finding an adequate solution of the problem of incest. The solution has already been found, and that long ago.

Confusion in this field of ethnological theory has been due to circumstances such as we have just described. Theorists who have sought biological or psychological explanations of incest tabus have been on the wrong track; they have only led us into blind alleys. Those who have sought a *culturological* explanation have succeeded fully and well.[18] The culturological point of view is younger and less widely known than the psychological or even the sociological. Although it was set forth simply and adequately by the great English anthropologist E. B.Tylor as early as 1871, in the first chapter of *Primitive Culture*—which was significantly enough entitled "The Science of Culture"—it has not become widely known or appreciated among social scientists, even among cultural anthropologists. There are some who recognize in the new science of culture only a mystical, fatalistic metaphysic that should be shunned like the Devil.[19] So habituated to psychological interpretations are many students of human behavior that they are unable to rise to the level of culturological interpretation. Thus, Goldenweiser looked to psychology for ethnological salvation:[20] "It seems hardly fair to doubt that psychoanalysis will ultimately furnish a satisfactory psychological interpretation of this 'horror of incest'." Professor William F. Ogburn observes that:

> Incest taboos and marriage regulations may be quite fully described historically and culturally, yet there is something decidedly strange about incest and about marriage prohibitions. One's curiosity is not satisfied by the cultural facts.[21]

And even men like Lowie and Wissler, who have done excellent work along culturological lines in other areas, have relapsed to the psychological level when confronted with the problem of incest. Thus Lowie once declared that "it is not the function of the ethnologist but of the biologist and psychologist to explain why man has so deep-rooted a horror of incest."[22] And Wissler is inclined to turn over all problems of

---

[18]Cf. White, 1947b.

[19]Cf. White, 1947a, especially pp. 189–205.

[20]Goldenweiser, 1922, p. 242; and 1937, p. 303.

[21]Ogburn, 1922, p. 175. What Professor Ogburn means apparently is that culturology cannot tell us *all* that we want to know about incest. This is true; psychology must be enlisted in the inquiry also. But one must insist upon a sharp and clear distinction between the psychological problem and the culturological problem. Psychology cannot account for the *origin* or the *form* of the prohibitions; only culturology can do this. But for an understanding of the way the human primate organism behaves—thinks, feels, and acts—within, or with reference to, one of these cultural forms, we must go to psychology. *See* White, 1947b, especially the closing pages.

[22]Lowie, 1920, p. 15.

cultural origins to the psychologist, leaving to the anthropologist the study of traits after they have been launched upon their cultural careers.[23]

The science of culture has, as we have already indicated, long ago given us an adequate explanation of incest prohibitions. We find it set forth simply and succinctly in an essay by E. B. Tylor published in 1888: "On a Method of Investigating the Development of Institutions, Applied to the Laws of Marriage and Descent:"[24]

Exogamy, enabling a growing tribe to keep itself compact by constant unions between its spreading clans, enables it to overmatch any number of small intermarrying groups, isolated and helpless. Again and again in the world's history, savage tribes must have had plainly before their minds the simple practical alternative between marrying-out and being killed out. (p. 267)

The origin of incest tabus greatly antedates clan organization, but a sure clue to an understanding of incest prohibitions and exogamy is given by Tylor nevertheless: primitive people were confronted with a choice between "marrying-out and being killed out." The argument may be set forth as follows:

Man, like all other animal species, is engaged in a struggle for existence. Cooperation, mutual aid, may become valuable means of carrying on this struggle at many points. A number of individuals working together can do many things more efficiently and effectively than the same individuals working singly. And a cooperative group can do certain things that lone individuals cannot do at all. Mutual aid makes life more secure for both individual and group. One might expect, therefore, that in the struggle for security and survival every effort would be made to foster cooperation and to secure its benefits.

Among the lower primates there is little co-

operation. To be sure, in very simple operations one ape may coordinate his efforts with those of another. But their cooperation is limited and rudimentary because the means of communication are crude and limited; cooperation requires communication. Monkeys and apes can communicate with one another by means of signs—vocal utterances or gestures—but the range of ideas that can be communicated in this way is very narrow indeed. Only articulate speech can make extensive and versatile exchange of ideas possible, and this is lacking among anthropoids. Such a simple form of cooperation as "you go around the house that way while I go around the other way, meeting you on the far side," is beyond the reach of the great apes. With the advent of articulate speech, however, the possibilities of communication became virtually unlimited. We can readily see its significance for social organization in general and for incest and exogamy in particular.

One might get the impression from some psychologists, the Freudians especially, perhaps, that the incestuous wish is itself instinctive, that somehow a person "just naturally" focuses his sexual desires upon a *relative* rather than upon a *non*-relative, and, among relatives, upon the closer rather than the remoter degrees of consanguinity. This view is quite as unwarranted as the theory of an "instinctive horror" of incest; an inclination toward sexual union with close relatives is no more instinctive than the social regulations devised to prevent it. A child has sexual hunger as well as food hunger. And he fixes his sex hunger upon certain individuals as he does his food hunger upon certain edible substances. He finds sexual satisfaction in persons close to him because they *are* close to him, not because they are his relatives. To be sure, they may be close to him because they are his relatives, but that is another matter. As a consequence of proximity and satisfaction the child fixates his sexual desires upon his immediate associates, his parents and his siblings, just as he fixates his food hungers upon familiar foods that have given satisfaction. He thus comes to have

[23]Wissler, 1927.
[24]Tylor, 1888.

definite orientations and firm attachments in the realm of sex as in the field of nutrition. There is thus no mystery about incestuous desire; it is merely the formation and fixation of definite channels of experience and satisfaction.

We find therefore, even in sub-human primate families, a strong inclination toward inbreeding; one strives to obtain sexual satisfaction from a close associate. This tendency is carried over into human society. But here it is incompatible with the cooperative way of life that articulate speech makes possible. In the basic activities of subsistence and defense against enemies, cooperation becomes important because life is made more secure thereby. Other factors being constant, the tribe that exploits most fully the possibilities of mutual aid will have the best chance to survive. In times of crisis, cooperation may become a matter of life or death. In providing food and maintaining an effective defense against foreign foes, cooperation becomes all-important.

But would primordial man be obliged to construct a cooperative organization for subsistence and defense from the very beginning, or could he build upon a foundation already in existence? In the evolutionary process, whether it be social or biological, we almost always find the new growing out of or based upon, the old. And such was the case here; the new cooperative organization for food and defense was built upon a structure already present: the family. After all, virtually everyone belonged to one family or another, and the identification of the cooperative group with the sex-based family would mean that the benefits of mutual aid would be shared by all. When, therefore, certain species of anthropoids acquired articulate speech and became human beings, a new element, an *economic* factor, was introduced into an institution which has up to now rested solely upon sexual attraction between male and female. We are, of course, using the term *economic* in a rather broad sense here to include safety as well as subsistence. The human primate family had now become a corporation with nutritive and protective functions as

well as sexual and incidentally reproductive functions. And life was made more secure as a consequence.

But a regime of cooperation confined to the members of a family would be correspondingly limited in its benefits. If cooperation is advantageous *within* family groups, why not between families as well? The problem was now to extend the scope of mutual aid.

In the primate order, as we have seen, the social relationships between mates, parents and children, and among siblings antedates articulate speech and cooperation. They are strong as well as primary. And, just as the earliest cooperative group was built upon these social ties, so would a subsequent extension of mutual aid have to reckon with them. At this point we run squarely against the tendency to mate with an intimate associate. Cooperation *between* families cannot be established if parent marries child; and brother, sister. A way must be found to overcome this centripetal tendency with a centrifugal force. This way was found in the definition and prohibition of incest. If persons were forbidden to marry their parents or siblings they would be compelled to marry into some other family group—or remain celibate, which is contrary to the nature of primates. The leap was taken; a way was found to unite families with one another, and social evolution as a *human* affair was launched upon its career. It would be difficult to exaggerate the significance of this step. Unless some way had been found to establish strong and enduring social ties between families, social evolution could have gone no further on the human level than among the anthropoids.

With the definition and prohibition of incest, *families* became units in the cooperative process as well as individuals. Marriages came to be contracts first between families, later between even larger groups. The individual lost much of his initiative in courtship and choice of mates, for it was now a group affair. Among many primitive peoples a youth may not even be acquainted with his bride before marriage; in some cases he may not even have seen her. Children may be betrothed in childhood or infancy—or even before they are born. To be sure, there are tribes where one can become acquainted or even intimate with his spouse before marriage, but the group character of the contract is there nevertheless. And in our own society today a marriage is still an alliance between families to a very considerable extent. Many a man has expostulated, "But I am marrying *her,* not her family!" only to discover his lack of realism later.

The widespread institutions of levirate and sororate are explainable by this theory also. In the levirate a man marries the wife or wives of his deceased brother. When a man customarily marries the unwed sister of his deceased wife the practice is called sororate. In both cases the group character of marriage is manifest. Each group of consanguinei supplies a member of the other group with a spouse. If the spouse dies, the relatives of the deceased must supply another to take his or her place. The alliance between families is important and must be continued; even death cannot part them.

The equally widespread institutions of bride-price and dowry likewise find their significance in the prohibition of incest to establish cooperation between family groups. The incest tabu necessitates marriage *between* family groups. But it cannot guarantee a continuation of the mutual aid arrangement thus established. This is where bride-price and dowry come in: they are devices for making permanent the marriage tie that the prohibition of incest has established. When a family or a group of relatives has received articles of value as bride-price or dowry, they distribute them as a rule among their various members. Should the marriage tie be broken or dissolved, they may have to return the wealth received at the time of the marriage. This is almost certain to be the case if it can be shown that the spouse whose relatives were the recipients of the bride-price or dowry was at fault. It very often happens that the relatives are reluctant to return the wealth if indeed they still have it. If it has already been consumed they will have to dig into their own pockets. It may already be

earmarked for the marriage of one of their own group. In any event, the return of dowry or bride-price would be an inconvenience or a deprivation. Consequently they are likely to take a keen interest in the marriage and to try to prevent their own relative from doing anything to disrupt it.

According to our theory the prohibition of incest has at bottom an economic motivation— not that primitive peoples were *aware* of this motive, however, for they were not. Rules of exogamy originated as crystallizations of processes of a *social system* rather than as products of individual psyches. Inbreeding was prohibited and marriage between groups was made compulsory in order to obtain the maximum benefits of cooperation. If this theory be sound, we should find marriage and the family in primitive society wearing a definite economic aspect. This is, in fact, precisely what we do find. Let us turn for summary statements to two leading authorities in social anthropology. Robert H. Lowie writes as follows.[25]

Marriage, as we cannot too often or too vehemently insist, is only to a limited extent based on sexual considerations. The primary motive, so far as the individual mates are concerned, is precisely the founding of a self-sufficient economic aggregate. A Kai [of New Guinea] does not marry because of desires he can readily gratify outside of wedlock without assuming any responsibilities; he marries because he needs a woman to make pots and to cook his meals, to manufacture nets and weed his plantations, in return for which he provides the household with game and fish and builds the dwelling.

And A. R. Radcliffe-Brown makes similar observations concerning the aborigines of Australia:[26]

---

[25]Lowie, 1920, pp. 65–66.
[26]Radcliffe-Brown, 1930, p. 435.

The important function of the family is that it provides for the feeding and bringing up of the children. It is based on the cooperation of man and wife, the former providing the flesh food and the latter the vegetable food, so that quite apart from the question of children a man without a wife is in an unsatisfactory position since he has no one to supply him regularly with vegetable food, to provide his firewood and so on. This economic aspect of the family is a most important one. . . . I believe that in the minds of the natives themselves this aspect of marriage, i.e., its relation to subsistence, is of greatly more importance than the fact that man and wife are sexual partners.

Turning to the colonial period in America we find the economic character of the family equally pronounced. According to William F. Ogburn:[27]

In colonial times in America the family was a very important economic organization. Not infrequently it produced substantially all that it consumed, with the exception of such things as metal tools, utensils, salt and certain luxuries. The home was, in short, a factory. Civilization was based on a domestic system of production of which the family was the center.

The economic power of the family produced certain corresponding social condi-

tions. In marrying, a man sought not only a mate and companion but a business partner. Husband and wife each had specialized skills and contributed definite services to the partnership. Children were regarded, as the laws of the time showed, not only as objects of affection but as productive agents. The age of marriage, the birth rate and the attitude toward divorce were all affected by the fact that the home was an economic institution. Divorce or separation not only broke a personal relationship but a business one as well.

And in our own society today, the economic basis of marriage and the family is made clear by suits for breach of promise and alienation of affections in which the law takes a very materialistic, even monetary, view of love and romance.[28] Suits for non-support, alimony, property settlements upon divorce, the financial obligations between parents and children, and so on, exhibit further the economic function of the family. Marriage for many women today means a greater economic return for unskilled labor than could be obtained in any other occupation.

It is interesting to note, in this connection, that Freud, who, according to popular belief, "attributes everything to sex," nevertheless declares that "the motivating force of human society is fundamentally economic."[29]

---

[27]Ogburn, 1933, pp. 661–662.
We recall, also, Benjamin Franklin's account of his proposal to marry a girl providing her parents would give him "as much money with their daughter as would pay off my remaining debt for the printing-house." He even suggested that they "mortgage their house in the loan-office" if they did not have the cash on hand. The parents, however, thought the printing business a poor risk and declined to give both money and girl. "Therefore," says Franklin, "I was forbidden the house, and the daughter shut up." (Franklin, 1940, p. 78.)

[28]One court ruling observes that "the gist of the action for alienation of affections is the loss of consortium. 'This is a property right growing out of the marriage relation'. . . ." (Supreme Court of Connecticut, Case of Maggay vs. Nikitko, 1933), quoted in Turano, 1934b, p. 295.
Another legal statement says that "the law generally takes the rather worldly view that marriage is a 'valuable' consideration; a thing not only possessing value, but one the value of which may be estimated in money, and therefore, in a sense, marriage engagements are regarded as business transactions, entered into with a view, in part, at least, to pecuniary advantage." (Ruling Case Law, Vol. 4, p. 143, quoted in Turano, 1934a, p. 40.)
[29]Freud, 1920, p. 269.

The notion that marriage is an institution brought into being to provide individuals with a means of satisfying their sex hunger is naive and anthropocentric. Marriage *does* provide an avenue of sexual exercise and satisfaction, to be sure. But it was not sexual desire that produced the institution. Rather it was the exigencies of a social system that was striving to make full use of its resources for cooperative endeavor. Marriage, as an institution, finds its explanation in terms of socio-cultural process rather than individual psychology. In primitive society there was frequently ample means of sexual exercise outside of wedlock. And in our own society the great extent of prostitution, the high incidence of venereal disease as an index of promiscuity, as well as other evidence,[30] show that the exercise of sexual functions is not confined to one's own spouse by any means. As a matter of fact, marriage very often restricts the scope of one's sexual activity. Indeed, monogamy ideally considered is the next thing to celibacy.

Nor is love the basis of marriage and the family, however fondly this notion may be cherished. No culture could afford to use such a fickle and ephemeral sentiment as love as the basis of an important institution. Love is here today but it may be gone tomorrow. But economic needs are with us always. Absence of love is not sufficient grounds for divorce. Indeed, one may despise and loathe, hate and fear one's mate and still be unable to obtain a divorce. At least one state in the Union will grant no divorce at all. And certain religious faiths take the same position. Marriage and the family are society's first and fundamental way of making provision for the economic needs of the individual. And it was the definition and prohibition of incest that

initiated this whole course of social development.

But to return to the definitions and prohibitions themselves. These vary, as we saw at the outset, from culture to culture. The variations are to be explained in terms of the specific circumstances under which cooperation is to take place. One set of circumstances will require one definition of incest and one form of marriage; another set will require different customs. The habitat and the technological adjustment to it, the mode of subsistence, circumstances of defense and offense, division of labor between the sexes, and degree of cultural development are factors which condition the definition of incest and the formulation of rules to prohibit it. No people known to modern science customarily permits marriage between parent and child. Brother-sister marriage has been restricted to the ruling families of a few advanced cultures, such as those of ancient Egypt, Hawaii, and the Inca of Peru. But this is not "royal incest," as Reo Fortune calls it,[31] or "sanctioned incest" to use Kimball Young's phrase.[32] Incest is by definition something criminal and prohibited. These marriages between siblings of royal families were not only not prohibited; they were required. They are examples of endogamy, as the prohibition[s] of brother-sister marriages are examples of exogamy. Solidarity is a source of strength and effective action in society, as cooperation is a way of achieving security. And endogamy promotes solidarity as exogamy fosters size and strength of mutual aid groups.

In view of the fact that a sure clue to the reason for the origin of prohibitions of incest was set forth by Tylor as early as 1888, it is rather

---

[30]"... virginity at marriage will be close to the vanishing point for males born after 1930, and for females born after 1940 ... intercourse with future spouse before marriage will become universal by 1950 or 1955." (Lewis M. Terman, *Psychologic Factors in Marital Happiness,* p. 323 [New York, 1938]), as quoted in Hohman and Schaffner, 1947, p. 502.

[31]Fortune, 1932, p. 622. R. H. Lowie also speaks of brother-sister marriage in Hawaii and Peru as "incest" (Lowie, 1940, p. 233). J. S. Slotkin, too, in a recent article (Slotkin, 1947, p. 613) appears to identify incest with certain specific forms of inbreeding rather than with a kind of union that is defined and prohibited as a crime.

[32]Young, 1942, p. 406.

remarkable that we should find anthropologists and sociologists today who juggle with "anti-incest responses" and who look to psychoanalysis for ultimate understanding. As a matter of fact, we find the reasons for exogamy set forth by Saint Augustine in *The City of God* (Bk. XV), more than 1400 years before Tylor:

> For it is very reasonable and just that men, among whom concord is honorable and useful, should be bound together by various relationships, and that one man should not himself sustain many relationships, but that the various relationships should be distributed among several, and should thus serve to bind together the greatest number in the same social interests. "Father" and "father-in-law" are the names of two relationships. When, therefore, a man has one person for his father, another for his father-in-law, friendship extends itself to a larger number.

He comments upon the fact that Adam was both father and father-in-law to his sons and daughters:

> So too Eve his wife was both mother and mother-in-law to her children . . . while had there been two women, one the mother, the other the mother-in-law, the family affection would have had a wider field. Then the sister herself by becoming a wife sustained in her single person two relationships which, had they been distributed among individuals, one being sister, and another being wife, the family tie would have embraced a greater number of persons.

Saint Augustine does not, in these passages at least, make explicit the advantages in security of life which would accrue to the group as a consequence of exogamy. But he makes it quite clear that community of social interest and "greater numbers of persons" in the group are the reasons for the prohibition of incest.

If an understanding of incest and exogamy is

as old in social philosophy as Saint Augustine and as early in anthropological science as Tylor, why is it that the subject is still so obscure and so little understood among scholars today? We have already suggested the answer: a preference for psychological rather than culturological explanations. Anthropomorphism is an inveterate habit in human thought. To explain institutions in terms of psychology—of wish, desire, aversion, imagination, fear, etc.—has long been popular. Explanations of human behavior in terms of psychological determinants preceded therefore explanations in terms of cultural determinants. But culturological problems cannot be solved by psychology. Preoccupation with psychological explanations has not only kept many scholars from finding the answer; it has prevented them from recognizing the solution when it has been reached by the science of culture. The sociological explanation, such as Kimball Young's "social interaction," is no better. As a scientific explanation it is not only inadequate; it is empty and meaningless. The sociologist's fixation upon "social interaction" keeps him, too, from appreciating a scientific interpretation of culture as a distinct class of phenomena.[33] Even men who have made notable contributions to culturology, such as Kroeber, Lowie, and Wissler, have failed to see the significance of Tylor's early discussion of exogamy. The following incident is remarkable and revealing. A. L. Kroeber and T. T. Waterman reprinted Tylor's essay, "On the Method of Investigating the Development of Institutions," in their *Source Book in Anthropology*[34] in 1920. But in a subsequent edition,[35] they cut the article down to conserve space, and omitted this highly significant passage!

Important contributions to science are sometimes made "before their time," that is, before the general level of scientific advance has

---

[33]Cf. White, 1947a, pp. 186 ff.
[34]Kroeber and Waterman, 1920, 1924.
[35]*Ibid.*, 1931.

reached a point where widespread appreciation becomes possible. There was really very little that was novel in the work of Darwin; most if not all of the ideas and facts had been presented before. But the broad front of the cultural process of biologic thought had not advanced sufficiently prior to 1859 to make a general acceptance of this point of view possible. So it is with the problem of incest. An adequate explanation has been extant for decades. But, because the problem is a culturological one, and because the science of culture is still so young and so few scholars even today are able to grasp and appreciate its nature and scope, an understanding of incest and its prohibitions is still very limited. As culturology develops and matures, however, this understanding as well as that of a host of other suprapsychological problems will become commonplace.

We do not wish to minimize the extent of this understanding today. Despite the ignorance and confusion of many scholars, there is a considerable number who do understand incest tabus. Thus Reo Fortune states that:[36]

A separation of affinal relationship from consanguineous relationship assures a wider recognition of social obligation. . . . Any incestuous alliance between two persons within a single consanguineous group is in so far a withdrawal of their consanguineous group from the alliance and so endangers the group's survival.

Malinowski, too, has illuminated the problem of incest tabus. Instead of emphasizing, however, the positive values that would accrue from alliances formed as a consequence of compulsory exogamy, he dwells upon the disruption and discord that the unrestricted exercise of sexual appetites would introduce into a small group of relatives or close associates. He writes:[37]

The sexual impulse is in general a very upsetting and socially disruptive force, [it] cannot enter into a previously existing sentiment without producing a revolutionary change in it. Sexual interest is therefore incompatible with any family relationship, whether parental or between brothers and sisters. . . . If erotic passion were allowed to invade the precincts of the home it would not merely establish jealousies and competitive elements and disorganize the family but it would also subvert the most fundamental bonds of kinship on which the further development of all social relations is based. . . . A society which allowed incest could not develop a stable family; it would therefore be deprived of the strongest foundations for kinship, and this in a primitive community would mean absence of social order.

B. Z. Seligman expresses somewhat similar views—as well as others that are less discerning.[38] A good statement on the nature and genesis of incest tabus is tucked away in a footnote in a recent monograph by John Gillin.[38a] William I. Thomas sees clearly the reasons for prohibitions of incest: "The horror of incest is thus plainly of social derivation."[39]

And Freud, apart from his drama of patricide, comes close to an understanding of incest tabus and exogamy. He says:

The incest prohibition, had . . . a strong practical foundation. Sexual need does not unite men; it separates them. . . . Thus there was nothing left for the brothers [after they had killed their father], if they wanted to live together, but to erect the incest prohibition.[40]

In another work he observes that:[41]

---

[36]Fortune, 1932, p. 620.
[37]Malinowski, 1930, p. 630. *See also, idem,* 1929a, Vol. 13, p. 407.

[38]Seligman, 1929, pp. 243–244, 247, 268–269.
[38a]Gillin, 1936, p. 93.
[39]Thomas, 1937, p. 197.
[40]Freud, 1931, pp. 250–251.
[41]*Idem.,* 1938, pp. 616–617.

KINSHIP AND SOCIAL ORGANIZATION

The observance of this [incest] barrier is above all a demand of cultural society, which must guard against the absorption by the family of those interests which it needs for the production of higher social units. Society, therefore, uses all means to loosen those family ties in every individual. . . .

The cultural function, if not the genesis, of incest tabus and of rules of exogamy seems to be very clearly seen and appreciated here. It is interesting to note, too, that Freud holds substantially the same view of the relationship between restrictions upon sexual gratification and social evolution that has been set forth earlier in this essay. One of the principal themes of *Civilization and Its Discontents*[42] is "the extent to which civilization is built up on renunciation of instinctual gratifications. . . . This 'cultural privation' dominates the whole field of social relations between human beings" (p. 63). He sees that "the first result of culture was that a larger number of human beings could live together in common" (p. 68); that "one of culture's principal endeavors is to cement men and women together in larger units" (p. 72). Thus, although he proceeds from different premises, Freud comes to essentially the same conclusions as ours.

There is, then, considerable understanding of incest and exogamy extant in the literature today. Yet, in a comparatively recent review of the whole problem a prominent anthropologist, John M. Cooper, has concluded that "the desire to multiply the social bonds [has] in all probability not been [an] important factor" in the origin of incest prohibitions.[43] How far he is from an understanding of the problem is indicated by the two "chief factors" which he cites: "(a) sex callousness, resulting from early and intimate association . . . ; (b) the distinctly social purpose of preserving standards of sex decency within the family and kinship circle." The first factor is contrary to fact; intimacy fosters incest rather

than callousness. The second explains nothing at all: what are standards of sex decency, why do they vary from tribe to tribe, and why is it necessary to preserve them?

The culturological theory of incest receives support from a comparison of primitive cultures with our own. The crime of incest is punished with greater severity in primitive societies than in our own, as Reo Fortune[44] has observed. Among the former the penalty of death is quite common; in our society punishment seldom exceeds ten years imprisonment and is often much less. The reason for this difference is not far to seek. In primitive societies, personal and kinship ties between individuals and families were more important than they are in highly developed cultures. The small mutual-aid group was a tremendously important social unit in the struggle for security. The very survival of the group depended to a considerable extent upon alliances formed by exogamy. In advanced cultures the situation is different. Society is no longer based upon kinship ties, but upon property relationships and territorial distinctions. The political state has replaced the tribe and clan. Occupational groups and economic organization also become important bases of social life. The importance of exogamy is thus much diminished and the penalties for incest become less severe. It is not to be expected, however, that restrictions upon inbreeding will ever be removed entirely. Kinship is still an important, though relatively less important, feature of our social organization and will probably remain so indefinitely. Rules of exogamy and endogamy will therefore continue to be needed to regulate and order this aspect of our social life.

In the various interpretations, both sound and unsound, of the definition and prohibition of incest we have a neat example of a contrast be-

---

[42]*Idem.,* 1930.
[43]Cooper, 1932, p. 20.

[44]Fortune, 1932, p. 620. Freud also remarks that "This dread of incest . . . seems to be even more active and stronger among primitive races living today than among the civilized." (Freud, 1931, p. 217)

tween psychological explanations on the one hand and culturological explanations on the other. The problem simply does not yield to psychological solution. On the contrary, the evidence, both clinical and ethnographic, indicates that the desire to form sexual unions with an intimate associate is both powerful and widespread. Indeed, Freud opines that "the prohibition against incestuous object-choice [was] perhaps the most maiming wound ever inflicted . . . on the erotic life of man."[45] Psychology discloses an "incestuous wish" therefore, not a motive for its prevention. The problem yields very readily, however, to culturological interpretation. Man, as an animal species, lives in groups as well as individually. Relationships between individuals in the human species are determined by the *culture* of the group—that is, by the ideas, sentiments, tools, techniques, and behavior patterns, [which] are dependent upon the use of symbols[46] and which are handed down from one generation to another by means of this same faculty. These culture traits constitute a continuum, a stream of interacting elements. In this interacting process, new combinations and syntheses are formed, some traits become obsolete and drop out of the stream, some new ones enter it. The stream of culture thus flows, changes, grows and develops in accordance with laws of its own. Human behavior is but the reactions of the organism man to this stream of culture. Human behavior—in the mass, or of a typical member of a group—is therefore culturally determined. A people has an aversion to drinking cow's milk, avoids mothers-in-law, believes that exercise promotes health, practices divination or vaccination, eats roasted worms or grasshoppers, etc., because [its] culture contains trait-stimuli that evoke such responses. These traits cannot be accounted for psychologically.

And so it is with the definition and prohibition of incest. From psychology we learn that the human animal tends to unite sexually with someone close to him. The institution of exogamy is not only *not* explained by citing this tendency; it is contrary to it. But when we turn to the cultures that determine the relations between members of a group and regulate their social intercourse we readily find the reason for the definition of incest and the origin of exogamy. The struggle for existence is as vigorous in the human species as elsewhere. Life is made more secure, for group as well as individual, by cooperation. Articulate speech makes cooperation possible, extensive, and varied in human society. Incest was defined and exogamous rules were formulated in order to make cooperation compulsory and extensive, to the end that life be made more secure. These institutions were created by *social* systems, not by *neuro-sensory-muscular-glandular* systems. They were syntheses of culture elements formed within the interactive stream of culture traits. Variations of definition and prohibition of incest are due to the great variety of situations. In one situation, in one organization of culture traits—technological, social, philosophic, etc.—we will find one type of definition of incest and one set of rules of exogamy; in a different situation we find another definition and other rules. Incest and exogamy are thus defined in terms of the mode of life of a people—by the mode of subsistence, the means and circumstances of offense and defense, the means of communication and transportation, customs of residence, knowledge, techniques of thought, etc. And the mode of life, in all its aspects, technological, sociological, and philosophical, is culturally determined.

## BIBLIOGRAPHY

COOPER, J. M.
    1932   Incest Prohibitions in Primitive Culture. *Primitive Man,* 5: 1–20.
DURKHEIM, E.
    1898   La prohibition de l'incest et ses origines. *L'Anée Sociologique,* 1: 1–70. Paris.

---

[45]Freud, 1930, p. 74.
[46]Cf. White, 1940.

FORTUNE, R.
    1932   Incest. *Encyclopedia of the Social
           Sciences,* Vol. VII. New York.
FRANKLIN, B.
    1940   *Autobiography.* Pocket Books, Inc., New
           York.
FREUD, S.
    1920   *General Introduction to Psychoanalysis.*
           New York.
    1930   *Civilization and its Discontents.* New
           York.
    1931   *Totem and Taboo.* The New Republic
           edition, New York.
    1938   Contributions to the Theory of Sex, in:
           *The Basic Writings of Sigmund Freud,*
           Modern Library edition. New York.
GILLIN, J.
    1936   The Barama River Caribs of British
           Guiana. *Papers, Peabody Museum,* Vol.
           XIV, No. 2. Cambridge, Mass.
GOLDENWEISER, A.
    1922   *Early Civilization.* New York.
    1937   *Anthropology.* New York.
HOHMAN, L. B. and B. SCHAFFNER
    1947   The Sex Life of Unmarried Men.
           *American Journal of Sociology,* 52:
           501–507
KROEBER, A. L., and T. T. WATERMAN
    1920, 1924   *Source Book in Anthropology.*
           Berkeley; New York (1931).
LINTON, R.
    1936   *The Study of Man.* New York.
LOWIE, R. H.
    1920   *Primitive Society.* New York.
    1933   The Family as a Social Unit. *Papers,
           Michigan Academy of Science, Arts and
           Letters,* 18: 53–69.
    1940   *An Introduction to Cultural Anthropology*
           (2nd ed.). New York.
MAHAFFY, J. P.
    1915   Cleopatra VI. *Journ. Egypt. Archeol.,*
           Vol. 2.
MALINOWSKI, B.
    1929a   Kinship. *Encyclopaedia Britannica,*
           14th ed.
    1929b   *The Sexual Life of Savages.* London.
    1930   Culture. *Encyclopedia of the Social
           Sciences,* Vol. IV.

MONTAGU, M. F. ASHLEY
    1937   Physiological Paternity in Australia.
           *American Anthropologist,* n.s., 39:
           175–183.
MORGAN, L. H.
    1877   *Ancient Society.* New York.
OGBURN, W. F.
    1922   *Social Change.* New York
    1933   The Family and its Functions, in: *Recent
           Social Trends in the United States*
           (one-volume edition). New York.
RADCLIFFE-BROWN, A. R.
    1930   The Social Organization of Australian
           Tribes. *Oceania,* Vol. 1.
SEGLIGMAN, B. Z.
    1929   Incest and Descent: Their Influence on
           Social Organization. *Journ. Royal
           Anthropological Institute,* Vol. 59.
SLOTKIN, J. S.
    1947   On a Possible Lack of Incest Regulations
           in Old Iran. *American Anthropologist,*
           n.s., 49: 612–617.
THOMAS, W. I.
    1937   *Primitive Behavior.* New York.
TURANO, A. M.
    1934a   Breach of Promise: Still a Racket.
           *American Mercury,* Vol. 32.
    1934b   The Racket of Stolen Love. *American
           Mercury,* Vol. 33.
TYLOR, E. B.
    1888   On a Method of Investigating the
           Development of Institutions; Applied to
           Laws of Marriage and Descent. *Journal
           of the Anthropological Institute,* 18:
           245–269.
WESTERMARCK, E.
    1921   *The History of Human Marriage.* 3 vols.
           London.
WHITE, L. A.
    1940   The Symbol: the Origin and Basis of
           Human Behavior. *Philosophy of Science,*
           7: 451–463.
    1947a   The Expansion of the Scope of Science.
           *Journal of the Washington Academy of
           Sciences,* 37: 181–210.
    1947b   Culturological vs. Psychological
           Interpretations of Human Behavior.

*American Sociological Review,* 12:
686–698.

WISSLER, C.
1927   Recent Developments in Anthropology,
in: *Recent Developments in the Social
Sciences,* E. C. Hayes, ed. Philadelphia.

1929   *An Introduction to Social Anthropology.*
New York.

YOUNG, K.
1942   *Sociology, a Study of Society and
Culture.* New York.

# 8

## THE INCEST TABOO AND THE MATING PATTERNS OF ANIMALS

*David F. Aberle, Urie Bronfenbrenner, Eckhard H. Hess, Baniel R. Miller, David M. Schneider, and James N. Spuhler*

*In this article, Aberle and his associates resurrect the notion that inbreeding is damaging in order to explain the origin of the incest taboo. In a review of other theories, they reject the idea suggested by Westermarck that primary relatives are not sexually interested in each other (if they are not sexually interested, what need is there for a taboo?) and White's cultural evolutionary theory (there are other ways people can form larger groups; why a universal ban on incest?). Instead, they suggest that the taboo is a cultural invention designed to prevent disruptive sexual competition within the family and the detrimental effects of inbreeding. In the preceding article, White down played the importance of inbreeding by saying that it was often as beneficial as it was detrimental. Adding new evidence from animal studies, the authors discredit White's contention and reestablish the position that inbreeding is perilous. They go on to accept White's argument for the extension of the incest taboo to other relatives on organizational grounds.*

We have noted a new wave of interest in the theoretical and empirical study of the incest taboo. This is manifested by Slater's (1959) paper and by three papers on the subject at the American Anthropological Association Annual Meetings in 1961: Margaret Mead, "A Re-Examination of the Problem of Incest," Peter J. Wilson, "Incest—A Case Study," and Melvin Ember, "The Incest Taboo and the Nuclear Family." We have felt moved by this activity to present the results of a work group which met in the Spring of 1956 at the Center for Advanced Study in the Behavioral Sciences at Stanford, to consider the problem of the origins of the incest taboo.

The group consisted of the authors and the late Alfred L. Kroeber. After several months of work, the seven members of the group presented a mutually acceptable theoretical formulation at a seminar for Fellows at the Center. We hoped to move on to a well-documented publication, but this has proved impossible.[1] We have been handicapped by our dispersion over several universities and have hitherto been hesitant to publish because we wished to assemble more materials on the limitations of inbreeding in animals and to construct various models of the population genetics of small, inbred groups. Although we have abandoned hope of more ample publication, we believe that the current interest in theories of incest justifies the publication of a schematic statement of the approach we developed in 1956. A few minor changes or elaborations of the 1956 seminar are specifically noted.

The incest taboo in any society consists of a set of prohibitions which outlaw heterosexual relationships between various categories of kinsmen. Almost always, it includes prohibitions on sexual relations between brother and sister, father and daughter, mother and son. Invariably, where any prohibitions are present, other, nonprimary relatives are tabooed as well. There are rare cases where the taboos seem to have been abandoned. In the main, these involve very small groups in some way or other isolated from other populations to a degree which makes it impossible to maintain the taboo if the group is to reproduce at all. There are other cases where sexual relations between brother and sister or father and daughter are permitted or prescribed for special categories (e.g. chiefs, kings), or under special circumstances (e.g. ritual). It must be emphasized, however, that in the very societies where these sexual relations are permitted to some people, or under some circumstances, they are forbidden to the bulk of people and under most circumstances. Incest prohibitions are not always obeyed, but we will not attempt here to discuss rates, causes, or consequences of transgressions.

Most theories about the incest taboo attempt to account for its origin and persistence, but especially for the origin and persistence of the taboo on sexual relationships with the nuclear family. (Here and elsewhere, the phase "sexual relationships within the nuclear family" will refer to sexual relationships between brother and sister, father and daughter, and mother and son.

The phrase "familial incest taboo" will refer to the prohibition of these relationships.) It is hard to provide satisfactory support for any theory which attempts to account for a universal phenomenon. (Thus far, almost no theory of the origin of the incest taboo which has any currency has attempted to utilize the exceptions to universality noted above to account for origins. For all practical purposes, virtually all theories treat the familial taboo as a universal in discussing origins. Fortune (1932) is an exception.) With a little ingenuity, virtually any universal phenomenon can be explained by, or be used to explain the existence of, any other universal phenomenon in the realm under discussion. There are no criteria save aesthetics and logical consistency for choosing among theories, since there is no possibility of demonstrating that A varies with B, if both A and B are universally and invariably present. Furthermore, most of the theories about the incest taboo provide a demonstration that in one or another sense it is adaptive, and thereby often confuse the question of origin and the question of persistence. It is not logically admissible to assert that a phenomenon has come to exist because it is adaptive: that men grew noses because they support spectacles. It can be said only that if something comes into existence which has superior adaptive potential, it is likely to be perpetuated or to spread. The question of the cause of its origin, however, remains unsolved.

Our concern, then, was to account for the origin of the incest taboo, and to find a range of phenomena such that the familial incest taboo need not be treated as a universal. This range of phenomena was the mating behavior of humans and certain other animals. Before this mating behavior is discussed, it is necessary to outline some of the theories respecting the origin and persistence of the incest taboo.

1. *The inbreeding theory.* This theory asserts that the mating of close kin produces bad results, such as abnormal, enfeebled, or insufficiently numerous offspring. The incest taboo is therefore adaptive because it limits inbreeding, and arose

on that account. [Westermarck (1894:352–53; 1929:36–37); Muller (1913) provides information on beliefs of this sort; Morgan (1907:69) seems to view inbreeding as deleterious, but assumes a prior stage when inbreeding did occur —hence inbreeding was not for Morgan an intolerable state of affairs.]

2. *The socialization theory.* This theory asserts that the regulation and control of erotic impulses is an indispensable element in socialization—that it serves to maintain the growing child's motivation to accept the roles that he is taught. These roles include extra-familial and society-wide roles as well as those in the nuclear family. Since societies must be larger than a single nuclear family to be viable, and since nonfamilial roles are different from family roles, these roles in the wider society must be learned by the child. In order for this learning to occur, the socializing agent must control but not directly gratify the child's erotic impulses. Therefore it is necessary that these impulses be frustrated and directed outside the nuclear family. The incest taboo does this (Parsons 1954; Parsons and Bales 1955:187–258).

3. *The family theory.* This theory asserts that unregulated sexual competition is disruptive for any group, that the family is a crucial group, and that the incest taboo is needed to maintain the family intact. The theory asserts that the incest taboo originated because it served this function. Freud, one of the proponents of this theory, made a vigorous effort to imagine the series of events which could have led from promiscuity and unregulated, lethal competition, to the final promulgation of nuclear family taboos (Freud 1950; Malinowski 1927; Malinowski 1931:630; Seligman 1929, 1950).

4. *The social and cultural system theory.* This theory asserts that, left to their own devices, human beings would prefer to mate within the family, but that the advantages of a wider group for mutual aid, collective economic security, internal peace, offense and defense, and of a wider group for the sharing of cultural innovations, make family and supra-family exogamy highly adaptive as a device for joining families or larger kinship groups. These advantages would be marked in any kinship-based society but were crucial in early human history. This is so because the first ordered human group to emerge was the family, and the incest taboo and exogamy permitted a society built on existing materials: these devices linked families by bonds developed within the family—the ties of parents and children and of siblings. Because of the strong tendency to mate within the family, the familial incest taboos were necessary to insure exogamy (Tylor 1888:267; Fortune 1932; White 1949, 1959:69–116; Murdock 1949:284–313). The general theory of the social advantages of exogamy for a culture-bearing animal is to be found in all these writers; the theoretical sequence of development from anthropoid to human social organization is White's (1959); Murdock has stressed the importance of the spread of cultural innovations through marriage ties between families. Fortune has utilized lapses of the taboo among chiefs and kings to support his argument.

5. *The indifference or revulsion theory.* According to this theory, the incest taboo is either a formal expression of the sexual indifference of kinsmen toward each other, or a formal expression of an instinctive horror of sexual relations among kinsmen. It is principally identified with Edward Westermarck (1894:352–53, and 1929: 36–37).

6. *The demographic theory.* This theory holds that for early man, the short life-span, small number of offspring to reach maturity, spacing of those offspring, and random sex ratio made intra-familial inbreeding a virtual demographic impossibility. Hence very early man bred out by necessity. Later, when technological improvements made for larger families and longer life, and intra-familial mating became possible, the already existing pattern of familial exogamy was given normative backing through the creation of the familial incest taboo. This taboo sustained a practice advantageous from the point of view of group cooperation. This theory, presented by Slater (1959), was not considered by the 1956 work group.

We omit various theories which center on the role of religious or mystical ideas in determining the specific prohibition on incest, such as those of Durkheim (1898) and Raglan (1933). We do not explicitly consider the numerous composite theories, most of which combine various elements from theories 1–4 to arrive at their conclusions.

We will now discuss various criticisms that have been, or might be directed at each of the six theories. The criticisms themselves are of three types. (1) The adaptive value claimed by the theory for the incest taboo may be rejected. (2) The adaptive value claimed by the theory for the incest taboo may be accepted, but the possibility that the adaptive quality gave rise to the taboo may be disputed. (3) The adaptive value claimed by the theory may be accepted, but the necessity to achieve this result through the incest taboo may be denied.

The inbreeding theory in its simplest form has been rejected for decades because it was thought to be wrong. In its pre-genetic form the inbreeding theory asserted that inbreeding caused a weakening or deterioration of the stock. The facts of genetics provided a simple corrective to this notion. It was found that inbreeding could not produce "deterioration" but could only bring to expression what was already present in the stock, by producing offspring homozygous for some recessive character. Therefore, it was argued, if deleterious recessives were present, they would appear with greater frequency as a result of inbreeding, but if advantageous recessives were present, they would also receive full expression. Thus the disadvantages of inbreeding were offset by the advantages.

This simple corrective, however, does not stand up in the face of new information from the field of population genetics (cf. Lerner 1958; Morton 1961; both of which appeared after the 1956 argument had been developed). First, it has become clear that the ratio of deleterious and lethal recessive genes to selectively advantageous genes is very high indeed. This results from the random character of mutation. Second,

as we move from (biologically defined) second cousin matings to first cousin matings to parent-child or sibling matings, both the models of population genetics and the experimental and observational evidence from animals indicate that the reduction of heterozygocity increases rapidly, and hence that the percentage of individuals homozygous for lethal or deleterious recessive genes also rises sharply. The same is true, of course, for adaptive recessive forms. Provided that the species in question can stand the loss of many offspring, close inbreeding can provide a superior strain—superior either from the point of view of adaptation to the environment or from the point of view of a human being practicing the selective breeding of some plant or animal domesticate. But where births are widely spaced, where the animal produces few offspring at a time, or only one, and where the animal reaches reproductive maturity only slowly, the closely inbred population may not be able to stand either culling or natural selection. The abortions, still births, animals incapable of surviving to reproductive maturity, and the animals whose breeding period or capacity to rear their young is drastically shortened, through the inheritance of homozygous disadvantageous recessive genes, may so reduce the total effective breeding population as to make its survival impossible, or as to result in its expulsion from its niche by an expanding, neighboring population. Close inbreeding of rats is possible over many generations; with chickens the process becomes more difficult; with cattle it seems to be impossible. Thus, in the perspective of population genetics, close inbreeding of an animal like man has definite biological disadvantages, and these disadvantages are far more evident as respects the mating of primary relatives than as respects other matings. Hence the biological advantages of the familial incest taboo cannot be ignored. (Ember, 1961, parallels this argument.)

It is difficult to see, however, how primitive man would come to understand the connection between familial inbreeding and low net reproductive rate or the production of monstrosities. We will return to this point.

It is often argued, however, that since many simple societies regard the marriage of first cross-cousins as highly desirable, the incest taboo by no means eliminates fairly close inbreeding. In this connection we must stress the fact that the familial incest taboo is virtually universal, and that familial inbreeding shows far more effects from the point of view of population genetics than cousin inbreeding.

The socialization theory is difficult to deal with. Fundamentally, it rests on psychoanalytic hypotheses of fixation and regression and regression which have not yet been fully demonstrated. For this reason we will not attempt to discuss it further here.

The family theory has certain empirical difficulties. It rests on the supposed acute conflict that would arise out of sexual rivalries between father and son over mother and sister, between mother and daughter over father and brother, between brothers over sisters, and sisters over brothers. Yet father and son, mother and daughter, brother and brother, sister and sister do in fact share sexual partners in a number of societies. With polyandry, father and son sometimes share the same wife (but not the son's mother), or brothers share the same wife (but not their sister). With polygyny, mother and daughter sometimes share the same husband (but not the daughter's father), or sisters share the same husband (but not their brother); there are a large number of instances of institutionalized sharing of sexual favors outside the marital bond, as well.

These objections to the family theory do not lead to the conclusion that the family could tolerate *unregulated* intra-familial sexual relations. There is ample evidence that sexual competition is disruptive. But there would seem to be two solutions to the problem of maintaining order within the family, rather than one. The first solution is, of course, the interdiction of sexual relations except for the parents: the familial incest taboo. The second, however, is the institutionali-

zation of sexual access in the family. This would define the time, place, and rate of access of each member of the family to every other. This institutionalization could not be a complete solution for all families. In some families there would be no male offspring, and in others no female. Cohabitation with the parent of opposite sex would temporarily solve this problem, but since children normally outlive their parents, the solution would be only temporary. Nevertheless, it would be possible to adopt this sort of institutionalization as the primary pattern, with secondary alternatives available. Thus, societies with other preferential, or even prescribed mating patterns, must ordinarily afford alternatives to these patterns, or redefine the groups suitable for prescribed alliances over time.

The family theory has one distinctive advantage. It is easy to see how human groups might evolve rules to deal with immediate and obvious potential sources of disruption of social life. If indeed jealousy threatened the integrity of the family, it is possible to conceive of the development of norms to cope with this. And the incest prohibitions of any society constitute a set of conscious norms.

The social and cultural system theory, especially in its evolutionary form, as stated by White, does not raise serious empirical difficulties. It is clear that the advantages postulated by White exist, and that, given a tendency to choose the most easily available mates, a complete prohibition on familial sexual relations is the simplest device for forcing ties between families. His theory seems to assert that because this shift was advantageous, it came into being. Yet, like the family theory, this theory requires a movement in opposition to certain strong trends. It requires the elimination of some younger members from the family, in spite of emotional attachments, and entrusting these members to groups where stable relationships do not yet exist. It also requires that primitive men understand the advantages of the exchange—or else must assume that familial exogamy and the familial taboo arose as a chance "mutation" and survived because of their adaptive character.

The indifference theory has both logical and empirical difficulties. It is hard to see why what is naturally repugnant should be tabooed, and the evidence for sexual attraction among kinsmen is quite adequate for rejecting the theory. We mention it only for the sake of completeness.

The demographic theory makes certain assumptions about the life-span, breeding period, etc., of very early man. If these assumptions are correct, most of the rest of what is said in this presentation is irrelevant and unnecessary. But if any of its assumptions about age of maturity or spacing of births or length of breeding period can subsequently be shown to be wrong, this theory would also face difficulties. It serves to remind us of the number of implicit or explicit assumptions about the time and conditions of the emergence of the incest taboo which are made in the case of each theory. Slater assumes a cooperative group and normal breeding population larger than the family; White and our work group assume a situation where family cooperative relationships have become reasonably firm, whereas inter-family relationships are fluctuating and unstable. Either approach, and various others, make assumptions about the biology and social life of our ancestors which cannot be fully validated at present. More primatological and archeological data may still make it possible to choose more carefully among these assumptions.

Thus far, for all of these theories except the demographic and the socialization theories, there are either empirical objections as regards their validity, or logical difficulties in understanding how the function that the taboo supposedly fulfills would have led to institutionalization of the taboo, or both. It should be noted that the empirical objections do not apply to the inbreeding theory or to the social and cultural system theory: in each case it seems fair to say that the advantages postulated would have resulted from the familial taboo, and that,

for primitive man, it is hard to see what other device might have been an effective alternative.

In order to broaden the range of phenomena to be considered, let us now turn to the realm of animal behavior. We will here restrict the term "animal" to birds and non-human mammals. There is a wide range of behavior as regards inbreeding among animals. At one end of the spectrum there is no restriction on matings except opportunity. At the other end, there is no intra-familial mating whatever, except for the parental pair. (An animal family will be defined as a relatively stable grouping of two generations of animals, of both sexes, including at least one sexual partnership, and smaller than a band of animals.) The most spectacular limitation on familial inbreeding is found in the case of the Canada Goose and the Graylag Goose. The behavior of the Canada Goose will be described here, based on observations by Eckhard H. Hess.

The young geese hatch in the spring. The following spring, they are not sexually mature, but are driven away from the family group while the parents rear the new brood. When the new brood is a few months old, the young from the previous year's brood rejoin the family group. During the next spring, the parents again drive off the older broods while they rear the current brood, and the older broods again join the family group a few months later. Hence, quite a large family develops. In the third year, the goslings from the first brood are sexually mature. They mate with individuals from other families. They will not mate with siblings or with the opposite-sex parent. The newly formed pairs may join either family of orientation, making one of the families even larger, or they may start their own family groups. Thus, in the Canada Goose, parents and children tend to remain in the same larger group after the young mature. These ties are very stable. Indeed, mating tends to be for life.

Experimental work on the Canada Goose indicates that this fastidious behavior is the result of sexual imprinting. It is necessary to emphasize that the reaction persists without external sanctions. The luckless breeder who takes a male and a female from the same brood to raise geese is doomed to disappointment: the pair will not mate even if no other partners are available. If, however, two members of the same brood are separated before hatching occurs and are subsequently re-introduced to each other, having been raised in different families, they may become mates.

There is no evidence to suggest that asexual imprinting occurs among mammals. There, the principal mechanism limiting inbreeding in animal groups with families—where there is such a mechanism—seems to take the form of competition between the parent and its same-sex child, when this child approaches or reaches sexual maturity. The older animal's superior size and strength normally result in the expulsion of the young animal from the family, so that it is forced to mate elsewhere. In the course of time, an older animal becomes enfeebled and may be overcome, so that some intra-familial mating will occur, but on a statistical basis this mechanism of intergenerational competition does ensure a large amount of outbreeding. It is particularly effective where most births are single births, so that two siblings of opposite sex rarely become sexually mature at the same time. The beaver seems to expel its sexually mature young and this may be true of the gibbon.

Among animals with apparent complete promiscuity may be mentioned the rat, the spider monkey, and the macaque. (By promiscuity we refer to patterns which result in the animal's mating indifferently with siblings, parents, or others. Since there are more "others," promiscuity involves a preponderance of outbreeding, as regards primary relatives. Promiscuity need not imply truly random mating. Size, strength, age, etc., always result in some departure from randomness, if only in the ordering of the sequence of copulatory partnerships.)

Sexual behavior among animals, as has been said, varies from complete promiscuity to complete elimination of familial inbreeding. Under what circumstances is elimination of familial in-

breeding likely to occur? It would seem that, on a cross-species basis, restriction of inbreeding, whether by competition or by asexual imprinting, is found among the larger, longer-lived, slower-maturing, and more intelligent animals. On a cross-species basis, these are also relatively late evolutionary products. Those species which limit inbreeding are among those which form families, although not all species that form families limit inbreeding. It would appear that a certain level of intelligence and length of life are necessary for animals to form stable attachments —that otherwise they will breed with kin or non-kin indifferently. When stable attachments are combined with familial groupings, however, they give rise to the potentiality for close inbreeding. Thus, there seems to be an empirical tendency for barriers against close inbreeding to be found where close inbreeding would otherwise be most likely to occur. Finally, it should be mentioned that among birds, asexual imprinting is particularly common in species which have both stable families and larger than familial groupings—a feature which we have not tried to account for.[2]

We will now bring the animal and human data into juxtaposition and define the range of mating behavior which we will attempt to explain. Some animals have no barriers which prevent parent-child, brother-sister matings. Some animals have barriers which reduce or prevent such matings. Humans drastically limit such matings through the familial incest taboo. Thus human beings share with some animals a limitation on familial inbreeding, even though the mechanism of limitation differs from those of all animal species. Only humans have any limitations on mate choice beyond the nuclear family: in no human society is the incest taboo limited to the nuclear family, whatever its range of variation may be.[3]

Let us first consider these facts in the light of the genetic theory. It has been suggested above that close inbreeding might not be deleterious to animals which mature quickly and have numerous offspring. It is in such cases that promiscuity is most likely, and promiscuity itself tends to reduce inbreeding, on a purely statistical basis. So even here, close inbreeding is unlikely. Where intensive inbreeding is most likely to occur, barriers are common. The more intelligent, slower-maturing animals living in family groups, where stable attachments are likely, and human beings, who also live in family groups where stable attachments are likely, manifest patterns which limit familial inbreeding: asexual imprinting, intergenerational competition, and the familial incest taboo. We suggest that with the emergence of culture, if not before, relatively stable family groupings in the human evolutionary line required *some* limitation on familial inbreeding. From this inference, alone, however, one cannot predict the familial incest taboo.

Asexual imprinting would be an equally effective mechanism—but it does not seem to occur in man, the apes, the monkeys, or even in more remote mammalian species. It is plausible to assume that this adaptive device was simply not available—not a part of the genetic equipment of man's ancestors or relatives. Intergenerational competition, however, would seem, at first blush, to be a feasible alternative. Competing with others to get and to keep mates is a widespread mammalian pattern, though not a universal one. Nothing is required to bend it in the service of limiting inbreeding except, that it be directed to maturing members of the family as well as to outsiders—and this does not represent a change in pattern, but merely the preservation of the mechanism as family life develops.

If, for any reason, a gap develops between the point at which the young animal is sexually mature and the point at which it is capable of fending for itself, expulsion becomes an unsuitable mechanism. There is such a gap in all known human groups—or at least in no known human group does the onset of sexual maturity coincide with *full* assumption of adult economic and social responsibilities. Even where marriage occurs at a very early age—indeed, especially where it does—the youthful marital partner, or pair, remains under the direction of senior members of

the kingroup. In early human or protohuman society, a gap of even a year between sexual maturity and the capacity to operate independently would create problems for a family unit which used intergenerational competition and expulsion to limit inbreeding. If expulsion continued, the young would be exposed to dangers —unless they could find acceptance in another group, which would presuppose no intergenerational competition in the other group. If expulsion were abandoned, the family unit would be exposed both to an increase of the impetus toward inbreeding and to unregulated sexual competition within the familial unit. A gap between sexual maturity and full capacity could occur either through changes of maturational pattern or through the development of culture and the consequent need for time to transmit cultural information, information about the local scene, etc., or both. The incest taboo is a cultural phenomenon, and we must therefore assume that it emerged concomitantly with, or subsequent to, the beginnings of culture. We cannot, however, be certain whether the gap between sexual maturity and full performance was a matter of culture, physical maturation, or both.[4]

What we seek is a situation which will result in the normative definition of the nuclear incest taboo. If, as can safely be assumed, unregulated sexuality is incompatible with a stable family unit, and if expulsion of the sexually maturing human animal is not possible, then the problem of maintaining order within the family posed by sexual competition would have to be solved. As has been said, two solutions are possible: institutionalized sexual access within the family, or the familial incest taboo. Either solves the competitive problem. Either is within the scope of a human animal with language and limited culture. The problem of order within the nuclear family would also be observable as a pressing problem, on a day-to-day basis, and the sources of the problem in sexual competition would be equally evident. Either mechanism might be adopted: regulation of sex, or its elimination from the family. But whereas either mechanism would solve the problem of order, only one mechanism, the familial taboo, would solve the genetic problem. Hence that group, or those groups of human beings which adopted a taboo on intra-familial mating would have an advantage both over those groups which could not solve the problem of order and over those groups which solved the problem by institutionalized intra-familial sexual activity, thereby encouraging close inbreeding. Hence, over time, only the familial incest taboo could survive, because of its superior selective advantages.

We suggest, then, that man, along with certain other animals, is particularly vulnerable to deleterious effects arising out of close and continuous inbreeding, and that he shares with these animals the characteristic of having a mechanism which limits or prevents inbreeding within the family. We suggest that this problem may have been the underlying cause for the development of the familial incest taboo, since man shares a limitation on familial inbreeding with other animals which are not cultural, which socialize their young far less elaborately than do humans, which do not have to educate them for role systems in a wider cultural order, and which do not have to cope with the problem of ordering the relationships of a number of potential sexual competitors in the same family. This suggestion of a common core shared by the various devices of animals and humans which limit familial inbreeding has the advantage of theoretical parsimony. It is also open to partial test, since there are a large number of studies of animals which could be carried out to demonstrate whether the variation we suggest on the basis of somewhat piecemeal evidence in fact occurs. But the human device, the familial incest taboo, is unique to humans, and is both required by, and made possible by culture. The incest taboo requires symbols, but it becomes significant only when expulsion from the family is impossible: a state of affairs largely, though perhaps not wholly dependent on the existence of a corpus of cultural tradition which must be fully transmitted for adequate functioning as an adult to occur.

The familial taboo has, of course, the *de facto* result of linking families, as well as of solving the problem of order within the family and the genetic problem. The stable attachments between individuals long associated in family units which make intra-familial mating so potent a possibility also create ties of interest and sentiment between members of an original family of procreation as they disperse. The advantages of ties between families have been clearly pointed out by Tylor, White, Fortune, and others: an enlarged circle of cooperation, sharing, offense, and defense. These advantages, in turn, generate the last phenomenon to be accounted for: the fact that in no animal group are there restrictions on inbreeding except for the family unit, whereas in no human group are incest taboos limited to the nuclear family. Once the familial taboo is in existence, extensions of the taboo to other categories of kin become a simple evolutionary step. Whether this step is made by stimulus generalization, planning, aesthetic reactions, or whatever, its adaptive value is such as to perpetuate the extensions, which increase the circle of cooperation still further.

Extensions of the incest taboo beyond the family sometimes involve permitted, preferential, or theoretically prescribed matings between first cousins. Hence the extensions may involve no further genetic advantage. Once again, we must point out that the results of familial inbreeding are genetically far more deleterious than those of first cousin matings.

Among animals, in the absence of symbolling, it is still conceivable that further restrictions on inbreeding might occur—e.g., through severe intergenerational sexual competition within a band, or through asexual imprinting such that the young would accept no members of the local group as mates. Such instances are, however, unknown. The genetic advantages of such a step would be considerably less than those of preventing familial inbreeding, and in the absence of culture the social advantages would also appear to be slight. This is so because cooperation in animals is limited in scope.

We might briefly query why a mechanism particularly suitable for maintaining the social and biological integrity of kinship-based societies is maintained not only in these societies but in complex societies as well. First, the problem of order within the family remains important, and the familial taboo, though not the only possible device for solving this problem, is the existing and well-institutionalized device. Second, for the bulk of pre-industrial complex societies, the functions of the incest taboo in its extended form remain important at the community level. There, the regulation of affairs is not impersonal and legal. On the contrary, the world remains divided into kinsmen, consanguine allies, and neutral or hostile groups. The nexus of social life and cooperation continues to be based on kinship to a significant degree, until societies with well-developed market economies appear. In just these societies, the scope of the incest taboo narrows, until in our own society its legal definition is often limited to primary relatives, secondary relatives, and the spouses of certain primary and secondary relatives. It is in such societies that participation on a relatively impersonal basis in a social system of considerable scope becomes significant, and it may be that under these circumstances the significance of the familial incest taboo in socializing individuals toward participation in this larger orbit increases. It is probable that if the nuclear family were to be dissolved, and to be supplanted by collective, non-kinship forms of life, the incest taboo would dissolve with it, provided that these new forms made close inbreeding statistically a rare phenomenon.[5]

In sum, we propose that the adoption of the familial incest taboo was adaptive primarily because of the genetic results of close inbreeding, and that man's familial taboo is to be considered part of the class of devices which limit familial inbreeding among intelligent, slow-maturing animals which bear few offspring at a time and which live in family units. The selection of the taboo, however, we hypothesize, occurred through efforts to solve the problem of sexual competition within the family in a cultural animal with an organized family life. Among the available mechanisms, the incest taboo solved this problem and the genetic problem. Other alternatives solved only one of these problems. Hence it had high selective value. We suggest that it might not have come into being as a response to needs for cooperation between families, but that, once it existed, it did promote this cooperation, which had an adaptive function of little significance for animals. Finally, the familial taboo could be extended, by a simple evolutionary step, to a wider group of kinsmen, with great selective advantages. To date, some combination of the various advantages inputed to the nuclear and more extended incest taboos has resulted in their perpetuation, even in post-industrial societies organized as states. The taboo in some form or other is likely to survive so long as the family remains a significant part of the social order.

## NOTES

1. Washburn's book (1961) has been consulted, but we have not tried to incorporate relevant new materials. Cohen's paper (1961) has not been read, although kindly made available to us by Cohen. Nor have we seen the papers read by others at the Symposium on Cross-Species Incest Behavior, held a few days after the first draft of the present paper had been completed.

2. The socialization theory would profit from the examination of animal cases where the young learn a fairly large part of their response repertory from their parents.

3. Here and at other points we must except those rare cases where the familial taboo has been partially or wholly abrogated for the sake of the propagation of the group.

4. The maturation argument has been elaborated here more fully than in the 1956 presentation—stimulated in part by Mead (1961).

5. This argument includes material on the future of

the incest taboo which was not a part of the 1956 presentation.

## REFERENCES CITED

COHEN, YEHUDI
1961 A hypothesis for the genetic basis of the universality of the incest taboo and its relation to kinship organization. Paper delivered at the annual meetings of the American Association for the Advancement of Science, Section H, Symposium on Cross-Species Incest Behavior, December 30, Denver, Colorado. Mimeo.

DURKHEIM, EMILE
1898 La prohibition de l'inceste et ses origines. L'année sociologique 1:1–70.

EMBER, MELVIN
1961 The incest taboo and the nuclear family. Paper read at the American Anthropological Association Annual Meetings, Philadelphia, November 16–19.

FORTUNE, REO
1932 Incest. Encyclopedia of the Social Sciences 7:620–622.

FREUD, SIGMUND
1950 Totem and taboo. Trans. James Strachey. London, Routledge, Kegan Paul, Ltd.

LERNER, I. MICHAEL
1958 The genetic basis of selection. New York, John Wiley and Sons.

MALINOWSKI, BRONISLAW
1927 Sex and repression in savage society. London, Routledge, Kegan Paul, Ltd.
1931 Culture. Encyclopedia of the Social Sciences 4:621–646.

MEAD, MARGARET
1961 A re-examination of the problem of incest. Paper read at the American Anthropological Association Annual Meetings, Philadelphia, November 16–19.

MORGAN, LEWIS HENRY
1907 Ancient society. New York, Henry Holt and Co.

MORTON, NEWTON E.
1961 Morbidity of children from consanguineous marriages In Arthur G. Steinberg, ed., Progress in medical genetics, vol. 1:261–291. New York, Grune & Stratton.

MULLER, H. F.
1913 A chronological note on the physiological explanation of the prohibition of incest. Journal of Religious Psychology 6:294–295.

MURDOCK, GEORGE PETER
1949 Social structure. New York, The Macmillan Co.

PARSONS, TALCOTT
1954 The incest taboo in relation to social structure and the socialization of the child. British Journal of Sociology 5:101–117.

PARSONS, TALCOTT AND ROBERT F. BALES
1955 Family, socialization and interaction process. Glencoe, The Free Press.

RAGLAN, F. R. S.
1933 Jocasta's crime. London, Methuen and Co., Ltd.

SELIGMEN, BRENDA Z.
1929 Incest and descent. Journal of the Royal Anthropological Institute 59: 231–272.
1950 The problem of incest and exogamy. American Anthropologist 52:305–316.

SLATER, MARIAM KREISELMAN
1959 Ecological factors in the origin of incest. American Anthropologist 61:1042–1059.

TYLOR, EDWARD B.
1888 On a method of investigating the development of institutions; applied to laws of marriage and descent. Journal of the Royal Anthropological Institute 18:245–269.

WASHBURN, SHERWOOD L., ed.
1961 Social life of early man. Wenner-Gren Foundation Publications in Anthropology, no. 31.

WESTERMARCK, EDWARD
  1894  The history of human marriage. London,
        The Macmillan Co.
  1929  Marriage. New York, Jonathan Cape
        and Harrison Smith.

WHITE, LESLIE A.
  1949  The definition and prohibition of incest.
        *In* Leslie A. White, The science of

culture: 303–329. New York, Farrar,
Strauss and Co.
  1959  The evolution of culture. New York,
        McGraw-Hill.

WILSON, PETER J.
  1961  Incest—a case study. Paper read at the
        American Anthropological Association
        Annual Meetings, Philadelphia,
        November 16–19.

# 9

## CHILDHOOD ASSOCIATION AND SEXUAL ATTRACTION: A FURTHER TEST OF THE WESTERMARCK HYPOTHESIS

*Arthur P. Wolf*

*With the exception of Edward Westermarck, theorists approaching the explanation of the incest taboo have assumed that primary relatives desire sexual relations with each other. They support this assumption logically by reasoning that there would be no use for the taboo if these relatives did not find one another sexually attractive. Westermarck, on the other hand, observed an absence of sexual desire among primary relatives, and it is this view that Arthur Wolf supports in this article, based on evidence from field work on Taiwan. There Wolf discovered that before 1900, about half the people married in the "minor form" of marriage. Boys were wed to girls, adopted as infants into their families with the idea of future marriage. Reasoning that a childhood spent growing up together would dull their sexual appetite, Wolf finds that later, when boys gained the power to influence whom they marry (a change that occurred after the arrival of the Japanese), they refused to marry their adopted sisters. They were also embarrassed by the thought of sex with one another, and in those cases where marriage did take place, sexual relations were often avoided. Citing these and some statistical measures based on a search of household records, Wolf challenges the notion that primary relatives desire one another sexually and suggests that the taboo is simply a cultural recognition of an emotional condition.*

In the view of most social theorists, the incest taboo is imposed on man for the sake of society. It is generally agreed that this taboo is necessary, but many reasons have been given to explain why. Edward Westermarck's suggestion to the contrary was widely criticized by his contemporaries and rarely receives favorable mention in more recent discussions of the subject. Not much more than supposition was needed to convict Westermarck of folly. With the exception of questionable evidence presented by psychoanalysts, the case against his hypothesis rests on Sir James Frazer's insistence that "the law only forbids men to do what their instincts incline them to do" (1910[4]:97). This criticism was quoted, as Westermarck himself wryly noted, "with much appreciation by Dr. Freud" (1922[2]:203) and is obviously the source of Leslie White's claim that "Westermarck's thesis . . . is not in accord with the facts in the first place and would still be inadequate if it were. Propinquity does not annihilate sexual desire, and if it did there would be no need for stringent prohibitions" (1948:420).

The reason for this ready acceptance of Frazer's critique of Westermarck is obvious. In explaining the incest taboo as the social means of achieving the advantages of mating and marrying outside of the family, anthropologists have had to assume that men are naturally inclined to mate and marry within the family. If intimate childhood association were sufficient to preclude sexual interest, as Westermarck hypothesized, the incest taboo would not be necessary to obtain the biological advantages of out-breeding. Mankind would not have been faced with those momentous choices pictured so vividly by White and Claude Lévi-Strauss. They would not have had to choose "between biological families living in juxtaposition and endeavoring to remain closed, self-perpetuating units, overridden by their fears, hatreds, and ignorances, and the systematic establishment, through the incest prohibition, of links of intermarriage between them," the condition of "a true human society" (Lévi-Strauss 1960:278). The tide that has run so long against Westermarck is drawn by the assumption that "the emergence of human society required some suppression, rather than a direct expression, of man's primate nature" (Sahlins 1960:77).

This tide has at last begun to turn. We now know that the social life of subhuman primates is not characterized by "selfishness, indiscriminate sexuality, dominance and brute competition" (Sahlins 1960:86). The chimpanzees observed in the Yerkes Laboratories engage in purposive cooperation and often evince "a capacity—or weakness—for developing a nondestructive interest in others" (Hebb and Thompson 1968:744). Recent field studies of Japanese and rhesus macaques show that the young males of the species do not commonly choose to mate with their mothers (Imanishi 1961; Kaufman 1965; Tokuda 1961–1962; Sade 1968). The purpose of this paper is to provide another example challenging the view that man's behavior in society is largely a creation of society. The data reported continue but do not conclude an argument initiated in an article published in this journal in 1966. They do not explain the incest taboo and do not tell us why childhood association and sexual attraction are antithetical; they only suggest that there is "a remarkable absence of erotic feelings between persons living very closely together from childhood" (Westermarck 1922[2]:vi).

The locale of my first study was a small Chinese village in northern Taiwan. It is situated near the town of Shulin on the west bank of the Tamsui River. Twelve miles upstream, on the edge of the central mountain range, is an old riverport known as Sanhsia, the commercial center of the area included in my second study. The native residents of both communities are Hokkien-speaking Chinese whose ancestors migrated to Taiwan from southern Fukien in the seventeenth and eighteenth centuries. Because of their common origins and frequent intermarriage, the people of the entire area, from Shulin at one end of the valley to Sanhsia at the other, support the same institutions and share similar expectations about the nature of family life. There is therefore no need to repeat here the background information provided in my two previous papers. I simply remind the reader that customary law in this area of China recognizes two distinct forms of virilocal marriage. One I term the major form of marriage: the bride enters her husband's home as a young adult, often not meeting the groom until the day of the wedding. The other I call the minor form of marriage: the bride is taken into her future husband's household in infancy or early childhood and raised as a member of his family. These two forms of marriage provide a unique opportunity to test the Westermarck hypothesis. The major form of marriage forges a conjugal bond between strangers; the minor form unites a couple whose experience of one another is as intimate as brother and sister.

In comparing reactions to these two forms of marriage we must always keep in mind the changes that have overcome this area of Taiwan in recent years. When Taiwan was ceded to Japan in 1895 as one consequence of the first Sino-Japanese War, life along the southern edges of the Taipei basin was as conservative as anywhere in China. Camphor and tea from the hills around Shulin and Sanhsia were poled down the Tamsui River to Taipei, where they were transshipped to foreign markets, but the foreigners and the influences they brought to China did not move upstream into the rural areas of the basin. The early years of the Japanese occupation did little to change this pattern. Although the new colonial government quickly extended police control into the villages and registered the land and the population, these changes did not challenge the authority of Chinese custom or create pressure for change. The full impact of the Japanese presence did not reach the rural areas until twenty years later when the government completed an improved transportation network and established schools in the villages and rural towns. Until that time people living outside of the city earned their livelihoods in agriculture or by means of small family businesses; they now sought employment in the coal mines opened along the edge of the basin and in new industries like the Hsulin winery. A few of the more fortunate graduated from local schools and then sought further education and employment in the city.

It was not long before these new opportunities began to have an effect on family life. Young married couples continued to live with their parents, as they do even today, but the internal structure of the family changed. Whereas young people had previously deferred to their parents in all important decisions, including decisions about their own marriages, they now began to demand more of a voice in family affairs, particularly the right to some influence in the choice of husbands and wives. The basis of their demand was economic. If a young man's parents tried to force him into an unsatisfactory marriage, he could leave the family and support himself by a job in the mines or in the city. The threat of desertion was usually enough to make the parents acquiesce. While the changes brought about by the Japanese occupation freed young people from a dependence on their parents, it did not free the parents from a dependence on their children. The new government did not offer pensions or open homes for the aged. Without children to support him in his old age a man was no better off in 1930 than he would have been in 1830.

One of the first consequences of this change of authority in the family was a sharp decline in the frequency of the minor form of marriage. In the first two decades of this century the minor form of marriage accounted for nearly half of all virilocal marriages; by the end of the Japanese occupation the proportion of minor marriages had dropped to less than ten percent of the total. This change was not a result of parents deciding that the minor form of marriage was no longer so advantageous as it had once been, but was rather a direct result of emancipated young people refusing to marry a childhood associate. This is evident in the fact that the frequency of this form of marriage began to decline a decade before the rate of female adoption (Wolf 1966:886). Parents continued to adopt girls to raise as wives for their sons until it became apparent that young people could no longer be forced to consummate these arrangements. Even today a few families raise girls in the hope of somehow persuading a son to marry in the minor fashion. They are always disappointed. One old man who had adopted a wife for his favorite grandson told me that he wanted them to marry "because that girl has always been very good to me, but I don't know whether they will or not. You just can't tell young people what to do anymore."

Were degree of childhood association the only difference between the two forms of marriage, this refusal of young people to marry a childhood associate would go a long way toward proving Westermarck's contention. But unfortunately this is not the only difference between the two forms of marriage. As I have pointed out in previous papers, the major form of marriage has advantages that might incline young people to prefer it to the minor form (1966:887–888; 1968:866–867). It is the right and proper way to marry, the prestigious way to take a wife, and it provides the new couple with a dowry and the advantages of dependable affinal ties. Anthropologists who are inclined to look for sociological explanations will immediately see that young people's dislike of the minor form of marriage may be motivated by practical rather than personal concerns. They may be seeking prestige and practical advantage rather than trying to avoid sexual intercourse with a childhood associate.

This explanation of the decline of the minor form of marriage sounds reasonable, probably because prestige and practical advantage are such common goals of human behavior. When I first encountered the problem, it did not occur to me to look for any other explanation, but talking to people about their attitude toward the minor form of marriage convinced me that this was a mistake. Chinese villagers, regardless of education, are articulate, socially sophisticated people; they understand many of the intricacies of their own society and are capable of verbalizing their insights. They can discuss at length the advantages and disadvantages of marrying a mother's brother's daughter and are well aware of the sociological consequences of the major and minor forms of marriage (Wolf 1968:871). They enjoy talking about the social calculations involved in deciding the appropriate value of wedding and funeral gifts. If young people objected

to the minor form of marriage because it is less prestigeful and entails certain practical disadvantages, I think they would say so. But of the many people I have talked to, not one has given me these reasons for not wanting to marry in this fashion. Asked why they do not want to marry a childhood associate, most informants blush and become inarticulate. All they say is that "it's embarrassing" or "uninteresting" or "difficult because people who are raised together know one another's hearts too well." They obviously are not thinking of the relative prestige of the two forms of marriage, the size of the dowry, or the value of affinal alliances.

These reactions give me confidence in the Westermarck hypothesis, but they will not do as proof of the hypothesis. The evidence rests too heavily on my impressions of the people I am studying. A better way of determining the relative importance of personal and practical concerns is to compare the conjugal relationships created by the two forms of marriage. If the resistance to the minor form of marriage is motivated by practical considerations, a couple raised together should be no less satisfied with one another than those who first meet as young adults. They may resent having their best interests sacrificed by their parents, but this is not likely to disrupt permanently their relations as husband and wife. If, on the other hand, the source of the resistance is a sexual aversion rooted in childhood association, it should persist and permanently mar the conjugal relationship. Couples raised together should be less intimate and more prone to marital discord than those brought together by the major form of marriage.

The problem becomes one of assessing the quality of the marital relationship. The ideal measure would be frequency of sexual intercourse and degree of sexual satisfaction, but it is difficult to obtain that kind of information in any society and next to impossible in China. Willing as they are to talk about the money a relative wastes on prostitutes and winehouse girls or the possibility that a neighbor is not his son's genitor, few Chinese will discuss the sexual act itself, and I doubt that any would be willing to talk about his experience with his own spouse. There is no point in even asking. Because the Chinese kinship system views the parent-child relationship as pivotal, the conjugal relationship is ideally distant and unemotional. Husband and wife must avoid displaying any sign of personal intimacy outside of the privacy of their own bedroom. Under these conditions couples who enjoyed the most blissful of relations would probably deny any interest in one another.

The only alternative is to look for the effects of marital dissatisfaction on other aspects of behavior. In my first study I made use of village gossip to identify men who commonly seek the company of prostitutes or neglect their wives in favor of mistresses. As one would expect if childhood association promotes sexual aversion, the majority of these men had married in the minor fashion (Wolf 1966:889–890). The problem I faced in returning to Taiwan last year was how to replicate this finding with a larger sample. Although I have since had occasion to doubt the wisdom of my choice, I decided to rely on the information available in the household registration records. Initiated by the Japanese at the turn of the century and maintained by the present Chinese government, these remarkable records contain a complete history of the composition of every family on the island. I made two predictions that could be tested by an examination of these materials. Assuming a weakening of the conjugal bond as a result of sexual aversion, I predicted a higher divorce rate among minor marriages than among major marriages. And assuming a tendency for couples subject to an aversion to avoid sexual relations for long periods of time, I also predicted a lower birth rate.

By the time this test of the hypothesis was formulated, I was already living in Sanhsia and had made the acquaintance of the officials in charge of the local household registration office. I therefore decided to use these records for a preliminary test and chose for this purpose two of the districts into which Sanhsia Chen is di-

vided. The two districts are located at the foot of the central mountain range on opposite sides of one of the tributaries of the Tamsui River. The district on one side of the stream includes four small hamlets, each clustered about a lineage hall; the district on the opposite side contains one large village with a number of small shops and a new temple. The majority of the men of both districts are descended from the ancestors enshrined in one or another of the four lineage halls; all but a few earn their livings as farmers, coal miners, laborers, or through a small family business. The differences between the wealthiest families and the poorest are too slight to support elaborate social distinctions. A local saying has it that the wealthy mix sweet potatoes with their rice while the poor mix rice with their sweet potatoes.

To avoid the complicating effects of social change I limited my sample to marriages contracted between 1900 and 1925. Since birth rates on Taiwan were rising at the same time that the frequency of minor marriages was declining, inclusion of marriages recorded after 1925 would produce an entirely spurious correlation between form of marriage and birth rates. There is also a danger that social change intensified the dissatisfaction of young people forced to marry a childhood associate. Those parents who insisted on the minor form of marriage after some had capitulated probably had to use exceptional means to see the arrangements consummated. If we included in our sample marriages contracted during the transitional period, the result would likely be a spuriously high rate of divorce among the minor marriages. As the reader can see by examining the information given in Table 1, the present sample avoids both these pitfalls. The relative frequency of major and minor marriages remains constant throughout the twenty-five-year period. Any differences we find between the two forms of marriage cannot be traced to rising birth rates or the resentment of young people who were allowed no choice in marriage after choice had become a possibility. The absence of a decline in the proportion of minor marriages argues that parents managed to preserve their traditional authority until sometime after 1925.

I also decided to limit my sample to marriages contracted by the end of the bride's twenty-fifth year. Since all second marriages are necessarily of the major form, this was done to keep the ages of the two halves of my sample roughly comparable. Even with this limitation the average age of women married in the major fashion is nearly two years older than the average age of those married in the minor fashion. Since this difference could affect both birth and divorce rates, it is important to note that these effects work against rather than for the hypothesis. If we find that minor marriages produce more divorces and fewer children, it is clearly not a consequence of the bride's youth. Women who marry earlier have more time to get a divorce and more time to bear children. This effect of the earlier age at which minor marriages are contracted may be offset by the bride's being too young to bear children and too much of a child to consider divorce. The important point is that the evidence presented in Table 2 suggests that there is little danger of our accepting the Westermarck hypothesis for the wrong reason.

The data reported in this paper were compiled for me by clerks in the household registration office. I spent my own time conducting a general ethnographic survey but naturally took advantage of every opportunity to inquire about reactions to the minor form of marriage. The

**TABLE 1**

Married Women by Type of Marriage and Year of Marriage

| Year of Marriage | Minor Marriage | Major Marriage | Total by Year |
|---|---|---|---|
| 1900–1905 | 26 | 38 | 64 |
| 1906–1910 | 17 | 31 | 48 |
| 1911–1915 | 22 | 34 | 56 |
| 1916–1920 | 29 | 34 | 63 |
| 1921–1925 | 38 | 34 | 72 |
| Totals | 132 | 171 | 303 |

**TABLE 2**

Married Women by Type of Marriage and Age at Marriage

| Age at Marriage | Minor Marriage | Major Marriage | Total by Age at Marriage |
|---|---|---|---|
| 13 | 1 | 2 | 3 |
| 14 | 7 | 4 | 11 |
| 15 | 27 | 11 | 38 |
| 16 | 23 | 20 | 43 |
| 17 | 31 | 34 | 65 |
| 18 | 18 | 26 | 44 |
| 19 | 11 | 24 | 35 |
| 20 | 6 | 16 | 22 |
| 21 | 3 | 9 | 12 |
| 22 | 5 | 9 | 14 |
| 23 | | 7 | 7 |
| 24 | | 4 | 4 |
| 25 | | 5 | 5 |
| Totals | 132 | 171 | 303 |
| Average age | 16.8 years | 18.4 years | 17.8 years |

stories and anecdotes I was given confirm the impressions formed during my first field study. There are at least five men in the town of Sanhsia who live with mistresses and are reputed to visit their wives and children only at the New Year. All five married a childhood associate. The most interesting aspect of these cases is the apparent lack of jealousy on the part of the two men whose wives responded to this treatment by taking lovers. Whereas the average Chinese husband would be outraged by a wife's infidelity, their neighbors claim that these two men "just don't care what their wives do." In one case the husband and his mistress and the wife and her lover live next door to one another in the same compound without any apparent friction. Perhaps the aversion that precludes interest in one another also precludes jealousy.

Consummation of a marriage of the minor type usually takes place on the eve of the lunar New Year. After locking up their doors and windows to exclude the malignant influences of a dying season, the family sits down to a large meal. It is usually at this meal that the head of the family tells his son and daughter that they are henceforth husband and wife. Whenever the opportunity offered, I asked my informants to describe the couple's reaction. One old man told me that he had to stand outside of the door of their room with a stick to keep the newlyweds from running away; another man's adopted daughter did run away to her natal family and refused to return until her father beat her; a third informant who had arranged minor marriages for both of his sons described their reactions this way: "I had to threaten them with my cane to make them go in there, and then I had to stand there with my cane to make them stay." These are exceptional rather than typical cases, but as evidence they carry a special weight. Most of the people I talked to had heard of at least one instance of a father's beating his son and adopted daughter to make them occupy the same bedroom. When I asked whether they had ever heard of this happening in the case of a major marriage, they just laughed.

But the new information I collected in the course of these interviews was not all encouraging. While it did confirm my confidence in the Westermarck hypothesis, it also raised doubts about my choice of a test of the hypothesis. Women whose husbands desert them to live with a mistress often take lovers or seek occasional sexual satisfaction with a neighbor. The problem is that the children are almost always registered as the husband's offspring. Even when the wife is loyal to a husband who prefers another woman, the registered children are not always the wife's progeny. One of the men who is reputed to visit home only once a year has registered three of his mistress's children as his wife's. A real difference in the number of children produced by the two kinds of marriage may be concealed by a combination of extramarital relations and falsification of the household registers.

My doubts about the test I had proposed were further aroused just by living again in a Chinese community. In the central room of every house, arranged on shelves generation by generation, are the family's ancestral tablets, mute but forceful reminders of every man's duty to perpetuate a line of descent. There must be heirs and descendants to inherit the family property and carry on the rites of ancestor worship. If there are no heirs to inherit, the work of many lifetimes is wasted; without descendants, the deceased members of the line are doomed to wander the world as hungry, homeless ghosts. Westermarck urged his readers to "not forget that a lack of desire, and even a positive feeling of aversion, may in certain circumstances be overcome" (1922[2]:201). He appears to have been thinking of situations in which there is no other opportunity for sexual gratification, but obviously the Chinese concern with perpetuating a line of descent would have the same effect. This concern may overcome and thereby conceal an aversion aroused by intimate childhood association.

There is also cause to worry about my use of divorce rates as a measure of marital dissatisfaction. No matter how dissatisfied a young couple may be with one another, for whatever reason, they cannot obtain a divorce easily. Divorce, like marriage, is under parental authority. Parents have the right to forbid a divorce that is not in the best interests of the family, and they also have the right to divorce a son's wife, with or without his consent. Because a major marriage requires payment of a bride price and expensive wedding feasts, it is rare for parents to initiate divorce proceedings. But it is not uncommon for parents to use their authority to prevent a divorce. By threatening to desert the family or by actually running away for a few months, young people sometimes persuade their parents to allow them to separate, but more often than not parental authority prevails. I know of a number of marriages in both Shulin and Sanhsia that would have ended in divorce if the couple's parents had not objected.

The role parents play with respect to divorce is relevant because it may introduce a bias against the Westermarck hypothesis. For reasons I have already discussed in detail elsewhere, a girl who is raised by her husband's family makes a better daughter-in-law than a girl who joins the family as a young adult (Wolf 1968:868–870). This is one of the reasons so many families choose to raise their sons' wives. Thus there is a possibility that parents will exert more pressure to preserve a minor marriage than a major one. The relative frequency with which the two forms of marriage end in divorce may not reflect relative marital satisfaction. Although the girl's early arrival in the minor form of marriage may preclude a close relationship with her husband, the problem may not be evident in divorce rates because of the girl's more satisfactory relationship with her husband's parents. Divorce may even be more common in the major form of marriage, not because of weaker conjugal ties, but because the husband's parents are more likely to be dissatisfied with their daughter-in-law.

These questions about the validity of my measures point up an important ambiguity in Westermarck's thesis. If the result of intimate childhood association is something as strong as "a positive aversion," the consequences of such association might be evident in birth and divorce rates despite contaminating circumstances. But if the consequences are only a mild distaste, as Westermarck suggests when he speaks of "an indifference," the effects of childhood association may be masked by other factors. My problem was to decide what conclusion to reach if the information from the household registers did not bear out my predictions. I could not argue that the failure to find any difference between the two forms of marriage indicates a mild aversion, but neither could I conclude that Westermarck's hypothesis is mistaken. The information I was collecting while the household registration data were being compiled argues that the minor form of marriage does create marital dissatisfaction and sexual avoidance.

I was beginning to look for another way to test the hypothesis when a young man who is known in the area as a petty racketeer and a confidence man asked me for a job. Because of his ties with people on whom my welcome in the community depended, I could not refuse his proposal, but at first I was at a loss as to how to make use of his talents. He suggested the answer when he told me a long, humorous story about his father's many escapades with prostitutes and winehouse girls. Here was a man who was charming, articulate, and completely without inhibition. He commanded respect because of his connections with important people, but his own reputation would not prevent free and easy conversation. Perhaps he could get people to talk about the adulterous affairs of their friends and neighbors. Our goal would be to identify those women who commonly sought sexual gratification outside of marriage. This would give me another way of testing the Westermarck hypothesis and would also allow me to correct some of the errors in the household registers.

After discussing the project with several of my friends and informal advisors, I decided to concentrate our attention on two men, one in each of the two districts from which my sample was drawn. These men are old enough to have known all of the women in the sample in their youth and are attuned to local gossip because they are often called upon to act as mediators and go-betweens. In outlining the nature of the project to my new assistant, who had had previous dealings of one kind or another with both men, I emphasized the need to explain the "scientific" nature of our interest. To credit my assistant's good manners, he listened politely; to credit his good sense, he ignored everything I said. He was a much better fieldworker than I will ever be. His first step was to invite one of our potential informants to my house for dinner. After we had eaten and toasted one another repeatedly, he initiated a joking conversation about prostitution and adultery. He always began by pointing out how common they are in the United States and Western Europe, illustrating his point with any table or chart that happened to be lying handy on my desk. "Look," he would say, pointing to an appropriate number in a table reporting crude death rates for selected prefectures, "this is the United States. More than a third of all the women in the United States sleep with other men. And look at this; this is France. In France almost all the women have lovers." At the end of this spiel came a question: "What about around here? Does this kind of thing ever happen here?" By this time our informant was usually impatient to contribute his favorite stories to the conversation; if he wasn't, or if he was still discreet about mentioning names, my assistant went on to his own family tree, explaining with gusto his own origin. "You know my father isn't really my father; he lived with another woman and my mother lived with a man from Yingke. And my grandmother was the same way." The result was that by the next time we got together, our informant was talking freely about the sex lives of his friends and relatives. We asked three questions about each woman in our sample: "Do you know this woman? Have you ever heard of her sleeping with other men? Do you think all her children are her husband's offspring?"

The reader will wonder about the accuracy of gossip concerning events that took place fifty years ago. I have no way of knowing how accurate it is, but I do not think the time factor is important. In the small communities in which my subjects and informants live, what people say about one another is not easily forgotten. In this world gossip is more than malicious talk; it is a part of a person's social identity, no more likely to be forgotten than the person himself. The gossip may be partially mistaken, consisting more of accusation than of fact, but even this does not disqualify it as evidence. There is no stereotype of women who marry in the minor fashion that contrasts their sexual behavior with that of women who marry in the major fashion. Whatever error occurs in the answers we were given is random with respect to the hypothesis we are testing. If we do not find the predicted difference between the two forms of marriage, it may be because the error is great or because the hypothesis is wrong. But if we do find the predicted difference, it can be taken as evidence. Critics may be able to account for the difference

in another way, but they cannot discount it. Random error does not produce significant differences.

We can now turn to the results of these various attempts to test the Westermarck hypothesis. Consider first the prediction that the minor form of marriage will end in divorce more often than the major form of marriage. As can be seen in the information reported in Table 3, my worries about the use of this measure of marital dissatisfaction were unfounded. There are clear and striking differences between the two forms of marriage. The one case in which a major marriage ended in divorce is one of those rare exceptions that does not detract from the rule. The woman in question had worked in Taipei as a prostitute for several years before her marriage. According to one of the couple's former neighbors, her husband was forced to divorce her "because she kept going back to work."

Table 3 also reports eight cases of permanent separation. This is part of the information collected by means of my unsolicited but invaluable assistant. We discovered two marriages that ended when the wife ran away to live with another man, another terminated by the wife's taking up a life of prostitution, and five others in which the husband permanently deserted his wife. Two of these five men ran away with local

**TABLE 3**
Number and Percent of Marriages Ending in Divorce or Separation

|  | Minor Marriage | Major Marriage |
|---|---|---|
| Total number of marriages | 132 | 171 |
| Number ending in divorce | 25 | 1 |
| Number of permanent separations | 7 | 1 |
| Percent ending in divorce or separation | 24.2 | 1.2 |

girls and are now living in mainland China. Although none of those marriages is registered as having ended in divorce, they can be taken as equivalent to divorce for our purposes. That seven of the eight are minor marriages makes the evidence in favor of the Westermarck hypothesis overwhelming. Perhaps these couples felt the same as the Somerset Maugham character who couldn't imagine Byron's taking an interest in his sister. "Of course she was only his half-sister, but just as habit kills love I should have thought habit would prevent its arising. When two persons have known one another all their lives and lived together in close contact I can't imagine how or why that sudden spark should flash that results in love" (Maugham 1934:787–788).

Of the 303 women in my sample, 286 were known to one or the other of my two informants. They claim that sixty of these women had sexual relations with other men while their husbands were alive. Some of those affairs were brief and involved only one other man, but for some of the women adultery was a way of life. One is said to have slept with "more than a hundred different men." "They used to come here all the way from Yingke and Sanhsia to sleep with that woman." Another woman "couldn't see men at home because her parents-in-law were very strict, but if you gave her ten cents she'd meet you anywhere you wanted." The most interesting case is that of a girl who avoided sexual relations with her "brother" by feeding him a potion concocted with juice extracted from pomegranate roots. This is said to have made the husband impotent. "After that she slept with dozens of other men. I don't know what was so different about that woman's bones; she just couldn't do without a man."

The relative frequency of adultery in the two forms of marriage is reported in Table 4. The sharp difference between the two strongly suggests a need for extramarital sexual gratification on the part of women who marry a childhood associate. That this is due to a distaste for sexual relations with their husbands is evident in my informants' characterization of the conjugal re-

TABLE 4
Number and Percent of Married Women Involved in Adultery*

| | Minor Marriage | Major Marriage |
|---|---|---|
| Total number of women | 127 | 159 |
| Number involved in adultery | 42 | 18 |
| Percent involved in adultery | 33.1 | 11.3 |

*Five minor marriages and twelve major marriages were dropped for lack of information.

lationship. About a third of the way through the interviews one of the informants insisted that a couple's four children were all the offspring of one or another of the wife's several lovers. When I asked him how he could be so sure, he answered, "Because she has never slept with her husband." After this I was careful to inquire about each woman's relations with her husband as well as her relations with other men. By the time the interviews were completed, twelve couples had been identified as having never engaged in sexual intercourse despite years of marriage. All twelve couples had been raised together. My informants say the reason for this remarkable abstinence is "embarrassment," but this is obviously only a euphemism for some more intense emotion. The example of those couples who meet for the first time on the day of their wedding argues that people can be embarrassed without being inhibited.

Although it is not at all unlikely that adultery is a common cause of divorce, the fact is that the twenty-six registered divorces in our sample include only six of the sixty cases of adultery. This is important because it says that our two tests of the Westermarck hypothesis are independent. The hypothesis is confirmed not only by the two tests but also by two independent sets of data. The significance of this can be seen in Table 5, which combines the two sets of data into one

**TABLE 5**

Number and Percent of Marriages Ending in Divorce and/or Involving Adultery by Wife

|  | Minor Marriage | Major Marriage |
|---|---|---|
| Total number of marriages | 132 | 171 |
| Number involving divorce and/or adultery | 61 | 18 |
| Percent involving divorce and/or adultery | 46.2 | 10.5 |

**TABLE 6**

Average Number of Children as Taken from Household Registration Records

| Years of Marriage (in five-year intervals) | Minor Marriage | Major Marriage |
|---|---|---|
| 1st | 1.27 | 1.81 |
| 2nd | 1.19 | 1.62 |
| 3rd | 1.12 | 1.54 |
| 4th | 1.06 | 1.23 |
| 5th | 0.54 | 0.75 |

overall measure of marital dissatisfaction. We now find evidence of dissatisfaction in nearly half of all the minor marriages as against only ten percent of the major marriages. The reader will not need statistical assurances to convince him that a difference of this magnitude is not likely to be due to chance.

By the time the data from the household registers were complete, I had all but given up the idea of using birth rates as a measure of conjugal sexuality. The Chinese concern with perpetuating a line of descent, the errors in the household registers, and the simple fact that birth rates are, at best, only a crude index of frequency of sexual intercourse had all combined to discourage me. One could only hope to find the predicted relationship if couples raised together avoided one another for periods of a year or more at a time. But again my pessimism was unfounded. Contrary to my expectations, but in line with my prediction, minor marriages do produce fewer children, far fewer than major marriages. The evidence is reported in Table 6. The intervals in this table are calculated separately for each woman; the first interval begins at the date of marriage. When a marriage is terminated by death or divorce the case is dropped from this and all subsequent intervals. If, for example, a woman marries and bears two children in the first five years, these two children are included in

the average of the first interval. If the woman then bears a third child in the sixth year of marriage but gets a divorce in the seventh year, this child and the case are not included in the averages of the remaining intervals. The method is imperfect, but it is the best that can be managed with a small sample.

The averages reported in Table 6 are based on the number of registered births. We have seen that some of these children are really the offspring of a mistress or children whose registered father is not their genitor. The information provided by my two informants allows us to correct at least the more obvious of these errors. We can discount children who were conceived while the husband was living with another woman in another part of the island, children who are known to be the progeny of one of the husband's mistresses, and the children of women who are said to have never slept with their husbands. The corrected averages, shown in Table 7, provide striking, indeed surprising, confirmation of the assumptions made in my original prediction. Throughout the first twenty-five years of marriage, minor marriages produce thirty percent fewer children than major marriages.

By now all but the most skeptical readers will be willing to concede the existence of substantial differences between the conjugal relationships created by the major and minor forms of marriage. But they will ask, with good reason,

TABLE 7
Average Number of Children as Corrected by Informants

| Years of Marriage (in five-year intervals) | Minor Marriage | Major Marriage |
|---|---|---|
| 1st | 1.06 | 1.74 |
| 2nd | 1.01 | 1.55 |
| 3rd | 0.97 | 1.51 |
| 4th | 0.94 | 1.21 |
| 5th | 0.49 | 0.75 |

whether there are other differences between the two forms of marriage that could produce these results. We must at least consider the fact that the girl who marries in the minor fashion is adopted. Although demographers have not as yet identified psychological factors that affect fertility, this is not to say they do not exist (Noyes and Chapnick 1964). Perhaps the trauma of adoption decreases a woman's chances of bearing children. The experience of being raised as an adopted daughter may also be relevant. Adopted daughters are often mistreated by their foster parents and are always expected to carry a heavier burden of household labors than the family's own daughters (Wolf 1968:871). Women who are raised as adopted daughters claim that they did not eat as well as the family's own children. This experience might also affect their ability to bear children and could even make it more difficult for them to adjust to marriage.

Because the desire to economize is one reason for choosing to raise a son's wife, minor marriages are probably more common among the poor than among the wealthy. Women who marry a childhood associate may be less fertile because they have to work harder on a less satisfactory diet. And if families choosing the major and minor forms of marriage do differ in wealth, they may also represent different strata of the society. While social status cannot vary greatly

in communities composed largely of farmers and laborers, there may be some variation, a difference between what some Americans call "good families" and "poor families." Perhaps divorce and adultery are more common among minor marriages because of the kind of family that chooses this type of marriage. The very fact that they choose to raise a son's wife indicates that these families are somewhat less concerned about prestige and public opinion than many of their neighbors.

There are reasonable replies to all of these objections, but fortunately my case does not have to rest on reason alone. The women in the sample who married in the major fashion include forty-two who were raised as adopted daughters. A few of them came from families who decided against the minor marriage after having made the necessary arrangements. The majority are women whose intended husbands died before they were old enough to marry. Their foster parents then had no choice but to allow them to marry out in the major fashion. Because the Chinese always look for a daughter-in-law among families of approximately the same social status, we can safely assume that these forty-two major marriages are drawn from the same social strata as the minor marriages in the sample. And since all of these women were raised as adopted daughters, a comparison of the two is the ideal way to test for the effects of social status and the experience of adoption. The only difference between them is that one group of women married childhood associates while the other married strangers met for the first time the day of the wedding.

Consider first the evidence on divorce and adultery. The one major marriage that ended in divorce did involve a woman raised as an adopted daughter, but this is an exceptional exception. The reader will remember that the woman was a prostitute before marriage. Her neighbors claim she became a prostitute to avoid marrying her foster brother. That marital dissatisfaction is not often the lot of adopted daughters who marry in the major fashion is evident in

Table 8. The likelihood of divorce or adultery among these women is only a fifth of what it is among adopted daughters who married a childhood associate. This is almost exactly the magnitude of the difference we found in comparing all major and minor marriages.

Major marriages involving an adopted daughter also produce more children than minor marriages. Table 9 reports the average number of registered children for the two groups; Table 10 includes the corrections made by my two informants. Again the difference between adopted daughters who marry in the major and minor fashions is almost exactly the same as the difference between all major and minor marriages. Although adopted daughters do experience trauma and deprivation and may represent a lower stratum of society, this is not the reason they bear fewer children, divorce their husbands, and sleep with other men. There is no evidence of unusual marital dissatifaction as long as they marry a stranger; problems arise only when they are forced to marry a childhood associate.

This paper begins a story that is still years away from its concluding paragraphs. When I found the results of my first search of the household registers so encouraging, I decided to

TABLE 8
Number and Percent of Marriages by Adopted Daughters Ending in Divorce and/or Involving Adultery by Wife

|  | Minor Marriage | Major Marriage |
|---|---|---|
| Total number of marriages | 132 | 42 |
| Number ending in divorce | 25 | 1 |
| Number ending in adultery | 42 | 4 |
| Percent involving divorce and/or adultery | 46.2 | 9.5 |

TABLE 9
Average Number of Children by Adopted Daughters as Taken from Household Registration Records

| Years of Marriage (in five-year intervals) | Minor Marriage | Major Marriage |
|---|---|---|
| 1st | 1.27 | 1.78 |
| 2nd | 1.19 | 1.77 |
| 3rd | 1.12 | 1.76 |
| 4th | 1.06 | 1.31 |
| 5th | 0.54 | 0.90 |

TABLE 10
Average Number of Children by Adopted Daughters as Corrected by Informants

| Years of Marriage (in five-year intervals) | Minor Marriage | Major Marriage |
|---|---|---|
| 1st | 1.06 | 1.73 |
| 2nd | 1.01 | 1.73 |
| 3rd | 0.97 | 1.76 |
| 4th | 0.94 | 1.31 |
| 5th | 0.49 | 0.90 |

copy the complete records for Shulin Chen and Sanhsia Chen, an area with a present population of approximately 80,000 persons. An analysis of these records will take at least five years and perhaps as long as ten. The goal of this project is to retest the propositions presented in this paper and at the same time to specify the vague term "intimate and prolonged childhood association." The household registers tell us when the parties to a minor marriage are brought into association and also the composition of the family in which they are raised. My hope is that this variation in the degree and quality of the association will allow me to isolate the conditions that produce lower birth rates and higher divorce rates. Raised like brother and sister, the parties to a minor marriage may come to think of themselves as brother and sister. They may be reluctant to marry because brother and sister never marry. Identifying the precise conditions that make some couples more averse to marrying than others will eliminate this alternative explanation and allow a more general formulation of the Westermarck hypothesis.

I began this paper by quoting questions raised by Westermarck's critics. It is appropriate to conclude by noting his response. When Frazer and then Freud criticized Westermarck for failing to recognize that the incest taboo is necessary, the law itself being sufficient evidence of man's inclination to commit the forbidden act, he replied: "The law expresses the general feelings of the community and punishes acts that shock them; but it does not tell us whether an inclination to commit the forbidden act is felt by many or by few" (1922[2]:203–204). Whether the feelings expressed by the incest taboo reflect an uncomplicated aversion, as Westermarck believed, or an anxiety created in reaction to strong desire, as Freud suggested on one occasion, or some other emotional consequence of family life remains to be determined. The only conclusion justified by the data presented in this paper is that there is some aspect of childhood association sufficient to preclude or inhibit sexual desire. This suggests that the taboo is not a response to the needs of the social order, instituted to suppress private motives, but that it is instead an expression of these motives, a formal statement of the feelings of the community, socially unnecessary but psychologically inevitable.

## REFERENCES CITED

FRAZER, SIR JAMES
1910 Totemism and Exogamy. 4 Vols. London: Macmillan and Co.
HEBB, D. O., and W. R. THOMPSON
1968 The social significance of animal studies. In The handbook of social psychology. 5 Vols. G. Lindzey and E. Aronson, eds. Reading, Massachusetts: Addison-Wesley.
IMANISHI, K.
1961 The origin of the human family—a primatological approach. Japanese Journal of Ethnology 25:119–130.
KAUFMAN, J. H.
1965 A three-year study of mating behavior in a free-ranging band of rhesus monkeys. Ecology 46:500–512.
LÉVI-STRAUSS, CLAUDE
1960 The family. In Man, culture and society. L. Shapiro, ed. New York: Oxford University Press.
MAUGHAM, W. SOMERSET
1934 The book bag. In East and west: the collected short stories of W. Somerset Maugham. Garden City: Garden City Publishing Company.
NOYES, ROBERT W., and ELEANOR M. CHAPNICK
1964 Literature on psychology and infertility: a critical analysis. Fertility and Sterility 15:543–556.
SADE, DONALD STONE
1968 Inhibition of son-mother mating among free-ranging rhesus monkeys. Science and Psychoanalysis 12:18–38.
SAHLINS, MARSHALL
1960 The origin of society. Scientific American 1960[48]:76–89.
TOKUDA, K.
1961–62 A study on the sexual behavior in the Japanese monkey troop. Primates 3:1–40.
WESTERMARCK, EDWARD
1922 The history of human marriage. 3 Vols. London: Macmillan and Co.
WHITE, LESLIE A.
1948 The definition and prohibition of incest. American Anthropologist 50:416–435.
WOLF, ARTHUR P.
1966 Childhood association, sexual attraction, and the incest taboo: a Chinese case. American Anthropologist 68:883–898.
1968 Adopt a daughter-in-law, marry a sister: a Chinese solution to the problem of the incest taboo. American Anthropologist 70:864–874.

# KINSHIP GROUPS

ISSUE   The definition of family: Is the family the universal building block of kinship systems?

If you were a visitor to the United States from some other part of the world and were to attend a university football game, you would probably be confused. Surrounding you would be thousands of people. Most would be located in a large terraced section with benches where you are; some would be found on a grassy area down below. Their dress would vary from a variety of everyday clothes to colorfully designed "uniforms." As you watched, you would notice that people's behavior varied in relatively systematic ways. People might cheer, then look glum; men would run, knock each other down, form a circle, and occasionally all run to a "bench." Others would march, blow on instruments or whistles, or sell food. If you stayed in this country long enough, attended many football games, and asked questions of participants in this activity, you would learn to identify how people organized and structured this complex activity.

Anthropologists face a similar task when they conduct field work, although their job is complicated by the large number of different events they observe and try to understand. They, too, observe organized behavior and attempt to understand it. Part of the understanding depends on a determination of the social structure of the actors.

*Social structure* refers to the culturally defined parts that make up a society or organized group. The structural description of a society is a little like the physiologist's description of the human body. The physiologist looks for distinctive parts of the body by carefully dissecting it. The results of his or her investigation can be found in any anatomy text. There, for page after page, are long descriptions of the body's parts, its bones, organs, muscles, and nerves. And along with the descriptions are extended discussions of how various parts are connected and related: how the organs are situated in relation to each other, how they contribute to bodily processes, how the muscles are attached to the bones, and how they work for the entire body.

In the same sense, anthropologists dissect societies, looking for their basic parts and relationships. Just as you would learn to discern social "parts" of the group present at the football game—the players, crowd members, hot dog vendors, officials, and marching band participants—so does the anthropologist look for the basic elements, such as neighborhoods, clubs, factories, friendship groups, and clans, into which a society is divided.

As part of this search for structural parts, many anthropologists have sought out basic, universal elements of social structure, the fundamental building blocks out of which other parts are constructed. The physiologist, for example, notes that the body's parts are all constructed of cells. The analysis of society also yields elements that appear to be universal. Social identities, for example, are the culturally defined positions in society, filled by members of groups when they interact with each other. Associated with identities are social roles, the rules for appropriate behavior. Terms such as "father," "boss," "private first class," and "president" label social identities and their associated roles in our society.

As we saw in the last section, kinship forms a basis of social structure in every society and is especially important for the organization of many non-Western peoples. Anthropological descriptions of kinship systems often talk about lineages, clans, phratries, moieties, septs, kindreds, and other kinship groups, the units into which kin are organized. Anthropologists have also sought the basic elements from which all other kinship groups are formed. A candidate for such a universal element is the nuclear family, made up of a husband and wife and their children.

But like all anthropological categories, this one presents empirical difficulties. It does not seem to apply in every society in the way its adherents claim. In this section, we include articles that deal with the nature and importance of the nuclear family as a basic building block of kinship. We begin with a chapter by Murdock from *Social Structure,* in which he argues that the nuclear family is universal because it is the only social group that can perform certain indispensable functions. The second article, by Levy and Fallers, calls Murdock's view into question, arguing that the nuclear family as Murdock defines it does not exist in every society but there are always groups that meet the functions Murdock assigned to the basic family group. In the last article, Adams argues that the basic building blocks of kinship are dyads, not the nuclear family. The issue of the nature and extent of the nuclear family illustrates clearly the difficulties anthropologists face as they attempt to classify culturally generated human social arrangements cross-culturally.

# 10

## THE NUCLEAR FAMILY

*George Peter Murdock*

*Any formal classification has fuzzy edges. Americans use the folk term "car" to refer to a class of motor vehicles that have four wheels and carry passengers. While they are fairly comfortable using this word (Americans know what they mean by the term "car"), there are still ambiguities associated with these vehicles as a class of things. For example, Chevrolet makes a four-wheeled vehicle called a "Suburban," which many people buy as a family car, yet mechanics often refer to the suburban as a "truck," another class of vehicles. One state solves the problem by calling the suburban a "car" when it has a back seat and a "truck" when it does not.*

*Anthropologists encounter the same problem with scientific definitions. Most definitions manifest ambiguities that detract from their power, yet remain necessary for the ethnological task of comparison. In this article, Murdock introduces his definition of the nuclear family as a group consisting of at least one married couple living in the same residence with their children and performing sexual, reproductive, economic, and educational functions. He also claims that the nuclear family is found in every society.*

The family is a social group characterized by common residence, economic cooperation, and reproduction. It includes adults of both sexes, at least two of whom maintain a socially approved sexual relationship, and one or more children, own or adopted, of the sexually cohabiting adults. The family is to be distinguished from marriage, which is a complex of customs centering upon the relationship between a sexually associating pair of adults within the family. Marriage defines the manner of establishing and terminating such a relationship, the normative behavior and reciprocal obligations within it, and the locally accepted restrictions upon its personnel.

Used alone, the term "family" is ambiguous. The layman and even the social scientist often apply it undiscriminatingly to several social groups which, despite functional similarities, exhibit important points of difference. These must be laid bare by analysis before the term can be used in rigorous scientific discourse.

Three distinct types of family organization emerge from our survey of 250 representative human societies. The first and most basic, called herewith the *nuclear family,* consists typically of a married man and woman with their offspring, although in individual cases one or more additional persons may reside with them. The nuclear family will be familiar to the reader as the type of family recognized to the exclusion of all others by our own society. Among the majority of the peoples of the earth, however, nuclear families are combined, like atoms in a molecule, into larger aggregates. These composite forms of the family fall into two types, which differ in the principles by which the constituent nuclear families are affiliated. A *polygamous*[1] *family* con-

---

[1] The terms "polygamy" and "polygamous" will be used throughout this work in their recognized technical sense as referring to any form of plural marriage; "polygyny" will be employed for the marriage of one man to two or more women, and "polyandry" for the marriage of one woman to two or more men.

sists of two or more nuclear families affiliated by plural marriages, i.e., by having one married parent in common.[2] Under polygyny, for instance, one man plays the role of husband and father in several nuclear families and thereby unites them into a larger familial group. An *extended family* consists of two or more nuclear families affiliated through an extension of the parent-child relationship rather than of the husband-wife relationship, i.e., by joining the nuclear family of a married adult to that of his parents. The patrilocal extended family, often called the patriarchal family, furnishes an excellent example. It embraces, typically, an older man, his wife or wives, his unmarried children, his married sons, and the wives and children of the latter. Three generations, including the nuclear families of father and sons, live under a single roof or in a cluster of adjacent dwellings.

Of the 192 societies of our sample for which sufficient information is available, 47 have normally only the nuclear family, 53 have polygamous but not extended families, and 92 possess some form of the extended family. . . .

The nuclear family is a universal human social grouping. Either as the sole prevailing form of the family or as the basic unit from which more complex familial forms are compounded, it exists as a distinct and strongly functional group in every known society. No exception, at least, has come to light in the 250 representative cultures surveyed for the present study, which thus corroborates the conclusion of Lowie:[3] "It does not matter whether marital relations are permanent or temporary; whether there is poly-

gyny or polyandry or sexual license; whether conditions are complicated by the addition of members not included in *our* family circle: the one fact stands out beyond all others that everywhere the husband, wife, and immature children constitute a unit apart from the remainder of the community."

The view of Linton[4] that the nuclear family plays "an insignificant rôle in the lives of many societies" receives no support from our data. In no case have we found a reliable ethnographer denying either the existence or the importance of this elemental social group. Linton mentions the Nayar of India as a society which excludes the husband and father from the family, but he cites no authorities, and the sources consulted by ourselves for this tribe do not substantiate his statement. Whatever larger familial forms may exist, and to whatever extent the greater unit may assume some of the burdens of the lesser, the nuclear family is always recognizable and always has its distinctive and vital functions—sexual, economic, reproductive, and educational— which will shortly be considered in detail. It is usually spatially as well as socially distinct. Even under polygyny a separate apartment or dwelling is commonly reserved for each wife and her children.

The reasons for its universality do not become fully apparent when the nuclear family is viewed merely as a social group. Only when it is analyzed into its constituent relationships, and these are examined individually as well as collectively, does one gain an adequate conception of the family's many-sided utility and thus of its inevitability. A social group arises when a series of interpersonal relationships, which may be defined as sets of reciprocally adjusted habitual responses, binds a number of participant individuals collectively to one another. In the nuclear family, for example, the clustered relationships are eight in number: husband-wife, father-son, father-daughter, mother-son, moth-

[2]Cf. M. K. Opler, "Woman's Social Status and the Forms of Marriage," *American Journal of Sociology,* XLIX (1943), 144; A. R. Radcliffe-Brown, "The Study of Kinship Systems," *Journal of the Royal Anthropological Institute,* LXXI (1941), 2.

[3]R. H. Lowie, *Primitive Society* (New York, 1920), pp. 66–7. Cf. also F. Boas *et al, General Anthropology* (Boston, etc., 1938), p. 411; B. Malinowski, "Kinship," *Encyclopaedia Britannica* (14th edit., London, 1929), XIII, 404.

[4]R. Linton, *The Study of Man* (New York, 1936), pp. 153 (quoted), 154–5.

er-daughter, brother-brother, sister-sister, and brother-sister. The members of each interacting pair are linked to one another both directly through reciprocally reinforcing behavior and indirectly through the relationships of each to every other member of the family. Any factor which strengthens the tie between one member and a second also operates indirectly to bind the former to a third member with whom the second maintains a close relationship. An explanation of the social utility of the nuclear family, and thus of its universality, must consequently be sought not alone in its functions as a collectivity but also in the services and satisfactions of the relationships between its constituent members.

The relationship between father and mother in the nuclear family is solidified by the sexual privilege which all societies accord to married spouses. As a powerful impulse, often pressing individuals to behavior disruptive of the cooperative relationships upon which human social life rests, sex cannot safely be left without restraints. All known societies, consequently, have sought to bring its expression under control by surrounding it with restrictions of various kinds. On the other hand, regulation must not be carried to excess or the society will suffer through resultant personality maladjustments or through insufficient reproduction to maintain its population. All peoples have faced the problem of reconciling the need of control with the opposing need of expression, and all have solved it by culturally defining a series of sexual taboos and permissions. These checks and balances differ widely from culture to culture, but without exception a large measure of sexual liberty is everywhere granted to the married parents in the nuclear family. Husband and wife must adhere to sexual etiquette and must, as a rule, observe certain periodic restrictions such as taboos upon intercourse during menstruation, pregnancy, and lactation, but normal sex gratification is never permanently denied to them.

This sexual privilege should not be taken for granted. On the contrary, in view of the almost limitless diversity of human cultures in so many respects, it should be considered genuinely astonishing that some society somewhere has not forbidden sexual access to married partners, confining them, for example, to economic cooperation and allowing each a sexual outlet in some other relationship. As a matter of fact, one of the societies of our sample, the Banaro of New Guinea, shows a remote approach to such an arrangement. In this tribe a groom is not permitted to approach his young wife until she has borne him a child by a special-sib-friend of his father. Certain peasant communities in Eastern Europe are reported to follow a somewhat analogous custom. A father arranges a marriage for his immature son with an adult woman, with whom he lives and raises children until the son is old enough to assume his marital rights.[5] These exceptional cases are especially interesting since they associate sexual rights, not with the husband-wife relationship established by marriage, but with the father-mother relationship established by the foundation of a family.

As a means of expressing and reducing a powerful basic drive, as well as of gratifying various acquired or cultural appetites, sexual intercourse strongly reinforces the responses which precede it. These by their very nature are largely social, and include cooperative acts which must, like courtship, be regarded as instrumental responses. Sex thus tends to strengthen all the reciprocal habits which characterize the interaction of married parents, and indirectly to bind each into the mesh of family relationship in which the other is involved.

To regard sex as the sole factor, or even as the most important one, that brings a man and a woman together in marriage and binds them into the family structure would, however, be a serious error. If all cultures, like our own, prohibited and penalized sexual intercourse except in the marital relationship, such an assumption might seem reasonable. But this is emphatically

---

[5]Cf. R. F. Kaindl, "Aus der Volksüberlieferung der Bojken," *Globus,* LXXIX (1901), 155.

not the case. Among those of our 250 societies for which information is available, 65 allow unmarried and unrelated persons complete freedom in sexual matters, and 20 others give qualified consent, while only 54 forbid or disapprove premarital liaisons between non-relatives, and many of these allow sex relations between specified relatives such as cross-cousins.[6] Where premarital license prevails, sex certainly cannot be alleged as the primary force driving people into matrimony.

Nor can it be maintained that, even after marriage, sex operates exclusively to reinforce the matrimonial relationship. To be sure, sexual intercourse between a married man and an unrelated woman married to another is forbidden in 126 of our sample societies, and is freely or conditionally allowed in only 24. These figures, however, give an exaggerated impression of the prevalence of cultural restraints against extramarital sexuality, for affairs are often permitted between particular relatives though forbidden with non-relatives. Thus in a majority of the societies in our sample for which information is available a married man may legitimately carry on an affair with one or more of his female relatives, including a sister-in-law in 41 instances. Such evidence demonstrates conclusively that sexual gratification is by no means always confined to the marital relationship, even in theory. If it can reinforce other relationships as well, as it commonly does, it cannot be regarded as peculiarly conducive to marriage or as alone accountable for the stability of the most crucial relationship in the omnipresent family institution.

In the light of facts like the above, the attribution of marriage primarily to the factor of sex must be recognized as reflecting a bias derived from our own very aberrant sexual customs. The authors who have taken this position have frequently fallen into the further error of deriving human marriage from mating phenomena among the lower animals.[7] These fallacies were first exposed by Lippert[8] and have been recognized by a number of subsequent authorities.[9]

In view of the frequency with which sexual relations are permitted outside of marriage, it would seem the part of scientific caution to assume merely that sex is an important but not the exclusive factor in maintaining the marital relationship within the nuclear family, and to look elsewhere for auxiliary support. One such source is found in economic cooperation, based upon a division of labor by sex.[10] Since cooperation, like sexual association, is most readily and satisfactorily achieved by persons who habitually reside together, the two activities, each deriving from a basic biological need, are quite compatible. Indeed, the gratifications from each serve admirably to reinforce the other.

By virtue of their primary sex differences, a man and a woman make an exceptionally efficient cooperating unit.[11] Man, with his superior physical strength, can better undertake the more strenuous tasks, such as lumbering, mining, quarrying, land clearance, and housebuilding. Not handicapped, as is woman, by the physiological burdens of pregnancy and nursing, he can range farther afield to hunt, to fish, to herd, and to trade. Woman is at no disadvantage, however, in lighter tasks which can be per-

---

[6] A cross-cousin is the child of a father's sister or of a mother's brother. The children of a father's brother and of a mother's sister are technically known as "parallel cousins."

[7] See, for example, E. Westermarck, *The History of Human Marriage* (5th edit., New York, 1922), I, 72; A. M. Tozzer, *Social Origins and Social Continuities* (New York, 1925), p. 145.

[8] J. Lippert, *Kulturgeschichte der Menschheit in ihrem organischen Aufbau* (Stuttgart, 1886–87), I, 70–4; II, 5.

[9] See, for example, R. Briffault, *The Mothers* (New York, 1927), I, 608; W. G. Sumner and A. G. Keller, *The Science of Society* (New Haven, 1927), III, 1495–8, 1517; P. Vinogradoff, *Outlines of Historical Jurisprudence*, I (New York, 1920), 203.

[10] See W. G. Sumner and A. G. Keller, *The Science of Society* (New Haven, 1927), III, 1505–18.

[11] *Ibid.*, I, 111–40.

formed in or near the home, e.g., the gathering of vegetable products, the fetching of water, the preparation of food, and the manufacture of clothing and utensils. All known human societies have developed specialization and cooperation between the sexes roughly along this biologically determined line of cleavage.[12] It is unnecessary to invoke innate psychological differences to account for the division of labor by sex; the indisputable differences in reproductive functions suffice to lay out the broad lines of cleavage. New tasks, as they arise, are assigned to one sphere of activities or to the other, in accordance with convenience and precedent. Habituation to different occupations in adulthood and early sex typing in childhood may well explain the observable differences in sex temperament, instead of *vice versa.*[13]

The advantages inherent in a division of labor by sex presumably account for its universality. Through concentration and practice each partner acquires special skill at his particular tasks. Complementary parts can be learned for an activity requiring joint effort. If two tasks must be performed at the same time but in different places, both may be undertaken and the products shared. The labors of each partner provide insurance to the other. The man, perhaps, returns from a day of hunting, chilled, unsuccessful, and with his clothing soiled and torn, to find warmth before a fire which he could not have maintained, to eat food gathered and cooked by the woman instead of going hungry, and to receive fresh garments for the morrow, prepared, mended, or laundered by her hands. Or perhaps the woman has found no vegetable food, or lacks clay for pottery or skins for making clothes, obtainable only at a distance from the dwelling, which she cannot leave because her children require care; the man in his ramblings after game can readily supply her wants. Moreover, if either is injured or ill, the other can nurse him back to health. These and similar rewarding experiences, repeated daily, would suffice of themselves to cement the union. When the powerful reinforcement of sex is added, the partnership of man and woman becomes inevitable.

Sexual unions without economic cooperation are common, and there are relationships between men and women involving a division of labor without sexual gratification, e.g., between brother and sister, master and maidservant, or employer and secretary, but marriage exists only when the economic and the sexual are united into one relationship, and this combination occurs only in marriage. Marriage, thus defined, is found in every known human society. In all of them, moreover, it involves residential cohabitation, and in all of them it forms the basis of the nuclear family. Genuine cultural universals are exceedingly rare. It is all the more striking, therefore, that we here find several of them not only omnipresent but everywhere linked to one another in the same fashion.

Economic cooperation not only binds husband to wife; it also strengthens the various relationships between parents and children within the nuclear family. Here, of course, a division of labor according to age, rather than sex, comes into play. What the child receives in these relationships is obvious; nearly his every gratification depends upon his parents. But the gains are by no means one-sided. In most societies, children by the age of six or seven are able to perform chores which afford their parents considerable relief and help, and long before they attain adulthood and marriageability they become economic assets of definite importance. One need only think here of the utility of boys to their fathers and of girls to their mothers on the typical European or American farm. Moreover, children represent, as it were, a sort of investment or insurance policy; dividends, though deferred for a few years, are eventually paid generously in the form of economic aid, of

[12]See G. P. Murdock, "Comparative Data on the Division of Labor by Sex," *Social Forces,* XV (1937), 551–3, for an analysis of the distribution of economic activities by sex in 224 societies.

[13]Cf. M. Mead, *Sex and Temperament in Three Primitive Societies* (New York, 1935).

support in old age, and even, sometimes, of cash returns, as where a bride-price is received for a daughter when she marries.

Siblings[14] are similarly bound to one another through the care and help given by an elder to a younger, through cooperation in childhood games which imitate the activities of adults, and through mutual economic assistance as they grow older. Thus through reciprocal material services sons and daughters are bound to fathers and mothers and to one another, and the entire family group is given firm economic support.

Sexual cohabitation leads inevitably to the birth of offspring. These must be nursed, tended, and reared to physical and social maturity if the parents are to reap the afore-mentioned advantages. Even if the burdens of reproduction and child care outweigh the selfish gains to the parents, the society as a whole has so heavy a stake in the maintenance of its numbers, as a source of strength and security, that it will insist that parents fulfill these obligations. Abortion, infanticide, and neglect, unless confined within safe limits, threaten the entire community and arouse its members to apply severe social sanctions to the recalcitrant parents. Fear is thus added to self-interest as a motive for the rearing of children. Parental love, based on various derivative satisfactions, cannot be ignored as a further motive; it is certainly no more mysterious than the affection lavished by many people on burdensome animal pets, which are able to give far less in return. Individual and social advantages thus operate in a variety of ways to strengthen the reproductive aspects of the parent-child relationships within the nuclear family.

The most basic of these relationships, of course, is that between mother and child, since this is grounded in the physiological facts of pregnancy and lactation and is apparently supported by a special innate reinforcing mechanism, the mother's pleasure or tension release in suckling her infant. The father becomes involved in the care of the child less directly, through the sharing of tasks with the mother. Older children, too, frequently assume partial charge of their younger siblings, as a chore suited to their age. The entire family thus comes to participate in child care, and is further unified through this cooperation.

No less important than the physical care of offspring, and probably more difficult, is their social rearing. The young human animal must acquire an immense amount of traditional knowledge and skill, and must learn to subject his inborn impulses to the many disciplines prescribed by his culture, before he can assume his place as an adult member of his society. The burden of education and socialization everywhere falls primarily upon the nuclear family, and the task is, in general, more equally distributed than is that of physical care. The father must participate as fully as the mother because, owing to the division of labor by sex, he alone is capable of training the sons in the activities and disciplines of adult males.[15] Older siblings, too, play an important role, imparting knowledge and discipline through daily interaction in work and play. Perhaps more than any other single factor, collective responsibility for education and socialization welds the various relationships of the family firmly together.

In the nuclear family or its constituent relationships we thus see assembled four functions fundamental to human social life—the sexual, the economic, the reproductive, and the educational. Without provision for the first and third, society would become extinct; for the second, life itself would cease; for the fourth, culture would come to an end. The immense social utility of the nuclear family and the basic reason for its universality thus begin to emerge in strong relief.

Agencies or relationships outside of the family may, to be sure, share in the fulfillment of any of these functions, but they never supplant the

[14]The term "sibling" will be employed throughout this work in its technical sense as designating either a brother or a sister irrespective of sex.

[15]Cf. R. Linton, *The Study of Man* (New York, 1936), p. 155.

family. There are, as we have seen, societies which permit sexual gratification in other relationships, but none which deny it to married spouses. There may be extraordinary expansion in economic specialization, as in modern industrial civilization, but the division of labor between man and wife still persists. There may, in exceptional cases, be little social disapproval of childbirth out of wedlock, and relatives, servants, nurses, or pediatricians may assist in child care, but the primary responsibility for bearing and rearing children ever remains with the family. Finally, grandparents, schools, or secret initiatory societies may assist in the educational process, but parents universally retain the principal role in teaching and discipline. No society, in short, has succeeded in finding an adequate substitute for the nuclear family to which it might transfer these functions. It is highly doubtful whether any society ever will succeed in such an attempt, utopian proposals for the abolition of the family to the contrary notwithstanding.

The above-mentioned functions are by no means the only ones performed by the nuclear family. As a firm social constellation, it frequently, but not universally, draws to itself various other functions. Thus it is often the center of religious worship, with the father as family priest. It may be the primary unit in land holding, vengeance, or recreation. Social status may depend more upon family position than upon individual achievement. And so on. These additional functions, where they occur, bring increased strength to the family, though they do not explain it.

Like the community, the nuclear family is found in sub-human societies, although here the father is less typically a member and, where he is, is usually less firmly attached. But man's closest animal relatives possess, at best, only a rudimentary division of labor by sex, and they seem to lack culture altogether. The universal participation of the father in the human family would thus seem to depend mainly upon economic specialization and the development of a body of traditional lore to be transmitted from one generation to the next. Since both are products of cultural evolution—indeed, amongst the earliest of such—the human family cannot be explained on an instinctive or hereditary basis.

This universal social structure, produced through cultural evolution in every human society as presumably the only feasible adjustment to a series of basic needs, forms a crucial part of the environment in which every individual grows to maturity. The social conditions of learning during the early formative years of life, as well as the innate psychological mechanism of learning, are thus essentially the same for all mankind. For an understanding of the behavior acquired under such conditions the participation of the social scientist would seem as essential as that of the psychologist. It is highly probable, for instance, that many of the personality manifestations studied by depth psychology are rooted in a combination of psychological and social-cultural constants. Thus the "Œdipus complex" of Freud seems comprehensible only as a set of characteristic behavioral adjustments made during childhood in the face of a situation recurrently presented by the nuclear family.[16]

---

[16]Unlike other psychological systems, that of Freud thus rests on cultural as well as physiological assumptions. See G. P. Murdock, "The Common Denominator of Cultures," *The Science of Man in the World Crisis,* ed. R. Linton (New York, 1945), p. 141.

# 11

## THE FAMILY: SOME COMPARATIVE CONSIDERATIONS[1]
*M. J. Levy, Jr., and L. A. Fallers*

*There are really two parts to Murdock's classic definition of the family: content and function. Content includes a minimum basis for membership of a married couple and one or more of their children, and common residence. Functions, the things the family unit does, are really universal requirements for the survival of society as a whole. For Murdock, these functions are the provision of legitimate sexual activity, reproduction, economic cooperation, and the socialization of children. In their article, Levy and Fallers argue that the family defined with the content Murdock proposed for it is not the exclusive or necessarily the most important author of these basic functions. Arguing that the functions are primary to the definition of the family, they suggest that any kinship unit that provides for sex, reproduction, economy, and education be called a family.*

In order to carry out comparative analysis, one clearly requires concepts on the most general level which are applicable to any society. The concept "family" is commonly used in this way; that is, it is commonly assumed that in every society there is something called "the family." We feel, however, that the concept as it is most often used is ill-adapted to comparative analysis. It is usually assumed, either implicitly or explicitly, that in every society there is a single social unit which is invariably associated with certain functions. It may even be assumed that this unit is everywhere structurally the same.

Now progress in the field of comparative analysis of societies has regularly involved clearer distinction between structure and function and between concrete social units and analytically distinguishable aspects of such units (Levy 1952). The political field provides a case in point. The term "political system" in its common-sense Western meaning refers to a series of specialized concrete social units (bureaucracies, legislatures, courts, parties) with particular structural forms (hierarchical in the case of bu-

reaucracies, collegial in the case of legislatures, and so on) and having particular functions with regard to the exercise of power and authority (adjudicating disputes, making decisions, securing consent). However, a concept like this is of little use comparatively. On the one hand, by this definition many societies simply do not have "political systems." In many societies a single social unit—perhaps a unilineal kinship group—may combine the functions of "church," "state," and "firm" and it will very likely differ greatly in structure from any of the specialized political units characteristic of the modern West. On the other hand, the above type of definition of "political system" tends to obscure as much as it reveals even within the systems to which it is indigenous. Even the specialized political units of the modern West have nonpolitical aspects, while other units, not of a specialized political nature, nevertheless have political aspects. It is only when these distinctions are recognized that the political systems of the full range of human societies become commensurable.

As applied to the political field or to most

other fields of comparative interest, distinctions of this kind are commonly made and, indeed, seem obvious, but in comparative studies of the family they seem to be considered unnecessary. Undoubtedly the reason for this is the apparent empirical ubiquity of small, kinship-structured domestic units having reproductive, socialization, and sex-regulation functions. In most other respects human society is empirically so variable that distinction between structure and function, between social units and analytically distinguishable aspects of them, comes quite naturally to the social analyst. But the family, it seems to be felt, is an exception because a particular set of functions is so regularly associated with a particular type of unit. Murdock, in what is certainly the most extensive and influential comparative study yet undertaken, feels able to assert at the outset, on the basis of data from his sample of 250 societies, that "Either as the sole prevailing form or as the basic unit from which more complex familial forms are compounded, [the nuclear family] exists as a distinct and strongly functional group in every society" and that it universally performs ". . . four functions fundamental to human social life—the sexual, the economic, the reproductive and the educational" (Murdock 1949: 2–3). Murdock's position has been widely adopted, perhaps most notably by Parsons and Bales (Parsons 1954; Parsons and Bales 1955).

It is not our purpose here to question the empirical ubiquity of small, kinship-structured domestic units with reproductive, sex-regulation, and socialization functions. That there are striking regularities in this sphere seems clear. Neither do we propose to take a stand on the question of whether or not these regularities are in any sense "biologically based." Rather we propose to argue that, in spite of such considerations—in a sense just *because* of the temptations to conceptual shoddiness to which apparent empirical regularities in the family sphere expose us—it is desirable to preserve in this field the conceptual distinctions which have

proved so necessary in the comparative analysis of other aspects of human society.

Let us assume, then, that small, kinship-structured units are universal—are indeed structural requisites of any society. Functionally, socialization would appear to be the heart of the matter. Parsons and Bales have argued with great cogency that socialization requires small units and that completely non-kinship-structured small units are unlikely to carry out the function effectively (although of course human ingenuity may devise alternatives). Of the other "universal functions" attributed by Murdock to the family, reproduction and sexual regulation would appear to be associated with, and probably secondary to, socialization. Parsons' argument here seems to us convincing (Parsons 1954). Murdock's remaining "universal function"—the economic—seems to us to be on an entirely different level. It is not so much that families universally fulfill economic functions vis-à-vis other units and the society at large; clearly, the degree to which and the ways in which they do so are subject to enormous variation. Rather, the point would seem to be that families, like other social units, must make provision for the distribution of goods and services —that, like other units, they have economic aspects. If families are universal, probably because of their usefulness as socialization devices, then indeed in every society they have economic functions. It would appear to be the socialization function, however, which lies at the root of the requisite nature of families.

But, assuming that small, kinship-structured units are structural requisites of any society, and assuming that they are so because socialization requires it, it does not follow either that (a) there is a single such unit in every society ("*the* family") which carries out every aspect of the socialization function and its associated or derivative functions or, still less, that (b) in every society this unit is the nuclear family. We do not believe that either Murdock or Parsons has shown these statements to be true. If they are not true, then it becomes seriously misleading to use the term "family" as a comparative concept on the most general level to refer to a concrete unit, to a particular structural type and to an invariant set of functions taken together. It becomes necessary to distinguish these elements so that the ranges of variation which are thereby admitted may be discussed.

Let us first consider the universality of the nuclear family as the unit for socialization. Murdock argues that, even where the nuclear family is "enveloped" in more extended domestic units, it is always clearly distinguished as a separate subunit and he rather implies that it is always the more fundamental unit vis-à-vis the "universal functions of the family." We would not deny that in most, if not all, societies persons are typically able to distinguish their own parents and siblings from other kinsmen. We do not believe, however, that extended family households always "consist" of aggregations of nuclear families—that in such households children are always socialized primarily in terms of the nuclear family subunit. This is essentially the point made by Linton in his distinction between "conjugal" and "consanguineal" families (Linton 1936: 159–160). We cannot in this paper undertake to test this notion on a wide range of empirical data, but we would cite data with which we are familiar from societies which are not particularly unusual in the relevant respects. One of us has pointed out that in the traditional Chinese family children are typically socialized in terms of the patrilineal extended family unit and that within this unit the nuclear family was by no means the "strongest" subunit for socialization purposes (Levy 1955). Among the Basoga of East Africa, the typical household is occupied by a nuclear family plus odd individual kinsmen. However, the solidarity of exogamous patrilineages is strong and nuclear families tend to be split by the conflicting loyalties of the spouses. Divorce is consequently very common and hence children are very often socialized in households where only one parent is present. More importantly, even where marriages remain

intact, the conflict of lineage loyalties results in a primary orientation on the part of children to the lineages of the two parents rather than to the nuclear family as a unit (Fallers 1957). The Hopi would appear to represent an analogous situation on the matrilineal side, while among the famous Nayar, apparently, the nuclear family disappears altogether in favor of the consanguineal unit (Eggan 1950:113–114; Gough 1952a, 1952b). (Thus the Nayar seem to us, not an ethnographic oddity, but merely an extreme extension of a quite widespread pattern.)

Secondly, there is the question of whether in every society there is a single small, kinship-structured unit which carries out the socialization function. Again, the traditional Chinese extended family would seem to represent a relatively common contrary case. Young children tend to be socialized almost exclusively by mothers and grandmothers; later the sexes divide, boys associating primarily with adult males and girls with adult females. Thus, at various times and with regard to the two sexes, different subunits emerge as primary for socialization. Among the matrilineal Ashanti of Ghana, it is quite clear from Fortes' material, the typical child is primarily oriented during one phase of socialization to a consanguineal unit centering upon its mother and her brother, while during another phase it is associated primarily with a conjugal unit based upon father and mother (Fortes 1949).

We are well aware that this brief discussion is far from doing justice to Parsons' complex psychoanalytic argument concerning socialization and the nuclear family. From a psychogenetic standpoint, the kernel of the problem is whether adequate socialization requires the "Oedipus situation" in its full sexual sense—that is, the regular presence in the domestic unit of a cohabiting pair or "conjugal family"—or whether the mere presence in the domestic unit of adult male and female role models—an adult brother and sister, for example—is sufficient. An attempt to deal more fully with the psychogenetic argument must await another occasion, but we do feel that considerations of the sort put forward here suggest a restatement of the problem along the following lines:

It seems to us untenable to assume that the socialization function is invariably carried out primarily within a single kinship-structured unit —the nuclear family or any other—even though we assume that small, kinship-structured units are structural requisites of any society and that their requisite nature is bound up with the socialization function. This being so, we suggest that the concept "family," to be useful for general comparative purposes, should be used to refer not to a single social unit in each society, but rather to any small, kinship-structured unit which carries out aspects of the relevant functions. We suspect that, using the term in this way, one would find in most societies a series of "family" units. We cannot systematically spell out the possibilities here, but one would want to distinguish, among others, units for socializing each of the two sexes and units associated with distinguishable aspects and temporal phases of socialization. We have noted above that, while the requisite and universal nature of small, kinship-structured units probably rests upon the socialization function, once such units exist other functions come into the picture. Thus, for example, one would have to distinguish units which fulfill the economic functions arising from the existence of the socialization units; there is no reason to assume that these units would be the same. In Ashanti, a child and its mother may commonly live in the household of the mother's brother, but the mother may nevertheless send food to her husband living in another household.

We suggest that the concept of the family presented here facilitates a more differentiated analysis of small, kinship-structured units and their functions; that it brings the study of such units into more systematic relationship with other kinship studies; and that it facilitates the systematic comparison of such units with non-kinship-structured units. There is clearly something special about "the family"; we argue only that the study of it deserves the same conceptual care that we customarily apply to the study of other aspects of society.

## NOTE

1. This is a slight revision of a paper presented at the 1957 meeting of the American Anthropological Association in Chicago, in a symposium on "Models for the Study of Kinship" organized by Harry W. Basehart.

## BIBLIOGRAPHY

EGGAN, FREDERICK
    1950 Social organization of the western pueblos. Chicago, University of Chicago Press.

FALLERS, L. A.
    1957 Some determinants of marriage stability in Busoga: A reformulation of Gluckman's hypothesis. Africa XXVII: 106–123.

FORTES, MEYER
    1949 Time and social structure: An Ashanti case study. *In:* Social structure: Studies presented to A. R. Radcliffe-Brown, Meyer Fortes ed. London, Oxford University Press.

GOUGH, KATHLEEN
    1952a Changing kinship usages in the setting of political and economic change among the Nayar of Malabar. Journal of the Royal Anthropological Institute 52:71–88.
    1952b A comparison of incest prohibitions and rules of exogamy in three matrilineal groups of the Malabar Coast. International Archives of Ethnography 46:81–105.

LEVY, M. J., JR.
    1952 The structure of society. Princeton, Princeton University Press.
    1955 Some questions about Parsons' treatment of the incest problem. British Journal of Sociology VI:277–285.

LINTON, RALPH
    1936 The study of man. New York, D. Appleton-Century.

MURDOCK, G. P.
    1949  Social structure. New York, Macmillan.
PARSONS, TALCOTT
    1954  The incest taboo in relation to social
          structure and the socialization of the

child. British Journal of Sociology
    V:101–117.
PARSONS, TALCOTT AND ROBERT F. BALES
    1955  Family, socialization and interaction
          process. Glencoe, The Free Press.

# 12

## AN INQUIRY INTO THE NATURE OF THE FAMILY

*Richard N. Adams*

*Unlike Levy and Fallers, Richard Adams returns to a consideration of the content or basic membership of the family in this article. He, too, notes that functions do not always fit the family unit as Murdock has defined it, and he points out that many societies lack a nuclear family unit. He specifically singles out evidence from Latin American societies, where so-called woman-headed families are relatively common. Here, he argues, despite the lack of true nuclear families, sexual, reproductive, economic, and educational functions are met. They are not necessarily met by the nuclear family, but by dyads or pairs of identities in the kinship system. Most important are the conjugal dyad formed by a man and woman, which provides for sexual and reproductive functions, and the maternal dyad of a woman and her children, which provides for economic and educational functions. Based on his analysis, Adams suggests that the basic building blocks of kinship structure are dyads, not the nuclear family, which is a group that is itself made up of dyads.*

*Science can study only what is.*

LESLIE WHITE,
in an Undergraduate Lecture, 1943

Literature on the human family appearing during the past decade has taken a decided swing away from the earlier simple classificatory goals of identifying lineality, locality, descent groups, and formal kin structures. The new direction, as has been noted by many persons active in the movement, has been towards examining the phenomenon within wider dimensions. No longer, for example, is it possible to speak simply and

securely of matrilocality or of patrilocality without extensive and adequate analysis of the precise configurations standing behind the activities of the members of the particular society concerned (Fortes 1949; Goodenough 1956). In a very real sense many of the formerly analytic terms have become heuristic and descriptive.

With respect to the form of the nuclear family, however, there has been little evidence of increased interest in fundamentals. Concern here is as ancient as any in the field of social organization, but treatments of it continue to be predominantly expressions of profound convictions, buttressed by more or less convincing logical arguments stemming from a variety of theoretical premises. A recent example of this may be found in Weston LaBarre's *The Human Animal* (1954), an absorbing and provocative though unconvincing argument for the absolute necessity and inevitability of a continuing nuclear family. A more rigorous argument with the same conclusion but based on different kinds of evidence is contained in G. P. Murdock's *Social Structure* (1949). Murdock claims, on the basis of an examination of 250 societies, that there are no cases where the nuclear family is not the fundamental unit or cell upon which all further familial and kin elaborations are based. Both before and after Murdock's study, exceptions to this picture were cited, specifically the Nayar of Malabar (Linton 1936; Gough 1952; Cappannari 1953), but in principle Murdock's judgment has met with general approval. Even an examination of the *kibbutz* led Spiro (1954) to conclude that whereas the *kibbutz* may have eliminated the nuclear family, it did so only through converting the entire community into a single large *gemeinschaft.*

The purpose of the present essay is to question whether some arguments in support of this general view are satisfactory and to do so through a review of selected cases in which the nuclear family is manifestly only one type of basic form. This is in accord with, but varies in focus from, the interest expressed by Marion Levy (1955) when he asked whether the nuclear family was "institutionalized" in all societies. Levy pointed out that even though the statuses of father, mother, spouse, sister, and brother may be present, they may not function as a nuclear family unit. He gave as an example the case of the traditional Chinese family. In the present paper the position is taken that social organization is flexible enough to permit different forms

of the family to exist simultaneously. These different forms may not even take care of the same general functional needs of the total society, and in many cases certain of the standard nuclear family statuses (that is, mother-wife, father-husband, unmarried children) may not function at all. So far as present evidence indicates, there is no question but that these statuses are present in the society; rather it is a question of how they are filled and how they function. The flexibility of social organization permitting the appearance of different family forms rests on the fact that there are more elemental forms of the family than the nuclear, and that different forms may function in relation to different aspects or characteristics of the total social structure.

The cases to be discussed are taken from contemporary Central and South America. We are intentionally treating only this material (and omitting the Nayar and similar cases) because it better illuminates the propositions we wish to explore. Studies in Latin America have increasingly indicated that while most contemporary family systems of that region reckon descent bilaterally, there are many instances where family forms other than the nuclear are operative. The nuclear family is generally replaced in these circumstances by a group based on what we will call the maternal dyad, a residential unit composed of a mother and one or more children. As is the case in many nuclear family residences, these dyad households may also have a variety of other members present, both kin and non-kin.

Our interest will focus on two dyad forms: the maternal dyad, just described; and an adult dyad, composed of a man and woman, which we shall clumsily call the sexual or conjugal dyad. This dyad may be based simply on the sexual act, or may be further sanctioned by marriage. There is a third dyad, the paternal (composed of father and one or more children) which we will not treat here. It is with no intent of minimizing the importance of this dyad in the world at large that it is minimized here, but simply because it does not appear in significant numbers apart from the nuclear family in our data.[1] The identification of the maternal dyad, as distinct from the nuclear family, is made on the basis of the fact that there is no husband-father regularly resident. The cases used here are based on a distinction made between households with a woman head and those with a man head. This identification in terms of the sex of household heads stems from the nature of census data from which much of the information is derived. While having both theoretical and practical disadvantages, it serves sufficiently well for present purposes. The presence of woman-headed households (in these bilateral societies) is being used here as an index to the prevalence of the maternal dyad family form, and man-headed households as an index to the prevalence of the nuclear family form. While some woman-headed households are doubtless due to widowhood, the percentage of widows seldom exceeds 5 per cent of the women in the society, and, of course, many widows are not heads of households. While some man-headed households may be paternal dyads and not nuclear families, the number is not significant in all cases where specific information is available.

## SOME CASES FROM LATIN AMERICA

In his recent monograph on the community of Villa Recôncavo, Bahia, Brazil, Harry W. Hutchinson (1957) defines an entire social class segment of his community in terms of the fact that it is composed of woman-headed households. Ninety (31 per cent) of the 290 house-

holds in the community were reported to be of this type in the 1950 census. Although Hutchinson says (1957:151) that, "The composition of these households almost defies classification," he promptly notes that 55 of them (19 per cent of the total number of families, and 61 per cent of the 90) are "composed of mothers and children, with the addition in some cases of relatives and an *agregado* as well as boarders." The other households in this class, Hutchinson describes as "left overs" from other families or marital unions. Although Hutchinson evidently feels that these families offer the scientist nothing but confusion, the fact that they were sufficiently distinct to move him to the extreme of categorizing them as an entirely separate "social class," and the fact that they do manifest a considerable consistency with respect to the presence of the dyad family indicate that they do not defy classification.

The Services, in their report on Tobatí, Paraguay (1954), indicate that what they call "incomplete" families form a prominent part of the community. Of a total of 292 families, only 133 (45.5 per cent) are complete nuclear families (with or without additional members); of the remainder, 113 (38.8 per cent of the total) are woman-headed households. This detailed report gives a somewhat higher woman-headed household rate than Emma Reh's earlier study (1947) of the Paraguayan community of Piribebuy where she estimated that 60 per cent of the families were complete and 33 per cent were headed by women. Since there are almost as many woman-headed households as man-headed households in Tobatí, there is little doubt that the maternal dyad is the basis of a highly significant portion of the household units.

Although national statistics for Brazil and Paraguay were not available to the writer, there is evidence from other areas that the presence of maternal dyad families is not a matter of limited or local significance. In Central America, 1950 census data are available for four countries concerning the relative number of families recorded as having women as heads of households:

[1]It would perhaps be well to note at this point that not only the paternal dyad, but many other forms both of family elements and artificial or pseudo-kin relationships are pertinent to the discussion as it progresses. In the interests of brevity, I am raising these principles for discussion, and am intentionally not pursuing here all the lines of exploration they suggest.

| Country | Number of Families | Per cent of Families with Woman Heads |
|---------|-----------|-----------|
| Guatemala | 561,944 | 16.8 |
| El Salvador | 366,199 | 25.5 |
| Nicaragua | 175,462 | 26.0 |
| Costa Rica | 143,167 | 17.2 |

Within this general picture for Central America, there is great variation both with respect to area and to ethnic types. Ethnically, there is a marked difference between Guatemalan departments (a department is equivalent to a U.S. state) where the population is heavily Mayan Indian, and departments occupied predominantly by Spanish Americans, called Ladinos. In the predominantly Indian departments (so classified because 70 per cent or more of their population was registered as Indian in the 1950 census) the total percentage of families with women as heads runs between 10 per cent and 20 per cent. Only two of the seven departments of this type had percentages greater than 15 per cent. Outside these departments, the percentage ran as high as 35 per cent. While the woman-headed household rate of the Ladino population is generally higher than that of the Indians, there is also a pronounced difference from one region to another within the Ladino area. In El Salvador a block of six departments (out of a total of thirteen) has percentages between 25 per cent and 30 per cent, while three Pacific coastal departments of Nicaragua run over 30 per cent. Although lack of data from Honduras (Honduras census data on heads of household were not tabulated by sex) makes a large blank in the Central American picture, the material from the aforementioned four countries makes it perfectly evident that woman-headed families are a widespread and common form in Ladino society. There is evidence from one area, El Salvador, that there is also a significant difference between urban and rural populations in this respect. (Urban is defined in the Salvadorean census as pertaining to a municipal or district capital town;

the population outside of these towns is rural.) While only 20.3 per cent of the Salvadorean rural families have women heads, 34.7 per cent of the urban families are of this type.[2]

The presence, then, of woman heads of households in Central America is not a confused and random situation but is definitely associated with the Ladino population, is concentrated in certain regions, and is probably more commonly associated with town dwellers than with rural populations (Adams 1957).

Another region from which there has been an increasing number of reports of dyad families is the Caribbean and the Guianas. Of the studies that have appeared in recent years one in particular has addressed itself to this issue and should concern us here. Raymond T. Smith (1956) studied three Negro towns in British Guiana in which the percentage of woman heads of households was as follows:

| Town | Number of Households | Percent of Households with Woman Heads |
|------|-----------|-----------|
| August Town | 275 | 37.1 |
| Perseverance | 103 | 16.5 |
| Better Hope | 71 | 29.2 |

Many accounts of West Indian societies have indicated the presence of these families (as in the work of Herskovits, Campbell, Simey, and Henriquez) but for present purposes we will restrict ourselves to the work of Smith.

These cases from Paraguay, Brazil, Central America, and British Guiana give ample evidence that in contemporary populations with

---

[2]While this urban-rural comparison superficially compares with the material cited by Franklin Frazier for Negro families of the United States, caution should be observed since the Salvador data do not make the same distinctions between "owners" and "tenants" and, more important, between "rural farm" and "rural non-farm," as Frazier makes. See Frazier (1939:570–1).

bilateral descent systems woman-headed households are quite common. We infer, especially from those cases which have been described in some detail, that this is an index to an almost equally high incidence of families that have the maternal dyad as their basic unit.


# THE UNIVERSAL FUNCTIONS APPROACH

The problem now is to arrive at a theoretical framework that will make these data intelligible. As literature on the family is extensive, we will restrict ourselves to a limited number of theories concerning the status of the nuclear family. The writers of particular interest to us here are Murdock, Parsons, and R. T. Smith.


## Murdock's Multiple-Function Approach

Murdock's major reasons for seeing the nuclear family as a universal and inevitable phenomenon are that it was present in all the societies in his original sample for *Social Structure* (1949), and that logically it seemed to him that the family fulfilled a number of functions better than any other conceivable agency. The four functions he regards as primary (although he would doubtless allow others for any specific society) are "fundamental to human social life—the sexual, the economic, the reproductive, and the educational." Murdock is quite explicit in saying that "Agencies or relationships outside of the family may, to be sure, share in the fulfillment of any of these functions, but they never supplant the family" (1949:10). The immediate issue that arises from Murdock's propositions is whether in fact other agencies have not frequently taken over the functions that he regards as being uniquely served by the nuclear family. In reading Murdock, one gathers that he is referring not only to the presence of a nuclear family

in all societies, but also to its pervasiveness among household groups in all societies. The implication is that its absence is considered by him to be an abnormal situation. When he says that "no society . . . has succeeded in finding an adequate substitute for the nuclear family, to which it might transfer these functions," one cannot help concluding that almost everyone in all societies must therefore rely on the nuclear family to fulfill these functions.

The cases cited earlier make it clear that large segments of some contemporary societies do not have functioning nuclear families, and that the nonnuclear family segments cannot fruitfully be cast aside as "abnormal" or "disorganized," but are regular, viable, family units in a regular, functioning society. With respect to the four functions listed by Murdock, we simply find that other social agents do in fact take over the functions for extended periods; precisely who may do it varies from one society to another. The educational function may be taken care of by the mother, other relatives, chums, schools, and so on. The rationale that a male child must have a resident father in order to learn to be a man does not hold in fact. The economic function may be handled by the mother and the children as they grow older; to this can be added grandparents, brothers, and other relatives who help either regularly or periodically. And, of course, the sexual function is handled well by other married men, boarders, visitors, friends, and so forth. The reproductive function does not need the father's presence; a midwife is more useful. While there is no denying the social necessity of the functions that Murdock has delineated, there is evidence that some families can achieve them without the presence of someone identified as a "father-husband."


## Parsons' Dual-Function Approach

In a recent collection of papers Talcott Parsons (1955) has expressed the opinion that the multiple-functions approach is not adequate to explain the basic necessity of the nuclear family. In its place, he offers another functional explanation. There are, he feels, two functions, and two functions only, that are necessary everywhere and account for the universal presence of the nuclear family. One of these concerns, which Murdock calls the "educational," is namely the necessity of providing socialization of the child. The other (not on Murdock's list, but again he probably would not deny its potential importance) consists of the constant development and balancing of the adult personality which is achieved because of the constant interaction between spouses. Parsons singles out this second function as being of particular importance in explaining the restrengthening of the American (U.S.A.) nuclear family today.

Since Parsons proposes these two functions as being essential everywhere, any documented instance in which they are not operative should be sufficient to cast doubt on his thesis. Such an instance is provided by R. T. Smith's detailed study of the British Guiana Negro family. While Smith would hold that the nuclear family does have universality in the sense that all the statuses therein are recognized, he makes it clear in his study that some households remain with women as heads for extended periods, often for the greater part of the adult life of the woman concerned. He adds, furthermore, that even when men are attached to the household, it is precisely during this period that the "men spend a considerable amount of time working away from home and they do not take any significant part in the daily life of the household. . . . There are no tasks allotted to a man in his role as husband-father beyond seeing that the house is kept in good repair, and providing food and clothing for his spouse and the children" (1956:112–113). The function of socio-psychological integration assigned by Parsons to the husband-wife relationship would have considerable difficulty operating if the husband were absent most of the time. The specific functions that Smith assigns to

the husband-father are economic. Parsons' argument for the universality of the nuclear family is basically no stronger than that of Murdock since the functions delineated by both can be taken care of by other agents in the society, or by other members of the family.

The fundamental weakness in Murdock's and Parsons' points of view is that they take functions that may be "imperatives," "universal functions," or "basic prerequisites" for a society, and try to correlate them with functions that are fulfilled by the nuclear family. Since it is mistakenly believed that the nuclear family form is found everywhere, that is, a universal, it must therefore be correlated with some universal requirement of human society. It is correct that there are social prerequisites, and that the nuclear family has numerous functions; but to correlate the two is a deduction that is not empirically supported.

## A STRUCTURAL APPROACH

Another approach to the problem of the significance of the woman-headed household and maternal-dyad families is taken up in Smith's study (n.d.). Following the lead of his mentor, Meyer Fortes, Smith regards the family as something to be studied empirically and within a temporal as well as spatial framework (Fortes 1949) and not a hard-shelled cell that forms the building unit of all kin-based social structure. Unlike Murdock and Parsons, Smith has approached the family from the point of view of the ethnographer and not the ethnologist or comparative sociologist, and studied a society where the dyad family and woman-headed households are normal. Much of Smith's work is of interest, but we will concentrate here on some major propositions referring to the woman-headed households.

Smith reports that the woman-headed household in British Guiana Negro society almost always goes through a stage during which there is a man attached to it.[3] A family starts in a nuclear form, and later develops into the maternal dyad form when the man leaves. Smith goes on to propose that there is a basic "matrifocal" quality in the familial relations so that it is relatively easy for a family to be reduced to the maternal dyad type; the husband-wife relationship and the father-child relationship are much less important than is the mother-child relationship. The weak character of the husband-father role is related to a situation in the general social structure in British Guiana. General social status is conferred through ascribed membership in an ethnic-class group. The specific occupation of the husband, in the lower class, confers no prestige, and hence the children have nothing to gain from their fathers in this matter. This is made more obvious by comparing the lower class Negroes with members of the higher class. In the latter, the occupation of the father is of importance for the general social status of the entire family, and the father is considered an indispensable part of the family. Smith correlates the presence of the woman-headed household with a social status system in which the father can achieve no superior status.

Smith's work provides an important structural analysis of the significance of the woman-headed household and shows that the maternal dyad can and does exist effectively in spite of the theoretical positions of Murdock and Parsons.

---

[3]This temporal difference was also noted in a survey of El Salvador in terms of residence pattern: "even though the patterned residence at the time of marriage or beginning to live together may be neo-local, the subsequent departure of the man of the family leaves it a domestic establishment based on the fact that the woman lives there. It is, if you like, matrilocality by-default." And further: "The solidarity of the Salvadorean nuclear family was reported in some places (Texistepeque and Chinameca) to be increased after the birth of children. This does not, however, seem to hold in all cases in view of the numerous cases in which the woman has retained her children and the man has gone elsewhere" (Adams 1957:460–461).

Parsons, who had access to Smith's study prior to the preparation of his own paper, failed to see the full implications of the Guiana material (Parsons 1955:13f.). The fact that the Guiana family may include a man long enough to get a household institutionalized in the local society and to undertake the procreation of children, does not mean that the man is present to fulfill either of the functions that Parsons tries to hold as being "root functions" that "must be found wherever there is a family or kinship system at all. . . ."

## THE ELEMENTAL FAMILY UNITS: DYADS AND NUCLEUS

In rejecting the propositions advanced by Parsons and Murdock in favor of a structural approach, their position concerning the elemental importance of the nuclear family is also cast into doubt. If "functions" do not explain the absence of the nuclear family in some situations, they can hardly be called upon to support the claim of universality for that form. No matter how fruitful this position has been in reference to other problems in social structure, we must seek an alternative view here.

The nuclear family comprises three sets of relationships that are identifiable as dyads. There is the relationship based on coitus between a man and a woman, and which may be identified as the sexual dyad until or unless it is recognized as a marital union, in which case it becomes a conjugal dyad. There is, second, the maternal dyad, composed of mother and child, that presumably begins at the time of conception but is not of great social significance as a dyad until parturition. And third, there is the paternal dyad, between father and child, that is identified specifically because of the relationship established by the sexual or conjugal dyad. Both the sexual and conjugal dyad, on the one hand, and the maternal on the other, have clear cut correlates in biological activity. The paternal does not. So no matter what importance it may hold in a given society, at the present level of analysis it must be looked upon as a dyadic relationship of a different order; it exists not by virtue of a biological correlate, but by virtue of other dyads. Once given these dyads (all three, the sexual-conjugal, maternal, and paternal) there are important economic functions that may be assigned them. Infant dependency through nursing is, after all, an economic relationship as well as a biological one. But the economic cooperation and interdependency that may be assigned beyond this level is clearly a socially defined activity with no immediate biological correlates.

If we reject the idea that the nuclear family is the fundamental "atom" in the social "molecule," or the irreducible unit of human kin organization, and take initially the two dyads with biological correlates as two distinct components which must each be present at certain times, but not necessarily always or simultaneously, we will be approaching a view of the elements of social organization which is less biased by contemporary social system philosophy. If we allow that the nuclear family is not the minimum model for the building of subsequent structures, then we can see that it is basically, as Lowie partially suggested (1948:215), an unstable combination of two simpler elements, each of which is also unstable and temporal. This allows us to look at more complex forms without the bias of assuming the nuclear family always to be present, and to seek excuses for its absence. There is a significance to be attached to the nuclear as well as the dyad forms, but it is distinctive. The conjugal or sexual dyad is particularly significant because it is the reproductive unit of the society; the maternal dyad is the temporal link between successive generations of adult dyads. While theoretically the two kinds of dyads can operate independently at all times, the society would be a sadly disjointed affair were they to do so. Their combination into a nuclear family provides generational relationships for all concerned. Since such combinations can be a short-lived activity for the individuals involved,

and actually may occupy only a limited time, most people are theoretically available most of the time to focus on the dyadic relationships.

The reason that human societies have supported the nuclear family in such abundance can be found at the level of social analysis. Like all animals, human beings live not only in families, but in larger aggregates which, following general usage, can generically be called *communities*. A community cannot maintain stability and continuity solely with such unstable and temporal forms as dyads for elemental units. Seen from this point of view, the nuclear family becomes one combination that, if on nothing more than a random basis, must inevitably occur from time to time. It is the simplest way of joining the two dyads. Since the mother is the only adult in the maternal dyad, and the wife is the only female in the sexual dyad, they can be jointed most readily by identifying the wife with the mother. Once this identification is made, the nuclear unit is created and can fulfill many potential functions. But while its occurrence is inevitable, its continuation is by no means inevitable because each of the dyads alone can also fulfill some functions, and there are, in addition, presumably other societal agents that can also fulfill them. The nuclear family therefore becomes only *one of the ways* the community maintains itself. For some functions and under some circumstances, individuals may be effective agents; for others the elemental dyads are more efficient; for yet others the nuclear family may serve, and still others find other kinds of groups more useful. There are, in short, *alternative* ways in which the basic kin units can be used and combined for continued maintenance of the community.

The social universals of human society are not, then, as has been held by many students, the nuclear family and the community, but rather the community and the two dyads. The nuclear family is, in a sense, a structural by-product of the nature of the dyads, but one which is almost inevitable, even if for the briefest period. However, beyond these, the dyads may be subject to a variety of combinations to further the continuity of the community. The case described by Spiro (1954) as existing in the *kibbutz* and the details of the woman-headed households of the British Guiana Negroes described by Smith should not be interpreted as being exceptions to a principle of nuclear family universality, but as positive illustrations of how dyads may and do operate outside of the nuclear family.

Before turning to the final points of the paper, we should deal briefly with other possible dyadic forms. Two candidates for basic forms are the paternal and sibling dyads. The appearance of a paternal dyad, as was mentioned earlier, is a result of the joining of the maternal and sexual dyads in the easiest way they can be joined. It is a logical derivative, a potential focus of social emphasis and available for further combinations itself. The sibling dyad is logically somewhat similar, being a derivative of the joining of two maternal dyads through the presence of a common mother. Again, once created it serves as a potential focus of emphasis and can combine with other dyads. While logically other dyads can be derived through further combinations, it is not within the scope of this essay to take the next step, and begin a logical and exhaustive construction of the possible combinations and derivative combinations of dyads, triads, quadics, and so on. It seems reasonable, however, to assume that such an analysis would lead us far in the creation of models of social structure, and offer insight into the actual forms that kin groups take in human society.[4]

It should not be thought that the concept of the dyad in social structure has gone unnoticed in social anthropology. Its significance, however, has usually been in descriptive terms rather than as an analytical tool. A. R. Radcliffe-Brown, certainly a pioneer in structural studies, pointed out on a number of occasions that the basic elements of social structure were dyadic:

I regard as a part of the social structure all social relations of person to person. For example, the kinship structure of any society consists of a number of such dyadic relations, as between a father and son, or a mother's brother and his sister's son. In an Australian tribe the whole social structure is based on a network of such relations of person to person, established through genealogical connections (1952a:191; see also 1952b: 52–53).

But Radcliffe-Brown's view was somewhat different from that proposed here, as he also held that, "The unit of structure from which a kinship system is built up is the group which I call an 'elementary family,' consisting of a man and his wife and their child or children, whether they are living together or not" (1952b:51). The nuclear family, as a constellation of statuses, served as the central block although, unlike Murdock and Parsons, Radcliffe-Brown did not hold that this unit must everywhere exist.

White Radcliffe-Brown saw in the "elementary family" three kinds of social relationships, "that between parent and child, that between children of the same parents (siblings), and that between husband and wife as parents of the same child or children" (1952b:51), he did not expressly project these as potential analytical units that could themselves be examined apart from the nuclear family context and considered as distinctive building blocks. On the other hand, Radcliffe-Brown did, in his principles of "the unity of the sibling group" and "the unity of the lineage," recognize the theoretical significance of a society's placing emphasis upon a given set of relationships that, in terms of the present discussion, we would see as a "sibling dyad" and either the maternal or paternal dyad. He did not carry it farther at the time of the essay in question to include the husband-wife dyad as also being a potential center of emphasis, nor did he distinguish between other maternal and paternal relations.

[4]Analysis based on triadic and quadic relations has already been started in communications research.

## THE WOMAN-HEADED HOUSEHOLD
## AND THE TOTAL SOCIETY

The thesis presented by Smith concerning the reasons for the appearance of the woman-headed household provides an analysis that on the surface fits well into the present argument. Over a single life cycle of Guiana Negroes the sexual or conjugal dyad tends to come into play strongly only at limited periods—for procreation and for support of the woman with infant. As a woman becomes free of dependent infants, the conjugal relation can and often does disappear or change its character. This dyad is weak because the members are part of an ethnically distinct, lower class community in which there is no status differentiation possible between males, and hence, little that one man can offer a family or son over what another can offer. According to this analysis we would expect to find similar developments in other similar situations. However, the data from Latin America do not support the extension of the analysis. Three examples will indicate the nature of the variations.

The first involves a comparison of the Guatemalan Indians and neighboring Ladinos. The former have predominantly nuclear families while the latter have a significantly high proportion of woman-headed households. The populations involved hold comparable positions within the total social structure, but the Indians in particular are similar to the Guiana Negroes in being a lower class ethnic group within which the status of the father does not necessarily give status to the son. There is some variation in this matter, and a situation comparable to that of the Guiana Negroes is to be found less among the more traditional Indians than among the more acculturated ones. Among both Indians and Ladinos some segments of the population work on plantations, some live in independent villages, and some are part-time subsistence farmers and part-time laborers. Both have the same general concept of land tenure, and both live within the same general national context. But, it will be remembered, in the predominantly Indian departments the percentage of households with women as heads is considerably lower than that of the Ladino departments.

Although Indians and Ladinos live under similar conditions, the Ladino family is much closer to the model Smith sets up for the British Guiana Negroes than is the Mayan Indian family. The difference lies in what Smith has referred to in the Guiana situation as the "marginal nature of the husband-father role" that gives rise to a "matrifocal system of domestic relations and household groupings." Shifting the theoretical focus from the structure of the family to the values associated with it is in one sense a shorthand method of indicating that somewhere the structure, in spite of overtly similar conditions, is different. Thus, presumably the Indians have within the structure of their total community certain features which stress the father-husband role, but they are not necessarily the same features whose absence causes the weak role in the Guiana Negro situation.

Smith reports another case in a later paper (n.d.) in which he says that the East Indian residents of British Guiana (like the Guatemalan Mayan Indians) have retained a strong father-husband role in spite of the similarity to the Negroes in their general circumstances. "Quite apart from their historical derivation the ideal patterns of [East] Indian culture and family life have themselves become an object of value in distinguishing Indians from their nearest neighbors in the ethnic status system, the Negroes." If Smith is interpreting his Guiana data and I my Guatemalan material correctly, the reasons behind women-headed households among the Guiana Negroes are relative to the structure of the particular society. Values associated with one phase or aspect of the social structural system may in fact conflict with or contradict values stemming from or associated with other aspects. Thus in many Guatemalan Indian situations, where the population works on coffee plantations, the nuclear family is not sustained through variable social status derived from the father, but is important economically. During the five or six months of harvest, the wife also brings in a significant income through picking coffee. This means that a man with a wife has access to a larger income than one without a wife.

Societies, in which families exist, offer many faces, and the form a specific family takes must integrate with as much of the total system as possible. Total systems are complex and seldom completely self-integrated, so some aspects will be more significant for the family form of some parts of the population, while other aspects prove to be more important for others. There is thus room for variation in the form a family may take simply because different families may be answering to different structural features.

The last case involves the Guiana Negroes and the Ladinos themselves, both societies in which two distinctive forms of the family appear within similar total structural situation. Smith reported, and the censuses for Central America show, that within these populations there are variations in the degree to which the woman-headed household occurs. If Smith's argument with respect to the relation between the dyadic Negro household and the total system is valid, we must then account for the presence of some continuous nuclear families. The answer here is probably the same as that just discussed. Within the total structure, there is room for variation, and we must assume that in spite of the structural features appearing to be the same, we are not identifying those features which the different family forms are answering to.

The evidence from the present cases does not provide us with a clear enough picture to delineate with precision why some families go one way and some go another. It is here that we must rest our case simply by preferring to place our confidence in the structural approach to solve the issue as over and against the "universal functions" preferred by other writers. We need to seek out facts pertaining to a number of situations:

1. We need to delineate the types of structural aspects which can differentially affect family forms within a single class or ethnic societal group, or both.

2. Given this, we need then to establish the principles which will hold for such relationships without any society.

## SUMMARY AND CONCLUSIONS

The preceding discussion has been exploratory, working on the hypothesis-building level. The following summary remarks are made in the light of the same approach.

1. The concept of "functions" as being activities necessary to the maintenance of the species, society, or individual personality is one which is not satisfactory to explain the various forms that the family may have in a given society. The economic, sexual, reproductive, and educational functions as outlined by Murdock, or the socialization and adult-personality-maintaining functions of Parsons may be taken care of by the nuclear family under some circumstances and not under others. We cannot agree with Parsons that there are "root functions" everywhere associated with the nuclear family. If there are such things, they would probably be better identified in terms of the community and the dyads. The search for universal functions has unfortunately become an activity not unlike the continuing search for human instincts: it is not that there are none, but that it is misleading unless it is correlated with structure.

2. A theoretical analysis of the human family must not start with the assumption that the nuclear family is a basic cell or atom, but rather that there are two distinct dyadic relations that go into the formation of the nuclear family as well as into other family forms. While the concept of the nuclear family is doubtless useful for many kinds of social analysis, the fact that it fails in analyzing some family forms means we must

look further. A full understanding of family form requires an analysis beginning with dyads. With this kind of approach, it may well prove that the nuclear family has not had the extensive ramifications which have been attributed to it heretofore. By adding other dyads, we are in a position to reanalyze kin and family structure as well as to pursue more analytically the nature of intrafamilial and other interpersonal relationships. It has been recognized that the nuclear family, as found among apes and men, is essentially a very primitive form. It is not surprising to find that man's culture elaborates on the dyadic possibilities of the family, and produces forms intricate and fantastic.

3. Smith's work among the British Guiana Negroes gives us a most important insight into the structural correlates of the woman-headed household in that society. It leads us to the next step, which is to seek the structural correlates which will explain why woman-headed households sometimes appear and sometimes do not within apparently a single structural system. One step in this explanation is to have recourse to the theoretical position that the other aspects of the total social structure may be working adversely to those which are producing a nuclear or a dyadic emphasis. The emphasis thus placed, however, must have structural correlates, even if they are merely reflective of some structural aspect that is about to disappear. In this case we need more research into the exact nature of form and structure relationships, both in a synchronic and a diachronic context.

4. The final general position to be derived from the preceding discussion is that it is neither necessary nor valid to attempt to find a single normal structural form for the family within a society. That there *may* be only one is possible; but the assumption that there *can* be only one is unfruitful. The conviction that there is only one right way is older than social science, but it continues to make itself felt today. Many sociologists and anthropologists have regarded the woman-headed household as an abnormal, incomplete, or disorganized form of the family.

This has contributed to the argument that the nuclear family is an indispensable, basic, stable, family type, and that its absence must therefore represent a breakdown. If we accept the notion, however, that the basic relational elements of the family are dyadic, and that the nuclear family is a more complex arrangement but one which is probably even less significant temporally than its dyad components, then we are in a position to see women-headed households as alternative or secondary norms rather than forms of disorganization. The assertion that the nuclear family successfully fulfills certain functions is perfectly valid. But the reverse assertion that other social forms can never suitably fulfill these functions is both empirically and theoretically invalid.

The denial of this reverse assertion is also important for our approach to other cultural forms. The search for a fundamental cell or building block of kin organization leads not only to a misplaced emphasis on the nuclear family, but towards a biased approach in the study of the entire family system. As Goodenough (1956) has pointed out with respect to residence, there are ethnographic ways of seeing things, and there are ethnological ways of seeing the same things. Just as the desire to discover cross-cultural regularities has led to forcing an ethnological straight jacket on a society's residence rules, so it has led to misleading assumptions concerning the identification of the nuclear family as the minimum structural form of family organization. If we look into other aspects of culture, it seems likely that we should assume that all cultural forms are alternatives (in the Lintonian sense) until a given form can be demonstrated to be universal by the ethnographers. To assume that a form, because it is a variant, is abnormal, is to evade the task before us. The first job of science is, after all, to study what *is,* not what might, or could, or should be.[5]

[5] I am indebted to William Davenport, Iwao Ishino, Raymond T. Smith, Nancie Solien de González, John Useem and the editors of this volume for critical readings of earlier drafts of this paper.

# BIBLIOGRAPHY

ADAMS, RICHARD N.
1957 "Culture Surveys of Panama—Nicaragua —Guatemala—El Salvador—Honduras." *Panamerican Sanitary Bureau, Scientific Publications,* 33.

CAPPANNARI, STEPHEN C.
1953 "Marriage in Malabar." *Southwestern Journal of Anthropology,* 9:263–267.

FORTES, MEYER
1949 "Time and Social Structure: An Ashanti Case Study." In *Social Structure; Studies Presented to A. R. Radcliffe-Brown,* ed. by Meyer Fortes, pp. 54–84. Oxford, Clarendon Press.

FRAZIER, E. FRANKLIN
1939 *The Negro Family in the United States.* Chicago, The University of Chicago Press.

GOODENOUGH, WARD H.
1956 "Residence Rules." *Southwestern Journal of Anthropology,* 12:22–37.

GOUGH, E. KATHLEEN
1952 "Changing Kinship Usages in the Setting of Political and Economic Change among the Nayar of Malabar." *Journal of the Royal Anthropological Institute,* 82:71–88.

HUTCHINSON, HARRY WILLIAM
1957 *Village and Plantation Life in Northeastern Brazil.* The American Ethnological Society. Seattle, University of Washington Press.

LABARRE, WESTON
1954 *The Human Animal.* Chicago, The University of Chicago Press.

LÉVI-STRAUSS, CLAUDE
1956 "The Family." In *Man, Culture, and Society,* ed. by H. L. Shapiro, pp. 261–285. New York, Oxford University Press.

LEVY, MARION J., JR.
1955 "Some Questions about Parsons' Treatment of the Incest Problem." *The British Journal of Sociology,* 6:277–285.

LINTON, RALPH
1936 *The Study of Man.* New York, D. Appleton-Century Company, Inc.

LOWIE, ROBERT H.
1948 *Social Organization.* New York, Rinehart & Company.

MURDOCK, GEORGE P.
1949 *Social Structure.* New York, The Macmillan Company.

PARSONS, TALCOTT
1955 "The American Family: Its Relations to Personality and to the Social Structure." In *Family, Socialization and Interaction Process,* by Talcott Parsons and Robert F. Bales, pp. 3–33. Glencoe, The Free Press.

RADCLIFFE-BROWN, A. R.
1952a "On Social Structure." In *Structure and Function in Primitive Society,* pp. 188–204. Glencoe, The Free Press.
1952b "The Study of Kinship Systems." In *Structure and Function in Primitive Society,* pp. 49–89. Glencoe, The Free Press.

REH, EMMA
1946 *Paraguayan Rural Life.* Washington, D.C., Institute of Inter-American Affairs.

SERVICE, ELMAN R., and HELEN S. SERVICE
1954 *Tobatí: Paraguayan Town.* Chicago, The University of Chicago Press.

SMITH, RAYMOND T.
1956 *The Negro Family in British Guiana: Family Structure and Social Status in the Villages.* London, Routledge and Kegan Paul.
n.d. "Family Structure and Plantation Systems in the New World." Paper presented at the Seminar on Plantation Systems of the New World, San Juan, Puerto Rico, 1957.

SPIRO, MELFORD E.
1954 "Is the Family Universal?" *American Anthropologist,* 56:839–846.

# RANK AND INEQUALITY

**ISSUE**  The status of woman: Do women have power, and what explains its cross-cultural variations?

Social rank is the estimation that some people and groups are more important than others. It results in some form of inequality in all societies. We see rank and inequality at work in the United States when we hear our parents urging children, "Work hard and make something of yourself." Rank underlies the view that doctors, lawyers, and bank presidents are more important than janitors, dishwashers, and secretaries. It tells us that there are "big" people to whom we must be polite and deferential. Doors seem to open readily to these individuals; everyone hurries to cash their checks; they are offered the best restaurant tables; they can frequent the white, sandy beaches and comfortable hotels of the most exotic vacation spots.

Rank and inequality may organize whole societies into groups, identifying individuals, regulating interaction, and assigning privileges. Some societies are stratified into ranked classes, groups defined by unequal access to both economic resources and prestige. Class systems are found in many societies and contain a particularly important feature. Members of classes may move up or down in the system by attaining attributes of higher or lower social value. In the United States, for example, it is possible, although not as likely as the "American dream" might predict, to increase one's rank. This process of social mobility usually begins with the acquisition of money through economic success. Money and wealth are marks of high status in this country, but by themselves they may not be enough to produce dramatic upward mobility. Newly wealthy people usually set about converting their money into other symbols of status, education at the best schools for their children, a house in a highly regarded neighborhood, a fleet of expensive automobiles, membership in exclusive clubs, and a variety of other status symbols. Although it will rarely be completed in a single generation, the rise in status can be achieved in class systems and marks them as a special kind of social stratification.

Caste systems are different. They, too, consist of ranked groups with unequal access to economic resources and prestige, but with one major proscription: membership in them is permanent. India is well known for its system of castes. Especially in rural India, people are born into named caste groups that are ranked in relation to one another. No matter what they do to attain the attributes of higher rank, their status will remain the same, assigned to them by an accident of birth. Many social scientists also feel that black and white people form castes in the United States.

One aspect of rank and inequality that is especially troubling for anthropologists and other social scientists is its empirical indicators. When is inequality present? How can it be recognized? Can its intensity be measured from one culture to the next? Part of the problem stems from different cultural definitions of the attributes of rank. In rural India, for example, economic success, although significant, is not as important as something called "ritual cleanliness" in conveying rank. A poor Brahmin priest outranks a successful moneylender. In an effort to measure rank cross-culturally, anthropologists have looked at several dimensions. As the definitions of class and caste suggest, economic resources and prestige are two of them. What people claim about rank may also be used as a measure. Recently, *relative power* has come into use as a measure of status.

One of the most important applications of the criterion of power has been in the cross-cultural study of female status. For years, anthropologists have held that men outrank women in every part of the world. (See the article by Divale and Harris that appears in Chapter IX for a statement and measurement of this assertion.) Even among hunter-gatherers like the !Kung of Africa, who otherwise lack formal systems of stratification, men hold formal authority over women and appear to have more prestige and privilege.

The articles in this chapter explore the question, Why do women lack public power and what accounts for increases in female public status? All three authors tie such status to women's economic role. Netting illustrates female power among the Kofyur of Nigeria and links its presence to their public economic endeavors. Sanday seeks to explain variations in female status as a function of women's importance in subsistence activities, particularly as these activities are shared with men. Sacks, using a theory first advanced by Engels, links a loss of female power to the fact that women were more difficult to exploit as public labor in stratified societies. This section nicely illustrates the attempts of anthropologists to discover and refine the important variables that account for a particular problem.

# 13

## WOMEN'S WEAPONS: THE POLITICS OF DOMESTICITY AMONG THE KOFYAR

*Robert McC. Netting*

*In this article, Robert McC. Netting clearly illustrates the perils of assessing women's status on the basis of formal public behavior and pronouncement. Basing his discussion on field work among the Kofyar of Nigeria, he notes that women do not hold formal political office, play a small part in patrilineal groups, do not own land, and are prohibited from participating in many religious rituals. Yet to conclude that they are powerless is a mistake. Women control valued goods, including elaborate two-storied houses, fields, and the crops and other goods they produce. Women form an essential part of the labor force. Divorce occurs frequently, and its threat gives women leverage over their husbands. In short, women hold a great deal of power in Kofyar society, especially over things that matter to them, such as work, sex, and the allocation of their time. Women's power probably stems from their important position in Kofyar economic activities.*

The Social position of African women is one of those compelling topics that allow the anthropologist to confront an invidious generalization and slay the stereotype of feminine oppression and subservience. He (or often she) can point out the variation in female roles and respect in neighboring societies (Talbot 1915:96–97) and show by a wealth of examples that divergence from a Western ideal of womanhood does not necessarily imply a lower status (Paulme 1963:4). But Evans-Pritchard (1965:41) has reminded us that any clarification of the status of women must be based on "imponderables" as well as on objective criteria. The following consideration of Kofyar women is an effort both to define criteria and to weigh some of the imponderables that figure in one version of the battle of the sexes.

The Kofyar are intensive agriculturalists living in dispersed settlements on the edge of the Jos Plateau in northern Nigeria. The women of this society have few institutionalized roles in political life or in patrilineal kin groups; they

marry virilocally so that about seventy-seven percent live away from their native villages; they do not own land or major productive tools; they are regularly excluded from performances of most ritual including sacrifices, prayer, and divinations; and yet they appear to wield a large measure of power in the society. They do not do this just in terms of influence, persuasiveness, cajolery, and universal feminine wiles, nor are they the aged whisperers behind the throne who have been noted in the huts of some African chieftains. Rather they are self-assured, independent women who give the impression of knowing what they want and how to get it. The question then is how women who lack lineage office or support, most kinds of property, and religious authority can protect their interests so effectively.

Perhaps I should not have subtitled this paper "the politics of domesticity." It implies a mixing of levels between the home where conflicts can be privately reconciled through kin ties and sentiments and the public arena where competing interests are revealed and community decisions of policy are hammered out. But Lucy Mair, to whom we owe this distinction, also noted that conflict and competition begin within the family (1962:10). The household may indeed deal with its own quarrels, but the *behavior* involved may be political. If the family and the household can be considered a social system, there is no doubt that Kofyar women participate in the "formulation and execution of binding or authoritative decisions" and that they "allocate valued things among two or more persons" (Easton 1959:226). Male-female conflicts are seldom acted out in public, but when they are, a set of far-reaching rights of women are publicly *recognized* and incorporated in jural proceedings. These rights apply chiefly to economic goods and to the marriage bond.

Valued economic goods are used, owned, and manipulated by Kofyar women with considerable freedom. Certain major types of property do not belong to women in the sense that they may be permanently occupied, alienated, or inherited, but female rights of use are clearly marked. A Kofyar adult wife may demand a house of her own. If nothing suitable is vacant in the homestead, her husband must build her a hut. Since traditional Kofyar women's houses are elaborate two-storied, mud-domed structures (Netting 1968a), this may involve the spouse in several months of work plus extra expense if an expert builder is hired. Once ensconced in such a house, the wife may cook and feed her children in secret, admit selected guests for drinking, and store her grain and valuables. If a tin door is present, the key is hers. A woman should receive some farming land from her husband, and if none is available, she may borrow or rent a field from a relative or friend. When a husband dies, his widow and children may continue to inhabit his homestead and use its resources for as long as they wish.

Perhaps more important are the goods women actually own. Crops produced in a woman's fields, groundnuts, sweet potatoes, vegetables, and even late millet may be distributed according to her desires. She may choose to use a portion to feed her family, but if she decides to sell all at the market, her husband cannot interfere. If a husband is unwise enough to appropriate some of his wife's food, she may demand its return and carry the case to court, where male judges may try to placate her and end by awarding her compensation considerably in excess of the amount stolen.

Women have other sources of income. They go on their own initiative to collect raffia palm leaves, firewood, and other sylvan produce. These they sell directly at markets. They raise animals, especially chickens but also dogs, goats, and even cows. Some of this domestic stock may be kept at home while the rest is given out to friends in an offspring-sharing arrangement. Manufactured items make perhaps the largest contributions to the female exchequer. During the dry season, quantities of cotton thread, grain-storage baskets, and clay pots are produced by women for sale. Every Kofyar woman knows how to brew, and beer always finds a ready market (Netting 1964). Enterprising women may buy grain or engage working parties to farm millet for them. The risk and the proceeds belong entirely to the woman who has made the beer. She malts, grinds, cooks, and ferments the brew in her own home and sells it there or at market.

Thus women both have cash on hand and speedy access to more. Seven budgets I collected gave annual expenditures of £1/14–£7/19 and averaged £3/17/1. Though this is only a little more than a third of male expenditures in the same village, women have fewer obligations to meet. They do not contribute to bride wealth, they pay no tax, and they need not purchase tools. Much male wealth is tied up in houses and land, which is not easily convertible, so that females often seem both more solvent and financially more liquid. Women have cash reserves and can pay for what they want—usually cloth, beer, salt, condiments, and adornments. Men are often reduced to borrowing cash from women. Repayment is assured by threats of legal action

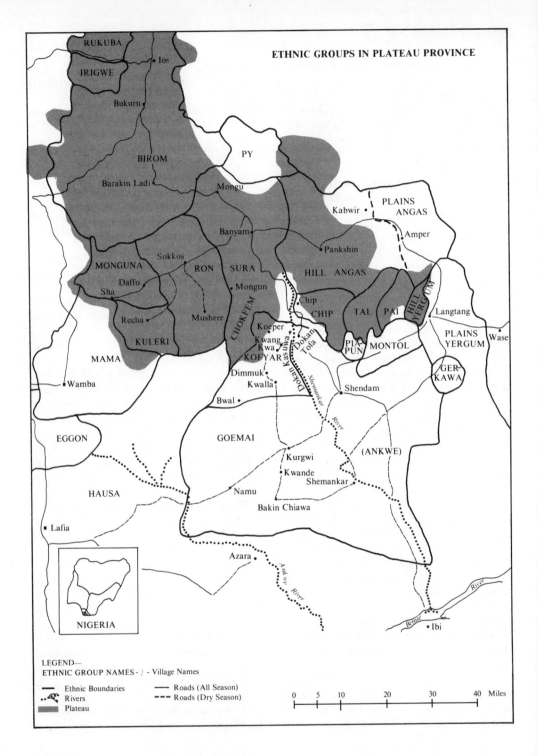

ETHNIC GROUPS IN PLATEAU PROVINCE

RUKUBA
Jos
IRIGWE
Bukuru
BIROM
Barakin Ladi
Mongu
PY
Kabwir
PLAINS
ANGAS
Amper
Banyam
Pankshin
SOKKOS
RON SURA
HILL ANGAS
MONGUNA
Daffo
Mongun
Chip
HILL YERGUM
Sha
CHOKFEM
CHIP
TAL PAI
Langtang
Recha
Mushere
Koeper
PLAINS
YERGUM
Wase
KULERI
Kwang Kwa
Dokan Kasuwa
PIA-
PUN
MONTOL
MAMA
KOFYAR
Dimmuk
Dokan
Tofa
GER-
KAWA
Wamba
Kwalla
Shemankar River
Shendam
Bwal
EGGON
GOEMAI
(ANKWE)
Kurgwi
HAUSA
Kwande
Namu
Shemankar
Lafia
Bakin Chiawa
Azara
Ankwe River
NIGERIA
Benue River
Ibi

LEGEND—
ETHNIC GROUP NAMES- / - Village Names

Ethnic Boundaries        Roads (All Season)
Rivers                   Roads (Dry Season)
Plateau

0    5   10        20          30         40  Miles

168

or, if the debtor is a close relative, refusal of all future requests for loans. A husband's rights over property of his wife are strictly defined—in the event of divorce, he gets half her chickens (because they fed on his grain) and half her groundnuts (because she farmed with his hoe).

Women also retain a large measure of control over their labor. Kofyar intensive agriculture requires a heavy labor input and full mobilization of the household work force (Netting 1968b:122–136). Women and men do the same tasks, hoeing, weeding, and harvesting side by side. A wife is the full partner of her husband in productive and maintenance activities. A husband needs his wife's contribution but he cannot compel it. A village chief who went on an errand with me one day was surprised and pleased to find that his three wives had continued to work on the homestead field in his absence. Obviously the choice was theirs. If a woman wishes to work on her own gardens, visit her parental home, or go about her own business, her husband cannot command her to do otherwise. The only time I ever saw women publicly censured for not working was when some individuals did not appear for a neighborhood thatching bee. They were scolded and ultimately fined, but the sanctions were imposed solely by other women.

The question remains, however, as to why masculine prerogatives are not more frequently asserted. Kofyar men are self-sufficient, tough, and stubborn. I believe that of the valuable things a woman controls, the most significant is herself, rights to her coresidence, her economic services, and her body. She may not originally assign these rights, but has the power to deny them. Marriage partners are always in short supply among the Kofyar. Every man would like to be a polygynist, but only a minority at any one time ever makes it. In a total of 489 families in a census of 15 villages, the average number of adult wives per husband was 1.75. The average per village ranged from 1.29 to 2.47 (see Table 1) and correlated well with relative village wealth. Fifty-five percent of the Kofyar men in the sample had one wife, and six percent had

four or more. In the total sample population of 2,587, the average ratio of males to females was 1:1.395.

Bride wealth is substantial, and comparisons of pre-1930, 1930 to 1950, and 1950 on indicate that it has not significantly changed over time. Since the institution of Native Authority courts, about nine out of ten cases have been concerned with divorce and bride wealth. The Kofyar claim that in the days of feuding warfare men postponed marriage until their thirties when their prime fighting years were over. Now that men marry in their early twenties and women about a year after the menarche, wives are objects of even greater competition and emphasis on early betrothal has increased.

Conventions governing marriage do not seem at first glance to give women much of a voice. As girls they are warned not to become pregnant in their father's house *(gam koepang)* and may be beaten if caught in compromising circumstances with a boy. The fault in such cases is the girl's, and in some villages her father is liable to a fine. The offending daughter is married off in embarrassed haste, sometimes with reduced bride wealth. Marriages are arranged by the fathers of bride and groom, but they clearly require the girl's consent and that of her mother. Her acceptance of courtship gifts during adolescence indicates her continued willingness to be married. A boy and a girl who are engaged, or who want to be, may tease each other, conduct elaborate verbal fencing, and intrigue through mutual friends. Marriage is celebrated with only a perfunctory dance of the women resident in the groom's neighborhood. Even after it is held, the bride is expected to move back several times for varying periods to her father's homestead. A girl can put off marriage, and if the groom loses patience he may send his friends to capture her. There is great kicking and screaming, storms of abuse, and small battles between women relatives of the girl and female lineage mates of the groom who are helping to carry her off. This satisfying hullabaloo usually ceases when the captured bride (who was undoubtedly expecting

**TABLE 1**
Kofyar Marriage Patterns

| Area/Village | Adult Married Men | Adult Married Women | Average Wives per Husband | No. of Men With | | | |
|---|---|---|---|---|---|---|---|
| | | | | One Wife | Two Wives | Three Wives | Four or More |
| Latok Hills | | | | | | | |
|   Mangbar | 37 | 50 | 1.35 | 26 | 9 | 2 | — |
|   Dep | 31 | 40 | 1.29 | 23 | 7 | 1 | — |
|   Gonkun | 22 | 30 | 1.36 | 15 | 6 | 1 | — |
|   Koepal | 16 | 21 | 1.31 | 13 | 1 | 2 | — |
|   Bong | 49 | 69 | 1.41 | 36 | 7 | 5 | 1 |
| Kofyar Hills | | | | | | | |
|   Kofyar | 61 | 115 | 1.89 | 33 | 15 | 7 | 6 |
|   Longsel | 25 | 47 | 1.88 | 10 | 9 | 5 | 1 |
|   Pangkurum | 25 | 55 | 2.20 | 8 | 8 | 5 | 4 |
|   Kopfuboem | 16 | 26 | 1.63 | 11 | 2 | 1 | 1 |
|   Bogalong | 50 | 101 | 2.02 | 18 | 17 | 13 | 2 |
|   Buumdagas | 15 | 37 | 2.47 | 3 | 7 | 3 | 2 |
| Kwa Plains and Foothills | | | | | | | |
|   Dunglong | 74 | 151 | 2.04 | 31 | 27 | 9 | 7 |
|   Mer | 28 | 40 | 1.43 | 19 | 7 | — | 2 |
|   Korom | 16 | 29 | 1.81 | 7 | 6 | 2 | 1 |
|   Wudai | 25 | 45 | 1.80 | 14 | 5 | 4 | 2 |
| Total | 489 | 856 | 1.75 | 267 | 133 | 60 | 29 |
| (% of total) | | | | (55) | (27) | (12) | (6) |

it) is safely immured in a house of the groom's lineage. However, if the girl is really opposed to the match, she may go on weeping and struggling for a few days, by which time everyone is convinced of her feelings and she is allowed to return home peaceably.

Kofyar women do not actively resist marriage in most cases, but they feel in no sense bound to stay married. They move into the married state gradually and unceremoniously, and they may leave it in the same way. Divorce frequencies as indicated in Table 2 suggest that about forty-four percent of all adult women have been divorced at least once. To leave her husband, a woman merely goes out to collect firewood or attend market and never returns home.

She may go to her parents or directly to another man who has expressed an interest in marrying her. The beginning of the rainy season sees a veritable spate of women leaving their husbands. The rationale is that they wish to farm where they will be eating next year. This incidentally deprives their husbands of female labor when they need it most for cultivation. A husband cannot keep his wife from leaving or bring her home by force. A physical attack on the wife stealer by the deserted husband is a punishable offense. He must deal with her father, brother, or guardian, enlisting the support of her relatives in persuading the woman to return.

Bride payments, say the Kofyar wearily, are never complete. To stay in the good graces of

TABLE 2
Kofyar Divorce

| Village | Married Women With No Divorces | Women With One Divorce | Women With Two Divorces | Women With Three or More Divorces | Total Women |
|---------|-------------------------------|------------------------|-------------------------|-----------------------------------|-------------|
| Bong    | 46 (61%) | 17 (22%) | 10 (13%) | 3   (4%)  | 76  |
| Kofyar  | 29 (53%) | 10 (18%) | 9 (16%)  | 7 (13%)   | 55  |
| Mangbar | 37 (54%) | 26 (38%) | 4   (6%) | 1   (1%)  | 68  |
| Total   | 112 (56%) | 53 (27%) | 23 (12%) | 11   (5%) | 199 |

in-laws, one must not only hand over an initial sum but one is forever subject to requests for loans (unrepaid), demands for hospitality (with beer *and* meat), and generalized sponging. If the husband wishes to retain his wife, he must satisfy her father or risk having him actively promote the woman's divorce and remarriage. Bride wealth unequivocally transfers only rights in a woman's offspring, and not all of those. Children belong to the husband who has paid bride wealth, and in former times the first one or two children born to a runaway wife (*la wa*, 'the child of going away') were returned to this man and affiliated to his kin group. What could not be purchased or contracted for were permanent rights of cohabitation and cooperation with a woman. Neither husband, kin, or village friends could keep her in a marriage she disliked. Pressure might be brought to bear by the former husband's withdrawal of a wife from one of the new husband's lineage mates, but it was agreed that nothing could prevail on a really determined woman.

Before the establishment of government courts, a woman who ran away permanently cost her husband any bride wealth he had paid. It was nonreturnable, and he could only hope, much as in the case of secondary marriage (Smith 1953), that she would someday come back to him. Bride wealth in these circumstances was often paid gradually and at intervals as the marriage appeared more permanent. A wife who leaves her husband is not felt to be necessarily in the wrong nor must she state grounds for di-

vorce. In modern courts, she says only that she has "had enough" of the marriage and wants out. She is not fined or censured and pays only minimal costs, usually provided by her new spouse. The real reason for divorce may be less clear, but a survey of thirty-eight divorces in which women would discuss the matter showed twenty cases due to barrenness or to the death of children. Refusal of the husband to pay her kin was mentioned six times and quarreling five. Table 3, based on the reproductive history of a sample of divorced women in two villages, shows that a total of eighty-six percent left marriages in which they had been childless or in which their children had died, while only fourteen percent left living children behind them (for similar findings see Baker 1954:372, 451). Thus a husband stands in more or less continuous danger of losing his wife. His best efforts may not be sufficient to secure her return, and he may be left with the long thankless tasks of (1) trying to get return of his bride wealth, which may necessitate further litigation, (2) trying to find another wife when most females are either betrothed or married, and (3) in the meantime performing in addition to his own chores the female jobs of fetching water, grinding, cooking, and child care.

If a Kofyar woman does not wish a divorce but is dissatisfied with her marriage, she has another alternative. She may take a *chagap*, a legitimate lover or cicisbeo who sleeps with her in her husband's homestead and with the knowledge and tacit consent of her husband. The rela-

**TABLE 3**
Divorce and Childlessness

| Village | Total No. Divorces | No. After Childless Marriage | No. After Loss of Children (miscarriage, stillbirth, early death) | No. After Living Children Produced |
|---|---|---|---|---|
| Bong | 64 | 31 (48%) | 26 (41%) | 7 (11%) |
| Kofyar | 42 | 23 (55%) | 11 (26%) | 8 (19%) |
| Total | 106 | 54 (51%) | 37 (35%) | 15 (14%) |

tionship may be with a married or unmarried man and is based on mutual attraction and affection. It is not considered adultery (*wat neer,* 'stealing the vagina') or wife-stealing, and a husband who demurs is considered a selfish man and accused of "having no shame." One household head who stripped and drove out a man caught sleeping with his wife was a figure of fun. A woman who took a lover without her husband's permission would perhaps be judged by her neighbors and fined a chicken. A husband who discovered his spouse's clandestine affair might merely remark mildly that he would not stop the pair and why shouldn't they be open about it and sleep together properly inside the homestead. It is possible that a wife might be jealous of her husband's *chagap,* but even if a quarrel ensued between the two women, the extramarital relationship would not be mentioned.

A wife may take a lover after being married a matter of six months. The lover usually comes from the same village and may be a near neighbor. He is no threat to the husband because there are strong sanctions against stealing the wife of a village coresident. He has no rights to any children born to the woman, even if he is known to be their genitor. A woman's husband and her lover may even cooperate in trying to get her back if she runs away to another village. The relationship may continue for years with the lover bringing occasional gifts and being especially entertained whenever the wife makes beer. He may visit her once or twice a week, and his

schedule is arranged so as not to conflict with that of the husband.

For a woman who is barren or has ceased to become pregnant, the *chagap* relationship offers certain advantages. She may enjoy the attentions of one or several lovers and use their gifts and assistance in the economic endeavors to which she increasingly turns her hand. Every woman would like children, which give her higher value in her husband's eyes, status in the community, and a guarantee of care in her old age. If she has no children, she may still become an influential figure by accumulating wealth and engaging in extramarital liaisons. A fertile woman, however, has less time for crafts and trade and is prohibited from having a lover during pregnancy. There is also a two year postpartum period of nursing when she has no sexual relations at all. Of twenty women in one village who had legitimate lovers, fourteen were childless and two had just conceived for the first time.

In things that matter to a Kofyar woman, she retains considerable control. Where she lives, when she works, and with whom she sleeps are subject to her own choice. She cannot be ordered to work, restricted in economic matters, regulated in extramarital affairs, or constrained from changing spouses. Her value to husband, lover, and indeed the whole community is high, and she can allocate this value in such a way that potential conflicts are settled in her favor. The Kofyar contend that every man wants wives and that no male would ever initiate a divorce. A woman can realize herself through the alternate paths of children and the home or through wealth and lovers.

If women's weapons are so potent, what do men do to keep their self-esteem and maintain a semblance of dominance, which they regard as desirable? There are very few important factors in the division of labor that distinguish the sexes. Few tasks demand superior physical strength or endurance. A man and his wife are equal partners in production. There is little overt social subordination, and male domineering is met by loud, public arguments from the distaff side. A man is left with precious few prerogatives and limited practical authority. His position is vulnerable, particularly to a wife's decision to leave him. Recent changes have, if anything, further eroded male status by depriving him of the warrior role while increasing market opportunities for his spouse. With the growing importance of cash, differences in physical strength and aggressiveness may become less socially significant. In 1961, a series of named and roughly age-graded male agricultural work groups were flourishing in Bong village. They specialized in rapid, competitive hoeing of large bush fields. They had completely disappeared by 1966, some of their recreational aspects and all their popular interest having been taken over by contribution clubs. Members put stipulated sums into a pool, which was then presented to each of them in turn at a festive beer party. Women who could pay the contributions were admitted on an entirely equal footing with men. The objective circumstances of female economic and marital independence and a blurred division of labor do not emphasize sexual distinctions or differences in social power, and I would suggest that Kofyar males assert their distinctness and their claim to social superiority largely in symbolic terms.

The sexual dichotomy is repeatedly stressed in more or less arbitrarily assigned conceptual oppositions. The right hand and the right side (gan wu mis) are considered masculine while the left are feminine, indicating relative strength. To go to the left means to go wrong, and to give something with the left hand is an insult. Women are to walk ahead of men on the path so that men can keep an eye on their wives. One of three binary oppositions used in interpreting divinatory signs is male vs. female. Traditionally Kofyar men wore a loin cloth or skin while married women wore bunches of leaves suspended fore and aft from a string around the waist. Older men and especially diviners might tie on a sheepskin (naar) so that it hung from waist to knees in back. It is said that when short cloth kilts were first introduced for women, a prominent chief strongly objected on the grounds that it made women look like men, and "Can a woman divine?" Women do not go hunting, an activity Kofyar men value highly although it is largely rewarding as sport rather than in game. Whatever meat is secured should be brought back home and shared with the family. The only exception to this rule is the eating of hares' ears by men in the bush. They insist that the morsels are especially tasty and salty, and in order to avoid giving a portion to women they maintain the transparent fiction that hares actually have no ears.

These rather minor symbolic signposts are multiplied and elaborated in magic and religion. Women cannot enter the sacred grove that belongs to each lineage. They may not prepare or partake of ritual meals and sacrifices. They may not doctor illnesses or perform curing ceremonies. Divination is a uniquely male occupation. Lineage and clan prayer meetings and grave libations exclude women. Certain granaries may not be entered by women, and their dangerous state during menstruation prohibits them from preparing food for their husbands or coming in contact with his medicines. The antifeminist bias is most clearly apparent in the periodic announcements of the kum or, 'the shouting spirit.' Men go secretly by prearrangement to the hilltops at night and utter a growling roar in which are audible certain warnings to women. They are told, for instance, to return home promptly from beer drinks so as to prepare food for their husbands. At the first sound, women

are enjoined to enter their huts and leave whatever food they were cooking on pain of illness.
Women appeared to observe these rules, but
they showed no particular anxiety over the voice
of the spirits. Perhaps they were merely going
along with the game. It appeared to me that the
village males were resorting to a "supernatural"
medium for conveying commands that they
could not utter to their wives' faces in the light
of day. An unbecoming spirit of revenge may
also be present in the diagnosis by a man of
serious female illness as due to *mang riin,* 'the
taking of her shadow,' usually by a spurned
lover.

Even in this masculine forest-preserve of
symbols, women are not wholly at a disadvantage. Though cut off from most ritual activity,
they may undergo possession, trembling and
thrashing, and speak in the voice of a dead father
or brother, demanding the performance of an
expensive funeral commemoration ceremony
*(maap).* This condition, called *nazhi,* may also
grant them second sight and allow them to chew
unharmed on a poisonous cactus. Women's accusations of witchcraft or confessions of witch
practices are as frequent and carry as much
weight as those of men. Even in the singing of
abusive songs at harvest time, when men poke
fun at the baldness of women's genitals, women
reply verse for verse, deriding the swollen scro-
tum of men and using gourds and sticks in spir-
ited pantomime. Women's sexual appetite is said
to be the equal of men's, and it is perhaps noteworthy that the physical position for Kofyar intercourse is side-by-side rather than male
superior.

Though it appears that males erect a considerable symbolic edifice in search of sexual identity and status, it is not clear just how well they
succeed. Perhaps a folktale best illustrates the
male dilemma. Rumor has it, according to the
story, that one of the wives of God has a penis.
God, who closely resembles a typically nonau-
thoritarian Kofyar village chief, decides to brew
beer and invite all the people to see for themselves. Each of his wives appears in turn, exposes

herself, and says, "Do you see me with a penis?
I have your thing," i.e., a vagina. At last the
tenth and most recent wife of God is summoned.
She responds slowly, getting out of bed, descending from her upper room, rattling her bracelet as
she pauses at her round house door. The audience calls her repeatedly and waits with mounting impatience and suspense. Only God knows
that the woman once had a penis which he himself in intercourse uprooted and got rid of. The
woman finally pokes her head out of the entrance hut, but God snatches her back into the
house and the people are left staring. The tale
concludes abruptly with the curiosity of the onlookers unsatisfied and the sex of God's wife
ambiguous.

When Kofyar men are confronted with the
very real weapons of women, as they must be
daily in the domestic round, their elaborate
shields of institutionalized symbols prove to be
a poor defense. The male can only fall back on
his physical difference, the seat of what is known
in Nigeria simply as his "power." At least he has
what no woman can hope to possess, his man-
hood, his penis. But behind this brave assertion
whispers the psyche of his society, the mythic
presentiment, that perhaps she has that, too.

## NOTES

Research on the Kofyar was sponsored by a Ford
Foundation Foreign Area Fellowship and a Social Science Research Council grant. An earlier
version of this paper was read at the 67th Annual
Meeting of the American Anthropological Association in Seattle, Nov. 22, 1968.

The survey of marital and maternal histories was conducted by my wife, Jacqueline Frazier Netting.
Her help in the collection of data and her insights
into female motivation are gratefully acknowledged.

The ever-piquant relativity of morals is demonstrated
by the shock and repulsion registered by Kofyar
women over the behavior of Fulani youths at a
dance who copulated promiscuously with unmarried and immature girls, did not ask permission of

the girl's father or fiancée, and went to the open fields for love making. On the other hand, a sophisticated member of Roman society, when told of the Kofyar *chagap* relationship, remarked with enthusiasm, "My, how very civilized."

## REFERENCES CITED

BAKER, T. M.
  1954  The social organization of the Birom. Unpublished Ph.D. dissertation, University College, London.

EASTON, DAVID
  1959  Political anthropology. *In* Biennial review of anthropology. B. Siegel, ed. Stanford: Stanford University Press.

EVANS-PRITCHARD, E. E.
  1965  The position of women in primitive societies and other essays in social anthropology. London: Faber and Faber.

MAIR, LUCY
  1962  Primitive government. Harmondsworth: Penguin Books.

NETTING, ROBERT McC.
  1964  Beer as a locus of value among the West African Kofyar. American Anthropologist 66:375–384.
  1968a  Kofyar building in mud and stone. Expedition 10(4):10–20.
  1968b  Hill farmers of Nigeria: cultural ecology of the Kofyar of the Jos Plateau. Seattle: University of Washington Press.

PAULME, DENISE (ed.)
  1963  Women of tropical Africa. Berkeley, University of California Press.

SMITH, M. G.
  1953  Secondary marriage in Northern Nigeria. Africa 23:298–323.

TALBOT, D. AMAURY
  1915  Woman's mysteries of a primitive people, the Ibibios of southern Nigeria. London: Cassell.

# 14

# FEMALE STATUS IN THE PUBLIC DOMAIN

*Peggy R. Sanday*

*Like the previous article by Netting, many anthropological studies draw on information about one or only a few societies. Such case studies and limited comparisons have an advantage: they can provide the contextual detail necessary to understand complex human behavior and to supply the insight required for theory construction. Their findings, however, largely apply to the societies from which the data were drawn. To remedy this limitation, many investigators employ a cross-cultural correlational approach. They develop an hypothesis, operationally define it (state it in a form that can be measured cross-culturally), and test it, using a large sample of different societies. Peggy Sanday employs the cross-cultural correlational approach in this article to test the relationship between the economic importance of women and public female power. She discovers that when women participate in a balanced way with men in subsistence activities, they are most likely to receive public status.*

In this cross-cultural analysis of female status, I have been guided by the need for an explanatory framework that includes both an explicit statement of relationships between phenomena and a specification of how these change as the relevant variables are altered. In the formulation that follows, I shall expand on a postulated model of the evolution of female status, described in detail elsewhere (Sanday, 1973). My emphasis will be on the ecological and demographic factors that influence a shift from a relative imbalance of power between males and females to a situation where power is more equally distributed between the sexes.

This model postulates that in the evolution of human culture social survival depends on the disproportionate expenditure of energy by males and females in three major activities: reproduction, defense, and subsistence. Since reproduction activity falls to the female, a constraint is imposed on the proportion of total female energy to be utilized in other activities. Such a constraint in turn increases the probability that the other two tasks draw more on the energy of males, thus placing men in a strategic position to gain control of resources. The question of interest here concerns the conditions under which the distribution and allocation of male and female energy change sufficiently that females can move into one or more of the other task activities in such a way as to alter what was initially an imbalance of power favoring males. However, before continuing with a discussion of these conditions and how they effect a change in other variables that are posited to co-vary with relative sex status, we must discuss the operational definition of female status to be employed.

## FEMALE STATUS: TWO DOMAINS AND THREE PARAMETERS

In developing an operational definition of female status, it is necessary to distinguish between the domestic and public domains and to decide whether to focus on the degree to which women are respected and revered in the domestic and public domains or to concentrate only on the degree to which women hold power and/or authority in one of these domains. Such considerations result in three possible, but not necessarily interrelated, parameters, which should be kept analytically distinct in the discussion of female status. Furthermore, the extent to which they are manifested in the domestic domain may be independent of their manifestation in the public domain.

The domestic domain includes activities performed within the realm of the localized family unit. The public domain includes political and economic activities that take place or have impact beyond the localized family unit and that relate to control of persons or control of things. The distinction between public and domestic realms, also drawn by Rosaldo and by Sacks, is important, since high status in one domain might conceivably preclude high status in the other, in some societies.

M. G. Smith (1960:18–19) defines power as "the ability to act effectively on persons or things, to take or secure favourable decisions which are not of right allocated to the individuals or their roles." Power, then, is de facto and not necessarily recognized. He defines authority as "the right to make a particular decision and to command obedience." In other words, authority is recognized and legitimized power. Rosaldo also discusses female power and authority using Smith's definitions. Since most ethnographers have little or nothing to say explicitly about female power in the public domain, Smith's definition provides a useful operational indicator for making inferences. Furthermore, it is important to recognize in dealing with the subject of female status that although female authority *may* imply power (I shall not explore that question here), female power does not necessarily imply authority. Consequently, one must make inferences about the degree of female power in assessing female status.

The degree to which women are respected and revered is the parameter most ethnographers have in mind when they say that women have high status or subordinated status. Western women in their often highly valued role as helpmate, sex object, the "driving force behind every successful man," etc., can be said to have relatively high status along this parameter. On the other hand, Nupe women, who occupy an economic position generally much better than that of their husbands but who are openly resented and feared by Nupe men (Nadel, 1960), would have to be defined as low in status according to this dimension alone. The same can be said of many African women who contribute heavily to the basic economy while the male activities, according to LeVine (1970:175), are much more prestigious. Brown (1970) makes a similar point when she notes that in one case high status may be inferred from deferential treatment, whereas in another high status may consist of an actual position of power over basic resources and important decisions. As she points out, the two need not coincide and should be considered separately. She describes in detail Iroquois women who were not accorded deferential treatment but who held considerable economic and political power. How deference relates to authority (does authority necessarily imply deference?) is another question we shall not get into here.

With these considerations in mind, female status is generally defined in terms of (1) the degree to which females have authority and/or power in the domestic and/or public domains; and (2) the degree to which females are accorded deferential treatment and are respected and revered in the domestic and/or public domains. An analysis of variation in female status and the causes of this variation in any one of these conceptual domains is a legitimate and interesting task. Even more interesting would be an analysis of the relationship between the domains. For example, it might be discovered that high female status in one domain precludes, or is antecedent to, high status in another domain.

In the empirical analysis of female status to be presented below, deferential treatment and respect will not be included in the operational definition of female status. The reason for this is

that while power and authority may form a single continuum, deferential treatment may be either independent or negatively related to these parameters. Consequently, deferential treatment is excluded until this possibility can be empirically explored. *I shall concentrate exclusively on female power and authority in the public domain.* The domestic domain will be excluded for two reasons. First, to include both domains at this point is likely to complicate matters, since it is conceivable that status in one domain may preclude status in the other.[1] Second, at this time a cross-cultural analysis of variation in female power and authority in the public domain is particularly appropriate in view of the current effort by Western women to remove barriers that have traditionally confronted them in the economic and political spheres. This effort has attracted widespread speculation, mostly unsubstantiated, about the causes of the status of women in general. A cross-cultural analysis of female public power and authority brings to attention societies in which women have achieved a relatively high status in the public domain, thereby contradicting the popular belief that women have been universally excluded from this domain. Such an analysis also provides the only format with which we can understand objectively the causes of variation in female public status. This may give activist Western women further insight into where to concentrate their efforts to bring about change in the imbalance of power between males and females.

## AN OPERATIONAL DEFINITION OF FEMALE STATUS IN THE PUBLIC DOMAIN

The general definition presented above is couched in terms of the *degree* to which women have de facto or recognized decision-making power that affects activities at the economic

---

[1]For a recent cross-cultural analysis of female domestic authority, see Schlegel (1972).

and/or political levels. I have further specified this definition so that data could be collected from a cross-cultural sample. In a pilot study of twelve societies (see Sanday, 1973), I selected four dimensions for coding female status in the public domain. These are:

I. *Female material control.* Females have the ability to act effectively on, to allocate, or to dispose of, things—land, produce, crafts, etc.—beyond the domestic unit.

II. *Demand for female produce.* Female produce has a recognized value either internally—beyond the localized family unit—or in an external market.

III. *Female political participation.* Females, even if only through a few token representatives, may express opinions in a regular, official procedure and may influence policy affecting people beyond the domestic unit.

IV. *Female solidarity groups devoted to female political or economic interests.* Females

group together in some regular way to protect or represent their interests, and are recognized and effectual in this activity.

When the data were collected, it was discovered that, using Guttman scaling procedures, it was possible to order the indicators into a continuously scaled measure of female status. The scale and the societies of the pilot sample are presented in Table 1. The coefficient of reproducibility is .92. The high reproducibility coefficient suggests that each indicator can be seen as a point on a continuum of female status. This continuum is of the general form presented in Figure 1.

The fact that the indicators could be scaled suggests, for the pilot sample at least, that the antecedent of female political authority is some degree of economic power, i.e. ownership or control of strategic resources. Whether economic power, noted in indicator I of the scale, includes economic authority, i.e. the recognized

**TABLE 1**
Scale of Female Status with Related Variables
(P = present; A = absent; ? = information not available or unclear)

| Society | I Female Material Control | II Demand for Female Produce | III Female Political Participation | IV Female Solidarity Groups | Scale Score | Percentage of Female Contribution to Subsistence | Percentage of Deities Who Are Female |
|---|---|---|---|---|---|---|---|
| Yoruba | P | P | P | P | 5 | 30 | 31.5 |
| Iroquois | P | P | P | P | 5 | 50 | 55.5 |
| Samoans | ? | P | P | P | 5 | 50 | 53.1 |
| Crow | P | P | P | A | 4 | 29 | 40 |
| Aymara | P | P | A | A | 3 | 52 | 46.2 |
| Tapirape | ? | P | A | A | 3 | 24 | 20 |
| Rwala | P | ? | A | A | 3 | 10 | 0 |
| Andamans | P | A | A | A | 2 | 50 | 43.8 |
| Tikopia | A | A | A | A | 1 | 75 | 60[a] |
| Azande | A | ? | A | A | 1 | 59 | 33.3 |
| Somali | A | A | A | A | 1 | 45 | 40[a] |
| Toda | A | A | A | A | 1 | 10 | 37.5 |

[a]Only 40 percent (Tikopia) and 20 percent (Somali) of female deities have general powers.

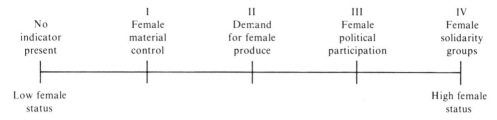

**FIGURE 1**
**Scale of female status.**

right to act effectively on things, is unclear. In some societies, such as the Yoruba, women have a clear and recognized title to the produce they trade. In this sense the Yoruba women can be said to have economic authority. In other societies women may have economic power but not authority. For example, among the Ibo (who were not included in the pilot sample) women made pots and traded, but the men controlled most of the income in the period before European contact (LeVine, 1970). After European contact the existence of certain other conditions aided Ibo women to mobilize their economic power and develop economic authority. The fact that female economic power precedes economic or political authority is not too surprising, since power over strategic resources has been frequently noted to be antecedent to or at least correlated with the development of economic and political authority.

The continuum of female status depicted in Figure 1 omits an important characteristic of political authority, i.e. the right to allocate or disburse political rights and power. This can be seen as a sixth step on the scale. It was excluded from the analysis because (it is conjectured) women do not seem to gain this right in many societies. If one accepts the assumption that female public status has evolved over time in response to a redistribution of male and female energy, then it would be expected that only a few societies would exhibit the sixth step on the scale. In the pilot sample, only the Iroquois show evidence of women's being accorded this right. As Brown notes (1970), Iroquois women

had the authority to veto the nomination of the chiefs, could decide the fate of prisoners of war, could participate in the deliberations of the Council through their male speakers, and had a voice concerning warfare and treaties. Even among the Iroquois, although female power was socially recognized and institutionalized, female authority was exercised indirectly through women's power to veto and to withhold food from war parties. Female political authority in some areas of Africa has reached a more advanced state. According to Hoffer (1972), within the Mende/Sherbro area in 1970 there were eighty-one chiefdoms, ten of which were headed by women. In 1914 in the same ethnic area, there were eighty-four chiefdoms, ten of which were headed by women. For further examples of advanced female political authority, see Lebeuf (1963); and for an example of an effective and powerful female solidarity group, see Leis [1974]. The question of concern now is the conditions under which women move into the public sphere along the continuum of female status discussed above.

## A THEORY OF FEMALE STATUS IN THE PUBLIC DOMAIN

The basic argument for the theory, presented in Figure 2, postulates that initially female energy is concentrated in the reproductive and child-rearing sphere, whereas male energy is concentrated mainly in the subsistence sphere.

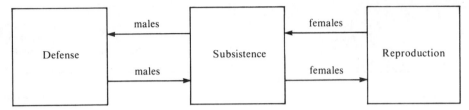

**FIGURE 2**
**The flow of male and female energy in three task activities.**

Over time the presence of human predators causes men to move out of the subsistence sphere and into the defense sphere. Depending on the nature of the warfare, its prolongation, and its interference with male subsistence activities, females move into the subsistence sphere to replace the displaced male energy. Females remain in the subsistence sphere according to whether males continue in warfare activities or become involved in other activities resulting in prolonged male absence. Even if men move back into the subsistence sphere, some women may remain. Over time their number may grow as men periodically flow in and out of the subsistence sphere (see Lipman-Blumen, 1972, for an interesting discussion of this process in the United States). This process may in time give rise to a condition of balanced division of labor, i.e. both sexes contribute to subsistence activities. The importance of balanced division of labor in the development of female public status will be discussed in detail below.

This is a simplified model, which includes the assumption, mentioned earlier, that initially female energy was concentrated primarily in the reproductive child-rearing sphere. Another implicit assumption is that females do not develop public power and authority unless at least some of their energies are employed in productive activities. The empirical relationship between female production and female status in the pilot sample will be presented below. As will be seen, this is not a simple linear relationship.

The basic argument, then, focuses on male absence and female contribution to production.

Male absence from the subsistence sphere forces women to enter this sphere if social survival is to be ensured. However, as noted elsewhere (Sanday, 1973), other conditions might also achieve the same result. Whereas defense or related activities increase the likelihood that females will enter the subsistence arena, this likelihood can increase independently when ecological conditions favor the successful utilization of female energy. In particular, when the mix between population density and the natural environment favors shifting agriculture or horticulture, women are more likely to engage in subsistence activities. An interesting but unanswered question is whether this also frees men to engage in warfare or to develop an exclusively male control sphere.

## FACTORS AFFECTING FEMALE CONTRIBUTION TO SUBSISTENCE

The model of female status, further elaborated in Figure 3, rests heavily on female contribution to production as an intervening variable. In this section I shall undertake a summary of the empirical correlates of female contribution to subsistence. The hypothesized factors affecting female contribution to subsistence are presented in Figure 3.

Using data drawn from the *Ethnographic Atlas* (see Sanday, 1973, for the details of this analysis), it was found that regional identification and type of agriculture explained most of the

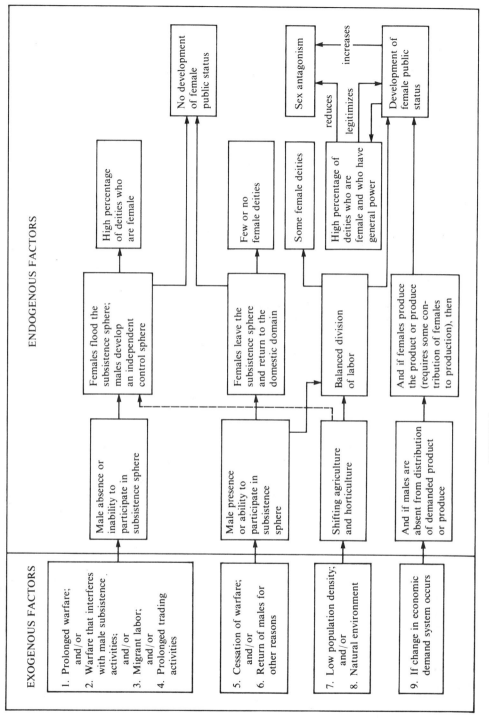

**FIGURE 3**
**Theory of female status in the public domain.**

181

variance in percentage of female contribution to subsistence. Women contribute more to subsistence in Africa and the Insular Pacific and in shifting agriculture or horticultural societies. These findings, although they present some contradictory results for South America, support the hypothesized relationship between type of environment (see exogenous factors 7 and 8 in Figure 3) and female contribution to production. I have discussed the relationship between population density and natural environment and type of agriculture in an earlier paper (Sanday, 1973), drawing on the work of Boserup (1970).

Ample evidence indicates a relationship between the effect of a certain type of warfare and female productive labor. Ember and Ember (1971) find support for the hypothesis that men do more in subsistence than women unless a certain type of warfare prevents them. Epstein (1971:11) discusses the increased utilization of women in the economies of the Communist-bloc countries caused by the huge wartime losses of manpower. In the Soviet Union, she notes that in spite of the wide base of female professionals, women are still not represented at the top of the Soviet professional and governmental hierarchy. The scale of female status presented here suggests that this is simply a matter of time and the development of female solidarity groups.

For the effect on female labor of other factors resulting in male absence and a drain of male labor, a study by LeVine is instructive. LeVine (1970:175–77) discusses a pattern of labor migration that developed in colonial Africa, resulting in rural African men leaving home to work far away for a period of years. Many tasks performed by men were relegated to their wives and children. According to LeVine, the absence of the men loosened the control over their wives' activities, but it did not result in increased status for women. What has resulted, LeVine suggests, is increased hostility by mothers toward their children due to the frustrations of the excessive work burden. LeVine goes on to say that these women, and other African women who shoulder a heavy work load in the absence of men, find

some emotional comfort in their subordinated status. I strongly disagree with this interpretation, and suggest instead that the frustration and hostility toward children is evidence that the women are not happy with their subordinated status. It is conceivable that the women in the societies LeVine refers to will assert their independence, with a consequent change in their status. LeVine's example, however, supports the contention that a drain on male energy will result in the redistribution of female energy. Ember and Ember (1971:579) have also stressed the absence of males as a key determinant. In addition to their warfare example, they allude briefly to the necessity for men to be away on long trading trips in parts of Micronesia and Melanesia as another determinant.

## RELATIONSHIP BETWEEN FEMALE STATUS AND FEMALE CONTRIBUTION TO SUBSISTENCE

The correlation between percentage contribution of women to subsistence and the scaled variable of female status in the pilot sample is negative ($r = -.16$). Plotting these two variables with data from Table 1 reveals a curvilinear relationship between these two factors (see Figure 4). This means that, when the percentage of female contribution to subsistence is either very high or very low, female status as measured by the scale depicted in Figure 1 is also low. In other words, when women contribute about as much as men, the value of the scaled variable is higher.

As would be expected from the graph presented in Figure 4, the correlation between female status and balanced division of labor by sex is high ($r = -.416$). The coefficient is negative because of the way the balanced division-of-labor variable was computed. The score for each society on this variable was determined by taking the absolute value of the difference from the overall mean percentage of female contribution to subsistence for the pilot sample. Thus a low value indicates more balance, and a high value imbalance. The correlation coefficient indicates, as does the graph in Figure 4, that the more balance there is in division of labor by sex, the higher the status score.

The overall mean percentage of female contribution to subsistence in the pilot sample is 40 percent. This is the same value found by Coppinger and Rosenblatt (1968) for a sample of sixty-nine societies, using a similar method for computing percentage of female contribution to subsistence. The fact that 40 percent is taken as representing balanced division of labor by sex is, according to these authors (p. 313), "a reasonable deviation from equal division considering that women must bear and nurse children." These authors found an association between balanced division of labor by sex and the absence of romantic love as a basis for marriage. They conjecture that the dependence of marriage partners on one another for subsistence is an important source of marital stability. They assume that some degree of marital stability is essential in reducing disruption, and that stable marriages need more than a private agreement between a man and a woman. Mutual dependence between

spouses for subsistence goods is one source of stability. In the absence of such dependence, an alternative bond must develop. They hypothesize (p. 310) that "romantic love is such an alternative bond, that where subsistence dependence between spouses is strong, romantic love is unimportant as a basis of marriage, while where subsistence dependence between spouses is weak, romantic love is important as a basis of marriage."

The findings of the pilot study indicate that balanced division of labor is also related to higher female status. This, and the results reported by Coppinger and Rosenblatt, raises two interesting questions. Is it the presence of romantic love that impedes women's acquisition of power and authority in the public domain, e.g. is romantic love a mechanism for keeping women in their place and happy with their lot? Or does the equal participation of men and women in the subsistence arena give women the impetus for moving into the public domain? It could be that when men and women experience mutual dependence in the subsistence arena, both are in a power position relative to each other, i.e. either one can obstruct the other's actions by withholding something the other needs. This fact may give men the experience of accepting female power when it is exercised in other capacities.

The above argument does not explain why women seem to have a relatively low status when they have a monopoly on the production of subsistence goods. When women produce most or all of the subsistence goods, it would be expected that they would have more power vis-à-vis men. However, it may be the case in such situations that women are far more dependent on men to meet nonsubsistence survival needs than men are on women to meet subsistence needs. For example, if men are engaged in warfare, women may depend on them for the protection of the family unit. When such warfare ceases, men may develop an independent control sphere, and expressive or actual mechanisms may be utilized to perpetuate female dependency. In the first case,

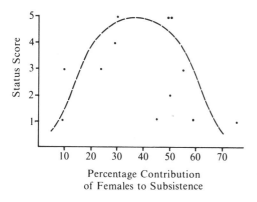

**FIGURE 4**
**Relationship between female status and female contribution to subsistence.**

romantic love may be one of the expressive means by which women are trained to maintain a subordinate stance and to be happy with such a position relative to men. In the second case, women may be treated as slave labor (as they are in the case of the Azande, to be discussed below) and forcibly maintained in a subordinated position.

These are interesting speculations for which there is little empirical support at present. Some of the above relationships are represented in the flow diagram of Figure 3, which shows a number of avenues by which women develop public status. It is clear from the above discussion that contribution to production is a necessary but not sufficient condition. An examination of some of the societies in the pilot sample supports some of the above discussion and supplies further insights.

In societies where control and production are linked and a competitive market exists, female power is likely to develop *if* females are actively engaged in producing valued market goods. In societies where control is based on a magical or religious title, female power is unlikely to develop unless some exogenous influence (such as the introduction of cash-cropping, famine, etc.) creates a new demand or results in a revaluation of female produce. Such exogenous influences can result in the development of a new control sphere based primarily on who has access to the valued product rather than on a magical or religious title to it.

The Tikopian, Azande, and Somali women provide examples of cases where women contribute predominantly to subsistence activities but have no status. Firth (1939:88) notes that whereas in modern European society control over the means of production is divorced from religious title to this control, in Tikopia production is controlled by chiefs whose political and economic influence rests on a religious basis. He also notes the absence of an external market, which means no external outlet for goods produced by women. Internally, the product of

female labor is not valued as much as that of male labor, because the main tasks of women demand few technical aids and much hard work. In contrast, male tasks are much more diversified and require more technical assistance. Firth concludes that "the subordinate position of the women as property owners is then to some extent to be correlated with the type of technical equipment and system of production in vogue in Tikopia" (1939:365).

Among the Azande, women are the main source of labor and are a symbol of wealth. Women are treated much like slaves and have traditionally been barred from the main source of power, which is through the exercise of magic. According to Evans-Pritchard (1937:284), the exclusion of women from any dealings with the poison oracle has been the most evident symptom of their inferior social position and the means of maintaining them in this position. This situation has changed among the Azande as contact with Europeans has created a demand for some Azande crops. According to De Schlippe (1956:145), under European rule women became emancipated, crops acquired cash value, war disappeared, hunting was reduced, and men were compelled to invest most of their effort in agriculture. It is interesting to note that when men moved into agricultural production they tended to favor the cash crops introduced by the Europeans, hence limiting the access of women to this new control sphere.

For Azande men, cash crops had a prestige value because of the hierarchical way of their introduction and because of their novelty (De Schlippe, 1956:145). This, of course, partially limited the access of women to a new control sphere based primarily on production. Had the important cash crops among the Azande not had this prestige value, the status of Azande women might have changed drastically in a short period of time, as it did for the Afikpo Ibo women in eastern Nigeria. According to LeVine (1970: 178), before European contact Ibo women made pots, traded, and farmed, but the men controlled most of the income and performed the prestige activities of yam farming and slave trading. The mobility of Ibo women was limited because of the prevalence of warfare. With the cessation of warfare, mobility became possible and trading increased. At the same time cassava was introduced, which Ibo men regarded with disdain, preferring to farm their prestigeful and ritually important yams. The women were allowed to grow cassava between the yam heaps and to keep the profits for themselves. As time went on, according to LeVine (1970:178):

> This despised crop eliminated the annual famine before the yam harvest and attained a high and stable market value. The Afikpo women became capable of supporting themselves and their children without aid from their husbands, and nowadays they even rent land independently for cassava cultivation. Once a woman becomes self-supporting in this way, she can say, in the words of an elderly Afikpo woman, "What is man? I have my own money" (Ottenberg, 1959:215). Afikpo husbands have found it increasingly difficult to keep their wives at home in their formerly subordinate position.

The Somali women were treated in much the same way as Azande women. The Somali regard their female children as stock, and in times of famine have sold them as slaves (Drake-Brockman, 1912:137–38). Women were forced, under threat of physical violence from their husbands, to perform all the menial and heavy work and were allowed to tend sheep and goats. Somali men considered it beneath their dignity to tend anything but camels, cattle, and ponies—the most valuable economic assets of the Somali. Here again we see a case where women perform much of the labor but are denied access to the valued produce and are kept in a subordinate position by external threat.

The social contexts of the Iroquois, Yoruba,

and Samoan women provide examples of the conditions under which women can achieve considerable economic and/or political power. Among the Iroquois the control of agricultural production was in the hands of a group of women in the village who formed a mutual aid society. Female control of agricultural production seems to have increased and been strengthened by the prolonged absences of males in warfare and trading activities (Noon, 1949). The literature on the Iroquois stresses the high position of women and their participation in political and religious activities. Women were able to influence decisions of the ruling council both directly and indirectly through the weight of public opinion. Since unanimity was necessary in decisions, any proposal unpopular with the women could be hindered by their disapproval. Women could also hinder or prevent the forming of a war party that lacked their approval by withholding supplies the warriors needed (Randle, 1951).

The Yoruba women are perhaps the most independent in Africa (LeVine, 1970:179). Traditionally these women maintained an autonomous economic role and a higher degree of mobility than, for example, the Ibo women, who were prohibited from moving about freely because of warfare. This suggests that, although warfare may function to increase female participation in production, it may also inhibit the development of female power in some societies (although not in all, as the case of the Iroquois clearly shows). The role of Yoruba women as independent market traders is, and has long been, highly institutionalized. The women have organized trade guilds, which regulate the conditions and standards of the craft and protect the interests of the members. These are powerful organizations whose leaders play an important role in political activities. Such organizations in many African societies are examples of the very real authority exercised by women in African political systems (Lebeuf, 1963).

The status of Samoan women before European contact was not as high as it is reported by Keesing (1937) after European contact. The new status of women was an outgrowth of their organizations and functions in the traditional system (Keesing, 1934:394). For example, there was an organization of the wives of chiefs and orators, which in modern Samoa developed into a female replica of the men's council, dealing with many matters other than those pertaining to women in earlier days (Keesing, 1937:9). The traditional women's committees in western Samoa also laid the basis for the later women's *Mau* movement, which gave women a strong taste for politics.

Data on the traditional economic activities of Samoan women indicate that on an informal level women played as active a part as the men in controlling economic arrangements (Mead, 1928:82). A woman's claim on her family's land rendered her as independent as her husband (Mead, 1928:108). In agriculture the heaviest work was done by men and the lighter and more detailed work by women. There was little feeling about the relative prestige of men's and women's work. Fine mats, which have been called the Samoan currency, were made by women and were highly valued (Mead, 1930:67–74). Thus, while traditional Samoan women did not seem to exercise the power that developed among Iroquois and Yoruba women, the basis for the later development of female power and authority seems to have existed.

## FEMALE STATUS, SEX ANTAGONISM, AND FEMALE DEITIES

In developing a theory of female public status, my emphasis has been on ecological and economic factors and the efficient distribution of human energy. An alternative explanation might emphasize magico-religious means by which women gain and maintain title to control. For example, women might gain power and authority in societies where maternity is viewed as

a sacred or magical function. As De Beauvoir (1953:67) has said, this can occur in early agricultural communities where there is frequently an association between maternity and fertility of the soil. In these belief systems the earth is seen as belonging to women, thus giving them religious title to the land and its fruits. Such beliefs are to be found in many societies. Among the Iroquois, for example, the female virtues of food providing and the fertility and bounty of nature are the qualities most respected and revered. Only women's activities are celebrated in the ceremonial cycle. There are no festivals to celebrate hunting or war, though they probably existed in the past. Most of the ceremonies are thanksgiving for the fertility of the earth, especially for the crops, which are women's chief concern (Randle, 1951: 172).

The problem with this type of explanation is that it can be considered an effect and not a cause of female status. A belief system emphasizing maternity and fertility as sacred may function to legitimize female status that develops because of ecological and economic factors. There is ample evidence in the ethnographic material, discussed above, that a change in female status is associated with a change in the productive system. Where this has occurred, as with the Ibo, it is interesting to note that sex antagonism develops or increases. Perhaps sex antagonism develops in the absence of a belief system that legitimizes and sanctions the power of women. Sex antagonism might be reduced in such societies when a belief system develops in which female power is attributed to the natural functions of women.

In order to investigate further the relationship between the belief system and female public status, I made a study of the sex and domain of authority of the deities, personified natural forces, and folk heroes in each of the societies of the pilot sample. The number in each category having clearly defined and general powers over a group were counted for each society. The percentage of these who were female was computed, as well as the percentage who were female and had clearly defined general power over both males and females (as opposed to power over females only, or males only). The data are displayed in Table 1. These two variables were then correlated with the female status scale and percentage female contribution to subsistence. Whereas there is a high correlation between percentage of deities who are female and female contribution to subsistence ($r=.742$), there is no correlation between the percentage of female deities and female status ($r=.039$). The correlation between the percentage of female deities with general powers over both males and females and female status is low but positive (.300). The correlation between female deities with general powers and female contribution to subsistence is slightly higher ($r=.547$). These pilot results are intriguing and can be interpreted in different ways. Clearly, more work must be done in this area. The flow chart of Figure 3 suggests that the belief system is a reflection and dramatization of female activities in the subsistence domain and that it also may serve to legitimize a change in female public status.

## CONCLUSION

There is no doubt from the data examined that there is a wide range of variation in female public status cross-culturally. In a few of the cases discussed, there is evidence that both men and women have power and authority in the public domain. However, in the majority of cases males clearly have higher public status. The question I have posed in this paper concerns the conditions under which the relative status of women changes in the direction of public equality. In answering this question I assumed that in the initial stages of human society—and probably throughout most of human history—

defense, subsistence, and reproduction were necessary activities for social survival and that male energy was more likely to be expended in subsistence and defense while female energy was devoted primarily to reproduction and secondarily to subsistence. If this was the case, it would suggest that males were in a better position to gain both access to and control over strategic resources.

Figure 3 presents the factors that were hypothesized to influence a change in the balance of power between males and females. The predominant emphasis in this schema has been on male absence, ecological factors, and change in the system of demand for female goods. Any condition of prolonged male absence can result in females invading the subsistence sphere if social survival is to continue. Certain ecological conditions can have the same effect. When females move into the subsistence sphere, the flow diagram in Figure 3 suggests three possibilities: women may occupy this sphere temporarily while males are absent; they may become the predominant laborers and remain in this sphere; or they may continue to occupy this sphere in conjunction with males, and a condition of balanced division of labor may result. In the first two cases the data indicate that the public status of women does not change, whereas in the latter case the data indicate that women develop economic and political power. Where females invade the subsistence sphere and remain there, the evidence indicates that males develop an independent control sphere, with the result that women are treated as slave labor. The schema depicted in Figure 3 further suggests that increased demand for certain goods produced by women will also result in the development of economic rights that can lead to an overall change in status.

Finally, it was hypothesized that when females develop economic and political power, this will be legitimized over time through the expressive cultural system. The existence or development of female deities who have general powers can be seen as a means for recognizing and accepting female power. This also can serve to reduce sex antagonism, which seems to develop when the status of women changes in such a fashion as to threaten male power and authority.

This has been, by and large, a programmatic and pilot effort. Although empirical support has been found for some of the relationships represented in Figure 3, the overall model requires empirical testing with an adequate cross-cultural sample. Only then will the theory meet the objections raised by Murdock (1971:19–20) concerning what passes as theory in anthropology. According to Murdock, anthropological theory "includes remarkably few propositions which meet the basic requirements of science, that is to say, which explicitly state relationships between phenomena, specify precisely how these change as relevant variables are altered, and support such statements with adequate validating evidence." It would be well to keep Murdock's criticisms of anthropological theory in mind when working in the area of relative sex status. Because this is an area prone to bias introduced by both ethnocentrism and sexcentrism, it is particularly important to seek the objectivity provided by the rigorous use of the scientific method.

## REFERENCES CITED

BOSERUP, ESTER. 1970. Women's Role in Economic Development. New York.

BROWN, JUDITH K. 1970. "Economic Organization and the Position of Women Among the Iroquois," Ethnohistory, 17 (3–4):151–67.

COPPINGER, ROBERT M., and PAUL C. ROSENBLATT. 1968. "Romantic Love and Subsistence Dependence of Spouses," Southwestern Journal of Anthropology, 24:310–19.

DE BEAUVOIR, SIMONE. 1953. The Second Sex. New York. Originally published in French in 1949.

DE SCHLIPPE, PIERRE. 1956. Shifting Cultivation in Africa: Azande System of Agriculture. London.

DRAKE-BROCKMAN, RALPH E. 1912. British Somaliland. London.

EMBER, MELVIN, and CAROL R. EMBER. 1971. "The Conditions Favoring Matrilocal Versus Patrilocal Residence," American Anthropologist, 73: 571–94.

EPSTEIN, CYNTHIA FUCHS. 1971. Woman's Place. Berkeley, Calif.

EVANS-PRITCHARD, EDWARD E. 1937. Witchcraft, Oracles and Magic Among the Azande. New York.

FIRTH, RAYMOND. 1939. Primitive Polynesian Economy. London.

HOFFER, CAROL. 1972. "Mende and Sherbro Women in High Office," Canadian Journal of African Studies, 6:151–64.

KEESING, FELIX M. 1934. Modern Samoa: Its Government and Changing Life. London.

———. 1937. "The Taupo System of Samoa," Oceania, 8:1–14.

LEBEUF, ANNIE M. D. 1963. "The Role of Women in the Political Organization of African Societies," in Denise Paulme, ed., Women of Tropical Africa. Berkeley, Calif.

LEVINE, ROBERT A. 1970. "Sex Roles and Economic Change in Africa," in John Middleton, ed., Black Africa. London.

LIPMAN-BLUMEN, JEAN. 1972. "Role De-Differentiation as a System Response to Crisis: Occupational and Political Roles of Women," Sociological Inquiry, 43:105–29.

MEAD, MARGARET. 1928. Coming of Age in Samoa: A Psychological Study of Primitive Youth for Western Civilization. New York.

———. 1930. "Social Organization of Manua," Bernice P. Bishop Museum Bulletin 76, Hawaii.

MURDOCK, GEORGE P. 1971. "Anthropology's Mythology: The Huxley Memorial Lecture 1971," Proceedings of the Royal Anthropological Institute of Great Britain and Ireland for 1971, pp. 17–24.

NADEL, S. F. 1960. "Witchcraft in Four African Societies: An Essay in Comparison," in S. Ottenberg and P. Ottenberg, eds., Cultures and Societies of Africa. New York.

NOON, JOHN A. 1949. "Law and Government of the Grand River Iroquois," Viking Fund Publications in Anthropology, No. 12, New York.

OTTENBERG, P. V. 1959. "The Changing Economic Position of Women Among the Afikpo Ibo," in W. R. Bascom and M. J. Herskovits, eds., Continuity and Change in African Cultures. Chicago.

RANDLE, M. C. 1951. "Iroquois Women, Then—

Now," in *Symposium on Local Diversity in Iroquois Culture,* Bureau of American Ethnology, Bulletin 149, Washington, D.C.

SANDAY, PEGGY R. 1973. "Toward a Theory of the Status of Women," *American Anthropologist,* 75:1682–1700.

SCHLEGEL, ALICE. 1972. Male Dominance and Female Autonomy: Domestic Authority in Matrilineal Societies. New Haven.

SMITH, MICHAEL G. 1960. Government in Zazau. London.

# 15

## ENGELS REVISITED: WOMEN, THE ORGANIZATION OF PRODUCTION, AND PRIVATE PROPERTY

*Karen Sacks*

*In 1891, Engels argued women held equal status to men in early communal classless societies, because both men and women produced for the group's use and the group, rather than the individual, owned property. With the advent of classes, men produced for exchange and came to own property; propertyless women lost public esteem. In this article, Karen Sacks reviews Engels's position and tests it against four African societies that range from a classless to a class organization. She concludes that there is a tendency for women in societies marked by class to lose public power, but not because of an inability to hold private property. Instead, she argues, men have been more easily exploited for their labor than women in class societies, and their contribution to public exchange has gained them higher status. Women, on the other hand, have not been able to translate their contribution to private family production into public esteem and have been denied adult public status. For equality, Sacks concludes, family labor and public labor must be merged so that women can have access to the same status measures as those for men.*

This paper reexamines Engels's ideas on the bases of women's social position relative to that of men. Engels is almost alone in providing an account based on a materialist theory—one that sees women's position as varying from society to society, or epoch to epoch, according to the prevailing economic and political relationships of the society. Though he made a number of specific ethnographic errors,[1] I think his main ideas are correct, and they remain the best way of explaining data gathered since he wrote— namely ethnographic and historical data showing that women's social position has *not* always, everywhere, or in most respects been subordinate to that of men.

Since capitalism has dominated and transformed the social orders of most of the world's people, it is useful to look to the past, as Engels has done, through ethnographic and historical reconstruction, both to understand the present state of affairs and to help shape the future. Looking at noncapitalist ways of organizing economic and political relations and how these affected the relative positions of men and women provided Engels with an answer to why women were subordinate to men in capitalist society, and what political and economic changes were needed to end sexual inequality.

*The Origin of the Family, Private Property and the State* (1891) is more than an analysis of women's status. It is a contrast between nonclass and class societies. Set in an evolutionary framework, it shows how private property originated, how once on the scene it undermined an egalitarian tribal order, creating families as economic units, inequality of property ownership, and, finally, exploitative class societies. Embedded in this picture is a description of how women's social position declined as private property gained strength as an organizing principle for society. Woven into this is an analysis of why such property had the effect it did; specifically, how it transformed women's work organization and, more generally, the relationship of property to class and sex.

The first part of this paper pulls together some of Engels's key points on how the sexual egalitarianism of preclass societies was undermined by changes in women's work, and by the growth of families as important economic units. It is a selective and somewhat interpretive summary. A brief second part reinterprets Engels's terminology and framework in the context of nonclass societies. The third part presents some ethnographic data as historical reconstruction to illustrate Engels's emphasis on the importance of public labor for determining women's social status, and to modify his ideas about women being social adults *or* wifely dependents. The final part suggests why class societies have used the family to circumscribe and subordinate women.

## WOMEN IN ENGELS'S THEORY A RECONSTRUCTION

Engels presents a historical dynamic by which women are transformed from free and equal productive *members of society* to subordinate and dependent *wives* and wards. The growth of male-owned private property, with the family as the institution that appropriates and perpetuates it, is the cause of this transformation. First I shall summarize the way Engels saw this evolutionary process, and then clarify some of Engels's terms.

In the early stages of society, productive resources were owned communally by the tribe or clan. Food had to be collected and cooked daily. Production was for use only, that is, to meet people's subsistence needs. There was no surplus produced for exchange.[2] The group consisting of husband, wife, and dependent children was neither a productive unit nor one for performing

---

[1] I have excluded enumeration of these partly for lack of space, but also because they are substantively secondary and are more than amply dealt with by others.

[2] Though Engels does not deal with this situation, people in many nonclass and noncapitalist societies do

housework—nor did it own property. Since Engels sees economic functions as key to the family, and since this group in no way was an economic unit, the family did not exist; it had not precipitated out of the larger household. The household, which was the basic social and economic unit, was communistic in that all food stores were held in common and all work was done for the household rather than for individual members or couples. Women did the housework and ran these households. "In the old communistic household, which embraced numerous couples and their children, the administration of the household, entrusted to the women, was just as much a public, a socially necessary industry as the providing of food by the men" (Engels, 1891:120).

At this stage the family, which Engels sees as a productive, consuming, and property-owning group, did not exist. Instead, the context of men's and women's life and labor was the tribe or clan. This was a communal property-owning group. Although individuals of both sexes owned tools and personal effects, on their death these passed to other members of their tribe or clan of the same sex, not necessarily to their own children. Decision making, both economic and political, involved the equal participation of all members, men and women. Both sexes were equal members of the group because both made crucial contributions to the economic life of the group.

Engels concluded that the absence of private property made men's productive work and women's household work of equal social significance. Men and women were simply involved in different stages of the production of the same *kinds* of goods—the production of subsistence.

All production was of the same kind: production for use. People worked for the communal household or clan rather than for individuals. Since all work was for social use and all adults were social producers, all adults were equal members of the group.

Engels focused on the public rights of women in the early stages of society: participation in political decision making, and their collective right to depose a chief (for the Iroquois). These rights came from membership in the clan, which in turn was based on performance of public or social labor. He was also impressed with the high status of a wife relative to her husband. This he attributed to the solidarity and kinship among the women, the core of the household.

The material base for the women's transformation from equal members of society to subordinate wives lay in the development of valuable productive resources, initially the domestication of large animals, as private property. For Engels, "private property" has a specific meaning. Only goods or resources with productive potential can be considered *property*. He was aware that people held personal goods individually. Though these are private, they are not property in the sense Engels means the word. In nonindustrial societies, the most important types of private property are domesticated animals and cultivated land. These are productive *resources.* Tools (productive means) are unimportant because the skills and materials for their manufacture are equally available to all. Engels is concerned with property that has productive potential. Other goods, for conspicuous consumption or display, are a result of economic and political inequality rather than a cause of it. When Engels speaks of private property, he is not referring to these goods.

Private property became possible in human history only when technological development and natural resources allowed a society to develop the skills needed to domesticate animals or to invest labor in land so that its productivity

in fact produce for exchange. The question of how production for exchange in these societies differs from that in capitalist societies is a complex one. Perhaps the best discussion of the fundamental differences involved can be found in Sahlins (1971).

lasted for an appreciable length of time. Engels believed that enduring productivity led to enduring private ownership.

Engels's usage of "private" is broader than the way it is used under capitalism—where there are almost no restrictions on what the owner can do with the property. For Engels, private seems to mean property owned by an individual, or by a family where rights to manage it are vested in one of the owners. It also means that these goods can be disposed of with *scme* leeway—that is, to acquire wives, clients, or service from others. Engels saw "gaining a livelihood" as always men's work, and the means of production as always owned by the user (with the stipulation that inheritance remained within the clan). From this, he reasoned that the earliest private productive property, which seemed to be domestic animals, must have been owned by men.[3]

Domesticated animals were assimilated into the older patterns of tool ownership; that is, they were privately owned. Yet animals were a qualitatively new kind of item: they met subsistence needs and they reproduced themselves—they were the first form of private property. The growth of private property shattered the communal political economy of the clan. The foundation for its egalitarianism had been collective ownership of productive property. Now that property was privately owned (by men), the family grew in importance and soon overshadowed the clan as the key economic and decision-making group. Unlike the clan, though, internal family structure was not egalitarian.

---

[3]It is worth noting that Engels saw these new items (domesticated animals, cultivated land) as being assimilated into an already existing social context: the pattern of owning personal effects. The qualitatively different nature of these new "effects"—that they could reproduce themselves and their fruits—led to the destruction of the communal political and economic order that had created them. Engels does not attribute the development of private property to a greedy male nature.

Families contained propertyless dependents (all women and children, and some propertyless men).

But private property transformed the relations between men and women within the *household* only because it also radically changed the political and economic relations in the larger *society.*

The new wealth meant that there was a surplus of goods available for exchange between productive units. With time, production by men specifically for exchange purposes became more developed and expanded, and came to overshadow the household's production for use. Industrial capitalism has now reached the stage where production is almost exclusively social, outside the household, and for exchange, leaving women's work as private maintenance for *family* use.

As production for exchange eclipsed production for use, it changed the nature of the household, the significance of women's work within it, and consequently women's position. Women worked now for their husbands and families instead of for society. Their labor was a necessary but socially subordinate part of producing an exchangeable surplus. Women became wards, wives, and daughters instead of adult members of society.

Private property made its owner the ruler of the household. Women and other propertyless dependents worked to maintain and augment the household head's property, for he was now engaged in competitive production and exchange with other heads of households.

Families perpetuated themselves through time by the inheritance of property. Thus changes took place in the definition of children. From new members of a societal group, they became either private heirs or subordinate, dependent workers. This meant that women's reproductive labor, like their productive work, also underwent a transformation from social to private. People and property became intertwined, and each became part of the definition of the other.

With the further development of technology and accumulation of wealth, the property owners separated themselves from their subordinate kinsmen and allied with other property owners to preserve and defend their holdings against the claims of the nonpropertied. This marked the end of kinship-based *productive* groups and the beginning of class society and the state.

## ENGELS'S THEORY AND NONCLASS SOCIETIES

To use Engels's concepts of social labor and production for exchange, I shall have to reinterpret them to be more in line with the ways nonclass societies are organized. Engels's usage of social or public labor in nonclass societies emphasizes work for and in the context of one's own corporate property-owning group. But marriage joins people from two groups; this generally means that at least one partner is not working for and in the context of his or her natal group. At the same time, he or she is not necessarily doing what Engels would call domestic work—work only for one's own household. Therefore, I shall stretch his concept of social labor to include any work done (singly or as part of a group) for use or appropriation by someone of another household. Some examples of social labor, illustrated in the next section, indicate the wide range of organizations it covers: participation in a cooperative work group, tributary labor for a chief, corvée, collective livestock raiding.

Production for exchange has to be expanded also. People do not spontaneously work to produce a surplus. There has to be some power forcing people to produce more than they themselves use. People in all societies give gifts, and gifts always put the recipient under an obligation to make a return. In a general way, as long as everyone has equal access to the means of subsistence, everyone has or can expect to have gifts by his own effort—and can thus make an equiva-

lent return. But when the means of subsistence are privately and unequally held, a recipient is often unable to make an equivalent return in goods. He is then expected to return the favor with service: he becomes a loyal dependent or client-follower.

Both situations are instances of exchange. But only the second situation gives one of the parties the ability to harness the labor power of others for his own ends. This kind of situation is production for exchange: the production of goods used to gain control over the services of others. By contrast, production for use is simply producing goods to meet consumption needs.

Perhaps the beginnings of production for exchange lay in the use of wealth to gain loyal followers, and then needing to use the labor of one's followers to create still more wealth to keep their loyalty. In any case, production for exchange goes hand in hand with private property and political and economic inequality.

For example, there is wealth inequality and clientage in nonclass societies with large domesticated animals. Not only do these animals contribute to subsistence, but they are necessary for a man in order to marry and to have political standing in the society. Thus, in much of East Africa prior to imperialist rule, men obtained cattle from kinsmen or from service to a chief or other wealthy man, to whom they then owed loyalty in exchange for the cattle. The production of cattle is then production for exchange. Loyalty and service are given for livestock, and are used to augment the wealth and power of the benefactor, whether kinsman or not. Regardless of various people's overlapping rights and obligations to the livestock, these are private property, because there is some choice in how they will be allocated and because an individual is empowered to make that choice.

Though Engels has an integrated theory, at the risk of some distortion I should like to separate two sets of ideas: (1) the immediate determinants or material bases of women's status—that social or public labor makes men or women adult citizens in the eyes of society and that men's ownership of private property establishes their dominance over women in the family and society; and (2) the evolutionary aspect—that women's status became solely subordinate and domestic with the development of male private property, production for exchange, and class society.

I shall discuss the immediate determinants of women's status by using illustrations from ethnography in the next part. This has the advantage of focusing first on the material bases of women's position. Even if Engels is right in a general way, that women are worse off in class than in nonclass societies, we still need to know what gives rise to this state of affairs. I do not believe that Engels's evolutionary explanation is valid as it stands. There is too much data showing that women are not the complete equals of men in most nonclass societies lacking private property. There are also many societies, with or without classes, where women do own and inherit property. Finally, I shall use some illustrations from class societies to suggest a different route to Engels's conclusions.

## WOMEN AS SOCIAL ADULTS AND WIVES: FOUR AFRICAN SOCIETIES

The following illustration is a reconstruction, mainly from ethnographies, of women's position in four African societies prior to the imposition of effective imperialist domination.[4] Using ethnographic reconstruction allows us to look at some of the variety in women's status in noncapitalist societies—nonclass as well as class—and to use the comparisons to illuminate Engels's ideas.

[4]Data come primarily from Krige and Krige (1943, Lovedu); Hunter (1936, Pondo); Turnbull (1965, Mbuti); and Roscoe (1966, Ganda). These societies were selected from the writings on East and South Africa primarily because the data on women were adequate and comparable. Thus many aspects—for example, concerning women in trade and marketing roles—though they are important, simply cannot be dealt with here.

The Mbuti of Zaire can be characterized as a band society, with subsistence based on communal net hunting and gathering of vegetable food. In South Africa, the Lovedu were principally hoe agriculturalists, whereas the Pondo combined agriculture with livestock. Ganda, a class society in Uganda, also based subsistence on hoe agriculture.

If we place these societies on a continuum from egalitarian society to class society, our rankings can be seen to hold in three principal respects. First, the Mbuti and Lovedu have economies of production for use; the Pondo have the beginnings of production for exchange centered around cattle; and in Ganda production for exchange bulks quite large. Second, in Mbuti and Lovedu, both sexes perform social labor in a use economy, and though this remains the organization of Pondo women's labor, Pondo men perform social labor at least in part in an exchange economy; whereas in Ganda women's work is individual domestic production for household use, while men work in groups, almost totally in production for exchange. Third, the Mbuti band owns the productive resources, whereas these are largely patrilineal family estates in Lovedu and Pondo; in Ganda the productive resources are in male hands, and less enmeshed in family obligations.

Among Mbuti, Lovedu, and Pondo, women's productive activities are social, and women have an adult social status. But in Ganda, where women's productive activities are domestic, the status of women is that of wife and ward only—despite the fact that women produce the bulk of the food. This suggests that Engels is right in seeing public or social labor as the basis for social adulthood.

But a more detailed look shows that women do not have to be characterized as *either* social adults *or* wifely wards. Rather, the data suggest that women can be both simultaneously. Women's status in a marital relationship seems to vary independently of their status in the larger society. But Engels seems correct in seeing the status of wife relative to husband as dependent on their relationships to the property of the

TABLE 1
Women's Social and Domestic Status Compared with Men's in Four African Societies

| Indexes of Women's Status | Discrimination Against Women's Participation | | | |
| | Mbuti | Lovedu | Pondo | Ganda |
| --- | --- | --- | --- | --- |
| SOCIAL | | | | |
| Mutual aid | n.a. | none | none | active |
| Self-representation | none | none | none | active |
| Socializing opportunity | none | none | none | active |
| Extramarital sex | none | none | none | active |
| Divorce | none | none | none | active |
| Social disposal of wealth | none | none | active | active |
| Political office | none | none | active | active |
| Extra-domestic dispute settlement | none | none | active | active |
| Extra-domestic mediation with supernatural | none | none | active | active |
| DOMESTIC | | | | |
| Wife's inheritance of marital estate | none | active | active | active |
| Wife's authority over domestic affairs | none | active | active | active |
| Wife as private reproducer (adultery compensation) | none | active | active | active |
| Menstrual and pregnancy restrictions | none | weak | weak | active |

NOTE: Ownership of major productive resources: the band in Mbuti, the family in Lovedu and Pondo, and the individual in Ganda. Collective social production by women, as against that by men: equal in Mbuti and Lovedu, unequal in Pondo, and absent in Ganda.

household; that is, the spouse who owns the property rules the household.

Table 1 summarizes some indexes of women's status in society and in the family, and their relationship to women's organization of productive activities and to property ownership.[5] Essentially, Mbuti and Lovedu women are the equals of men, whereas Ganda women are subordinate and Pondo women fall somewhere between. The first five variables, which I have labeled social adulthood, involve egalitarian relations with people outside the household. A look at mutual aid relationships suggests that

social adulthood is based on performing collective social labor. Lovedu men and women both have some sort of age groupings. These are mobilized to work for the district head and queen. For women at least, a neighborhood age group may take collective action against the group of a person who has offended one of its members. Pondo women of a neighborhood work together and cooperate in the performance of girls' initiation ceremonies, and women of the same household cooperate in arranging extramarital sexual affairs. Women's collective action is recognized by men when men collectively punish women and girls for what men deem to be sex offenses.

Self-representation in legal proceedings indicates that a woman is regarded as able to be wronged or to do wrong in the eyes of society, and is practiced among the Mbuti, Lovedu, and

[5]The variables and their categorization, rather than being determined in advance by a logical scheme, emerged as a result of comparing the positions of women in these four societies.

Pondo. A Ganda woman, by contrast, requires a male guardian (generally husband or father) to bring her case to court; the guardian is held responsible for her acts and receives compensation for wrongs done to her.

Though Mbuti, Lovedu, and Pondo men and women both participate in most of the same social activities, in the latter two societies young wives are kept busy at domestic work, which significantly restricts their ability to enjoy these events. But as older wives, as sisters visiting their own kinsmen, and as diviners, women attend social events as freely as do men. In Ganda, many of the social activities are patron- or state-oriented; women are excluded from these.

Although marital and social status are closely related, the ease of divorce for men versus women indicates their relative importance for each. In Ganda a husband can effectively end a marriage by simply ignoring his wife, but a woman must contend not only with her husband but with her brother, who as partial guardian generally acts to preserve the marriage.

Mbuti and Lovedu have a single standard regarding extramarital sexual affairs. Pondo women view their extramarital affairs as right and proper, but the men do not. A Ganda husband may kill his wife for real or suspected adultery, but a wife has little recourse against her husband. Men may use the courts to deal out severe punishment to their wives' lovers. In general, Ganda restricts extramarital sexual activity much more than do the other societies. Exceptions are made for high-ranking men who have affairs with peasant women, but men and women in the reverse situation are punished severely. Cohen's (1969) point seems borne out here, that restricted sexual activity serves to strengthen the marital bond at the expense of bonds that could serve as a basis for rebellion in class societies.

Being able to give and receive food and items of social exchange is the material basis for exercising political power. Engels suggests that real power develops only with production for exchange and private property. In societies without these—that is, in societies based on production for use—the performance of social labor gives a person the right to join with other adults in making political decisions and settling disputes. This is because political decision making and dispute settlement are responsibilities of adult members of an egalitarian society.

Among Mbuti and Lovedu both sexes give and receive food. Lovedu women give and receive cattle and may marry a wife with them; they become, in effect, husbands. But Pondo women, though they are social producers, cannot dispose of the most important exchange item: livestock. Perhaps the explanation lies in the nature of Pondo production for exchange. Women's agricultural work is for use; work is geared over the long and short run to the needs of the household. But men's organization for livestock raiding involves them in production for exchange; over the short run, warfare is geared more to the power need of a chief than to household needs; a chief keeps a following over the short run by having cattle to distribute. Over the long run, a chief keeps power by actually distributing cattle more or less widely. The chief owns the cattle captured in warfare, but sooner or later he distributes them among the warriors by virtue of their role in raiding. These livestock are the chief's to allocate. They are the most important item of exchange (in bridewealth, loans, and feasts) and of establishing long-term relationships (marriage and service). Because Pondo women do not participate in production for exchange (raiding), they cannot dispose of the property that establishes power relationships. Thus they do not hold overt political power.

Lovedu women hold political office, enter the decision-making arenas of the society, and predominate in officiating in religious rituals on behalf of their lineages. Ganda peasant women are barred from even the minimal access to political positions available to peasant men. Yet the mother and one sister of the king do hold important offices and exercise some power. This is predicated on their relationship to the king.

A wife's position vis-à-vis her husband is

based on her ownership, or lack of it, of the marital estate. In Lovedu, Pondo, and Ganda, productive resources are inherited patrilineally. Here, there is a contradiction, or opposition, in the fact that production is organized in a social or public way, but families or individuals appropriate and inherit the productive resources. A wife does not participate in the ownership of resources of her marital household. On the other hand, the Mbuti's appropriation for *use* by families seems to me qualitatively different from appropriation for inheritance and exchange, as in the other societies. Mbuti resources are owned by the territorial band as a whole. Residence entitles a person to use these, and there is no inheritance. Thus, Mbuti husbands and wives have the same relationship to the band resources.

Lovedu, Pondo, and Ganda wives labor for their husband and his patrikin, but do not belong to the group that appropriates the product of their labor. Wives provide heirs, raise children, and do the bulk of the domestic work under the authority of the husband and his kin. They do not represent the household to outsiders. By contrast, Mbuti marriage carries no restrictions on a woman's authority over her work, children, or socializing. Her fertility cannot be said to be private, since her husband receives no compensation for her extramarital sexual relationships.

Menstrual and pregnancy restrictions on women's activities among Lovedu, Pondo, and Ganda seem to operate to separate women's reproductive functions from contact with the social production of exchange goods; that is, from contact with warriors, cattle, craft, and some medical practices. In these three societies children are potential heirs; they inherit property and continue the family line. Regardless of how women's productive activities are organized, their reproductive potential is private. But among the Mbuti, where children are social members rather than private heirs, menstruation and pregnancy are not surrounded by any such restrictions. This contrast suggests that men-

strual and pregnancy restrictions are based on private property, and that they serve to symbolize a contradiction between social production of exchange goods and private or familial appropriation. Since men too are involved in the reproductive process and are subject to the same contradiction, logically they should—and actually they do—face analogous restrictions. Lovedu, Pondo, and Ganda men must separate sexual relations from their participation in social production for exchange. By contrast, Mbuti regard the collective hunt as an ideal time for sexual liaisons.

A final point remains. Though Ganda is a class society, I have not dealt with the differences between women of ruling families and women of peasant families. There are several privileges accorded to wives, sisters, and daughters of the king. Each category of ruling-class women shares some privilege with ruling-class men: freedom from productive labor for some wives; sexual freedom for sisters and daughters; political and economic power for the queen mother and sister. In these they are distinguished from peasants. But none of these women have all the privileges of men of their class. This seems to reflect the contradictory position of ruling-class women: they are of a privileged class but of a subordinate sex. I have not dealt with them in depth because their existence does not really change the generalizations made on the basis of peasant women. This should not be surprising if we recall Queen Victoria and her times in England. But it should make one wary of generalizations based on a few women holding prominent positions.

Though I have separated women's position as wives from their position as social beings, in reality the two are very much related. Wifely subservience reduces the ability of Lovedu and Pondo women to exercise their social prerogatives. They are held back from social activities to the extent that they work under the authority of the husband and his kin. Similarly, Pondo women may become diviners, and most diviners are women. This allows women opportunities for travel, socializing, and financial reward—but a woman may not be initiated to practice without her husband's consent.

Yet things can work the other way also. If a woman is socially regarded as an adult, this can limit the extent to which she can be subordinated as a wife. Thus, although a Pondo woman's fertility may be said to belong to her husband, and although he may claim compensation for her extramarital sexual affairs, this is a matter between men. A woman regards extramarital sexual relations as proper, and is assisted in arranging them by her husband's own kinswomen. Moreover, should a woman choose to end a marriage, or visit her own kin, there is little her husband can do to prevent it.

I have suggested, then, that there are two aspects to women's position—women as social adults, and women as wives—and that these can vary somewhat independently. What determines how, or whether, women are regarded as adults is not the same thing as what determines their positions vis-à-vis their husbands. Basically, women are social adults where they work collectively as part of a productive group larger than or separate from their domestic establishment. The meaning and status of "wife," though, depend on the nature of the family in much the way Engels suggests. Where the estate is familial, and the wife works for it but does not share in its ownership, she is in much the same relationship to her husband and his kin as is a worker to his boss. Where there are no private estates, or perhaps where the family estate is jointly owned, the *domestic* relationship is a more egalitarian one (Friedl, 1967). This last point is overstated, since the domestic and social spheres of life are not really independent. On the basis of the American experience, it is difficult to conceive of a completely egalitarian domestic relationship when only the male partner is regarded as fully adult beyond the bounds of the household.

## WOMEN IN CLASS SOCIETIES: A REINTERPRETATION

When we note how the position of women declined from Mbuti and Lovedu to Ganda in this illustration, and since this is correlated with the domestication of women's work and the development of production for exchange and private property, it is tempting to conclude that Engels was right after all—that private property and production for exchange lead to women's domestication and subordination. Many anthropologists accept something like Engels's view of the relationship between private property and the growth of social inequality and classes. I too suspect that women in general stand in more equal relationship to men in non-class societies than in class societies.

But I do not think that male property ownership is the basis for male supremacy in class societies. First, not all males own productive property. Second, in many class societies women as well as men own productive property—even in societies with a strong pattern of male dominance. In the latter case, a wife's ownership of property does give her a substantial amount of domestic power in relation to her husband (Friedl, 1967). But class societies result in a sharp dichotomy between the domestic and public spheres of life, and this domestic power is not translatable into social power or position in the public sphere. Moreover, in class societies the economic and political autonomy of a household is quite restricted. Thus, in necessary dealings in the public sector women are at a disadvantage. This probably militates against even domestic equality.

It seems likely, then, that in class societies the subordinate position of women derives not from domestic property relations but from something outside the household that denies women adult social status. The question then becomes, why do class societies have male public power and ideals of male social dominance? For an explanation, the focus must shift from the domestic to the societal level.

We have seen that public or social labor is the material basis for adult social status. It follows that a society would have to exclude women from public labor to deny them social adulthood for any length of time. This seems to have been the case, at least for precapitalist agrarian states of Eurasia (Boserup, 1970). Leaving aside for the moment the obvious exception of industrial capitalism, what were the circumstances that may have led class societies to exclude women from social production?

Class societies are exploitative, which means that many people must work for the benefit of a few. Whereas tithes and taxes on domestically produced goods can serve this end, even agrarian societies do not rely exclusively or, I think, mainly on this form of production. Corvée for public works (both sumptuary and productive), conscription and predatory war, and collective agricultural or wage work for the rulers—all collective forms of social or public labor—are important productive activities in class societies. Although these may not necessarily bulk large from the local viewpoint, they are crucial nationally for creating the "surpluses" by which rulers and their states are maintained.

Though women may or may not engage in domestic agriculture, they do not seem to participate in these large-scale forms of social production. It seems that class societies tend to socialize the work of men and to domesticate that of women. This creates the material and organizational foundations for denying that women are adults, and allows ruling classes to define them as wards of men.

But why would this happen in a class society? With the development of socialized production for a ruling class, domestic production for subsistence becomes more precarious, forcing people into greater reliance on production for exchange—laboring for the rulers in exchange for their subsistence (alternatively, rulers can force people to work for them as a condition of

access to subsistence resources). Ruling classes select men as social laborers partly because they are more mobile, but probably more significantly because they can be more intensively exploited than women, not having to nurse and rear children.

Clark (1968) provides rather gruesome data from seventeenth-century England, a period *preceding* and setting the social conditions for later industrialization. Peasants were being forced off the land and were swelling a class of rural, landless laborers. The idea of wages as something paid for a task was not yet fully institutionalized. This belief contended with the earlier notion that an employer was in some way obligated to meet the subsistence needs of his workers. Yet payments were so low that a landless family was barely able to survive. A man or woman without children could survive, but prevailing remuneration did not allow for reproduction and rearing of the next generation of laborers. Indeed, they did not reproduce themselves. Clark shows that the laboring class grew in size only from constant new recruits from the peasantry. Women and children were deliberately excluded from wage work by employers, who felt an obligation to their workers but could not or would not bear the burden of supporting nonproductive dependents. In human terms the results were an abandonment of women and their early death, and in organizational terms a largely male public labor force.

Once such a dichotomy is made—women in domestic work for family use; men in social production for exchange—there is an organizational basis for a sexual divide-and-rule policy. Whether such policies are conscious or not, debates about motivation or conscious conspiracy are irrelevant here. The *effect* of state legal systems and other aspects of ideology developed mainly by ruling classes has been to convert differences between men and women in terms of their roles in production into a system of differential worth. Through their labor men are social adults; women are domestic wards.

Men are more directly exploited, and often collectively so—a situation where the possibility exists that they can act collectively to change it. Women's field of activity and major responsibility is restricted to the household, which neither produces nor owns the means of production for more than domestic subsistence—a level of organization at which little can be done to institute social change in a class society. This situation has several consequences. First, women are relegated to the bottom of a social pecking order (a *man's* home is his castle). Second, because of their isolation and exclusion from the marketplace, women can be used as a conservative force, unconsciously upholding the status quo in their commitment to the values represented by home, family, and children. Finally, the family is the sole institution with responsibility for consumption and maintenance of its members and for rearing children—the future generation of exchange workers. It is necessary labor if the system is to be perpetuated, but women are forced to perform it without compensation.

Modern capitalism has maintained this pattern of exploiting the private *domestic* labor of women, but since industrialization women have been heavily involved in public or wage labor. Meeting the heavy labor burden that capitalism places on the family remains socially women's responsibility. Responsibility for domestic work is one of the material bases for present barriers to women working for money and for placing them in a more exploitable position than men in the public labor force. As Benston shows (1969), this domestic work is not considered "real" work because it has only private use value and no exchange value—it is not public labor. Women's greater exploitability in the modern wage labor force may even derive from a preindustrial adaptation to being excluded from public labor (ironically, because women were *less* exploitable in a prewage milieu). Only after they had been defined as inadequate for public labor were the conditions right for industrial capitalism to discover women as a source of cheap labor.

In short, what I am suggesting is that inten- sive exploitation in social production by and for ruling classes favored making this men's work. In turn, ruling classes capitalized on the situation, legitimizing the division of labor by a thoroughgoing system of differential worth. In return for the loss of economic autonomy, they conferred on men exclusive social adulthood and guardianship of women. Under these circumstances, even if women own property, the state intervenes to limit what they can do with it publicly, and to subordinate the household to the larger society. The key aspect, then, of women's position, especially in class societies, is social adulthood, and this comes from participation in social production.

This brief examination of the bases of women's domestic and social status suggests some tentative conclusions about the kinds of economic and social changes necessary for full sexual equality. Although property ownership seems important for women's domestic position vis-à-vis a husband, the exercise of domestic power, particularly in class societies, is limited by whether or not women have adult status in the social sphere. This in turn is determined by their participation in social production. But the dichotomization of family and society, which is especially strong in class societies, makes women responsible for the production of private use value and makes men responsible for the production of exchange value. The distinction between production for use and production for exchange places a heavy responsibility on women to maintain themselves as well as exchange workers and to rear future exchange and maintenance workers. In this context wage work becomes an additional burden and in no way changes women's responsibility for domestic work. For full social equality, men's and women's work must be of the same kind: the production of social use values. For this to happen, family and society cannot remain separate *economic* spheres of life. Production, consumption, child rearing, and economic decision making all need to take place in a single social sphere— something analogous to the Iroquois gens as described by Engels, or the production brigades of contemporary China. That is, what is now private family work must become public work for women to become full social adults.

## REFERENCES CITED

BENSTON, MARGARET. 1969. "The Political Economy of Women's Liberation," *Monthly Review,* 21: 13–27.

BOSERUP, ESTER. 1970. Women's Role in Economic Development. New York.

CLARK, ALICE. 1968. Working Life of Women in the Seventeenth Century. London.

COHEN, YEHUDI. 1969. "Ends and Means in Political Control: State Organization and the Punishment of Adultery, Incest and the Violation of Celibacy," *American Anthropologist*, 71: 658–88.

ENGELS, FRIEDRICH. 1891. The Origin of the Family, Private Property and the State, 4th ed. Moscow.

FRIEDL, ERNESTINE. 1967. "The Position of Women: Appearance and Reality," *Anthropological Quarterly,* 40: 97–108.

HUNTER, MONICA. 1936. Reaction to Conquest. London.

KRIGE, E. J., and J. D. KRIGE. 1943. Realm of a Rain Queen. London.

ROSCOE, JOHN. 1966. The Baganda. New York.

SACKS, KAREN. 1971. "Economic Bases of Sexual Equality: A Comparative Study of Four African Societies." Ph.D. dissertation, University of Michigan.

SAHLINS, MARSHALL. 1971. Stone Age Economics. Chicago.

TURNBULL, COLIN. 1965. Wayward Servants. New York.

# CULTURAL ECOLOGY

ISSUE   India's sacred cows: Does religious belief create a cattle surplus in India?

People from most industrial societies believe they control nature, shaping it to make life more secure and comfortable. And on the surface this view seems reasonable. We are surrounded by evidence of human mastery over nature. Cities dot the countryside, covering immense areas with pavement, houses, and tall buildings. Highways cross-cut the nation, showing little respect for hills, valleys, or rivers. Open land divides into large manicured fields with neat rows of weed-free standing crops.

We like to think of these things as achievements, as the hard-earned results of an indomitable American spirit. Many anthropologists, on the other hand, see the cities, roads, and buildings as a cultural adaptation to an ever-growing population in a world of limited resource. The study of this adaptive process and of the resulting relationship between humans and the animal and natural features of their environment, is called *cultural ecology*.

Culture is a remarkable device for adaptation, as we noted in Chapter II. While most animals adjust to changes in their environment genetically, requiring many generations to develop new adaptive strategies and forms, humans can invent new responsive behaviors and make them part of their culture within a single generation. The flexibility of culture and the rapidity with which it can change have worked exceptionally well for our species. We

202

manage to live almost anywhere in the world, and we have been able to multiply our numbers by exploiting our environment more and more effectively.

The increase in population, however, has set in motion an interesting process. For millions of years our hunter-gatherer ancestors harvested the natural products of the land. Evidence indicates that many of them enjoyed a well-rounded and dependable diet without disturbing their environments too much. But success gradually resulted in a population increase; eventually the land could no longer support everyone. Agriculture was the cultural invention by which people coped with the new problem. But agriculture created a new difficulty by permitting even larger populations to live off smaller areas of land. Since the invention of agriculture over 10,000 years ago, people have been in a technological race with their own numbers. The large, complexly organized, mechanized societies like ours are the result. And, of course, the problems of population and overexploitation continue to require further technological invention and cultural adjustment.

The articles on India's sacred cattle included in this chapter reflect one kind of situation anthropologists look at as they study cultural ecology. India's population exceeds 600 million people; its total area is about one-third that of the United States. Although some years are more productive than others, hunger is a common feature of life for many Indian peasants, and starvation, while largely prevented by more effective food distribution, may surface in the slower form of malnutrition. Given this grim ecological picture, many anthropologists and economists have questioned the utility of the approximately 120 million cattle in India. They argue that Indian cattle compete with people for precious food supplies and give little by way of return. The reason for the surplus, they note, is the Indian religious value called *ahimsa,* which prohibits the taking of life, especially that of cattle. Ahimsa is ecologically irrational and potentially dangerous according to these critics.

The following articles both challenge and support the view that Indian behavior toward cattle is a detriment. Harris argues that sacred cattle are useful in India, that they inhabit an important ecological niche and play an essential role in the production of food and fuel. Heston points out that Harris' ecological objectives could be met with many fewer cows (not bulls), implying that the surplus in cows is due to the religious proscription on slaughter. Freed and Freed comment on both positions using carefully gathered data from a single village. They conclude that the number of cattle largely fit farmers' needs.

# 16

## THE CULTURAL ECOLOGY OF INDIA'S SACRED CATTLE
*Marvin Harris*

*Cultural materialism in anthropology argues that culture is largely shaped by people's material needs. Cultural institutions, including religion, should reflect the material imperative and facilitate human ecological adaptation. Marvin Harris, who is closely identified with the cultural materialist position, applies this point of view to an ecological analysis of India's cattle. He argues that far from being competitors for scarce food, cattle are essential to the Indian productive enterprise. They draw the plows that cultivate virtually all of India's farmland, provide some milk, are eaten by some low-caste people, and supply manure for cooking fires and crop fertilization. Cattle graze on wasteland and do not compete with humans for food. Although they do not slaughter cattle, Indians do cull their herds of unwanted cows through neglect. In short, India's cattle population is in balance with her ecological system.*

In this paper I attempt to indicate certain puzzling inconsistencies in prevailing interpretations of the ecological role of bovine cattle in India. My argument is based upon intensive reading—I have never seen a sacred cow, nor been to India. As a non-specialist, no doubt I have committed blunders an Indianist would have avoided. I hope these errors will not deprive me of that expert advice and informed criticism which alone can justify so rude an invasion of unfamiliar territory.

I have written this paper because I believe the irrational, non-economic, and exotic aspects of the Indian cattle complex are greatly overemphasized at the expense of rational, economic, and mundane interpretations.

My intent is not to substitute one dogma for another, but to urge that explanation of taboos, customs, and rituals associated with management of Indian cattle be sought in "positive-functioned" and probably "adaptive" processes of the ecological system of which they are a

part,[1] rather than in the influence of Hindu theology.

Mismanagement of India's agricultural resources as a result of the Hindu doctrine of *ahimsa*,[2] especially as it applies to beef cattle, is frequently noted by Indianists and others concerned with the relation between values and behavior. Although different anti-rational, dysfunctional, and inutile aspects of the cattle complex are stressed by different authors, many agree that *ahimsa* is a prime example of how men will diminish their material welfare to ob-

---

[1]The author (1960) suggested that the term "adaptive" be restricted to traits, biological or cultural, established and diffused in conformity with the principle of natural selection. Clearly, not all "positive-functioned," i.e., useful, cultural traits are so established.

[2]*Ahimsa* is the Hindu principle of unity of life, of which sacredness of cattle is principal sub-case and symbol.

tain spiritual satisfaction in obedience to nonrational or frankly irrational beliefs.

A sample opinion on this subject is here summarized: According to Simoons (1961:3), "irrational ideologies" frequently compel men "to overlook foods that are abundant locally and are of high nutritive value, and to utilize other scarcer foods of less value." The Hindu beef-eating taboo is one of Simoons' most important cases. Venkatraman (1938:706) claims, "India is unique in possessing an enormous amount of cattle without making profit from its slaughter." The Ford Foundation (1959:64) reports "widespread recognition not only among animal husbandry officials, but among citizens generally, that India's cattle population is far in excess of the available supplies of fodder and feed. . . . At least 1/3, and possibly as many as 1/2, of the Indian cattle population may be regarded as surplus in relation to feed supply." Matson (1933:227) writes it is a commonplace of the "cattle question that vast numbers of Indian cattle are so helplessly inefficient as to have no commercial value beyond that of their hides." Srinivas (1952:222) believes "Orthodox Hindu opinion regards the killing of cattle with abhorrence, even though the refusal to kill the vast number of useless cattle which exist in India today is detrimental to the nation."

According to the Indian Ministry of Information (1957:243), "The large animal population is more a liability than an asset in view of our land resources." Chatterjee (1960) calculates that Indian production of cow and buffalo milk involves a "heavy recurring loss of Rs 774 crores. This is equivalent to 6.7 times the amount we are annually spending on importing food grains." Knight (1954:141) observes that because the Hindu religion teaches great reverence for the cow, "there existed a large number of cattle whose utility to the community did not justify economically the fodder which they consumed." Das and Chatterji (1962:120) concur: "A large number of cattle in India are old and decrepit and constitute a great burden on an already impoverished land. This is due to the

prejudice among the Hindus against cow killing." Mishra (1962) approvingly quotes Lewis (1955:106): "It is not true that if economic and religious doctrines conflict the economic interest will always win. The Hindu cow has remained sacred for centuries, although this is plainly contrary to economic interest." Darling (1934:158) asserts, "By its attitude to slaughter Hinduism makes any planned improvement of cattle breeding almost impossible." According to Desai (1959:36), "The cattle population is far in excess of the available fodder and feeds."

In the *Report of the Expert Committee on the Prevention of Slaughter of Cattle in India* (Nandra, *et al.* 1955:62), the Cattle Preservation and Development Committee estimated "20 million uneconomic cattle in India." Speaking specifically of Madras, Randhawa (1961:118) insists, "Far too many useless animals which breed indiscriminately are kept and many of them are allowed to lead a miserable existence for the sake of the dung they produce. Sterility and prolonged dry periods among cows due to neglect add to the number of superfluous cattle. . . ." Mamoria (1953:268–69) quotes with approval the report of the Royal Commission on Agriculture: ". . . religious susceptibilities lie in the way of slaughter of decrepit and useless cattle and hence the cattle, however weak and poor are allowed to live . . . bulls wander about the fields consuming or damaging three times as much fodder as they need. . . . Unless the Hindu sentiment is abjured altogether the Indian cultivators cannot take a practical view of animal keeping and will continue to preserve animals many of which are quite useless from birth to death." Despite his own implicit arguments to the contrary, Mohan (1962:54) concludes, "We have a large number of surplus animals." The National Council of Applied Economic Research (1963:51) notes in Rajasthan: "The scarcity of fodder is aggravated by a large population of old and useless cattle which share scant feed resources with working and useful cattle."

The Food and Agriculture Organization (1953:109) reports, "In India, as is well-known, cattle numbers exceed economic requirements by any standard and a reduction in the number of uneconomic animals would contribute greatly to the possibilities of improving the quality and condition of those that remain." Kardel (1956:19) reported to the International Cooperation Administration, "Actually, India's 180 million cattle and 87 million sheep and goats are competing with 360 million people for a scant existence." According to Mosher (1946:124), "There are thousands of barren heifers in the Central Doab consuming as much feed as productive cows, whose only economic produce will be their hides, after they have died of a natural cause." Mayadas (1954:28) insists "Large herds of emaciated and completely useless cattle stray about trying to eke out an existence on wholly inadequate grazing." Finally, to complete the picture of how, in India, spirit triumphs over flesh, there is the assertion by Williamson and Payne (1959:137): "The . . . Hindu would rather starve to death than eat his cow."

In spite of the sometimes final and unqualified fashion in which "surplus," "useless," "uneconomic," and "superfluous" are applied to part or all of India's cattle, contrary conclusions seem admissible when the cattle complex is viewed as part of an *eco-system* rather than as a sector of a national price market. Ecologically, it is doubtful that any component of the cattle complex is "useless," i.e., the number, type, and condition of Indian bovines do not per se impair the ability of the human population to survive and reproduce. Much more likely the relationship between bovines and humans is symbiotic[3] instead of competitive. It probably represents the outcome of intense Darwinian pressures acting upon human and bovine population, cultigens, wild flora and fauna, and social structure

and ideology. Moreover presumably the degree of observance of taboos against bovine slaughter and beef-eating reflect the power of these ecological pressures rather than *ahimsa;* in other words, *ahimsa* itself derives power and sustenance from the material rewards it confers upon both men and animals. To support these hypotheses, the major aspects of the Indian cattle complex will be reviewed under the following heading: (1) Milk Production, (2) Traction, (3) Dung, (4) Beef and Hides, (5) Pasture, (6) Useful and Useless Animals, (7) Slaughter, (8) Anti-Slaughter Legislation, (9) Old-Age Homes, and (10) Natural Selection.

## MILK PRODUCTION

In India the average yield of whole milk per Zebu cow is 413 pounds, compared with the 5,000-pound average in Europe and the U.S.[4] (Kartha 1936:607; Spate 1954:231). In Madhya Pradesh yield is as low as 65 pounds, while in no state does it rise higher than the barely respectable 1,445 pounds of the Punjab (Chatterjee 1960:1347). According to the 9th Quinquennial Livestock Census (1961) among the 47,200,000 cows over 3 years old, 27,200,000 were dry and/or not calved (Chaudri and Giri 1963: 598).

These figures, however, should not be used to prove that the cows are useless or uneconomic, since milk production is a minor aspect of the sacred cow's contribution to the *eco-system.* Indeed, most Indianists agree that it is the buffalo, not the Zebu, whose economic worth must be judged primarily by milk production. Thus, Kartha (1959:225) writes, "the buffalo, and not the Zebu, is the dairy cow." This distinction is elaborated by Mamoria (1953:255):

---

[3]According to Zeuner (1954:328), "Symbiosis includes all conditions of the living-together of two different species, provided both derive advantages therefrom. Cases in which both partners benefit equally are rare." In the symbiosis under consideration, men benefit more than cattle.

[4]The U.S. Census of Agriculture (1954) showed milk production averaging from a low of 3,929 pounds per cow in the Nashville Basin sub-region to 11,112 pounds per cow in the Southern California sub-region.

Cows in the rural areas are maintained for producing bullocks rather than for milk. She-buffaloes, on the other hand, are considered to be better dairy animals than cows. The male buffaloes are neglected and many of them die or are sold for slaughter before they attain maturity.

Mohan (1962:47) makes the same point:

For agricultural purposes bullocks are generally preferred, and, therefore, cows in rural areas are primarily maintained for the production of male progeny and incidentally only for milk.

It is not relevant to my thesis to establish whether milk production is a primary or secondary objective or purpose of the Indian farmer. Failure to separate emics from etics (Harris 1964) contributes greatly to confusion surrounding the Indian cattle question. The significance of the preceding quotations lies in the agreement that cows contribute to human material welfare in more important ways than milk production. In this new context, the fact that U.S. cows produce 20 times more milk than Indian cows loses much of its significance. Instead, it is more relevant to note that, despite the marginal status of milking in the symbiotic syndrome, 46.7% of India's dairy products come from cow's milk (Chatterjee 1960:1347). How far this production is balanced by expenditures detrimental to human welfare will be discussed later.

## TRACTION

The principal positive ecological effect of India's bovine cattle is in their contribution to production of grain crops, from which about 80% of the human calorie ration comes. Some form of animal traction is required to initiate the agricultural cycle, dependent upon plowing in both rainfall and irrigation areas. Additional traction for hauling, transport, and irrigation is provided by animals, but by far their most critical kinetic contribution is plowing.

Although many authorities believe there is an overall surplus of cattle in India, others point to a serious shortage of draught animals. According to Kothavala (1934:122), "Even with . . . overstocking, the draught power available for land operations at the busiest season of the year is inadequate. . . ." For West Bengal, the National Council of Applied Economic Research (1962:56) reports:

However, despite the large number of draught animals, agriculture in the State suffers from a shortage of draught power. There are large numbers of small landholders entirely dependent on hired animal labour.

Spate (1954:36) makes the same point, "There are too many cattle in the gross, but most individual farmers have too few to carry on with." Gupta (1959:42) and Lewis and Barnouw (1958:102) say a pair of bullocks is the minimum technical unit for cultivation, but in a survey by Diskalkar (1960:87), 18% of the cultivators had only 1 bullock or none. Nationally, if we accept a low estimate of 60,000,000 rural households (Mitra 1963:298) and a high estimate of 80,-000,000 working cattle and buffaloes (Government of India 1962:76), we see at once that the allegedly excess number of cattle in India is insufficient to permit a large portion, perhaps as many as 1/3, of India's farmers to begin the agricultural cycle under conditions appropriate to their technoenvironmental system.

Much has been made of India's having 115 head of cattle per square mile, compared with 28 per square mile for the U.S. and 3 per square mile for Canada. But what actually may be most characteristic of the size of India's herd is the low ratio of cattle to people. Thus, India has 44 cattle per 100 persons, while in the U.S. the ratio is 58 per 100 and in Canada, 90 (Mamoria 1953:256). Yet, in India cattle are employed as a basic instrument of agricultural production.

Sharing of draught animals on a cooperative basis might reduce the need for additional animals. Chaudhri and Giri point out that the "big farmer manages to culitvate with a pair of bullock a much larger area than the small cultivators" (1963:596). But, the failure to develop cooperative forms of plowing can scarcely be traced to *ahimsa*. If anything, emphasis upon independent, family-sized farm units follows intensification of individual land tenure patterns and other property innovations deliberately encouraged by the British (Bhatia 1963:18 on). Under existing property arrangements, there is a perfectly good economic explanation of why bullocks are not shared among adjacent households. Plowing cannot take place at any time of the year, but must be accomplished within a few daylight hours in conformity with seasonal conditions. These are set largely by summer monsoons, responsible for about 90% of the total rainfall (Bhatia 1963:4). Writing about Orissa, Bailey (1957:74) notes:

As a temporary measure, an ox might be borrowed from a relative, or a yoke of cattle and a ploughman might be hired . . . but during the planting season, when the need is the greatest, most people are too busy to hire out or lend cattle.

According to Desai (1948:86):

. . . over vast areas, sowing and harvesting operations, by the very nature of things, begin simultaneously with the outbreak of the first showers and the maturing of crops respectively, and especially the former has got to be put through quickly during the first phase of the monsoon. Under these circumstances, reliance by a farmer on another for bullocks is highly risky and he has got, therefore, to maintain his own pair.

Dube (1955:84) is equally specific:

The cultivators who depend on hired cattle or who practice cooperative lending and borrowing of cattle cannot take the best advantage of the first rains, and this enforced wait results in untimely sowing and poor crops.

Wiser and Wiser (1963:62) describe the plight of the bullock-short farmer as follows, "When he needs the help of bullocks most his neighbors are all using theirs." And Shastri (1960:1592) points out, "Uncertainty of Indian farming due to dependence on rains is the main factor creating obstacles in the way of improvements in bullock labor."

It would seem, therefore, that this aspect of the cattle complex is not an expression of spirit and ritual, but of rain and energy.

## DUNG

In India cattle dung is the main source of domestic cooking fuel. Since grain crops cannot be digested unless boiled or baked, cooking is indispensable. Considerable disagreement exists about the total amount of cattle excrement and its uses, but even the lowest estimates are impressive. An early estimate by Lupton (1922:60) gave the BTU equivalent of dung consumed in domestic cooking as 35,000,000 tons of coal or 68,000,000 tons of wood. Most detailed appraisal is by National Council of Applied Economic Research (1959:3), which rejects H. J. Bhabha's estimate of 131,000,000 tons of coal and the Ministry of Food and Agriculture's 112,000,000 tons. The figure preferred by the NCAER is 35,000,000 tons anthracite or 40,-000,000 tons bituminous, but with a possible range of between 35–45,000,000 of anthracite dung-coal equivalent. This calculation depends upon indications that only 36% of the total wet dung is utilized as fuel (p. 14), a lower estimate than any reviewed by Saha (1956:923). These vary from 40% (Imperial Council on Agricultural Research) to 50% (Ministry of Food and Agriculture) to 66.6% (Department of Education, Health and Lands). The NCAER estimate of a dung-coal equivalent of 35,000,000 tons is therefore quite conservative; it is nonetheless an impressive amount of BTU's to be plugged into an energy system.

Kapp (1963:144 on), who discusses at length the importance of substituting tractors for bullocks, does not give adequate attention to finding cooking fuel after the bullocks are replaced. The NCAER (1959:20) conclusion that dung is cheaper than coke seems an understatement. Although it is claimed that wood resources are potentially adequate to replace dung the measures advocated do not involve *ahimsa* but are again an indictment of a land tenure system not inspired by Hindu tradition (NCAER 1959:20 on; Bansil 1958:97 on). Finally it should be noted that many observers stress the slow-burning qualities of dung and its special appropriateness for preparation of *ghi* and deployment of woman-power in the household (Lewis and Barnouw 1958:40; Mosher 1946:153).

As manure, dung enters the energy system in another vital fashion. According to Mujumdar (1960:743), 300,000,000 tons are used as fuel, 340,000,000 tons as manure, and 160,000,000 tons "wasted on hillsides and roads." Spate (1954:238) believes that 40% of dung production is spread on fields, 40% burned, and 20% "lost." Possibly estimates of the amount of dung lost are grossly inflated in view of the importance of "roads and hillsides" in the grazing pattern (see Pasture). (Similarly artificial and culture- or even class-bound judgments refer to utilization of India's night soil.) It is usually assumed that Chinese and Indian treatment of this resource are radically different, and that vast quantities of nitrogen go unused in agriculture because of Hindu-inspired definitions of modesty and cleanliness. However, most human excrement from Indian villages is deposited in surrounding fields; the absence of latrines helps explain why such fields raise 2 and 3 successive crops each year (Mosher 1946:154, 33; Bansil 1958:104.) More than usual caution, therefore, is needed before concluding that a significant amount of cattle dung is wasted. Given the conscious premium set on dung for fuel and fertilizer, thoughtful control maintained over grazing

patterns (see Pasture), and occurrence of specialized sweeper and gleaner castes, much more detailed evidence of wastage is needed than is now available. Since cattle graze on "hillsides and roads," dung dropped there would scarcely be totally lost to the *eco-system,* even with allowance for loss of nitrogen by exposure to air and sunlight. Also, if any animal dung is wasted on roads and hillsides it is not because of *ahimsa* but of inadequate pasturage suitable for collecting and processing animal droppings. The sedentary, intensive rainfall agriculture of most of the subcontinent is heavily dependent upon manuring. So vital is this that Spate (1954:239) says substitutes for manure consumed as fuel "must be supplied, and lavishly, even at a financial loss to government." If this is the case, then old, decrepit, and dry animals might have a use after all, especially when, as we shall see, the dung they manufacture employs raw materials lost to the culture-energy system unless processed by cattle, and especially when many apparently moribund animals revive at the next monsoon and provide their owners with a male calf.

## BEEF AND HIDES

Positive contributions of India's sacred cattle do not cease with milk-grazing, bullock-producing, traction, and dung-dropping. There remains the direct protein contribution of 25,000,000 cattle and buffalo which die each year (Mohan 1962:54). This feature of the *eco-system* is reminiscent of the East African cattle area where, despite the normal taboo on slaughter, natural deaths and ceremonial occasions are probably frequent enough to maintain beef consumption near the ecological limit with dairying as the primary function (Schneider 1957:278 on). Although most Hindus probably do not consume beef, the *eco-system* under consideration is not confined to Hindus. The human population includes some 55,000,000 "scheduled" exterior or untouchable groups (Hutton 1961:VII), many of whom will consume beef if given the opportunity

(Dube 1955:68–69), plus several million more Moslems and Christians. Much of the flesh on the 25,000,000 dead cattle and buffalo probably gets consumed by human beings whether or not the cattle die naturally. Indeed, could it be that without the orthodox Hindu beef-eating taboo, many marginal and depressed castes would be deprived of an occasional, but nutritionally critical, source of animal protein?

It remains to note that the slaughter taboo does not prevent depressed castes from utilizing skin, horns and hoofs of dead beasts. In 1956 16,000,000 cattle hides were produced (Randhawa 1962:322). The quality of India's huge leather industry—the world's largest—leaves much to be desired, but the problem is primarily outmoded tanning techniques and lack of capital, not *ahimsa*.

## PASTURE

The principal positive-functioned or useful contributions of India's sacred cattle to human survival and well-being have been described. Final evaluation of their utility must involve assessment of energy costs in terms of resources and human labor input which might be more efficiently expended in other activities.

Direct and indirect evidence suggests that in India men and bovine cattle do not compete for existence. According to Mohan (1962:43 on):

... the bulk of the food on which the animals subsist ... is not the food that is required for human consumption, i.e., fibrous fodders produced as incidental to crop production, and a large part of the crop residues or by-products of seeds and waste grazing.

On the contrary, "the bulk of foods (straws and crop residues) that are ploughed into the soil in other countries are converted into milk" (p. 45).

The majority of Indian cattle obtain their requirements from whatever grazing is available from straw and stalk and other residues from human food-stuffs, and are starved seasonally in the dry months when grasses wither.

In Bengal the banks and slopes of the embankments of public roads are the only grazing grounds and the cattle subsist mainly on paddy straw, paddy husks and ... coarse grass ... (Mamoria 1953:263–64).

According to Dube (1955:84), "... the cattle roam about the shrubs and rocks and eat whatever fodder is available there." This is confirmed by Moomaw (1949:96): "Cows subsist on the pasture and any coarse fodder they can find. Grain is fed for only a day or two following parturition." The character of the environmental niche reserved for cattle nourishment is described by Gourou (1963:123), based on data furnished by Dupuis (1960) for Madras:

Il faut voir clairement que le faible rendement du bétail indien n'est pas un gaspillage: ce bétail n'entre pas en concurrence avec la consommation de produits agricoles. ... ils ne leur sacrifient pas des surfaces agricoles, ou ayant un potential agricole.

NCAER (1961:57) confines this pattern for Tripura: "There is a general practice of feeding livestock on agricultural by-products such as straw, grain wastes and husks"; for West Bengal (NCAER 1962:59): "The state has practically no pasture or grazing fields, and the farmers are not in the habit of growing green fodders ... livestock feeds are mostly agricultural by-products"; and for Andhra Pradesh (NCAER 1962:52): "Cattle are stall-fed, but the bulk of the feed consists of paddy straw. ..."

The only exceptions to the rural pattern of feeding cattle on waste products and grazing them on marginal or unproductive lands involve working bullocks and nursing cows:

The working bullocks, on whose efficiency cultivation entirely depends, are usually fed with chopped bananas at the time of fodder scarcity. But the milch cows have to live in a semi-starved condition, getting what nutrition they can from grazing on the fields after their rice harvest (Gangulee 1935:17).

At present cattle are fed largely according to the season. During the rainy period they feed upon the grass which springs up on the *uncultivated* hillsides. . . . But in the dry season there is hardly any grass, and cattle wander on the *cropless* lands in an often halfstarved condition. True there is some fodder at these times in the shape of rice-straw and dried copra, but it is not generally sufficient, and is furthermore given mainly to the animals actually *working* at the time (Mayer 1952:70, italics added).

There is much evidence that Hindu farmers calculate carefully which animals deserve more food and attention. In Madras, Randhawa, et al. (1961:117) report: "The cultivators pay more attention to the male stock used for ploughing and for draft. There is a general neglect of the cow and the female calf even from birth. . . ." Similar discrimination is described by Mamoria (1953:263 on):

Many plough bullocks are sold off in winter or their rations are ruthlessly decreased whenever they are not worked in full, while milch cattle are kept on after lactation on poor and inadequate grazing. . . . The cultivator feeds his bullocks better than his cow because it pays him. He feeds his bullocks better during the busy season, when they work, than during the slack season, when they remain idle. Further, he feeds his more valuable bullocks better than those less valuable. . . . Although the draught animals and buffaloes are properly fed, the cow gets next to nothing of stall feeding. She is expected to

pick up her living on the bare fields after harvest and on the village wasteland. . . .

The previously cited NCAER report on Andhra Pradesh notes that "Bullocks and milking cows during the working season get more concentrates. . . ." (1962:52). Wiser and Wiser (1963: 71) sum up the situation in a fashion supporting Srinivas' (1958:4) observation that the Indian peasant is "nothing if he is not practical":

Farmers have become skillful in reckoning the minimum of food necessary for maintaining animal service. Cows are fed just enough to assure their calving and giving a little milk. They are grazed during the day on lands which yield very little vegetation, and are given a very sparse meal at night.

Many devout Hindus believe the bovine cattle of India are exploited without mercy by greedy Hindu owners. *Ahimsa* obviously has little to do with economizing which produces the famous *phooka* and *doom dev* techniques for dealing with dry cows. Not to Protestants but to Hindus did Gandhi (1954:7) address lamentations concerning the cow:

How we bleed her to take the last drop of milk from her, how we starve her to emaciation, how we ill-treat the calves, how we deprive them of their portion of milk, how cruelly we treat the oxen, how we castrate them, how we beat them, how we overload them. . . . I do not know that the condition of the cattle in any other part of the world is as bad as in unhappy India.

## USEFUL AND USELESS ANIMALS

How then, if careful rationing is characteristic of livestock management, do peasants tolerate the widely reported herds of useless animals? Perhaps "useless" means one thing to the peasant and quite another to the price-market-oriented agronomist. It is impossible at a distance to judge which point of view is ecologically more valid, but the peasants could be right more than the agronomists are willing to admit.

Since non-working and non-lactating animals are thermal and chemical factories which depend on waste lands and products for raw materials, judgment that a particular animal is useless cannot be supported without careful examination of its owner's household budget. Estimates from the cattle census which equate useless with dry or non-working animals are not convincing. But even if a given animal in a particular household is of less-than-marginal utility, there is an additional factor whose evaluation would involve long-range bovine biographies. The utility of a particular animal to its owner cannot be established simply by its performance during season or an animal cycle. Perhaps the whole system of Indian bovine management is alien to costing procedures of the West. There may be a kind of low-risk sweepstakes which drags on for 10 or 12 years before the losers and winners are separated.

As previously observed, the principal function of bovine cows is not their milk-producing but their bullock-producing abilities. Also established is the fact that many farmers are short of bullocks. Cows have the function primarily to produce male offspring, but when? In Europe and America, cows become pregnant under well-controlled, hence predictable, circumstances and a farmer with many animals, can count on male offspring in half the births. In India, cows become pregnant under quite different circumstances. Since cows suffer from malnutrition through restriction to marginal pasture, they conceive and deliver in unpredictable fashion. The chronic starvation of the inter-monsoon period makes the cow, in the words of Mamoria (1953:263), "an irregular breeder." Moreover, with few animals, the farmer may suffer many disappointments before a male is born. To the agriculture specialist with knowl-

edge of what healthy dairy stock look like, the hot weather herds of walking skeletons "roaming over the bare fields and dried up wastes" (Leake 1923:267) must indeed seem without economic potential. Many of them, in fact, will not make it through to the next monsoon. However, among the survivors are an unknown number still physically capable of having progeny. Evidently neither the farmer nor the specialist knows which will conceive, nor when. To judge from Bombay city, even when relatively good care is bestowed on a dry cow, no one knows the outcome: "If an attempt is made to salvage them, they have to be kept and fed for a long time. Even then, it is not known whether they will conceive or not" (Nandra, et al. 1955:9).

In rural areas, to judge a given animal useless may be to ignore the recuperative power of these breeds under conditions of erratic rainfall and unpredictable grazing opportunities. The difference of viewpoint between the farmer and the expert is apparent in Moomaw's (1949) incomplete attempt to describe the life history of an informant's cattle. The farmer in question had 3 oxen, 2 female buffaloes, 4 head of young cattle and 3 "worthless" cows (p. 23). In Moomaw's opinion, "The three cows . . . are a liability to him, providing no income, yet consuming feed which might be placed to better use." Yet we learn, "The larger one had a calf about once in three years"; moreover 2 of the 3 oxen were "raised" by the farmer himself. (Does this mean that they were the progeny of the farmer's cows?) The farmer tells Moomaw, "The young stock get some fodder, but for the most part they pasture with the village herd. The cows give nothing and I cannot afford to feed them." Whereupon Moomaw's *non sequitur:* "We spoke no more of his cows, for like many a farmer he just keeps them, without inquiring whether it is profitable or not" (p. 25).

The difficulties in identifying animals that are definitely uneconomic for a given farmer are reflected in the varying estimates of the total of such animals. The Expert Committee on the Prevention of Slaughter of Cattle estimated 20,000,000 uneconomic cattle in India (Nandra, *et al.* 1953:62). Roy (1955:14) settles for 5,500,000, or about 3.5%. Mamoria (1953:257), who gives the still lower estimate of 2,900,000, or 2.1%, claims most of these are males. A similarly low percentage—2.5%—is suggested for West Bengal (NCAER 1962:56). None of these estimates appears based on bovine life histories in relation to household budgets; none appears to involve estimates of economic significance of dung contributions of older animals.

Before a peasant is judged a victim of Oriental mysticism, might it not be well to indicate the devastating material consequences which befall a poor farmer unable to replace a bullock lost through disease, old age, or accident? Bailey (1957:73) makes it clear that in the economic life of the marginal peasantry, "Much the most devastating single event is the loss of an ox (or a plough buffalo)." If the farmer is unable to replace the animal with one from his own herd, he must borrow money at usurious rates. Defaults on such loans are the principal causes of transfer of land titles from peasants to landlords. Could this explain why the peasant is not overly perturbed that some of his animals might turn out to be only dung-providers? After all, the real threat to his existence does not arise from animals but from people ready to swoop down on him as soon as one of his beasts falters. Chapekar's (1960:27) claim that the peasant's "stock serve as a great security for him to fall back on whenever he is in need" would seem to be appropriate only in reference to the unusually well-established minority. In a land where life expectancy at birth has only recently risen to 30 years (Black 1959:2), it is not altogether appropriate to speak of security. The poorest farmers own insufficient stock. Farm management studies show that holdings below 2/3 of average area account for 2/5 of all farms, but maintain only 1/4 of the total cattle on farms. "This is so, chiefly because of their limited resources to

maintain cattle" (Chaudhri and Giri 1963: 598).

## SLAUGHTER

Few, if any, Hindu farmers kill their cattle by beating them over the head, severing their jugular veins or shooting them. But to assert that they do not kill their animals when it is economically important for them to do so may be equally false. This interpretation escapes the notice of so many observers because the slaughtering process receives recognition only in euphemisms. People will admit that they "neglect" their animals, but will not openly accept responsibility for the *etic* effects, i.e., the more or less rapid death which ensues. The strange result of this euphemistic pattern is evidenced in the following statement by Moomaw (1949:96): "All calves born, however inferior, are allowed to live until they die of neglect." In the light of many similar but, by Hindu standards, more vulgar observations, it is clear that this kind of statement should read, "Most calves born are not allowed to live, but are starved to death."

This is roughly the testimony of Gourou (1963:125), "Le paysan conserve seulement les veaux qui deviendront boeufs de labour ou vaches laitières; les autres sont écartés . . . et meurent d'epuisement." Wiser and Wiser (1963:70) are even more direct:

Cows and buffaloes too old to furnish milk are not treated cruelly, but simply allowed to starve. The same happens to young male buffaloes. . . . The males are unwanted and little effort is made to keep them alive.

Obviously, when an animal, undernourished to begin with, receives neither food nor care, it will not enjoy a long life (compare Gourou 1963:124). Despite claims that an aged and decrepit cow "must be supported like an unproductive relative, until it dies a natural death" (Mosher 1946:124), ample evidence justifies belief that "few cattle die of old age"[5] (Bailey 1957:75). Dandekar (1964:352) makes the same point: "In other words, because the cows cannot be fed nor can they be killed, they are neglected, starved and left to die a 'natural' death."

The farmer culls his stock by starving unwanted animals and also, under duress, sells them directly or indirectly to butchers. With economic pressure, many Indians who will not kill or eat cows themselves:

are likely to compromise their principles and sell to butchers who slaughter cows, thereby tacitly supporting the practice for other people. Selling aged cows to butchers has over the centuries become an accepted practice alongside the *mos* that a Hindu must not kill cattle (Roy 1955:15).

Determining the number of cattle slaughtered by butchers is almost as difficult as determining the number killed by starvation. According to Dandekar (1964:351), "Generally it is the useless animals that find their way to the slaughter house." Lahiry (n.d.:140) says only 126,900 or .9% of the total cattle population is slaughtered per year. Darling (1934:158) claims:

All hindus object to the slaughter and even to the sale of unfit cows and keep them indefinitely . . . rather than sell them to a cattle

_____

[5]Srinivas (1962:126) declared himself properly skeptical in this matter: "It is commonly believed that the peasant's religious attitude to cattle comes in the way of the disposal of useless cattle. Here again, my experience of Rampura makes me skeptical of the general belief. I am not denying that cattle are regarded as in some sense sacred, but I doubt whether the belief is as powerful as it is claimed to be. I have already mentioned that bull-buffaloes are sacrificed to village goddesses. And in the case of the cow, while the peasant does not want to kill the cow or bull himself he does not seem to mind very much if someone else does the dirty job out of his sight."

dealer, who would buy only for the slaughter house, they send them to a *gowshala* or let them loose to die. Some no doubt sell secretly, but this has its risk in an area where public opinion can find strong expression through the *panchayat.*

Such views would seem to be contradicted by Sinha (1961:95): "A large number of animals are slaughtered privately and it is very difficult to ascertain their numbers." The difficulty of obtaining accurate estimates is also implied by the comment of the Committee on the Prevention of Slaughter that "90% of animals not approved for slaughter are slaughtered stealthily outside of municipal limits" (Nandra, *et al.* 1955:11).

An indication of the propensity to slaughter cattle under duress is found in connection with the food crisis of World War II. With rice imports cut off by Japanese occupation of Burma (Thirumalai 1954:38; Bhatia 1963:309 on), increased consumption of beef by the armed forces, higher prices for meat and foodstuffs generally, and famine conditions in Bengal, the doctrine of *ahimsa* proved to be alarmingly ineffectual. Direct military intervention was required to avoid destruction of animals needed for plowing, milking, and bullock-production:

During the war there was an urgent need to reduce or to avoid the slaughter for food of animals useful for breeding or for agricultural work. For the summer of 1944 the slaughter was prohibited of: 1) Cattle below three years of age; 2) Male cattle between two and ten years of age which were being used or were likely to be used as working cattle; 3) All cows between three and ten years of age, other than cows which were unsuitable for bearing offspring; 4) All cows which were pregnant or in milk (Knight 1954:141).

Gourou (1963:124–25), aware that starvation and neglect are systematically employed to cull Indian herds, nonetheless insists that destruction of animals through starvation amounts to an important loss of capital. This loss is attributed to the low price of beef caused by the beef-eating taboo, making it economically infeasible to send animals to slaughter. Gourou's appraisal, however, neglects deleterious consequences to the rural tanning and carrion-eating castes if increased numbers of animals went to the butchers. Since the least efficient way to convert solar energy into comestibles is to impose an animal converter between plant and man (Cottrell 1955), it should be obvious that without major technical and environmental innovations or drastic population cuts, India could not tolerate a large beef-producing industry. This suggests that insofar as the beef-eating taboo helps discourage growth of beef-producing industries, it is part of an ecological adjustment which maximizes rather than minimizes the calorie and protein output of the productive process.

## ANTI-SLAUGHTER LEGISLATION AND GOWSHALAS

It is evident from the history of anti-slaughter agitation and legislation in India that more than *ahimsa* has been required to protect Indian cattle from premature demise. Unfortunately, this legislation is misinterpreted and frequently cited as evidence of the anti-economic effect of Hinduism. I am unable to unravel all the tangled economic and political interests served by the recent anti-slaughter laws of the Indian states. Regardless of the ultimate ecological consequences of these laws, however, several points deserve emphasis. First it should be recalled that cow protection was a major political weapon in Ghandi's campaign against both British and Moslems. The sacred cow was the ideological focus of a successful struggle against English colonialism; hence the enactment of total anti-slaughter legislation obviously had a rational base, at least among politicians who seized and retained power on anti-English and anti-Moslem

platforms. It is possible that the legislation will now backfire and upset the delicate ecological balance which now exists. The Committee on the Prevention of Slaughter claimed that it

> actually saw in Pepsu (where slaughter is banned completely what a menace wild cattle can be. Conditions have become so desperate there, that the State Government have got to spend a considerable sum for catching and redomesticating wild animals to save the crops (Nandra, *et al.* 1955:11).

According to Mayadas (1954:29):

> The situation has become so serious that it is impossible in some parts of the country to protect growing crops from grazing by wandering cattle. Years ago it was one or two stray animals which could either be driven off or sent to the nearest cattle pound. Today it is a question of constantly being harassed day and night by herds which must either feed on one's green crops, or starve. How long can this state of affairs be allowed to continue?

Before the deleterious effects of slaughter laws can be properly evaluated, certain additional evolutionary and functional possibilities must be examined. For example, given the increasing growth rate of India's human population, the critical importance of cattle in the *eco-system,* and the absence of fundamental technical and environmental changes, a substantial increase in cattle seems necessary and predictable, regardless of slaughter legislation. Furthermore, there is some indication, admittedly incomplete but certainly worthy of careful inquiry, that many who protest most against destructiveness of marauding herds of useless beasts may perceive the situation from very special vantage points in the social hierarchy. The implications of the following newspaper editorial are clear:

> The alarming increase of stray and wild cattle over wide areas of Northern India is fast

becoming a major disincentive to crop cultivation.... Popular sentiment against cow slaughter no doubt lies at the back of the problem. People prefer to let their aged, diseased, and otherwise useless cattle live at the expense of *other people's crops* (Indian Express, New Delhi, 7 February 1959, italics added).

Evidently we need to know something about whose crops are threatened by these marauders. Despite post-Independence attempts at land reform, 10% of the Indian agricultural population still owns more than 1/2 the total cultivated area and 15,000,000, or 22%, of rural households own no land at all (Mitra 1963:298). Thorner and Thorner (1962:3) call the land reform program a failure, and point out how "the grip of the larger holder serves to prevent the lesser folk from developing the land.... Quite possibly, in other words, the anti-slaughter laws, insofar as they are effective, should be viewed as devices which, contrary to original political intent, bring pressure to bear upon those whose lands are devoted to cash crops of benefit only to narrow commercial, urban, and landed sectors of the population. To have one's cows eat other people's crops may be a very fine solution to the subsistence problem of those with no crops of their own. Apparently, in the days when animals could be driven off or sent to the pound with impunity, this could not happen, even though *ahimsa* reigned supreme then as now.

Some form of anti-slaughter legislation was required and actually argued for, on unambiguously rational, economic, and material grounds. About 4% of India's cattle are in the cities (Mohan 1962:48). These have always represented the best dairy stock, since the high cost of feeding animals in a city could be offset only by good milking qualities. A noxious consequence of this dairy pattern was the slaughter of the cow at the end of its first urban lactation period because it was too expensive to maintain while awaiting another pregnancy. Similarly, and by methods previously discussed, the author calf was killed

after it had stimulated the cow to "let down." With the growth of urban milk consumption, the best of India's dairy cattle were thus systematically prevented from breeding, while animals with progressively poorer milking qualities were preserved in the countryside (Mohan 1962:48; Mayadas 1954:29; Gandhi 1954:13 on). The Committee on the Prevention of Slaughter of Cattle (Nandra, *et al.* 1955:2) claimed at least 50,000 high-yielding cows and she-buffaloes from Madras, Bombay, and Calcutta were "annually sent to premature slaughter" and were "lost to the country." Given such evidence of waste and the political potential of Moslems being identified as cow-butchers and Englishmen as cow-eaters (Gandhi 1954:16), the political importance of *ahimsa* becomes more intelligible. Indeed, it could be that the strength of Gandhi's *charisma* lay in his superior understanding of the ecological significance of the cow, especially in relation to the underprivileged masses, marginal low caste and out caste farmers. Gandhi (p. 3) may have been closer to the truth than many a foreign expert when he said:

Why the cow was selected for apotheosis is obvious to me. The cow was in India the best companion. She was the giver of plenty. Not only did she give milk but she also made agriculture possible.

## OLD-AGE HOMES

Among the more obscure aspects of the cattle complex are bovine old-age homes, variously identified as *gowshalas, pinjrapoles,* and, under the Five-Year Plans, as *gosadans.* Undoubtedly some of these are "homes for cows, which are supported by public charity, which maintain the old and derelict animals till natural death occurs" (Kothavala 1934:123). According to Gourou (1963:125), however, owners of cows sent to these religious institutions pay rent with the understanding that if the cows begin to lactate they will be returned. The economics of at least some of these "charitable" institutions is, therefore, perhaps not as quaint as usually implied. It is also significant that, although the 1st Five-Year Plan called for establishment of 160 *gosadans* to serve 320,000 cattle, only 22 *gosadans* servicing 8,000 cattle were reported by 1955 (Government of India Planning Commission 1956:283).

## NATURAL SELECTION

Expert appraisers of India's cattle usually show little enthusiasm for the typical undersized breeds. Much has been made of the fact that 1 large animal is a more efficient dung, milk, and traction machine than 2 small ones. "Weight for weight, a small animal consumes a much larger quantity of food than a bigger animal" (Marmoria 1953:268). "More dung is produced when a given quantity of food is consumed by one animal than when it is shared by two animals" (Ford Foundation 1959:64). Thus it would seem that India's smaller breeds should be replaced by larger, more powerful, and better milking breeds. But once again, there is another way of looking at the evidence. It might very well be that if all of India's scrub cattle were suddenly replaced by an equivalent number of large, high-quality European or American dairy and traction animals, famines of noteworthy magnitude would immediately ensue. Is it not possible that India's cattle are undersized precisely because other breeds never could survive the atrocious conditions they experience most of the year? I find it difficult to believe that breeds better adapted to the present Indian *eco-system* exist elsewhere.

By nature and religious training, the villager is unwilling to inflict pain or to take animal life. But the immemorial grind for existence has hardened him to an acceptance of survival of the fittest (Wiser and Wiser 1963).

Not only are scrub animals well adapted to the regular seasonal crises of water and forage and general year-round neglect, but long-range selective pressures may be even more significant. The high frequency of drought-induced famines in India (Bhatia 1963) places a premium upon drought-resistance plus a more subtle factor: A herd of smaller animals, dangerously thinned by famine or pestilence, reproduces faster than an equivalent group of larger animals, despite the fact that the larger animal consumes less per pound than 2 smaller animals. This is because there are 2 cows in the smaller herd per equivalent large cow. Mohan (1962:45) is one of the few authorities to have grasped this principle, including it in defense of the small breeds:

> Calculations of the comparative food conversion efficiency of various species of Indian domestic livestock by the writer has revealed, that much greater attention should be paid to small livestock than at present, not only because of their better conversion efficiency for protein but also because of the possibilities of bringing about a rapid increase in their numbers.

## CONCLUSION

The probability that India's cattle complex is a positive-functioned part of a naturally selected *eco-system* is at least as good as that it is a negative-functioned expression of an irrational ideology. This should not be interpreted to mean that no "improvements" can be made in the system, nor that different systems may not eventually evolve. The issue is not whether oxen are more efficient than tractors. I suggest simply that many features of the cattle complex have been erroneously reported or interpreted. That Indian cattle are weak and inefficient is not denied, but there is doubt that this situation arises from and is mainly perpetuated by Hindu ideology. Given the techno-environmental base,

Indian property relationships, and political organization, one need not involve the doctrine of *ahimsa* to understand fundamental features of the cattle complex. Although the cattle population of India has risen by 38,000,000 head since 1940, during the same period, the human population has risen by 120,000,000. Despite the anti-slaughter legislation, the ratio of cattle to humans actually declined from 44:100 in 1941 to 40:100 in 1961 (Government of India 1962:74; 1963:6). In the absence of major changes in environment, technology or property relations, it seems unlikely that the cattle population will cease to accompany the rise in the human population. If *ahimsa* is negative-functioned, then we must be prepared to admit the possibility that all other factors contributing to the rapid growth of the Indian human and cattle populations, including the germ theory of disease, are also negative-functioned.

## REFERENCES CITED

ANSTEY, VERA. 1952. *The economic development of India.* New York: Longmans, Green.

BAILEY, F. G. 1957. *Caste and the economic frontier.* Manchester: University of Manchester Press.

BANSIL, P. C. 1958. *India's food resources and population,* p. 104. Bombay: Vora. p. 97 (if 1959).

BHATIA, B. M. 1963. *Famines in India.* New York: Asia Publishing House.

BLACK, JOHN D. 1959. Supplementary to the Ford Foundation team's report: India's food crisis and steps to meet it. *The Indian Journal of Agricultural Economics* 14:1–6

CHAPEKAR, L. N. 1960. *Thakurs of the Sabyadri.* Oxford: Oxford University Press.

CHATTERJEE, I. 1960. Milk production in India. *Economic Weekly* 12:1347–48.

CHAUDHRI, S. C., and R. GIRI. 1963. Role of cattle in India's economy. *Agricultural situation in India* 18:591–99.

COTTRELL, FRED. 1955. *Energy and society.* New York: McGraw-Hill.

DANDEKAR, U. M. 1964. Problem of numbers in cattle development. *Economic Weekly* 16:351–355.

DARLING, M. L. 1934. *Wisdom and waste in a Punjab village.* London: Oxford University Press.

DAS, A. B., and M. N. CHATTERJI. 1962. *The Indian economy.* Calcutta: Bookland Private.

DESAI, M. B. 1948. *The rural economy of Gujarat.* Bombay: Oxford University Press.

———. 1959. India's food crisis. *The Indian Journal of Agricultural Economics* 14:27–37.

DISKALKAR, P. D. 1960. *Resurvey of a Deccan village Pimple Sandagar.* Bombay: The Indian Society of Agricultural Economics.

DUBE, S. C. 1955. *Indian village.* Ithaca: Cornell University Press.

DUPUIS, J. 1960. *Madras et le nord du Coromandel; étude des conditions de la vie indienne dans un cadre géografique.* Paris: Maisonneuve.

FOOD AND AGRICULTURE ORGANIZATION. 1953. *Agriculture in Asia and the Far East: Development and outlook.* Rome: FAO.

FORD FOUNDATION. 1959. *Report on India's food crisis and steps to meet it.* New Delhi: Government of India, Ministry of Food and Agriculture and Ministry of Community Development and Cooperation.

GANDHI, M. K. 1954. *How to serve the cow.* Edited by Bharaton Kumarappa. Ahmedabad: Navajivan Publishing House.

GANGULEE, N. 1935. *The Indian peasant and his environment.* London: Oxford University Press.

GOUROU, PIERRE. 1963. Civilization et economie pastorale. *L'Homme* 123–29.

GOVERNMENT OF INDIA. 1956. *Second five-year plan.* Planning Commission. New Delhi.

———. 1957. *India.* Ministry of Information and Broadcasting. New Delhi.

———. 1962. *Statistical Abstract of the Indian Union* 11. Cabinet Secretariat. New Delhi.

———. 1963. *India.* Ministry of Information and Broadcasting. New Delhi.

GUPTA, S. C. 1959. *An economic survey of Shamaspur village.* New York: Asia Publishing House.

HARRIS, MARVIN. 1959. The economy has no surplus? *American Anthropologist* 61:185–99.

———. 1960. Adaptation in biological and cultural science. *Transactions of the New York Academy of Sciences* 23:59–65.

——. 1964a. *The nature of cultural things.* New York: Random House.

HOPPER, W. DAVID. 1955. Seasonal labour cycles in an eastern Uttar Pradesh village. *Eastern Anthropologist* 8:141–50.

HUTTON, J. H. 1961. *Caste in India,* p. VII. London: Oxford University Press.

KAPP, K. W. 1963. *Hindu culture, economic development and economic planning in India.* New York: Asia Publishing House.

KARDEL, HANS. 1956. *Community development in agriculture: Mysore State, India,* Washington, D.C.: International Cooperation Administration.

KARTHA, K. P. R. 1936. A note on the comparative economic efficiency of the Indian cow, the half breed cow, and the buffalo as producers of milk and butter fat. *Agriculture and Livestock in India* 4:605–23.

——. 1959. "Buffalo," in *An introduction to animal husbandry in the Tropics.* Edited by G. Williamson and W. J. A. Payne. London: Longmans, Green.

KNIGHT, HENRY. 1954. *Food administration in India 1939–47.* Stanford: Stanford University Press.

KOTHAVALA, ZAL R. 1934. Milk production in India. *Agriculture and Livestock in India* 2:122–29.

LAHIRY, N. L. n.d. "Conservation and utilization of animal food resources," in Proceedings of symposium on food needs and resources. *Bulletin of the National Institute of Sciences of India* 20:140–44.

LEAKE, H. MARTIN. 1923. *The foundations of Indian agriculture.* Cambridge: W. Heffer.

LEWIS, OSCAR, and VICTOR BARNOUW. 1958. *Village life in northern India.* Urbana: University of Illinois Press.

LEWIS, W. A. 1955. *The theory of economic growth.* Homewood, Ill.: R. D. Irwin.

LUPTON, ARNOLD. 1922. *Happy India.* London: G. Allen & Unwin.

MAMORIA, C. B. 1953. *Agricultural problems of India.* Allahabad: Kitab Mahal.

MATSON, J. 1933. Inefficiency of cattle in India through disease. *Agriculture and Livestock in India* 1:227–28.

MAYADAS, C. 1954. *Between us and hunger.* London: Oxford University Press.

MAYER, ADRIAN. 1952. *Land and society in Malabar.* Bombay: Oxford University Press.

MISHRA, VIKAS. 1962. *Hinduism and economic growth.* London: Oxford University Press.

MITRA, ASHOK. 1963. "Tax burden for Indian agriculture," in *Traditions, values, and socio-economic development.* Edited by R. Braibanti and J. J. Spengler, pp. 281–303. Durham: Duke University Press.

MOHAN, S. N. 1962. Animal husbandry in the Third Plan. *Bulletin of the National Institute of Sciences of India* 20:41–54.

MOOMAW, I. W. 1949. *The farmer speaks.* London: Oxford University Press.

MOSHER, ARTHUR T. 1946. *The economic effects of Hindu religion and social traditions on agricultural production by Christians in North India.* Unpublished Ph.D. dissertation, University of Chicago. (Also microfilms T 566.)

MUJUMDAR, N. A. 1960. Cow dung as manure. *Economic Weekly* 12:743–44.

NANDRA, P. N., et al. 1955. Report of the expert committee on the prevention of *slaughter of cattle in India.* New Delhi: Government of India Press.

NATIONAL COUNCIL OF APPLIED ECONOMIC RESEARCH. 1959. *Domestic fuels in India.* New York: Asia Publishing House.

——. 1960. *Techno-economic survey of Madhya Pradesh.* New Delhi.

——. 1961. *Techno-economic survey of Tripura.* New Delhi.

——. 1962a. *Techno-economic survey of Andhra Pradesh.* New Delhi.

——. 1962b. *Techno-economic survey of Punjab.* New Delhi.

——. 1962c. *Techno-economic survey of West Bengal.* New Delhi.

——. 1963. *Techno-economic survey of Rajasthan.* New Delhi.

OPLER, MARVIN K. 1956. Review of *The art of Indian Asia,* by H. Zimmer, as edited by J. Campbell (New York: Pantheon Books, 1955). *Philosophy and Phenomenological Research* 17:269–71.

RAM, L. 1927. *Cow-protection in India.* Madras: South Indian Humanitarian League.

RANDHAWA, M. S. 1962. *Agriculture and animal hus-*

bandry in India. New Delhi. Indian Council of
Agricultural Research.

RANDHAWA, M. S., et al. 1961. Farmers of India. 2
vols. New Delhi: Indian Council of Agricultural
Research.

ROY, PRODIPTO. 1955. The sacred cow in India. Rural
sociology 20:8–15.

SAHA, M. N. 1956. Fuel in India. Nature 177:923–
24.

SCHNEIDER, HAROLD. 1957. The subsistence role of
cattle among the Pakot and in East Africa. American Anthropologist 59:278–300.

SHAHANI, K. M. 1957. Dairying in India. Journal of
Dairying Science 40:867–73.

SHASTRI, C. P. 1960. Bullock labour utilization in agriculture. Economic Weekly 12:1585–92.

SIMOONS, F. J. 1961. Eat not this flesh. Madison: University of Wisconsin Press.

SINHA, R. P. 1961. Food in India. London: Oxford
University Press.

SPATE, OSKAR HERMANN. 1954. India and Pakistan: A
general and regional geography. London: Methuen.

SRINIVAS, M. N. 1952. Religion and society among the
Coorgs of South India. Oxford: Oxford University
Press.

————. 1958. India's cultural values and economic
development. Economic Development and cultural change 7:3–6.

————. 1962. Caste in modern India. New York: Asia
Publishing House.

THIRUMALAI, SHRI. 1954. Post-war agricultural problems and policies in India, p. 38. New York: Institute of Pacific Relations.

THORNER, DANIEL, and ALICE THORNER. 1962. Land
and labour in India. New York: Asia Publishing
House.

U.S. CENSUS OF AGRICULTURE. 1954. "Dairy producers and dairy production." in Farmers and
farm production in the United States 3, part 9,
chap. V.

VENKATRAMAN, R. B. 1938. The Indian village, its
past, present, future. Agriculture and Livestock in
India 7:702–10.

WILLIAMSON, G., and W. J. A. PAYNE. 1959. An introduction to animal husbandry in the Tropics. London: Longmans, Green.

WISER, WILLIAM H., and C. V. WISER. 1963. Behind
mud walls: 1930–1960. Berkeley: University of
California Press.

ZEUNER, F. E. 1954. "Domestication of animals," in
A history of technology. Edited by C. Singer, et al.,
pp. 327–52. New York: Oxford University Press.

# 17

# AN APPROACH TO THE SACRED COW OF INDIA

## Alan Heston

*Alan Heston is an economist and India specialist. In this paper, he disagrees with Harris's
position on the overall utility of cattle in India by challenging two of Harris's conclusions.
First, argues Heston, Indian cattle do compete with people for precious food resources.
Using Indian government statistics as well as data collected by other researchers, he points
out that cattle consume about 2.5 percent of India's human food supply. Second, he
asserts that the number of bullocks now found in India could be produced by far fewer
cows. With their numbers reduced, the smaller population of animals would be healthier,
produce just as much manure, and still be available for work. On this basis, the Indian
religious proscription against killing cows does result in an excess population of females.*

The large cattle population of India has long interested travelers, social reformers, district officers, commissions of inquiry, orthodox Hindus, nonvegetarians, and the Editors of *Life*. To many, reverence for the cow is the "one thing" that has led to the impoverishment of India (though to others the "one thing" is land fragmentation, caste, use of ghi, or, recently, human population). While most Western observers and many Indians view the cattle population as excessive, expert groups, like the Ford Foundation team (1959:66), have argued that any policy must take account of the strong religious attitudes which have affected the cow population. In contrast, Harris (1966) has made a strong attack on both the view that cattle are in excess and the view that religious attitudes towards cattle are useful in explaining characteristics of the Indian cattle population. Harris attempts to show that, viewed in the large context of the balance between cattle, land and crops, and humans, most features of the cow population in India can be explained in terms of adjustment to their environment. To him, the "cultural ecology of India's sacred cattle" does not appear out of balance.[1]

Although he argues that India's cattle economy is in ecological balance, Harris vehemently denies (1967:253) that this balance produces optimal results. Evolutionary development in Indian agriculture, he asserts, will lead to better uses of cattle. He does not deny, however, and apparently affirms, that the Indian cattle population is the best possible configuration under present conditions. If his argument is an empirical assertion about the Indian economy, then he must consider the possibility that alternative cattle complexes might exist under present conditions; that the present cattle population might be

in some way poorly adapted to the environment and the goals of Indians; and that the present population might be explained in part by religion. If for Harris there is one and only one adaptation of the cattle population to present ecological conditions, then of course his is not an empirical assertrion, since the circumstances under which it would be false can never be realized. While much of Harris' discussion sounds deterministic, and indeed he says that it is (Harris 1968:4), I cannot accept this interpretation. It would, for one thing, make his article unnecessary, since there could never have been doubt about whether the Indian cattle population was in balance. Secondly, it would leave no grounds upon which economists and cultural ecologists could carry on discussion; and since I feel that they have much to learn from each other I would like to believe that there is a basis for a meaningful exchange of ideas.

My own approach to the cattle question in India is an economic one and is, I believe, more useful than that of Harris. What Harris does is find that for most aspects of the Indian cattle population there are sensible explanations that do not need to fall back on custom or religion. Most of these observations, while not generally wrong, are either not specific enough or not relevant to the question of whether the cattle population is in excess. An illustration of the lack of specificity is the fact that Harris makes no real attempt to discuss the relative numbers of males and females, which, as I will show, is at the center of the problem. The lack of relevance of most of Harris' remarks is due to his particular framework. It is perfectly possible that individual peasants are sensible in their handling of cattle and that the sum of their individual actions nevertheless adds up to a poor allocation of cattle for the economy as a whole. Since Harris does not look at the specific facts at the farm level, let alone the overall figures for India, he is evidently led to believe that because the peasant has reasons for what he does with cattle, the existing number of cattle is appropriate for present conditions.

The approach of the economist to the ques-

---

[1]Harris' article received a number of responses; I have relied on several of these, particularly that by Bennett (1967). I also acknowledge a large intellectual debt to Brown (1964) for his doctrinal article on the cow, to Dandekar (1964) for his paper on what might be called cow economics, and to Arnold Green for very useful comments on an earlier draft of the paper.

tion is to ask whether alternative cattle populations (or alternative uses of the resources embodied in the population) under the present rural conditions could increase the satisfaction of the society.[2] I argue that in India, if cow slaughter were allowed, the cattle population could be substantially reduced, the output of the cattle could be increased, and land would be freed for production of other crops. Further, I show that even with no cow slaughter at all (this is not a part of Harris' argument; he apparently believes that the appropriate number are slaughtered), the cattle allocation under existing institutions could be improved by presently known methods. As a part of this presentation I also show that the present Indian cattle complex appears to be definitely influenced by the Indian tradition of *ahimsa* (nonviolence) and the Hindu reverence for the cow.

# I

Cattle, while producing power, milk, and other products, are also competitors with humans for land. If cattle did not compete for land or other resources with man or with other pro-

ductive animals (as may be the case in hilly tracts), they could not be in excess from the economic point of view. On this point Harris makes what I think is a major misinterpretation of the Indian scene. He says (1966:55): "Direct and indirect evidence suggests that in India men and bovine cattle do not compete for existence." He goes on to say that most cattle feed in India comes from grain by-products, for which the alternative is not human consumption but, at best, mulch. He points out, further, that many of India's scrawniest cattle are not fed at all, but are left to chew stubble remaining in the field or otherwise scrounge for their feed. Harris notes that for the individual cultivator it may make sense to let females, which might possibly breed sometime, scrounge for their feed. It costs the peasant nothing, and the gains are some dung, a hide, and perhaps a work animal—or the cow might perchance be hit by a car, and the driver, Indian or foreigner, made to compensate the owner for the loss of such a valuable animal.

While none of what Harris says about feed and use of waste products by cattle is wrong, it does not follow that cattle do not compete with humans. India devotes 5% of her acreage to fodder crops. Feed for all livestock was valued in 1958–59 at Rs. 5.74 billion. Stalks, straw, husk, sugarcane tufts, and bran represented slightly more than half of this amount, Rs. 2.93 billion (Government of India 1961:61–63). These feeds are by-products of grain, sugar, and other crops, and while they have alternative uses, including export, they are not directly consumed by humans. The remaining feed is fodder crops, cereals, pulses, and concentrates that directly use land that could be planted to crops for human consumption. In addition, several rotations of Indian crops include grains with a large amount of feed by-product—because people will pay for rice bran or jowar grass. The value of the milk and power of bullocks and cows justifies spending money to feed some fraction of the cattle population, but another significant proportion is left to graze where it can. Because

---

[2]Satisfaction here is measured by the money value of goods and services produced in a given time period. Clearly, in treating cattle in India the outputs should go beyond power, milk, and hides, since part of the production is the presence of cows themselves. Conventionally, for instance, the output of pets and zoos in the United States can only be approximated by the expenditure on cat food, fish tanks, zoo keepers, etc. With productive animals, however, the cost of their feed is customarily subtracted from the gross value of milk and other agricultural products to arrive at output net of the cost of maintaining milk and work animals. To the extent that cattle are also maintained partly as pets, the value of their presence, as approximated by the cost of their feed, might be included in national income, contrary to present practice.

pasture for grazing is in short supply, many of the animals left to themselves die off, though not from old age.

If a large fraction of the cattle population were not allowed to graze freely but were somehow (to be discussed below) removed, there would be more cattle feed available to the remaining cattle. Less land would be needed for fodder crops, and hence more land would be available for human uses. It is in this sense that the cattle population competes with the human population. It is not that the marginal cow is eating feed that humans want, but that she eats feed that other productive animals could eat, and these latter animals are using resources, like fodder acreage, in direct competition with humans. However, competition of cattle with man for land need not imply that the cattle population is in excess; to deal with this question we must turn to a discussion of cattle, both male and female.

## II

The cow in India is worshipped as a symbol of warmth and moisture, as earth mother, and as producer of milk and indirectly ghi, so essential in sacrifices. She is also protected because of the principle of nonviolence to living things *(ahimsa)*. The Indian respect for the cow has many specific characteristics, but also shows similarities to beliefs found in some African societies, where cattle are sometimes called the "gods with the wet noses" (Southworth and Johnson 1967:219).[3] Though cow protection in

India refers to the "cow and her progeny," and Nanda and other bulls are important minor deities, there are additional sanctions which single out the female cow for special consideration. *Go,* "cow," refers to both male and female, but when a Hindu says, *"Go hamārīe mātā hai,"* he is likening the female cow, not the bull or bullock, to our mother. The special consideration shown females, which as we shall see, are in excess if any cattle are, is illustrated by the slaughterhouse statistics. In 1958–59, for example, 122,000 bullocks and only 10,000 cows were slaughtered in Maharashtra State (Dandekar 1964:352). Even if sex is grossly misreported, this shows less reluctance to slaughter, or report the slaughter of, the economically valuable bullock than the cow. Similarly, in 1952–53, of the licensed slaughterhouses in Uttar Pradesh none could slaughter youngstock, one could slaughter cows, and five could slaughter bullocks (Government of Uttar Pradesh 1955:38).

The Indian buffalo is not considered sacred. Rather, to the ardent cow protectionist the buffalo is a target for criticism because the female is a better milker than the cow. Both cattle and buffaloes adapt to most of the subcontinent, though their relative distribution is uneven, depending in part on local breeds and the type of agricultural work to be done. The male buffalo is used as a work animal, particularly in wet paddy cultivation, except in eastern India and East Pakistan. He is also adaptable to heavy tasks like pressing bales of hay or turning a wheel. However, the bullock is the predominant work animal, because he can do dry and wet ploughing and pull a cart. In India in 1956, 88.4% of the working cattle and buffaloes were bullocks, 2.6% cows, and 9% buffaloes (90% of these male), while in Pakistan buffaloes account for under 6% of the bovine work animals. For milk, however, the buffalo is often preferred. Thus for all of India in 1956, buffaloes were 14% of all cattle and buffaloes, but buffaloes in milk were as much as 37% of all female cattle and buffaloes. Since the average yield of milk per buffalo is about double that

---

[3]Although one associates the sacred cow with India, it is doubtful whether the life of the Indian peasant is nearly as involved with cattle as the life of an African pastoralist. Judging by the accounts of Evans-Pritchard (1940) or Dupire (1965), for example, cattle play a much larger role in Africa than in India.

of cows, buffaloes provide India over half its milk.[4]

Because the buffalo is a better milker, there is discrimination against the cow. Table 1, which gives the age and sex distribution of cattle in India for the last two censuses, shows the effects of this discrimination. In the age groups up to three years, the ratio of the sexes is about equal; after that, the ratio of females to males declines markedly. If there were no discrimination among the sexes, we would expect the ratio of females over three to males over three to be 1.0. Only in Rajasthan, Jammu and Kashmir, Himachal Pradesh, and Kerala, however, does this ratio exceed 1.0, whereas for all India it was .77 in 1956.[5] Ironically, the state with the lowest ratio of females to males, .49, is Uttar Pradesh, which generates the most rhetoric about cow protection but apparently neglects them most. (It can be assumed that the low ratio is explained not by export or import of cattle or slaughter, but by neglect of females and their premature death.)

---

[4]The National Sample Survey (1963:24) estimates production of buffalo milk at 29,000 tons and cow milk at 20,000 tons per day, though other estimates put cow milk relatively higher. Per animal, the daily yield of buffaloes is around twice that of a cow, but they lactate more days; buffaloes are estimated to produce 1,018 lbs of milk per lactation, and cows 428 lbs. (National Sample Survey 1963:11). Estimates of profitability vary widely by region, but usually the cost per pound of buffalo milk (which usually commands a slightly higher price per pound) is less than that of cow milk. It is often argued that improvements in treatment of cows could improve their yield to compete with the buffalo, but it is not clear in these comparisons whether the conditions, such as feed, of the buffalo are also to change. Chatterjee (1962) and Chaudhuri and Giri (1963), in arguing for more use of cattle, discuss these issues.

[5]Adult females exceed males in Rajasthan probably because it is a cattle-exporting area. In mountainous areas like Jammu and Kashmir and Himachal Pradesh, the noncultivated area is sufficient to allow all cattle enough pasture.

Given the desire to preserve cows, a major dilemma is posed in the areas where both buffaloes and cows can thrive. The peasant wants bullocks and female buffaloes; or, to put the matter negatively, cows are needed principally to produce bullocks, and male buffaloes are needed even less. A commonly offered solution to this problem is to breed cows that are better milkers. This, for example, was a hope of the Gosamvardhan (cow protection) Enquiry Committee of Uttar Pradesh in 1955 in its discussion "Cow versus Buffalo" (Government of Uttar Pradesh 1955:10–15). But even if the cow were to become the preferred milker, there would remain, as Dandekar (1964) has so clearly pointed out, a problem of numbers in Indian cattle development.

The problem is this: To stay in milk, a cow must calve every one or two years, so that in her lifetime a cow with normal feeding would produce, say, six adults. If only two-thirds of the adult females (a low rate) could successfully breed, each adult female and male would be replaced by four (2/3 X 6) new adults, a doubling of the cattle population every 10–15 years. (India has clearly not allowed this situation). If it is desired to maintain a given number of bullocks, the ratio of adult breeding females to bullocks must be one-third or less. That is, two of every three females born must (1) never reach maturity, or (2) never reproduce, if allowed to mature. This particular case, which is an equilibrium of sorts, I would like to refer to as the *stationary bullock solution*. If it should be desired to maintain a bullock population of 300 and at the same time to have more than 100 females, say 150, as milch animals, there would be even more surplus animals to be disposed of; for 150 females in milk will produce 450 males and 450 females, resulting in 150 extra males and 300 extra females.

If, on the other hand, the main purpose of the cattle population is milk production (and here I assume, contrary to fact for India, that the cow is the superior milker, for if only milk were desired, India could just use the buffalo), then 100

TABLE 1
Indian Cattle Population, 1956 and 1961, by Age and Sex[a] (figures in millions)

|  | 1961 | 1956 |
| --- | --- | --- |
| Cattle over three years | 126.7 | 114.8 |
| Males | 72.5 | 64.9 |
| Females | 54.2 | 49.9 |
| Youngstock one to three years old | 25.9 | 23.0 |
| Males | 12.3 | 11.2 |
| Females | 13.6 | 11.8 |
| Youngstock under one year | 22.9 | 20.8 |
| Males | 11.5 | 10.5 |
| Females | 11.4 | 10.3 |

[a]Figures for 1956 are from the *Indian Livestock Census, 1956* (Government of India 1960); figures for 1961 are from Chaudhuri and Giri (1963). The two sets of figures are not strictly comparable, the increase from 1956 to 1961 being probably in part due to improved coverage. The National Sample Survey (1960) conducted a sample verification of the 1956 census and found that total cattle were underreported by 3.7%, total males by 4.4%, though cows in milk were over-estimated somewhat.

milk cows, who must be breeding, will produce 300 milk cows and 300 males, an excess of 500 animals, give or take a prize bull or two. Under the *stationary milch cow solution,* typical of countries using considerable mechanical power in agriculture, the surplus animals are usually bred for slaughter. If slaughter is unacceptable, tremendous conflict results, since five of every six cattle are surplus and competing for scarce food.

India sits somewhere between these two extremes, allowing most adult females to procreate, as in the stationary milch cow case, but desiring a given stock of bullocks for agricultural work. The problem of numbers is inevitable, then, even without the buffalo. It might be argued that the competition of the buffalo as a milker leads to more neglect of cows and therefore less progeny, creating less conflict over sur-

plus cattle than would otherwise exist. A final point about our examples: if it is desired that the cattle population grow each year the situation is not basically changed, though it is eased the higher the growth rate desired.

III

In what sense is the Indian cattle population in excess? Let us consider first the case in which the slaughter of females is culturally acceptable and the goal is to maintain a given stock of bullocks, as in the stationary bullock solution. India has excess cattle in the sense that the present adult male population of 72.5 million would require for maintenance only 24 million breeding females, as opposed to the actual 54 million The extra 30 million females could be slaughtered or, as is now being suggested, exported to other countries without reducing the output of milk and other products; for one cow fed on the feed that would keep two cows alive produces more than twice the milk, more than twice the dung, and probably a hide of more value than the hides of two poorly fed cows.

The argument here is in part based on the fact that larger animals use feed more efficiently. Harris (1966:59) has argued against applying this idea to Indian cattle on the grounds that emaciated Indian breeds may be particularly well adapted in their metabolism to scrounging for feed. No evidence is offered for this. Evidence is available, on the other hand, for the position taken here. Estimated responses of milk yield to increased feeding are given for 12 milk production areas in different parts of India by Whyte and Mathur (1968:155–212). Milk yield per lactation for a cow is held to vary from 750 to 3,000 lbs. with various combinations of concentrates, green fodder, and hay. In general, milk yield rises proportionately or more than proportionately with feed. For example, in the Maharashtra Deccan, milk yield doubles (from 1,000 to 2,000 lbs. per lactation) when groundnut cake and other concentrates rise 50% (from 800 to 1,200 lbs per year) and when green fodder and hay rise 70% (from 19,200 to 32,500 lbs. per year) (Whyte and Mathur 1968:192–93). This means that one cow will produce a given amount of milk for less feed than it would take to maintain two cows that together would produce the same amount of milk. Furthermore, during youth and periods not in milk, one well-fed cow will require even less feed than that. Dung output will probably be higher from the one cow. The quality of the hide might also be improved, since it depends partly on timely removal from the animal and better-fed animals tend to be skinned sooner than neglected ones. If slaughter were allowed, then, or cattle were exported, India could have all the products it now has (except the presence of those slaughtered) and free land for other uses. All of this could be done with existing breeds of cattle.

Thus far, I have argued that the number of cattle in India is in excess because there are more females than necessary to maintain the present (and, I assume, needed) male population and to produce the present milk, hide, and dung supply. I have further shown that extra cattle are a real cost to the economy because the use of land for cattle feed competes with alternative human uses. In other words, and still assuming slaughter is culturally acceptable, there are alternative cattle populations that would better use India's resources, given the present technology. Or, in Harris' terms, the cultural ecology of India's sacred cattle is not in balance.

Let us turn to the more realistic case, namely that a significant group within Indian society values positively the presence of cows and negatively their slaughter. Harris has argued that the sacredness of Indian cattle is not important in explaining the Indian cattle population; I shall argue that he is wrong here. The case I now discuss assumes, contrary to Harris, that cattle are valued in part as pets, so that one cannot summarily slaughter 30 million cows

and leave Indian welfare unchanged. The following exercise will in part show that the present cattle population in India is in excess in terms of "the system's own objectives" (Bennett 1967).

These objectives could be better served by allowing fewer cattle to be born. The institutions for this control exist in many localities: all but breeding males are castrated, and the service of bulls can be, and often is, regulated. The advantage of lowering cattle births is that the feed now used to support those cattle which eventually die of starvation could be transferred to milking and work cattle.

The practice of allowing surplus cattle to starve to death is reflected in Table 1, which shows, in addition to high mortality of females after age three, high mortality among the youngstock of both sexes. Rather than being close to double the number of cattle under one year, the number in the one- to three-year age group is just slightly greater, indicating that almost half the one-year-olds die in the next two years. I suspect that the age reporting may produce some of this high mortality, since it seems surprising that females in the one- to three-year age group exceed males, only to drop so drastically after age three. However, the general pattern of high mortality of youngstock of both sexes occurs in all states and territories, and the high mortality of females after three years occurs in most states, lending broad support to this pattern.

In Figure 1, the broken line indicates the age and sex distribution of cattle that would be necessary to maintain the bullock population at the 1961 figure, 70 million, under the assumption of no slaughter or neglect of females. I estimate that the maintenance of this population would require that 8 million males (and 8 million females) be born each year. Assuming adequate feed for these cattle (though the 30 or so million breeding or working females would, of course, get more feed than the 35 million or so idle adult females), the number of males and females at all ages would be the same, as is indicated by the solid line.

The area within the solid line, representing the model population, may be contrasted with the area within the broken line. As drawn—and again I emphasize the conjectural nature of the figure—there are three areas of overlap, labeled A1, A2, and B. In A1 and A2, the model population is less than the actual population, indicating that at present there is an excess of cattle births and very high mortality in the early years. In area B, the model population exceeds the actual population, because the model does not allow females to die prematurely of neglect and starvation.

Under the model regime, the cattle in areas A1 and A2 would not need to be fed. On the other hand, since the model regime provides green pastures, or at least a maintenance ration for nonbreeding and nonworking adult females,

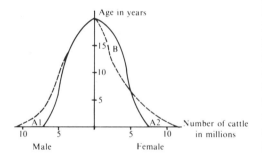

FIGURE 1

Distribution of cattle by age and sex necessary to maintain the bullock population at the 1961 figure, 70 million, assuming no slaughter or neglect of females, with adequate feed for all cattle (solid line) and without it (broken line). Since there is no data on the year-by-year age distribution of cattle in India and not much is known about mortality at a given level of food intake at various ages, the distribution is conjectural; it is based on what is known about the age and sex distribution of Indian cattle (shown in Table 1) and on some crude demographic considerations.

the cows in area B would require feed (and yield welfare) beyond that at present. Would enough feed be freed by the cattle in areas A1 and A2 to provide for the cattle in area B, allowing for the fact that many of the former are young and require less feed than the latter? Assuming that the ration for animals in areas A1 and A2 is 60% of that of nonworking and nonbreeding females in area B, it would seem that the answer is yes, and further that there would be feed left over for use by cattle in all age classes. The 60% figure is calculated on the basis of data from a survey conducted by Panse, Singh, and Murty (1964: 140–44), which shows that milk cows consume 23 lbs. of fodder per day, cows not in milk 14 lbs. per day, and youngstock about 8 lbs. per day, and the fact that there are 13 to 14 million animals in area B compared to about 25 million animals in areas A1 and A2 taken together.[6]

This means that with its present feed, India could support a cattle population that better fulfilled its objectives of better feeding the existing cattle population and feeding all adults. Since dung production from one animal weighing 500 lbs. is greater than from two animals each weighing 250 lbs. and requires less feed, the model population in the figure produces more organic manure and fuel. As discussed earlier, milk production too would tend to be higher, and hide quality would be improved. This exercise, then, has suggested a regime in which, with the present use of resources, India could have more physical output from its cattle without slaughter and without neglect of useless cattle. Such a regime would operate to improve welfare.

---

[6]While I think these calculations are reasonable, it is not essential to my main position that areas A1 and A2 are nearly twice as large as area B. The fact that areas A1 and A2 exist and could be eliminated within the existing rural framework is sufficient to indicate that the present cattle population represents a nonoptimal arrangement.

## IV

While a religious belief may sanction or be consistent with a set of practices, it need not be seen as *explaining* those practices where other explanations—such as rational self-interest—are available. This view is consistent with the idea that religious belief is a projection of the social structure and practices of a society. Morris (1967) has examined the Hindu value system in this respect and found that, contrary to Weberian tradition, religion and values were unnecessary as an explanatory device for, or were even at odds with, the reality of economic change in India in the 19th century. In this context one might argue, as does Harris, that one need not have recourse to the beliefs of Hindus in explaining the cattle complex of India. This argument against invoking religion as an explanatory variable might be extended to the 1966–67 demonstrations and agitation against cow slaughter in New Delhi and elsewhere. These demonstrations might be considered as political, not religious, movements employing certain convenient symbols. In this view cow slaughter was one of a number of symbols that could be used against those in power; the fact that it was chosen over the others is unimportant.

I maintain, nevertheless, that the composition of the cattle population of India is affected by the high regard given to the cow by Hindus, Jains, and other groups in India. If my view is correct, we can expect that if one of two adjacent areas with similar physical environments has a large number of Hindus, it will have a higher ratio of adult female to adult male cattle. India and Pakistan naturally recommend themselves as suitable areas for testing this hypothesis, because in Pakistan the proportion of Hindus is very low, and in India very high. I shall compare parts of East Pakistan with Assam and West Bengal, West Punjab with East Punjab, and Sind with Rajasthan and Gujarat. The test is not as simple as it may at first appear, because the proportion of female to male cattle also varies with

other factors, including the use of females for work and the extent to which an area exports cattle.[7]

In the comparison of the predominantly Muslim Chittagong and Dacca Divisions of East Pakistan with the State of Assam, we are faced with three problems. First, in these East Pakistan areas adult female (3.37 million) outnumber adult male cattle (2.98 million) because female animals are used for work (1.77 million females work versus 1.60 million milch). In the previous section I did not consider the case in which the female is a work animal, and indeed this is not the usual case in the subcontinent. But where it

---

[7]After completing this paper, I learned of an excellent discussion by Raj (1969) of some of the issues raised in the first two sections of this paper. Raj also argues that religion is unimportant in explaining the Indian cattle composition. His international analysis is less detailed than the above. His interstate analysis for India cites Kashmir, with its large Muslim population, and Kerala, with its sizable Christian and Muslim population, both areas having ratios of females to adult male cattle greater than the Indian average, as indication that religion plays no role. The case of Kerala is special, but I would guess it is the cropping pattern that leads to the female/male composition there. Kashmir is a hill area; all hill areas tend to have more grazing area, so adult females do not easily starve. Finally, Raj analyzes eight districts of the state of Uttar Pradesh, including traditionally Hindu districts like Benares and traditionally Muslim districts like Aligarh, showing there is little difference in the ratio of females to males. In this case, I believe Raj is misled by the districts chosen. My own analysis of all 54 districts of Uttar Pradesh shows that the correlation between the percent of total population Muslim in 1961 and the ratio of adult female to adult male cattle in 1961 was –.48. The obverse of this correlation is that in highly Hindu districts in Uttar Pradesh more females are retained relative to males than in other districts. But I would qualify this finding by stating that many of the hill districts of U.P., which as I argued for Kashmir would have a high proportion of females to males because they are hill districts, happen to have few Muslims, which in this case provides spurious support for our hypothesis.

is possible the problem of cattle slaughter or neglect need rarely arise.[8] Second, the feed situation for cattle is very much better in Assam than other areas so these is less likelihood that the excess females will die in early adulthood. Finally, Assam is not in the mainstream of movements for cow protection because of its very heterogeneous population and fairly independent past. Thus, although in the Muslim areas of East Pakistan the ratio of females to males is 1.13 while in Assam the ratio is .93, this seems best explained by the use in East Pakistan of the female as a work animal, and does not bear on the issue of religion and cattle.

Similarly, in West Bengal adult females are .82 of adult males, while in the Rajshahi and Khulna Divisions of East Pakistan the figure is .96, but the main reason is that in Rajshahi and Khulna 30% of the adult females are used as work animals, while only 1% are so used in West Bengal. One might argue that use of females as work animals is in itself evidence that Muslims use their cattle more rationally than Hindus. I know of no evidence that would confirm or negate this argument. Of using female cattle as work animals, the *Indian Livestock Census* of 1956 (Government of India 1960:vii) says,

Cows are generally not put under yoke. For reasons of economy this is, however, done in areas where milk yield is very poor. The largest number of such cows is found in Madras (558 thousand) followed by Bihar and Mysore with 300 thousand and 267 thousand respectively.

My source for Pakistan, the 1960 Agricultural Census (Government for Pakistan 1962), does not discuss the subject. My own conclusion is that comparisons of Assam and West Bengal with East Pakistan offer no evidence bearing on religion and the cattle complex, though they raise questions of the circumstances in which the female will be used for work.

In the western portion of the subcontinent, on the other hand, the comparison produces remarkably clear results. In the predominantly Muslim districts in West Pakistan bordering on East Punjab we find that the adult females total only .33 of adult male cattle, while in Hindu and Sikh East Punjab adult females are .76 of the adult male cattle.[9] Although both divisions of the Punjab have been leading areas of growth for India and Pakistan, and the Punjabi farmer, whether Hindu, Muslim, or Sikh, is noted as a rational sort, there appears to be only one explanation of the high proportion of female cattle in East Punjab: the Hindu regard for the cow. This comparison is the more convincing when we contrast individual adjacent districts in Pakistani and Indian Punjab. In all Pakistani districts the ratio of female to male adult cattle is lower than its Indian counterpart and lower than in any district in East Punjab.

A comparison of Sind districts of West Pakistan with equivalent districts in Rajasthan and Gujarat yields similar results.[10] The Sind-Rajas-

---

[8]Returning to the model, we see that if, say, 500 male and female animals are desired for work, this may be achieved by 100 females producing 600 animals, of which 200 females and 300 males work, and 100 females breed and give milk. This would be an equilibrium with no surplus animals. However, in most of the subcontinent the female is not desired as a work animal, so this solution is unavailable.

[9]The districts compared in West Pakistan were Gujarat, Lyllapur, Sialkot, Gujranwala, Sheikhupur, Lahore, and Montgomery. If Multan is added to this group, the relation is not affected. The Indian districts considered were Amritsar, Ferozepur, Gurdaspur, Bhatinda, Kapurthala, Jullundur, Hissar, and Ludhiana (Government of Punjab 1964).

[10]Ratios were calculated for the districts of Dadu, Larkana, Sukkur, Bahawalpur, Bahawalanagar, Rahimya Khan, Khairpur, Nawabshah, Sanghar, Hyderabad, Tharparkar, and Thatta in Pakistan (Government of Pakistan 1962) and for Gujarat (Government of Gujarat 1964).

than comparison is not as helpful as it might be because the Rajasthan districts of Barmer, Bikaner, Ganganagar, Jaisalmer, and Jodpur all export cattle (Government of Rajasthan 1963: 100) and would be expected to have more adult female than adult male cattle for that reason alone. A better comparison is provided by the Sind districts, where adult females are .60 of adult males, and the Rajkot division of Gujarat, where adult females are .79 of adult males. Even stronger support for the hypothesis may be seen in the fact that two of the Sind districts involved, Thatta and Tharparkar (the name is also a cattle breed), are famous for the cattle they export. Thus beliefs about cow slaughter in Gujarat seem a reasonable explanation for the higher ratio of female to male cattle in Gujarat than in Sind.

## V

I have provided evidence that the sanctity of the cow for Hindus is a belief that is useful in explaining the composition of the Indian cattle population. I have argued that to the extent that India does try both to prevent cow slaughter and to produce livestock products it does not do so very well. I have said that changes within the present institutions of rural India could produce more output than is now obtained from the resources devoted to cattle. If we are willing to follow Harris and ignore the sanctity of the cow, then the Indian cattle complex is even more decidedly out of balance. In supporting the use of traditional economic analysis, it has not been my intention to deny either the contributions of cultural ecology or its comparative advantage in dealing with some problems of peasant and other economies (for example, see Geertz 1963). However, I would also insist that the traditional tools of economic analysis will provide for certain problems—including the sacred cattle of India—at least as useful a framework.

## REFERENCES CITED

BENNETT, JOHN W. 1967. On the cultural ecology of Indian cattle. *Current Anthropology* 8:251–52.

BROWN, W. NORMAN. 1964. The sanctity of the cow in Hinduism. *Economic Weekly* (Bombay) 16:245–55.

CHATTERJEE, I. 1962. Towards a single species cattle economy. *Agricultural Situation in India* 17:764–84.

CHAUDHURI, S. C., and R. GIRI. 1963. Role of cattle in India's economy. *Agricultural Situation in India* 18:591–99.

DANDEKAR, V. M. 1964. Problem of numbers in cattle development. *Economic Weekly* (Bombay) 16: 351–56.

———. 1969. India's sacred cattle and cultural ecology. *Economic and Political Weekly* (Bombay) 4:1559–67.

DUPIRE, MARGUERITE. 1965. "The Fulani—peripheral markets of a pastoral people," in *Markets in Africa*. Edited by Paul Bohannan and George Dalton, pp. 93–129. Graden City: Doubleday.

EVANS-PRITCHARD, E. E. 1940. *The Nuer.* Oxford: Oxford University Press.

FORD FOUNDATION. 1959. *Report on India's food problem and steps to meet it.* New Delhi: Government of India, Ministry of Food and Agriculture and Ministry of Community Development and Cooperation.

GEERTZ, CLIFFORD. 1963. *Agricultural involution.* Berkeley: University of California Press.

GOVERNMENT OF GUJARAT. 1964. *Season and crop report, Gujarat State, 1960–61.* Baroda: Government Press.

GOVERNMENT OF INDIA. 1954. *Agricultural labour enquiry.* New Delhi: Bureau of Labour, Government of India.

———. 1956. *Report on the marketing of cattle in India.* New Delhi: Directorate of Marketing and Inspection, Ministry of Food and Agriculture, Government of India.

———. 1958. *Studies in the economics of farm management in Madhya Pradesh. Report for 1955–56.* New Delhi: Ministry of Food and Agriculture, Government of India.

————. 1960. *Indian livestock census, 1956. Vol. I: Summary tables.* New Delhi: Economic and Statistical Adviser to the Government of India, Directorate of Economics and Statistics, Ministry of Food and Agriculture.

————. 1961. *National income statistics. Proposals for a revised series of national income estimates for 1955–56 to 1959–60.* New Delhi: Central Statistical Organization, Department of Statistics, Government of India.

————. 1962. *Studies in the economics of farm management in Bombay. Report for 1954–55 to 1956–57.* New Delhi: Ministry of Food and Agriculture, Government of India.

————. 1963a. *Studies in the economics of farm management in Uttar Pradesh. Report for 1954–55.* New Delhi: Ministry of Food and Agriculture, Government of India.

————. 1963b. *Studies in the economics of farm management in West Bengal. Report for 1954–55 to 1956–57.* New Delhi: Ministry of Food and Agriculture, Government of India.

GOVERNMENT OF PAKISTAN. 1962. *Pakistan census of agriculture, 1960. Vol. I: Final Report, East Pakistan; Vol. II: West Pakistan Report 3.* Karachi: Agricultural Census Organization, Ministry of Agriculture and Works, Government of Pakistan.

GOVERNMENT OF PUNJAB. 1964. *Punjab livestock census of 1961.* Chandigarh: Department of Land Records, Punjab State.

GOVERNMENT OF RAJASTHAN. 1963. *Statistical abstract, Rajasthan, 1961.* Jaipur: Directorate of Economics and Statistics, Rajasthan State.

GOVERNMENT OF UTTAR PRADESH. 1955. *Report of the Gosamvardhan Enquiry Committee.* Allahabad: Animal Husbandry, State of Uttar Pradesh.

HARRIS, MARVIN. 1966. The cultural ecology of India's sacred cattle. *Current Anthropology* 7:51–60.

————. 1967. Reply to: "On the cultural ecology of Indian cattle," by John W. Bennett, *Current Anthropology* 8:252–53.

————. 1968. *The rise of anthropological theory.* New York: T. Y. Crowell.

MORRIS, MORRIS D. 1967. Values as an obstacle to economic growth in South Asia: An historical survey. *Journal of Economic History* 27:588–607.

NATIONAL SAMPLE SURVEY. 1960. *No. 25: Sample verification of livestock census: 1956* Delhi: The Cabinet Secretariat, Government of India.

————. 1962. *No. 65: Tables with notes on animal husbandry.* Delhi: The Cabinet Secretariat, Government of India.

————. 1963. *No. 72: Tables with notes on milk production.* Delhi: The Cabinet Secretariat, Government of India.

PANSE, V. G., DAROGA SINGH, and V. V. R. MURTY. 1964. *Sample survey for estimation of milk production.* New Delhi: Indian Council of Agricultural Research.

————. 1969. Investment in livestock in agrarian economies: An analysis of some issues concerning "sacred cows" and "surplus cattle." *Indian Economic Review* 4:1–33.

SOUTHWORTH, H. M., and E. F. JOHNSTON. Editors. 1967. *Agricultural development and economic growth.* Ithaca: Cornell University Press.

WHYTE, R. O., and M. L. MATHUR. 1968. *The planning of milk production in India.* Calcutta: ORIENT Longmans.

# 18

## CATTLE IN A NORTH INDIAN VILLAGE[1]

*Stanley A. Freed and Ruth S. Freed*

Anthropologists often look at theory in the context of small, focused studies of communities. In this article, Stanley and Ruth Freed look at both Harris's and Heston's views in the context of the economy of Shanti Nagar, a village of 799 people northwest of Delhi. They report that the number of bullocks (castrated males) in the village is optimal for working village land holdings, a point that supports Harris. They also suggest that although there are more cows than would be required to maintain the village bullock population at the proper level, the excess females bear calves that people export, adding cash to the village economy. Villagers do let cows die through neglect, but they keep large enough herds of them to provide for this export. Finally, the Freeds confirm the fact that Indians feed their cattle food that can also be eaten by people, but that the practice may be looked at as a farming expense for such food goes to bullocks when they require extra calories for the work of plowing and to cows in lactation.

Recent debate about cattle[2] in India has focused on the issues of whether India's cattle population is too large, whether there are useless or uneconomic animals that compete with humans for scarce food, and if these questions are answered affirmatively, whether the Hindu reverence for the cow and the general Hindu reluctance to slaughter any cattle are largely responsible. On the one hand, Marvin Harris and others who to some extent share his views hold that the technological and environmental framework in which Indian farmers operate adequately explains the characteristics of India's cattle population. When India's cattle are analyzed from this point of view, one finds, according to Harris, that there is no excess but rather a shortage of bullocks, that the so-called "useless" cattle are in fact useful, and that the general policy of not slaughtering cattle that is today derived from religious beliefs has many positive economic functions and no negative ones. Heston and others of similar views argue,

on the other hand, that the cattle population is too large, that there are uneconomic animals that compete with humans for food, that this situation is due at least in part to the religious veneration of the cow and the reluctance to slaughter cattle, and that a smaller cattle population with different demographic characteristics could adequately perform all of the functions of the present population (except providing the pleasure that the former owners derived from their missing cattle) at less cost (Heston 1971; Dandekar 1969; Raj 1969; Bennett 1967; and Harris 1966).

We propose to approach some of these questions through an analysis of the cattle population of Shanti Nagar, an all-Hindu village of 799 people located about eleven miles northwest of Delhi in the Union Territory in Delhi. In the context of the village, we shall deal with the questions of whether or not there is a shortage of bullocks; which components of the cattle population are in excess, if any; and the contribution of religious beliefs to the demographic characteristics of the cattle population.

## CATTLE IN GENERAL

The people of Shanti Nagar own 200 zebu cattle: 95 bullocks, 47 cows, and 58 calves. They own 190 water buffaloes: 111 cows and 79 calves. There are no adult male buffaloes in the village. The bull that services the water buffaloes is shared with another village, as is the zebu bull; both wander freely and are owned by no one. Thus, the people of Shanti Nagar have full title to 390 cattle (see Table I).

In addition to these, there are eleven water buffaloes and one zebu cow in Shanti Nagar under an arrangement whereby the ownership of the animals is shared with people living outside the village. In Shanti Nagar and the surrounding region, some people do not want to care for a cow or buffalo that is not giving milk; they give such an animal to a second party, who is required to have it impregnated if it is not already pregnant, to feed it until delivery, to pay the delivery expenses, and to keep it until the owner comes for it. For these services, the owner and the second party agree that the latter will receive half (more rarely, one-third) of the market value of the animal when the owner reclaims it. In the meantime, the second party is entitled to all the milk and dung that the animal produces. If there is a disagreement about the market value of the animal, the one that values it more highly keeps it and pays the other the appropriate share. Under such an arrangement, the original owner effectively transfers a share of the animal to the person who cares for it. Thus the villagers of Shanti Nagar can be said to own an additional half zebu cow and five and one-half water buffaloes or a total of 396 cattle. There are 402 cattle physically present in Shanti Nagar. In the analysis that follows, we ignore the 12 cattle partially owned by people outside of Shanti Nagar. Cattle given on shares by one villager to another are credited to the original owner.

## BULLOCKS

The farmers of Shanti Nagar use bullocks for plowing, sowing, threshing, turning sugar cane mills and Persian wheels, and pulling carts. These activities do not overlap to any significant extent; a farmer is not plowing at the same time that he is threshing or crushing his sugar cane. Thus the most demanding work that is required of bullocks, which is plowing, is the principal factor in the number of bullocks that a farmer keeps.

The villagers say that a yoke of bullocks can adequately work a maximum of 12.63 acres. An appraisal of the adequacy of the bullocks of Shanti Nagar on a village-wide basis can be made by comparing the number of bullocks with the area of cultivable land. There are 591.05 acres of currently cultivable land in the village. For cultivating this land, there are, in addition to the bullocks, one tractor owned by a man with 12.21 acres and a camel owned by a man with 44.21 acres. The amount of land that must be cultivated by bullocks is the total cultivable land less 12.21 acres for the tractor and 9.47 acres for the camel (villagers say that one camel is the equal of 1.5 bullocks), in short, 569.37 acres. The 95 bullocks are capable of cultivating 600.40 acres (95 bullocks times 6.32 acres). On a village-wide basis, therefore, the fit of cultivable land and bullocks is very close. If village lands were held as one large estate and all bullocks were well and strong, the land could be cultivated by 90 bullocks; the actual situation in the village thus departs from the most efficient condition to the extent of five bullocks, a surplus of only 6 per cent.[3]

Although there is a good balance of land and bullocks from the village-wide point of view, the land of Shanti Nagar is not cultivated as a single

**TABLE 1**
Number and Type of Cattle by the Landownership of Families*

|  | Landowning Families | | Landless Families | |
|---|---|---|---|---|
|  | Number of Cattle | Average per Person | Number of Cattle | Average per Person |
| All cattle | 307 | .63 | 83 | .27 |
| Zebu cattle | 173 | .35 | 27 | .09 |
| Bullocks | 92 | .19 | 3 | .01 |
| Cows | 36 | .07 | 11 | .04 |
| Calves | 45 | .09 | 13 | .04 |
| Water buffaloes | 134 | .27 | 56 | .18 |
| Cows | 83 | .17 | 28 | .09 |
| Calves | 51 | .10 | 28 | .09 |

*There are 59 landowning families with 490 members and 51 landless families with 309 members.

unit; rather, it is divided among 59 families, and each of these individual farms can be managed independently of the rest. We may, therefore, look at each farm to see whether there is a shortage or an excess of bullocks in relation to the cultivable land. Instead of landowning families, however, we shall deal with cultivating families (N = 58), for a few landowning families do not cultivate, and a few landless families cultivate land on shares.

Table 2 tabulates the cultivating families by number of bullocks and amount of land cultivated. If one adopts the position that the minimum complement of bullocks for a cultivating family is two, for it takes two bullocks to draw a plow, then one might argue that ten families are short two bullocks apiece and twelve families are short one, for a total village shortage of 32. To this we might add another five to provide the owners of three bullocks with two complete yokes. If individual farmers base their decisions upon a presumed need for a yoke of bullocks no matter how much land they cultivate, then, from the point of view of the cultivable land, there would be an excess of bullocks on the order of 47 per cent. However, it is not necessary to own a yoke of bullocks to get one's plowing done;

other arrangements are commonly made. Men can and do hire others to plow their fields at a fixed rate per acre, or two men (often brothers or lineage members) each owning one bullock may arrange to share animals. Because such arrangements are possible, cultivators do not have to own two bullocks without regard to the size of their landholding. If, in a farmer's estimation, the cost of bullocks exceeds the benefits derived therefrom, he can manage without them or with only one. A farmer has several options, and his decision rests on an appraisal of costs *versus* benefits; in the case of bullocks, the overriding benefit is drawing a plow. That the system is effective is indicated by the good balance of bullocks and land in the village.

We can anticipate that farmers with very small holdings will own no bullocks, those with 6.32 acres will own one, those with 12.63, two, and so on. An examination of Table 2 shows that the situation in Shanti Nagar approximates these expectations. The average holding of cultivators with no bullocks is 1.4 acres. If these farmers each owned a pair of bullocks, they would have something like 10 times the bullock power that they need. Farmers who own one bullock, or "half a plow" as the villagers say,

**TABLE 2**
Cultivating Families by Number of Bullocks and Amount of Land Cultivated

| Number of Families | Bullocks per Family | Acreage Cultivated per Family (standard deviation in parentheses) |
|---|---|---|
| 10 | 0 | 1.40   (.86) |
| 12 | 1 | 4.28   (2.88) |
| 28 | 2 | 11.23  (8.44) |
| 5 | 3 | 20.58 (13.29) |
| 3 | 4 | 28.91  (6.86) |

cultivate an average of 4.28 acres. These farmers have 50 percent more bullock power than they need. Farmers who own a "plow," that is, two bullocks average very close to the appropriate landholding. Those with three bullocks are also very close to expectations on the basis of their landholding. The few cultivators with four bullocks have land somewhat in excess of their bullock power. It should be noted that the standard deviations are fairly large.

One conclusion that may be drawn from the figures in Table 2 is that the ownership of bullocks is fairly well adjusted to size of landholdings and that not too much adjustment by sharing or hiring is necessary to get the village land plowed. For example, the total holding of the ten families without bullocks is only fourteen acres, the equivalent of slightly more than one plow. However, ten individual agreements must be negotiated to effect the necessary transfers of bullock power even if no single agreement involves the use of bullocks for more than a few days. This could be considered a nuisance and would be a factor in a farmer's decision to buy his first bullock a bit sooner than might be justified on strictly financial grounds. Thus an examination of the holdings of farmers with no bullocks and those with one bullock suggests that the decision to buy a bullock is made with a landholding of about 2.95 acres. Of the ten cultivating families that own no bullocks, none has a landholding as large as 2.95 acres, whereas nine of the twelve families owning one bullock have a landholding that large or larger.

We suggest that the distribution of bullocks among farmers is best understood in terms of appraisals of costs *versus* benefits by individual farmers. This assumes that any farmer can find the means to own a bullock if he is willing to bear the costs. On the other hand, one might argue that farmers without bullocks have none because they are poor and unable to obtain the necessary capital, or possibly can do so only by mortgaging their land and running the risk of losing it. We believe that this argument is untenable with regard to Shanti Nagar. First, a farmer in need of money to buy cattle can borrow it within the village. The requisite sums are not large in terms of the village money-lending business; the common rate of interest is 1.5 per cent per month. Second, bullocks vary in price. A farmer with a small landholding need not buy 100-dollar bullocks; 30-dollar bullocks may be quite adequate for his holding of an acre or two. Of course, the interest that he must pay on his loan is an additional factor to be considered in deciding whether or not to buy at all.

In addition to the interest, he must consider other factors in borrowing money. Money-lending in Shanti Nagar traditionally establishes a relationship between lender and borrower that may to some extent obligate the borrower to help the lender occasionally at inconvenient times. However, a borrower no longer has to worry about losing his land as security for a loan, for the Delhi Land Reforms Act, 1954 (Delhi Administration, Law and Judicial Department 1960:82) forbids the mortgage of land where ". . . possession of the mortgaged land is transferred or is agreed to be transferred in [the] future to the mortgagee as security for the money advanced. . . ." In short, a man with a small farm can obtain the necessary services of bullocks more economically with arrangements other than ownership.


## MALE WATER BUFFALOES

Aside from one bull that Shanti Nagar shares with a neighboring village, there are no adult male water buffaloes in Shanti Nagar. The villagers do not use water buffaloes as draft animals, and they do not ordinarily eat buffalo meat. Consequently, the male animals are not useful and are not kept. Because of the sentiment against killing cattle, the useless males cannot be slaughtered. Villagers let them die of neglect, turn them loose to wander, or sell them to outsiders who propose to use them as draft animals but who in some cases doubtless slaughter them. Villagers say that they will not knowingly sell an animal for slaughter. They are aware that an unknown buyer may deliver an animal to the slaughterhouse, but they often choose to ignore this possibility.

We did not ascertain the sex of calves and hence do not know how many male buffalo calves there are in the village. Although there may be a few that are old enough to be sold for a few dollars, the fact that villagers generally prefer to dispose of them as soon as possible, often without any attempt at selling them, suggests that they are of little value and also that religious sentiments concerning cattle slaughter may inhibit people from attempting to realize even the small sums that could be obtained in a sale. In this view, death by deliberate neglect is preferable to slaughter. In any case, we believe that a male water buffalo found in the village or wandering in the fields, aside from the needed bull, is best considered a surplus animal that is allowed to live largely because of the religious prohibition of cattle slaughter.


## BUFFALO AND ZEBU COWS

The question of whether or not bullocks and male water buffaloes are in short supply or in excess can be discussed in terms of the functions of the animals within the village setting. The most demanding function of the bullock is plowing, and one can calculate how many bullocks are needed to plow the cultivable land of the village. Hence, one has a criterion for appraising the adequacy of the bullock population. Male water buffaloes have no function other than impregnating females, and a single male is apparently adequate for the village. There is again a criterion for deciding whether or not there are excess animals. In both cases, a reasonably satisfactory analysis can be made by treating Shanti Nagar as a closed system and ignoring the larger marketplace.

With regard to milch cows, however, we may not treat Shanti Nagar as if it were a closed system. Milk is readily marketable, and, from the point of view of the village, the large city of Delhi provides a market that can absorb almost any quantity of surplus milk that the village might produce. The principal product of the bullock, draft power, is not readily marketable outside of Shanti Nagar. Furthermore, people own cattle not only for their products but also because they hope to realize a profit by buying and selling them in the marketplace. A profit may be realized in two ways. First, prices in the market constantly fluctuate and one can earn a profit by buying and selling at favorable moments. Second, an animal may change in value owing to its stage in the reproductive cycle. In this regard, there is an important difference between cows and water buffaloes on the one hand and bullocks on the other. In general, a dry cow or water buffalo is worth less than when it is producing milk. One can take advantage of this fact by acquiring a dry animal and selling it after it gives birth. (One can also lose money if the cost of the dry animal and delivery expenses exceed the selling price.) Bullocks do not undergo such price fluctuations based upon reproductive considerations, and there is consequently much more trading of cows and water buffaloes than of bullocks. Bullocks are bought for use; cows and water buffaloes are bought for the products they provide and also for speculation.

Since the functions of milch cows are so closely connected with large markets outside of Shanti Nagar, it is difficult to judge whether or not there are too many or too few of them from the point of view of their functions within the village. However, it is possible to discuss whether or not there might be a surplus of zebu cows, for, although both buffaloes and cows produce milk and dung, there are important differences between the two animals. In the Shanti Nagar region, the buffalo is the superior milk producer; villagers testify that the buffalo gives twice as much milk as the cow. The buffalo is also the better dung producer. Why therefore, keep cows at all except for the fact that bullocks, unlike male buffaloes, are essential in agriculture? If we accept the suggestion of Heston (1971: 193) that a stable bullock population requires at most one cow to three bullocks, we have a techno-environmental criterion for judging the appropriateness of the number of cows.

Applying this criterion to Shanti Nagar, we find that there are 47 cows whereas only 32 would be required to maintain a bullock population of 95. May we then say that there is an excess of 15 cows (47 per cent)? We have seen that the buffalo is the superior milk and dung producer. If milk and dung were the only considerations in choosing milch cattle, the rational villagers would replace their cows in excess of reproductive needs by buffaloes. Do the "excess" cows represent the need of individual farmers to breed bullocks for their own use? This

argument is untenable for much the same reason as is the argument that every cultivator needs to own a yoke of bullocks. Just as one can arrange to have one's fields plowed without owning two bullocks, so too, one can acquire bullocks without raising them oneself. They can be bought rather than raised, and this is in fact the usual mode of acquisition in Shanti Nagar.

The bullock-producing function of cows relates more to their trading value than to the need of individual owners to produce bullocks for their own use. Of the 95 bullocks in Shanti Nagar, only three are owned by landless families, and these families cultivate land on shares. Thus the owner of a bullock uses the animal on his land; if he does not cultivate, he owns no bullocks. Of the 47 cows, nine are owned by landless noncultivators and two by landless families that cultivate. If we calculate a ratio of cattle per person, bullocks are nineteen times as frequent among landowners as among the landless, whereas cows are only slightly more than twice as frequent (see Table 1). A landless man generally would have no more economic need for a cow (assuming that he could acquire a buffalo for milk and dung) than for a bullock were it not for the possibility of realizing a profit from the former.

The fact that landless people own as many cows as they do suggests that the cow may be a superior trading animal for them. One advantage for poor people is that cows cost much less than buffaloes, so that a man can enter the cattle business with less capital by buying a cow. However, an examination of the distribution of cows and buffaloes, does not support this. If cows are economically more advantageous for landless people than for landowners, then they should constitute a higher proportion of the milch animals of the former. The actual proportions of cows among the milch animals of the two groups, however, are very similar: 28 per cent for the landless and 30 per cent for the landowners. Furthermore, we doubt that either cows or buffaloes could have a clear advantage as a trading animal for very long, for if such an advantage were to develop the forces of the marketplace would soon produce an equilibrium. We recorded only a very few statements by villagers on the relative trading merits of cows and water buffaloes, and opinion was evenly divided as to which animal is superior.

Because an appraisal of techno-environmental and economic factors does not appear to account for the number of cows in Shanti Nagar, one must consider whether or not the Hindu religious doctrine of the sacredness of cows contributes to their apparent excess. The force of this belief cannot be discounted; it is one of the most prominent elements in the Hinduism of the village. One of the questions we asked a random sample of 67 men and 47 women was: "What is the best thing in the Hindu religion?" The single most common response, given by eighteen men (27 per cent) and eight women (17 per cent) was "the cow." Furthermore, with regard to selling cows, the village may intervene to punish improper behavior, even if inadvertent. We recorded a case in which a village council fined a man five dollars, a heavy fine by village standards, because he sold a cow to a man suspected of being a Muslim.

Within Shanti Nagar, there is no non-Hindu group whose cattle population could be compared to that of the Hindus. Such a comparison involving similar villages, groups, or regions could provide an indication of the influence of Hindu religious beliefs upon cattle populations. Heston (1971: 196) makes several such comparisons, but the results are not entirely clear owing to the difficulty of finding regions differing only in religion. His most convincing evidence that apparently shows a higher proportion of female cattle among Hindus than among Muslims comes from a comparison of West Pakistan and East Punjab, regions relatively close to Shanti Nagar. Despite the fact that we cannot make a comparison of Hindu and non-Hindu groups in Shanti Nagar, it is nonetheless of interest that only zebu cows appear to be in excess of village needs (we cannot judge female water buffaloes in

these terms) and that this is the animal considered sacred by Hindus.

## DIET OF CATTLE

Excess cattle are a problem principally to the extent that they compete with humans for food. Much of the diet of cattle comes from the chaff of wheat and other grains, the tufts of sugar cane, cotton seeds, oil-cake (the residue of seeds after oil has been pressed from them), and grass growing in fallow fields, on waste land, and on the village common land. None of these foods are consumed by people. However, a part of the diet of cattle consists of fodder crops grown in fields that could, in many cases, be used to raise food for people. In addition, villagers feed gram and *gur* (a brown sugar) to bullocks when they are being used intensively and to milch animals during the last weeks of pregnancy and when they are giving milk. Wheat may be used as a dietary supplement during the last few weeks of pregnancy. Some people habitually feed their cows a piece of bread every day. Gram, *gur* and wheat are all important human foods.

Some idea of the extent to which village resources are used to support its cattle population can be obtained from a detailed budget kept by a farmer for one year. This farmer lived with his wife, mother, and two small children. He owned one water buffalo throughout the year and two bullocks for the last seven months of the year. He cultivated 6.11 acres of which 2.53 (41 per cent) were used to raise food for his livestock. He had cash expenditures of $572 during the year. He bought his bullocks for $189. Of the remaining $383, he spent $125 (33 per cent) on his livestock, principally to buy gram, oil-cake, and cotton seeds. This farmer is a moderately well-off landowner who has a yearly salary in addition to his income from farming, and he probably provides his livestock with a better diet than average. The diet fed to cattle varies with the economic circumstances of the owner; poor, landless people feed their cattle less well than do rich landowners. However, most of the village cattle are owned by landowners.

In brief, the belief that buffaloes and cattle do not compete to any great extent with humans for food because they live from grazing in fallow fields and on waste land, or eat the residue from the processing of grain and sugar cane, does not appear tenable in the relatively densely populated Shanti Nagar region. The village livestock consume a considerable amount of gram, wheat, and *gur* that could otherwise be eaten by people, and many acres of land have to be devoted to fodder crops. It is also worth noting that, although the dietary supplements of oil-cake and cotton seeds are not human foods, they nonetheless cost money.

The fact that any village resident can graze his livestock in fallow fields, on waste land, and on village common land free of charge offers the landless man the opportunity of getting into the cattle business at relatively little cost to himself if he or his wife has the time needed to collect bits of fodder here and there in the fields and along paths and roads. The existence of village common land carries with it the danger of over-exploitation (Hardin 1968). It is unlikely that a weak, landless man would attempt to graze an excessive number of livestock at village expense, for the privilege of free grazing could be withdrawn by the landlords. For example, one of the traditional privileges of the village, that of collecting dung that falls from cattle in fallow fields and on village common land, was withdrawn by the village council while we were in Shanti Nagar. The rights to this dung were auctioned with the proceeds going to the village council, and, as a result, one of the village potters could not practice his trade because he depended upon free dung for firing his pots. Excessive exploitation of village resources is more likely from a powerful, well-to-do man. This possibility was exemplified just before we left Shanti Nagar when one man took some eighteen head of livestock on shares from a neighboring village. Were this to become common, poorer people might find the owner-

ship of livestock increasingly expensive, for they could depend upon free fodder less than formerly.

## NOTES

1. We thank the Social Science Research Council and the National Science Foundation for the postdoctoral fellowships that supported our field research in India from 1957 to 1959, and Mr. Kenneth W. Payne who assisted us while supported by the Undergraduate Research Participation Program, National Science Foundation (grant number 8A GY 8924).

2. We use cattle to refer to both bovine cattle and buffaloes.

3. The fit of bullocks to land is not quite this good because a few farmers hire a man with a tractor from a neighboring village to give their fields their first plowing. After that, they use bullocks. The first plowing is the most strenuous. Most crops require several plowings; for example, eight plowings is considered the minimum for wheat. Other factors that might be taken into account in calculating the fit of bullocks to land are: (1) the fact that a field of sugar cane is good for four years before it must be replanted, (2) crop rotation often results in a field's lying fallow for one of the growing seasons, and (3) the different number of plowings required by each crop. Such a calculation would be rather complicated and would, in any case, require detailed records, which we lack, of the crops grown by each farmer throughout the year.

## BIBLIOGRAPHY

BENNETT, J. W. 1967. On the Cultural Ecology of Indian Cattle. Current Anthropology 8:251–252.

DANDEKAR, V. M. 1979. India's Sacred Cattle and Cultural Ecology. Economic and Political Weekly 4:1559–1566.

DELHI ADMINISTRATION, LAW AND JUDICIAL DEPARTMENT. 1960. The Delhi Code, V. 2. Delhi.

HARDIN, G. 1968. The Tragedy of the Commons. Science 162:1243–1248.

HARRIS, M. 1966. The Cultural Ecology of India's Sacred Cattle. Current Anthropology 7:51–66.

HESTON, A. 1971. An Approach to the Sacred Cow of India. Current Anthropology 12:191–209.

RAJ, K. N. 1969. Investment in Livestock in Agrarian Economies. Indian Economic Review 4:53–85.

# THE ECONOMIC SYSTEM

**ISSUE**   The potlatch: Why do Northwest Coast Indians give away their wealth?

Imagine a friend has just bought a Yamaha XS 750 E motorcycle for $1995.00 from a local dealer. You know that your friend has been riding a smaller motorcycle for several years, is bothered by engine vibration, likes to tour with his wife, and has a moderate income. The machine he has bought is smooth, designed for the open road, and has comfortable springing and plenty of power for "two-up" riding. Its price, moreover, is $400 below list. With the knowledge that your friend has been saving for a new machine, it is not surprising to hear that he has bought this particular motorcycle at this time.

But another event may be harder to understand. When your friend was married, his wife's father paid for an elaborate wedding. He invited hundreds of guests, hired expensive caterers for a wedding reception that was held at an exclusive country club, and gave his daughter a $10,000 wedding gift. It was rumored that all together he spent over $30,000 on the wedding. Although you know this man is wealthy, it is hard to imagine why he would use his money in this way.

For most anthropologists, these two very different events are connected: both are economic processes. The economic system is the process of providing goods and services to meet biological and social wants. The study of economic systems cross-culturally involves everything from the investigation of production, including the allocation of resources, ownership, technology, and the division and organization of labor, to strategies for distributing goods. Of special interest are the factors that motivate people to participate in the economic process.

The motivation behind the purchase of a motorcycle is not so hard for us to understand. Motorcycles are fun for many people. When a motorcycle meets the right personal requirements and its cost is reasonable by comparison with the price of other motorcycles, the economic exchange makes sense. Anthropologists identify this sort of purchase as *market exchange*. It is defined as the transfer of goods and services on the basis of price, supply, and demand. Behind the notion of market exchange is the motivation to economize, to get the greatest value for the least expenditure. The motorcycle buyer consciously considered the need to be economical when he made the purchase.

The motivation behind the wedding expenditure is more difficult to analyze. By giving a feast for guests, providing them with entertainment, and transferring money to his daughter, the father of the bride engaged in an economic transaction. But the event does not seem to involve economizing in quite the same way as does buying a motorcycle. The act of giving (not the act of buying goods and services to be given) does not seem to involve getting value for the least expenditure. Instead, it appears to occur because it is customary for fathers of brides to hold weddings. Such an expected economic transaction, based on one's role obligation rather than on a desire for particular goods or money, is called *reciprocal exchange*. Christmas giving, dinner parties, borrowing among neighbors, and many other arrangements fall into this classification. Some hunter-gatherer and horticultural societies depend on reciprocal exchange for the transfer of goods, with money and market exchange absent altogether.

The example of the wedding poses a second problem, however. Why does the event to involve so many guests and cost so much when obligation does not demand such opulence? The answer to this question is more difficult and probably relates directly to more general social processes. Most would argue that such an expenditure involves the rank or status of the giver.

It is the problem of giving in the form of an institution called the "potlatch" that concerns the articles presented in this section. Potlatches are rituals held by the Indians of the Northwest Coast of North America. Potlatching gained the attention of anthropologists because its central purpose was the giving away of vast amounts of wealth. Canadian authorities were appalled by the potlatch because it violated Western values on saving and frugality. At one point they actually banned the ritual altogether although it is again legal today.

The articles reprinted in this section attempt to account for the origin and the causes of the potlatch. Suttles argues that the potlatch served to redistribute food through exchange among different groups of Indians. Piddocke carries this argument further by asserting that such ritual giving prevented starvation. Drucker and Heizer reject both views, arguing instead that the potlatch functioned to validate status and tie different groups together by means of reciprocal exchange.

# 19

## AFFINAL TIES, SUBSISTENCE, AND PRESTIGE AMONG THE COAST SALISH[1]

*Wayne Suttles*

*In this article, Wayne Suttles accounts for the potlatch among the Coast Salish, one of the Northwest Coast Indian groups, by tying the ritual to the redistribution of basic foods. He points out that on the coast, different foods are produced in different places, and that food quantities vary from one year and place to the next. The results were occasional shortages of food for most local groups in the past. The Salish, however, practiced a visiting custom among affinal (kin through marriage) relatives. One local group would travel to the location of another and be fed as a matter of hospitality. In return, the visiting group would offer gifts of prestige goods as a matter of courtesy. But people who ran short of food found themselves too busy to manufacture prestige goods. Thus, it was possible for well-fed groups to acquire wealth with their food while poor ones would run out of both, ending their ability to make visits. The potlatch, which occurred regularly, ensured that groups with wealth would redistribute it, thus keeping the visiting pattern alive. The adaptive advantage of the system lay in the continued availability of food for those who were short of it.*

The nature of Northwest Coast social stratification and the nature of the institution most intimately related to it, the potlatch, are problems of widely recognized importance. Yet attempts at solving these problems have not been wholly satisfactory. Generalizations about social stratification have been betrayed by failure to give sufficient weight to all of the differences in social structure that existed among the various Northwest Coast tribes. Explanations of the potlatch have been only partial ones, finding its function in the expression of the individual's drive for high status or in the fulfillment of society's need for solidarity. Relating these functions to man's other requirements for survival has often been inhibited by an assumption that the satisfaction of alimentary needs through the food quest and the satisfaction of psychological needs through the manipulation of wealth form two separate systems, the "subsistence economy" and the "prestige economy." Or if a relationship between the two is hypothesized, the hypothesis usually makes the "prestige economy" depen-

dent upon the "subsistence economy"; it is assumed that a rich habitat provides an abundance of food which in turn supports the prestige economy which in turn maintains social stratification. I believe, however, that it is more reasonable to assume that, for a population to have survived in a given environment for any length of time, its subsistence activities and prestige-gaining activities are likely to form a single integrated system by which that population has adapted to its environment. I will try to show how this may be true of one group of Northwest Coast tribes, the Coast Salish of Southern Georgia Strait and the Strait of Juan de Fuca,[2] and in particular I will try to show that in the socio-economic system of these tribes a role of crucial importance was played by the ties established through intercommunity marriage.

Native social organization in this area was characterized by a seeming looseness. Kinship was reckoned bilaterally. Residence was usually, but not always, patrilocal. The nuclear families of brothers, cousins, and brothers-in-law formed extended families ($x^w \partial n\partial \acute{c} \acute{e} l \partial w \partial m$), occupying great cedar-plank houses and claiming rights to certain local resources and to certain inherited privileges. One or more such extended families formed a village or community. The community was linked through ties of marriage and kinship with other communities and these with still others to form a social network with no very clear boundaries. Groups of villages like the Lummi and Cowichan were linked by common dialect and traditions as "tribes" but in recent generations these village groupings were certainly not separate "societies."

Within most communities there seem to have been three distinct social classes—a majority identified as "high class," a somewhat smaller group identified as "low class," and a still smaller group of slaves. The slaves lived in the households of the upper class; the lower class often occupied separate houses in its own section of the community or in a location sufficiently separate so that it might be regarded as a lower class community subservient to an upper class group. In native theory the lower class consisted of people who "had lost their history," that is, people who had no claim to the most productive resources of the area and no claim to recognized inherited privileges, and who furthermore "had no advice," that is, they had no private knowledge and no moral training.[3]

For the upper class the most proper and usual sort of marriage was one arranged between families of similar social standing in different communities. The arrangements usually included preliminary negotiations by members of the prospective groom's family, a vigil kept by the young man at the girl's house, and an exchange of property between the two families. This exchange was the wedding itself. It was held in the bride's house. The groom's family brought wealth for the bride's family; the bride's family gave wealth, perhaps nearly an equal amount, to the groom's family; and the bride's father also gave, if possible, an inherited privilege or privileges, such as a name or the right to

use a rattle or mask, to the couple for their child or children. After the wedding the couple usually went to live with the groom's family. The two families could continue to exchange property as long as the marriage endured. And the marriage might be made to endure longer than the life of one party to it, for if one or the other died the family of the deceased might provide another spouse for the survivor.

The kinship terms seem to indicate something of the nature of these relationships. The terms for blood kin form a system in some respects like the English, bilateral with lineal and collateral kin distinguished in parents' and children's generations, the most important difference being that the sibling terms distinguish older and younger siblings and are extended to cousins to distinguish senior from junior lines of descent.

But the affinal terms form an entirely different system. For the relationships indicated by the English terms "father-in-law," "mother-in-law," "son-in-law," "daughter-in-law," "brother-in-law," sister-in-law," there are four native terms: $s\check{k}^w\acute{i}t\partial w$ (spouse's parent, wife's brother), $sc\partial wt\acute{e}\ell$ (child's spouse, man's sister's husband), $sm\acute{e}t\partial x^w t\partial n$ (man's sister-in-law, woman's brother-in-law), $sx^w\acute{e}t\partial x$ (woman's sister-in-law). Thus the affinal terms, quite unlike the consanguineal terms, may lump persons of different generations and distinguish by sex of speaker. The English affinal terms form a structure that mirrors that formed by the consanguineal terms; the native affinal terms form an entirely different sort of structure. The key to this structure seems to be that it shows the "direction of the marriage," that is, the direction of the movement of women as wives, and it shows the possibility of secondary affinal marriage. A man calls by the term $s\check{k}^w\acute{i}t\partial w$ his wife's father and brother, that is, the men from whom he received her, and he is called $sc\partial wt\acute{e}\ell$ by them. And, conversely, he uses the term $sc\partial wt\acute{e}\ell$ for his sister's husband and daughter's husband, that is, the men who have received women from him, and they of course call him $s\check{k}^w\acute{i}t\partial w$. Siblings-in-law of the opposite sex, that is, men and women who might marry through the operation of the levirate or sororate, call each other *smétəxʷtən*. Sisters-in-law call each other *sxʷʔɬax*, which means literally "one who functions as sister." If a spouse dies, his or her relatives are all called by a single term *čέyʔɛ* by the widow or widower. To marry one's *čέyʔɛ* is called *čέyʔɛm*. If this is done the former terms are again used.

The most important remaining affinal kinship term is *sk̓ʷɬlwəs*, child's spouse's parent. Since there is no usual English term for *sk̓ʷɬlwəs*, I propose to use a term of my own, "co-parent-in-law." This relationship is one of the most important in the whole social system. Co-parents-in-law are people linked by the marriage of their children. These are the people who exchange wealth at the wedding and who may continue to make exchanges as long as the marriage lasts. After the death of one party to the marriage they become *čɬxέɛm* ("those who weep together") until the marriage is reconstituted.

According to informants from several tribes in the area, a man could at any time take food to a co-parent-in-law and expect to receive wealth in return. To make such a trip was called *íst* (literally "to paddle") or *ɬəwέn* in Straits, *ʔə́xət* or *k̓ʷəlwəsέɛn* in Halkomelem. The person taking food invited members of his community to help him take it; these people were called *šq̓áʔwət*. The person or family receiving the food then invited members of their own community to share the food in a feast (*sx̌ɛ́xən*, from *x̌έxən* "to invite"). At this time they hired a speaker (*šqʷíʔqʷέl'*) to "pay the paddles" and to "thank" the co-parent-in-law. To "pay the paddles" ( *q̓ɛ́ʔwəl'wɛʔs*, from *q̓ɛ́ʔwət*, "to pay for services," and -*əl'wɛʔs*, "paddle") meant to pay each of the *šq̓áʔwət* who had helped bring the food, and also to make payments for the canoes themselves, the paddles, and even the bailers. The Swinomish, Lummi, and Katzie seem to have spoken of "paying" the co-parent-in-law for the food, using the verb (in Halkomelem) *náwnəc*, "to pay for something

bought." A Lummi informant stated that on Vancouver Island people did not pay their co-parents-in-law. My Musqueam informants likewise stated that they and the Cowichan did not pay for the food. But then they explained that you had to "thank" ( *číɬ* ) your co-parents-in-law. The Vancouver Island people still do this—at Cowichan "you ought to thank them with between ten and twenty dollars." The difference then is only in the terms used. Everywhere one can take food and expect to receive wealth.

This sort of exchange is not confined to co-parents-in-law; it may take place between father-in-law and son-in-law or between brothers-in-law, or between cousins in different communities as well. But informants usually speak of the exchange first in relation to co-parents-in-law, probably because this is the relationship of the two families who have established the tie through marrying their children to one another and who begin the series of exchanges. Exchanges between other relatives are, I believe, simply the continuation of exchanges begun by co-parents-in-law.

Several informants indicated that the exchanges of food and wealth between affinals could become competitive. The amount of wealth extracted from an in-law could be increased by increasing the amount of food taken and by increasing the number of fellow villagers invited to help take it. But if the amount of wealth required were very great, the recipient of the food might "pay for it with a song," that is to say, he might sing an inherited song ( *səyəwənəm* or *shəy̓wíʔnaqʷ* ) or (perhaps only among the Klallam) a spirit song bestowed by a wealth spirit ( *yólməx̌* ). If the recipient of the food had such a song which he might sing at this time as additional payment, the bringer of the food might then feel obliged to thank him for this performance with a gift of wealth, or to treat him in the same fashion when the situation was reversed.

Two things must be made clear. First, this sort of exchange between affinals is not simply a repayment of the bride price or a balancing out of the exchanges that took place at the wedding. Historically it may be derived from this, or in individual cases it may begin with this, but families seem to have continued and developed the series of exchanges long after the original connection was established. Second, this sort of exchange is not to be confused with the potlatch. The potlatch ( sx̣ánəq ) is an occasion when the host or hosts invite members of other communities to the host community to receive gifts of wealth to validate changes of status and exercise of inherited privileges. The sponsor may be an individual, but it seems that more often a number of persons in the host community pooled their occasions for the validation of claims to high (or at least new) status and invited guests at the same time so that the community as a whole served as host.

As I said earlier, I believe the exchange between affinals that I have just described plays an important part in the native socio-economic system. First, it is an important link in the relationship between food, wealth, and high status, a relationship that has not been very thoroughly explored for any Northwest Coast society.

Among the Coast Salish of the area I am describing food and high status are directly related. High status comes from sharing food. The variety of native subsistence techniques and property rights, together with individual differences in skill (generally interpreted in native ideology as resulting from differences in supernatural support), made for considerable differences in productivity. And, of course, the man who produced more than others was honored. A man was expected to share food with his close relatives and housemates. Certain types of food, such as sea mammals, were usually shared at feasts ( sx̣éxən ) at which someone from each family was served and given a portion called máqaθ to take home. And, as I have indicated, a man used food brought by his co-parents-in-law for a feast for his own people, so that having productive affinals meant being a food provider yourself—as long as you could thank your affinals properly for their gifts.

People also shared food with neighbors and relatives from other communities by sharing access to their techniques and/or resources. One conjugal family working alone had the instruments for and equal access to most types of resources within the territory of its community. But some of the most productive techniques required the cooperation of several persons. Moreover, access to some of the most productive sites was restricted by property rights. Not all, but the best camas beds, fern beds, wapato ponds, and clam beds were owned by extended families with control exercised by individuals. Most duck-net sites were so owned; deer-net sites were not, but the investment of material and labor in the nets was such that only a few hunters had them, and the same was probably true of seal nets. Weirs and traps for salmon seem usually to have been built by a whole community, perhaps under the direction of the head of an extended family, but with no distinction in access. However, the houses standing at the weir sites, which were necessary for smoking the catch, were owned by individuals or extended families. Some other types of fishing were more restricted by property rights. The sturgeon traps of the Musqueam belonged to extended families. The reef-net locations of the Straits tribes (Lummi, Saanich, Songish) were owned by individuals. But in one way or another access was shared, both within the community and among communities. The director of a Musqueam sturgeon trap might give permission to members of other extended families to help take fish from it for a share. The owner of a Straits reef-net location might "hire" a crew from members of other extended families or even other communities. Some Cowichans fished in the summer on reef nets belonging to Saanich and some of the Saanich, who had no important stream in their territory, went to the Cowichan River for the fall runs of fish caught at weirs. The Katzie were hosts to people from up and down the Fraser when it was time to take wapato from their ponds or pick berries on their bogs.

High status also comes from directing food

production. Perhaps every kind of joint enterprise had a director in the owner of the gear or the "owner" of the site. The actual degree of control given to an individual probably varied with the complexity of the process and the responsibility required of him. The Straits reef net was a complex device that had to be carefully made and skillfully operated; the reef-net location was always said to be "owned" by one man or at most two brothers, who evidently had considerable authority over it. On the other hand, the Musqueam sturgeon trap was simply a kind of tidal pond from which fish could be easily drawn out at low tide; members of the extended family that had built the trap were its "owners" and were free to come and take fish at any time without consulting the director—it being expected they would share the fish; while the only responsibility of the director was to see that the trap was repaired once a year and to give permission to nonmembers to participate in the taking of fish. But even the Katzie wapato ponds and berry bogs had an "owner" who gave permission to outsiders to collect there. Thus, for some subsistence techniques there may be technical reasons for control by a director while for others there are not. But with such widespread sharing of access to resources, there are surely social reasons why there may be an "owner" even when technical reasons are minimal, simply in order to show outsiders that *somebody's* permission had to be asked.

The potlatch very likely played an important part within this system of sharing access to resources. By potlatching, a group established its status vis-à-vis other groups, in effect saying "we are an extended family (or a village of several extended families) with title to such-and-such a territory having such-and-such resources." And when a leading member assumed a name that harked back to the beginning of the world when the ancestors of the group first appeared on the spot, this not only demonstrated the validity of the group's title but perhaps also announced in effect "this is the man in charge of our resources." But could not any sort of spectacle

serve the same ends? It seems to me that these functions are not sufficient to explain that feature which is most typical of the potlatch—the lavish giving of wealth.

The relationship between wealth and high status is quite clear. As in other Northwest Coast societies, by giving wealth at a potlatch a man validates a claim to noble descent and inherited privilege and thus converts wealth into high status. It might be argued then that the relationship of wealth and high status only parallels that of food and high status, but the argument is convincing only if food and wealth are unrelated.

Food and wealth are indeed separate categories of goods in native culture. "Wealth" ( *áwk̓ʷ* ) consisted of blankets, shell ornaments, fine baskets, hide shirts, bows and arrows, canoes, slaves—items of varying utility but all relatively imperishable. Blankets were the most important such item, especially since they could be ripped apart and the wool rewoven time after time. Food was not classed as "wealth." Nor was it treated as wealth. There is some evidence that food was seen as a gift from the supernatural; *χέ' χε síləŋ* , "holy food," a Semiahmoo informant called it. It should be given freely, he felt, and could not be refused. Food was evidently not freely exchanged with wealth. A person in need of food might ask to buy some from another household in his community, offering wealth for it, but food was not generally offered for sale.

Food and wealth were *indirectly* related in one important way. A man who could produce more food could release some of the members of his household from food-producing activities and let them produce wealth and he could attract more food-producing and wealth-producing persons to his household as wives for himself (polygyny being permitted) and for his sons, brothers, and nephews, and as sons-in-law (residence with wife's family being permitted). Thus food could be indirectly converted into wealth. But of course a larger household means more mouths to feed at all times and conditions of production must have set limits to the size of a household.

And finally, as described above, food could be taken to affinal relatives and wealth received in return. This then appears to have been the most important mechanism for *directly* converting food into wealth. The relationship of food, wealth, and high status is complete. They all form a single system.

Thus the first thing I want to point out about the food-for-wealth exchange between affinals is its importance within the total system of food, wealth, and high status. The second is that through it the total system is an adaptive one.

The environmental setting of native culture was characterized by four significant features: 1) *variety of types of food,* including sprouts, roots, berries, shellfish, fishes, waterfowl, land and sea mammals; 2) *local variation* in the occurrence of these types, due to irregular shore lines, broken topography, differences between fresh and salt water, local differences in temperature and precipitation; 3) *seasonal variation,* especially in vegetable foods and in anadromous fishes; 4) *fluctuation from year to year,* in part due to the regular cycles of the different populations of fish, in part to less predictable changes, as in weather.

The first three of these four environmental features are no doubt closely related to the clearly patterned yearly round of subsistence activities. In the spring the different families occupying the sections of a big house left the community, perhaps separately, to spend a good part of the year moving from place to place accumulating stores of food. But this food quest was not at all a random movement. People knew quite well where and when they were likely to find what food and so they generally exploited a certain place at a certain time for a certain thing. Their choice was determined largely by the first three of the environmental features just mentioned, together with technological and social factors suggested earlier. But the fourth of the environmental features, fluctuation from year to year, must have demanded versatility and adaptability. While these environmental features were

characteristic even of the small territory identified with each community, they were of course of greater significance for the whole area under consideration. The rather pronounced differences in resources among communities, plus year-to-year fluctuation in quantities, must have put a premium on intercommunity cooperation.

The sharing of access to resources was a form of intercommunity cooperation that must have made for greater efficiency in the exploitation of the environment. But this form of cooperation was probably one that required some planning, as when a Saanich reef-net captain hired Cowichan net pullers or when a Musqueam family decided to visit their Katzie relatives at wapato harvesting time, and worked out best for predictable differences in resources. But the availability of food was clearly not always predictable; there were temporary unforeseen shortages and surpluses. Under all of these conditions any mechanism by which members of one community could "bank" a temporary surplus of some particular item of diet with members of another community would be advantageous. The exchange between affinals was such a mechanism. If one community had a sudden oversupply of, say, herring, its members could take canoeloads to their various co-parents-in-law, receive mountain-goat wool blankets in exchange, with which they might later "thank" their co-parents-in-law for gifts of camas bulbs or dried sturgeon. Wealth then was credit for food received. Wealth was a part of this adaptive system.

Looking now at that most famous institution, the potlatch, I find that *within this total socioeconomic system,* its most important function is to be found neither in the expression of the individual's drive for high status nor in the fulfillment of the society's need for solidarity, neither in competition nor in cooperation, but simply in the redistribution of wealth. Wealth has been accumulated by various means—producing it within one's own household, receiving it for services, receiving it as gifts validating the status of donors at previous potlatches, and receiving it in thanks for food taken to one's in-laws in other communities. Since wealth is indirectly or directly obtainable through food, then inequalities in food production will be translated into inequalities in wealth. If one community over a period of several years were to produce more food than its neighbors, it might come to have a greater part of the society's wealth. Under such circumstances the less productive communities might become unable to give wealth back in exchange for further gifts of food from the more productive one. If amassing wealth were an end in itself the process of sharing surplus food might thus break down. But wealth, in the native view, is only a means to high status achieved through the giving of it. And so the community that has converted its surplus food into wealth and now has a surplus of wealth gets rid of its wealth by giving it away at a potlatch. And this, though the participants need not be conscious of it, by "restoring the purchasing power" of the other communities, enables the whole process to continue. The potlatchers have converted their surplus wealth into high status. High status in turn enables the potlatchers to establish wider ties, make better marriages with more distant villages, and thus extend the process farther.

This interpretation of the potlatch among this particular group of tribes suggests that it serves as a regulating mechanism within the total socioeconomic system. The drive to attain high status emerges from this interpretation as a prerequisite to the sorts of behavior that keep the system operating. Satisfying this drive is a "function" of the potlatch only in a secondary or instrumental sense (i.e. it serves an end that is only a means to another end); by satisfying the individual potlatcher's and the community's drive to attain high status, the potlatch provides the rewards necessary to keep others striving to rise. The drive for high status is itself a part of the total system. Since it is necessary to the system, we may assume that values stimulating and supporting it have developed at the expense of values inhibiting it. Some of the values stimulating and supporting the drive to attain high status are

seen in native ethical theory, which insists that knowledge of good behavior is the monopoly of the "good" families and that the lower class are "without advice" (i.e. without properly enculturated values), and some are seen in native supernaturalism, which insists that success in any practical activity is achieved with supernatural support and thus gives the seeker for supernatural power both the confidence and the incentive to succeed in the practical. These values are given to the individual early in life and are reaffirmed until the end. They provide a constant stimulation to the drive for high status, which finds its greatest satisfaction in the potlatch.

But the drive to attain high status is clearly not the explanation of the potlatch. Nor is the production of surplus. Nor the cooperation achieved by the potlatching community. The potlatch is a part of a larger socio-economic system that enables the whole social network, consisting of a number of communities, to maintain a high level of food production and to equalize its food consumption both within and among communities. The system is thus adaptive in an environment characterized by the features indicated before—spatial and temporal variation and fluctuation in the availability of resources. Values, drives, surpluses, competition, and cooperation—all of these may be as much effects as causes. The whole has probably developed through a process of variation and selection, within the limitations of environment and cultural means, that can be best described by the term "cultural evolution."

The foregoing is an interpretation of the culture of one Northwest Coast society as an adaptive system. The data on which it is based are not always as clear as I would like but I offer it with the strong feeling that, seen in this fashion, more of native culture makes better sense than it does otherwise. I do not offer it as an interpretation of the whole Northwest Coast culture area except in a general way. In its details it may not even apply to the Coast Salish north of the Squamish and south of the Skagit. And certainly the other subareas within the Northwest Coast differ greatly in several features of social organization and they very likely differ in features of ecological setting as well. The relationship between these two sets of variables remains to be worked out.

# NOTES

1. This paper was presented in somewhat shorter form at the 12th Annual Northwest Anthropological Conference held at Portland State College in April, 1959. The field research upon which it is based has been done at various times over the last twelve years and has been supported successively by the University of Washington, a Wenner-Gren Pre-doctoral Fellowship, the University of British Columbia, and the Leon and Thea Koerner Foundation. The interpretation presented here has evolved from one presented in my Ph.D. dissertation (1951), modified by later work on the Lower Fraser, and further developed and broadened by collaboration with Dr. A. P. Vayda and discussion with our students at the University of British Columbia.

2. There is no general term for the tribes of this area. They are all speakers of two closely related Coast Salish languages, Halkomelem and Straits (Lkungeneng). Dialects of Halkomelem are spoken by the Stalo tribes, including the Chilliwack, Katzie, Kwantlen, Musqueam and others on the Lower Fraser, and by the Nanaimo, Chemainus, and Cowichan of Vancouver Island. Straits dialects are spoken by the Semiahmoo, Lummi, and Samish on the mainland south of the Fraser and by the Saanich, Songish, and Sooke on Vancouver Island. The Klallam, on the south shore of the Strait of Juan de Fuca and at Becher Bay on Vancouver Island, speak a more divergent dialect of Straits. There are few significant cultural differences among these tribes. That they have some kind of social unity is suggested by the fact that the system of kin terms described here is identical

in Straits, Halkomelem, and Nooksack, but different in structure to the north and to the south. The system of affinal exchange described here, however, seems to have extended somewhat beyond this area, but my data are not sufficient to permit me to draw any neat boundaries.

My data are mainly from work done with informants of the Straits tribes and of the Katzie and Musqueam. The personal recollections of the oldest of these people did not take them back earlier than the 1870's and 80's, though traditional genealogies and bits of history allow for some inferences about conditions during the first half of the 19th century. The present paper is thus an interpretation based on an ethnographic reconstruction.

Portions of this area have been covered in the published ethnographic works of Boas, Hill-Tout, Jenness, Gunther, Stern, Barnett, and Duff. I have used these as guides for enquiry, but the material this paper is based on is almost wholly my own field notes.

Native terms have been transcribed in the system of phonetic symbols used in the more recent publications on this area. Unless otherwise indicated, native terms are given in the Musqueam dialect of Halkomelem. Dr. W. W. Elmendorf and I are preparing a comparative study of Halkomelem dialects to be presented elsewhere.

3. I have discussed this in greater detail in "Private Knowledge, Morality, and Social Classes among the Coast Salish" (1958).

# REFERENCES CITED

SUTTLES, WAYNE

1951 The economic life of the Coast Salish of Haro and Rosario Straits. Unpublished Ph.D. dissertation, University of Washington.

1958 Private knowledge, morality, and social classes among the Coast Salish. American Anthropologist 60:497–507.

# 20

## THE POTLATCH SYSTEM OF THE SOUTHERN KWAKIUTL: A NEW PERSPECTIVE

*Stuart Piddocke*

*Stuart Piddocke takes a more extreme view of the economic function of the potlatch. Analyzing the ritual among the Southern Kwakiutl, a second Northwest Coast Indian group, Piddocke argues that regional variation in food production could have really serious consequences for the survival of local Indian communities. Food could be exchanged for wealth and the potlatch redistributed the wealth so that its exchange for food could continue. Prestige was a motivating factor in the system and resulted from the need to exchange wealth for food.*

This paper[1] is, first, an attempt to reconstruct the potlatch system of Southern Kwakiutl society around the last decade of the eighteenth century, i.e. at the beginning of direct contact with Occidental civilization; and, second, an argument that in aboriginal times the potlatch had a very real pro-survival or subsistence function, serving to counter the effects of varying resource productivity by promoting exchanges of food from those groups enjoying a temporary surplus to those groups suffering a temporary deficit.[2] In making this reconstruction, I find myself forced by the data to depart from the orthodox portrait of the Kwakiutl potlatch and to develop another based on data rather neglected in the literature. At the same time, there is no need to reject the orthodox picture as at least an approximately accurate description of *later* Kwakiutl potlatching, because the later form can be deduced from the proposed model of the aboriginal potlatch when certain actual historical processes, i.e. the events of the contact period, are fed in as conditions disturbing the original state of equilibrium specified in the model. Therefore, although this paper is not intended as a reconstruction of Kwakiutl history, it does provide an explanation for some of the responses that actually occurred in the historic period.

In particular, I wish to present evidence for the following propositions:

---

[1]This inquiry into the ecological relationships of the Kwakiutl potlatch was first started in 1959–60 as part of a seminar on Northwest Coast cultures conducted at the University of British Columbia by Dr. Wayne Suttles and Dr. A. P. Vayda, who must be regarded as the joint inspirers of this paper and for whom its first version was written. A second version was read in the late fall of 1960 at the London School of Economics seminar on anthropological theory conducted by Professor Raymond Firth, whose criticism has greatly benefited both this paper in particular and my own thinking in general. Reference to this unpublished second version is also made in a 1961 paper by Dr. Vayda; and the preparation and publication of this final version is therefore in the nature of a somewhat belated fulfillment of a scholastic obligation.

[2]Compare Suttles (1960:296–305), where he shows how the Coast Salish potlatch, status rivalry, subsistence activities, variations in production within the Coast Salish resources, and their system of exchanges between affinal relatives were all linked together as parts of a single socioeconomic system.

(a) The Kwakiutl have been commonly described as having a "fantastic surplus economy" distinguished by a great abundance of food and other natural resources further maximized by efficient methods of exploiting and storing the various products; this great abundance, preserved in summer, fed the people throughout the winter, during which season an abundance of leisure time enabled the people to develop their extraordinary potlatches and winter ceremonials (Codere 1950:4–5, 14, 63–64, 68, 126; Ford 1941:8). What I hope to show is that, however true such a picture of abundance may have been for the Kwakiutl as a whole, it was less than true for the various individual local groups. For these latter, scarcity of food was an ever-present threat, depending on the varying productivity of sea and land; and without the distribution of food from wealthier local groups to poorer ones, the latter would often have died of hunger.

(b) The potlatch was in aboriginal times confined to the chiefs or headmen of the various localized kin-groups or numayms that made up the tribes or winter-village groups, and hence the series of potlatches between the various chiefs were in effect exchanges of food and wealth between tribes and numayms. Through this exchange system, the effects of variations in productivity were minimized, and a level of subsistence was maintained for the entire population.

(c) In this system food could be exchanged for wealth objects, such as blankets, slaves, and canoes; and wealth objects exchanged in turn for increased prestige.

(d) The desire for prestige and the status rivalry between chiefs directly motivated potlatching and so indirectly motivated the people to continue the system of exchanges; and the continuation of these practices ensured the survival of the population.

Kwakiutl history may be divided into four periods: the Aboriginal or Pre-Contact period, extending from the indefinite past to 1792; the Early Contact period, 1792 to 1849; the Potlatch

period, 1849 to the early 1920's; and the Post-Potlatch period, from the early 1920's to the present. What I have here separated as the Aboriginal and Early Contact periods corresponds to the Pre-Potlatch period distinguished by Codere (1961:434); the two later divisions follow Codere exactly. In 1792, European civilization, in the persons of Captain Vancouver and his expedition, first made direct contact with the Kwakiutl at the place known as "Cheslakee's Village" (Vancouver 1801:268–73).[3] European influence thenceforward slowly but steadily increased until in 1849 the Hudson's Bay Company established their trading post of Fort Rupert (Dawson 1887:66), and shortly thereafter the four Kwakiutl tribes later to be known as the Fort Rupert tribes settled hard by the post. This marks the appearance in Kwakiutl country of a direct non-traditional source of wealth, as contrasted with indirect trade through Nootka or relatively inconstant trade with trading ships. And with this new source of wealth there came changes in Kwakiutl society, notably an intensification of status rivalry and an increase in the frequency and volume of potlatching, so much so that the potlatch became the predominant Kwakiutl institution. This Potlatch period ended in the early 1920's when the beginning of an economic depression for the Kwakiutl coincided with the first notable successes in the Government's campaign to stop the Indians from potlatching.

## SUBSISTENCE

Sea-fishing, river-fishing, berry picking, and the hunting of land and sea animals were the chief subsistence activities. Reviewing the list of the fish, animals and plants eaten, one gets at first glance an impression of abundance: salmon, salmon-spawn, herring, herring-spawn, eulach-

---

[3]Identified by Dawson (1887:72) with the Nimkish village of Whulk, at the mouth of the Nimkish River.

en or candle-fish (notable for its oil), halibut, cod, perch, flounder, kelp-fish, devil fish, sea-slugs, barnacles, and winkles; seals, porpoises, and the occasional beach-stranded whale; mountain goats; elderberries, salalberries, wild currants, huckleberries, salmon-berries, viburnum berries, dogwood berries, gooseberries, and crab-apples; clover roots, cinquefoil roots, sea-milk-wort, bracken roots, fern-roots, erythronium roots, lupine roots, wild carrots, and lily-bulbs; eel-grass and some sea-weeds. Of these, some would be eaten in summer, and the rest preserved for use in winter (Boas 1921:173–514).

This impression of abundance is, however, not sustained by further examination. For instance, the various roots and berries did not grow everywhere. Good crabapples could be picked in only two places; elsewhere they were "rotten." Viburnum berries could be picked only at the end of summer at the head of Knight Inlet (Boas 1921:213, 216). And berries and roots, generally, could be picked only in season.

Similar restrictions governed the supply of fish. The several varieties of salmon ran only at certain seasons of the year and did not spawn in every stream. Herring did not spawn everywhere. The eulachen ran in spring (Boas 1921:198), and, according to Curtis (1915:22–23), in three streams only, namely those on Kingcome River, at the head of Knight Inlet, and at the head of Rivers Inlet; furthermore, "this fish cannot be taken for its oil above tidal water." Curtis (1915:24–25) also informs us that only the following groups specialized in halibut fishing (though others might fish for halibut also, their fishing was only occasional): four tribes of Quatsino, two tribes (one now extinct) at Cape Scott, the Newettee of Hope Island, the Goasila of Smith Inlet, the Naquoqtoq of Seymour Inlet, and the Owikeno of Rivers Inlet; the principal halibut banks were near Hope Island, Galiano Island, the Gordon group, and certain islands of the larger inlets. Flounders had to be caught in calm weather, when the tide was coming in (Boas 1921:413). Winkles were collected only when they spawned (Boas 1921:509). Kelp-fish

were not caught in large numbers, and there was in any one catch usually only enough for a family (Boas 1921:397, 400, 405, 408). Of this apparent abundance of products, only a few were staples; the rest were additions, very welcome and very necessary to the Kwakiutl, but still only supplementary to the main diet. These staples were salmon, herring, eulachen, berries, and, to a somewhat lesser extent, goats, seals, and porpoises.

The Kwakiutl quarrelled and fought amongst themselves over rights to hunting grounds, fishing stations on rivers, use of fish weirs and traps, and berrying grounds; trespassing was a frequent cause for conflict (Boas 1921:1345–1348; Curtis 1915:22). Wars were waged "to take the land away from people" (Boas 1935:60, 66–67).

Starvation was no stranger to the Kwakiutl. Stories of starvation were more numerous among the tribes living on the islands in Queen Charlotte and Johnstone Straits, but all experienced hunger. Reasons given for such starvation included prolonged periods of bad weather which prevented hunting and fishing, and the failure of fish runs. The tales emphasized the especial dependence of the people on the salmon (Boas 1935:24). People would eat fern-roots when they were hungry and lacking in other food or when they had to camp for a long time in bad weather. The lupine root when eaten caused dizziness and sleepiness; yet it would be eaten in spring "when the tribes are hungry" before the eulachen arrived in Knight Inlet (Boas 1921:196, 198). As we would expect in such circumstances, they wasted very little of what food there was; for instance, recipes are given for salmon tails and roasted salmon backbone (Boas 1921:329).

This evidence can only lead, I think, to the conclusion that the abundance of the resources of the Kwakiutl has been somewhat overestimated and its significance misinterpreted. It was great enough to support a population larger than the usual size reported for hunting and gathering societies; but this population lived sufficiently close to the margins of subsistence so that variations in productivity which fell below normal could threaten parts of the population with famine and death from starvation.

Thus the evidence in the ethnographic record. It describes the localization of Kwakiutl subsistence resources and indicates—but does not document—variations in productivity. Further evidence for variation, however, is to be found in fisheries statistics concerning production of salmon and herring.

*Herring*

Statistics on herring show great variations, some spawning grounds apparently not being continuously used. Times of spawning vary from place to place. Changes in population abundance, says Outram (1956:7; 1957:7; cf. also 1958), are due primarily to variations in environmental conditions which cause variations in the "relative strengths of the contributing year classes" rather than to inadequate spawning or over- or under-fishing.

The Kwakiutl ate both herring and herring-spawn, and caught both at the spawning grounds. Besides the variation from year to year in the absolute number of herring spawn deposited (measured in miles of spawn at some standard intensity of deposition), the intensity of spawn varied from ground to ground, and we might expect this to have some effect on the catch made by Kwakiutl.

*Salmon*

Considerable year-to-year variation is likewise shown in the statistics on the packs of canned sockeye and other salmon taken at Rivers Inlet from 1882 to 1954 (Cobb 1921:172–174; Godfrey 1958a:333; cf. also Hoar 1951, for a general survey of variations in abundances of pink salmon on the British Columbia coast). These variations in salmon packs are traced to variations in the actual size of the salmon populations, variations which are in turn due to several causes. Notable among these causes are variable water levels and temperatures in the spawning streams, variations in the permeability of the stream beds, occasional extreme floods, variable temperatures and salinity in the ocean, and the variable freshwater runoffs and the action of tides, currents, winds, and deep-water upwelling in the estuarine and inshore waters that are the habitat of the young salmon for weeks or perhaps months before they reach the open seas (Godfrey 1958b; Neave 1953, 1958; Rostlund 1952:16; Wickett (1958). These causes are likely to have operated in previous centuries as well as in the present, and therefore indicate the existence of variations before statistics began to be kept on the fish population.

Rostlund (1952:16–17) has suggested that Indian fishing, before the advent of commercial fishing, helped to maintain the optimum salmon population by preventing over-crowding of the salmon streams. This may have been so, and it is a possibility to be taken into account when evaluating the productivity of subsistence resources for the Kwakiutl. But the effect of the Indian fishing would nevertheless not eliminate variations due to the causes enumerated above.

In addition to the variation in actual numbers of fish and game available for food, we must take into consideration the effects of the weather in hindering or preventing hunting and fishing expeditions. This has already been referred to as one of the reasons for starvation among the Kwakiutl.

The evidence is, I think, sufficient. For the various local groups of the Kwakiutl, scarcity of food was an ever-present threat, depending on the varying production of sea and land. Oftentimes it fell out that a local group would have died of starvation if it had not acquired food from other groups. The remainder of this paper will now be devoted to showing how the exchange system of the Kwakiutl ensured a continual movement of food from those groups enjoying a temporary abundance to those groups suffering privation, and so contributed to the survival of the whole population involved in the exchange system.

## SOCIAL UNITS

The basic unit of Kwakiutl society was the numaym, which may be summarily described as a named group associated mythologically with a traditional place of origin; it owned property consisting of fishing locations, hunting territory, and one or more houses in a winter village; and it was headed by a chief or headman descended, at least in theory, in the most senior genealogical line from a founding ancestor.[4] The members of the numaym consisted of people related, sometimes closely, sometimes distantly, usually patrilineally, but often through their mothers or wives, to the chief. There would at any time probably be a number of visitors dwelling with the people of the numaym, and some of the members of numaym would also likely be away visiting. The numaym was in pre-contact times the potlatching unit, resource-exploiting unit, and the unit of social control.[5]

---

[4]Succession to the chief's position could apparently go to a woman, if she were a chief's eldest child and on condition that she resided in her father's numaym. We can perhaps best describe the succession as one of primogeniture with a patrilineal bias and a residence qualification. Since marriage seems to have been generally virilocal, at least for persons of high status, the residence qualification would tend to have ruled out most daughters, barring uxorilocal exceptions (which, of course, occurred). See also the section on rank, below.

[5]The whole question of the nature of the Kwakiutl numaym is still a thorny one. This brief sketch, based on Boas (1889:832; 1897:332–338; 1920:112ff; 1921:795ff; 1925:57–58, 91, 101; 1935:173), Curtis (1915:28, 132), and Ford (1941:15) should be considered still only approximate and provisional and should also be considered in relation to the portrait of Kwakiutl ranking (see below).

The next larger unit of Kwakiutl society was the tribe. This was composed of a number of numayms which shared a common winter village site. In summer the villages dispersed and the various numayms departed for their fishing stations. As these summer grounds, groups living in separate winter villages would meet. This seasonal migration was an important feature of Kwakiutl life, and it involved both intertribal meetings and some sharing of access to resources (Curtis 1915:21–23, 108; Dawson 1887:64, 72).

## CHIEFTAINSHIP

The position of the chief or numaym head among the Kwakiutl was described by the people themselves as "the office of giving potlatches among the tribes" (Boas 1925:91, 99, 105), an expression which points out the position of the chief as representative of his numaym and his special task of potlatch giving. In former times, potlatching was a chiefly prerogative. Dawson (1887:79) has a significant passage on this point:

Mr. George Blenkinsop, who has been for many years among the Kwakiool, informs me that the custom [of the potlatch] was formerly almost entirely confined to the recognized chiefs, but that of late years it has extended to the people generally, and become very much commoner than before. The Rev. A. J. Hall bears testimony to the same effect. With the chiefs, it was a means of acquiring and maintaining prestige and power. It is still so regarded, but has spread to all classes of the community and become the recognized mode of attaining social rank and respect.

By the time Boas was making his studies of the Fort Rupert Kwakiutl and collecting and editing George Hunt's texts, the potlatch was no longer a chiefly prerogative alone, and it had also, perhaps, been modified with respect to the job it was performing in society. This change seems to have been due to the advent of European traders, bringing sources of wealth beyond those traditionally provided for by Kwakiutl culture, and to the decline of population, which led to some groups having more "seats" (see below) than members (cf. Codere 1961; Drucker 1955:121–122, Wike 1952:98–99).

The chief was the custodian or manager of the resources of the numaym. As such, it was his duty to perform the necessary rituals concerning the exploitation of these resources at the appropriate season. In this position, he received a certain portion (sometimes called "tribute" in the texts) of the fish, seals, goats, etc., caught by the men. His wife similarly received a portion of the berries and roots collected by the women. With this supply the chief could hold potlatches (though not always without further assistance) and could pay for the carving of totem poles, the construction of canoes, and the building of a new house (Boas 1921:1333–1340; 1925:311ff, 331; Curtis 1915:28).[6]

### Rank

Three status levels have been distinguished among the Kwakiutl and are termed in the literature "nobles," "commoners," and "slaves." But the distinctions between them are not of the same sort. Slaves were not, writes Boas (1897:338), strictly part of the numaym but

---

[6]It should be noted that the term "chief" in the literature denotes sometimes simply "numaym head" and at other times "numaym head and other high ranking nobles," but it is not always clear which usage is intended. That there is a distinction between the "numaym head" and the other "chiefs" seems to be indicated by the tenor of the various relevant texts. However, it does not matter much for my argument if nobles other than the headmen occasionally gave inter-numaym or even intertribal potlatches, as it is clear they gave them on behalf of their numayms. Nor would such other nobles constitute a very great part of the "nobility" as a whole.

were, rather, captives taken in war or people obtained by purchase; they might change ownership like any other piece of property, being, for instance, given away as marriage gifts (Boas 1921:856, 865–866, 881), presented to guests as a potlatch (Boas 1921:1027), or used as part of the purchase price of a copper (Boas 1921:1024). Indeed, according to one ancient account, a woman-slave was once killed and eaten in the cannibal dance (Boas 1921:1017). Marriages between free persons and slaves were possible, but they were considered disgraceful; and the stigma of having had slaves among one's ancestors descended to the children and grandchildren of the marriage, and beyond (Boas 1921:1094ff, 1104ff). Not even the accumulation (in later, post-contact times) of wealth and of names could remove it.

The distinction between "nobles" and "commoners" is of a different kind than that between free persons and slaves. Codere (1957:474–475) has summed it up in the following words:

"Commoner" in Kwakiutl refers to a person who at the moment of speaking is either without a potlatch position, chief's position, or standing place—all these bring interchangeable but "noble" terms—or applies to one who has low rank which is nevertheless a "standing place" or position. The man referred to at that moment might have passed on his position just the moment before, or he might just the next moment be a successor to a position. "Commoners" in Kwakiutl society cannot be considered a class, for they have no continuous or special function; they have no identity continuity, or homogeneity as a group, and no distinguishing culture or subculture. Individuals can at will become commoners by retirement from potlatch positions, and they customarily did so; individuals are raised from a common to a noble position at the will of others; individuals chose to consider "common" the lower positions of noble social rank; brothers and sisters of the same parents were given positions greatly varying in social rank and the younger ones might receive a position so lowly as to be "common."

These potlatch positions, or "seats" as Boas (1897:338) called them, were ranked in serial order, the chief of the numaym occupying the position of highest rank. Boas described these seats as each having associated with it a tradition of origin ("which almost always concerns the acquisition of a manitou"), certain crests, and certain privileges which the holder of the seat may enjoy; the rank was recognized in the order of seating the holders at potlatches, whence the position with its privileges came to be referred to as a "seat." Curtis (1915:137–138) describes the properties of the seat as including "names, crests, special ceremonial privileges, and territorial rights as to fishing and gathering vegetal food."

Succession to rank was by succession to the name and crest and complex of associated privileges, which of course also included its ranking. According to Curtis (1915:139), this succession was

ordinarily reckoned directly through the male line from father to eldest son; but a childless man may transfer his rank to a younger brother by adopting him as a son. More commonly, if he has a daughter his seat goes to her eldest son, or to her in trust for her infant or expected son. Less important names, along with ceremonial privileges, are regularly given to the son-in-law as a part of the dowry, in trust for his children; in fact, the acquisition of titles and privileges for children yet unborn is the most important consideration in arranging a union. But the principal name and rank never thus pass out of the direct succession unless there is no direct male heir. If a man dies while his eldest son is too young for man's responsibilities, the seat may be given in trust to an elder sister of the boy, or to an uncle.

Though Boas in his earlier work (1897:338–340) does not mention this distinction between names

and positions which could go out of the numaym and those which could not, he does recognize it in his later paper (1920:121) reviewing Kwakiutl social organization. The distinction is also repeatedly affirmed by the Kwakiutl themselves in the texts collected by Boas (1921:786–787, 824, 231; 1925:91, 101, 105), that only those names acquired from one's father-in-law can be given to one's son-in-law, and that certain names and positions, including that of headchief of the numaym, cannot be given away or go out of the numaym, daughters therefore inheriting when sons are not available. The distinction was sharper in principle than in practice, for, as might be expected, a few exceptions to the rule also did occur.

The numaym may be seen, then, not only as a kinship unit (as it was described earlier) but also as a collection of ranked positions, their incumbents, and persons related to these incumbents. As Codere (1957:479) has put it:

A numaym is a lineage group consisting of a series of ranked social positions, plus children and adults who do not have one of the ranked positions but who may receive one as a relative of someone who has one to pass on to or who may have held one and retired from it.

The numayms within a tribe were also ranked in serial order, the head of the highest-ranking numaym being reckoned the head chief of the tribe or village. This seems also to have been true in aboriginal times. There is no evidence, however, that the villages or tribal groups were ranked prior to European contact; the ranking of villages is a later nineteenth century development (cf. Codere 1961:445).

Thus far in this paper we have examined subsistence, the basic social units, chieftainship, and rank, demonstrated the first of the four propositions of this paper, and laid the foundation for demonstrating the remaining three. If in aboriginal times only chiefs potlatched (the chiefs being the numaym headmen and possibly one or two other leading men in each numaym as well), and if chiefs were supported in their potlatching by their numayms and potlatched on behalf of their numayms, then potlatches could only be between different numayms and were in effect exchanges of gifts between these numayms. The evidence for the first part of the antecedent in this proposition has been given in the section on "Chieftainship," and the second part of the antecedent implicitly supported there also. The numaym has been described and its resource-exploiting function noted. Kwakiutl ranking and its relation to the numaym have also been described, and something of its importance to the social structure suggested. What remains to be described is the system of exchanges, the conversions between food, wealth, and prestige, and the motivating factor of "status rivalry." These come to a focus in the institution of the potlatch, and to this we must now turn.

## THE POTLATCH

What may be called the orthodox[7] view of the kwakiutl potlatch is based largely on the summary and analysis given by Helen Codere in *Fighting with Property* (1950:63–80), following in turn the interpretation given by Boas in his early study of Kwakiutl social organization and "secret societies" (1897:341–358). As Codere has herself admitted (1950:89), however, her reconstruction does not apply to the *aboriginal* potlatch but to the potlatch of the later contact period. Between the aboriginal potlatch and the potlatch of Codere's reconstruction there are several very important differences.

The first point of difference concerns Codere's setting the potlatch "in the context of a fantastic surplus economy" (1950:63). There seems no valid reason to doubt the appearance among the Kwakiutl in the last quarter of the

nineteenth century of a great surplus beyond the needs of subsistence. But in aboriginal times such a surplus did not exist. Earlier in this paper I assembled evidence to indicate that the "fantastic surpluses" of the Kwakiutl have been overestimated, and that they were much closer to the margins of survival than has commonly been thought. The appearance of great wealth and "surpluses above any conceivable need" in later, post-contact times was probably due (a) to the drastic population decline from smallpox, venereal diseases, etc., ensuring that the productivity of sea and land, variable or not, was more than ample for the survivors' needs; and (b) to the increase in wealth coming from the sale of sea-otter furs to the fur traders and, later, to other non-traditional sources of wealth made possible by the contact situation. In aboriginal times, no such source of wealth was available, and it may also be presumed that the population was then at the limit of subsistence. Hence the threat of starvation, and in turn a very real pro-subsistence function for potlatch exchanges.

Secondly, Codere's account emphasizes not merely the giving away of gifts in the potlatch and the consequent accrual of honor to the giver, but also the obligation on the recipient to give a return potlatch or else lose prestige. She particularly writes (1950:68–69):

The property received by a man in a potlatch was no free and wanton gift. He was not at liberty to refuse it, even though accepting it obligated him to make a return at another potlatch not only of the original amount but of twice as much, if this return was made, as was usual, in a period of about a year. This gave potlatching its forced loan and investment aspects, since a man was alternately debtor and creditor for amounts that were increasing at a geometric rate.

This passage links the obligatory nature of the return potlatch to the institution of borrowing-and-lending-at-interest. Following Boas (1897:341), Codere sees borrowing-and-lending-at-interest as an integral, indeed essential, part of

---

[7]It has, for instance, been followed by Herskovits (1952:165, 225, 306) in his now classic work on economic anthropology, and by Bohannan in his recent textbook (1963:253–259).

potlatching, and a consequent continuous increase in the size of potlatch gifts as therefore also integrally part of the whole system.

This interpretation has, however, been vigorously denied by Curtis (1915:143–144) whose account has been curiously neglected in the study of the Kwakiutl potlatch:[8]

It has been said of the potlatch that "the underlying principle is that of the interest-bearing investment of property." This is impossible. A Kwakiutl would subject himself to ridicule by demanding interest when he received a gift in requital of one of like amount made by him. Not infrequently at a potlatch a guest calls attention to the fact that he is not receiving as much as he in his last potlatch gave to the present host; and he refuses to accept anything less than the proper amount. Even this action is likened to "cutting off one's own head," and results in loss of prestige; for the exhibition of greed for property is not the part of a chief; on the contrary he must show his utter disregard for it. But to demand interest on a potlatch gift is unheard of. Furthermore, a man can never receive through the potlatch as much as he disburses, for the simple reason that many to whom he gives will die before they have a potlatch, and others are too poor to return what he gives them. Thus, only a chief of great wealth can make a distribution in which all the tribes participate and every person receives something; but all except a very

few of these members of other tribes will never hold an intertribal potlatch, and consequently the man who gives presents to them cannot possibly receive any return for them. As to those who die, it may be said that theoretically a man's heir assumes his obligations, but he cannot be forced to do so, and if they far exceed the credits he is likely to repudiate them.

The potlatch and the lending of property at interest are two entirely distinct proceedings. Property distributed in a potlatch is freely given, bears no interest, cannot be collected on demand, and need not be repaid at all if the one who received it does not for any reason wish to requite the gift. When the recipient holds a potlatch he may return an equal amount or a slightly larger amount, or a smaller amount with perhaps the promise to give more at a future time.

The feeling at the bottom of the potlatch is one of pride rather than greed. Occasionally men have tried to accumulate wealth by means of the potlatch and of lending at interest, but the peculiar economic system has always engulfed them, simply because a man can never draw out all his credits and keep the property thus acquired. Before his debtors will pay, he must first call the people together and inaugurate a potlatch, thus ensuring an immediate redistribution.

This is a very different picture of the potlatch system. The practice of borrowing-and-lending-at-interest is both clearly distinct from and subordinated to the potlatch proper. The appearance of its being part of the potlatching is clearly due to the fact that debts were paid and could be called in only in connection with potlatching, often (Curtis 1915:144) only on the day of the potlatch itself.

The whole tone of the potlatch is different in Curtis' account—"one of pride rather than greed." This picture is much more consistent with data provided by Codere (1956:334ff) on the "amiable side" of Kwakiutl potlatching and

---

[8] It is very odd that though Codere in *Fighting with Property* (1950) relies very heavily on Curtis' accounts of Kwakiutl warfare, she makes absolutely no reference to Curtis' description of the potlatch, even though it is in the same volume as the war histories. According to his book, Curtis gathered his data intermittently between 1910 and 1914 and was assisted by George Hunt; his inquiry was also facilitated by Boas' earlier work, especially *Social Organization and Secret Societies* (1897). Curtis' book contains Kwakiutl material which cannot be found in any other published source.

by Boas himself (1925:249) in texts published at a later date, indicating that a chief should not be too proud or arrogant. The inability of creditors to enforce their claims unless they were intending to put on a potlatch—in which case their claims would be reinforced by public opinion—is in perfect accord with the lack of developed institutions of social control among the Kwakiutl. This institution of borrowing-and-lending-at-interest was, furthermore, by no means a universal Northwest Coast institution, apparently being confined to the Southern Kwakiutl (Barnett 1938:349ff; Olson 1940:173).

Curtis' report of potlatch gifts as not increasing in size but remaining about the same is, ironically, supported by Codere's own analysis of aboriginal potlatches (1950:90–94; 1961:446), where she notes that during the one hundred twenty years previous to 1849 the potlatches recorded in the texts involved relatively small distributions and showed no tendency to increase in size.

Finally, Curtis' account is more consistent with Dawson's report, already quoted in the section on chieftainship, that formerly only chiefs potlatched. In aboriginal times only chiefs would be able to assemble the wealth with which to hold a potlatch. For most people in the numaym the importance of having a position of rank would be in the receiving of gifts at potlatch distributions, not in having to validate these positions by potlatch giving—note Curtis' remark that many if not most of the persons receiving gifts in a potlatch, especially an intertribal one, would not be able to give potlatches in return.

For these reasons, the viewpoint followed in this paper in reconstructing the aboriginal potlatch is Curtis' rather than Boas' and Codere's.

Thirdly, we must also raise doubts about the aboriginal existence of the sacrifice potlatch, an institution which looms large in all the accounts of our authorities (Boas, Codere, *and* Curtis) on the post-contact potlatch. The sacrifice potlatch and the grease feast are not mentioned in Kwakiutl mythology, nor does their presence in aboriginal times seem indicated by any other

evidence. Concerning the destruction of property in the context of public assemblies or feasts Boas (1935:68), in summing up Kwakiutl culture as reflected in mythology, has only the following to say:

> In myths the destruction of property occurs only in connection with the cannibal ceremony when the cannibal devours his own slaves or is given slaves to eat. Canoe breaking during a potlatch occurs in a tale on which the person who breaks canoes owned by others makes them whole again by his magical powers. A man pushes a copper under a mountain during a feast.

No sacrifice potlatch or grease feast here!

The destruction of property in aboriginal times is, however, clearly indicated in connection with the dead or dying. For example, food is burnt and so sent to a spirit in order to persuade him to spare the life of the dying child; spoons must be burnt by a woman visiting the ghost-country in order that the spirits of the dead may receive the gifts; and when a man has died, bundles of dried salmon, along with oil, fishing hooks, clothing and his canoe, are burnt to provide him with travelling provisions (Boas 1921:705–711, 1329). What we have, then in historic times is a spread of the idea of the destruction of property from a funeral context to a context of potlatching and active status rivalry, with the idea of honoring the dead perhaps providing the semantic link between the two contexts, and the new wealth consequent upon contact providing the means. This would be part of the religious changes suggested by Wike (1952) as having taken place on the Northwest Coast during the nineteenth century, namely a transfer of interest and concern from practices linked with the dead to a more secular manipulation of wealth and prestige.

How, then, may we describe the potlatch of aboriginal or precontact times, taking into consideration the points debated above?

The kwakiutl potlatch, during those early

times, may be described as the giving by a numaym, represented by its chief or headman, of a feast and presents to other numayms and their chiefs, often from other villages. At these distributions the more generous the host was, the more prestige he received; and if his generosity was not matched by the guests when they gave their potlatches, the host and his numaym increased in prestige at the expense of the guests. Hence there was a competitive element necessarily present in the potlatch.

Potlatches were held on several occasions: following or during funerals, by the deceased's successor when he entered formally into his new position; when a man wished to make a public announcement of his successor; whenever a name was changed or a person took on a new status in the community, as when a boy attained puberty or a girl first menstruated; when a marriage was contracted, and at several points thereafter during the marriage cycle; during the winter ceremonials, when dances were given; when persons were initiated into the "secret societies" or dance-fraternities; at "house-warmings," given when one's new house had been completed; when a copper was sold or bought; whenever a man, having accumulated a lot of property, wished to do something for the honor of himself and his numaym; when a man wished to humiliate his rivals and elevate his rank at their expense; and, sometimes, when persons on ill terms with one another decided to make peace (Boas 1921:691; 1925:135–357; Curtis 1915:142; Ford 1941:17, 19–23, 31, 36ff, 49, 169, 184–185, 218ff).[9] Potlatching, that is to say, was not so much a special social event (though such purely potlatch events did occur) as an aspect or accompaniment of many social happenings.

At these potlatchings a great many people would be present, and these spectators would act as witnesses to the changes of status thus an-

nounced and to whatever other transactions also went on. Such memorable events therefore served the function of marking and validating changes in social status; in fact, Barnett (1938) saw in this task the especial function and underlying principle of the potlatch. In the old days, a numaym member who did not himself have sufficient wealth to hold a potlatch (and most numaym members would be in such a predicament) would give such wealth as he did have to the chief of his numaym, and the latter would put on the potlatch for him (Drucker 1955:125, 129).

In potlatching, a chief was assisted by the members of his numaym, who gave food, blankets, and other property in amounts dependent upon their means. They did not expect him to return to them what they had given him, but they would receive recognition of their services in intangible but no less important returns (Boas 1921:1340–1344; Drucker 1955:124–125, 129). This was in addition to the wealth received by the chief as "tribute"; and if he still did not have as much as he wanted, he could obtain it by borrowing from his friends and relatives in other numayms or by calling in what was owed him.

Blankets, as already intimated, were not the only gifts given in the potlatches. The guests were heavily feasted, the food being formally reckoned as worth a hundred blankets (Boas 1925:205); and the food they did not eat they would take home with them (Boas 1935:38) or their hosts take them afterwards, often with the very feast dishes as well (Boas 1921:768, 775). Canoes might be given away with or instead of blankets. "The potlatch which took place upon the occasion of the marriage payment by the bride's family a few years after the wedding invariably involved the distribution of such household articles as provisions, wooden boxes, mats, blankets. . . ." (Ford 1941:19). At another form of the potlatch, known as the "grease feast," boxes of eulachen oil were given away.

Potlatches were given by one numaym to other numayms, or by one tribe to other tribes. In the light of the data presented on subsistence,

---

[9]Many of the occasions named here would be more important in the lives of nobles and their immediate relatives rather than in the lives of commoners. Potlatching was a responsibility of aristocrats.

the utility of intertribal distributions of food and wealth will be readily obvious. But the utility of distributions between the various numayms *within* a single tribe may not be obvious at first glance. However, the numaym and not the tribe was the land-owning, resource-exploiting unit, and in summer the various numayms of the tribe dispersed to different places. It might easily happen, therefore, that some of the numayms within the tribe had a more fruitful year than did the others; and in such circumstances, distributions of food and wealth between the numayms even within the same tribe would be advantageous to all.

The potlatch had no one essential function, but several. It redistributed food and wealth. It validated changes in social status. It converted the wealth given by the host into prestige for the host and rank for his numaym, and so provided motivation for keeping up the cycle of exchanges. The potlatch was, in fact, the linch-pin of the entire system.

## BUYING AND SELLING

But blankets, canoes, and boxes cannot be eaten. A starving numaym would find it very awkward if it could not convert into food the wealth it had received in potlatches. I have shown how, through the potlatch, wealth could be converted into prestige. Could food be exchanged for wealth, so that a starving numaym could sell blankets for the food it needed in order to subsist, and a wealthy numaym sell food in return for the blankets necessary to potlatch?

The answer is yes. In preparing to give a potlatch, the host, if he did not have sufficient food to feed his guests, could buy it with blankets (Boas 1897:342). I have already noted that food given in a potlatch was reckoned as being worth one hundred blankets. In a short summary of accounts of buying and selling in the texts which he collected, Boas (1935:67) wrote:

When a man catches many herrings at his beach, he sells them for slaves and becomes a rich man. People go out in canoes and buy food from another tribe. A chief goes out and buys many cherries from the neighbouring tribe. Starving people pay for food with dressed elkskins, slaves, canoes, and even their daughters.

## CONCLUSIONS

In the beginning of this paper I set forth four propositions linking (a) variable productivity of food sources, (b) potlatch exchanges, (c) interconvertibility of food, wealth, and prestige, and (d) status rivalry among the Kwakiutl. The rest of the paper has been devoted to presenting the evidence in support of these propositions. It remains simply to explain the picture of aboriginal Kwakiutl society that results.

Let us first consider a simplified system made up of only two numayms, A and B. This simplification is not wholly artificial, since the total Kwakiutl potlatch exchange system may be considered as being made up of combinations of such overlapping pairs. Let our pair, furthermore, start out evenly balanced in resources, food supply, wealth, and prestige. Both, however, are pressing in numbers upon the margins of their resources, so that a poor harvest for either one would result in its going hungry and, if the poor harvests continue, in eventual starvation, certain diminution, and possible extinction. Since the initial amount of wealth possessed by each is the same, at the end of a potlatch cycle each numaym has still about the same amount of wealth as it began with, and the prestige of the two numayms also remains alike.

Let A suffer a severe failure in food supply. To feed themselves, the members of A sell blankets to B in exchange for food. This increment of wealth enables B either to hold potlatches more frequently or to give bigger gifts in their potlatches. And B does so, giving wealth to A in batches larger than before and so gaining increased prestige in return. Thus through the potlatch A recovers its wealth in return for granting more prestige to B. With this wealth A can either hold a return potlatch and regain its prestige by giving equally large gifts or use the wealth to purchase more food. If A uses some of this wealth to purchase more food, it will not be able to give a return potlatch of generosity equal to B's potlatch, and the increment in B's prestige will be more firmly established. If, sometime later, B suffers a deficiency in food supply, it can buy food from A, and this cycle will be repeated with the roles reversed.

Two consequences stand out from the above model: (a) if a numaym continually suffers from a failure of food supply, it will not be able to respond in potlatching with gifts of value equal to what it has received, and its prestige will steadily decline. Because the potlatch-system is also tied in with other aspects of society, such as marriage and war,[10] such a steady decline of prestige would probably have the effect of forcing the numaym in time out of the system entirely as an independent unit: it would either literally die out, or it would become a permanent dependency of its wealthy partner. (b) There will be, over time, a steady increment in the absolute size of potlatch gifts, regardless of which partner suffers food deficiencies. In fact, the more frequent such deficiencies are, the greater the rate of incrementation is likely to be. This does not, however, necessarily entail an increase in the number of actual wealth objects; tally sticks,

---

[10]Codere (1950) has shown how in historic times warfare declined as potlatching increased. We may further add that comparisons of the war histories and the marriage accounts suggest a tendency for the groups with which a given numaym warred not to be those with which it inter-married; war and marriage were alternate means of gaining new crests. Establishing new marriage links would also have had the effect of increasing the number of relatives, both affines and kinsfolk, with whom oneself and one's children and other relatives could visit.

such as the Kwakiutl did in fact use (e.g. Boas 1897:352), would serve the purpose adequately.

The institution of borrowing and lending can be seen as another way of acquiring blankets with which, in times of economic distress, to maintain one's level of potlatch giving and so maintain one's prestige.

This system would be more efficient the more units were involved. With many numayms selling food, the increment in wealth received by them would be for each much smaller than that if only one numaym was the seller, and the temptation to increase potlatch gifts would be correspondingly reduced. Consequently, with many numayms in the system, the rate of increase in sizes of potlatch gifts would be reduced. Further, the chances of many numayms all suffering deficient harvests simultaneously would be considerably less than the chances for two numayms being thus afflicted together.

If the food deficiencies be *short-term, intermittent,* and *not sustained,* the relative ranking of the numayms involved will over the long-run remain constant, whether or not one numaym is given to suffering more deficiencies than another. If the deficiencies be *long-term and sustained,* however, as pointed out above, the numaym so marked out will be forced in the long run out of the system.

However, even a long-term run of bad luck, with continually deficient food supply and declining prestige, may be offset if the wealthier partner in its turn suffers a long-term deficiency while the food supply of the poorer improves, provided of course that the poorer numaym's run of misfortune has not been so prolonged as to drive it out of the system altogether. In such circumstances the *long-term* relative ranking of the numayms will oscillate about a constant level.

The model presupposes, therefore, an overall balance of resource productivity among the numayms involved in the system. No numaym, or at most only a few, suffers from long-term, sustained resource deficiencies which would take it out of the system: variations in resources tend to be short-term and intermittent. All groups are pressing on their resources, so that times of low productivity menace their existence; but the population/resource ratio for each is substantially the same. Indeed, we may suspect that a rough equality in population/resource ratios between numayms is necessary for this system to work.

This system, coping successfully with variable productivity and by its exchanges of food and wealth enabling a larger population to live in the Southern Kwakiutl country than would otherwise have lived there, is nevertheless vulnerable to the following:

(a) A change in the pattern of resource exploitation such that some numayms increase their food production consistently relative to the remainder: This change will change their population/resource ratio, enable them to sell more food for more wealth, and so, as has already been explained, by increased potlatching gain more prestige than can be matched by poorer numayms. Such a resource discrepancy may occur through some numayms decreasing their food production, through some increasing theirs, or through population decline in some numayms and not in others so that the former no longer press so closely on their resources. Changes in food production could in turn be due either to changes in the natural environment beyond human control or intent, or to changes in techniques of resource exploitation.

(b) The entry into the system of a new, non-traditional source of wealth: The general effect of this factor would be to promote more frequent potlatches and bigger potlatch gifts, and to permit persons other than the traditional chiefs to engage in potlatching. This in turn would promote an increase in competitive or rivalrous potlatching. Exchanges would become less between numayms and more between prestige-seeking individuals. The balance between food, wealth, and prestige would, I think, become more

precarious, but, provided the effects were distributed evenly over the whole system, the system would still survive, though at a higher level of activity. Destruction of wealth, if adopted, would serve to take some of this new wealth out of the system and so serve to inhibit the increase in the velocity of circulation. And, finally, if the influx were only for a short time, the system could probably survive it without much change.

But if the influx of wealth were unevenly distributed among the numayms, benefiting some more than others, not only would potlatch rivalry be accentuated, but some groups would rapidly gain an ascendancy over the others, and the balance of the system would be upset. The groups having lost prestige would in one way or another eventually be forced out of the system. And through the decline in the number of potlatching social units, the system itself would become increasingly unstable. This instability would be further heightened by the increase in potlatching rivalry and by a concurrent increasing individualization of potlatching. The end result would, in time, be to destroy the system beyond recovery.

(c) A general decline in population, with the consequence that the population no longer presses on the margins of its resources, and the threat of starvation resulting from reduced harvests is removed: Assuming that the amount of wealth in the total system remains constant, this change would both free more wealth from food-purchasing for use in potlatching and increase the per capita wealth among the Kwakiutl. Frequency and size of potlatches would increase, and with this increased wealth the chances of more persons being engaged in it would also be increased. The effects of population decline would therefore be similar to those of the influx of new wealth.

In post-contact times we find the latter two changes taking place together and in marked degree, viz., an influx of new wealth, first from the fur-trade and later from other non-traditional sources, and a drastic decline in population, both prolonged for about a hundred years. The result was as would be expected if the construction proposed in this paper is correct: an increase in the size and frequency of potlatches, a general spread of potlatching to most persons in the Kwakiutl communities, an increase in rivalrous potlatches with a concomitant individualizing of potlatches, and the appearance of the "fantastic surplus economy" so marked in the later ethnographic record.

## BIBLIOGRAPHY

BARNETT, H. G.
   1938   The Nature of the Potlatch. *American Anthropologist* 40:349–358.
BOAS, FRANZ
   1889   First General Report on the Indians of British Columbia. *Report of the British Association for the Advancement of Science*, pp. 801–893.
   1897   The Social Organization and the Secret Societies of the Kwakiutl Indians. *Report of the U.S. National Musuem for 1895*, pp. 311–738.
   1920   The Social Organization of the Kwakiutl. *American Anthropologist* 22:111–126.
   1921   Ethnology of the Kwakiutl. *Thirty-Fifth Annual Report of the Bureau of American Ethnology, 1913–1914*, pp. 41–1581.
   1925   *Contributions to the Ethnology of the Kwakiutl.* New York: Columbia University Press.
   1935   *Kwakiutl Culture as Reflected in Mythology.* American Folklore Society, memoir 28.
BOHANNAN, PAUL
   1963   *Social Anthropology.* New York: Holt, Rinehart, and Winston, Inc.
COBB, JOHN N.
   1921   Pacific Salmon Fisheries, 3rd edition, appendix I. *U.S. Bureau of Fisheries: Report of U.S. Commission of Fisheries for the Fiscal Year 1921.*

CODERE, HELEN S.
   1950   *Fighting with Property.* American Ethnological Society, monograph 18.
   1956   The Amiable Side of Kwakiutl Life: The Potlatch and the Play-Potlatch. *American Anthropologist* 58:334–351.
   1957   Kwakiutl Society: Rank without Class. *American Anthropologist* 59:473–486.
   1961   "Kwakiutl," in *Perspectives in American Indian Culture Change* (ed. by E. H. Spicer), pp. 431–516. Chicago: University of Chicago Press.
CURTIS, EDWARD S.
   1915   *The North American Indian, Volume X. The Kwakiutl.* Norwood (Mass.): The Plimpton Press.
DAWSON, GEORGE M.
   1887   Notes and Observations on the Kwakiool People. . . . *Transactions of the Royal Society of Canada*, sect. ii.
DRUCKER, PHILIP
   1955   *Indians of the Northwest Coast.* New York: McGraw-Hill Book Co. Inc. for the American Museum of Natural History.
FORD, CLELLAN S.
   1941   *Smoke from Their Fires.* New Haven: Yale University Press for the Institute of Human Relations.
GODFREY, H.
   1958a   A Comparison of Sockeye Salmon Catches at Rivers Inlet and Skeena River, B.C., with Particular Reference to Age at Maturity. *Journal of the Fisheries Research Board of Canada* 15:331–354.
   1958b   Comparisons of the Index of Return for Several Stocks of British Columbia Salmon to Study Variations in Survival. *Journal of the Fisheries Research Board of Canada* 15:891–908.
HERSKOVITS, MELVILLE J.
   1952   *Economic Anthropology.* New York: Alfred A. Knopf.
HOAR, W. S.
   1951   The Chum and Pink Salmon Fisheries of British Columbia 1917–1947. *Fisheries Research Board of Canada*, bulletin 90.

NEAVE, FERRIS
1953 Principles Affecting the Size of Pink and Chum Salmon Populations in British Columbia. *Journal of the Fisheries Research Board of Canada* 9:450–491.
1958 "Stream Ecology and Production of Anadromous Fish," in *The Investigation of Fish-Power Problems—A Symposium Held at the University of British Columbia April 28 & 30, 1957* (ed. by P. A. Larkin), pp. 43–48. Vancouver: U.B.C. Institute of Fisheries.

OLSON, RONALD L.
1940 The Social Organization of the Haisla of British Columbia. *Anthropological Records 2.*

OUTRAM, D. H.
1956 *Amount of Herring Spawn Deposited in British Columbia Coastal Waters in 1956.* Fisheries Research Board of Canada, Pacific Biological Station, Nanaimo, B.C., circular 42.
1957 *Extent of Herring Spawning in British Columbia in 1957.* Fisheries Research Board of Canada, Pacific Biological Station, Nanaimo, B.C., circular 46.
1958 *The 1958 Herring Spawn Deposition in British Columbia Coastal Waters.* Fisheries Research Board of Canada, Pacific Biological Station, Nanaimo, B.C., circular 50.

ROSTLUND, ERHARD
1952 *Freshwater Fish and Fishing in Native North America.* University of California Publications in Geography 9.

SUTTLES, WAYNE
1960 Affinal Ties, Subsistence, and Prestige among the Coast Salish. *American Anthropologist* 62:296–305.

VANCOUVER, GEORGE
1801 *A Voyage of Discovery to the North Pacific Ocean . . .,* vol. 2. London: John Stockdale.

VAYDA, ANDREW P.
1961 A Re-Examination of Northwest Coast Economic Systems. *Transactions of the New York Academy of Sciences,* series II, 23:618–624.

WICKETT, W. P.
1958 Review of Certain Environmental Factors Affecting the Production of Pink and Chum Salmon. *Journal of the Fisheries Research Board of Canada* 15:1103–1126.

WIKE, JOYCE
1952 "The Role of the Dead in Northwest Coast Culture," in *Indian Tribes of Aboriginal America: Selected Papers of the XXIXth International Congress of Americanists* (ed. by Sol Tax), pp. 97–103. Chicago: University of Chicago Press.

# 21

## TO MAKE MY NAME GOOD: A REEXAMINATION OF THE SOUTHERN KWAKIUTL POTLATCH

*Philip Drucker and Robert F. Heizer*

*In 1967, Philip Drucker and Robert Heizer published an extensive review of Kwakiutl potlatching of which the following is the final chapter. They reject both Suttles's and Piddocke's economic determinist positions, arguing that while the food supply did vary from one place and time to another on the Northwest Coast, shortages never became serious enough to threaten life. Furthermore, visiting often occurred during the time when food was most plentiful and had to be eaten by guests on the spot. Food received from visits could hardly have tided over starving guests when they returned home for a lean winter. Instead, the authors argue, potlatching had important social functions. The ritual permitted chiefs to validate (not attain) their high social status, and it served to bind together local groups that intermarried in a perpetual reciprocal system of gift exchange.*

As we have presented our data and discussions, we have tried to develop the thesis defined in the early pages of this paper: that the potlatch of the Southern Kwakiutl in its social functions, economics, and mechanics conformed to the basic pattern of the complex in the area, as clarified in Barnett's (1938; n.d.) studies. Features previously regarded as anomalous may be seen on analysis to resolve into expressions of areal patterns or, as in the case of the infinitely compounding double return, prove not to have been actual native custom. The true rivalry potlatch, which has been interpreted by others as being socially disintegrative and even as a manifestation of psychic abnormality, we have shown to be basically a technique for resolving conflicting claims of presumptive heirs. In a broad sense, it was simply a process at civil law. It likewise provided a channel for emotional release by the parties in conflict. To let off steam in controlled surroundings appears to have made possible the preservation of a very important behavioral value standard, one that strongly opposed intragroup physical violence in conflict situations. The rivalry gesture seems to have operated consistently as the same sort of a release mechanism. Our position, therefore, is that these specializations of the potlatch complex were not significant as deviants from the areal norms. One might even interpret them as highly consistent with the fundamental function of the institution, that toward social integration.

## MOTIVATIONS

The potlatch did not give, or create, social status. Present data make abundantly clear that this was as true of the Southern Kwakiutl as it was of other northwest coast groups. No matter how many potlatches a chief gave, he did not alter his formal rank one whit beyond that to which he was legally entitled through heredity or acquisition of rights in marriage. For example, although Mr. Whonnuck derived great satisfaction from his performance in the flour feast episode and regarded it as a moral victory, he did not thereby alter his formal status vis-à-vis his arch rival; In any potlatch given in the old fashioned manner, in which the precedence order was signalized, Mr. Johnson, o'woxalagilis, would still be the first of the Kwagyut eagles to receive a gift, and Mr. Whonnuck would remain in second place. And it was precisely the precedence order that was of most importance in the Southern Kwakiutl social system.

The misconception so often encountered in anthropological literature that an Indian gained social status by potlatching, or potlatched to gain social status, comes in part from the Indians themselves; it is thus one of the categories of ethnographic fact mentioned in earlier pages, what people say they do. The Southern Kwakiutl and their neighbors as well liked to say, in effect, "So-and-so was a great chief because he gave many potlatches." Close analysis reveals that the reverse was actually true: So-and-so gave many (read "several major") potlatches because he was a great ("highly ranked") chief. The distinction between *acquiring* status through potlatching—the popular misinterpretation—and *confirming* or *validating* hereditary status is not a minor one. It is crucial to understanding the whole system. The only exceptions to this rule, and they were few indeed, were those who in relatively recent times, by potlatching and by otherwise establishing good personal relationships with the chiefs, were able to persuade the chiefs to create eagle places for them. And even these eagle places once established had a precedence order that no amount of potlatching could change.

At the same time it must be specified that reference is to the formal structure of hereditary status and rank, the precedence order of the occupants of the seriated positions in the namima and tribal role systems. Quite apart from this, there did exist a factor of informal prestige inextricably linked to potlatching; the key word here is "informal." Interest in this factor had a motivational significance affecting individual behavior. This informal prestige is essentially the element that Barnett (1938:354–355; n.d.:95–100) refers to as "esteem"—the self-esteem of the potlatch giver and the esteem accorded him by his guests.

Barnett's analysis both puts the "esteem" or informal prestige feature of the potlatch in proper perspective in relation to the formal social structure, and develops the theme of its significance as an incentive to the individual (particularly in n.d.: 95–100). We accept his conclusions on this matter; what we shall do here is to draw on our Southern Kwakiutl data to sort out some of the major constituent forces of the "esteem."

First of all, occupying the conspicuous position of giver of the potlatch was a source of ego gratification, especially since so doing implied recognition of hereditary right, which was to the Kwakiutl the highest value of all. One does not have to be a megalomaniac to respond pleasurably to such recognition. The flowery speeches of gratitude by the guest chiefs were designed to heighten this effect. As Barnett has pointed out, the guests on their part received a complementary gratification in the host's recognition of their statuses, not only by his gifts but by his adherence to the rules of precedence in giving and use of the guests' formal titles.

Another element of the self-esteem was obviously the solid satisfaction any person in any culture finds in the adequate performance of the duties of his social role. The data emphasize that the Indians regarded potlatching as an obligation of the chiefs. They were quite aware that a potlatch did not just happen, like spontaneous combustion. A potlatch was staged properly only after long and careful planning, not only in the assembling of the wealth goods, notifying debtors, decisions made as to the amount to be given to each guest, and other financial details arranged; but the privileges to be shown had to be selected, ceremonial paraphernalia refurbished, dancers rehearsed, songs made and taught to the singers, speeches planned, arrangements made with fellow chiefs regarding their participation, the invitation party organized and dispatched, and a host of other preparations made. The chief did not do all these things himself; like any good executive he delegated them to his namima brothers and fellow tribesmen. But he had to see to it that all these things were tended to. (Reference is to a chief potlatching in his own right, not a youngster whose potlatch was really managed by his father or other elder relative.) Giving a potlatch, in short, was a demonstration of a certain administrative competence. This was the work of the chiefs, as the Kwakiutl would say. A man who accomplished all this had a right to a certain pride in his performance.

Another complex of factors involved the subtle nuances in gift-giving, a subject explored in considerable detail by Blau (1964:106–114). In broad terms the potlatch giver publicly and conspicuously affirmed or reaffirmed his position relative to his peers, and that relative to his inferiors, at the same time that he distributed valuables to gain the good will of his guests (normal amicable situations are being discussed here; rivalry gestures are in a different category). That this sort of situation is emotionally rewarding is obvious.

A final motivational factor with strong derivative satisfactions to which we invite attention is what has been called "gamesmanship." This was certainly a major constituent of the rivalry gestures, particularly in the case of the hereditary rivalries, although it was also a factor in the true rivalries. In the latter, however, the aggressive-defensive reaction previously discussed as a result of the invasion of right was the major motivating factor.

It is clear also that these several factors had differing motivational weights for different individuals. For instance, Mr. Nowell unquestionably found his major satisfaction in the meticulous performance of his traditional obligations, whereas Mr. Whonnuck patently enjoyed the gamesmanship aspects of his potlatch relationships.

## FUNCTIONS AND ORIGINS

Speculation as to origins of social institutions does not invariably contribute to the understanding of the institutions concerned. In the present case, however, it seems worthwhile to give brief consideration to the matter of origins for two reasons. First, the potlatch has a superficial appearance of being a cultural anomaly, or at least it has been so presented by some writers; and second, our present data and certain other materials on record suggest that it should be possible to factor out certain concepts in Southern Kwakiutl, and then general Northwest Coast culture, that seem to have provided the basis on which the potlatch complex developed. The essential purpose here is to stress the interpretation of the potlatch as a fairly rational development rather than as a cultural monstrosity, understandable only in terms of psychologic aberrations among its partisans.

Fairly recently Suttles (1960a, b) has contributed two papers on certain features of culture of Coast Salish divisions of lower Vancouver Island and opposite mainland shores, groups included in the linguistic groupings Lkongeneng and Halkomelem.[1] From his data he has drawn conclusions as to the function and origin of the potlatch among these groups

and, by extension, to the origin of the potlatch in Northwest Coast areal culture. His study represents the first new approach to the subject since Barnett's analysis. While we do not accept certain of Suttles' conclusions, we agree with a part of his interpretation as indicating a functional factor in the probable origin of the potlatch. We shall therefore use his work as a springboard to clarify our views.

Suttles' approach to the Coast Salish potlatch and its underlying factors is in terms of economic determinism; this is a part of his interpretation with which we are not in accord. He regards the potlatch itself as a device for redistributing wealth goods that tended to concentrate in the hands of certain especially favored or fortunate local groups. He stresses the fact that Coast Salish subsistence economy was derived from a region characterized by great variability in natural resources, a variability manifested both geographically—basic foodstuffs having spotty distributions in the several localities and biotic zones—and temporally, according to season and in regard to salmon from year to year in accordance with greatly varying spawning cycles. Thus, at any given time, as Suttles depicts the situation, some Coast Salish groups would be enjoying abundance while others were on short rations. These inequities were countered by a special social custom, according to which surplus food products were taken to affinal kindred as gifts. Such food gifts, however, obligated the recipients to make a return gift of "wealth goods." Suttles distinguishes wealth in food from that in more durable materials. It was not actually a barter system, but it operated like one. Suttles presents it as a commercial sort of transaction through which groups temporarily possessing food surpluses acquired credits in the form of durable wealth goods with which they, in their time of scarcity, would discharge their obligations when they were similarly presented with food gifts. At this point Suttles emphasizes the importance of the network of affinal relationships that interconnected all the local groups of the linguistic entities of his study. These affinal

---

[1]For convenience Suttles refers to these groups simply as "Coast Salish."

relationships provided the basis for all social contact beyond that of the local group of blood kin.

As the next step, he envisages certain groups, through greater industry, luck, or skill, as having more frequent surpluses of food than their affinal kin, so that they had a favorable balance of trade leading to acquiring wealth goods over and above their needs for repaying food gifts. Hence the wealth goods tended to accumulate in their hands. The potlatch served to remedy the stagnation of the wealth system that would otherwise have resulted by providing a mechanism for redistributing this wealth, so that the essential process, the exchange of food for wealth goods which leveled off the inequalities of the natural resources, might continue indefinitely.

In extending his consideration beyond the Coast Salish territory, Suttles proposes the same function for the potlatch, subject to differences in group composition resulting from the seriation of social rank among the Wakashan-speaking peoples, so that the potlatch also becomes "the means by which individuals and local groups establish and maintain rank within the series," and to differences imposed by the most rigid group definition of all, that of the unilateral descent groups of the northern portion of the coast.

Discussion of Suttles' hypothesis must necessarily begin with consideration for the food-for-wealth exchange system between affinal kin. As a sort of side issue, Suttles posits a comparable diversity of local resources north of Salish territory to that of the Coast Salish, which would necessitate similar subsistence distribution mechanisms. He challenges generalizations as to the basic uniformity of Northwest Coast natural resources by way of substantiating his view.

Now, it is to be doubted that anyone who is reasonably familiar with the Northwest Coast and its native culture patterns would deny that there was considerable local diversity in natural resources. Such diversity ranged from gross environmental differences—as for example, the semi-inland habitats of groups such as the

Chilkat Tlingit, the Gitksan, the Bella Coola, and various small units like the Nootkan a'minqasath as compared with the habitats of their neighbors of the outer coast and off-shore islands —to local variations in resources resulting from specialized distributions of certain species of fish and game—the fact that olachon run in certain rivers only, as do sockeye salmon, and that there were no deer on the Queen Charlotte Islands and no red cedar in the Chilkat country. Pages could be filled with items of this sort. What the generalizations on uniformity of resources really mean is that throughout the area there was one important food source, salmon, which though seasonal lent itself to preservation for storage by use of a fairly simple technique. It may be stressed here that two species regarded by both Indians and ourselves as inferior in flavor, chums and pinks (colloquially, "dog salmon" and "humpbacks"), were of major importance to the natives, since both species ceased feeding for a considerable period prior to entering fresh water and hence were leaner and kept better than fat species such as spring salmon or coho. The same is probably true of sockeye taken in fresh water. While Suttles stresses the marked year-to-year difference in size of Frazer River sockeye runs, it may be doubted that primitive precommercial demands were so heavy that the smaller runs produced serious hardship. In any event, the year-to-year fluctuations in salmon were not characteristic of parts of the area other than those occupied by Coast Salish. The result of the natural features of the salmon fishery, in cultural terms, was an annual period of intensive economic activity by the natives, comparable in a broad sense to the busy harvest season of agricultural peoples.

Another important food source for all except riverine groups like the Gitksan was shellfish. Ethnographic accounts do not develop the importance of this humble, unspectacular resource, and Suttles incorrectly surmises that it may have been sparse and sporadic north of Salish territory. But one has only to observe the amazingly numerous and large midden deposits, composed chiefly of shell along the coast, to realize the utility of local mollusca in native economics (Drucker, 1943). There is a myth current in certain anthropological circles to the effect that there are no extensive midden sites in Tlingit territory. This, like other myths, is factually incorrect.

In addition, there were other aquatic resources. Some were seasonal, like herring and, in certain mainland rivers, olachon; and others were available throughout the year. There were also marine mammals—hair seal, sea lion, sea otter, porpoise, and whale. As a result, fishing and sea mammal hunting were major forms of economic activity. Concomitant with this economic pattern was a stress on water transport, and habitation patterns reflected this use of canoes, a favorable beach for landing being a most important consideration in the choice of a site throughout the area. Land hunting was less important in terms of subsistence, although mountain goat wool, marmot hides, and in historic times peltries were important valuables. This emphasis on river and sea as more important than the land in the food quest is an aspect of the broad uniformity of Northwest Coast native economy. The fact that the Nootkan staff of life was dog salmon, while the Haida wintered on dried humpbacks, does not materially alter the picture.

North of Salish territory,[2] the intergroup distribution of sporadically occurring food products was accomplished through barter. The most prominent center for barter was the Coast Tsimshian and Niska olachon fishing camps on the

lower Nass, where Tlingit and Haida assembled to trade. But there was other trade, apparently in short steps, between neighboring groups through which special foods like olachon grease as well as wealth goods were disseminated. The general impression one receives of this trade, however, is that both "wealth items" and foodstuffs involved in the exchanges were in the category of luxury goods and, contrary to Suttles' picture of the Coast Salish exchange system were not basic necessities for groups short of supplies. The Haida who came to the Nass to trade for olachon grease did not, it is true, have streams in their islands from which olachon could be taken. If, however, they actually needed all the animal fats they like to consume, they had local sources in the abundance of hair seal and sea lion, which they were highly skillful at hunting; the grease-rich "black cod"; and other fish, including the spring salmon taken by trolling. In other words, the olachon grease they acquired at the Nass was over and above their actual dietetic needs. Some southern Tlingit, such as those having access to olachon fishing in the Unuk and Stikine rivers, went to the Nass for grease because the Nass olachon were reputed to have a superior flavor. We might justifiably compare them to people in our own culture who willingly pay a premium price for allegedly country-cured Virginia ham in preference to the standard Chicago packing-house variety. There can be little doubt about the luxury aspect of such commerce.

The nearest approach to the formal Coast Salish food-for-wealth interchanges between affinally related groups among the non-Salish was the feast pattern. It is true that the Indians of the coast invariably distinguish between feasts and potlatches, both in terminology and in formal procedure, but it is likewise true that feasts and potlatches were intrinsically related conceptually. Both forms involved a host group and formally invited guest group or groups; both had elaborate etiquette patterns and were tied into the system of protocol of rank. The Wakashan-speaking groups from whom we have detailed

---

[2]In contrasts between Coast Salish and non-Salish groups in the present discussion, it must be understood that we use "Coast Salish" precisely as Suttles does, that is, to refer to the Lkongeneng and Halkomelem dialectic entities; and furthermore, since in cultural terms the Bella Coola were highly similar to their Heiltsuk neighbors, we include them with the non-Salish, despite the fact of their actual linguistic affiliation, to avoid cumbersome special mention in each case of reference.

information, and probably all their neighbors as well, announced certain hereditary rights at feasts, comparable to those announced at potlatches. In the case of feasts, such rights included special feast names; and when the food had come from hereditarily owned tracts (fishing places, berry grounds, hunting areas, and so forth), that fact and the genealogical route of transmission to the current possessors were announced. Where the food did not come from owned areas but had been taken through inherited knowledge, both practical and magical—as, for instance, in the case of Nootkan whaling—the source and line of descent of such knowledge was recounted, just as at a potlatch the origin and inheritance of a mask, a dance performance, and the like were formally presented before the guests. Finally, both feasts and potlatches involved consumption and distribution of surpluses assembled by the host chief with the aid of his group. We are referring here to the pattern described as the older one by Southern Kwakiutl informants prior to the development of individual giving of potlatches. At feasts, food was typically served not only for consumption on the spot, but in sufficient amount so that the guests would have plenty to take home. A chief might be given a very large amount so that he could distribute it to members of his group who had not been able to attend the formal affair. He was expected to explain to them the rights and so forth claimed by the giver and any other circumstances of the feast.

Feasts were normally given among groups that were in frequent, friendly contact: the several groups sharing a winter village or neighbors within a well-marked physiographic region, such as an inlet. These were essentially the groupings referred to by Southern Kwakiutl informants as those within which potlatches were given in former days. These were the groupings most frequently linked by intermarriage. There was no closely calculated system of reciprocity, but over the long haul feasts were returned, guest groups sooner or later inviting their former hosts. Among the matrilineal descent groups of

the northern coast, guests had to be from a division with which the rule of exogamy permitted marriage.

There are two points that this summary of feast usages brings out. One is that there is no indication among Wakashan or northern groups of any rigorously formalized food-for-wealth system of food giving or feast giving. The other is that, similarly, there is no hint from any of these groups that the guests were hardship cases. Northwest Coast feasts were not CARE packages; the guests normally had food in plenty in their own storage boxes and baskets. One highly significant fact, insufficiently stressed in most of the literature, that does inevitably appear from informants' accounts is that feasts had considerable diversion value. They were usually occasions for jollity in contrast to potlatches, which were as a rule more formal and serious even when not directly part of mortuary observances.

If we return to Suttles' construct in terms of the general areal picture, then we must of necessity reach one or the other of two possible conclusions. The first possibility is that the Coast Salish had developed a highly specialized food distribution system, distinct from all other feast and food-giving customs of the area. The other possible conclusion is that Suttles' informants may have oversystematized their descriptions of this phase of native culture; they were members of groups that along with their congeners of Puget Sound and the Chinook have the longest history of intensive acculturation on the coast, dating back to the days of the crown colony of Vancouver Island, with a consequent awareness of white concepts of sale of commodities. This does not mean that such transactions were not made, particularly during the historic period, but that they may have been less commercialized. That is, groups with food surpluses may not have consistently singled out affinal kin who were suffering scarcity as recipients of the gifts in order to exact payments of wealth goods. As a matter of fact, Barnett, who had a couple of decades advantage in regard to Coast Salish informants, describes as customary a food-wealth exchange that went in part in the opposite direction from that reported by Suttles.[3] According to his account, in the Coast Salish equivalent of what we have referred to among the Kwakiutl as the "repayment of the bride price," the father of the bride took food gifts, or wealth goods that could be exchanged for food, as well as the wealth goods for the bride-price repayment. The food was given to the son-in-law or to his sponsor, so that the recipient might give a feast in honor of the occasion to announce the rights and privileges being transferred by the father-in-law. The wealth goods that constituted the bride-price repayment had been transferred prior to the feast. When the father-in-law made ready to depart several days later, the son-in-law and his kin provided canoes loaded with food, which the father-in-law took to give a feast at his own home, announcing the food as a gift from his son-in-law. Derivatively he thereby acknowledged his own compliance with his obligation to repay the bride price.[4]

This description of a common expression of Coast Salish gift exchange between affinal relatives deserves a little closer examination, for Barnett makes clear that food gifts were made with the specific purpose that the recipient give a feast with the food received, at which he would inform the guests from whom and why he had received the food, thus publicizing and emphasizing the relationship between the two groups. This was not a Salish peculiarity. The use of food gifts we noted among the Southern Kwakiutl, and it was a fundamental Northwest Coast concept. Food gifts in quantity were to be redistributed by the recipient within his group at a feast and were never intended to be hoarded for

rationing out in hard times. Thus, if we score the operation as described by Barnett, noting that it is more acceptable in terms of areal ideals and values than Suttles' interpretation, we find the following gains in calories: father-in-law, zero; son-in-law, zero. In terms of our thrift-biased economic reckoning, both actually lost, for the food each gave the other for feasts might have been stored away for use when supplies were short instead of being gormandized in the season of plenty. But what the persons in the exchange really gained was the strengthening of their formal affinal bond, and the informal but important public esteem that accrues to one in any culture who is punctilious in compliance with his social obligations.

Another problem that arises in connection with Suttles' interpretation of food-for-wealth exchanges between Coast Salish groups that served to counterbalance abundance and scarcity of natural resources relates to the prehistoric and even early historic intergroup relationships. It is obvious that to have the economic effect described by Suttles the exchanges had to be between distant groups, at least between groups inhabiting different biotic zones, depending on different spawning cycles of salmon, etc. Variable as the Coast Salish habitat may have been, adjacent villages must have suffered the same scarcities and enjoyed the same abundances, so that food gifts to close neighbors could scarcely have had the effect posited. Yet Barnett (1955:182, 267 ff.) makes clear that, while certain enclaves of adjacent groups usually maintained friendly relations among themselves, hostility was usual between more remotely situated units. He suggests that it was probably the enforcement of order by white authorities that led to the "abandonment of aboriginal group isolation" (p. 182). What we infer from this is that the situation among these groups was closely comparable to that among the Southern Kwakiutl, where small, exclusive groupings of neighboring social units gave feasts and potlatches only among themselves until relatively late historic times. That Suttles regards his "Coast Salish" as biologically a single popu-

[3]Reference is to Barnett (1955:180 ff., esp. 191–192). Suttles was apparently unfamiliar with this important source on the groups he studied since he does not refer to it.

[4]Barnett (1955:192–193) makes the point that the term "bride price" is not in accord with the Salish concepts of the transfers accompanying marriage. While accepting his qualification, we continue to use the term for convenience.

lation and culturally a single people, and that even aboriginally they may have established occasional affinal ties between distant units, are not significant factors. The Southern Kwakiutl were surely biologically and culturally a single people, and occasionally arranged marriages of state between scions of chiefly lines of remotely situated groups, but nonetheless they fought bitterly among themselves in ancient days. The same is known of the Nootkan tribes, of the Heiltsuk, where the groups that came to be known as the Bella Bella savagely persecuted their linguistic and cultural kindred, the Awikeno and the Xaihaid; and identical situations prevailed among the northern divisions of the coast. It is quite obvious that long-range, peaceful intercourse was nowhere part of the areal pattern. Thus, the network of affinal relationships linking all the Coast Salish that Suttles postulates could not very well have provided the channels for the sharing of the food wealth.

The next step proposed by Suttles, the concentration of wealth goods in few hands as the result of the postulated exchanges, would not follow in any case unless it could be shown that there were certain garden spots in Coast Salish territory that always had surpluses; and in that case it would be expectable that only certain of the Coast Salish would indulge in giving potlatches. Their less fortunate affinal kindred would have had to dedicate all the wealth goods they could acquire to the repayment of the hypothetical food gift obligations. There is, however, no evidence at all to show that certain Salish groups only were hosts at potlatches, while the rest were chronically guests.

Significant error is introduced into Suttles' considerations regarding potlatch function by his reliance on the fallacious assumption that the giving of potlatches and feasts created high status.[5] In Barnett's general study of the potlatch, he made clear that this was not so; and in

his descriptive account of Coast Salish cultures, including most of the same ethnic entities treated by Suttles, he demonstrates that among those people, as with others of the Northwest Coast, high social rank and control of wealth, food resources, and the personnel whose cooperation was essential to potlatching and feast-giving were simultaneous attributes of noble birth —that is, of inheritance of high status (Barnett, 1938; 1955:241–249, 250–266). Our present data from the Southern Kwakiutl make the same fact clear; even when, as informants asserted, in recent times lesser chiefs of the namima began to give potlatches, they did so on the basis of their recognized social rank. The only persons not originally hereditarily entitled to special status who were permitted to participate prominently in the potlatching were the eagles, and they had places artificially created for them. It is worth noting that even the eagle places were fitted into the mold of hereditary right; the places *became* hereditary privileges and were strictly regulated by the real chiefs who refused to permit more than a limited number of them to be established.

Suttles' observation that the potlatch was a means by which wealth was redistributed is valid, but we do not accept that it ever served, as he maintains, to accommodate local group economies to variation and fluctuation in natural resources. As we have indicated, aboriginal and early historical potlatching involved groups in geographical propinquity, so that there would rarely be significant variation in resources among them; and in addition, both potlatching and feasting, as well as other forms of foodgiving, were matters of manipulating surpluses, not basic necessities. One way in which the Indians themselves express this latter point is in their insistence that in aboriginal times potlatches were of relatively infrequent occurrence whereas feasts were common. What they mean is that, prior to the introduction of the plethora of trade goods that came to be integrated into their wealth system (blankets, and so forth), accumulation of a surplus adequate for even a modest potlatch was a slow and painstaking process. The same principle operated in modern times

---

[5]Suttles (1960a:299) states, "high status comes from the sharing of food"; and (1960a:303) "wealth . . . is a means to high status achieved through the giving of it."

among the Southern Kwakiutl. As the earning power of these people expanded with the growth of the canned salmon industry, their potlatching burgeoned, despite severe administrative pressures against it. There was, however, a lull during the Depression years; only a few chiefs who had been saving potlatch capital for years previous could give feasts and potlatches during this period. Another lull followed the financially disastrous fishermen's strike in 1936, when most Southern Kwakiutl, at the end of what should have been their major earning season, found themselves not only with scant funds but heavily in debt. We may surmise that correspondingly in ancient times an occasional failure of a salmon run or other basic resource would have inhibited the giving of feasts; and if there had been access to provisions by barter, this use would have cut into the accumulation of surpluses of wealth goods also.

While we disagree sharply with Suttles' interpretation of the potlatch as a device for leveling off inequities in natural resources among the tribes, it is only proper to recognize that he presents in reasonable terms his data on the diversity, permanent and occasional, of food resources in the Coast Salish habitat. Such is not the case in Piddocke's (1965) attempt to apply the same hypothesis to Southern Kwakiutl potlatching.

Piddocke (an early draft of whose proposition was followed by Vayda [1961]) carries Suttles' appraisal of economic diversity as a factor contributory to the potlatch to extremes by asserting that the Southern Kwakiutl lived constantly on the verge of starvation, warded off only by the food-for-wealth exchanges from which he derives the institutionalized potlatch. That these or any other Northwest Coast people lived with the specter of starvation perpetually leering over their shoulders is absurd.

To begin, Suttles' thesis of diversity of resources in Coast Salish country derives in part at least from the circumstances that the Coast Salish occupied in the main two specialized biotic regions that differed climatologically and in flora

and fauna from the rest of the British Columbia coast. We do not accept these differences as forming the basis for the origin of the potlatch, as does Suttles, but they certainly were reflected in Coast Salish economy. The "Coast Forest Biotic Area" (all Vancouver Island west of Sooke and north of Comox and the mainland north of Burrard Inlet) differed in various ways. Suttles (1960b) has elucidated these differences. While there were rather less edible vegetal products available to the natives, there is no evidence of the drastic cyclic fluctuations in the fisheries recorded for the "Gulf Islands Biotic Area." Fluctuations in fish populations do occur, but they are random, less frequent, and proportionately smaller than in the pink and sockeye salmon runs in Salish territory. This suggests that variability of water temperatures on the spawning grounds and the other environmental conditions that ichthyologists cite are more stable in the Coast Forest zone, so that reproduction-and-survival rates quickly reestablish affected populations. The obvious corollary is that the enormous demand of modern commercial fishing is of more significance in creating annual variation with occasional seasons of poor fishing in Kwakiutl territory and to the northward rather than in the Coast Salish region; hence in pre-commercial times years of scarcity must have been even less common than in modern days.

Thus, in short, Piddocke's construct of the famine-ridden Kwakiutl does not make sense. The classical anthropological picture of the Northwest Coast as a region prodigal in foodstuffs for its primitive inhabitants must stand as essentially correct. The idea of the potlatch as a sort of intertribal AID program to combat starvation does not fit the ecological facts.

This is not to deny that there were now and again times of food shortage in the midst of this plethora of abundance. But these were short periods of skimpy rations and discomfort but not of abject starvation. Men's bellies rumbled, small children cried, but no one actually starved to death. Drucker (1951:36–37) has reported such situations among the Nootkans, caused often by mismanagement of provisions—spectacular waste in feasting on winter stores—followed by stormy weather that made ground fishing (for cod, halibut, etc.) and sea hunting impossible. Land game in such periods lies low in such shelter as it can find and is difficult to encounter. The Nootkans whose habitat was more exposed to the lash of the tremendous seas of southeasterly storms—the principal source of heavy weather on the Northwest Coast—suffered more from such weather than did most of their neighbors, except for the Kwakiutl Quatsino Sound groups and those of storm-beaten Cape Scott. But there was always something to be found even in such periods. "Those were the times when people walked the beaches looking for codfish heads, spurned by seals and sea lions, and storm-killed herring, and pilchard. They collected and ate the tiny mussels of the inner coves and bays, and similar molluscs disdained in normal times" (Drucker, 1951). A tough, rank-flavored seagull may be nothing to make a gourmet's eyes glisten, but it will sustain life in a pinch. These birds congregate in sheltered coves in bad weather. The Indians shot them with arrow, clubbed them, or caught them on small fishhooks baited with shallow water molluscs.

The point of this argument is to develop a series of facts that combine to invalidate Piddocke's theory of the potlatch as a defense against starvation:

1. Periods of food shortage among the Indians of the Coast Forest Biotic Area were infrequent and limited principally to periods of heavy storms, when winter stores were exhausted so that the people depended on day-to-day food procurement.

2. Even at such times there were food sources, not tasty perhaps, but sufficient to stave off abject starvation.

3. When one group was subject to such hardship conditions, stormbound in other words, all their neighbors were too—southeasters are general storms on the coast, not local—so that groups having surplus provisions could not have come to the rescue of neighbors in short supply.

In addition there is no evidence whatsoever of ceremonious food-for-wealth exchanges among the Southern Kwakiutl. For certain products of limited natural occurrence like olachon (specifically, the grease derived from them) or of special local abundance like the Cape Scott halibut, the concept of buying and selling ("bartering" would be more precise) existed, that is, of transfers in a mercantile, not ceremonial, context. Piddocke himself, cites various passages from Boas' writings to this effect. This "interconvertibility of food, wealth, and prestige" does not provide a *source* for the institutionalized potlatch, hence Piddocke is eventually forced to assume the existence of the potlatch (1965: 259 ff.).

Finally, the point made in connection with Suttles' interpretation of the Coast Salish situation regarding feast and ceremonious food-gift patterns (as distinct from mercantile barter) applies to Piddocke's food distribution for survival: food given at feasts and in ceremonious distribution was not given to be hoarded by recipients against hard times but to be expended promptly by them—gormandized—in feasting. The obvious import of this is that food gifts were surpluses, not necessary to survival, to both the donors and the recipients. Piddocke's construct, in fine, in no way conforms to the facts of Southern Kwakiutl life.

Thus far we seem to have been highly critical of Suttles' views. His emphasis on the importance of the affinal relationship, however, provides a significant lead as to conceptual sources contributing to the base on which the potlatch complex seems to have developed. This very special social relationship had not been given adequate attention previously. It is a kinship behavior form that is more subtle than a joking relationship or mother-in-law avoidance, but it was quite as real and, moreover, had far-reaching significance in the total configuration of Northwest Coast society.

Suttles sought to contrast the effects of the affinal relationship among the Coast Salish with what he calls "seriation" among Wakashan-speaking groups, because data on this point from these latter peoples were not available, although Drucker (1951) gave the matter mention in dealing with Nootkan society. However, present data from the Southern Kwakiutl show that this aspect of kinship behavior was significantly operative among them also, as among their neighbors. The informant Whonnuck's appeal to the recalcitrant tawitsis, that they alter their plans so as to permit completion of his father's potlatch, revolved about this relationship. It was the intimate bond between father-in-law and son-in-law that made the elder Whonnuck's trick, through which he made a son-in-law bend double and thus symbolically break a copper for the man's own father-in-law, especially malicious and insulting to both men. The giving of a potlatch to the entire tribe from which the wife came, as a form of payment of the bride price—thus making her entire tribe, rather than just her namima, affinal kind—was another Kwakiutl way of expressing the store that they set on this relationship. The ancient potlatching groups were simultaneously the normally intermarrying groups, although even in ancient times some unions were arranged between distant groups by chiefs bold enough and with a large enough supporting force of warriors to dare to approach remote, unfriendly villages openly. It was just these old, long-range affinal ties that were seized upon to justify expansion of the potlatch groupings when white-enforced peace began to make distant visits safe. In brief, our data show plainly that the affinal relationships were just as socially significant among the Southern Kwakiutl as among Coast Salish.

Suttles is on firm ground once more when he points out the important functional relationship between the unilateral descent system of the northern peoples where the affinal groupings were in effect crystallized by the clan and moiety organizations and the potlatch reciprocity. That he suggests derivation of the unilateral descent

system from potlatch reciprocity is something else again—the argument deteriorates into something comparable to that as to the priority of the chicken or the egg—but there is no question at all but that the two institutions have a high degree of functional compatibility. In fine, throughout most of the area of distribution of the potlatch complex—all of that region from which we have reasonably complete data—we find marked accent on importance of affinal relationships and potlatch reciprocity between groups standing in such relation to each other.

In an attempt to point to function factors contributing to the development of the potlatch, the present writers would trace the pattern of formal relationships with affinal kin one step farther back; that is to say, to the establishment of such bonds by gift exchanges that formalized marriage. The marriage established the affinal bonds; the gift exchange set a behavior pattern for the newly linked social units.

Payment of some sort of bride price to legitimatize marriage, even though at times it was but a token, was a widespread enough practice in native North America so that its occurrence on an earlier phase of Northwest Coast culture might be assumed without much hazard. It is necessary only to point to certain qualifying precautions. One is, of course, that while terms such as "bride price" and "marriage by purchase" are often met with in the literature and are convenient, short designators, they are rarely if ever precise descriptions of the situation; for it seems clear that there was always a distinction between "purchase" of a wife and purchase of a chattel. It might be possible to argue on purely hypothetical grounds that the "repayment" of the bride price as practiced by the Wakashan-speaking groups and most Coast Salish represented a defense against what we might call a strictly commercialized transaction. Be that as it may, the gift exchanges manifestly defined a pattern for the future relationships of the two groups involved.

A second precaution is that, for an interpretation of the significance of such gift exchanges as providing part of the structural base of the potlatch, it becomes necessary to assume in addition the prior existence of a wealth system consisting of food surpluses and of utilitarian and/or nonutilitarian objects regarded as worth possessing. Such an assumption does not seem to offer major difficulty in view of the various forms of wealth systems that we know to have been developed in various parts of the world, even though no two of them may have been quite alike in meaning and function.

The final major factor, the one which we believe must have been present in order that the preceding concepts be structured into the rudiments of the potlatch, is a little more complex. The gift exchanges could have been little more than a casual and inconsequential kinship usage unless this practice was linked to a concept of inheritance of rights and an equation of possession of such rights with social status. The invariable purpose of the potlatch, that of presenting claims to hereditary rights, manifestly means that such a concept was basic. We can go a bit further and suggest that the early form of the potlatch may well have been that at which the deceased chief was replaced by his successor, providing the basis through which, in the northern section of the coast, the mortuary and memorial aspects of the affair seem at times to outweigh the presentation of the heir—although invariably the heir formally claimed his inheritance at the occasion. As guests, the affinal kindred saw the heir, in whom they had a direct interest, presented as the claimant to the rights that they knew were his due. The potlatch gifts distributed to them may be considered a repetition of the "bride price," representing a desire to continue the friendly bond between the two groups. Or, a little more imaginatively, those gifts may have been the final payment of the transaction; perhaps the heir was what his father's group was really "buying" when they first began to arrange the marriage. That this idea is not as far-fetched as it might seem at first glance is suggested by the Nootkan emphasis on an heir or heirs as essential to the completion of the marriage arrangements. If a married couple separated or had no issue, the various wealth goods payments were not returned, that is, there was no cash refund; but, and this is the significant point, all rights and privileges formally bestowed by the bride's father at the time of the bride-price repayment reverted to him (and his group).

What we have been trying to say in these final pages is this: We do not accept economic determinism as the origin of the potlatch; we do not believe that it was devised to assist distant hostile groups in solving their subsistence problems, nor to keep wealth goods circulating. Neither do we believe that it could have sprung into being full-blown as a technique for conspicuous consumption by paranoiacs. Rather we believe that the complex probably developed gradually through a fusion of certain simpler concepts mutually compatible in function. As possible basic components, we have pointed to gift exchange at marriage, leading into a continuing special relationship between affinal kin, a wealth system, the concept of inheritance of rights associated with social status, and the formal presentation of the heir at the mortuary rites in honor of a deceased chief. These concepts themselves may have been expanded as the new complex grew, and thus explain the rights elaborated by fancies lifted from mythologies, or the statuses increased in number and seriated in rank. We believe that this hypothesis offers a modicum of intelligibility into possible origins of the potlatch, which was, after all, a rather peculiar social institution.

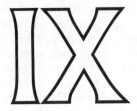

# SYSTEMS OF POLITICS AND LAW

**ISSUE**    Human warfare: Why do people fight?

A city manager and police chief watching an ant farm might envy its inhabitants. The queen rests in her protected chamber, the object of busy attention by countless workers. Other workers cooperate to excavate a tunnel, forage for food, tend young larvae, and see to the other needs of the colony. Conflict is absent; each ant seems to know what to do, cooperating with the others for the common good. If they knew something about biology, the human observers would realize that the ants are genetically programmed to work together. The cooperation and amity are automatic; ants do what they are born to do.

The human inhabitants of a city behave in a different fashion. There is certainly organized interaction visible in such a community, but conflict and lack of cooperation are also evident. There is regular disagreement over what kinds of common activity should occur. Disputes often punctuate the flow of social activity. Although discord is probably more prevalent in crowded cities and complex societies, it occurs in every human society, for unlike genetically programmed ants, people, as we have already seen, organize culturally, and culture permits more flexibility and the expression of competitive individual and subgroup interests. The city manager and police chief must try to deal with the potential social disruptions caused by the conflict of interests. They do so by means of two cultural systems, politics and law.

The political system defines the process of making and carrying out public policy. The political process outlines the way plans for action are formulated and instituted (and often enforced) for the group of people (the public) affected by them. In every society there must be structures that facilitate the political process, leadership, authority, and decision-making groups. Support must be generated for public decisions in order to ensure public compliance.

The legal system is the process used by people to settle disputes, when that process involves agents who have the recognized authority to effect settlements. In our society we culturally define both a set of disputes that can be settled legally (robbery, murder, and rape, etc.), and agents with the legitimate right to settle these disputes (judges, police officers, etc.).

Some disputes are not legal in this sense. They are infralegal, or below the level of a legal dispute. Two neighbors who regularly insult one another verbally, for example, are parties to a dispute. They may shout at each other daily, impugning one another's virility and legitimate ancestry; so long as this is all they do, their dispute will not be legal. Members of the society do not define insults as a matter requiring the intervention of agents with the right to settle the matter.

Wars and feuds also fall outside the legal process and are usually classed as extralegal disputes. Wars occur between the largest political units of which people are members, and feuds take place inside such units. Both wars and feuds involve violence that can lead to death. Neither can be settled by the intervention of a legal agent.

Anthropologists have been interested in the nature and causes of war for a long time, but as Netting points out in his article included in this chapter, the investigator's task has been difficult. Most people whom anthropologists visit in the field have already been "pacified" by the intervention of colonial governments. By the time the anthropologist arrives, wars have ceased and the culture surrounding them has begun to fade. The articles by Vayda and Netting that appear in this chapter are attempts to reconstruct the culture of primitive war based on ethnohistorical techniques. Both authors are more interested in accounting for the particular rhythm and outcomes of fighting than they are in the general explanation of why war occurs to begin with. Divale and Harris, on the other hand, present a massive cross-cultural study linking war to the pressures of human population and a male supremacist cultural complex.

# 22

## PHASES OF THE PROCESS OF WAR AND PEACE AMONG THE MARINGS OF NEW GUINEA[1]

*Andrew P. Vayda*

*War often seems formless and chaotic; it appears to represent the absence of the usual rules that control social interaction and maintain order. Yet even in war, cultural rules exist that shape the fighting, define the sides, and limit the outcomes. In this article, Andrew Vayda describes how clan clusters, the largest political units in the Maring region of New Guinea, were drawn into war with each other about once each decade. Wars started over such things as murder, poaching, crop thefts, territorial encroachments, and sorcery, but they were in no sense chaotic. Sides would repair to a special fighting ground where they might "nothing fight" by standing safely behind large shields or "truly fight" by moving into close quarters with clubs and stabbing spears. Wars generally ended when one side, its strength far superior than that of its opponent's on a particular day, routed the enemy. Victors killed anyone found in the vanquished village, and burned it to the ground. But Vayda points out that the loser's land will be redistributed only when population pressures are high.*

This paper is a sequel to an earlier one showing that fighting for revenge, as illustrated by materials on the Maoris of New Zealand, can be part of a multiphase process including also a phase of attempted territorial conquests and serving to regulate the territorial expansion and dispersion of populations (Vayda, 1970). The present paper provides materials for exploring interpretations that are possible when fighting for revenge and various other practices characteristic of some phases of the total process are found among populations which, unlike the Maoris in pre-European times, are not manifestly expanding. The data used here are derived almost wholly from field work among the Maring people of the Bismarck Mountains of eastern New Guinea, but the kind of interpretation to be offered should be applicable also, as will be suggested in a concluding section, to the study of warfare and ecological processes among other populations of primitive farmers and warriors.

### THE MARING REGION AND PEOPLE

The Maring region is used here as the designation for a rugged forested area of about 190 square miles within which live some 7,000 people sharing certain cultural characteristics and

[1]This paper was presented at the seventieth Annual Meeting of the American Anthropological Association in New York City in 1971. I thank William C. Clarke, Mark D. Dornstreich, Paula Brown Glick, Mervyn Meggitt, Roy A. Rappaport, and Cherry Lowman Vayda for reading a draft and commenting on it. The map was prepared by William C. Clarke and Ian Heyward, who used a base map drawn by Ian Hughes. Another version of the paper is planned as a chapter in a book tentatively entitled *War, Peace, and the Structure of Adaptive Response Processes* that I am writing on war and peace as an ecological process.

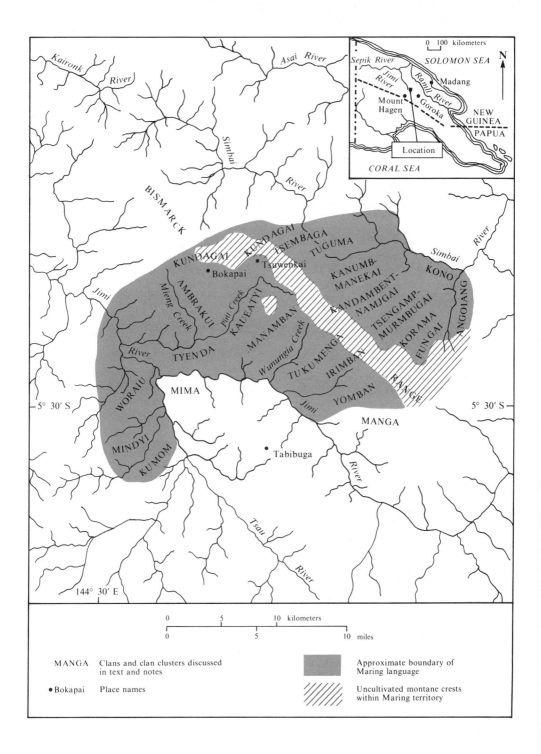

MANGA   Clans and clan clusters discussed in text and notes

● Bokapai   Place names

Approximate boundary of Maring language

Uncultivated montane crests within Maring territory

speaking the Maring language, which has been classified as belonging to the Central Family in the Eastern New Guinea Highlands stock (Wurum and Laycock, 1961; Bunn and Scott, 1963). Cutting across the region is the Bismarck Range, flanked by the Simbai River to the north and the Jimi River to the south. About 2,000 of the Marings live in the Simbai Valley and the rest are in the Jimi Valley. Subsistence activities throughout the region are the traditional ones of slash-and-burn farming of tuberous staples and other crops, pig husbandry, pandanus tree cultivation, and some gathering of wild plant foods and hunting of feral pigs, small marsupials, and birds.

Population is unevenly distributed, becoming less dense where the Simbai and Jimi Rivers reach lower altitudes—at the eastern end of Maring settlement in the Simbai Valley and the western end in the Jimi Valley. Gross contrasts in density correlate with some differences in the organization of local populations. In the more densely settled areas, which have either close to 100 people or many more per square mile of land under cultivation or in secondary forest, clan clusters are the largest named groups with recognized territory boundaries and with members that act together in war and in ceremonies. The core of each of these groups consists of men who belong to local clans, which are units with members putatively, although often not actually, related through patrilineal descent. Each clan in a cluster is an exogamous unit, but the cluster itself is not. There are about a dozen clusters in the more densely settled Maring areas. If we use the term clan cluster population to refer to all the people, whether agnates or non-agnates, who live and garden continually on the lands of the clans of a cluster, we can say that the size of clan cluster populations ranges from some 200 to some 850 people.[2]

The same kind of integration of clans into clusters is absent from the less densely settled areas. Sometimes in warfare here, there were alliances of clans that had adjacent territories, and it is possible to devise definitions whereby any allied clans may be regarded as constituting a clan cluster.[3] However, it needs to be emphasized that these alliances rarely last for more than a generation, and, even while they are still in force, the allied clans do not necessarily have all friends and enemies in common, and they perform separately (and sometimes as hosts and guests rather than as co-hosts) the main ceremonies of the long sequence of rituals that follow warfare.[4] For purposes of the present article, it makes sense to refer to allied clans simply as allied clans and to reserve the clan cluster designation for the more highly integrated named multi-clan groups of the more densely settled Maring areas.

A further contrast between these areas and the lower-density ones lies in the shape and location of group territories. In the former areas most clusters, and many clans within them, occupy territories that extend in irregular bands, from the mossy forests by the crest of the Bismarck Range at an altitude of 6,000–7,000 feet to lands at about 2,000 feet at or near the bottom

---

[2]The imprecision in my statement of the number and size of the clan cluster populations in the more densely settled parts of the Maring area is mainly a result of my being uncertain whether some of the groups whose densities could not be estimated (be-

cause usable air photographs of their territories had not been made) are to be regarded as being in the more densely settled parts or not. As discussed in Lowman-Vayda (1968:202–203), it was possible to make estimates of densities in the territories in which almost half the total population resides.

[3]Before being fully aware of the importance of the differences between the more densely and less densely settled groups, I described all Marings as belonging to clan cluster populations (Vayda and Cook, 1964). For examples of the broad definitions that permit this usage, see Clarke, 1968:53; Lowman-Vayda, 1968:205. Contrasts similar to those between the more and less densely settled Maring groups have been observed by Meggitt (1957b:37ff. and 1965:272) between the Ipili and Mae Enga peoples.

[4]This sequence has been described in detail by Rappaport (1967) from the vantage point of the Tsembaga clan cluster.

of the Simbai or Jimi Valleys.[5] Some clans in the less densely settled areas also have territories dropping from the top of the Bismarck Range, but others have their lands only on small mountains and spurs between the Simbai or Jimi River and its tributaries and in basins formed by these tributaries.

At the time of our initial field work in the Maring region in 1962,[6] the Maring people in general, and especially those in the Simbai Valley, had had hardly any impact yet from missions, trade stores, or labor recruiters. Indeed, although steel axes and bush knives had been introduced along native trade routes in the 1940's, some Maring groups had not been contacted by any white men until four years before our arrival, and had not been brought under Australian administrative control until 1960. The last wars between Maring local groups had been fought no more than half a dozen years before our arrival, and the enmities persisting from these wars were still strong among the people in 1962.

The nature of these wars, as reconstructed from informants' accounts, will be indicated in succeeding sections as part of the description of the multi-phase process operating among the Marings.

## ANTECEDENTS OF FIGHTING

In considering the Maring process, we need not dwell at great length on the peaceful phase immediately preceding the outbreak of fighting. I have suggested elsewhere that a corresponding phase among other peoples—for example, the Maoris (Vayda, 1970:564–66)—involved increase in the pressure exerted by a group upon

its existing territory so that the members were stimulated to commit offenses against other groups and to commit more and more of them, or more and more severe ones, as population pressure increased. The provocations to warfare were cumulative. By contrast, although the provocations in the Maring case were offenses similar to those characteristic of the pre-war phase among the Maoris, the available evidence gives no indication that the offenses had a cumulative effect in provoking war or that their commission correlated with the pressure of particular Maring groups upon their land.

Let us note at this point what the offenses provoking war were. Informants were able to specify the proximate causes of 39 Maring wars for me, and in almost every case some offense by the members of one group against the members of another was involved. Murder or attempted murder was the most common, and occurred in 22 of the cases. Other offenses mentioned included poaching, theft of crops, and territorial encroachment; sorcery or sorcery accusations; abducting women or receiving women who had eloped; rape; and insults.[7] Sometimes these led directly to war and sometimes to homicide first.

It is possible to argue on *a priori* grounds that almost all of those offenses, along with the provocations to commit them, should have increased, among the Marings as among other peoples, with population pressure, which entails a heightening of tensions and of competition over resources. However, it is also possible that the Marings needed less of an accumulation of grievances to incite them to war than did such other peoples as the Maoris. This would be consistent with the fact that among the Marings the account kept of all offenses that one's group made against others and that others made against the group was not as strict as among the Maoris.[8]

---

[5]Similar distributions of territories have been reported both from other parts of the world and from elsewhere in New Guinea (Brookfield and Brown, 1963:170.)

[6]Conducted by R. and A. Rappaport, C. Lowman-Vayda and myself under a National Science Foundation grant (No. G23173).

[7]The cases of territorial encroachment are referred to in a later section.

[8]On the Maori practice in this regard, see Vayda, 1960:45.

More significantly, it would also be consistent with the fact that for each Maring group there were recurrent periods of years when warfare was ritually proscribed. That is to say, if the Marings tended not to undertake wars while the ritual proscriptions were in force, then perhaps they could fight on the basis of fewer provocations than did the Maoris and still not fight so frequently as to jeopardize their survival.[9] The proscriptions became effective after wars and applied to members of the groups that had been the main belligerents and were able to maintain themselves on their own territories. When warfare ended, the men of these groups performed certain rituals. These involved thanking the ancestor spirits for their assistance in the fight, sacrificing for them whatever mature and adolescent pigs were on hand, and promising them many more pigs, commensurate with the help received, to be sacrificed when the group had a herd large enough for holding a festival—something of the order of 170 pigs for a festival hosted by about 200 people.[10] Until the festival,

warfare was not to be undertaken because, in the Maring view, there would be no help forthcoming from either spirits or allies until they received their just rewards. The periods required for raising herds considered sufficiently large thus corresponded as a rule to periods of nonaggression. Moreover, these periods, which lasted usually some 10 years, tended to be marked not only by an absence of open fighting between groups but also by an absence of provocations or offenses between them. This is because, as will be discussed later, the use of land in places where there was likelihood of contact with members of other groups tended to be avoided by people as long as they could not feel secure in having the support of their ancestor spirits when potentially hostile outsiders or their potentially malefic magic were encountered. In other words, until the spirits were appeased with pig sacrifices, intergroup offenses were unlikely simply because intergroup encounters were avoided. Obversely, as soon as the outstanding obligations to spirits and allies had been met, people were more readily disposed to repair to the borderlands of their territories so that encounters with members of other groups and, concomitantly, disputes with them were likely to take place. Informants gave accounts of wars that broke out within two or three months or even

---

[9]This is a view presented in detail by Rappaport in his book (1967) on Maring ritual and ecology; he also notes that there have been violations of the ritual proscriptions. Three cases of what may have been violations are known to me: the Kauwatyi raid on the Tyenda in 1955, the fighting initiated by the Manamban against the Kauwatyi in 1956, and the Tukumenga attack on the Manamban in 1956. Details of these hostilities are given later in this paper.

[10]The figures are based on the pigs and people involved in the festival held by the Tsembaga clan cluster population in 1962–63, as described by Rappaport (1967). Groups smaller than the Tsembaga and with smaller territories held festivals with considerably fewer pigs, while larger groups are said to have held festivals with several hundred pigs. Elsewhere (Vayda, in press) I have made the following observations: ". . . the people tend to hold the festivals when they can afford to—when they have had good fortune for a number of years and when, accordingly, pigs may have become 'too much of a good thing' for them. Indeed, there is evidence that when pig herds become large they also become burdensome and cause people

to agitate for pig festivals, for expanding pig populations increasingly compete with human beings for garden food, and their care calls for larger and larger outlays of energy by the pig-keepers" (cf. Rappaport, 1967:153–65; and Vayda, Leeds and Smith, 1961). One Simbai valley group, the Kanumb-Manekai, with a resident population of 91, was beginning its festival in March, 1963, and informants from the group told me that they had originally planned to wait for the return of some of their young men from coastal employment before holding their festival, but then had had to decide to go ahead without them—because there were "too many pigs destroying gardens." When I made a census of Kanumb-Manekai pigs in June, 1963, prior to the wholesale killing of pigs in the festival, I found 62 adult pigs (23 males and 39 females) and 26 piglets.

within weeks after the termination of a pig festival.[11]

There is, moreover, no evidence that provocations to war and then warfare itself ensued less quickly after pig festivals among the Maring groups exerting least pressure upon their land. Some of the smallest Simbai Valley clan populations, living at the edge of a vast expanse of unoccupied forest extending eastwards along the Bismarck Range, fought as often as did some of the large clan cluster populations of the central Maring area, where there are not only higher population densities but also such other indicators of greater pressure upon resources as shorter fallow periods for garden plots, more painstaking harvests from the gardens, and, as a result of more intensive land use in a few places, some tracts of permanent grassland and degraded secondary forest, both of which are rare in the low-density territories.[12] Most Maring groups seem to have averaged one or two wars per generation, and it is in the wars themselves and their aftermaths and not in the antecedents of fighting that we must look for mechanisms operating in response to demographic factors.

---

[11]The most recent war in which a main belligerent was the Tsembaga clan cluster studied by Rappaport (1967:218) began within three months of the end of a Tsembaga pig festival. In the case of the last war between the Yomban and Manga clusters of the Jimi Valley, the first provocation to fight was made while the Yomban were still engaged in their pig festival. Their old enemies, the Manga, shouted at them, "You're not men—you're women. We killed some of you, but you didn't kill us. So what are you making a festival for?" The incensed Yomban concluded their festival and then quickly repaired to Manga territory, where they killed one man and four women in a garden by first spearing them and cutting them up with axes. The war was on.

[12]This comparison is based on Clarke, 1966:348–52. Further discussion of differential pressure on the land is presented below.

## TWO PHASES OF WAR: NOTHING FIGHTS AND TRUE FIGHTS

All Maring groups sometimes took part in engagements that they called small fights or nothing fights. In these, the warriors repaired each morning from their homes to prearranged fight grounds at the borders of the lands of the two main belligerent groups. The opposing forces took up positions close enough to each other to be within the range of arrows. Thick wooden shields, as tall as the men and about two feet six inches wide, afforded protection in combat.[13] With the bottoms of the shields resting on the ground, warriors darted out from behind them to shoot their arrows. Some men also emerged temporarily from cover in order to taunt their foes and display bravery by drawing enemy fire. At the end of each day's fighting, the men returned home. Although these small bow-and-arrows fights sometimes continued for days and even weeks, deaths or serious injuries were rare. Indeed, Rappaport (1967:121–23), in his discussion of the fights as described to him by warriors of the Tsembaga cluster, suggested that rather than serious battles they were, among other things, settings for attempts at conflict resolution by non-violent means. They brought the antagonists, as he noted, "within the range of each other's voices while keeping them out of the range of each other's deadlier weapons." Sometimes the voices at the fight ground uttered insults, but there also were times when moderation was counseled (especially by men who came as allies of one belligerent group but also had ties with the other) and when settlements of disputes were negotiated so as to obviate escalation of the fighting to a more deadly phase.

When there was escalation, the Maring pattern was for it to be to a phase involving what informants called true fights—fights in which not only bows and arrows and throwing spears

---

[13]For descriptions of Maring shields and their use, see Lowman-Vayda, in preparation.

but also axes and jabbing spears, the weapons of close combat, were used. While the small fights were still going on, advocates of escalation as well as the Maring equivalents of doves were speaking out. Whether the hawks would prevail depended upon a variety of factors—for example, the fighting strength of the enemy as displayed in the nothing fight, the casualties if any, and the nature of previous relations between the antagonists. Sometimes a group chose to escalate a fight in order to attempt to even the score with the enemy in killings, while at other times a group abandoned a fight because it had already suffered too many deaths.[14] It is possible that the enemy's show of force in the nothing fight was sometimes sufficient to induce a group to flee without submitting to any further test of arms; accounts that Rappaport (1967:124) received from some Tsembaga informants suggest this. The nothing fights may be said to have had what some authors would describe as an epideictic aspect (Rappaport, 1967:195; Wynne-Edwards, 1962:16–17). And, as in the case of other epideictic phenomena, what the fights disclosed to the participants about the size of their rivals' groups could lead to behavior changing the size or dispersion of the groups involved.

If a consensus in favor of escalation to a phase of true fights did develop on both sides, the antagonists, after shouting to each other that the time had come for more serious warfare, withdrew to make elaborate ritual preparations for it for at least two days.[15] When they returned to the fight ground, they took up positions in formations several ranks deep. While men in the opposing front ranks fought duels with one another from behind their huge shields, they were provided with cover by bowmen who were in the

ranks further to the rear and who shot at any enemy warrior exposing himself. Front positions were exchanged for rear ones from time to time in the course of battle, and sometimes individual men temporarily withdrew from combat in order to catch their breath. Most fatalities in these true fights seem to have occurred when an enemy arrow or throwing spear brought down a man in the front ranks so that he could be finished off with axes in a quick charge from the enemy front line. Because of the protection that the shields afforded and because the fighting was from static positions rather than involving any appreciable tactical movements, the warfare could proceed for weeks and even months without heavy casualties. Each morning when there was to be fighting, the able-bodied men who were the warriors assembled near their hamlets and went *en masse* to the fightground for their day's combat, while the women remained behind to attend to routine gardening and domestic tasks. The men themselves did not fight daily. When it rained both sides stayed in their houses, and, by mutual agreement, all combatants sometimes took a day off to re-paint their shields, to attend to rituals in connection with casualties, or simply to rest. There could even be intervals of as long as three weeks during which active hostilities were suspended and the men worked at making new gardens.

It must be emphasized that these truces had to be agreed to by both sides. If only one side absented itself from the fight ground, this was in effect a signal to the other side to consider escalating to another kind of military action: what is to be described below as routing. Although this was an action that characteristically lasted but a few hours at the most, it can be usefully discussed as a separate phase in the process of war and peace. Before turning to it, however, we must consider what role allies could have in bringing about routs and what alternative there could be to nothing fights and true fights as the phases of hostilities antecedent to routing.

---

[14]There are illustrations of both kinds of decisions in informants' accounts of warfare—for example, fights between the Irimban and Yomban clusters and between the Manamban and Tukumenga clusters.

[15]A description of these preparations is given in Rappaport, 1967:125–38.

## ALLIES

The prelude to a group's being routed could be a reverse at the fight ground, and this could, as Rappaport (1967:139) noted in his account of the last war between the Tsembaga and Kundagai clusters in the Simbai Valley, come about through the failure of allies to appear in force. It should be understood that a Maring war characteristically had two groups as the main belligerents and that allies were men belonging to other groups and participating in the fighting because of individual ties between them and the members of the two main belligerent groups. The longer that fight-ground hostilities dragged on, the more difficult it became for the main belligerents to maintain the support of allies, who, naturally enough, had their own affairs to attend to. In the case of the Tsembaga, the greatest number of their allies belonged to the neighboring Tuguma cluster, and it was on the day when the Tuguma did not come to the fight ground that the Kundagai, still supported by their own allies and aware of their numerical advantage, mounted a charge in which the Tsembaga suffered heavy casualties. The routing of the Tsembaga ensued.

There also were times when a group learned in advance that needed allies were withdrawing their support. Instead of fighting and dying in a lost cause, the group fled to refuge immediately and its adversaries were left with houses and gardens to destroy but no people to slaughter. The Kanumb group is said to have fled in this manner in its last war with the Tuguma cluster (Rappaport, 1967:139).

In view of the importance of allies for success, it must be understood that whether their support in sufficient numbers and for long enough time would be forthcoming was not a capricious matter. Those from whom help might come were non-agnatic kinsmen living elsewhere and also other men recruited by such non-agnatic kinsmen. Of the two main belligerent groups in a war, the larger one would thus be likely to have its numerical advantage magnified

by having more allies. Being larger, it would as a rule have formed more numerous ties with other groups through marriage. Also, other things being constant, the group that was doing a better job of using its land and growing crops and pigs on it would have an advantage for receiving support, for it would have been better able to make prestations of pigs and other valuables so as both to maintain the allegiance of existing kinsmen in other groups and to create new ties through new marriages.

It needs to be emphasized that merely having kinsmen in other groups was not sufficient to ensure their support. If relations with them had not been kept active through prestations of goods and through services such as helping the kinsmen in their own wars and acting as intermediaries for them in trading goods over long distances, the kinsmen were not likely to be quick to give military assistance. Indeed, a number of Marings that we met had refused to give such assistance to affines who they felt had slighted them. Moreover, it should be noted that the principle of helping kinsmen often left latitude as to where aid should be rendered at a particular time, for one was apt to have kinsmen engaged in different wars simultaneously or in a single war on opposing sides. Under such circumstances calculations of self-interest were a factor in decisions about aid. Thus one redoubtable warrior from the Fungai clan initially helped his affines in the Murmbugai clan, but when he felt himself to have been insufficiently requited for his efforts he switched to the side of the Murmbugai's enemies, the Korama, a clan that also contained some of his kinsmen.

The Kauwatyi cluster of the Jimi Valley, never routed from its territory and with some 850 in the cluster population, is an example of a large, aggressive, successful, and centrally-located group whose side it was advantageous to be on. The Kauwatyi got even more help than they wanted or needed from their many kinsmen in almost all groups on both sides of the Bismarck Range. According to Kauwatyi infor-

mants, the superfluous allies were tolerated at
the nothing fights and duly rewarded with pork
on subsequent ceremonial occasions, but were
not asked to join in the more deadly fighting in
which any deaths suffered by allies would have
had to be recompensed profusely—with brides
among the prestations—by the Kauwatyi themselves. No doubt it was an advantage to the
Kauwatyi not to have these allies helping the
enemy, even if their direct aid could be dis-
pensed with.

The last war that the Kauwatyi fought was
against the Manamban cluster in 1956, and it
was a war in which the Kauwatyi did seek allies
—but they were allies from a specific group,
recruited for a specific tactical operation. Some
of the antecedents and consequences of the involvement of these allies, men from the Tukumenga cluster, in the war are worth recounting
here, for they nicely illustrate the kinds of hard-
headed strategic considerations that could be
operative in decisions about launching attacks
and becoming allies. Initially, while the Kauwatyi-Manamban war was going on, most of the
Kauwatyi Tukumenga allies were involved in
hostilities elsewhere. Tukumenga territory is
bordered on the west by the territory of the Manamban and on the east by that of the Yomban,
and one or the other of these clusters has been
the enemy in all but one of the six recent wars
in which the Tukumenga have been one of the
main belligerents.[16] At the beginning of 1956 the
Tukumenga were not themselves the main belligerents in any war, although large numbers of

Tukumenga men were helping the Manga cluster, a non-Maring group, in fight-ground battle
against the group that had been their own enemy
in their last war: the Yomban.[17] Since the Yomban cluster, of more than 700 people, was about
twice the size of the Manga, the substantial help
received by the Manga from the Tukumenga was
no doubt of critical importance to the Manga
cause. When hostilities broke out between the
Kauwatyi and the Tukumenga's other traditional enemy, the Manamban, the war was already on between the Yomban and the Manga
and it was to the Manga that the Tukumenga
men continued to give their help. Each morning
they went by a track near the Jimi River, far
from the Yomban settlements, to the Manga-
Yomban fight ground and, after a day of combat,
they returned home each evening the same way.
This had been going on for many weeks when in
late April or early May two of the Kauwatyi
leaders came secretly to the Tukumenga houses
(but not to those where men with Manamban
affines might betray the plans) and asked for
help in a concerted attack upon the Manamban
to take place on the following morning. Part of
the proposal was that after defeating and routing
the Manamban the Kauwatyi and Tukumenga
would attempt to take over the Manamban territory, with the new boundary between the
two victorious groups to consist of Wunungia
Creek in the center. The Tukumenga agreed to
the plan; the Yomban-Manga war had been
dragging on to no effect, whereas here there
was a prospect of a quick and advantageous
victory. The Kauwatyi leaders returned to their
homes, while the Tukumenga warriors collected their weapons, performed certain pre-fight ri-

[16]The exception consisted of a war in which the
Tukumenga stayed on the north bank of the wide and
deep Jimi River and their adversaries, the Mima,
stayed on the south bank. Actual fighting was limited
to shooting arrows across the water. After more than
a month of this, and with nobody killed, some Tukumenga said: "It is no good to fight distant enemies. Our
bellies are still angry; so let us kill some people
nearby." They found two Manamban men doing garden work and killed them. The Tukumenga then abandoned the war against the Mima and fought the
Manamban (cf. Vayda, 1967:134).

[17]The Yomban are the easternmost Maring group
in the Jimi Valley. The Manga are the next group to
the east and are Narak-speakers but have customs in
warfare hardly different from those of their Maring
neighbors (see Cook, 1967). Adopting the terminology
favored by some anthropologists (e.g. Salisbury,
1963:257–58), we could say that the Yomban and the
Manga belonged to a single "league."

tuals,[18] and then made their way to the forests high above their settlements. Here they arranged their shields to form makeshift houses, made fires in the middle of these, and then slept. At dawn they moved along the top of the Bismarck Range and then descended to the Kauwatyi-Manamban fight ground so as to come upon the enemy's rear and take him by surprise. The Manamban were easily routed. After joining in the work of destroying the houses and gardens, the Tukumenga went with the Kauwatyi to the houses of the latter and then returned towards the evening to their own houses via the tracks down near the river. On their way back, they could see to the east the smoke and fire which were issuing from the settlements of the Manga: the Yomban had taken advantage of the one-day absence of the Tukumenga. They had mounted a charge which took the lives of five Manga warriors and had followed this up with the routing of the Manga and setting fire to their houses.

## AN ALTERNATIVE PHASE: RAIDS

The Tukumenga and Manamban cluster each comprised some 600 people, and the size of the Kauwatyi and Yomban was, as previously noted, even greater. Only one other Maring group, the Kundagai of the western part of the Maring region in the Jimi Valley, approached these four clusters in size. In the case of the much smaller groups of the less densely settled Maring areas, warfare could be conducted essentially in the manner already described, although, obviously, on a much smaller scale. However, among these groups another mode of fighting, employed only rarely among the large clusters, also seems to have been common and to have constituted an alternative to nothing fights and

---

[18]Including those described in Rappaport, 1967:152, citing accounts that I obtained in 1966 from Tukumenga participants in the fighting.

true fights as antecedents of routing. This was raiding and consisted usually of stealing in the night to the houses where the men of an enemy clan slept—the 30 or so men in a clan would have their sleeping quarters distributed among perhaps four or five houses. At dawn the raiders made fast the doors of as many of these as possible and then shot their arrows and poked their long spears through the leaf-thatched walls. If the men inside succeeded in undoing the doors, they were picked off by raiders waiting behind the fences. With a numerical advantage on the side of the raiders these tactics could annihilate the manpower of an enemy clan. This is what may have happened to the Woraiu, a now extinct Maring group that had been living on the south side of the Jimi River, where it was attacked by an alliance of the Mindyi and Kumom clans. However, in the accounts that I received from informants in the low-density Maring areas in the eastern Simbai Valley rather than in the Jimi, the raiding force never seems to have been large enough to take care of all of the enemy men's houses. The raiders in all cases, after killing a few, were forced to retreat because of counter-attacks by warriors from houses other than those raided.

These eastern Simbai accounts underscore that this mode of fighting could as a rule be effective only when the enemy group attacked was small. Otherwise the position of raiders deep in enemy territory could be extremely perilous, for warriors might rise up against them from all sides before they could make good their retreat. In the light of these considerations, it is not surprising that raiding should have been uncommon among the large populations. Indeed, I was told of only one clear case in which the fighting force of such a population attacked the enemy in his settlements without previously having tested him in fight-ground battle, and it is significant that the attack was made by the Kauwatyi, the largest of the Maring populations, against the Tyenda, a group less than half its size. The Kauwatyi men had gone during the night to Tyenda territory and, at dawn, appeared *en*

*masse* and fully armed at the Tyenda settlements. The Tyenda just ran while the Kauwatyi
wrought death and destruction. This attack took
place in 1955. The Kauwatyi suffered no fatalities and the Tyenda, a group of about 300, lost
23. It is hardly likely that a similar attack by the
Tyenda against the Kauwatyi swarm would
have been successful.


## ROUTS AND THEIR AFTERMATH

The phase designated here as routing consisted, as already suggested, of going to the
enemy settlements, burning the houses there,
killing indiscriminately any men, women, or
children found in the settlements, and, after having put the survivors to flight, destroying gardens, fences, and pandanus groves, and defiling
the burial places. These proceedings sometimes
took place immediately after the enemy warriors
had broken ranks and fled in response to a
charge at the fight ground. That is to say, the
fleeing warriors would rush to their hamlets,
gather their women and children, and then flee
to seek refuge, while the routers wreaked as
much death and destruction as they could. This
is what happened in the war in which the
Kauwatyi and Tukumenga jointly routed the
Manamban. At other times the routing did not
take place until the day after losses at the fight
ground; the side that had suffered them would
fail to appear and its antagonists would there-
upon proceed to the settlements to burn and to
kill. A Yomban-Tukumenga fight had this outcome.

Routing was not an inevitable consequence of
the true wars of the Marings. It was possible,
before events moved into the routing phase, for
both sides to opt for an armistice whereby there
could be no warfare between them until after a
massive pig festival such as was referred to earlier. Rappaport (1967:143) suggested that armistice was the more likely course when the number
of killings between the antagonists was equal or

when both agreed that, regardless of any disparities in the homicide score, the pressure of subsistence tasks made it impractical to continue
hostilities. This may well be. However, on the
basis of information about warfare involving either the Tsembaga or Tuguma cluster, Rappaport (1967:142) has made the further
suggestion that true wars ended most frequently
with armistice. This suggestion is not in accord
with the accounts that informants gave me concerning the termination of 29 such wars. Nineteen of these ended with the routing of people
and the destruction of their houses and gardens.
The important point is that the phase of true
wars, like that of nothing fights, was one from
which there could be either a return to peace or
else escalation leading to further testing of the
antagonists. That this was testing of the belligerents' capacity not only to defend themselves but
also to defend and use land can be seen in the
aftermath of routs.

The routs themselves did not necessarily
have a decisive effect on these capacities. The
Woraiu, as noted in the preceding section, may
have had their manpower effectively destroyed
when they were raided by the Mindyi and Kumom, but such annihilation of the fighting force
of a group cannot have been common. The Marings, unlike such other peoples as the Maoris,
did not customarily pursue an enemy beyond his
settlement. To have done so would have been,
according to informants, inviting death; so, as
already indicated, the victors stayed behind and
burned houses, ravaged gardens, and performed
other destructive acts. The two Maring wars in
which informants belonging to defeated groups
claimed to have suffered the heaviest losses were
the ones fought against the Kauwatyi by the
Tyenda and the Manamban in the mid-1950s.
When some 300 Tyenda were routed following
the Kauwatyi's surprise raid, 14 Tyenda men,
six women, and three children were killed. The
600 Manamban lost only eight men and three
women in the course of being routed by the combined forces of the Kauwatyi and Tukumenga
(although there had been 20 other Manamban

deaths at the fight ground previously). If these figures indicate the heaviest mortality suffered in Maring wars, it may be questioned whether routs in general were effective in decisively altering the capacity of groups to defend and use land.

Let us consider, then, the testing of the antagonists in the aftermath of routs. First of all, during the period or phase which may be described as that of refuging by the routed group. The first opportunity that such a group had to show its mettle in this period was in the selection of a place of refuge. I have accounts of 21 routs. In seven of these the groups did not even leave their own territory and took refuge in portions of it at some distance from the borderlands where the enemies had engaged them. Among the 14 other cases the members of some routed groups fled across the Bismarck Range or the major rivers, but there were others where they remained closer and, indeed, sometimes continued to maintain a claim to their territory by going to it for food.

In the case of groups taking refuge outside of their own territories, a major test versus the enemies lay in making the return. Rappaport's discussion of routs suggested that defeated groups often failed to do this (Rappaport, 1967:145). However, in 13 of my 14 cases the routed groups did, indeed, return; the one exception involved the Woraiu, who, as noted earlier, may have had their manpower effectively destroyed when they were raided by the Mindyi and Kumom. Unfortunately, the interpretation of these data is made difficult by the fact that the routed groups in seven of the cases referred to made their returns after the Australian administration had established its presence. It may be—as indeed Rappaport (1967:145) suggested it was—that some of the groups, especially after having fragmented for the sake of obtaining refuge in one or another of the places where there were kinsmen or friends of individuals, would not have reconstituted themselves and repossessed their territories if not for the security and protection that the Australian presence afforded. There is, unfortu-

nately, no evidence on which firm conclusions about this may be based. It seems likely, however, that Australian intervention did enable some groups to return to their territories more quickly and to rebuild their settlements in closer proximity to those of their enemies than would have been the case otherwise. This was most notably so in the case of the Manga. After being routed by the Yomban in 1956, they fled across the Jimi to friends and kinsmen living around a place called Tabibuga. From there, word of the Manga defeat was carried south across the Wahgi-Sepik divide to Minj, the Government subdistrict headquarters. The Assistant District Officer there had visited the Yomban-Manga area previously with armed patrols—in 1953 and 1955. When an aerial survey confirmed the destruction of the Manga settlements, a new patrol was organized and marched along the tracks to the area some time in May, less than a month after the routing of the Manga. The Manga themselves were first taken back to their land by the patrol, which then proceeded to move against the Yomban. The ambushes that Yomban warriors armed with axes had prepared were unsuccessful, but they nevertheless continued to shower arrows upon the patrol and finally fled only after six of their number had been shot dead by police. This intervention, however, was quickly followed by what was to have a more continuous impact. A Patrol Post was established at Tabibuga with an Australian in charge and a complement of armed native police to extend *Pax Australiensis* into the Jimi Valley. Tabibuga is but a couple of hours' walk from the Manga settlements, so the people now had the security to devote themselves to rebuilding their houses on their former sites and to using their lands once more.[19]

---

[19]My account of the routing of the Manga is based upon information from Yomban informants and written résumés of the official patrol reports. The latter were kindly supplied in 1963 by Mr. J. K. McCarthy, then Director of the Department of Native Affairs, Territory of Papua and New Guinea. Other reports of

Members of some other groups, perhaps partly because of their greater distance from Tabibuga, were more hesitant about leaving their refuges, but eventually all the Jimi Valley groups, with varying degrees of help and supervision from Tabibuga, were repatriated. From July through to October of 1956 there were monthly visits to the disturbed areas by Australian officials. Among the instructions given to the people were that they were to rebuild their houses and gardens, to report any raids to the patrol officer, and to keep their own noses clean unless they wished to be very severely dealt with. Weapons also were collected and burned publicly. By early October the officer, Barry Griffin, stated that all the recently routed Maring groups of the Jimi Valley—the Ambrakui, the Manamban, and the Tyenda—had, like the Manga, been restored to their lands.

Actually the statement, at least in October 1956, could not be made accurately without qualifications that are suggestive as to what might have been the aftermath in the absence of intervention. While all the groups had been restored to some degree, there were, it must be noted, variations. Thus the Ambrakui, who had been routed some time around 1954 as a result of fighting that began with land encroachments by the Kundagai,[20] had taken refuge on the south side of the Jimi River, mainly on the lands of the Mima cluster, which included numerous affines and friends. From Mima territory, some of them accompanied a patrol led by Griffin at the end of September, 1956, to their abandoned territory north of the river. He instructed them to re-settle there and left a few police in the

general area to help in the work. He also held discussions with both Kundagai and Ambrakui about their lands and then affirmed boundaries which, according to what I was told by Ambrakui informants in 1963, corresponded to the ancestral ones between the lands of the two groups. However, when he revisited the territory in June of 1957 he saw that the resettlement, averred in October of the previous year, was still far from complete: the men had, in effect, simply been visiting their old lands, while the women, children, and pigs had, for the most part, not even been doing that; they had remained in their Mima refuges. New gardens had not been made in the old lands. Only with increased police supervision and with further warnings to the Kundagai was the full return finally effected later in 1957. Less than five years later there were new land encroachments by the Kundagai. In response to the complaints of the Ambrakui, the patrol officer (a successor of Griffin) sent police to destroy Kundagai plantings on Ambrakui land and to arrest the offenders and bring them to Tabibuga. These incidents show that the 250 Ambrakui, one of the smallest of the Maring cluster populations, still had in the Kundagai a powerful enemy that was ready to act aggressively unless stopped by superior force. Any Ambrakui skittishness about being repatriated is perhaps not surprising.

In contrast, members of the large and powerful Manamban cluster, after having fled for refuge to at least 10 different groups on both sides of the Bismarck Range, began drifting back to their own territory within a week or two of having been routed by the Kauwatyi and Tukumenga in late April or early May of 1956. When the patrol from the sub-district headquarters at Minj arrived to confront the Yomban, some Manamban were already back on their land and a delegation of them went to Yomban territory to meet with the Australian officer. A Government patrol that included Manamban territory in its itinerary in July, 1956, reported that the Manambans had not yet returned but that a fair gathering of them assembled. According to the

---

government contacts with Maring groups, including those on which the next four paragraphs are based, were kindly made available by the Simbai and Tabibuga Patrol Officers in 1963 and 1966. Published accounts of the patrol post at Tabibuga and some of the work done from there include Attenborough, 1960: Chapter 5, and Souter, 1964:235.

[20]See below.

head count made there were 239 people. This constitutes about 40%. When Griffin arrived 16 days later to make a census, he saw 305 people and recorded their names. The return of the remainder proceeded smoothly thereafter.

The third people, the Tyenda, seemed to have been intermediate in their readiness to be repatriated—less timid than the Ambrakui, less bold than the Manamban. Not a large group, they nevertheless had had support even in refuge from numerous allies among the powerful Kundagai and Manamban. The former was the group that most of the Tyenda had been refuging with following their rout at the hands of the Kauwatyi in 1955, and they had continued to go to their own lands for food. Indeed, on one occasion they had killed four Kauwatyi men pursuing a pig deep into Tyenda territory, and the Kauwatyi were thereafter afraid to go far beyond the old boundary between the two groups. As for the Manamban, their support had been demonstrated by the response to a Tyenda kinsman's pleas for revenge against the Kauwatyi who had killed his children and brothers; the Manamban had gone *en masse* to challenge their old enemies by killing a Kauwatyi man. This had led to the Kauwatyi-Manamban war ending with the Manamban rout in 1956. The enmity between the Kauwatyi and the Manamban had been of long standing, but this very fact points up a difference between the position of the Tyenda and that of the Ambrakui, for the latter had no strong group to which they could turn to make common cause against the foe that had routed them. It is consistent with this that when the Ambrakui were still remaining close to their Mima refuge in June, 1957, the Tyenda were found by Griffin to be going ahead well with resettlement and to have prepared extensive new gardens in their territory. On the basis of the variations in the tempo of resettlement even with government support, it may be supposed that, in its absence, the Ambrakui would not have returned but the Manamban would have, and so perhaps, at least to a part of their land, would have the Tyenda.

Groups failing to return would, in effect, be leaving their territories for others eventually to annex. This would mark the end of a cycle of testing of the capacity to defend and use the land. New multi-phase cycles could then begin with fresh outbreaks of hostilities and with new sets of contending groups.

If, however, routed groups did return, the cycle of testing did not end with repatriation. What happened to groups and their lands after warfare in which no group had been permanently routed? This is the question with which we must now deal.

## TWO KINDS OF PEACE: WITH AND WITHOUT LAND REDISTRIBUTION

Usually the defeated groups, whether they had been routed or not, made new settlements further than their old ones from the borders with the enemies who had beaten them. In the Maring view, the rationale for this course of action was not only to avoid the enemies but also to avoid their malefic magic, thought to infest the borderlands where the fighting had taken place. The worse the defeat had been, the more the enemy and his magic were to be feared, and, in extreme cases, new settlements of a group were made deep within the forests that had previously been used for hunting rather than for gardens or long-term residence.[21] At times the new settlements were made not even in the group's own territory, although that continued to be used for making gardens and for other economic activities. Houses were constructed on the land of a neighboring group that was friendly. This con-

---

[21]The Manamban and the Manga in the Jimi Valley and the Kono and the Angoiang in the Simbai Valley have done this. After the officer and his police had demonstrated the power of their magic by shooting six Yomban dead, some of the Yomban went to hunting grounds north of the crest of the Bismarck Range and made settlements there.

stitutes in effect the same pattern of settlement and land use as operated among the Tyenda while they were refuging with the Kundagai. The pattern is noted here again because it was put into effect by some groups like the Tsembaga (see Rappaport, 1967:145) and the Murmbugai of the Simbai Valley not when in their original places of refuge after having been routed but rather when they had returned from those places to use their own territories even if not to live on them. The Murmbugai were still following this pattern in 1963, some seven or eight years after they had been defeated by the Kandambent-Namigai group. This was not the first time that the Murmbugai had done this. The Korama clan had destroyed their houses in an earlier war, and they had made new ones on the Tsengamp clan territory, whence they issued forth in due time to destroy the Korama settlements.

Some defeated groups succeeded in rehabilitating themselves fully. The gardens that they made on their lands grew well, their pig herds increased, their allies stood by them, and they accumulated the wherewithal to make the appropriate sacrifices to appease the ancestor spirits. The members of such groups eventually felt strong enough and secure enough to stand up to the old enemies and their magic and, some 10 years after the warfare, they would return to the borderlands, utter spells to chase the enemy spirits and the corruption caused by them back to enemy territory, and then would plant new boundary stakes where the old ones had been.[22] This last action signified that the *status quo ante bellum* was to be restored as far as territories were concerned—that there was to be peace without land redistribution. The stake-planting would be followed by a pig festival in which, as previously noted, the outstanding obligations to allies and ancestor spirits would be met and their help in future encounters with enemies would thus, most beneficially for morale, be secured.

But not all defeated groups that gained subsistence from their own lands after warfare had their confidence—and the grounds for confidence—restored to this same high degree. For some groups, perhaps with the loss of men and destruction of resources suffered in warfare compounded by post-bellum adversities such as diseases affecting themselves or their pigs, the borderlands where the enemy, his spirits, and his magic were thought to lurk continued to be places of fearsome peril. If a group did not rehabilitate itself sufficiently to be able to assert itself at its old boundaries by planting stakes there, it might simply leave some territory to be annexed by enemies. Informants stated this as a possibility but were unable to cite any recent examples.[23] They did, however, refer to certain dispositions by the Tyenda as an example of an alternative that groups not strong enough to confront their old enemies at the borderlands might have recourse to. The dispositions occurred after the last defeat of the Tyenda at the hands of the Kauwatyi and consisted of giving to the Kundagai groups of Bokapai and Tsuwenkai about 1.8 square miles in the higher altitudes in the northern part of Tyenda territory. This land, running as a band from the crest of the Bismarck Range down to the Pint River and, in its lower reaches which are best suited for gardens, bordering Kundagai territory on the west and Kauwatyi territory on the east, comprised about 30–40% of the total territory of the Tyenda. By giving the land to their Kundagai friends, including those who had provided them with refuge after their rout by the Kauwatyi, the Tyenda were requiting help in the past, making future help from them more likely, and, perhaps most importantly, arranging to have friends at the boundary between the land that the Tyenda were relinquishing and the land to which they were holding on. It must be added that in this last regard the Tyenda were not completely suc-

---

[22]Rappaport (1967:166 ff.) gives details of the stake-planting ceremonies.

[23]An example not from a recent war but rather from the early years of this century is discussed by Rappaport (1967:171).

cessful, for the Kauwatyi quickly appropriated for their own agricultural use some of the ground in question before the Kundagai had a chance to occupy it. As a result the Kundagai, kept by the *Pax Australiensis* from seeking redress through the traditional recourse to arms, were planning to bring the Kauwatyi before the Government courts over the matter. These effects can be argued also to have been advantageous for the Tyenda insofar as they were diverting the hostility and aggressions of the Kauwatyi from the Tyenda themselves. In any event, a more densely settled group–whether the Kundagai or the Kauwatyi–was getting land from the Tyenda, which had relatively low population density before bestowing the northern territory upon the Kundagai.[24] The example suggests that there may have been a variety of ways in which land redistribution following routing and refuging took place and that some of these ways may themselves have been multi-phase processes. The fact that in our exposition here we have distinguished not multiple post-refuging phases involving land redistribution but rather only a single phase designated as peace with land redistribution may well constitute an oversimplification of processes that actually took place in the past. If, however, this should be the case, it must be said that the oversimplification is unavoidable, since the post-refuging redistribution processes have hardly been operating recently, and details about them are, accordingly, hard to come by.

By regarding peace without land redistribution and peace with it as alternative phases antecedent to new rounds of fighting, we may be guilty of further oversimplification. Some hazy accounts of events that took place long ago suggest that redistribution could be a slow post-

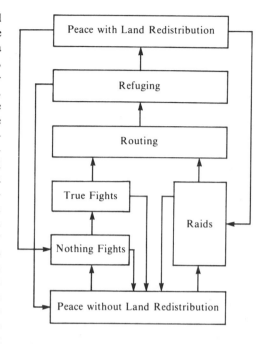

bellum process involving groups that had appeared initially not to have relinquished any of their lands. An example of such an account concerns an original autonomous group—either clan or clan cluster—called the Kombepe. Towards the end of the last century, before any of our informants had been born, these people had their own discrete territory in the low altitudes between the Mieng and Pint Creeks, were neighbors of the Kundagai and the Ambrakui, and had a number of affines in both. When a dispute arose between some Kundagai and Kombepe, the Kundagai took their affines among the Kombepe home to their settlements for safety and then made an attack upon the remaining Kombepe. Of these the ones surviving went as a group to live with the Ambrakui and now constitute a clan of that cluster. In other words, the Kombepe split into two groups and ceased to exist as a single autonomous group. They did not, however, thereby cease to maintain their rights to

---

[24]Here, as before, I am defining as more densely settled those groups that have either close to 100 people or many more per square mile of land under cultivation or in secondary forest. Tyenda density prior to the land transfers was only about 60 people per square mile of such land.

their ancestral ground. Some of this continued as the land of the Kombepe staying with the Kundagai and the rest of it as the land of the Kombepe affiliated with the Ambrakui. But the two groups of Kombepe made grants of usufruct to their respective hosts. In the case of the Kundagai Kombepe, their failure to have many descendants resulted in the eventual complete absorption of themselves and their lands by the Kundagai. Informants were unable to provide any details of the process.

But regardless of possible, even if largely unknown, complexities in post-bellum redistribution, the fact remains that most groups in recent decades have held on to their own lands after warfare.

## DISCUSSION: POPULATION PRESSURE AND THE PERSISTENCE OF SYSTEMIC PROCESSES

Why did the cycle of phases in recent times so often end before escalation to territorial conquests? A possible answer is that population decline has left each group with numbers which, on the one hand, could be sustained adequately on its existing land and, on the other, were insufficient for effective exploitation of additional areas. Although detailed demographic and ecological data for substantiation of this possibility are lacking, various observations in accord with it may be made. Thus, we do have evidence that, at the time of our field work, the Maring population as a whole had been declining for some years, apparently mainly because many people had not yet developed resistance to diseases introduced by Europeans. A dysentery epidemic carried off at least 20% of some groups in the late 1930's or early 1940's, and in more recent years, the average rate of decline has been about 1% annually. This is a preliminary estimate from census data now being subjected to detailed analysis by Georgeda Buchbinder.

There can of course have been population decline without its having been of such magnitude and generality as to have eliminated any appreciable pressure to which the territories of particular groups may have previously been subjected. The fact is, however, that when we were doing our field work in the 1960's we could find no clear evidence of such pressure anywhere in the Maring region except in Kauwatyi and Kundagai territory, where there were tracts of permanent grassland and degraded secondary forest. Apart from this, the indicators of pressure and concomitant environmental deterioration such as are to be found in more intensively exploited parts of the highlands were absent—no sediment-laden streams and no rill wash or sheet erosion except on trails, bare clay houseyards, and occasional landslides (compare Street, 1969:105, on the Chimbu region, with Street, n.d.:4–5, on the Maring region).

An absence of pressure is suggested also by the amount of land which is in primary forest (P.F. for short).[25] Air photographs of territories of groups containing 3,240 people, almost half the total Maring population, are available (see footnote 2); these territories constitute an area of 55 square miles, of which 40% is P.F. Overall population density per square mile of P.F. in this area is 150, and only one group, with 800 people per square mile of such forest, seems to have less

---

[25]It should be noted that with regard to P.F. used as hunting grounds there was not always clear definition of what was within a group's territorial boundaries and what was not. I plan to devote another article to a consideration of the significance of the varying nature of rights to hunting grounds. Here, for the purpose of calculating the size of group territories and the extent of P.F. within them, I have followed two arbitrary rules: (1) to regard as being within a group's territory all the forest which the members of only that group described as being theirs; and (2) to regard as not belonging to any group those portions of the forest to which members of more than one autonomous group claimed rights.

than it needs. No other groups have more than 245 people per square mile of P.F. The groups with ample P.F. could subsist from new gardens made in some of it when they were compelled by warfare or other circumstances to abandon their garden sites and settlements in secondary forest tracts.[26]

Significantly, the group with the proportionately least amount of P.F. is the Kauwatyi. According to informants from the group, they have imposed upon themselves a taboo whereby no gardens may be made in the little more than a square mile they have of P.F. It must be noted that such forest is an important resource area in its own right for game, firewood, building materials, and various wild food plants.[27] The Kauwatyi, like other groups, had to keep some land in P.F. in order to have access to these resources. The unavailability of Kauwatyi land for what might be called "internal pioneering" —a group's conversion of P.F. within its own territories into garden land—may have been an important factor promoting the land encroachments and aggressions by these people against their neighbours.[28] Only one other group in recent times committed land encroachments that led to warfare. This was the Kundagai of Bokapai, who, in the mid-1950's, fought the Ambrakui after having begun to make gardens on their land. The Kundagai are not among the groups whose land in P. F. can be estimated

from the available air photographs, but local informants told me that they were short of such land. It is noteworthy that they are the one large group which, as suggested earlier, might have succeeded in permanently displacing another and taking over its territory if the administration had not intervened.

What is important in the present context is not so much the indication of pressures for the Kauwatyi and the Kundagai but rather the absence of it for the other groups. Does this mean, however, that these latter groups were not suffering from pressure which might be conducive to conquest? The answer must be not necessarily; as I have argued elsewhere (Vayda, 1961:353–54), it is unjustified to assume that a group will take land from neighbors only when the source of pressure is its having numbers as great as or possibly even greater than its existing territory can support under a given system of land use. Food supplies diminishing slowly as the size of a group increases might, for example, predispose members to territorial conquests long before they attain numbers equivalent to the maximum which their original territory can carry and long before there is readily visible environmental deterioration (cf. Birdsell, 1957:54; Vayda, 1970:564–65). Unfortunately we do not have the data that might indicate how far such a process of diminution of food supplies had gone, if it was operating at all, among particular groups at particular times. And while Rappaport (1967:87–96 and Appendix 10) has made some calculations of the carrying capacity of Tsembaga territory and has tentatively concluded that Tsembaga numbers were well below capacity, we have no adequate basis for making reliable estimates of just how much below the carrying capacities of their territories were the sizes of various groups at different times and in different parts of the Maring region. Such estimates would have to be based on ecological investigations more lengthy and comprehensive than those which have been made throughout the Maring region or throughout any other re-

---

[26]Some of the groups that were converting portions of their P.F. into farmed land after warfare are specified in footnote 21. A constraint that should be noted here is that almost all groups had some P.F. located on land too high (and therefore too cold or too often covered by clouds) for effective cultivation of root crops by Maring techniques.

[27]P.F. resources utilized by the Marings are included in the lists provided in Clarke, 1968: Appendices A and C, and Rappaport, 1967: Appendix 8.

[28]This was first suggested to me by C. Lowman-Vayda.

gion where there has been primitive warfare in recent times (see Street, 1969). In short, we cannot argue categorically that absence of population pressure explains the non-escalation to territorial conquests in recent Maring warfare.

Nevertheless, even if there were significant pressure of which we are not aware, it is clear enough that there was nothing comparable in magnitude to the pressure associated with territorial conquests among such people as the Central Enga, whose region is much more densely settled and intensively exploited.[29] As noted by Meggitt (1957a: 135–36; 1965:82, 218; n.d.:31), when population increase was adding to the pressure on the resources of centrally located Enga clans, there was no unoccupied arable land for their extra members to use and the conquests of the territories of other clans had to be attempted. Enga warfare regularly featured the destruction of weaker clans and resulted in a continual redistribution of arable land between groups.

Such contrasts to the Maring situation make it reasonable to hypothesize that there are certain thresholds of pressure that groups such as those of the Maring and Enga regions must reach before they undertake territorial conquests and, further, that Enga and other highlanders[30] were attaining these thresholds in recent times while Maring groups, with the pos-

sible exception of the Kauwatyi and Kundagai, were not. In the absence of more precise quantitative data, we can regard this only as a working hypothesis—which, it would be hoped, would lead to further field investigations. However, certain questions raised by the hypothesis are appropriate for consideration here. These relate to the persistence of systemic processes.

Recent Maring warfare as I have described it here and early nineteenth century Maori warfare (Vayda, 1970) were similar in having features that could be interpreted as no longer doing something they had formerly done, i.e., as no longer leading to territorial conquests as an adaptive means of reducing disparities between groups in their man/resource ratios. Does this mean, then, that the conclusion reached about the Maoris after their adoption of muskets must apply also to the Marings; namely, that their traditional system had been disrupted and that the persistence of fighting among them was a case of non-adaptive cultural lag? The answer is no, for, as suggested by the hypothesis just discussed, recent Maring warfare may have been operating in a manner which was both appropriate to the prevailing demographic and ecological conditions and also in keeping with the traditional functioning of the larger system of population dispersion and land redistribution in which Maring fighting, routing, refuging, and returning from refuge were components. In other words, even if territorial conquests had been only an infrequent rather than a regular aftermath of Maring warfare for a considerable time, the warfare remained the kind that could, through an already institutionalized systemic process, lead again to the adjustment of man/resource ratios whenever demographic and ecological conditions changed sufficiently to make it appropriate for this to happen.[31] Moreover, sig-

---

[29]Population density of the 55,000 Central Enga "averages about 110 to 120 per square mile" and some Enga groups have densities of over 300 people per square mile (Meggitt, 1962:158 and n.d.:2). Density in the Maring region as a whole averages less than 50 per square mile, and no Maring group has a density exceeding an average of 85 per square mile of a group's total territory. For contrasts in intensity of land use between Maring areas and a location in the Tairora-speaking region of the eastern part of the highlands, see Clarke, 1966. See also Brookfield's table (1962:244–45) presenting data on 25 highland localities.

[30]For example, the Chimbu as described by Brookfield and Brown (1963:79) and by Vial (1942, especially p. 8).

---

[31]When, if ever, such conditions obtained throughout the Maring region is problematic. Stanhope (1970:38) has tentatively suggested that malaria and the limitations on food production imposed by the steep slope of the land have made Maring areas in the

nificant change in the conditions was a continuing possibility in the Maring region: new crops or new diseases could be introduced; the size of a population could be swelled by the arrival of refugees from elsewhere (cf. Watson, 1970); the demography of particular local groups could be drastically altered as, in the course of shifting their garden sites and residences in accordance with the requirements of swidden agriculture, they unwittingly moved either into a malarial zone or out of it. The adaptiveness of the institutionalization and persistence of a multi-phase process of war and peace with regulated escalations from phase to phase may be argued to derive from this changeability in demographic and ecological conditions.

I suspect that similar changeability obtained in both New Guinea and the rest of the world in places from which we have reports of modes of hostilities similar to recent Maring warfare. Conclusions from such reports to the effect that the warfare of the people studied—for example, the Dani and Jalé of West Irian (Heider, 1967:838; Koch, 1970a and 1970b:43 ff.) or the headhunters of north-east India (Fürer-Haimendorf, 1968:28)—was unrelated to the adjustment of man/resource ratios need to be re-examined in light of the possibility suggested here.[32] In

other words, just as about the Marings, it needs to be asked also about these other peoples whether their reported warfare might not have constituted only the first phases of a systemic process that would regularly escalate to territorial conquests and adjustments under some recurrent conditions, even if not under the conditions that obtained at the time of the hostilities which the ethnographers have described.

## BIBLIOGRAPHY

ATTENBOROUGH, D. (1960): *Quest in Paradise*, London.

BIRDSELL, J. B. (1957): "Some Population Problems Involving Pleistocene Man," *Cold Spring Harbor Symposia on Quantitative Biology*, Vol. 22, pp. 47–68.

BROOKFIELD, H. C. (1962): "Local Study and Comparative Method: An Example from Central New Guinea," *Association of American Geographers, Annals*, Vol. 52, pp. 242–54.

BROOKFIELD, H. C., and BROWN, P. (1963): *Struggle for Land*, Melbourne.

BUNN, G., and SCOTT, G. (1962): *Languages of the Mount Hagen Sub-district*, Ukarumpa, Eastern Highlands, Territory of New Guinea: The Summer Institute of Linguistics.

CLARKE, W. C. (1966): "From Extensive to Intensive Shifting Cultivation: A Succession from New Guinea," *Ethnology*, Vol. 5, pp. 347–59.

CLARKE, W. C. (1968): *The Ndwimba Basin, Bismarck Mountains, New Guinea: Place and People*, unpublished Ph.D. dissertation in geography, University of California, Berkeley. (To be published

---

Simbai Valley a part of an ever-dying periphery into which populations spilled over from ever-expanding centers in the highlands. What Stanhope calls his model does not, however, rule out major population pressures in the past in the Simbai areas, for it does not specify either the time of arrival of malaria or the extent to which populations spilling over from the centers moved into the periphery by means of expansive warfare.

[32]While I have made no careful study of the data on warfare in these other regions, I can refer to some specific information which is in accord with the suggested possibility. Thus, in the case of the headhunters in north-east India, it is known that there were times when their warfare did lead to the taking of land (Shakespear, 1912:3–8; Soppitt, 1885:19–20). In the case of the Dugum Dani, Heider (1970: Chapter 3) found that, between his first period of field work in the

---

early 1960's when he observed the ritualistic warfare depicted in the well-known film *Dead Birds* and his return visit in 1968, warfare had escalated to a secular phase which could lead to territorial conquests and which the Dani ethnographers had not previously known to be the kind of recurrent phase described by Heider in his latest work. Unfortunately, the data on Dugum Dani demographic and ecological conditions are inadequate for any rigorous testing of hypotheses about the role of warfare in adjusting man/resource ratios.

302

SYSTEMS OF POLITICS AND LAW

as *Place and People: An Ecology of a New Guinean Community*, Berkeley.)

COOK, E. A. (1967): *Manga Social Organization*, unpublished Ph.D. dissertation in anthropology, Yale University, New Haven.

FÜRER-HAIMENDORF, C. VON (1968): "Violence: Can We Break the Habit?" (review of *War: The Anthropology of Armed Conflict and Aggression*, edited by M. Fried *et al.*), *Saturday Review*, June 1, pp. 27–29.

HEIDER, K. G. (1967): "Speculative Functionalism: Archaic Elements in New Guinea Dani Culture," *Anthropos*, Vol. 62, pp. 833–40.

HEIDER, K. G. (1970): *The Dugum Dani*, Viking Fund Publications in Anthropology No. 49, New York.

KOCH, K.-F. (1970*a*): "Cannibalistic Revenge in Jalé Warfare," *Natural History*, February, pp. 40–51.

KOCH, K.-F. (1970*b*): "Warfare and Anthropophagy in Jalé Society," *Bijdragen tot de Taal-, Land- en Volkenkunde, Anthropologica*, Vol. 12, pp. 37–58.

LOWMAN-VAYDA, C. (1968): "Maring Big Men," *Anthropological Forum*, Vol. 2, pp. 199–243.

LOWMAN-VAYDA, C.: *Art and War in a New Guinea Society* (in preparation, to be published by the Museum of Primitive Art, New York).

MEGGITT, M. J. (1957*a*): "Enga Political Organization: A Preliminary Description" *Mankind*, Vol. 5, pp. 133–37.

MEGGITT, M. J. (1957*b*): "The Ipili of the Porgera Valley, Western Highlands District, Territory of New Guinea," *Oceania*, Vol. 28, pp. 31–55.

MEGGITT, M. J. (1962): "Growth and Decline of Agnatic Descent Groups Among the Mae Enga of the New Guinea Highlands," *Ethnology*, Vol. 1, pp. 158–65.

MEGGITT, M. J. (1965): *The Lineage System of the Mae-Enga of New Guinea*, Edinburgh.

MEGGITT, M. J. (n.d.): "Pigs Are Our Hearts!: The Te Exchange Cycle Among the Mae Enga of New Guinea," paper for publication in a symposium, ed. A. Strathern, concerning systems of exchange in the New Guinea highlands.

RAPPAPORT, R. A. (1967): *Pigs for the Ancestors*, New Haven.

SALISBURY, R. F. (1963): "Ceremonial Economics and Political Equilibrium," *VIᵉ Congrès International des Sciences Anthropologiques et Ethnologiques, II. Ethnologie*, Vol. 1, Paris: Musée de l'Homme.

SHAKESPEAR, J. (1912): *The Lushei-Kuki Clans*, London.

SOPPITT, C. A. (1885): *A Short Account of the Kachcha Nâga (Empêo) Tribe in the North Cachar Hills*, Shillong.

SOUTER, G. (1964): *New Guinea: The Last Unknown*, Sydney.

STANHOPE, J. M. (1970): "Patterns of Fertility and Mortality in Rural New Guinea," *People and Planning in Papua and New Guinea*, ed. M. W. Ward, New Guinea Research Bulletin No. 34, Canberra.

STREET, J. M. (1969): "An Evaluation of the Concept of Carrying Capacity," *Professional Geographer*, Vol. 21, pp. 104–107.

STREET, J. M. (n.d.): "Soil Conservation by Shifting Cultivators in the Bismarck Mountains of New Guinea," unpublished paper.

VAYDA, A. P. (1960): *Maori Warfare*, Polynesian Society Maori Monographs No. 2, Wellington.

VAYDA, A. P. (1961): "Expansion and Warfare Among Swidden Agriculturalists," *American Anthropologist*, Vol. 63, pp. 346–58.

VAYDA, A. P. (1967): "Research on the Functions of Primitive War," *Peace Research Society (International), Papers*, Vol. 7, pp. 133–38.

VAYDA, A. P. (1970): "Maoris and Muskets in New Zealand: Disruption of a War System," *Political Science Quarterly*, Vol. 85, pp. 560–84.

VAYDA, A. P.: "Pig Complex," *Encyclopaedia of Papua and New Guinea*, Melbourne (in press).

VAYDA, A. P., and COOK, E. A. (1964): "Structural Variability in the Bismarck Mountain Cultures of New Guinea: A Preliminary Report," *New York Academy of Sciences, Transactions*, Vol. 26, pp. 798–803.

VAYDA, A. P., LEEDS, A., and SMITH, D. B. (1961). "The Place of Pigs in Melanesian Subsistence," *Proceedings of the 1961 Annual Spring Meeting of the American Ethnological Society*, ed. V. E. Garfield, Seattle.

VIAL, L. G. (1942): "They Fight for Fun," *Walkabout*, Vol. 9, No. 1, pp. 5–9.

WATSON, J. B. (1970): "Society as Organized Flow: The Tairora Case," *Southwestern Journal of Anthropology,* Vol. 26, pp. 107–24.

WURM, S. A., and LAYCOCK, D. C. (1961): "The Ques-

tion of Language and Dialect in New Guinea," *Oceania,* Vol. 32, pp. 128–43.

WYNNE-EDWARDS, V. C. (1962): *Animal Dispersion in Relation to Social Behaviour.* Edinburgh.

# 23

## KOFYAR ARMED CONFLICT: SOCIAL CAUSES AND CONSEQUENCES

*Robert McC. Netting*

*At times anthropologists cannot actually witness the behavior they wish to study. Most often this occurs when social change has rendered past activities nonadaptive or, in the case of the Kofyar, illegal following the intervention of British colonial government. When this occurs, anthropologists can employ ethnohistorical techniques by interviewing older people (and seeking out any available records) about the actions of the past. This is the approach taken by Robert Netting in this article on Kofyar armed conflict. In it he describes the events that could lead to war, the fighting with spears, knives, and clubs, and the rules prescribing tactics and eventual settlement. He notes that above all, Kofyar war involves breaches of obligation within the kinship system that ties Kofyar villages together. The outcome is to make the territorial unit more important than the one based on kinship.*

The factual study of primitive warfare has never had a fighting chance in anthropology. A condition of doing field work by means of intensive participant observation usually has been that the subject population was suitably "pacified" or under sufficient military control so that little threat to an outsider's life and limb was presented. The rise of anthropology coincided with the fall of independent native polities, and the first power to be appropriated by a colonialist regime or an expanding state was the power to prohibit settlement of quarrels by force of arms. Even the

nature of past fighting was popularly stigmatized as "savage" or "barbaric" to the point where conquered peoples were sometimes unwilling to discuss their traditional military activities in detail. Perhaps more crucial to the neglect of this topic has been the frequent theoretical bias of the social scientist toward evidence of social solidarity, functional integration, and conflict resolution (Turney-High 1971:21). Killing, looting, and subjugation suggested a breakdown of orderly social processes and a disturbance of the postulated equilibrium system so necessary to functional analysis.[1] This view of conflict as an integrative or evolutionary mechanism was developed by sociologists following Marx or Simmel, and anthropologists confined themselves to such general questions as the relative importance of aggression in *Homo sapiens* or the influence of warfare on state formation. Specific data on who fought whom over what, with details of battles, raids, casualties, and peace terms, are regrettably scanty in the literature.[2]

In those few cases where anthropologists have brought adequate field research to bear on the problem of warfare, explanations have often foundered on the old dichotomy of economic versus psychological causes (cf. the attempts of Vayda [1968, 1969] to reconcile these two approaches) or latent as opposed to manifest functions. Those less sanguine about the possibility of a genuine social science would abandon the entire functionalist effort in disgust (Hallpike 1973). A more productive approach might seek the systemic interrelations of ecologic and material variables empirically involved in conflict behavior while at the same time regarding native explications of war's genesis and consequences as crucial to its understanding. The connection between what measurably *is* and what it *means* to people is the heart of the anthropological enterprise, and our sectarian squabbles over the etic and the emic or the behaviorist as opposed to mentalist position should not obscure this

fact. Rappaport (1971:247–248) has suggested that the "operational model" of physical process in a scientifically observed ecosystem must be integrated with the "cognized model" of knowledge and belief held by cultural insiders about their environment. These two approximations of reality may appear radically unlike, grounded as they are in the divergent epistemological assumptions and theories of cause and effect of the ethnographer and the native. If the cognized model indeed produces behavior which confers some selective advantage on the actors, its underlying principles must be compatible at some level with the systemic explanations of the investigator. Rather than regarding folk understandings as either endogenous determinants of culturally patterned activity or ecologically naive and irrelevant notions, we need to ask by what means operational and cognized models articulate.

I have elsewhere (Netting 1973) discussed Kofyar warfare as a regulator of man-land interaction, increasing in severity as a function of population pressure, and resulting in resettlement, changes in agricultural land use, and exposure to epidemic disease that may have had demographic implications. This complex causal chain, if indeed it does exist in the postulated form, is not directly perceived by the people affected. Lacking demographic records, comparative measures of nutrition, and an awareness of insects as vectors of disease, there are no accurate means for appraising significant variations in the local ecosystem. Yet there remain indications that Kofyar explanations of the genesis of conflict reflect, through a kind of social analogy, some of the disruptive consequences of population pressure and the relative severity of conflict. They also appear to foreshadow a restructuring of social relations that is congruent with an altered ecological situation and that leads ultimately to a reduction in warring activity.

The following ethnohistoric account of recent conflict and its stated causes pertains to the Kofyar who live along the southern escarpment

---

[1]Consider, for example, Radcliffe-Brown's (1952: 181) remarks on the role of conflict: "... a social system ... has a certain kind of unity, which we may speak of as a functional unity. We may define it as a condition in which all parts of the social system work together with a sufficient degree of harmony or internal consistency, i.e., without producing persistent conflicts which can neither be resolved nor regulated."

[2]There are, however, several recent first-hand accounts of combat giving direct insights into the nature and functions of warfare as well as interpretations of its meaning to participants. Cf. the observations on the South American Yanomamö by Chagnon (1968), on the New Guinea Dani by Heider (1970), and on the Philippine Tausug by Kiefer (1970).

of the Jos Plateau in Benue-Plateau State, Nigeria. It covers 37 armed encounters which took place from approximately 1870 to 1942. Informants were for the most part directly involved as participants or spectators, but earlier clashes were reported on the basis of accounts passed on by an elder male relative of the informant.[3] The Kofyar area (then designated the Kwolla District) was known to British colonial officers by 1907 but conquest did not begin until 1909 on the plains, and in 1930 an armed uprising in the hills was forcibly suppressed. Control remained somewhat loose, especially in the more isolated hill villages, and sporadic internecine disturbance continued into the early 1940s.[4] Specifically, I will review the methods of fighting, the nature of participating groups, the reasons given for initiating conflict, and certain features of the conceptual frame of kinship relations used by the Kofyar as a rationale for their most serious wars.

---

[3]Accounts of fighting were collected in 1960–1962 and 1966–1967 during fieldwork supported by a Ford Foundation Foreign Area Fellowship and a Social Science Research Council Grant. Specific investigations of warfare were also carried on with a questionnaire form prepared by the Ethnocentrism Project of Robert LeVine and Donald Campbell. Twenty-five informants from 11 different villages provided the bulk of the information on which this paper is based; it was possible in many cases to compare reports from different individuals on the same conflict situation. I am especially grateful to Ellen and Keith Basso as well as to John Pfeiffer for their close and sympathetic reading of this manuscript. I have incorporated a number of their suggestions in matters of both interpretation and style, but the responsibility for content and final form is, of course, my own. The map used in Figure 1 was prepared by Charles Sternberg.

[4]Information on the suppression of Kofyar armed conflict is contained in Fitzpatrick (1910), Ames (1934), and various unpublished administrative reports from the provincial offices in Jos and the district headquarters at Shendam. The material is summarized in Netting (1968b:48–49).

## HOW THE KOFYAR FOUGHT

### Weapons and Equipment

Every adult Kofyar male owned certain basic weapons, spears *(kop)* and clubs *(dugul)*, that were used for both hunting and warfare. They were often kept in a hut near the entrance to the homestead where the man and his older sons slept. Spear points were made from locally forged iron and were fitted to a light wood shaft counterweighted with strips of metal wound around the base so that they could be thrown. Three named styles were used: (a) a small leaf-shaped point followed by a double row of barbs along the shaft (the most common type); (b) a larger flat blade; (c) a smooth bullet-shaped point with a single hooked tang. Each man carried two or three such spears when hunting for bush cow, antelope, leopard, baboon, or wild pig, and when going into combat. Each man also had one or more rough wooden clubs *(dugul)* about three feet long with a knob at one end which could be used as clubbing or throwing instruments. At his belt or in his goatskin knapsack he had a sheath knife *(chuk)*, pointed like a dagger and hafted in a wood grip covered with tanned hide. Stones picked up on the field of battle for throwing at the enemy were an important part of the arsenal. Men of the Bwal village hurled stones a longer distance by use of the sling *(luwang)*. As a defense against projectiles and stones, warriors carried square topped, round based shields *(gwat)* on the left arm. Such shields of thick, stiff bush-cow hide reddened with ocher were a valued heirloom which not every family possessed. The same weapons were used by mounted warriors from the plains village clusters of Kwalla, Dimmuk, and Mernyang, where open, level land allowed cavalry manoeuvres. Only a few of the Kofyar villages including Fogol, Lardang, Kwanoeng, Moeduut, Koedut, and Kofyar-Dimmuk had the bow.

Special accessories were worn into battle. Though men were clothed only in loincloths of cotton or leather, a woven cotton sash *(zal)* was tightly wound many times around the waist. It was said to stop hunger and give some protection against spear thrusts. The knapsack *(doom or kuluk)* was of whole goatskin, hair-side out or, more impressively, of leopard. It held the club, knife, and a sideblown war trumpet *(feer)* made of water buck horn lengthened with a section of cow horn. Some men wore red cloth caps *(dagar ko* "cock's comb"), while others tied on a cotton head band decorated with upright white and blue feathers. A horse's tail was often carried into the fray, stuck into the sash or waved at the enemy during the fighting. All of these items, with the exception of headgear, are still in evidence among the Kofyar during the mock charges which are a feature of *maap* funeral commemoration ceremonies.

## Training

Young men formerly practiced the arts of warfare in neighborhood clubs *(jeb moe riang)*. Beginning at age 15 to 19, unmarried youths would live together during the post-harvest dry season in simple stone-walled huts on the outskirts of the hill villages. They would work as a group for individuals, receiving porridge, meat, or beer in return. One informant recounted how his group of nine contemporaries wrestled among themselves and fought other neighborhood clubs. In one game they formed lines and threw foot-long sticks at one another, protecting themselves with sorghum stalk shields. Variations of the fight *(lek)* called for hurling clods of earth against palm leaf shields or, when close enough, beating the other side with short poles. People claimed that such fighting made the boys strong. Older men watched and reproved cowardly behavior. There were occasional injuries. The clubs were discontinued after warfare became a thing of the past.

## Defenses

Each dispersed Kofyar homestead is designed to provide basic protection. Huts are set close together and joined by stone walls so that all must be entered from a corridor with a single opening. The exterior walls have almost no openings. Though this arrangement defended the household livestock and possessions from thieves, it could not effectively halt attackers, who simply set fire to the thatched roofs.

A few Kofyar villages did have stone walls *(gan)* built on undefended approaches. Undressed rocks were laid without mortar, enclosing a core of packed earth (Netting 1968a, photograph p. 13). One wall almost 400 feet long and averaging six feet in height guarded the eastern flank of Bong village. The people of Bong claim that to build it required two years of intermittent work, during which time they were aided by several settlements to the south. Another wall above Bong at the base of a conical volcanic core was used as a citadel; huts within it sheltered the villagers during a months-long siege. Remains of a similar low wall of volcanic boulders are visible on the plain in Kwanoeng village. Most fighting seems to have occurred, however, in open treeless areas between settlements.

## ADVERSARIES

### The Village as Fighting Unit

The village is the largest independent political entity among the Kofyar (Netting 1968b:153–156). It is a clearly bounded territorial unit within which agricultural cooperation, ceremonial observance, and peaceful dispute settlement takes place. On the plains, the village (e.g., Mernyang, Dimmuk, and Kwalla, Fig. 1) contains a number of large contiguous named neighborhoods represented by ward leaders under a single chief; it was considered by British administrators as a tribe. Hill villages have smaller neighborhoods, and often hamlets that are geographically distinct but politically incorporated in the village. Conflict between villages was the only type of dispute in which resort to force was regularly possible. Individual fights, rare cases of homicide, land disputes, and other quarrels were mediated within the village. Any argument which reached the stage of blows was halted immediately, elaborately investigated, and resolved by a series of later moots. Because of scarcity of farmland and the lack of important intervillage descent groups, individual men or groups could not easily form new settlements or gain entrance to other communities. The defense of village territory or offensive activities were always treated as matters involving the entire group. This was true even though raiding or ambush parties at times included only a few village men, and the decision to stage a raid was sometimes taken against the advice of the chief and some of his elders. On the other hand, there are no accounts of rival lineages within a village fighting each other, nor did any segment of a village's population apparently ally itself with an enemy.

Kofyar conflict often occurred between two villages or two groups of allied villages. At any one time there seems to have been a possibility of armed hostility with *any* village sharing a common boundary. Of ten conflicts in which Bong village was involved, five were with Kofyar villages immediately adjoining it (Mangbar, Gonkun, Zugal, Dung, and Longsel, Fig. 1), while two were with Chokfem Sura villages which also bordered Bong (cf. Fig. 1). The remaining engagements were with the villages one tier away, i.e., separated from Bong by only one intervening village territory, as in the cases of Koenji and Lardang. Of all other hill and plains conflicts recorded, 21 were with directly adjacent groups, eight with villages once removed, and only one seems to have been with an ethnic group at some distance from the Kofyar area

(Mernyang versus Moefan, which may have been 15 miles away on the other side of the Shemanker valley).

## Intra versus Interethnic Conflict

Not only did Kofyar tend to fight with their nearest neighbors rather than with distant villages, but they also were involved in more frequent and more serious conflicts within the ethnic group than outside it. The designation "Kofyar" is in fact a rather loose way of referring to a number of village groupings which share a myth of common origin, a number of cultural traits, and certain dialectal similarities, but which lack both political unity and an inclusive name for themselves (Netting 1968b:35–43). The Kofyar emphasize the ethnic distinctiveness of several adjoining hill villages by labelling them collectively Chokfem. Though separated from the Kofyar area by the deeply cut Li river valley, Chokfem is within hailing distance, and frequent contact is maintained by visiting, trading, and reciprocal ceremonial participation. Social separation is most clearly marked by the absence of intermarriage, a restriction justified on both sides by unflattering stereotypes of the others' personal habits.[5] In the majority of cases Kofyar marry women from other villages, though there is some tendency for hill and plains people to limit marital choices to their geographic subdivisions. Both warfare and marriage are focused on the nearest Kofyar settlements and decline in direct proportion to distance and geographic

---

[5] Kofyar regarded the Chokfem penis sheath and narrow G-string with good-natured derision and expressed repugnance for their neighbors' supposed body odor, manner of defecation, dirtiness, immodesty, red-painted faces, and position adopted in sexual intercourse. Chokfem in turn stigmatized the Kofyar as thieves and carriers of venereal disease (Netting 1969:36–47, 104–111).

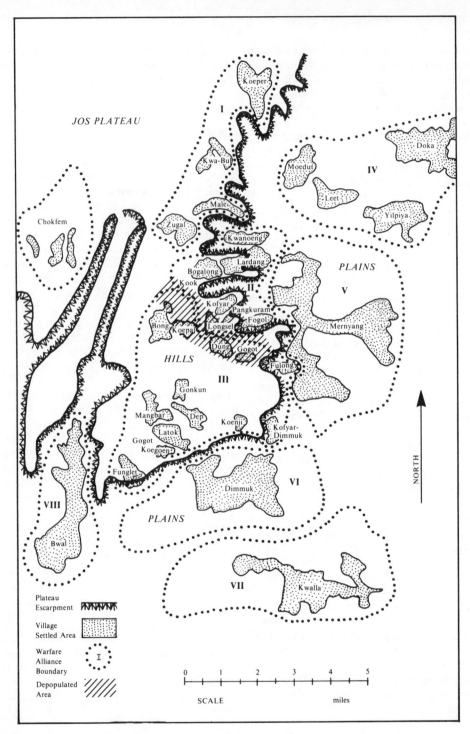

JOS PLATEAU

Koeper

I

Kwa-Bul

Chokfem

Male

Zugal

Kwanoeng

Lardang

Bogalong

Kook

II

Kofyar

Pangkuram

Bong

Koepal

Longsel

Fogol

Mernyang

Dung

Gogot

HILLS

Fulong

III

Gonkun

Mangbar

Dep

Koenji

Latok

Kofyar-
Dimmuk

Gogot
Koegoen

Funglet

VIII

Dimmuk

VI

PLAINS

Bwal

VII

Kwalla

Moedut

Leet

Doka

IV

Yilpiya

PLAINS

V

NORTH

Plateau
Escarpment

Village
Settled Area

Warfare
Alliance
Boundary

I

Depopulated
Area

| 0 | 1 | 2 | 3 | 4 | 5 |

SCALE                    miles

accessibility.[6] Of seven recorded encounters between Kofyar villages and Chokfem, five (#1, 2, 3, 6, 9 on Table 1) were brief and quickly settled; one (Chokfem-Zugal #26) was longer but involved very little damage to either side. Only the hazy account (#37) of a long war of attrition in the semi-mythical past pitted a major Chokfem force against the Kofyar and resulted in significant Kofyar depopulation. The larger plains villages seem to have confined their warfare in most instances to fighting with each other.

*Alliances*

Though fighting might take place with any of the surrounding villages, the Kofyar recognized warfare alliances (*sar gwat* "shield arm") which united certain contiguous villages. Alliances I, II, and III (Fig. 1) were centered in the hills, though they included some villages with both hill and plains segments (e.g., Lardang, Funglet) and other villages occupying the narrow valleys which reached into the escarpment (e.g., Kwanoeng, Fogol, Fulong, and Kofyar-Dimmuk). Ties existed between the plains Mernyang and the adjacent hill alliance II, also known as *Gankogom* ("the side of the harmattan wind"). This did not mean that the hillmen were obligated to take part in plains wars or vice versa. Individuals might join if they wished, and it is probable that communities situated on the lower portion of the escarpment often accompanied their close plains neighbors in forays. Villages could seek voluntary support from within their alliance but could not depend on assistance being provided. There is no evidence of central direction or even *ad hoc* councils of chiefs. A man or group of men within each alliance were recognized as outstanding warriors, but

they seem never to have acted as military commanders. Villages fought as separate units, deciding independently when they should join battle and when they should leave the field. When a village was overrun, there was sometimes suspicion that erstwhile allies may have taken advantage of the confusion to join in the looting.

If trouble broke out between villages in the same alliance, men might be killed but heads were not taken. This provision might be extended to the nearest village of an opposing alliance. Thus Lardang and Bogalong did not carry on headhunting against Zugal because they were "brothers." Care was taken in battle to avoid hostile contact with relatives, mainly affinal kin, on the other side. A man might change his place in line if he found himself opposite a *koen* (MoBr), or he might purposely miss a kinsman with his weapon. Expressions of friendship and approval of other villages seem to have depended little on whether they were members of the same alliance. For example, Latok held a low opinion of nearby Gonkun and classed Bong with Bwal as major enemies. Bong, on the other hand, regarded their opponents in Lardang as outstanding in bravery, but criticized their allies in Latok as selfish and in Gonkun as cowardly. Charges of being quarrelsome, dishonest, lazy, or cruel were leveled against some neighboring villages and not others, with no regard to alliance affiliation.

## CASUS BELLI

*Stated Reasons for Fighting*

Kofyar are careful to offer a fairly precise cause for every occasion of inter-village violence mentioned. Causes may be grouped under the following headings: (1) Individual arguments leading to a fight with weapons; (2) individual theft and the treatment of a captured thief; (3) hunger, leading to raiding for food; (4) territo-

[6]For a useful discussion of social units defined by a similar combination of geographical and marital criteria, see Bradfield's chapter on the commune (1973:151–189).

**TABLE 1**
Kofyar Armed Conflicts

| No. | Combatant Groups | Estimated Date | Duration | Stated Cause | Dispute Type | Casualties |
|---|---|---|---|---|---|---|
| 1 | Chokfem vs. Funglet | ? | brief | Hunting argument | Fight | 2 killed including 1 as compensation |
| 2 | Latok vs. Chokfem | ? | brief | Latok guest at *maap* wounded, fought and killed Chokfem man with knife | Fight | 1 wounded 1 killed |
| 3 | Chokfem vs. Bong | 1920's | brief | Bong guest at *maap* offended hosts, driven away; Bong man caught stealing from house where hidden, killed | Fight and theft | 1 killed |
| 4 | Mernyang vs. Kwalla | 1890's | 2 days | Kwalla men stole goat from Mernyang | Theft | ? |
| 5 | Latok group vs. Bwal | 1928 | ½ day | Thieves from Funglet and Koenji caught in Bwal, mutilated | Theft | 4 Latok wounded, 38 houses burned, minor looting |
| 6 | Latok group vs. Chokfem | 1926 | brief | Mangbar thief killed in Chokfem, cannibalism suspected, Latok ambushed Chokfem | Theft | 1 Mangbar killed, 1 Chokfem |
| 7 | Zugal vs. Lardang | 1917 | 1 day | Lardang thief stole goat in Zugal, pursued and caught in Lardang territory | Theft | 15 Zugal houses burned, plundered |
| 8 | Latok vs Gogotkoegoen | ? | brief | Thief from Gogotkoegon caught in Latok, refused to pay fine | Theft | 0 |
| 9 | Zugal vs. Chokfem | 1893 | 1 day | Zugal stole goat from Chokfem, returned carcass, Chokfem attacked Zugal | Theft | 0 |
| 10 | Zugal vs. Kwa-Bul | 1920's | brief | Zugal men at beer drink decided Kwa-Bul had stolen goat (no evidence) | Theft | 1 Kwa-Bul killed, 3 houses plundered |
| 11 | Zugal vs. Bong | 1870's | several years | Bong thief stole dog from Zugal | Theft | Casualties? Bong destroyed, nine month seige of refugees |

TABLE 1
(Continued)

| No. | Combatant Groups | Estimated Date | Duration | Stated Cause | Dispute Type | Casualties |
|---|---|---|---|---|---|---|
| 12 | Bong vs. Dung | 1880's | ? | Bong boy exiled for witchcraft returned to steal goat, in pursuit Bong routed Dung, Dung with neighbors laid seige to Bong | Theft | 1 Dung killed, 1 Bong killed, Bong destroyed |
| 13 | Mernyang vs. Leet | 1906 | brief | Mernyang hungry in October-November, raided Leet for food | Food raid | 0 |
| 14 | Mernyang vs Pangkurum | ? | brief | Mernyang crops destroyed by locusts, raided Pangkurum for food | Food raid | 0 |
| 15 | Fogol vs. Pangkurum | ? | brief | During famine, Fogol raided Pangkurum for food, alleged Pangkurum had killed Fogol ancestors | Food raid | 0 |
| 16 | Bong vs. Gonkun | 1940 | brief | Gonkun cutting thatch on Bong territory | Trespass | 1 Bong killed, 1 Gonkun killed |
| 17 | Chokfem vs. Lardang | 1930's | brief | Lardang cutting Chokfem's thatch, Lardang robbed and chased Bong and Zugal bypassers | Trespass | 0 |
| 18 | Lardang vs. Bong, Chokfem | 1942 | brief | Lardang cutting thatch in Bong and Chokfem territories | Trespass | 0 |
| 19 | Lardang-Bogalong vs. Zugal | 1933 | 2 days | Lardang cutting thatch in Zugal territory, Zugal threat followed by fight, Lardang returned 11 months later for vengeance | Trespass | 2–4 Lardang killed 75 Zugal houses plundered, 2 Zugal men 1 woman killed |
| 20 | Lardang vs. Kofyar | ? | brief | Lardang killed leopard in Kofyar territory | Trespass | 0 |
| 21 | Latok vs. Gogotkoegoen | 1917 | brief | Land dispute between two individuals | Property | 0 |
| 22 | Dep, Latok vs. Gonkun | ? | brief | Old Latok man helped in Gonkun thatching, was refused food | Property | Gonkun looted |
| 23 | Funglet, Latok, Dimmuk vs. Bwal | pre-1900 | ? | Bwal retained strayed horse from Funglet, Funglet did same, then attacked with neighbors | Property | Bwal routed, "many" killed, Bwal looted |

TABLE 1
(Continued)

| No. | Combatant Groups | Estimated Date | Duration | Stated Cause | Dispute Type | Casualties |
|-----|------------------|----------------|----------|--------------|--------------|------------|
| 24 | Latok vs. Bwal | 1920's | brief | Bwal refused to return Latok horse, Latok attacked Bwal | Property | Minor looting of Bwal |
| 25 | Bwal vs. Mangbar, Latok, Dimmuk, Bong | 1890–1900 | 10 years; intermittent | Dispute over use of farm belonging to Mangbar man relocated in Bwal | Property | Many wounded, Bwal houses, palms destroyed |
| 26 | Kwanoeng vs. Lardang | pre-1930 | brief | Kwanoeng man wanted return of child from Lardang, took hostage from Lardang, Lardang attacked Kwanoeng | Property | 1 Lardang killed, 1 Kwanoeng given as compensation |
| 27 | Zugal vs. Chokfem | 1910–1914 | 4 years; intermittent | Chokfem accused Zugal of capturing and selling Chokfem children as slaves | Property | No casualties from battles on boundary |
| 28 | Kwalla vs. Mernyang | 1910–1913 | 3 years | Kwalla kidnapped Mernyang woman in Dimmuk territory | Vengeance | ? |
| 29 | Kwalla vs. Mernyang | 1918–1920 | 2 years | Mernyang man lured by offer of trade, killed and beheaded by Kwalla on Dimmuk land | Vengeance | "Many" Kwalla killed, two neighborhoods destroyed |
| 30 | Dimmuk vs. Kwalla | 1912 | 1 year (ca. 7 battles) | Dimmuk man killed by Kwalla | Vengeance | 1 Kwalla neighborhood burned, 3–4 Dimmuk, 1 Kwalla killed in one battle |
| 31 | Kwalla vs. Dimmuk | 1900 | 1 day | Kwalla killed Mernyang boy, Dimmuk supported Mernyang, claimed murder was on Dimmuk territory | Vengeance | "Many" Dimmuk killed |
| 32 | Lardang-Bogalong vs. Bong | 1900 | 1 year | Boys from Lardang and Bong wrestling at boundary, Lardang boy clubbed, Bong boy killed in retaliation | Vengeance | 1 Bong killed, 2 Mernyang killed |
| 33 | Zugal vs. Male | 1925 | 1 day | Zugal woman married in Male killed by husband | Vengeance | 3 Zugal killed, Male plundered |
| 34 | Bong vs. Latok group (III) | 1921 | 2 days | Affine of Fulong killed by lightning in Bong, Latok group raided Bong twice | Vengeance | 1 Latok killed, 3 Mangbar killed, 2 Bong killed, 25–30 Bong houses destroyed |

TABLE 1
(Continued)

| No. | Combatant Groups | Estimated Date | Duration | Stated Cause | Dispute Type | Casualties |
|-----|-----------------|----------------|----------|--------------|--------------|------------|
| 35 | Kofyar alliance (II) vs. Bong alliance (III) | 1902–1925 | 23 years | Longsel boy died mysteriously, Fulong affines claimed homicide, Fulong attacked Lonsel, Lonsel attacked Bong | Vengeance | Documented killings: 6 Longsel, 1 Fulong, 7 Bong, 2 Male 2 Kofyar, 3 Lardang, 1 Fogol, Destruction and desertion of Longsel, Koepal, Gogot, Dung, Kook |
| 36 | Mernyang vs. Moefan | 1904 | 2 years | Moefan killed one Mernyang in Moefan territory | Vengeance | "Many" Moefan killed and heads taken |
| 37 | Chokfem vs. Bong | semi-mythical past | ? | Chokfem seized Kofyar territory including several hill villages, finally driven out when hero killed | Conquest | ? |

rial trespass and illicit appropriation of natural resources; (5) disputed ownership of property; (6) unpunished murder or unnatural death of a relative requiring vengeance.

All cases of arguments resulting in fights involved Kofyar visitors to Chokfem. The cultural signals which operated to head off violence among Kofyar obviously did not function well in the somewhat alien environment of Chokfem. Lacking marital ties, kinship restraints also were less effective. In one case (#1) an argument about hunting between parties of Funglet and Chokfem men led to one death. (Numbers in parentheses refer to the cases described briefly in Table 1.) The Kofyar class hunting with fighting, use the same word *(lek)* for assaulting a man or a dangerous beast, and generate similar emotional excitement in both situations. It is probable that the hunting squabble took place in intermediate bush-covered waste land over which both Kofyar and Chokfem ranged. The dispute was quickly settled by providing a victim to be killed in compensation by the side suffering the initial loss. On another occasion (#2), a Latok man attending a Chokfem funeral commemoration (at which martial exploits are celebrated and re-enacted) was speared, turned on his assailant, and killed him with a knife. A Bong guest at a similar celebration (#3) offended his Chokfem hosts and was driven away with his fellows. Even then, no serious harm would have resulted if another Bong man had not attempted to steal from the homestead where he was hiding and been killed in the attempt. Each incident was promptly adjusted and produced no continuing hostilities.

Simple theft might lead to hostilities if the thief was identified as a member of another village; thus, Kwalla men caught stealing a goat from Mernyang triggered two days of fighting (#4). More often the issue was not the theft but the nature of the punishment meted out to the miscreant. When thieves from Funglet and Koenji were caught in Bwal (#5), they were mutilated; this action provoked a pillaging raid from their home villages, which were joined by Latok and other adjacent settlements. Similarly, on another occasion (#6), a thief from Mangbar was caught in Chokfem and killed. Chokfem refused to return the corpse. It was strongly suspected that the unlucky thief had been eaten, and this provoked an ambush of Chokfem people. In another case, a known thief from Lardang pilfered a goat in Zugal (#7), and was caught after he had crossed the Lardang border. Lardang admitted that the thief had been guilty, but felt the violation of their territory merited a partial plundering of Zugal. When the home village of a thief would not make restitution for his crime, the village of the victim might engage in a brief show of force, as when Gogotkoegoen refused to pay a fine for a villager caught stealing in Latok (#8). If compensation was agreed to, the matter was considered at an end. Thus, when Zugal returned the carcass of a stolen goat to Chokfem (#9), they did not expect to be attacked later and responded as to unprovoked aggression. Sometimes theft was an excuse for punitive looting; for example, some Zugal men decided (without evidence) at a beer party that Kwa-Bul had stolen a goat, and proceeded to plunder three houses and kill a man who resisted (#10).

All of these occurrences gave rise to brief conflicts which seldom lasted more than a day or two. Occasionally a more serious sequence of events would be triggered, apparently when the opposing forces were grossly unequal. The theft by Bong of a dog from Zugal supposedly resulted in raids over several years by the more populous Zugal (#11). These attacks destroyed Bong and forced the residents to take refuge behind their defensive wall for at least nine months. In the years following this defeat, a Bong boy exiled to Gogot for witchcraft returned to steal a goat (#12). In pursuing him, Bong drove the innocent people of Dung from their homes. Dung gathered its allies, razed Bong, and laid seige again to its inhabitants.

Raiding for food typically pitted densely populated plains villages against relatively weak villages which were sparsely settled on flat lands or the crest of the escarpment. Mernyang went to Leet (#13) in the hungry period of October and November just before the sorghum harvest to get grain, goats, and chickens. Leet was too isolated to mobilize its allies quickly. When its crops were destroyed by locusts, groups of Mernyang regularly raided little Pangkurum (#14), though the plains chiefs tried to stop such activities. Fogol demanded food from Pangkurum under similar circumstances, threatening the people on the basis of an old grudge (#15).

In the dry season fighting frequently erupted over cases of trespass as men of one community entered the bush lands of a neighboring village to cut thatching grass. These forays took place in January, at the conclusion of the agricultural year, when men were relieved of normal farming tasks. Since Kofyar norms permitted the cutting of grass beyond village borders if the owning village had filled its need for thatch, it is probable that trespass was a deliberate provocation in some cases. Many of the villages provide examples of fighting over tresspass. A brief fight took place after Gonkun cut grass in Bong territory (#16); one man on each side was killed. When Chokfem disputed a grass cutting incursion by Lardang (#17), innocent bystanders from Bong and Zugal were robbed and driven away by Lardang men. As late as 1942, skirmishes occurred between Lardang trespassers on the lands of Bong and Chokfem (#18). These encounters sometimes erupted into more severe fighting. Thus, when armed men from Zugal tried to prevent Lardang from taking grass (#19), Lardang drove them back to their village and plundered some 75 homesteads. In the course of the looting several men from Lardang were killed; in revenge ten months later, Lardang ambushed Zugal harvesters, slaying two men and a woman.

Attempts to punish trespass were also made when big game with ritual value, such as bush cow and leopard, were taken in a rival territory (#20).

Fighting might also involve property disputes between members of different sovereign village units. Quarrels developed over land ownership (#21), and over the failure to give customary payment for work (#22) or to return a strayed horse (#23, 24). One case hinged on the unusual permanent migration of a Mangbar man to Bwal (#25), combined with his insistence that he should continue to have the use of his old farm in Mangbar. Sometimes the property in question was a person. A Kwanoeng man wanted a child born of his former wife who had left him without return of bridewealth (#26). Though entitled to the child, the man was not empowered to take a hostage from Lardang to enforce his claim, and a fight ensued. At another time, a series of formal battles followed Chokfem's claim that Zugal had captured children and sold them as slaves (#27).

Murder seemingly was rare among the Kofyar. When it occurred, the village of the killer was expected to turn him over to the affinal kin of the victim who could then bash his brains out.[7] Alternatively, a payment of blood wealth might be arranged. Cases in which a Mernyang woman was kidnapped by Kwalla (#28), and a Mernyang man lured into a trap by Kwalla, then killed and beheaded (#29), both led to extended periods of warfare. Fighting was considered the only recourse in the absence of an agreement by Kwalla to punish the criminals. Another Kwalla homicide of a Dimmuk brought a year of ven-

---

[7]For the positive statistical relationship of fraternal interest groups as indicated by patrilocal residence and polygyny with the blood feud in a cross-cultural sample, see Otterbein and Otterbein (1965). Though fraternal interest groups are assuredly present in Kofyar patrilineal, patrilocal descent groups, it is the nonresident affines who had the sole responsibility for avenging a murder or a death under suspicious circumstances.

geance raids and plundering (#30). Dimmuk once attacked Kwalla because Kwalla allegedly had killed a Mernyang boy on Dimmuk soil (#31). Hostilities between Bong and Lardang-Bogalong (#32) followed a wrestling bout between boys from both villages at their common border. A Lardang boy had been clubbed, a youth from Bong killed in retaliation, and Lardang refused responsibility for the death. When a Zugal woman was murdered by her husband in Male, Zugal joined Kwa, home of the victim's mother, in pillaging Male (#33).

Perhaps the most serious conflicts in the eyes of Kofyar informants were those arising from an "unnatural" death blamed by the affines of the victim on the deceased's agnates. Kofyar regard the physical well-being of an individual as the responsibility of his near patrilineal kin. This group typically lives in the same village and cooperates in both economic and ritual activities (Netting 1968b:143–152). The patrilineage—specifically the nearest male agnates—are answerable to an individual's real or classificatory mother's brother. Because of the predominance of village exogamy, the mother's brother often resides in another village. This kinsman watches over the welfare of his sister's son and, in the case of serious illness, supervises the divinations. The sick person may be suffering from his agnates' witchcraft, and his mother's brother is charged with protecting him against such threats, if necessary by publicly accusing the agnates of bewitching their brother. Thus, a mysterious death may be credited to the evil activities of the victim's patrilineage and their co-villagers, and vengeance may be exacted by matrilateral kin who usually reside in another village.

Detailed accounts were available of the so-called "thunder war" *(dyel naantoeng)* which happened in December, 1921, according to official records (#34). It was precipitated by a bolt of lightning in Bong which struck four people and killed one of them, a young man called Kaganbe. The death was duly reported to his MoBr, Doewus of Bong, and to his MoMoBr,

Dajeng of Zugal. Only the FaMoBr, Daswar of Gogot, refused to accept the account. He was angry, contending that lightning did not usually kill people and the reason for its destructiveness must lie with the people of Bong. He warned the messengers that he would "come after them" (equivalent to a challenge), and raised the war cry which brought men running from Fulong, Gonkun, Dep, and Mangbar. They assembled at the wall east of Bong, and Daswar shouted his charges, both to declare war and to acquaint his allies with the reason for fighting. An estimated 40 Bong defenders faced 120 attackers who burst into the nearest neighborhood of the village and plundered three houses. In the melee, three men from Mangbar were speared, two of whom later died. Bong could not understand why their allies should turn on them: Dung had remained neutral, and only Koepal came to help Bong. Because the attackers were members of the same warfare alliance as Bong, the latter did not attempt to take heads. After conducting a divination which promised victory if another raid was made, Gogot returned in six days with reinforcements from the more distant villages of Koenji, Latok, Gogotkoegoen, and Funglet. Bong, fighting alone and vastly outnumbered, retreated into the village. Twenty-five or 30 homesteads in three neighborhoods were burned. The advance stopped in the center of the village because the attackers feared being outflanked. The raid lasted from approximately 9 A.M. till midafternoon. Two Bong men died as a result of injuries and one man each from Mangbar and Latok were killed. The British administration later forced the invaders to return the goods they had carried off.

By far the most disruptive Kofyar war began as vengeance for a young man named Daman (#35). Accounts from informants in Kofyar, Longsel, Bong, and Lardang differ in details but it appears that Daman from Longsel was en route to visit his father, who had been accused of bewitching his wife and exiled to Gogot. Daman disappeared, and was later found either hung from a locust bean tree or drowned in a shallow pool at the base of the tree. The death was reported by Longsel to the MoBr of the deceased at Fulong. The MoBr insisted that the young man had been seized by Dyambong of Longsel who tried to sell him as a slave and later killed him, attempting to make the victim's demise appear as suicide. Contrary explanations in Longsel and Kofyar were that Daman had either fallen from the tree or had an epileptic attack and drowned. Fighting began with a raid by Fulong on Longsel in which three were killed and four wounded. The conflict escalated with an effort by Longsel to outflank Fulong by thrusting through Bong. Bong and its allies counterattacked and drove the inhabitants of Longsel from their village. When some Longsel villagers returned to sleep in their houses, enemies surrounded the village at night, killed several people, and cut off one man's ear. The mutilation angered Lardang and initiated headhunting between alliances II and III. Longsel was forced to take permanent refuge in Kofyar, while neighboring Koepal fled in the opposite direction to Bong. Gogot and Dung were deserted, with the refugees going to Fulong, Gonkun, and Bong. Inhabitants of Kook, a hamlet on the Bong-Bogalong border, scattered and joined both opposing groups. A no-man's-land was formed and the entire boundary area between the alliances was depopulated. Evidence of the ensuing destruction remains in the shorter (i.e., younger) oil palms of Longsel and Koepal. These communities were not only destroyed, but their lands were left idle and burned annually so that all trees of economic value were wiped out. Isolated groves outside Bong mark sites where refugees established permanent homesteads. One account mentions that 33 households with 40 adult men from Dung, Koepal, and Kook settled in Bong. Even one exposed neighborhood of Bong itself was abandoned.

Efforts by the chiefs of Dung, Gogot, and Kofyar to establish peace were unsuccessful, and the war may have continued with sporadic battles, raids, and ambushes for more than 20 years. Formal battles were staged near the site of Longsel, or between Bogalong and Bong. These could take place as often as several times a year, and reports usually mention a single killing during each encounter. Raids and ambushes were frequent: Lardang killed a Bong man on the Zugal road; two Bong men making a foray into Kofyar were discovered and killed one of their pursuers with stones; three men from Bong went at night to burn a house in Bogalong and carry off goats; Kwanoeng killed a Bong man from ambush, and two men from Male were slain by Lardang. Lardang and Kofyar took a horse from Bong but missed an opportunity to steal a child. A party of 20 from Bong raided Kofyar, and one man who retreated more slowly was wounded by a spear. During a night attack, a Kofyar killed his neighbor by mistake.

## Effects of Endemic Warfare

The long war between alliances acted to restrict severely many Kofyar activities. Shifting cultivation in the bush fields beyond the settled perimeter of the village was curtailed by the danger of ambush. With the added burden of refugee populations, food was scarce. An informant claimed that only the chief of Bong had enough to eat. Children cried with hunger and ate unripe corn, though no one starved.[8] Contacts between certain villages ceased. The duties of kinship, such as reporting a death to a mother's brother, could not be performed if travel into enemy territory was necessary. New trade networks were required to secure salt and iron. Men delayed marriage until they were over 30, because they believed that sexual relations with women made one weak and unfit for war.

---

[8]For an analysis of the effects on population of evacuation and restricted agriculture with resulting increase in exposure to sleeping sickness carried by tsetse fly, see Netting (1973).

## Attitudes toward Warfare

Attitudes toward war were mixed. The excitement was valued, but death was feared. Violent aggression was celebrated in a triumphant public *kwagal* dance in which the trophy head was displayed. Enemy skulls, as well as those of leopards, were stored in shrines within sacred precincts. Bravery was encouraged by public honors: men who took heads were granted a title, special rights to beer, and an elaborate funeral commemoration with mock battle charges and war dances. It was said that many men liked fighting and considered it their profession. Children were not allowed to see wounded men, since Kofyar believed that the sight could lead them to fear fighting. Nevertheless, chiefs and older men often counseled against raiding and warfare, and young men might not undertake a raid if divination performed by their elders gave an unfavorable omen for the day. Women disliked war and feared for the safety of their husbands. One of the most serious accusations against a witch was that he had started a war. A man killed in battle was suspected of having been magically "pushed" to his death by one of his own brothers. People laughed at cowards but often advised retreat as the better part of valor. Exaggerated bravery was regarded as an inborn trait of certain men who fought "as if they never want to eat again." An informant would freely describe himself in panicked flight from a threatening enemy, and such a story provoked gales of laughter from his audience. The general attitude seemed to be that fighting would have been the best of fun if the risk of death had not been involved.

## THE SOCIAL IDIOM OF WARFARE

The Kofyar cognitive model of warfare presented two different types of explanation for the causes of warfare and the consequences of hostilities. The first recognized a set of quite obvious crimes against property and persons. These have been classified as fights, theft, food raids, trespass, property disagreements, and vengeance for murder. Though no courts existed for adjudicating such intervillage disputes, there was in each case a clear, relatively simple breach of a legal norm and the corresponding potential for redress of grievances. Such conflicts were for the most part sporadic, evenly distributed among contiguous villages, and involved no permanent break in social relations. Fighting was limited and local with few casualties. A second, contrasting statement was offered by the Kofyar to explain long-term conditions of hostility which involved depopulation of territory, the formation of alliances, greater loss of life, headhunting, and the decisive interruption of social contacts. Causation was traced to unusual deaths, often credited to witchcraft, and by implication to the contradictions inherent in the obligations of agnatic and affinal kin with respect to the individual victim. Long, complex stories with variant versions explored the initial breaking of kinship norms and the progressively more serious violations of expected interpersonal behavior. Conventional methods for ending warfare seemed useless in such cases, and only outside intervention could restore peace.

The most intractable conflict (#35) remembered by the Kofyar was rooted in breaches of the moral order exemplified by kinship. As mentioned above, the father of Daman of Longsel had been exiled for witchcraft, possibly at the behest of his co-resident patrilateral kin to whom he was potentially dangerous. This initial violation of lineage solidarity was compounded when the alleged witch's son, Daman, died mysteriously on the way to visit his father in Gogot. Another man from Longsel (and therefore a putative agnate of both Daman and his father) was accused of attempting to sell the young man as a slave and then murdering him under circumstances that would make it appear to be an accident or suicide. Daman's mother's brothers in Fulong, already convinced that their sister

had been injured by witchcraft, were now confronted with the unnatural demise of that same sister's son. Their suspicions were strengthened when the agnate who reported the death to Daman's MoBr disrespectfully stopped on his way home to drink beer in Gogot. Daman's affines, joined by the Gogot affines of Daman's father, were moved to vengeance against the village of Longsel which appeared to be driving out and killing its own sons. Thus the kinship responsibilities of affines were mobilized to punish the presumed sins of the agnatic next-of-kin.

The conflict between the father's people and mother's people of Daman developed with a kind of tragic inevitability. Each killing increased the grievance, but it was mutilation that marked a symbolic break in kinship. Lardang people became so incensed when their opponents cut an ear from a corpse that they claimed they could no longer be "brothers" with the members of alliance III.[9] In other contexts, alliance III (Ganguk) was referred to as the "child" of alliance II (Gankogom). Whereas neighboring villages, even as enemies, had usually avoided headhunting, after the taking and parading of heads was initiated, ties of brotherhood were further damaged. Later in the conflict the same man accused of murdering Daman was said to have danced with the intestines of an enemy in his teeth. Such treatment of a man as if he were an animal was reflected in the instant withering of the tree on which the intestines were displayed, and the perpetrator emerged as a monster.

As borders hardened, it became impossible to maintain contact with kin—usually affines—on the other side, and a number of individuals must

[9]The Kofyar word for brother is more accurately translated as sibling. It is applied to males and females and is extended to a wide variety of kin in collateral and descending generations following a modified system of Crow terminology (Netting 1968b:235). Brotherhood in this context seems to be a synonym for kinship and does not necessarily reflect shared agnatic links.

have been separated from an important source of affection, material support, and magico-religous protection. The mother's brother played an important role in divinations held to determine the cause of sickness or injury affecting his sister's child. Specified portions of game, small economic services, and a substantial part of the funeral meats conventionally passed from sister's child to mother's brother, while these prestations were reciprocated by licensed stealing and gifts at marriage (Netting 1968b:151–152). Individuals who had confessed to witchcraft or been accused of this crime by divination conventionally sought sanctuary with a mother's brother in a different community. The individual's only refuge from the strains of the corporate descent group was traditionally through the assertion of claims on the basis of alliance. Endemic fighting also made the mandatory formal announcements of death and the participation of mother's brother in funeral commemoration ceremonies impossible in some cases. Warriors tried to avoid injuring kin in battle, but the opposing pulls of loyalty to agnates and affines must have been felt by some participants. Though lineage and clan mates tended to be concentrated in single localities, important affinally linked males designated by the reciprocal mother's brother term could be found in two villages in the two ascending generations and as many as 9 other villages in the two descending generations (Netting 1968:234–235). Thus affinal kinship represented for Kofyar the most important and widely ramifying network of supra-local relationships. Moreover, new kin ties with the opposition could not be created. Marriages were out of the question, because, as one informant said, if he ventured into enemy territory, they would have been after him "like dogs after duiker."

Efforts to settle the conflict were also played out in kinship terms. At one point a chief of Gogot stood on the battlefield midway between the opposing forces and sacrificed a goat, throwing the head toward Longsel as the father of Daman and the hind quarter toward the mother's brother's people from Fulong. These are the portions of a sacrificed animal traditionally allotted to the major relatives at a funeral commemoration ceremony. The gesture was unsuccessful, indicating that the reciprocal kinship roles were refused or that the escalating fighting had involved so many groups in the cycle of terror and vengeance that efforts at conciliation of restricted local kin groups were no longer meaningful to the participants. A temporary peace following the sacrifice was broken because men from Kofyar feared to report a death to the appropriate mother's brother in Fulong, thus violating a kinship responsibility.

It is possible that the war which began as vengeance for Daman represented a qualitative shift in Kofyar conflict. Its history of many years duration, increased casualties, headhunting, village evacuation, and virtual insolubility (it ended only after a show of force by British colonial troops and the killing of a number of hill Kofyar in their first contact with rifle fire) all suggest that the old patterns of fights and raids, of states of temporary hostility with a variety of neighboring villages, were at an end. Perhaps more important, the warfare alliance of a number of autonomous hill communities emerged as a significant social unit. The long war emphasized incorporation into a supra-village unit on the basis of common defense. Refugees mixed the population within the alliance and provided a focus for sentiments of deprivation and hostility. (It is perhaps significant that the best known leaders of both sides in the Daman war came from adjoining evacuated villages, Longsel and Koepal.) If either alliance was to achieve real advantage, there was at least the possibility of structural change, uniting villages under a paramount chieftaincy and coordinating their activities by new and more centralized political mechanisms. On the other hand, individual affiliations outside the alliance were minimized, with the breaking of at least some affinal ties. The functionally specific associations based on patrilineal kinship, contiguity, and military alliance were stressed at the expense of diffuse and multidirectional relationships arising from marriage and kinship through women. Serious fighting was conceptually rooted in and itself exacerbated some of the ambivalence or disjunction inherent in the kinship system.

The idea that violations of kinship obligations may lead to a tragic severing of fundamental relationships is a universally moving theme of dramatic literature. By framing their explanation for the most serious warfare in kinship terms, the Kofyar reduce the impossible complexities of group conflict to a simple determinate set of oppositions known and understood by all members of society. The effects of incommensurable ecological factors have been translated into the restricted, highly organized language of kinship (Leaf 1973). Though this might seem at first glance an inappropriate cognitive model, it accurately reflects the social dimensions of the emergence of new population groups. By emphasizing the breaking of cross-alliance affinal bonds and the interdiction of further marital connections, the Kofyar explanation gives social significance to the geographical separation caused by endemic fighting and the creation of an enduring no-man's land. To the extent that competition for scarce resources continues to characterize an areal eco-system, more clearly defined internal territories maintained by the conventional competition of occasional formal battles may paradoxically act to *reduce* the general level of conflict.[10] The establishment by counterposed alliances of two reproductively isolated groups from a single, formerly interbreeding population may be a first step in differentiating ethnic units. The contrast between the minor, brief, easily adjusted fights of the Kofyar with the ethnically distinct Chokfem and the severe, interminable struggle among Kofyar settlements suggests the possible functions of ethnic boundaries in mitigating conflict.

It may also indicate the need to consider processes engendering ethnic diversity *within* a group along with the more familiar study of the maintenance of ethnic difference *between* groups of separate origin brought into contact by conquest or migration.[11]

Kinship categories are not an accidental or illogical framework for thinking about social conflict. For the Kofyar, the idiom of kinship serves as a means of organizing information about warfare. It communicates in terms of a structure whose ties and cleavages are presumably familiar to all the society's adult members. Moreover, since relations are involved (in kinship among persons in warfare among village groups), the idiom functions as a calculus in terms of which relations at one level can be dealt with by analogy with relations at another. The basis of the analogy may be hidden or disguised and is thus metaphorical. The Kofyar seem to be saying that kinship causes warfare, whereas in fact kinship shares certain formal features with warfare and their similarity suggests an approach to understanding the relatively opaque and perplexing nature of conflict. A reciprocal interaction of the two domains of experience is also implied by the fact that warfare in reality interrupts or even negates important kin ties. "It may be, then, that the kinds of 'fit' that we shall find between 'physical models' and 'cognized models' can best be discussed in metaphorical terms" (K. Basso, personal communication).[12]

Whatever the real relevance of the Kofyar metaphor of sundered kinship to the fact of warfare, it is plain that the idiom was an emotional-

---

[10]An interesting parallel from animal ethology is the contention that territorial definition and defense by means of ritual confrontation is more advanced in terms of evolutionary level than is genuine fighting (Clapham 1973:74).

[11]Dialectal differentiation within a single original speech community might develop along similar lines, with the linguistic isolation brought about by warfare and a cessation of intermarriage resembling that introduced by geographical barriers. The evidence of contiguous, related, but highly divergent languages makes such a process plausible, though we lack demonstrations of this kind of microevolution at work.

[12]For the ideas in this paragraph, I owe a great deal to the perceptive comments of Keith Basso.

ly expressive response to their situation. The Kofyar appear to have been aware of radical disorder affecting their social system. The disturbance of the kinship balance was contrary to the natural course of things, just as were deaths by epilepsy, lightning, witchcraft, and madness. All suggested a kind of animal inhumanity as opposed to brotherly responsibility and mutual protection. War for the Kofyar was not a conflict with strangers; it was not a response to threat or attack by enemy foreigners. Instead it was essentially civil strife, a struggle among equals who shared a single culture and knew the names of their opponents. Its primal poignancy and bitterness arose from its violation of the ideology of kinship. When brother lifts his hand against brother, an unquestioned support of the social universe is fractured. The pruning away of some kinship ties and the substitution for them of territorial political relationships is an honorable theme in social anthropology. It was this process, as catalyzed by warfare, which gives significance to the Kofyar idiom of kinship in conflict.

## BIBLIOGRAPHY

AMES, C. G.
1934 Gazetteer of Plateau Province. Jos: Jos Native Authority.

BRADFIELD, RICHARD MAITLAND
1973 A Natural History of Associations: A Study in the Meaning of Community, vol. 1. London: Duckworth.

CHAGNON, NAPOLEON A.
1968 Yanomamö Social Organization and Warfare. Pp. 109–159 in War: The Anthropology of Armed Conflict and Aggression (ed. by M. Fried, M. Harris, and R. Murphy). Garden City: Natural History Press.

CLAPHAM, W. B.
1973 Natural Ecosystems. New York: Macmillan.

FITZPATRICK, J. F. J.
1910 Some Notes on the Kwolla District and Its Tribes. Journal of the African Society 10:16–52, 213–221.

HALLPIKE, C. R.
1973 Functionalist Interpretations of Primitive Warfare. Man 8:451–470.

HEIDER, KARL G.
1970 The Dugum Dani. Chicago: Aldine.

KIEFER, THOMAS M.
1970 Modes of Social Action in Armed Combat: Affect, Tradition and Reason in Tausug Private Warfare. Man 5:586–596.

LEAF, MURRAY
1973 Peasant Motivation, Ecology, and Economy in Panjab. Pp. 40–50 in Contributions to Asian Studies 3 (ed. by K. Ishwaran). Leiden: Brill.

NETTING, ROBERT McC.
1968a Kofyar Building in Mud and Stone. Expedition 10, no. 4:10–20.
1968b Hill Farmers of Nigeria: Cultural Ecology of the Kofyar of the Jos Plateau. Seattle: University of Washington Press.
1969. Ethnocentrism Fieldnotes for the Kofyar of Northern Nigeria (ed. by Marilynn B. Brewer). Manuscript of the Cooperative Crosscultural Study of Ethnocentrism, Northwestern University, Evanston, Illinois.
1973 Fighting, Forest, and the Fly: Some Demographic Regulators Among the Kofyar. Journal of Anthropological Research 29:164–179.

OTTERBEIN, KEITH F., AND
CHARLOTTE SWANSON OTTERBEIN
1965 An Eye for an Eye, A Tooth for a Tooth. A Cross-Cultural Study of Feuding. American Anthropologist 67:1470–1482.

RADCLIFFE-BROWN, A. R.
1952 Structure and Function in Primitive Society. Glencoe: Free Press.

RAPPAPORT, ROY A.
1971 Nature, Culture, and Ecological Anthropology. Pp. 237–267 in Man, Culture, and Society (ed. by Harry L. Shapiro). New York: Oxford University Press.

Turney-High, Harry H.
  1949 Primitive War. Columbia: University of
       South Carolina Press (1971).
Vayda, Andrew P.
  1968 Hypotheses about Functions of War. Pp.
       85–91 in War: The Anthropology of

Armed Conflict and Aggression (ed. by
M. Fried, M. Harris, and R. Murphy).
Garden City: Natural History Press.
  1969 The Study of the Causes of War, with
       Special Reference to Head-hunting Raids
       in Borneo. Ethnohistory 16:211–224.

# 24

## POPULATION, WARFARE, AND THE MALE SUPREMACIST COMPLEX

*William Tulio Divale and Marvin Harris*

*Both Vayda and Netting, in the two previous papers, note the close relationship between population density and the likelihood of hostilities, but they limit their observations to the particular cases of war they describe. In this article, William Divale and Marvin Harris present a broad cross-cultural study to test a series of hypotheses. Using reports on particular societies as a sample for their test, they demonstrate that population size, a male supremacist complex, and warfare are related. Specifically, they argue that the male supremacist complex is commonly found in world societies and that because males are biologically better suited for fighting, the complex is related to war. These two factors are connected to population control through the institution of infanticide (the killing of babies). Where the male supremacist complex is strong, female infanticide and neglect leading to the death of female children is high. The limitation of the size of the female population is the surest way to keep population size in check in the absence of other birth control techniques. Thus war is related to population control not through battlefield casualties, but through limits on the number of women of bearing age.*

In this paper[1] we (1) confirm the existence of a pervasive institutionalized material and ideological complex of male supremacy in band and village societies; (2) identify the practice of pre state warfare as the most important cause of this complex; (3) explain the perpetuation and propagation of warfare among band and village societies as a response to the need to regulate population growth in the absence of effective or less costly alternatives; (4) relate the complex of warfare and male supremacy to additional widespread cultural phenomena. By warfare we mean all organized forms of *intergroup* homicide involving combat teams of two or more persons, including feuding and raiding.

The primary ethnological evidence for the existence of a pervasive institutionalized complex of male supremacy consists of asymmetrical frequencies of sex-linked practices and beliefs which on logical grounds alone either ought not to be sex-linked or ought to occur with equal frequency in their male-centered and female-centered forms. Certain aspects of this complex are well-known; others are less well-known or have hitherto been viewed as isolated phenomena.

Among the more familiar parts of the complex are the male-centered postmarital locality practices and descent ideologies. Three quarters of 1,179 societies classified by Murdock (1967) are either patrilocal or virilocal while only one tenth are matrilocal or uxorilocal (Table I). Postmarital residence is closely associated with control over access to, and the disposition and inheritance of, natural resources, capital, and labor power. The best comparative evidence for male dominance in these spheres consists of the skewed distributions of descent rules. Thus patrilineality occurs five times more frequently than matrilineality (Table I).

The interpretation of the statistical imbalance in sex-linked residence and descent rules as evidence for male dominance of the decision-making process responsible for the allocation of domestic resources, capital, and labor power, is strengthened by two remarkable facts: in matrilineal societies avunculocality occurs more frequently than matrilocality, and the logical opposite of avunculocality does not occur at all. The logical opposite of avunculocality is called amitalocality (Murdock 1949:71). It would involve, if it existed, postmarital residence with wife's father's sister rather than as in the case of avunculocality, residence with husband's mother's brother.

The high frequency of avunculocality and patrilocality in matrilineal societies—they are the prevailing residence pattern in 58% of matrilineal societies—is best explained by the following theory: In matrilineal societies no less than in patrilineal societies, males dominate the allocation of domestic resources, labor, and capital. Matrilineal societies therefore tend to revert

to patrilocal, patrilineal systems. Avunculocality is a phase in the cycle that leads back to patrilocality (Divale 1974a, 1974b; Murdock 1949; Schlegel 1972).

In contrast, there is no basis for interpreting most cases of matrilineality as a phase in a cycle that begins with matrilineality, passes through a patrilocal phase, and then reverts to matrilocality. Such an alternative interpretation would be valid only if evidence existed to indicate that patrilocal, patrilineal systems passed through an amitalocal phase. As we have just said, amitalocality does not exist.

Equally strong evidence for the pervasiveness of male dominance in the domestic sphere is provided by the distribution of marriage forms. Polygyny occurs 141 times more frequently than polyandry (Table II). Logically, there should be some advantages in having several males simultaneously provide food and services for one woman and her children. Such an arrangement would seem to be at least as efficient as having one husband provide food and services for several women and their children. Polyandry is also remarkably underrepresented when its potential for regulating population growth is considered. Polygyny encourages the rearing of female infants in order to provide plural wives, whereas polyandry, in theory at least, is better suited for societies that rely on female infanticide to regulate population growth. Such populations are extremely common (Table IV). Therefore, the fact that polygyny is so much more common than polyandry implies the existence of powerful adaptive advantages associated with polygyny.

The nonexistence of the female-centered opposite of another widespread marriage-related institution, brideprice, has received less notice but is no less puzzling. Brideprice occurs in 57% of the societies in the *Ethnographic Atlas,* but groom price, the logical opposite of brideprice, is as nonexistent as amitalocality. This fact has been obscured by the frequent juxtaposition of dowry with brideprice. Brideprice is an economic compensation given to a bride's family for

TABLE 1
Frequency of Residence Patterns by Type of Descent

| Predominant Residence Pattern | All Types | | Patrilineal | | Matrilineal | | Ambilineal | | Double Descent | | Bilateral | |
|---|---|---|---|---|---|---|---|---|---|---|---|---|
| | Freq. | % | Freq. | % | Freq. | % | Freq. | % | Freq. | % | Freq. | % |
| Patrilocal or virilocal | 823 | 70.9 | 563 | 97.0 | 30 | 19 | 31 | 68 | 39 | 93 | 160 | 48 |
| Matrilocal or uxorilocal | 132 | 11.3 | 1 | .2 | 50 | 33 | 5 | 11 | — | — | 73 | 22 |
| Avunculocal | 67 | 5.7 | — | — | 62 | 39 | 2 | 4 | 3 | 7 | — | — |
| Bilocal | 81 | 7.0 | 5 | .9 | 6 | 4 | 8 | 17 | — | — | 62 | 19 |
| Neolocal | 52 | 4.5 | 8 | 1.4 | 6 | 4 | — | — | — | — | 38 | 11 |
| Duolocal | 7 | .6 | 3 | .5 | 4 | 2 | — | — | — | — | — | — |
| No information | 17 | — | 8 | — | 3 | — | — | — | 2 | — | 4 | — |
| Totals | 1,179 | 100.0 | 588 | 100.0 | 164 | 100 | 46 | 100 | 44 | 100 | 337 | 100 |

Based on Murdock (1967).

324

**TABLE II**
Frequency of Marriage Forms

| Marriage Form | Frequency | % |
|---|---|---|
| Monogamy | 171 | 14.6 |
| Limited Polygyny (424) | | |
| General Polygyny (565) | 989 | 84.8 |
| Polyandry | 7 | .6 |
| No Information | 12 | — |
| Totals | 1,179 | 100.0 |

Based on Murdock (1967).

the loss of her valuable productive and reproductive services (Goody and Tambiah 1973:6). Dowry often is compensation given to the groom's family, but it is seldom given for the loss of the groom's valuable productive and reproductive services. Rather, it is given as compensation for the cost of maintaining an economically burdensome woman or as payment for the establishment of political, economic, caste, or ethnic alliances valuable to the bride's family. Almost all cases (83%) of brideprice and dowry are associated with patrilocal, patrilineal systems. Groom price, if it existed, ought to be associated with matrilocal, matrilineal systems.

The theory that best explains why groom price does not occur in matrilineal systems is that marriage in such systems does not entail the permanent transfer of the productive and reproductive services of males from one corporate unit to another. On the contrary, as is well-known, marriage in most matrilocal, matrilineal systems is notoriously fragile and is made and unmade with little ritual. Husbands in matrilocal, matrilineal systems in other words, do not occupy a position analogous to wives in patrilocal, patrilineal systems; they are not incorporated into their wives' domestic group and they do not surrender control over their natal domestic affairs to their sisters; hence there is no groom price paid to their sisters. This also explains why 15% of matrilocal or uxorilocal societies continue to have brideprice (Table III).

Male dominance is also implicit in the widespread asymmetry of the sexual division of labor. Women in band and village societies are usually burdened with drudge work, such as seed grinding and pounding, fetching water and firewood, and carrying infants and household possessions. Hunting with weapons is a virtually universal male specialty.

Male supremacy is even more directly displayed in the asymmetry of political institutions. Headmanship occurs widely in band and village societies; headwomanship, in a strictly analogous sense, is no more common than polyandry, if it exists at all. Control over redistributive systems in pre-state societies is seldom if ever vested in women. The institution of "big man" which occupies a critical position in the evolution of class stratification is not matched anywhere by a comparable institution of "big woman." Shamanic leadership is also male-centered; female shamans do occur, but they are almost always less numerous and less prominent than male shamans. When the total number of occupations in a society are considered, women always have fewer economic roles open to them (M. Naroll n.d.), and even when they exercise some control over the economic process their status remains lower than males (Divale 1976; Sanday 1973: 1682).

Central to the sexual distribution of power is the fact that almost everywhere men monopolize the weapons of war as well as weapons of the

**TABLE III**
Modes of Marriage by Types of Residence

| Mode of Marriage | All Types | | Patrilocal or Virilocal Only | | Matrilocal or Uxorilocal Only | |
|---|---|---|---|---|---|---|
| | Freq. | % | Freq. | % | Freq. | % |
| Extensive brideprice | 673 | 57 | 560 | 68 | 19 | 15 |
| Bride service | 118 | 10 | 55 | 7 | 30 | 23 |
| Gift exchange | 61 | 5 | 49 | 6 | 3 | 2 |
| Exchange of women | 34 | 3 | 32 | 4 | 1 | 0.8 |
| Dowry | 31 | 3 | 21· | 3 | 1 | 0.8 |
| Not Important | 253 | 22 | 102 | 12 | 76 | 58.4 |
| Totals | 1,179 | 100 | 823 | 100 | 132 | 100 |

Based on Murdock (1967).

hunt. Nowhere in the world do women constitute the principle participants in organized police-military combat. In many band and village cultures women are not even permitted to handle the weapons which males employ in combat. The male police-military specialty is closely associated with sexually differentiated training for fierce and aggressive behavior. Here another link in the male supremacist complex is forged: the combat effectiveness of males is enhanced through their participation in competitive sport such as wrestling, racing, dueling, and many forms of individual and mock combat. Women seldom participate in such sports and to the best of our knowledge, almost never compete with men.

The material, domestic, political, and military subordination of women is matched in the ritual and ideological spheres by pervasive beliefs and practices that emphasize the inferiority of females. Menstruating women are almost universally regarded as ritually unclean (Simmons 1937:495); menstrual blood pollutes, whereas semen is used widely in rituals aimed at improving production, health and well-being. While a belief in witches is usually accompanied by a belief in warlocks, witches are regularly regarded as the more evil of the two. Although female gods occupy important positions in the pantheons of

many ecclesiastical religions, male supreme gods greatly outnumber female supreme gods (Gangloff n.d.), and legendary heroes greatly outnumber legendary heroines (Simmons 1937). Throughout the world, males menace women and children with bull-roarers, masks, and other sacred paraphernalia. Men's houses, in which these sacred items are stored, are also part of the same complex. Women seldom menace men in general in their religious activities and there are few communal women's houses reported in the literature known to us. Also, there are instances of funeral suttees for widows, but we know of no instance where husbands are grave escorts for their wives.

But the most important component in the male supremacist complex remains to be mentioned. A widespread cultural preference exists for male children among preindustrial societies. In Simmons' (1937) study, male children were strongly preferred in 66% of the cases. This preference is often explicit and sometimes embodied in a rule that the firstborn *must* be a male. More significantly, the actual demographic profile of the majority of band and village societies prior to modern contact is heavily unbalanced in favor of male infants and children. Demographic analysis of 160 band and village populations, censused prior to modern contact and while they still practiced warfare, shows an average sex ratio in the age group 14 or under of 128 boys per 100 girls (Divale 1972). The average sex ratio of humans at birth is 105.5 males per 100 females (Thomlinson 1965:429; Thompson 1942:49). The only way in which sex ratios as high as 128:100 can be achieved, is through postpartum selection (Lorimer 1954: 151; Birdsell 1968:229). Infanticide involving strangling, blows to the head, exposure, and other direct acts, is correlated with the sex ratio as Table IV shows. Nonetheless, preferential overt female infanticide must be reckoned as only the tip of the iceberg. Many cultures with markedly skewed junior age-sex ratios deny that they practice any infanticide at all. Hence it can be inferred that the sexual imbalance in favor of males is achieved as much through covert infanticide, including clandestine aggression and various forms of malign and/or benign neglect that adversely affect the survivability of female infants (Neel and Weiss 1975:32; Bahadur, Jammu, and Sharma 1931).[2]

What accounts for the scope, persistence, and distribution of the male supremacist complex? The most obvious explanation is that institutionalized male supremacy is a direct product of genetically determined human sexual dimorphism which endows males with taller stature,

heavier musculature, and more of the hormones that are useful for aggression. But this hypothesis accounts for only part of the complex under consideration. It accounts for why males rather than females dominate domestic, political, religious, economic, and military institutions. Yet it cannot satisfactorily account for the preference for male children as objectified in the unbalanced sex ratios. Indeed to the extent that there is polygyny, competition for women, and the exploitation of female labor, simple biological determination leads one to expect that more females than males would be reared to reproductive age. Infrahuman primate populations do not have comparable sex ratios. Since women are exploited by men, one would expect girls to outnumber boys just as slaves outnumber masters, serfs outnumber feudal lords, and proletarians outnumber capitalists. Several recent studies have shown that even in hunting societies, per capita, women are productively more valuable than men (Lee 1972; Morren 1973). And polygyny confirms the great value which men place on women. Thus polygyny stands in mysterious contradiction to the high frequency of the practice of female infanticide. Polygyny renders most males superfluous as far as replacement of population is concerned. Since males control domestic and political institutions, one would expect

**TABLE IV**
Sex Ratios of Children by Frequency of Infanticide[2]

| Ethonographer's Report of the Frequency with which Infanticide is Practiced | Sex Ratio of Age Group 14 Years or Younger (Males per 100 Females) | Number of Populations Censused |
|---|---|---|
| 1. Commonly practiced | 117:100 | 179 |
| 2. Occasionally practiced | 117:100 | 29 |
| 3. Not commonly practiced | 104:100 | 94 |
| 4. Not practiced | 108:100 | 91 |
| Total | | 393 |

*T* tests for significance of difference between the average percent of males for each group: 1 vs. 2, P = n.s.; 2 vs. 3, P = .05; 3 vs. 4, P = n.s.; 1 & 2 vs. 3 & 4, P = .01.

the number of females per male to be maximized. Instead, we find female infanticide limiting the number of females, and polygyny exacerbating the shortage.

There is one distinctively human cultural practice, the presence of which can be used to predict all of the components of the male supremacist complex, and which seems capable of explaining the apparent contradiction involved in combining polygyny and the exploitation of female labor with the rearing of more males than females. Wherever preindustrial warfare occurs, we suggest that a premium survival advantage is conferred upon the group that rears the largest number of fierce and aggressive warriors (Sipes 1973; Otterbein 1970; Naroll and Divale 1976). Given warfare, males rather than females are trained to be fierce and aggressive because in hand combat with muscle-powered weapons the average height and weight advantage of males is decisive for individual and group survival. Despite the fact that some women are physically better suited for warrior training than some males, there is an advantage in making such training the exclusive prerogative of males and in establishing a male monopoly over military weapons. (Male monopoly over hunting weapons may be seen as a functional corollary of the monopoly over military weapons.) The advantage is that sex can be used as the principle reinforcement for fierce and aggressive performances involving risk of life. Sex, rather than other forms of reinforcement such as food or shelter, is used to condition warlike behavior because sexual deprivation does not lead to the impairment of physical fitness, whereas deprivation of food and shelter would cripple fighting capacity. Furthermore, if women are to be the reward for military bravery, women must be reared to be passive and to submit to the decisions concerning the allocation of their sexual, productive, and reproductive services. Polygyny is the objectification of much of this system of rewards. At the same time, polygyny intensifies the shortage of females created by the postpartum manipulation of the sex ratio, producing

positive feedback with respect to male aggressivity and fierceness, and encouraging combat for the sake of wife capture.

In an attempt to rear passive and submissive women, males enlist aid of the supernatural. Hence, women are intimidated by bull-roarers, masked male dancers, and male religious specialists. When intensive warfare is practiced between closely related neighboring bands and villages, it leads to the establishment of, or reinforces the prior existence of, solidary groups of males who have a joint interest in the exploitation and defense of a common territory. Patrilocality is the cross-generational objectification of these male-centered interest groups; and patrilineality is the appropriate kinship ideology for enhancing the sentiments of solidarity within the co-resident core of sons, fathers, and brothers. We note in passing that recent quantifications of subsistence practices have largely invalidated the hypothesis that locality practices are determined by which sex plays a predominant role in production (Divale 1974a, 1974b). Indeed, something of an inverse relationship may exist. Women probably produce more calories per capita in most band and village societies. Women probably tend to be more thoroughly exploited and to produce an even more disproportionate share of goods and services in direct proportion to the intensity of the male supremacist complex (Sanday 1973; Ember and Ember 1971; Divale 1973; Witkowski n.d.). On the other hand, a shift from internal forms of warfare can be used to explain many of the shifts from patrilocal, patrilineal systems to matrilocal, matrilineal systems (Divale 1974a, 1974b). Thus, the hypothesized causal thread connecting warfare with the various aspects of the male supremacist complex, not only also helps to explain the development of matrilocality but also why males remain dominant in matrilocal, matrilineal systems.

Our use of warfare to resolve the apparent contradictions in the male supremacist complex does not dispose of the possibility that the male supremacist complex is the direct expression of human-sexual dimorphism. It may still be argued that warfare itself is the direct product of biologically determined aggressive impulses. However, we believe that the most parsimonious explanation for the prevalence of warfare in band and village societies is that war was formerly part of a distinctively human system of population control. The principle component in this system was the limitation of the number of females reared to reproductive age through female infanticide, the benign and malign neglect of female infants, and the preferential treatment of male children. Warfare functions in this system to sustain the male supremacist complex and thereby to provide the practical exigencies and ideological imperatives for postpartum cultural selection against female infants. The relationship between female infanticide and war is shown in Table V. For the 160 band and village populations that were censused while warfare was still practiced, the sex ratio of those 14 years or younger is 128 boys per 100 girls due to female infanticide, and the sex ratio of those 15 years or older is almost equal (101:100) due to male mortality in warfare. For the 236 populations that were censused a generation (5 to 25 years) after warfare had been stopped (usually by colonial authorities), the sex ratios among young and adults are 113 boys and 113 men per 100 girls and women. The increase in the ratio of adult men from 101:100 when war was present to 113:100 when war had been recently stopped is probably due to the survival of males who previously would have been killed in warfare. This change in the sex ratios with the cessation of warfare is strong evidence that warfare and not some other variable is responsible for these demographic effects.

The sex ratios are even more extreme when both the frequency of infanticide and the presence of warfare are controlled for. Table VI lists the sex ratios for 448 populations for which information on both warfare and the frequency of infanticide is available. For the 110 populations where warfare was still practiced at the time of census, and where ethnographers report that infanticide is commonly or occasionally practiced, the sex ratio among the young is 133 boys per 100 girls. But among the adults, it declines to 96 men per 100 women. For the 102 populations

TABLE V
Sex Ratios of Children and Adults by Presence of Warfare at Time of Census[2]

| Presence of Warfare at the Time Population Was Censused | Sex Ratio of Age Group 14 Years or Younger | Sex Ratio of Age Group 15 Years or Older | Number of Populations Censused |
|---|---|---|---|
| | (Males per 100 Females) | | |
| 1. Warfare present at time of census | 128:100 | 101:100 | 160 |
| 2. Warfare stopped 5 to 25 years before population was censused | 113:100 | *113:100 | 236 |
| 3. Warfare stopped 26 or more years before population was censused | 106:100 | 92:100 | 165 |
| Total | | | 561 |

*Increase in this ratio of adult males is probably due to survival of males who previously would have been killed in warfare.

T tests for significance of difference between the average percent of males for each group:
Young Age Group: 1 vs. 2, P = .005; 2 vs. 3, P = .05; 1 vs. 3, P = .0005.
Adult Age Group: 1 vs. 2, P = .0005; 2 vs. 3, P = .0005; 1 vs. 3, P = .01.

where warfare had been stopped 26 or more years prior to the census, and where infanticide was reported as not common or not practiced, the sex ratio among the young is 104 boys per 100 girls and 92 men per 100 women. The sex ratios of these latter groups are not markedly different from the sex ratios at birth. Thus in band and village societies, we are most likely to find unbalanced sex ratios when warfare is present. T tests on the major geographical regions and in the 112 cultures which compose the 561 populations show that the differences in the percentages of boys to girls in the young generation are significantly different (and always in the same direction—more boys than girls) when warfare is present than when warfare has been suppressed (Tables VII and VIII).

We suggest that postpartum selection against female infants is an unavoidable consequence of the absence of effective or safe prenatal contraceptives or abortion techniques. Extremely low rates of population growth have been characteristic of most of human history. The rate was probably no more than .00015% per annum for most of the Paleolithic, and about .036% for most of the Neolithic (Hassan 1973; Carneiro and Hilse 1966; Coale 1974). Part of the indicated control over fertility was probably achieved by the effect of low female body fat to body weight ratios on the postponement of menarche, and the postponement of the resumption of the menstrual cycle after birth (Frisch and McArthur 1974). The Bushmen are reported to maintain a .5% rate by prolonging lactation, which slows the buildup of body fat in nursing females (Kolata 1974). This rate, how-

TABLE VI
Sex Ratios of Children and Adults by Presence of Warfare *and* Frequency of Infanticide[2]

| Presence of Warfare at Time of Census and Frequency of Infanticide as Reported by Ethnographers | Sex Ratio of Age Group 14 Years or Younger | Sex Ratio of Age Group 15 Years or Older | Number of Populations Censused |
|---|---|---|---|
| | *(Males per 100 Females)* | | |
| 1. Warfare present at the time of census *and* Infanticide is reported as either commonly or occasionally practiced | 133:100 | 96:100 | 110 |
| 2. Warfare stopped 5 to 25 years before population was censused | 133:100 | *113:100 | 236 |
| 3. Warfare stopped 26 or more years before population was censused *and* Infanticide is reported as either not common or not practiced | 104:100 | 92:100 | 102 |
| Total | | | 448 |

*Increase in this ratio of adult males is probably due to the survival of males who previously would have been killed in warfare.

*T* tests for significance of difference between the average percent of males for each group:
  Young Age Group: 1 vs. 2, P = .0005; 2 vs. 3, P = .025; 1 vs. 3, P = .0005.
  Adult Age Group: 1 vs. 2, P = .0005; 2 vs. 3, P = .0005; 1 vs. 3, P = n.s.

**TABLE VII**

Geographical Breakdown of Sex Ratios by Presence of Warfare[2]

| Presence of Warfare at Time of Census | Sex Ratio of Age Group 14 Years or Younger | Sex Ratio of Age Group 15 Years or Older | Number of Populations Censused |
|---|---|---|---|
| | *(Males per 100 Females)* | | |
| AFRICA | | | |
| 1. Warfare present | 133 : 100 | 69 : 100 | 10 |
| 2. War stopped 5 to 25 years | 85 : 100 | 88 : 100 | 46 |
| 3. War stopped 26 or more years | 104 : 100 | 79 : 100 | 16 |
| Subtotal | | | 72 |
| ASIA | | | |
| 1. Warfare present | 150 : 100 | 108 : 100 | 28 |
| 2. War stopped 5 to 25 years | 122 : 100 | 138 : 100 | 1 |
| 3. War stopped 26 or more years | 112 : 100 | 127 : 100 | 2 |
| Subtotal | | | 31 |
| NORTH AMERICA | | | |
| 1. Warfare present | 127 : 100 | 92 : 100 | 30 |
| 2. War stopped 5 to 25 years | 96 : 100 | 114 : 100 | 2 |
| 3. War stopped 26 or more years | 104 : 100 | 104 : 100 | 19 |
| Subtotal | | | 51 |
| OCEANIA | | | |
| 1. Warfare present | 127 : 100 | 117 : 100 | 41 |
| 2. War stopped 5 to 25 years | 122 : 100 | 122 : 100 | 186 |
| 3. War stopped 26 or more years | 122 : 100 | 92 : 100 | 29 |
| Subtotal | | | 256 |
| SOUTH AMERICA | | | |
| 1. Warfare present | 122 : 100 | 96 : 100 | 51 |
| 2. War stopped 5 to 25 years | 108 : 100 | 96 : 100 | 1 |
| 3. War stopped 26 or more years | 104 : 100 | 92 : 100 | 99 |
| Subtotal | | | 151 |
| Grand total | | | 561 |

$T$ tests for significance of difference between the average percent of males were run for each region comparing the war present groups with the combined average of the two war stopped groups. This was for both generations. The difference between the war present and the war stopped groups was statistically significant (at least the .05 level) in four of the five regions for the young generation (the difference was not significant in Oceania). Among the adult generations the difference was significant in all regions but Oceania and South America.

331

TABLE VIII
Sex Ratios of Children and Adults by Presence of Warfare Using Averages for Societies Rather than Local
Populations[2]

| Presence of Warfare at the Time Populations in the Society Were Censused | Sex Ratio of Age Group 14 Years or Younger | Sex Ratio of Age Group 15 Years or Older | Number of Societies Censused |
|---|---|---|---|
| | *(Males per 100 Females)* | | |
| 1. Warfare present at time of censuses | 127:100 | 100:100 | 55 |
| 2. Warfare stopped 5 to 25 years before censuses were taken | 104:100 | 104:100 | 34 |
| 3. Warfare stopped 26 or more years before censuses were taken | 108:100 | 96:100 | 23 |
| Total | | | 112 |

$T$ tests for significant differences in the average percent of males for each group:
Young Age Group: 1 vs. 2, P = .01; 2 vs. 3, P = n.s.; 1 vs. 3, P = .01.
Adult Age Group: 1 vs. 2, P = n.s.; 2 vs. 3, P = n.s.; 1 vs. 3, P = n.s.

ever, amounts to a doubling every 139 years. Had this rate been typical of band and village societies during the past 10,000 years, there would now be $2^{79} = 604,463,000,000,000,000,-000,000$ people in the world. Hence, even spacing of children to four or five year intervals by means of prolonged lactation cannot be regarded as the major means of population control for band and village societies. Moreover, village populations apparently cannot rely on nursing to prolong the birth interval much beyond 18 months (Van Ginneken 1974).

A moderately healthy population, for example, one that has a life expectancy at birth of 47 years, will become stationary if about one third of all females born never survive to reproductive age, and if each female who survives to reproductive age has on the average three live births. If the average woman in a population has four live births, about half of all the females born cannot live to reproductive age if the population is to remain stationary. Such a population will have an average life expectancy at birth of about 33 years (Coale 1974:45).

Since the reproductive potential of most sexually reproducing species is determined largely by the rate of female survivorship (Cavalli-Sforza 1971:670), the most effective mode of population control is to reduce the percentage of the population which consists of sexually active fertile females (Dickeman 1975a, 1975b). Outright suppression of sexual activity of fertile females was (and is) difficult to achieve. Abortion was widely practiced, but it affected the sex ratio only by shortening the life expectancy of adult women. While preferential female infanticide and preferential benign and malign neglect of female infants seem cruel and wasteful, it had two conspicuous advantages over abortion among band and village societies: (1) male fetuses could be brought to term and selectively reared to adulthood; (2) the death of babies was less costly in an emotional, structural, and economic sense, than the death of mothers.

If the last point is true with respect to the alternative of lowering the life expectancy of adult females, why then should there be a preference for rearing additional numbers of males to adulthood, only to see them killed in battle? Would it not be less costly simply to rear the same number of males and females? Why didn't the cost of battle in pain and suffering dampen the system and force an end to the emphasis on rearing fierce and aggressive males? We suggest that male combat deaths were less costly emotionally and structurally than adult female deaths associated with abortion techniques that induce general body trauma. The decisive difference is that the agents responsible for male combat deaths are not part of the domestic or local group. Combat deaths are blamed on the enemy, and this enhances the solidary sentiments of the domestic and local groups, whereas adult female deaths from induced abortions destroy solidary sentiments.

Because of war's adaptively advantageous demographic and ecological feedback, war was self-perpetuating. Once introduced, its diffusion could not be resisted. Band and village societies which failed to attain stationary populations suffered cuts in their standard of living and were threatened by hunger and disease. Societies which achieved stationary populations by means other than the male supremacist-warfare complex were routed and destroyed by their more aggressive neighbors. Note that we are not suggesting that once in existence warfare simply perpetuated and propagated itself by inertia. Rather, we are saying that warfare perpetuated and propagated itself because it was an effective method for sustaining the material and ideological restrictions on the rearing of female infants.

Note also that we are rejecting the theory that war achieved its adaptive value by limiting population growth directly through combat deaths. The high death rate from combat deaths attests to the seriousness of war in band and village societies, but most combat deaths were males. In societies which practice serial monogamy or plural marriage, high rates of male combat deaths will not produce stationary or near stationary populations (Livingston 1968).

It follows that a single theory cannot account for warfare in band and village, as well as state-level, societies. Among state-level societies, warfare represents a systemic attempt to solve production deficiencies through perpetual territorial and demographic expansion (Naroll and Divale 1976; Carneiro 1970). Among the former, warfare represents a systemic attempt to achieve stationary or near stationary populations (Divale 1970, 1971, 1972; Harris 1972, 1975:264). Obviously, however, the two forms are evolutionarily related, perhaps in some cases through the development of matrilocal, matrilineal varieties of external warfare as a result of migration into an inhabited region (Divale 1974b:19–63).

It is not essential for our theory that the precise cause of the first instance of an outbreak of war in a given region be known. Rather it suffices to show why war would tend to be perpetuated and propagated among band and village societies. In general, however, we predict that the intensity of warfare and the rate of its spread, will vary inversely with the ability to achieve stationary populations by means other than female infanticide and benign and malign neglect of female infants. Band societies with diets high in protein but low in fats and carbohydrates can be expected to rely more on birth-spacing effects of prolonged lactation than on the male supremacist-war complex. Band and village societies with high-calorie, low-protein diets cannot rely on prolonged lactation and hence will depend more on the war complex. Hence, we predict an intensification of warfare (measured in terms of frequency of combat and relative number of deaths per capita due to combat) in association with the Neolithic and the spread of starchy diets. Moreover, with the development of permanent settlements, standing or stored crops, and domesticated animals, warfare more often led to territorial routs and pursuit with the intent to maximize enemy deaths, and expropriation of capital investments.

Some evidence already exists which supports these predictions. Leo Simmons' (1937) study shows that warfare is significantly associated with many variables found in village horticultural and agricultural societies: an increase in the frequency of warfare is correlated with agriculture, permanency of residence, durability of dwellings, use of grain as food, mining and smelting of metals, and pottery. In other words, warfare is infrequent when horticulture is absent or only casual, and warfare is frequent when horticulture is extensive. The frequency of warfare is also associated with many variables of the male supremacy complex. Frequent warfare is significantly correlated with patrilocal residence, patrilineal inheritance, polygyny, marriage by capture, brideprice, postmarital sex restrictions on women, property rights in women, male secret societies, male age grades, and men's houses. It is also significant that frequent warfare is negatively correlated with polyandry (Table IX).[3]

One hypothesis which flows from our theory and remains untested is that any sudden shift from high-protein, low-calorie diets to low-protein, high-calorie diets, should produce a spurt of population growth, followed by an increase in female infanticide and the intensification of warfare. The Yanomamo of Amazonia may be the classic case. Expansion of their investment in banana and plantain gardens proba-

bly provided the starchy calorie supply for a 2–3% per annum population explosion among the central villages (Lizot 1971). This expansion may have adversely affected the fragile animal-protein ecology typical of interriverine Amazon habitats (Gross 1975). Female infanticide produced junior-age sex ratios of 148:100 for 11 Yanomamo villages in the intensive warfare zone, and an intense male supremacist-warfare complex developed. But in 12 Yanomamo villages that were peripherally located, junior-age sex ratios were only 118:100 and warfare was less intense. This contrast is even more marked in two villages studied by Lizot: the peripheral Karohi-teri have a ratio of 77:100; the war-making Ihirubi-teri, 260:100 (Chagnon 1973, 1974). Since bananas and plantains are perennials, recently fissioned groups fought each other for possession of jointly cleared garden sites, as well as for possession of the proportionately decreasing number of women and protein resources (Harris 1974, Gross 1975; Ross and Ross n.d.; Chagnon 1974).

By accounting for the male supremacist com-

TABLE IX
Correlates of Warfare Frequency and Selected Traits[3]

| Traits | Gamma | Probability | N |
|---|---|---|---|
| Permanency of residence | .57 | .001 | 66 |
| Durability of dwellings | .41 | .022 | 66 |
| Men's houses | .59 | .028 | 50 |
| Agriculture | .71 | .001 | 65 |
| Use of grain as food | .51 | .006 | 61 |
| Mining and smelting of metals | 1.00 | .001 | 55 |
| Pottery | .82 | .001 | 60 |
| Secret societies | 1.00 | .001 | 39 |
| Patrilocal residence | .47 | .027 | 61 |
| Age grades | .75 | .003 | 22 |
| Polyandry | −.48 | .053 | 52 |
| Marriage by capture | 1.00 | .007 | 50 |
| Brideprice | .55 | .003 | 62 |
| Postmarital sex restrictions on women | .88 | .001 | 58 |
| Property rights in women | .79 | .009 | 34 |

Adapted from Simmons (1937).

plex without direct appeal to biologically programmed aggression, we suggest that our theory
has important implications beyond the scope of
this paper. The hypothesized causal chain that
links the various parts of the male-supremacist
complex to warfare subsumes, in more parsimonious form, the causal chain established by
John Whiting and his associates linking protein
deficiencies with prolonged nursing and special
training for aggression in males such as initia-
tions, mutilations, ordeals, and vision quests
(Ember 1974). Our theory challenges the use of

the Freudian Oedipus complex as an independent variable in the explanation of intergenerational conflict and sex roles. We reverse the
direction of the Freudian derivation of war and
intergenerational conflict. Intergenerational hostility between males is an integral part of the
male supremacist complex. Our theory points to
the derivation of intense Oedipal conflicts from
war and allows for the possibility that war, Oedipal strife, and the entire masculine supremacist
complex, may be an evanescent phase in the evolution of a stationary world population.

## APPENDIX
List of Societies Used in Tables IV–VIII (including percent of boys and adult men)

| No. | Society | Date of Census | Average Percent of Boys | Average Percent of Adult Males | No. Pop. Censused | Infanti-cide | Warfare |
|---|---|---|---|---|---|---|---|
| | | | ASIA | | | | |
| 1. | Andamanese | 1901 | 62 | 53 | 15 | 1 | 1 |
| 2. | Lepcha | 1937 | 57 | 48 | 1 | 1 | 1 |
| 3. | Miao | 1940 | 56 | 48 | 1 | 1 | 1 |
| 4. | Nicobarese | 1886 | 64 | 54 | 8 | 1 | 1 |
| 5. | Toda | 1870 | 54 | 56 | 3 | 1 | 2 |
| 6. | West Tibet | 1847 | 56 | 45 | 2 | 1 | 1 |
| | | | AFRICA | | | | |
| 7. | Dorobo | 1938 | 53 | 61 | 3 | 1 | 2 |
| 8. | Edo | 1910 | 55 | 47 | 1 | 5 | 1 |
| 9. | Fang | 1951 | 47 | 44 | 3 | 1 | 3 |
| 10. | Ibo | 1912 | 56 | 48 | 3 | 1 | 1 |
| 11. | Katab | 1947 | 53 | 45 | 21 | 1 | 2 |
| 12. | Kukuruku | 1910 | 55 | 46 | 1 | 5 | 1 |
| 13. | Kung | 1952 | 40 | 44 | 19 | 1 | 1 |
| 14. | Lokko | 1931 | 51 | 47 | 1 | 5 | 3 |
| 15. | Mende | 1931 | 49 | 45 | 1 | 5 | 3 |
| 16. | Ngonde | 1931 | 53 | 24 | 2 | 1 | 2 |
| 17. | Nupe | 1934 | 50 | 44 | 3 | 5 | 3 |
| 18. | Tiv | 1929 | 50 | 47 | 14 | 1 | 2 |
| | | | NORTH AMERICA | | | | |
| 19. | Airilik Eskimo | 1907 | 64 | 43 | 1 | 1 | 1 |
| 20. | Alaskan Eskimo | 1839 | 56 | 50 | 3 | 1 | 1 |

| No. | Society | Date of Census | Average Percent of Boys | Average Percent of Adult Males | No. Pop. Censused | Infanti-cide | Warfare |
|---|---|---|---|---|---|---|---|
| | | NORTH AMERICA (continued) | | | | | |
| 21. | Athapascans | 1858 | 37 | 26 | 2 | 1 | 1 |
| 22. | Barren Grounds Esk. | 1929 | 58 | 44 | 5 | 2 | 1 |
| 23. | Bernard Harbor | 1922 | 54 | 52 | 1 | 1 | 1 |
| 24. | Central Eskimo | 1883 | 56 | 49 | 9 | 1 | 1 |
| 25. | Copper Eskimo | 1916 | 25 | 44 | 9 | 1 | 1 |
| 26. | Ponca | 1874 | 49 | 52 | 1 | 4 | 1 |
| 27. | Omaha | 1884 | 48 | 47 | 1 | 4 | 2 |
| 28. | Flatheads | 1884 | 53 | 50 | 1 | 5 | 3 |
| 29. | Greenland Esk. | 1901 | 38 | 35 | 4 | 4 | 2 |
| 30. | Iroquois | 1845 | 49 | 47 | 1 | 2 | 3 |
| 31. | Kaska | 1944 | 46 | 53 | 3 | 1 | 3 |
| 32. | Kutchin | 1858 | 60 | 55 | 3 | 1 | 1 |
| 33. | Netsilik Esk. | 1902 | 68 | 49 | 1 | 1 | 1 |
| 34. | Nootka | 1863 | 51 | 50 | 3 | 5 | 1 |
| 35. | Ogibwa | 1955 | 55 | 49 | 1 | 5 | 3 |
| 36. | Plateau Yumans | 1919 | 49 | 59 | 1 | 2 | 2 |
| 37. | Sauniktumiut | 1902 | 55 | 44 | 1 | 1 | 1 |
| 38. | Seri | 1955 | 52 | 48 | 1 | 5 | 3 |
| 39. | Sinamiut | 1902 | 63 | 50 | 1 | 1 | 1 |
| 40. | Tewa | 1790 | 48 | 52 | 2 | 5 | 3 |
| 41. | Yucatec Maya | 1929 | 53 | 51 | 5 | 3 | 3 |
| | | OCEANIA | | | | | |
| 42. | Aitape | 1914 | 26 | 31 | 2 | 5 | 2 |
| 43. | Amwie Island | 1926 | 48 | 50 | 1 | 5 | 2 |
| 44. | Apui | 1926 | 67 | 77 | 1 | 5 | 1 |
| 45. | Arawa | 1929 | 44 | 56 | 1 | 5 | 2 |
| 46. | Aslingbun | 1926 | 64 | 50 | 1 | 5 | 1 |
| 47. | Aus Island | 1922 | 51 | 72 | 1 | 5 | 1 |
| 48. | Auti | 1926 | 63 | 63 | 1 | 5 | 1 |
| 49. | Baitsi | 1929 | 54 | 56 | 4 | 5 | 2 |
| 50. | Bali Island | 1926 | 50 | 54 | 1 | 1 | 2 |
| 51. | Banoni | 1929 | 62 | 49 | 6 | 5 | 2 |
| 52. | Biawaria | 1927 | 51 | 53 | 2 | 5 | 2 |
| 53. | Buka Island | 1914 | 34 | 20 | 2 | 1 | 2 |
| 54. | Dani | 1962 | 49 | 39 | 1 | 4 | 1 |
| 55. | Dukdukno | 1926 | 50 | 57 | 1 | 5 | 2 |
| 56. | Easter Island | 1878 | 47 | 54 | 2 | 5 | 2 |
| 57. | Emira Island | 1925 | 61 | 50 | 4 | 5 | 2 |
| 58. | Flores Island | 1949 | 52 | 49 | 1 | 5 | 3 |
| 59. | Groote Eylandt | 1960 | 53 | 62 | 1 | 1 | 2 |
| 60. | Iban | 1950 | 62 | 50 | 1 | 2 | 1 |

| No. | Society | Date of Census | Average Percent of Boys | Average Percent of Adult Males | No. Pop. Censused | Infanti- cide | Warfare |
|-----|---------|---------|---------|---------|---------|---------|---------|
| | | | OCEANIA (continued) | | | | |
| 61. | Kapauku | 1954 | 49 | 48 | 5 | 4 | 1 |
| 62. | Lamani | 1927 | 53 | 56 | 1 | 1 | 1 |
| 63. | Maori | 1891 | 57 | 54 | 2 | 2 | 2 |
| 64. | Maring | 1963 | 60 | 54 | 1 | 3 | 1 |
| 65. | Marshall Islands | 1907 | 48 | 48 | 5 | 1 | 1 |
| 66. | Matty Island | 1922 | 51 | 56 | 1 | 5 | 2 |
| 67. | Mismis | 1927 | 53 | 52 | 1 | 1 | 1 |
| 68. | Mokalonglo | 1926 | 78 | 63 | 1 | 5 | 1 |
| 69. | Molbun-Mikeni | 1926 | 100 | 80 | 1 | 5 | 1 |
| 70. | Molo | 1926 | 67 | 54 | 1 | 5 | 1 |
| 71. | Mortlock Islands | 1922 | 60 | 54 | 2 | 5 | 2 |
| 72. | Nagovisi | 1929 | 53 | 55 | 14 | 5 | 1 |
| 73. | So. New Britain | 1926 | 49 | 52 | 8 | 5 | 2 |
| 74. | New Ireland | 1929 | 51 | 56 | 71 | 4 | 2 |
| 75. | Nukumanu | 1922 | 62 | 50 | 1 | 5 | 2 |
| 76. | Peregnen | 1926 | 50 | 81 | 1 | 5 | 1 |
| 77. | Pintubi | 1957 | 55 | 44 | 1 | 5 | 1 |
| 78. | Pukapuka | 1935 | 56 | 50 | 1 | 4 | 3 |
| 79. | Repu | 1927 | 44 | 46 | 1 | 1 | 1 |
| 80. | Romonum Island | 1947 | 54 | 52 | 1 | 1 | 3 |
| 81. | Rook Island | 1926 | 51 | 48 | 1 | 5 | 2 |
| 82. | Samoa | 1920 | 54 | 49 | 4 | 4 | 2 |
| 83. | Santa Cruz | 1960 | 53 | 49 | 1 | 5 | 3 |
| 84. | Siwai | 1928 | 55 | 49 | 33 | 5 | 2 |
| 85. | Solomon Islands | 1938 | 51 | 51 | 1 | 2 | 2 |
| 86. | St. Matthias | 1925 | 54 | 53 | 16 | 5 | 2 |
| 87. | Tasmania | 1800 | 50 | 42 | 1 | 1 | 1 |
| 88. | Telei | 1927 | 62 | 54 | 29 | 5 | 2 |
| 89. | Tikopia | 1928 | 56 | 51 | 2 | 1 | 3 |
| 90. | Truk Islands | 1946 | 58 | 46 | 10 | 1 | 3 |
| 91. | Walbiri | 1957 | 54 | 47 | 1 | 5 | 1 |
| 92. | Waria | 1927 | 64 | 46 | 1 | 1 | 1 |
| 93. | Woleai | 1903 | 56 | 46 | 3 | 4 | 1 |
| 94. | Yangman | 1957 | 45 | 53 | 1 | 5 | 1 |
| 95. | Yap | 1948 | 55 | 53 | 2 | 2 | 3 |
| 96. | Zia | 1927 | 49 | 59 | 1 | 5 | 2 |
| | | | SOUTH AMERICA | | | | |
| 97. | Aymara | 1953 | 54 | 51 | 5 | 2 | 3 |
| 98. | Bacairi | 1884 | 56 | 59 | 1 | 2 | 1 |
| 99. | Bush Negroes | 1958 | 50 | 50 | 1 | 4 | 3 |
| 100. | Caraja | 1908 | 51 | 47 | 2 | 2 | 1 |
| 101. | Cuna | 1929 –40 | 51 | 48 | 92 | 2 | 3 |

APPENDIX
(Continued)

| No. | Society | Date of Census | Average Percent of Boys | Average Percent of Adult Males | No. Pop. Censused | Infanti-cide | Warfare |
|-----|---------|--------|--------|--------|--------|--------|--------|
| | | SOUTH AMERICA (continued) | | | | | |
| 102. | Guana | 1918 | 57 | 47 | 2 | 1 | 1 |
| 103. | Jivaro | 1946 | 46 | 41 | 3 | 2 | 1 |
| 104. | Siriono | 1941 | 45 | 29 | 2 | 2 | 1 |
| 105. | Tapirape | 1935 | 59 | 53 | 2 | 1 | 1 |
| 106. | Trumai | 1938 | 80 | 52 | 1 | 1 | 1 |
| 107. | Uru | 1942 | 44 | 40 | 1 | 5 | 1 |
| 108. | Warao | 1954 | 50 | 48 | 1 | 2 | 3 |
| 109. | Yanomamo | 1966 | 57 | 50· | 26 | 1 | 1 |
| 110. | Yauro | 1947 | 50 | 40 | 4 | 5 | 3 |
| 111. | Yupa | 1954 | 61 | 47 | 2 | 5 | 1 |
| 112. | Yuruna | 1884 | 45 | 52 | 6 | 5 | 1 |

Infanticide codes: 1 = commonly practiced, 2 = occasionally, 3 = not common, 4 = not practiced, 5 = no information.

Warfare codes: 1 = war present at time of census or stopped within 5 years, 2 = war stopped from 5–25 years before census was taken, 3 = war stopped 26 or more years prior to the census.

## NOTES

1. An earlier version of this paper was presented before the New York Academy of Sciences on 15 October 1974.

2. The data for Tables IV through VIII come from a sample of 561 populations comprising 112 different cultures (see Appendix). Societies were included in the sample if data were available on (1) the age-sex structure of one or more populations and (2) the presence of warfare, or, if absent, how many years had it been stopped prior to the census date. Data were collected by an unsystematic search of the literature and by examining the entire 300 societies processed in the Human Relations Area Files. While the sample is not random, we feel it is generally representative of the universe of preindustrial societies because (1) its large size greatly reduces the likelihood of sampling error, (2) the universe of HRAF societies is reasonably representative of the world's major geographical regions, and (3) no society encountered was dropped from the sample if information were available on the number of boys, girls, and adult men and women in a given population.

The percentage of boys and adult men were calculated for each population, and averages were computed for each of the warfare and infanticide categories in Tables IV through VIII; these percentages were then transformed into sex ratios of males per 100 females. We do not doubt that coding errors have been made. However, we feel that overall the data are reliable and our results are not due to systematic error bias. Some of the census data, including date of census, percentage of young and adult males, number of populations censused, and codings on infanticide and warfare for each society in the sample have been published elsewhere (Divale 1970, 1972). A listing of all the data used in this paper appears by society in the Appendix.

3. Simmons (1937) provides information on warfare frequency and 108 cultural practices and beliefs for a sample of 71 societies. We do not defend his sample or codings and have used them only because they permit a preliminary test of some hypotheses deduced from our theory. Simmons' variables are measured on a four-point ranked scale, but analysis suggests that his data do not warrant more than a two-point ordinal scale. The scales were thus collapsed, and one of his traits, "Prevalence of Warfare," was correlated with the relevant variables.

# REFERENCES CITED

BAHADUR, RAI, ANANT RAM JAMMU, and J. SHARMA
1933 Jammu and Kashmir State. *In* Census of India, 1931, Vol. 24, Pt. 1.

BIRDSELL, JOSEPH
1968 Some Predictions for the Pleistocene Based on Equilibrium Systems among Recent Hunter-Gatherers. *In* Man the Hunter. Richard B. Lee and Irven DeVore, eds. Pp. 229–249. Chicago: Aldine.

CARNEIRO, ROBERT L.
1970 A Theory of the Origin of the State. Science 169:733–738.

CARNEIRO, ROBERT L., and DAISY F. HILSE
1966 On Determining the Probable Rate of Population Growth during the Neolithic. American Anthropologist 68:177–181.

CAVALLI-SFORZA, L. L., and W. BODMAN
1971 The Genetics of Human Populations. San Francisco: W. H. Freeman.

CHAGNON, NAPOLEON
1973 The Culture-Ecology of Shifting (Pioneering) Cultivation among the Yanomamo Indians. *In* Peoples and Cultures of Native South America. Daniel R. Gross, ed. Pp. 126–142. New York: Natural History Press.

1974 Studying the Yanomamo. New York: Holt, Rinehart and Winston.

COALE, AUSLEY
1974 The History of Human Populations. Scientific American 231(3):41–51.

DICKEMAN, MILDRED
1975a Demographic Consequences of Infanticide in Man. Annual Review of Ecology and Systematics 6:107–137.

1975b Female Infanticide and Hypergamy: A Neglected Relationship. Paper presented at the 74th Annual Meeting of the American Anthropological Association, San Francisco.

DIVALE, WILLIAM TULIO
1970 An Explanation for Primitive Warfare: Population Control and Significance of Primitive Sex Ratios. New Scholar 2:173–192.

1971 Ibo Population Control: The Ecology of Warfare and Social Organization. California Anthropologist 1(1):10–24.

1972 Systemic Population Control in the Middle and Upper Palaeolithic: Inferences Based on Contemporary Hunter-Gatherers. World Archaeology 4:222–243.

1973 Warfare in Primitive Societies: A Bibliography. Santa Barbara: American Bibliographic Center-Clio Press.

1974a Migration, External Warfare, and Matrilocal Residence. Behavior Science Research 9:75–133.

1974b The Causes of Matrilocal Residence: A Cross-Ethnohistorical Survey. University Microfilms No 75–7742. Ann Arbor: University Microfilms.

1976 Female Status and Cultural Evolution: A Study in Ethnographer Bias. Behavior Science Research. (in press).

EMBER, MELVIN
1974 Warfare, Sex Ratio and Polygyny. Ethnology 13:197–206.

EMBER, MELVIN, and CAROL R. EMBER
1971 The Conditions Favoring Matrilocal versus Patrilocal Residence. American Anthropologist 73:571–594.

FRISCH, ROSE, and JANET MCARTHUR
1974 Menstrual Cycles: Fatness as a Determinant of Minimum Weight for Height Necessary for Their Maintenance or Onset. Science 185:949–951.

GANGLOFF, DEBORAH
n.d. Sex Bias in Primitive Religions. Manuscript, York College, City University of New York.

GOODY, JACK, and S. T. TAMBIAH
1973 Bridewealth and Dowry. Cambridge: Cambridge University Press.

GROSS, DANIEL R.
1975 Protein Capture and Cultural Development in the Amazon Basin. American Anthropologist 77:526–549.

HARRIS, MARVIN
1972 Warfare Old and New. Natural History 81(3):18, 20.

1974  Cows, Pigs, Wars and Witches: The Riddles of Culture. New York: Random House.

1975  Culture, People, Nature. Second ed. New York: Crowell.

HASSAN, FERKI
1973  On Mechanisms of Population Growth during the Neolithic. Current Anthropology 14:535–540.

KOLATA, GINA
1974  !Kung Hunter-Gatherers: Feminism, Diet, and Birth Control. Science 185:932–934.

LEE, RICHARD B.
1972  The !Kung Bushmen of Botswana. In Hunters and Gatherers Today. M. G. Bichiere, ed. Pp. 327–367. New York: Holt, Rinehart and Winston.

LIVINGSTON, FRANK
1968  The Effect of War on the Biology of the Human Species. In War: The Anthropology of Armed Conflict and Aggression. Morton H. Fried, Marvin Harris, and Robert F. Murphy, eds. Pp. 3–15. New York: Doubleday.

LIZOT, J.
1971  Aspects economique et sociaux du changement cultural chez les Yanomamis. L'Homme 11:2–51.

LORIMER, FRANK, et al.
1954  Culture and Human Fertility. Paris: UNESCO.

MORREN, GEORGE E. B., JR.
1973  Woman the Hunter. Paper presented at the 72nd Annual Meeting of the American Anthropological Association, New Orleans.

MURDOCK, GEORGE P.
1949  Social Structure. New York: Free Press.

1967  Ethnographic Atlas. Pittsburgh: University of Pittsburgh Press.

NAROLL, MAUD
n.d.  Attila's Sister: Women's Occupations in Pre-Industrial Society. Manuscript, State University of New York, Buffalo.

NAROLL, RAOUL, and WILLIAM TULIO DIVALE
1976  Natural Selection in Cultural Evolution: Warfare versus Peaceful Diffusion. American Ethnologist 3:97–128.

NEEL, J. V., and K. M. WEISS
1975  The Genetic Structure of a Tribal Population, the Yanomama Indians. American Journal of Physical Anthropology 42:25–51.

OTTERBEIN, KEITH
1970  The Evolution of War. New Haven: HRAF Press.

ROSS, J., and E. ROSS
n.d.  Untitled manuscript, Columbia University.

SANDAY, PEGGY R.
1973  Toward a Theory of the Status of Women. American Anthropologist 75:1682–1700.

SCHLEGEL, ALICE
1972  Male Dominance and Female Autonomy. New Haven: HRAF Press.

SIPES, RICHARD G.
1973  War, Sports and Aggression: An Empirical Test of Two Rival Theories. American Anthropologist 75:64–86.

SIMMONS, LEO W.
1937  Statistical Correlations in the Science of Society. In Studies in the Science of Society. George P. Murdock, ed. Pp. 495–517. New Haven: Yale University Press.

THOMLINSON, RALPH
1965  Population Dynamics. New York: Random House.

THOMPSON, W.
1942  Population Problems. New York: McGraw-Hill.

VAN GINNEKEN, J. K.
1974  Prolonged Breastfeeding as a Birth Spacing Method. Studies in Family Planning 5:201–208.

WITKOWSKI, STANLEY
n.d.  Environmental Familiarity and Models of Band Organization. Manuscript, Northern Illinois University.

# RELIGIOUS SYSTEMS

Culture gives people confidence. By providing them with knowledge, beliefs, and customs, culture facilitates a sense of control, a feeling of familiarity with what is going on. Most of our culture concerns everyday things, the people, places, actions, and events that regularly occupy our time. It allows us to interpret our world and act in an appropriate way. But occasionally our actions fail to work as they should. Things go wrong; other people succeed, while we fail using the same cultural plan. In short, there are events and conditions that usual cultural formulas cannot explain. Religion has been the cultural answer to such anomalies.

*Religion* refers to the beliefs and practices related to the supernatural that we use to cope with the ultimate problems of our existence. People everywhere wonder about the basic problems of existence: life's meaning, death, and evil. Why are we alive? What is the significance of what we do? What is death? Why do death and disease strike so unevenly? To answer these questions, people in many societies believe in a supernatural system, a variety of gods, spirits, or powers that seem "beyond the natural" and that account for the origin of the world and the outcome of activities in it.

Religious systems vary immensely. Some, like the Judeo-Christian tradition of the West, focus on personal salvation. God is creator and master of the world. People work within his world and are saved for a more perfect existence by faith in him and by the moral conduct of daily life. Mbuti pygmies have no concept equivalent to salvation. Their divine world is equal to their natural one, the Ituri Forest in which they live and hunt. Their religious objective is to identify with the forest, to keep it, their world, happy and balanced. There are no supernatural beings active in their lives.

But in many societies where anthropologists have conducted field work, religion involves a host of supernatural beings and powers. There are usually superior gods and goddesses, creators and controllers of the world. There are also numerous other supernatural beings who live among people and who act there to affect the outcome of daily events. Unfortunate luck, sickness, an abundant crop, untimely death, all can be explained by the intervention of these beings.

It is not surprising to find that people attempt to communicate with spirits who play such an immediate role in their daily lives. In religious systems such as these, we often find divination, the act of posing and receiving answers to questions through supernatural intervention. Spirit possession also is a common feature of these systems. Possession occurs when spirits inhabit a person's body, controlling his or her actions and communicating directly with human observers. People who are possessed appear to be in what Western observers call a trance, and what they say and do is supposed to reflect the personality of the possessing supernatural being.

In some cases, people look forward to possession. Special mediums become possessed by supernatural beings so that the spirits' help can be requisitioned or other matters discussed. In possession, such spirits talk to people, warning them of transgressions and complimenting them on proper ritual performance. They may take responsibility for troubles and, depending on their inclination, agree to help when things go wrong. Possession cults are found in many societies around the world.

Demonic possession, or spirit possession by evil supernatural beings bent on harming their hosts, is often found alongside mediumistic possession. If supernatural beings possess mediums to communicate, why can't malevolent beings do the same thing? But malevolent possession is not found in every society where supernatural beings are close at hand, nor does it affect everyone in societies where it does occur. From a scientific standpoint, how can we explain the presence of such a negative and potentially frightening custom?

The articles presented in this section deal with this question. Drawn from field work in India and Ceylon, where demonic possession is common (it is also found in many other parts of the world), these articles look at the nature and distribution of possession in an effort to discover its functions for people. Opler points out the relationship between possession and the special strains that some Indians endure. Freed and Freed show a relationship between possession and both internal and external anxiety. Stirrat treats possession as a collective representation.

# 25

## SPIRIT POSSESSION IN A RURAL AREA OF NORTHERN INDIA

*Morris E. Opler*

*In every society, people endure stress caused by the context of their lives. In the United States, we undergo pressure associated with such events as examinations, changed jobs, heart attacks, and rejection by others. In India, people also encounter stress. Young women become anxious about moving into their husband's household upon marriage. Rural boys, many of whom must go at least temporarily to cities for work, find life there frightening. Low-caste people resent having to pay deference to those of higher station. Many feel powerless in the presence of disease. It is stressful situations such as these that Morris Opler links to demonic spirit possession in this article. He sees possession as a device through which people can express and project their anxieties and enlist the aid and support of others. It is a way Indians manage to meet their psychological needs.*

It is widely believed in India, especially among the rural folk and the less educated, that misfortune and epidemic or persistent sickness are in actuality punishment and persecution visited upon the locality, the family, or the individual by a displeased god or goddess or a malevolent ghost. Consequently, in order to right matters, it is necessary to determine what deity or ghost is involved, why the supernatural attack has been launched, and what is required to pacify the deity or banish the ghost. Often the identity of the troublesome supernatural power can be established rather readily. A specific goddess is identified with smallpox, and if an epidemic of smallpox rages it is quite certain that the smallpox goddess is displeased and has grievances or unfulfilled demands. It is, however, less easy to learn the cause of the goddess' ire and what must be done to hasten her departure. Often, too, it is rather easy to guess that a certain malevolent ghost is at the root of a personal misfortune, for the difficulty may have arisen soon after a weird or unpleasant experience at a place where some person met a violent and untimely death and where his restless spirit is reputed to hover. But

why the shade should pick the particular victim and what must be done to force it to release its baneful hold is, again, much harder to settle.

Obviously the surest guide to all these questions, and especially to the more subtle ones, will be the words of the deity or ghost itself. And pronouncements from these sources are precisely what are sought. In order to obtain the explanations and directions of the supernaturals involved, a state of trance and possession develops or is induced in which the deities enter and speak through their devotees or those they have possessed, or during which the malevolent spirit speaks through the victim it has "caught" and from whose body it must be ousted. In instances where a malevolent ghost has entered the body of the sufferer and speaks through him, the shaman or religious practitioner acts to hasten the trance state, questions the possessing spirit and argues with it, pits his tutelary gods against the invading spirit, and either persuades it to leave or sets a trap for it which will force departure, capture, or transfer.

It is not the intention here to describe the phenomenon of possession in detail and at length. For the purposes of this article it is not necessary to dwell upon the recruitment of devotees and shamans or to discuss their procedures. The emphasis will be, rather, on the areas of anxiety that are suggested by the nature of the illnesses and misfortunes and by the identity of the spirits or individuals who are held responsible for the onslaught. For it must be remembered that in these cases of possession it is the victim through whom the invading or troublesome spirit speaks. Consequently the victim has an unusual opportunity to identify anyone whom he believes has sent the ghost to persecute him, and to air any opinion he has concerning why this was done. Such cases, considered in their general social and psychological setting, may point to the conditions that stimulate possession and to the functions that spirit possession serve, at least in the region from which the data come.

The widow of a man who had recently been beaten to death as a result of a political and intercaste feud suddenly began to curse and snap at those around her, shouting that she would bite and eat them. Her diatribes were directed particularly at a woman of her own caste with whom she had quarreled and at members of another, higher caste who had been involved in the assault on her husband. Normally she would have been expected to show respect and deference to members of the latter caste. The woman, who was now recognized as being possessed, started to run away, but was caught and held down. A shaman who was working in a nearby field was summoned and began to carry out his ritual for her. When he demanded to know who the spirit possessing the woman was, the spirit, using the voice of a woman, identified itself as a *churain* or malevolent female ghost. It was the usual voice of the woman that was heard, except that the words were uttered somewhat more slowly and deliberately. After further ministrations of the shaman the ghost announced: "I am going; I am going." The shaman acidly expressed his disbelief that the ghost was really departing and demanded that the ghost lick its own spittle as

an earnest of its intention. At this the woman spat in her hand and licked up the saliva. The ghost then announced: "I am leaving." The woman now seemed to recover and spoke in a normal and calm manner to those around her. She professed to have no recollection of what happened during the period of active possession. This woman, who is short-tempered and moody at best, had more than enough cause for smoldering anger. It is possible to interpret this attack as a case of hysteria associated with attempts to master an overwhelming urge toward overt aggression, something unseemly in a woman and socially unacceptable when directed toward those of higher status, but understandable and forgivable as the activity of a malevolent and reckless ghost.

A villager met a violent death and therefore it was expected that he would become a vengeful ghost. Another villager who had quarreled with the dead man about the ownership of a piece of land was visited one night by the ghost of the deceased, which demanded that he surrender the land. This he refused to do. Soon after, he became ill and it was only a few weeks before he, too, was dead. It was accepted that the ghost had entered his body and laid him low. That this man had a guilty conscience in regard to the land transaction is very clear, and it is also certain that the circumstances of his rival's death aggravated this feeling. To what extent the fear and despondency arising from this contributed to his sickness and death is not known, for he had no adequate medical examination and treatment. But whatever the origin of his sickness, the despair and the terror induced by the attentions of his rival's ghost did him no good.

A young man of untouchable caste, a Hindu, left the village and found employment in a mill in a city. He was told that a path he took from his place of residence to the mill was infested with ghosts of Muslims, but he laughed at such tales and continued to take this route. Then he had a severe and persistent case of boils and had to leave his job and return to the village. In the village he became violent and abusive and was constantly in trouble. He would speak out against the high-caste landlords and tell them he was a Muslim spirit and couldn't be harmed by them. He narrowly escaped a beating at the hands of these indignant prominent villagers. It was apparent to his kinfolk that he was in the clutches of a ghost, and a shaman was brought to treat him. At first the spirit or spirits which had entered him would not reply to the shaman's questions, though they caused his body to move convulsively and with great violence. It turned out that there were four Muslim spirits within him, who identified themselves and made their wishes known after three days of ceremony. When the ceremony had been concluded and the offerings for which the spirits asked had been given, the patient began to recover.

Villagers who go to urban industrial establishments to work ordinarily live in cramped, unhygienic quarters and have a very inadequate diet. Often, as in this case, they fall sick and have to return to their homes. But often, too, the greater social freedom and anonymity enjoyed in the city make it more difficult for them upon their return to accept the more rigid caste and status restrictions of the rural environment. In this case the young man apparently scoffed at the tales of evil spirits of Muslims (in the city to which he went there was a large Muslim population and considerable tension between Hindus and Muslims) until he himself became sick. Then he became thoroughly frightened and was convinced that evil influences were working against him. Possession allowed him to objectify these causes of fear and make them available for treatment. Possession and the attribution of what he said and did to the invading Muslim spirits also allowed him to vent his feelings with a minimum of danger on the proud high-caste group for whom his own caste have been traditional servants.

A woman who was sure she was being persecuted by a ghost was told by a shaman whom she consulted that her tormentor was the spirit of her husband's first wife. The first wife had been attacked by ghosts while in Calcutta and had come back to the village to die. Having been killed by ghosts, she herself became one and now made difficulties for her successor. There are two interesting facets to this situation. It will be noted that the first wife was attacked by ghosts and sickened when she joined her husband who was working in a city far from their home. Villagers, and especially village women, are often lonely and unhappy in such circumstances and live under conditions that invite sickness. Such an illness, contracted in a strange place and in frightening circumstances, is then frequently attributed to ghosts unless another origin is very obvious or the malady yields readily to ordinary treatment. The other matter which deserves attention is that the dead woman caused difficulty for the second wife of the man to whom she had been married. A woman who marries a widower is expected to honor and worship the deceased wife. Any laxity or reluctance in this, or anything that gives cause for belief that the dead woman has become a ghost, is likely to result in psychological uneasiness.

A young man attributed violent attacks from which he suffered and during which he spoke abusively to those around him and sought to strike them, to the activities of a number of ghosts of Muslims who had "caught" him when he was working in an industrial center some distance away from the village. It took several people to hold him down when he had such seizures and not even close relatives, such as his mother and sister, were immune from his invective. The attacks had continued for about a year when he gave his account, and he had suffered an attack about twenty days before he was interviewed. Shamans had identified three of the ghosts while he was possessed; but a fourth one had not yet spoken through him, and this elusive and resistant spirit presumably was the cause of his continued trouble. This case presents some familiar features. The affliction begins when the youth is employed in the city. Muslim ghosts cause him to be rancorous toward his Hindu relatives and neighbors. He is abusive toward persons to whom he normally shows respect. It might be mentioned that these events occurred during a period when there was quite a bit of tension between India and Pakistan and between Hindus and Muslims in India. The young man was undoubtedly impressed by the difference in the attitudes toward such matters in the village, which is almost entirely Hindu and in which the Muslims are submissive and unimportant, and the city, where the Muslims were a sizable group and where strained relations existed for a time. Some unconscious scapegoating on the part of this young man, in which Muslim ghosts conveniently serve to mask his own aggressions and adequacies, can be inferred.

Eight of ten children born to a village woman died in infancy. Finally a shaman was called. He traced the cause of the deaths to a ghost and named a family which he said had sent the unfriendly spirit. Since the sufferer was of the same caste as those who had sent the ghost, a caste assembly was called. The evidence concerning the ghost and its provenience was reviewed, and the accused family was ordered to take back its ghost. This they agreed to do. In this instance the early death of so many children gave rise to the suspicion that ghosts and some kind of sustained attack were involved. One of the most common fears among women is that ghosts will impair their childbearing capacities or destroy their infants, and a good many precautions are taken to prevent such occurrences. Also, it is generally believed that ghosts are seldom destroyed or reformed; they are most often merely transferred. Usually a shaman can persuade a ghost to leave its host only if he provides or promises to provide another "vehicle." Often the transferral is accomplished without malice. The ghost is secured by the shaman in some ritual objects which are then buried at a crossroad. The first vulnerable person who passes this place becomes the new host for the spirit. Or the ghost may be imprisoned by the shaman in a clove or a flower which he touches to the garment of almost any person at some large gathering. In such a case he may not even know the person to whom the ghost is being transferred. But

whether the ghost is specifically intended for them or not, the family to which it becomes transferred will be indignant and will be aggressive in their demands that the ghost be recalled by its former owners.

An epidemic of smallpox was raging in a hamlet of the village. Two outsiders were invited to the hamlet to use ritual means to arrest the sickness. During their stay they were being provided for and paid by contributions from the inhabitants of the hamlet. One of these visitors was a devotee of the smallpox goddess, a person who had directed so much ritual attention and propitiation to the goddess that he had a special relation to her, received messages from her, and was believed to have influence over her. The second person was a gardener and flower seller, a member of a caste which traditionally is involved in the curing of smallpox. One family head refused to contribute to the cause, on the grounds that the sickness was continuing unabated and the visitors were accomplishing no good. Then thirteen members of this man's extended family caught the disease. The villager still refused to contribute, for he suspected that it was the devotee, angered by his attitude, who had sent the smallpox goddess (the disease) to his house. Instead he himself made ritual offerings to the goddess, who is the personification of the disease. Early one morning, when he was carrying out a fire ritual or sacrifice to the goddess, his youngest son, who was one of those ill with smallpox, spoke to him disrespectfully, an evidence that the boy was possessed and that in reality it was the smallpox goddess who was speaking. The goddess continued to speak to him through his son. She praised him for his ceremonial offerings, advised him about future offerings to her, and informed him that she would respond if he would carry out such ceremonies whenever smallpox or cholera spread. Following this all of his family members recovered and this man himself became a devotee of the smallpox goddess. It is interesting that the onset of possession and the appearance of the goddess was signaled in this case by the breakdown of inhibition and social convention, by the disrespect shown by the son for his father. The deities so often display attitudes forbidden by convention to man!

In May, 1953, during a cholera epidemic, this new devotee played a prominent part in attempting to pacify the sickness goddess. He and others arranged and purified an outdoor site for a ceremony and kindled a fire of mango leaves there. While a drum was beaten and the names of various gods and goddesses were uttered, he and another man ladled clarified butter into the fire. One of the group of men present lit a stick of incense in the fire and stared at it fixedly as prayer and the mention of the names of the deities continued. Finally he leaped up, jumped forward and backward, extended his arms and then fell to the ground. When he arose his forearms and hands were shaking violently. It was evident that he was possessed by a spirit. In a restrained and respectful voice the devotee asked him who he was. He answered that he was Sitala, one of the personified aspects of the disease goddess, in fact the aspect usually associated with smallpox. The devotee drew out the information that the goddess was visiting the village in the terrible guise of disease because she was dissatisfied with the offerings made to her. She wanted certain songs to be sung in her honor and a band provided for the music. Hastily women were summoned to sing the required songs. At that the possessed man recovered, stopped shaking, and sat down and looked into the fire. During the singing of the songs still another man became possessed, leaped into the air, and fell writhing to the ground. Soon he rose to his knees, shook his hands back and forth, and invited the devotee to ask him who he was. It was learned that he was possessed by a different aspect of the disease goddess who demanded still more singing and a brighter ceremonial fire. At this the women sang with increased vigor. The fire was fed again and the possessed person stopped shaking and resumed his place. No sooner was he relaxed than the man who had first been possessed showed evidence of agitation. The de-

votee requested that he identify himself and the disease goddess spoke through him, issuing some general and vague warnings. She said that the people were overproud of their hamlet and of its increase in size and had become too self-satisfied. When asked what specific things they should do to regain her favor, she would say no more than that they should be careful and should remember that she lives everywhere and goes anywhere she likes. She admitted that she was pleased with the ceremony but warned them again to be careful unless they wished to be obliged to spend a great deal of money in corrective ceremonies. Now drumming and singing were resumed and a procession which circled the hamlet counterclockwise was begun. During the march ritual objects were left at the four cardinal directions, beginning with the north. The devotee was one of the leaders of the procession and a director of the ritual acts which punctuate it. Two days later a very similar rite of possession and divination was held in another hamlet of the village.

About ten days after these appearances of the disease goddess in public rituals, she possessed and spoke through the body of a woman of the grain-parcher caste. The hands of the woman began moving back and forth, her face became expressionless, she fell to the ground and rolled back and forth rhythmically as her hair fell around her in disorder. Frequently she would scream in a high-pitched voice and announce that she was the disease goddess. Her husband and a caste-fellow sought to induce the goddess to leave her body by offering a sacrificial fire and repeating prayers. The unhappy husband, who was not at all pleased with the visit of the goddess to his home, kept repeating, "You are not the disease goddess, you are my wife." A brahman priest had been sent for, and his first act upon arrival was to offer still another fire sacrifice to the goddess. The possessed woman tried several times to brush glowing coals from the fire into the folds of her garment, and her husband was kept busy brushing them away and restraining her. The ability to handle fire and hot objects is often considered a sign of the presence of a deity or of a grant of supernatural power. A group of men and women had gathered by this time, and some of them began to ask the "goddess" questions. One high-caste woman repeatedly inquired about the nature of the sickness of her daughter-in-law. This apparently annoyed the goddess, for the possessed low-caste woman slapped the questioner, something that a woman of her caste could never do with impunity in normal circumstances. Yet in this setting the rebuff was taken calmly. Another woman asked whether her son, who was reported to be sick in Bombay, would recover. The answer was in the affirmative. Whenever the goddess spoke through the possessed woman, those who were present would bow reverently and touch the earth. Finally the brahman's prayers and sacred fire ceremony achieved their purpose, for the possessed woman collapsed on the ground and slowly returned to her normal state. It was mentioned by someone present that the possessed woman's father had been a well-known devotee of the disease goddess and that she herself had had a similar experience of possession only a year before.

When a certain woman of the village married, she and her husband took up residence in her parents' home. The usual custom is for the woman to accompany her husband to his father's village and home at marriage. Since the young man was more or less cut off from his patrilineal kin by this move, he made no efforts to worship the family gods of his paternal line regularly. Matters continued like this until the oldest son of this couple was about fifteen years old. This boy then began to act strangely. He would disobey his parents, curse them, and remain away from home for long periods. A diviner was hired who told the parents that the boy was possessed by a displeased goddess who expected homage from members of the father's line. A shaman of a nearby village was next consulted and, during the ritual which he conducted, the goddess spoke through the son and complained of neglect. When the mother

pointed out that the father's family worshiped not one but three family deities and that the two others would be angry if this goddess alone were honored, the goddess spoke through the son to say that she would prevent the other godlings from causing difficulty to the family. This greatly relieved the mother, for ceremonies of this kind are expensive, involving as they do the sacrifice of animals and much else. And so the goddess was formally installed as a family deity of this branch of the line. Once every three years the family arranges an impressive ceremony in her honor, during which the son becomes possessed, makes known the will and prophecies of the goddess, and, while still possessed, puts the sacrificial fire out with his bare hands without suffering any burns.

A village boy of about thirteen years of age was staying in Bombay with his father and father's brothers who were working in the city as grain parchers and venders. The father went back to the village to visit, leaving the boy in the custody of the uncles. Soon after the departure of the father the boy's "brain became hot." He talked wildly and incessantly, saying that all people around him were evil and crazy. He repeatedly ran away. The unhappy uncles took the boy to shamans in Bombay, who told them the boy was possessed by three types of ghosts of deceased Muslims. They were not successful in inducing all three to leave the boy at once and so the boy did not fully recover. He was therefore brought back to the village and to his parents, where other ceremonies conducted by a religious practitioner of another village proved effective.

When the news of the ceremonies to be conducted for this boy spread, a young man with broadly similar but even more acute complaints was brought for treatment at the hands of the same imported religious practitioner. This young man, who was also of the grain-parcher caste, had been living in Bombay too. His father was dead and his mother asked the boy's married sister who lived in the city to make room for him in her household. The young man found employment in a Bombay mill. But the boy and his brother-in-law disliked one another, and the situation was soon very unpleasant. One day the boy began to act strangely. He made obeisance to donkeys on the street. He began to sprinkle the urine of cattle and his own urine on his head and body. He showed symptoms of great fear and declared that a ghost in a nearby tree was trying to devour him. His delusions had a political note, for, though he is a Hindu, he shouted that Pakistan is going to beat India, that Muslims are fine people, and declared that he would shoot Gandhi and Nehru. Gandhi, incidentally, had been assassinated six years before. It did not take his brother-in-law long to decide to send him back to his mother. At the ceremony arranged by his mother the shaman cuffed the boy around rather harshly. This was intended as punishment of the possessing spirits and a means of making them uncomfortable and willing to leave. Such forthright methods are not uncommon in shamanistic practice when possession is certain. The shaman determined that the boy was possessed by two malignant spirits, both of Muslim origin. One, a result of black magic which his brother-in-law had had worked on him, had attacked him while he was at the latrine and this accounted for his unsavory behavior with urine. The other was able to enter his body because he stole and ate sweetmeats which a woman was carrying to a temple. It was because of this spirit that he extolled Pakistan and voiced threats against India's leaders. Once these troublesome spirits were ousted, the youth became quiet and respectful and was able to leave for his home village with his mother and younger brother.

It is to be noted that in both these cases the young men were far from home and unhappy when the evil spirits entered their bodies. Partition of India between Pakistan and India and resulting difficulties and riots between Hindus and Muslims were part of the childhood memories of the youths. Continued tension between the two countries and between Hindus and Muslims in India was a theme of which they heard a great deal in the new urban surroundings. It is little wonder that the ghosts which bothered these Hindus, by a process of projection and scapegoating, took on a Muslim coloring.

In early April, 1954, during a nine-day period especially devoted to the worship and propitiation of the goddess of disease, the house of a shaman, as was usual during this period, was filled with women seeking aid from troublesome spirits who had "caught" or possessed them. The shaman sang a type of song associated with the goddess and beat a monotonous rhythm on his drum until a woman who was seated in the back showed signs of the activity of the ghost within her. He had her come forward to the sacrificial fire and squatted before her. Her hands, palms pressed together, were before her, and her head was shaking back and forth.

The shaman addressed the ghost and demanded to know where it had seized the woman. The ghost, speaking through the voice of the afflicted woman, replied that it had "caught" her when she was returning to her husband's house and village from her father's home. The shaman then asked who had sent the ghost to the woman. The ghost refused to reveal this. Next the shaman wanted to know the caste of the person responsible for the assault. This, too, the ghost refused to reveal. To the question, "How many other ghosts are with you?" the ghost who was conversing with the shaman answered, "Four or five." The shaman then asked the ghost, "Has any other shaman looked at you?" and the ghost replied, "Several, but they didn't make her speak." The shaman next asked bluntly, "Will you leave her?" The response was, "Only if I get another vehicle like her." The shaman then sought to persuade the ghost to leave. He told it that the woman was very poor and hardly a fit vehicle for it. He promised the ghost that at a certain religious fair garlands of flowers, ornaments, coconut, and other offerings would be made to it. He also promised the ghost that at the same time he would provide it with another vehicle; that is, that he would make it possible for the ghost to enter some other victim.

During the dialogue, when the ghost was refusing to answer some of the questions, other women sitting around urged that the ghost be induced to become more "active" so that the woman could be more violently possessed and tell everything. The shaman agreed to ask the ghost to become more active. The ghost explained that it could possess her more violently but that, if it did, the patient would die. In the end the shaman took a flower, placed it on the ground, and asked the ghost to descend from the woman's body and enter the blossom. He said that the ghost would have to live with his tutelary godling, the deified spirit of a brahman, until he could transfer him to another person. It should be mentioned that the woman who was treated, like most of the other women who came for help, was comparatively young.

The factor to which particular attention should be called in this case is that the ghost, speaking through the victim, established the onset of the trouble during the journey from the parents' home to the husband's home. In this connection it should be kept in mind that village exogamy is practiced in this part of India and that residence after marriage is patrilocal. Marriage also entails for the woman many restrictions on movement and behavior in her husband's village and many special forms of avoidance and polite usage to her husband's kinsmen, and, by extension, to his fellow villagers, particularly the males. This contrasts markedly with the comparative freedom a girl enjoys in her father's home and as a "daughter" of her father's village. Since marriage is ordinarily hypergamous, with the husband's family belonging to a superior section of the same caste, at marriage a woman enters a family which considers itself higher in status than the one from which she has come. As a new bride she comes as the most junior and subordinate member of the family and only with time, with the arrival of new brides, and with the birth to her of sons, is her comparative position likely to improve to any extent. In story, proverb, and song, the society has from her earliest years reminded her of

the sharpness of the transition at marriage, and of the possible hostility of the mother-in-law and sisters-in-law.

If it is a joint or extended family with a number of sons to which she goes, she will find there other wives from different villages and family backgrounds with whom she must live at close quarters and with whom she may or may not get along well. She comes as a stranger, for it would be most unseemly for her to have known her husband or his family beforehand. If she has grievances, it would do her little good to complain to her husband, for he is expected dutifully to support his parents in their decisions, and would be most likely to command his wife sternly to obey his elders. Actually her main recourse is to get word to her own parents and brothers of any great unhappiness or mistreatment and have them intervene on her behalf.

Because of the sharp break in the life of the newly wed woman, and because she is often so young at marriage, the society has provided for frequent and prolonged visits of the married woman to her parents' home, especially during the early period of matrimony. If the girl is fearful, uncertain of her ability to cope with the situation, or unhappy about her husband or his family, the return trip to the husband's house after the relaxed atmosphere during a visit to the parental home and village may be an anxious period. It is not unusual, therefore, for a girl, as in the case just described, to be "caught" by a ghost on the journey from her parents' home to that of her husband and to become ill after her arrival.

It may be well to mention here other acute anxieties which not infrequently are associated with the early years of the married state. A woman who does not conceive, who suffers miscarriage, or who does not bear a son after some years of wedded life may have reason to fear for her status and happiness in the family circle. It is almost certain that she, and her husband's family too, will wonder if a ghost or malignant spirit is not at the root of her trouble.

One other potential cause of anxiety and distress in the early phase of marital life might be added to the list. A girl who has been a "pet" of her father's household (and often the knowledge that a girl will be under strict surveillance and will have to work hard in her husband's household is the rationalization for leniency and permissiveness in the parental home) may find the restrictions and obscurity of her new role difficult to accept. Possession by ghosts and spirits calls attention to the young woman, fosters a more solicitous attitude toward her, and makes her the center of dramatic ritual activity.

It must be remembered, too, that the claim of possession by ghosts may be a punishment unconsciously meted out by a young woman to those about her for real or fancied grievances. A ghost or malignant spirit has a habit of persecuting a whole family, once it enters the circle of a home through an individual, and consequently its presence is most unwelcome to the whole group. Also, its eradication or pacification is an expensive undertaking and often a lengthy one. It may cause still other marriage difficulties, because few families want to enter into marriage negotiations that will result in receiving a ghost in addition to a new member. A number of shamans have pointed out that a large percentage of their clients are young women who were "caught" soon after joining their husband's families. A knowledge of the social and marital practices and the points of tension they involve goes far to explain the concentration of hysteria, possession, and trance states in this group.

The importance of marital and child-bearing functions in situations of shamanism and possession can be gathered from the following observations. Six ailing women were present on an occasion when one of our observers visited a shaman. All of them were sure that they were possessed by ghosts, and this was verified in each case by the shaman. One woman was subject to fits and was probably an epileptic. Another suffered from acute menstrual pains and irregularity. Still another had not conceived, although

she had been married for a number of years. The shaman told her that a family godling, who was not being worshiped by certain households since the separation of the large family, was angry, had possessed her, and was denying progeny to the women of her line. A fourth woman had twice been the victim of miscarriage in the fourth month of pregnancy. The particular difficulties of the fifth woman were not ascertained, but the sixth, too, had been unable to conceive. She was a woman in her thirties, who had been hopefully coming to the shaman for years. Thus four of the five cases about which we have information appear to show complaints which are associated with the physiological functions of the female.

The part played by domestic tragedy in notions of persecution by evil spirits and ghosts can be gathered from a few examples, also. A girl of the potter caste had been married to a man who deserted her for another woman. Against the advice of her mother she went to the place where her former husband and the other woman were staying. A very unpleasant scene resulted, but she made no progress in regaining her mate. Soon she had acute feelings of persecution and sought relief in a shamanistic ceremony. During the ceremony she became actively possessed, beating her hands and even her head on the ground in front of her. So violent were her exertions that she collapsed twice and had to be placed in sitting position again. In an effort to identify the ghost which was bothering her, the shaman recited caste names, one after the other. The ghost responded through the woman when the correct caste was named. Before the end of the session both the unsympathetic mother and the woman who had stolen the husband were accused of sending evil spirits to distress the patient.

In another case, where neglect seems to have depressed the patient, the ghost, when it was asked why it had entered the woman, replied, "Before, I was given every comfort—nice meals, sweets. I was respected, admired, massaged with oil. But now I'm denied all this." An association between the clash of wills and possession by ghosts is reflected in many other accounts. A woman brought an ailing daughter of about fourteen years of age to a shaman. When the shaman informed her that the girl's illness could be traced to possession by a ghost of an aborted fetus, the old woman cried out: "Oh, it's true. She went against my wishes one day with a Chamain [a woman of the untouchable caste from whom midwives are recruited] to help her carry mud from a tank to the house. She fell ill and told us many secrets of the family. We couldn't understand how she knew these things so suddenly. She broke out in boils and since then has not been well." Here the defiance of this high-caste girl in associating with the untouchable and her raking up of unsavory family secrets, suggest a situation of tension and conflict. The mother may be fairly close to the truth, after all, in connecting these matters with the girl's physical symptoms.

Not infrequently ghosts and possession serve as a convenient explanation for extreme or violent behavior. A woman who is well known for her moody nature and uncertain temper was found by another woman trying to hang herself. She was led to an adjoining house and there she showed signs of being possessed. She announced that she was a godling which was worshiped by her family. Shamans were called to learn the will of the godling and discovered that a ceremony and animal sacrifice were demanded. As soon as the ceremony was promised the woman became calm and seemed normal. Later, when she was asked why she had attempted suicide, she denied memory of such an act. She asked rhetorically why she would do a thing like that, when she has four children to look after. She took the position that whatever happened was due to the intrusion into her body of an irritated godling who had not been given sufficient ritual attention.

When a supernatural attack is assumed and the person responsible is being sought, the thinking often moves along traditional channels. It is proverbial that the daughters of the household and their sisters-in-law, who enter the household through marriage, do not always get along well together. The feelings of suspicion and resentment may persist even after the daughters themselves leave the home in marriage. Charges that were raised in the summer of 1956 will illustrate what can happen. The sister of a villager was married and went to live in her husband's village. No sooner had she arrived than she became sick. A shamanistic rite revealed that the ghost of a dead brahman had been sent to possess her. It also was alleged that her brother's wife was responsible for this. The basis for the fear was the knowledge on the part of the afflicted woman that the household from which she had come did have a ghost of a deceased brahman attached to it. However, this household asserted that it had kept the *brahm* pacified and harmless by constant offerings, and stoutly denied that any woman of the household had directed the spirit toward the married kinswoman.

When a woman is both childless and quarrelsome, if her barren state is attributed to unfriendly ghosts, she is likely to be greatly feared. The possibility that a possessed person may persuade a ghost to enter another "vehicle" is always present, and it is believed that a self-centered and strong-minded woman will not hesitate to take this step. One such woman came to the village some years ago as a bride. For a long time she bore no children and it was whispered about that this was because she was possessed by a vengeful ghost of a deceased brahman. Actually it was this woman's mother who had first drawn the ire of the ghost. The mother had neglected to pay a debt to a brahman and after his death was persecuted by his shade. When the daughter came to the village, the *brahm* was transferred to her and came along. The daughter was accused more than once of trying to pass the ghost along to others. So bad did her reputation become that even after she bore a son it was said that she had managed to transfer the family ghost to a young girl who was leaving the village to marry. As a result all kinds of misfortunes plagued the husband and his family as soon as the bride arrived. For one thing, the husband went blind—seemingly a case of hysterical blindness. The bride was returned to her father's home without delay.

More that one ghostly attack has been traced to compunctions of conscience over unpaid debts. A Muslim cotton carder of the village died without leaving issue. One of the villagers had never repaid fifty rupees which he owed this man. When the debtor developed stomach pains and diarrhea, he wondered whether he were not being persecuted by the ghost of the Muslim. He consulted a shaman who verified this, and the matter was resolved by going to the spot where the Muslim was buried, placing a coin in the ground as a symbolic payment, and making other offerings there.

It is obvious that possession and the state of being a channel for the voice of the gods can be an attention-getting device for men as well as women. A villager who was unmarried, asthmatic, and not particularly highly regarded became a devotee of the high god, Shiva. When he was not in a religious setting, he gave the impression of a person who lacked assertiveness and confidence, and yet who desired attention. In December, 1955, he arranged to have a brahman carry on a ceremony for him in honor of Shiva. As the rite progressed he became increasingly excitable and very impatient with the brahman. It was not long before he was moving his head to and fro. Then Shiva spoke through the possessed man chiding him for not serving him better by prophesying that he would do so in the future. Shiva also called upon him to protect the Hindu religion and to protect cows. During the ritual this man was possessed in addition by Hanuman, Vishnu, and Parvati, the divine wife of Shiva—all very important deities of the Hindu pantheon. When the possessed man became the spokesman of Hanuman, he called to his religious teacher in an argumentative tone, "Oh, you think I'm not as great as Shiva, don't you? I'll show you my power!" By the time the

ritual was over a rather good-sized group had gathered, and most of the onlookers were ultimately quite impressed.

At a time of epidemic sickness, possession is encouraged by fear that the disease will spread and strike and by desire to know what acts of worship will mollify the disease goddess. During a smallpox epidemic in February, 1955, a gardener, belonging to a caste whose members act as ritualists at such a time, heard that a woman of the potter caste was sick and went to visit her. She told him that she had been possessed by the disease goddess and that the goddess had voiced her displeasure at having been given an offering of unclean curd and had threatened to take five lives in the village. The gardener began to sing and make offerings, and the woman became possessed again. Then the gardener conversed with the goddess through the person of the possessed woman. The goddess asked for songs and offerings of a certain type and advised that a full-scale ceremony should be carried out on behalf of the woman at a given time. When she was asked whether she were "going to manifest herself on the body of the woman" (that is, whether the woman were going to contract the disease), she answered in the affirmative, but added that it would be a mild case and that "everything will be all right." It is probable that at this time the possessed woman thought that she had caught or was getting the disease. Actually her fears were groundless; she was not stricken with it during this epidemic.

Evidences of fear and wishful thinking also characterize a case of possession of an eight-year-old girl during this same period. The mother of the girl had asked her to perform some task. The girl stretched out her hands saying, "Don't you see my hands. You are asking me to work?" There were pox marks on her hands. Soon the girl was possessed and the intruding spirit identified itself as the godling of a shrine in another village of the area. Through the little girl it scolded the audience, saying, "Because I'm at a distance you people of this village have forgotten me. You don't offer ceremonies to me. Unless you worship me, you'll all be in great trouble." She also assured her hearers, "There won't be any trouble in this house. There won't be any smallpox." Just then a woman of a caste much higher than that of the child appeared, and the godling, speaking through the little girl, upbraided the woman in these words, "Go away from here. You promised that you would offer me a ceremony and fried bread if a boy would be born to your nephew. But when a girl was born, you didn't do it. You completely forgot me at that time."

Despite the youth of the girl many women accepted the authenticity of the possession, were much concerned at the displeasure voiced by the godling, and forthwith planned a trip to his shrine. Yet, contrary to the promises of the godling, two cases of smallpox did develop in the family of the possessed girl, something that caused much puzzlement and comment among the villagers.

The fear of ghosts can lead to hysterical symptoms at even more tender ages than this. A woman recalls that a place in the village of her birth was haunted by a female ghost of a certain type, a type noted for its unclean habits. The very branch of the tree in which the ghost was reputed to live was pointed out to the child, and she was told that she was in imminent danger of being caught by this unwholesome spirit. She was three or four years old when she learned about this. She began to be incontinent at night and was at first punished for it. She protested to her mother that she never defecated at night. Her mother asked the child's grandfather about it. This man was a shaman and pronounced what was happening to be the work of a ghost. He conducted a ceremony over the child and ordered the ghost to leave. After that the child had no trouble of this kind. Apparently, either because of a feeling of hopelessness at being in the grip of a defiling force, or because of projection of unpleasant responsibilities upon the ghost, the child had regressed in its toilet-training habits.

Concern over the consequences of impiety or contact with forbidden or dangerous ritual objects may also lead to seizures, possession, and the need for ceremonial aid. After a ceremony to rid the village of epidemic disease, a shaman buried a covered pot filled with flowers in the waters of a tank at the edge of the village. A villager who was bathing in the tank and who had forgotten the event, felt the pot with his foot and retrieved it. When he realized that it was the symbol of the disease which had been captured and banished from the village which he had disturbed and recovered, he was terror-stricken and began to vomit. He made his way to his home with difficulty and took to his bed. It took at least two specialists and considerable ritual to restore him to health.

There is one other activity of the ghost that should be mentioned. Some ghosts make a practice of appearing to persons of the opposite sex and possessing them by engaging in sexual intercourse with them when they are asleep or dreaming. Ghosts are said to appear to young widows at night in the form of their deceased husbands and to have connection with them. More disturbing still, ghosts sometimes appear in the guise of men other than the husband to "tease" and frighten a woman by such activities. The ghost of a young man who fell into a well and drowned has a reputation of this kind of knavery.

Female ghosts tantalize men in a comparable manner. One villager described how a ghost took the form of an attractive young woman, the wife of another man, who had just returned to the village from a visit. This apparition visited him at night and was having intercourse with him. Just as he was about to ejaculate, he woke up and rushed out to the side of the field. It is apparent from these and other accounts that illicit and socially unacceptable desires which cannot be repressed are rationalized as the work of shameless ghosts.

In summary we can say that cases of spirit possession do not occur in a random fashion throughout the society. Except when a shaman or devotee calls upon the gods he worships to

enter him and speak through him, spirit possession is almost inevitably interpreted as an unhappy incursion into the human body in order to
cause sickness or misfortune. Consequently
those who believe that their sickness and misfortune are due to evil forces of the outer world for
which they are the targets are prone to spirit
possession. And it is those who are particularly
vulnerable or in a precarious social position who
tend to decide that any reverse is a sign of spirit
possession. The young married woman, beset by
homesickness, anxious for acceptance by her rel-
atives-in-law, fearful that she may not be able to
present sons to her husband and his family, may
label her woes a form of ghost possession. If she
has been ignored and subordinated, the spirit
possession may take even more dramatic and
strident form as a compensation for the obscurity under which she has labored. Also there
seems to be a large number of cases of possession
among young men who leave the village for urban areas and who either fail to make an adequate adjustment to that environment or who
encounter difficulties upon their return. Possession seems to be correlated also with repressed
aggression among low-caste persons and
younger people, for it allows the individual,
through the haughty spirit within, verbally to
castigate his superiors or seniors with impunity.

On the individual level possession often can
be traced to unresolved interpersonal conflict.
Unpaid debts and ungracious acts tend to reap-
pear after the death of one of the principals as
intrusive ghosts. In this sense ghosts can be said
to represent the standards and conscience of the
community and, derivatively, of that of its individuals.

There is a rather prominent amount of projection and scapegoating in spirit possession.

Not only is there a reflection of the animosities
that the victim believes are directed toward him,
but he tends to reveal his suspicions and unfavorable attitudes toward other groups and individuals: ill-feeling toward minority groups and
intercaste rancor are sometimes mirrored in his
conception of his troubles. The ghosts of deceased Muslims were exceedingly active in persecuting Hindus in the troubled days following
partition. Persons of high caste tend to be persecuted by large, dark, low-caste spirits. And
in speaking about scapegoating and projection,
the tendency to attribute unmanageable and socially reprehensible sexual desires to the activities of the ghosts of others should not be
forgotten.

Above all, a prevailing health anxiety is suggested by the data regarding ghost and spirit
possession. I would venture to say that the material on this topic strongly challenges the notion
that the Indian villager meets sickness and death
with fatalism, resignation, and composure.
There is, on the contrary, a determined effort
through possession to anticipate and forestall
disease, to deal with it when it is present, and to
learn why it claimed its victims. And this is
reasonable, for health and survival are the foundation upon which so much else rests. The
mother is in terror of losing her child. It is often
not only a life but her very status and future
which are at stake. The family heads tremble
lest the sons be stricken by epidemic disease and
the line become extinct. Ghosts do not wander
aimlessly though Indian village culture. They
gather at points of stress and they attack the
soft spots of the social order. To follow their
movements is to learn a good deal about that
social order.

# 26

## SPIRIT POSSESSION AS ILLNESS IN A NORTH INDIAN VILLAGE[1]

*Stanley A. Freed and Ruth S. Freed*

*In this article Stanley and Ruth Freed analyze a detailed case of possession from a village in North India. Identifying spirit possession as a form of hysteria, they show that the subject of possession, a young girl, displayed sexual anxiety. She also experienced an uncomfortable relationship with her new husband's older brother. Possession resolves the internal conflict surrounding sexual anxiety by permitting its expression and projection on an outside malevolent spirit and by generating secondary external support. Relatives and friends attempt to drive the possessing spirit from the girl's body, paying special attention to her and helping reduce some of the anxiety caused by life with strangers in her new household. Additional cases of possession confirm the conclusion that possession works to reduce anxiety associated with both internal and external stress.*

The possession of a person by a ghost or godling which results in somatic or psychological illness is widespread in India. This paper discusses spirit possession as illness in Shanti Nagar, a north Indian village near Delhi, and briefly compares spirit possession in Shanti Nagar and other parts of northern India. First we describe in detail the case for which we have the fullest data: that of a young bride named Daya. During a two-week period in which Daya suffered a series of possessions, we interviewed her several times in an attempt to gain some indication of why she should become possessed. We report Daya's testimony at length after the description of her possession and treatment by shamans. Second, we describe several other cases of spirit possession in Shanti Nagar. Third, we analyze spirit possession in Shanti Nagar as a psychological and cultural phenomenon. The behavior of persons possessed by spirits closely resembles hysteria. Daya's testimony and the social circumstances of Daya and others suffering from possession suggest that spirit possession, like hysteria, has two conditions: a basic condition due to the individual's intra-psychic tension and a precipitating condition due to an event or situation involving unusual stress or emotion. The basic condition of spirit possession is psychological. The precipitating conditions are cultural events or situations which exhibit two general characteristics: (1) the victim of spirit possession is involved in difficulties with relatives within the nuclear or joint family, and (2) he is often in a situation where his expectations of aid and support are low. Finally, we analyze spirit possession in Shanti Nagar as compared with eastern Uttar Pradesh and Calcutta. The comparison indicates that spirit possession as illness is a basically uniform pattern in northern India, although regional variations do occur.

## DAYA'S POSSESSION

Daya was fifteen, married, and a member of the Chamar caste, who are leatherworkers and laborers ranking close to the bottom of the caste hierarchy of Shanti Nagar. On the day we observed her possession we visited her family for

357

another purpose and paid no particular attention to the girl, who was quietly sewing on a machine which was part of her dowry. Young brides are expected to be inconspicuous. Daya's mother-in-law, husband's older brother, husband's sister, and several other Chamar men, women, and children were present.

The conversation immediately preceding the possession seems, in the light of later analysis, to have some significance, for Daya could interpret some of the comments and behavior as subtle and indirect reflections on her good character. The husband's older brother was teasing Daya. He told us he could do this because he was the older brother of the husband. (The relationship is fictive; see Freed 1963 for a discussion of fictive kinship in Shanti Nagar.) We replied that we thought it was the husband's younger brother who could tease the bride and not the husband's older brother. (Ideally, the relationship of the husband's older brother and the younger brother's wife is one of respect. The wife covers her face before him and does not address him. The husband's younger brother and the older brother's wife have a warm, joking relationship.) The Chamars avoided answering directly and pointed to another man and said, "He's also a husband's older brother and never says anything."

Then the husband's older brother who had been teasing Daya said, "Say what you will, this business of tailoring is suitable only for men." We asked, "Why shouldn't a woman do it if she has the skill?" A woman said, "He's just ignorant and can't do anything." The husband's older brother replied that the woman's family was ignorant. He said that if a man is a tailor, he can get anyone's measurements, but a woman can't do this. For a woman to sew clothes for members of her family or lineage has recently been accepted in Shanti Nagar, and a sewing machine as part of a dowry carries considerable prestige. Daya was the first low-caste girl to bring a sewing machine. Although Daya's activities were perfectly proper, the aggressive teasing of her husband's older brother, from which she

could not defend herself, and the fact that this was a breach of the traditional relationship could have disturbed her.

Abruptly the mother-in-law changed the subject and began telling us about an illness that was plaguing the new bride. Apparently Daya emitted subtle cues before her possessions, and the mother-in-law was aware of the impending possession a few minutes before we noticed anything amiss. The first really noticeable symptoms of spirit possession were when Daya complained of feeling cold and began to shiver. She was moaning slightly and breathing hard. The mother-in-law and one of her daughters helped Daya lie down and piled about six quilts on her. She moaned and talked under the quilts; then she lost consciousness. The ghost had come.

The husband's older brother brought some burning cow dung. The mother-in-law, husband's sister, and husband's older brother helped Daya sit up and wafted some dung smoke into her face. All at once she started to jerk violently. The three relatives grabbed Daya to restrain her. They shouted, "Who are you? Are you going?" The ghost, speaking in normal Hindi through the girl, said, "Yes, I am going." Then the three relatives released Daya and she remained sitting. Suddenly she fell backward unconscious; the ghost had returned. This time the relatives revived her by putting some water from a hookah in her eyes while pulling her braids. When she began to return to semi-consciousness, she made a high wailing sound which seemed to announce the presence of the ghost. The three relatives again had the girl sit up. The mother-in-law asked, "Who are you?" The ghost replied, "No one." The relatives repeated the question, and then the ghost said, "I am Chand Kor." They asked the ghost what it wanted. The ghost said it would not leave until it had taken Daya with it.

Daya sat for a time and then once more fell unconscious. This time she was brought back to a semi-conscious trance state by putting rock salt between her fingers and squeezing them together. She again emitted the highpitched wailing, and the ghost was ready to talk. By this time several other Chamar women had gathered and began conversing with the ghost. The ghost complained that it had been promised noodles (a delicacy eaten in summer) that morning but that the mother-in-law had given it none. A woman then said that she would give the ghost cow dung to eat. The ghost said, "In the morning the girl was fed noodles, but I wasn't given any." The woman repeated that she would give the ghost cow dung. The ghost said to the woman, "You stop talking rot." The woman said, "You mother-in-law [an insult], you eat cow dung." The ghost said, "You eat cow dung." The woman retorted, "You mother-in-law, you bastard, you eat cow dung."

Daya sat quietly for a while, and it seemed as if the ghost had gone; but it returned, and Daya once more lost consciousness. Again they put salt between her fingers, but the ghost said that it was leaving before they had a chance to squeeze the fingers together. Daya, however, asserted that she could see the ghost standing in the next room. Her mother-in-law and the other women tried to convince her that there was nothing in the next room but a trunk. Then Daya fell back again and lay still. This time no effort was made to revive her, and the spectators drifted away. Daya remained unconscious for several hours until a shaman was summoned who revived her.

Although the mother-in-law was quite distressed during the possession and on one occasion cried, none of the others present gave the impression that they thought the possession was strange or unusual. They all seemed to know just what to do. During the lulls in the possession, they speculated as to the ghost's identity and discussed ways of driving off the ghost. Much of the conversation with the ghost, beside the insults, was to determine the ghost's identity. The ghost said its name was Chand Kor, who was a woman from Daya's mother's brother's village. Daya had lived with her mother's brother for some time, and she and Chand Kor had become close friends. Chand Kor drowned in a well and, having died an untimely and violent death, became a ghost. The ghosts of women who die in this fashion do not keep their promises. On previous occasions when the ghost possessed the girl, it promised not to return. One of the women present during the possession kept repeating that the ghost was a "widow [an insult] who did not keep her promises." In the last conversation between the ghost and the women, the ghost changed its name saying, "You can never get hold of me." The women decided that the ghost had been lying about its earlier identity but were not convinced that the new name was correct.

Among the remedies suggested for driving off the ghost were putting hookah water in the girl's eyes or squeezing rock salt between her fingers while pulling her braids, the smoke of burning cow dung or pig's excreta, a copper coin, a shaman, and beating the girl. The daughter struck Daya once; but a man of the Jat caste (farmers) who came in about midway during the possession protested, saying that the girl had some ailment and that no ghost was present. Most of the methods used by the villagers to exorcise ghosts involve shock (beating, pulling, and squeezing) and/or unpleasantness (e.g., burning pig's excreta and verbal insults). Certain substances such as salt and cow dung are inimical to evil spirits (see Crooke 1894: 147–148, 194, 198, 201; Lewis 1958:295–299).

## CURES BY SHAMANS

Daya's frequently repeated possesssions indicated that a permanent cure was beyond the powers of the villagers; consequently shamans were summoned from outside of Shanti Nagar. Several treatments by different shamans took place before the ghost was banished, and no one could be really sure that the ghost would not again return. On at least one occasion, two shamans treated Daya together. We never saw any of the shamans at work, but we interviewed one the day after he treated the girl.

This shaman told us he had stayed in Shanti Nagar a night and a day, apparently waiting in vain for Daya to be possessed. Then he spent a day in Delhi, and upon his return he found the villagers waiting for him at the bus stop with the news that the girl was possessed. The shaman claims he has considerable power. His major source of power is Hanuman, a popular Hindu diety, who the shaman claims is his *guru* (spiritual teacher). He also has power from the "conjurer *(jadugar)* of dacca [in Bengal]," from Sayyid Pir (a Muslim saint), from a spirit called Barwari who lives at a fruit *(ber)* tree, and from the goddess Kalka of the cremation ground. The ghost identified itself as Prem, a girl from Daya's village, and said it wanted to take Daya. The shaman asked why, and the ghost replied, "I just do." The shaman then inquired, "Is there anything else you want in place of her?" The ghost answered in the negative. The shaman said: "You still have a chance. I haven't called my powers yet, and you can choose something else. If I call my powers you won't be able to go even one step." The ghost still refused.

Then the shaman called one of his minor powers, the minister of Hanuman. He thought of Hanuman, said some words in his heart, and asked the minister to catch the ghost. The minister then caught the ghost, which kept trying to escape. The shaman held Daya's braids so that the ghost could not escape and made the ghost promise to leave the girl alone. However, the shaman told the ghost that its promises were worthless and threatened to call his *guru*. The ghost said, "No, no; let me go, and I won't come again." The shaman asked the ghost when it was going, and the ghost said it would leave Shanti Nagar in the company of the shaman. The shaman replied that he had people at home and could not take the ghost with him, but the ghost insisted that it wanted to go with the shaman. According to the shaman, all this talking is a joke and superficial; the real process of catching the ghost goes on in the heart.

The ghost then asked for several presents which the shaman felt were too expensive. The shaman and the ghost finally settled on an offering of Rs. 1.25 (26 cents), a length of red cloth, and a coconut to be taken to Kalka temple in Chirag Delhi near Delhi. The shaman asked the ghost who would make the offering, and the ghost said it would. When the shaman pointed out that only a man could make the offering, the ghost instructed the shaman to do it. But the shaman said he could not because his *guru* would become angry. So the shaman and the ghost decided that someone from Daya's family should make the offering at a fair which is held twice a year at the temple. As a parting threat, the shaman told the ghost that if it came again he would summon his *guru*, Hanuman. The shaman claimed that the ghost departed and Daya was cured. However, six days later she was again possessed, and her family called two shamans. (For a similar shamanistic cure see Lewis 1958:297–298.)

Other remedies used by various shamans were the following: to recite sacred verses (mantras) and tie a blue band around the girl's neck; to cut some of her hair and throw it in a fire; to cut a little of her hair, tie it in a cloth, and carry it away; and to make an offering of sweets. Shamanistic cures seem to emphasize spells, offerings, and the transference of the ghost from the victim to something or someone else, not infrequently the shaman. The remedies involving physical shock used by the villagers are not prominent in shamanistic curing. Both styles of curing involve considerable conversation, during which the ghost can complain and insult to its heart's content. This might have a therapeutic effect upon the one suffering the possession.

## INTERVIEWS WITH DAYA

Daya's testimony is presented in the following order: her symptoms and mood, recent history, comparison of her parents' and husband's houses, relations with her affinal relatives, relations with her husband, and who the ghosts were and what had been her relationships to them. These were obvious areas to investigate. Since Daya had never been possessed before arriving in Shanti Nagar, her comments about life in Shanti Nagar and in her parents' house seemed essential in exploring the reasons for her possession. Because Daya and one of the girls whose ghost possessed her had been as close as sisters, we thought that some features of this girl's life or personality or some aspect of the relationship of the two girls might be relevant. Two themes dominated the interviews: Daya's expressed fear of sexual relations with her husband, and her interest in the illicit sexual adventures of her girl friends.

Ruth Freed, through an interpreter, interviewed Daya because we felt that the girl would talk more freely with a woman. The interpreter was a man, but he did an excellent job of effacing himself. At the beginning of the interview, Daya addressed a few remarks to the interpreter, but she soon was looking at the interviewer and talking directly to her. The interpreter was reduced to a mouthpiece, and he played this difficult role perfectly. Daya was encouraged to talk freely with a minimum of stimulus through direct questions. The interviews were unusually easy. The girl obviously identified with the interviewer (she said she was used to schoolteacher types) and was eager to talk to someone congenial. Daya was cheerful and co-operative, spoke freely, and impressed the interviewer as quite intelligent. Daya's mother-in-law was very helpful in being willing to leave the interviewer alone with Daya, for she knew that Daya could not talk freely in her presence. The mother-in-law gave the impression that she thought the attention Daya was getting and the opportunity for her to talk would be good for her. The interviewer recorded Daya's remarks in a notebook during the interviews. Regarding her physical and mental symptoms, Daya said:

My legs, arms, and whole body ache. Sometimes I feel giddy as though I were going to fall, and sometimes I feel sick to my stomach. I sleep too much. Sometimes when I am just lying on a cot, I fall asleep, even when I don't want to. Sometimes I think I hear someone calling, "Daya, sleep, sleep." I feel very hot, even at night, yet I don't perspire.[2] Then I have the feeling that I am being suffocated, that weights are pressing on my body, legs, feet, and chest. When I'm sitting I have difficulty breathing, and I feel a queer sensation in my stomach as if it is becoming larger and larger. I don't feel like working, only like sleeping; yet I was quite active and did all sorts of work in my parents' house. [Daya frequently dreams that she is passing through the village and that all the boys are quarreling with her.]

Four or five days before the observed possession, Daya arrived in Shanti Nagar for a stay with her husband's family. This was her third visit to her husband. The first, during which the bride and groom traditionally have no sexual intercourse, took place at the time of the marriage ceremony. The second occurred a few months later, and, as is customary, Daya and her husband had their first mating. The first two visits are always brief, but the third is usually an extended stay. Because Daya had reached her menarche a few months before her marriage, her second and third visits to her husband followed soon after the marriage ceremony. This sequence of events is normal for villages in the Delhi region. Villages are exogamous, and women move to their husbands' villages, but the shift of residence takes place gradually. In the early years of marriage, women frequently returned to their parents' villages for considerable periods and usually spend more time with their parents than with their husbands. The Chamars generally send brides to their husbands for the second time within six months of marriage if the girl has reached the menache. In the few days following the beginning of Daya's third visit to Shanti Nagar, she was possessed three times.

Daya emphasized the prestige her family enjoys in their own village. Her father is in military service, and one uncle is a bus conductor. Among the Chamars any steady job carries some prestige, and military service is considered a desirable occupation by many people of all castes. In addition, Daya's family owns two or three acres of land, a matter of considerable pride among the predominantly landless Chamars. This contrasts with her husband's family, who are landless, have only one wage earner in a low-paying factory job, and live primarily as agricultural laborers. With regard to her new life in Shanti Nagar, Daya said:

I feel lonesome and restricted here. In my parents' village, I was free and could do as I liked. In Shanti Nagar I must cover my face from older men and not leave the house unaccompanied. I don't feel at ease with my face covered. Sometimes I forget, and then people remind me. I have no one to talk to, and so I stitch clothes or just sleep when I finish my work.

Daya's relationships with her relatives by marriage and her feelings about them are the normal ones for young brides. She says that for a day or two she disliked all of her affines but realized that she would have to get used to them. Her husband's younger brothers, who are young boys, tease her. She feels at home with them. This is the traditional, warm joking relationship between the husband's younger brother and the older brother's wife. She is afraid of her father-in-law because she must tell him if anyone talks or jokes with her. The relationship of the father-in-law and daughter-in-law is one of respect and avoidance on the part of the daughter-in-law and of authority and avoidance on the father-in-law's part. Daya and her mother-in-law like each other. This relationship is traditionally one of tension and antagonism, but these feelings

often develop after the daughter-in-law is older and has sons of her own. When the daughter-in-law first comes to her husband's family she is quite young, and in the early years the relationship with the mother-in-law can be warm. Daya says that her mother-in-law goes everywhere with her and protects her. If the mother-in-law is not available, a small female child accompanies her. She complains that the boys of the village joke with her. She did not mention her husband's older brother's wife except to note that this woman told her what to do when her husband visited her at night. This was the wife of her husband's real brother, not the husband's brother who had been teasing her. The husband's older brother's wife is often the one to tell newly married people how to have sexual intercourse. She did not discuss her husband's sisters or older brother.

Daya says that she is terrified of her husband when he comes in the night, but that he is quite gentle and tells her not to be afraid. He says he will do whatever she likes; he won't even touch her. She has become less frightened than she was at first. Her mother-in-law and the wife of her husband's older brother are no help to her when she is afraid. She says she learned about sexual relations from listening to her older married friends, that is, girls from her village who had married and returned home for a visit. They told her what would happen to her and that she would become annoyed and start crying. When she came to her husband's house, her husband's older brother's wife explained sexual relations to her. She says that she was afraid and told her husband's older brother's wife that she would sleep only with her. The husband's older brother's wife merely said that, when her husband joined her, she must be quiet and not scream— that it is only natural and is how her mother and father had children. Nevertheless, she slept with her husband's older brother's wife, who, however, moved away during the night; when Daya awoke in the morning, she found her husband had joined her. When she came for her most recent visit, she slept with her husband three or four days and had sexual intercourse. Then she was visited by the ghost and did not sleep with her husband for two weeks. When her husband again asked her to sleep with him, she said she was too weak. However, when she awoke in the night she found him there. He said he was staying with her only because she was alone; they did not have sexual relations.

Daya discussed in some detail the sexual adventures and subsequent misfortunes of two girls she had known. Both died violently a few years before Daya's possession, and one, Chand Kor, became a ghost and possessed her. According to Daya, Chand Kor was forced to commit suicide by her family because of a premarital pregnancy. Chand Kor was pregnant when she was sent to her husband's family, who therefore rejected her and returned her to her parents. Her father was very angry. Chand Kor begged forgiveness, but her father replied: "I won't keep you. Go jump in a well." Chand Kor's parents continued to abuse her for several days, telling her to commit suicide by jumping in a well. So one day when Chand Kor was playing with a group of girl friends, she excused herself and ran and jumped in a well.

The events which befell Chand Kor are typical of the way premarital pregnancies are handled in Shanti Nagar and nearby villages. A pregnant, unmarried girl or a married girl who has not had sexual intercourse with her husband is such a grievous blow to a family's prestige that she will not be allowed to live. If such a girl is married, she will be sent to her husband's family, for she belongs to that family and her natal family can take no action until the husband's relatives have indicated their wishes. Moreover, the girl's parents hope against hope that the husband's family will be gentle and forgiving people and will keep the girl. However, we never heard of a case where this happened; the girl is always returned to her parents, which means she is not wanted. The fact that the girl was sent to the husband and then returned readies village opinion for what is to follow. The villagers feel that the girl's father has done everything possible to

save her life and that he cannot avoid the next step. The father and other relatives may either force the girl to commit suicide, or the father may simply kill her. Village opinion will solidly support the family which takes this drastic step. The death will be reported to the police as an accident, suicide, or result of illness. When Daya told us the story of Chand Kor, she began by saying that the fall into the well was an accident but quickly switched to the story of suicide. Villagers like to pass off the deaths of women in wells as accidents; but all such events are suspect, and they more often are suicides.

Girls are well aware of the risks they run through premarital sexual intercourse. Daya knew that Chand Kor was having relations with a man and warned her that, if her father or husband found out, they would not let her live. Daya also told Chand Kor that she could not be too friendly any longer. Gossip starts so quickly in Indian villages that Daya may have thought her character could be destroyed if she continued her close association with Chand Kor. When we witnessed Daya's possession, the ghost of Chand Kor seemed to be the principal one involved although there was some switching of names toward the end. In a later possession, a shaman identified the ghost of Prem.

Daya had another friend whose premarital sexual activities resulted in her death. Daya mentioned this girl, named Santara, while discussing her schooling. Daya attended school for only five grades. Her parents refused to let her go further because Santara, one of her classmates, was molested by one of the male teachers. Villagers are reluctant to send older girls to study with male teachers. Considerable unfavorable gossip about the character of local school teachers is current in Shanti Nagar and presumably in other villages; and, while most such gossip is undoubtedly groundless, parents nonetheless usually insist upon female teachers for older girls. Daya says that one of the teachers had sexual relations with Santara. One day a boy saw the teacher touch Santara's breast, and the news spread quickly. Santara's father was furious. According to Daya, the father took Santara into the fields a few nights later, had sexual relations with her, cut her throat, and threw her into a well. The father said that Santara was his daughter and he had every right to do with her as he liked. He was never punished, although Daya said he had to give the police a bribe so that the murder would not be investigated. Daya's account of this case departs from the usual procedure only in the statement that the father had sexual relations with his daughter.

The ghost of Santara did not come to trouble Daya. Prem, the other ghost which possessed Daya, was a girl from Daya's village who died of illness and about whom Daya had little to say. We believe that the ghost of Chand Kor was uppermost in Daya's mind and that Prem served principally to confuse the identification. Deception and confusion about the ghost's identity hold the interest of spectators and prolong the curing procedure through several sessions. Thus the person possessed gains additional attention and has greater opportunity for expressing himself through the ghost.

## OTHER CASES OF SPIRIT POSSESSION

Four other villagers had attacks of spirit possession or were suffering its aftereffects while we were in Shanti Nagar. These cases add to our knowledge in showing that (1) spirit possession affects both men and women of varying ages;[3] (2) it is related to difficulties and tension with close relatives; (3) it often affects persons whose expectations of aid and support are low; and (4) while the victim usually recovers, the condition can develop into a different and apparently permanent psychological affliction. Much of our data about the possessions of these four villagers come from interviews with their relatives and other persons. We briefly interviewed three of the four and observed one of the attacks.

Bhim Singh, a Brahmin man in his fifties, suffered a series of ghost possessions lasting about ten days. He was possessed by the ghost of a sweeper (Chuhra) who had died in Shanti Nagar during an epidemic. The sweeper was born in another village and was moving from place to place. Because he died an untimely death, he became a ghost. He is one of the three ghosts permanently resident in Shanti Nagar and is considered the strongest of the three, being credited with causing a death about twenty years ago.

The cure followed the usual method of determining the ghost's identity and then driving it out. Identifying the ghost was no problem, for it kept shouting its name and asking for sweet things to eat. The ghost of the sweeper was known to have a fondness for sweets. The ghost also asked for a hookah to smoke and, when offered a Brahmin's hookah, refused it, insisting on a sweeper's hookah. Then the villagers were certain of the ghost's identity. (In general, each caste smokes the hookah only with others of the same caste.) Exorcising the ghost was relatively simple: the villagers went to a neighboring village and procured a liquid which, when thrown in a fire, produces a smoke which banishes ghosts. Some villagers said the liquid was put in Bhim Singh's nostrils and eyes.

Bhim Singh is a widower and has no children. He lives in a joint family with his two brothers and their descendants. He has a history of spirit possession. One informant told us that Bhim Singh was possessed some twenty years ago because an elderly woman of the family died over some dispute. The informant was not sure of the details of the woman's death but implied it was murder or suicide. Bhim Singh's family has more than the normal share of troubles. One man in the family has only one good eye, and one-eyed men are considered inauspicious. This one-eyed man married a widow, thereby causing a great scandal since Brahmin widows are not supposed to remarry. The scandal is still alive in village gossip even though the couple live away from Shanti Nagar. The family is relatively poor for a high-caste family, having only three acres of land for eleven people, and the family's sole wage earner recently lost his job. The sons and daughters-in-law of Bhim Singh's brothers have been suggesting that the joint family separate into three nuclear families. The separation of a joint family is a serious step and may involve considerable tension.

We believe that Bhim Singh's latest possession was precipitated by family problems, especially the possibility of a division of the joint family which would isolate Bhim Singh and place him in a difficult situation. Because he has no wife or sons, he would have no woman to cook for him and no relatives to help in his agricultural work. One informant said that Bhim Singh's possession was because he asked his younger brother's wife to have sexual intercourse with him and she refused. This opinion was based on no more than the generally appreciated fact that men without wives have almost no opportunities for sexual relations with women and are therefore likely to be frustrated. Most villagers, in discussing Bhim Singh's possession, generally dealt with its most superficial features. They said Bhim Singh became possessed because he ate sweet food, for which the ghost has a fondness, and then walked through the area frequented by the ghost.

Santosh, a woman of the beggar (Bairagi) caste in her middle forties, was possessed by the ghost of her older brother. She said she had gone to a garden to get some fruit. On the way she jumped across a ditch. She thinks that this was when the ghost caught her, for her knees began to behave badly and she came home. She lost consciousness. Her two sons, one of whom lives in a separate family, tried to banish the ghost. One son held her hair and asked, "Who are you?" The ghost replied that it was Santosh's older brother. This brother had been close to Santosh and had always helped her. The son asked the ghost why it had come, and the ghost answered, "Why does my brother-in-law hurt my sister?" The son told the ghost to go away and not hurt his mother; he promised that in the future Santosh's husband would not trouble her. The next day a second spirit possessed Santosh,

and the village shaman was called. Apparently he cured Santosh, for her possessions ceased.

Because of the remarks of the ghost, we believe that Santosh's possession was related to difficulties with her husband. We are not certain as to what the trouble was, although we knew Santosh and her husband well. The husband was a very mild mannered person and at least fifteen years older than she, his second wife. We noticed no particular tension between them. However, we suspect that Santosh was having a sexual affair with a powerful Jat landlord who is a widower. If this were true, it would certainly have led to trouble between Santosh and her husband. A noteworthy feature of Santosh's possession is that it was by an older brother, a relative with whom a sister has very warm ties and from whom she expects gifts, sympathy, and support. The possession indicates that Santosh may have felt a lack of such support.

One day early in our residence in Shanti Nagar we were called to aid a Brahmin woman, named Chameli, who had lost consciousness. We arrived to find her lying on a cot, completely limp, with her eyes closed. Her jaws were together, but her lips were slack. Her mother-in-law, one son, and one daughter were present. We gingerly shook her by the shoulder, but this failed to revive her or to have any effect whatsoever. Chameli's son and mother-in-law seemed entirely unconcerned. Her daughter, who had summoned us, was mildly disturbed. We could think of no way to help and, as nothing was being done to aid Chameli, we left. We learned later that Chameli remained unconscious for about 45 minutes. Chameli later told us that just before she lost consciousness she had seen the ghost of one of her husband's father's brother's sons and his wife, who said, "Come with us." The next time Chameli had an attack, a swami (who was a curer) was called from a neighboring village. This man was not a shaman, but apparently he treated her successfully, for she had no more attacks while we were in Shanti Nagar.

Chameli was 42 years of age and had seven living children, two boys and five girls, all unmarried except one daughter. We knew her very well, for we lived only a few steps from her house. Chameli's health was not good, and she was going through the menopause. Her relations with her husband and mother-in-law were very unsatisfactory. Chameli and her husband had not engaged in sexual relations for several months. The principal reason was probably the desire on the part of the husband and his mother to avoid the birth of another daughter, for she would be an added economic liability due to marriage and other ceremonial expenses. Chameli desired normal relations with her husband, and when he occasionally did not come home at night because of business or visits to relatives, she accused him of having other women. The mother-in-law, who as senior woman in the house controlled the stores of food, refused to give Chameli ghee (clarified butter) for her bread. Chameli said that her mother-in-law wanted her to die. Dramatic quarrels between Chameli on the one hand and her husband and mother-in-law on the other frequently broke out. Chameli and her mother-in-law traded insults. The husband complained that Chameli was killing him (by creating extreme tension in the household) and told her that she would have to live at the feet of her mother-in-law. For two months he refused to accept food or water from her hands.

Except for her oldest daughter, who occasionally sided with her, none of Chameli's children supported her in her quarrels with her husband and mother-in-law. Moreover, she constantly fought with her sister, who lived next door and was married to her husband's brother (i.e., her husband's father's brother's son); even in these disputes she could not always count on the support of her family. She complained bitterly about this, saying that she was fighting her family's battles alone.

Chameli's attack of spirit possession seems clearly related to the tense relations with her husband and mother-in-law. It is particularly noteworthy because of the response of the other members of the family; they made no effort to induce the state of trance in which the ghost can be identified and persuaded to leave. Nevertheless, Chameli's illness was not entirely ignored, for a curer was summoned after the next attack. A few months after Chameli's possession she and her husband resumed sexual relations and tension in the house subsided considerably.

The fourth case of spirit possession differs from the others because of its psychological aftermath: the woman never recovered and apparently developed a permanent psychological illness. She was Bhagwani, a sweeper (Chuhra) in her forties. Her possessions began about three years before our visit. Her early attacks were similar to other spirit possessions: she saw the ghost and would point it out to the spectators. However, the ghost was apparently absent from her later attacks, which featured abuse of relatives, even her husband, and destructiveness.

Bhagwani's appearance and behavior differ from the others who suffered spirit possession. During our interview she crooned, muttered, moaned, and acted as if she were falling asleep. She was withdrawn and sullen or hostile. She showed almost no physical energy. She sat in a semi-reclining position and occasionally plucked at things. She seemed irritated by noises, conversation, and at having to do anything. Whenever the conversation turned to her husband or sons, she flared up in an irritable manner. Her eyes were inattentive and never seemed to focus.

Bhagwani told us she feels depressed and often cries. She says that she can never be cured and that this knowledge makes her irritable. She wants to commit suicide and says that everyone watches her so that she will not kill herself. When she lies down, she sees animals and insects moving before her eyes. When this happens, she is terrified; she cannot close her eyes and sleep; she yawns, shrieks, and feels that she will die. Bhagwani said that her illness was because someone put something in her food and that she would kill the person if she could find him.

According to Bhagwani's relatives, her possession involved difficulties with one of her daughters-in-law named Sita. We think that this is probably accurate as far as it goes but that Bhagwani's changed relationships with her son and possibly her husband due to Sita's arrival also entered into the possession. Sita's husband gave us the following account. Bhagwani and Sita do not get along well, although when Sita first came to Shanti Nagar the two were very affectionate. One would not take her meals without the other. Sita had two children, the second about three years ago. After the birth of each, Sita suffered attacks of spirit possession. Her husband says that these attacks occurred two to five times a day for about a month. Bhagwani's husband is a shaman and attempted, unsuccessfully, to cure Sita. While he was attempting the cure, he became involved in a dispute with Sita. She spoke to him, which she should not have done as a daughter-in-law, and he abused her, apparently making uncomplimentary remarks about her mother. (Something occurred between Sita and her father-in-law, but we doubt that this is exactly what happened.) Because Bhagwani's husband could not affect a cure, Sita returned to her parents' village. Her father had been a shaman, and although he was dead, his disciple was active and possessed considerable power. The disciple cured Sita. While in her parents' village, Sita mentioned that she had been insulted by her father-in-law. She stayed in her parents' village for about three years and returned to Shanti Nagar only quite recently. Shortly after Sita left Shanti Nagar, Bhagwani suffered a possession. Sita's husband said that the disciple had sent spirits to possess her, and this opinion was shared by all with whom we talked. Sita's husband said that his mother's attacks were the reason Sita stayed in her parents' village so long.

## PSYCHOLOGICAL AND CULTURAL ANALYSIS

Almost all who have written on spirit possession regard it as a form of hysteria. A concise and exhaustive definition of hysteria is not possible, for a large number of symptoms and etiological factors have been ascribed to this condition. Abse (1959:274) states that the possible symptoms are so numerous that a discussion of all of them would assume encyclopedic proportions. Parker (1962:93, n. 2) uses the term hysteria "to cover such phenomena as temporary states in which there is a loss or clouding of consciousness, manifestations of convulsive, hyperexcitable, or 'freezing' behavior, and which involves no progressive psychic deterioration such as is often associated with schizophrenia." Abse (1959:274) says the typical clinical features are: (1) "physical symptoms without an ascertainable structural lesion"; (2) complacency in the presence of physical disability; and (3) episodic disturbances in which "an ego-alien homogeneous constellation of ideas and emotions occupies the field of consciousness." Pain is the most common complaint (Abse 1959:279). Dramatic somatic symptoms include convulsions and other conversion reactions such as deafness, dumbness, and blindness. Globus hystericus, "a sensation of contraction of throat or a globular mass rising from the stomach into the esophagus" (Warren 1934:116), is a noteworthy symptom. Dizziness may occur. Abse (1959: 276) notes that attacks of convulsive hysteria occur only in the presence of spectators and that the victim does not fall in a dangerous situation.

In his survey of the literature on hysteria, Abse (1959:274, 276, 283, 285) frequently notes sexual disturbances, among which are guilt feelings arising from infantile incestuous attachments, as conditions of hysteria. "When traced to its roots," says Abse (1959:283), "hysteria in all its forms is predominantly related to the climax of infantile sexuality, the Oedipus situation, with its struggle to surmount incestuous genital-sexual and hostile strivings." Chodoff and Lyons (1958:735), in discussing characteristics of the hysterical personality, mention, among other things, sexual frigidity, intense fear of sexuality, and sexual apprehensiveness. FitzGerald (1948: 710) also notes the sexual frigidity of hysterics.

The dependency cravings and strong need for love and approval which Parker (1962:80) mentions as being frequently ascribed to hysterics seem to be derived from emotional attachments to the parents which the hysteric is unable to replace with a normal adult sexual relationship (Abse 1959:285–286; FitzGerald 1948:710–714). Tension due to intrapsychic conflict can be thought of as the basic condition of hysteria.

Events or situations involving unusual stress or strong emotions precede hysterical attacks (Abse 1959:276–277; Yap 1960:121–122; Fitz-Gerald 1948:702; Parker 1962:78). These events are the precipitating conditions of hysteria. The stresses of war, dangerous situations encountered while hunting, and difficulties with parents and employers are examples of situations which can precipitate hysterical attacks. Such events can also precipitate other forms of psychiatric disturbance. Opler (1958) lists a number of precipitating events for possessions in a rural area of eastern Uttar Pradesh: the murder of a husband in a feud, difficulties involving urban employment, quarrels over land, the problems of young brides, and others.

Abse (1959:283–284) distinguishes primary and secondary gains for the individual's psyche from an hysterical attack. He describes the primary gain as follows: "The symptoms consist of an autoplastic attempt to discharge the tension created by intrapsychic conflict, and express drive and defense simultaneously, short-circuiting conscious perception of conflict related to the Oedipus complex." The secondary gain, the importance of which Abse believes is often underestimated, involves the individual's use of his symptoms to attract attention, gain sympathy, and manipulate other people and his current life situation. Other studies mention these secondary gains (e.g., Yap 1960:130–132; Parker 1962:80). It is not difficult to see a close connection between the secondary gains of hysteria and the crisis which precipitated the condition. Opler's (1958) discussion of spirit possession in Indian villages emphasizes precipitating conditions and secondary gains.

The possession of Daya was clearly a case of hysteria, as defined by Abse and Parker. Her attack involved loss of consciousness, shivering, and convulsions. It occurred before an audience. She fell unconscious in surroundings presenting no physical dangers. She complained of physical symptoms: pains in her body, dizziness, and a sensation as if her stomach were swelling (possible globus hystericus). However, she seemed quite cheerful and unconcerned about her condition. She recently moved from the warm, supporting environment of her parents' house to her husband's house, where she lived under considerable tension and could count on little support from her affines. She experienced no spirit possession before coming to Shanti Nagar. Her testimony stressed fear of sexuality and a concern with sexual episodes involving incest between father and daughter and/or severe punishment by the family, especially the father.[4] Daya's remarks indicated that, in accord with Abse's analysis of hysteria, tension and conflict related to the Oedipus complex were the underlying condition of her possession. The precipitating condition was her new role as a wife.

Daya achieved substantial secondary gains through her possessions. She became a center of attention. She aroused sympathy and concern among all her affines. Her husband reduced his sexual demands. Daya's parents and other consanguineal relatives rallied to her support. Her father came to see her and, thinking she might be weak, brought some vitamins and arranged for a series of vitamin injections. Even unsophisticated villagers have considerable faith in injections, and the girl's father, who was in military service, no doubt favored modern medicine. Daya is the only daughter in her nuclear family, and therefore many of her relatives, including all of her male relatives, came to see if she were all right. They spoke of arranging a marriage between Daya's younger sister, of whom she is quite fond (actually the daughter of her father's younger brother who lives in a joint family with Daya's father), and her husband's younger brother.

Although the other cases of spirit possession in Shanti Nagar contribute little to our knowledge of its symptoms and psychic conditions, they do aid in better understanding the precipitating events and secondary gains; and one of them, the case of Bhagwani, is especially important in showing the possibility of a transition from hysterical spirit possession to a psychological condition which resembles schizophrenia.[5] In the case of Bhim Singh, the precipitating event was most likely tension in his joint family, especially over whether or not to separate. In the event of a separation, Bhim Singh would be all alone in a separate family. One villager, a bit of a gossip, suggested a sexual rebuff from his brother's wife as a precipitating factor. While this can not be substantiated, sexual frustration should not be overlooked in Bhim Singh's case. The precipitating condition in Santosh's case was probably tension with her husband, possibly regarding a sexual relationship with a powerful Jat landlord. Her possession brought her sons to her aid, saying they would not permit their father to trouble their mother. Chameli's attack was clearly brought on by considerable tension with her husband and mother-in-law. Although Chameli had many children and a sister living next door, she received little support in her troubles. The three latter victims recovered.

The possession of Bhagwani involved difficulties with her daughter-in-law and probably also with her son and husband. At first Bhagwani's possession conformed to the normal pattern. However, she failed to recover, and gradually her behavior changed. Her later attacks featured abuse of relatives and destructiveness instead of spirit possession with its loss of consciousness, trance, and conversion symptoms. Delusions of persecution were present: she believed that her condition was caused by someone's putting something in her food and said that she would kill the person if she found him. She had hallucinations, seeing animals and insects moving before her eyes. Her attention was impaired. Talking to her was somewhat difficult because of her muttering and seeming to be on the verge of falling asleep. Bhagwani's symptoms resemble an early state of schizophrenia of the paranoid type as described by Arieti (1959:459–461, 466–467). Abse (1959:275, 284) notes that transitions between hysteria and schizophrenia occur. In discussing Bhagwani, one astute villager said, "Formerly she was possessed by a ghost and behaved like Daya [the Chamar girl] pointing and saying the ghost is there and there; but now she is mad."

One tentative inference from the Shanti Nagar data is that events precipitating spirit possession are likely to be difficulties involving relatives of the nuclear or joint family and that the victim is often in a position where he can expect little support. These conditions pertain much more frequently to married women than to males or unmarried girls, and this is reflected in the preponderance of married women among those suffering possession. Spirit possession may be thought of as a means of controlling relatives. Other common situations of stress do not seem to call forth hysteria: for example, the considerable tension surrounding the statewide examinations for college and high school degrees, loss of employment, disputes with people of other families or castes, disputes or lawsuits over land, and financial reverses such as crop failure, theft, and the death of valuable animals.

## SPIRIT POSSESSION AS ILLNESS ELSEWHERE IN NORTHERN INDIA

Spirit possession as illness appears basically uniform from Punjab to Calcutta (Temple 1884–1886: ii, 164; iii, 202–203; Lewis 1958:295–299; Majumdar 1958: 234–236; Opler 1958). The general elements of the pattern are as follows. A person begins to act in an odd manner or contracts an illness which does not respond to ordinary remedies. Often events involving unusual stress precede the attacks. Spectators or a shaman suspect spirit possession and use a variety of methods to force the spirit to reveal itself. The spirit is most often the ghost of a person who has died an untimely death. The patient is cured by exorcising the ghost, which can be done in a variety of ways: ritual offerings, transferring the ghost to another person or thing, and various measures designed to make the ghost uncomfortable such as beating, cursing, and smoking with burning dung. Complete recovery seems to be the rule.

Within the basic pattern, the particular details of the precipitating events, behavior during the attack, diagnosis, and treatment show considerable variety. Three broad features of this variation appear noteworthy with regard to possible regional differences. The first concerns the typical behavior during an attack; the second involves spirit possession as a mechanism of controlling others; and the third pertains to differences in the readiness with which people attribute a wide variety of illnesses and misfortunes to spirit possession.

The typical attack in Shanti Nagar involves loss of consciousness, trance, and conversion symptoms. In eastern Uttar Pradesh and Calcutta, attacks are characterized by aggression and threatened or actual physical violence. Loss of consciousness does not always occur or may occur only after the shaman has begun the cure. Opler (1958:554–556, 559, 563) briefly describes several cases of spirit possession in eastern Uttar Pradesh in which aggression and threatened physical violence seem to dominate the attack. A woman "suddenly began to curse and snap at those around her, shouting that she would bite and eat them"; a young man "became violent and abusive and was constantly in trouble"; a young man had "violent attacks . . . during which he spoke abusively to those around him and sought to strike them"; a boy "would disobey his parents, curse them, and remain away from home for long periods"; and a woman "who is well-known for her moody nature and uncertain temper was found by another woman trying to hang herself." Temple (1884–1886: iii, 202–203) reports a case from Calcutta in which a woman attacked her husband and tried to

strangle him. He escaped and gave the alarm to his family. This made the woman furious and she screamed nearly all night.

These descriptions indicate that the features of spirit possession typical of Shanti Nagar are not necessarily typical elsewhere. In Shanti Nagar, the victim shivers, moans, or feels weak, loses consciousness, goes into a state of trance, and eventually recovers. In eastern Uttar Pradesh and Calcutta, the victim suddenly lashes out at those around him; then a shaman induces a trance, the ghost is exorcised, and recovery follows. Although we have only a few cases, many of which are described very briefly, the apparent contrast between aggressive possessions in Uttar Pradesh and nonaggressive possessions in Shanti Nagar may be significant.

As a means of social control, spirit possession in Shanti Nagar and in eastern Uttar Pradesh shows two noteworthy differences. When the precipitating condition of spirit possession is tense interpersonal relations, the people involved, in Shanti Nagar, are always close relatives, whereas in eastern Uttar Pradesh they may frequently be nonrelatives (Opler 1958:554–555, 557, 562); consequently, spirit possession in eastern Uttar Pradesh is a more general form of social control than in Shanti Nagar. Second, spirit possession in Shanti Nagar does not typically involve accusations of witchcraft, whereas in eastern Uttar Pradesh such accusations are common (Opler 1958:556–557, 562–563). The witchcraft accusations and the typically aggressive behavior of spirit possession in eastern Uttar Pradesh and their lack in Shanti Nagar seem to indicate that spirit possession is a generally more aggressive behavior pattern in the former area.

The third regional difference is the tendency of the villagers of eastern Uttar Pradesh, especially women, to attribute a considerable variety of illnesses and misfortunes to spirit possession, whereas the people of Shanti Nagar are much less inclined to do so. This difference may partly be due, we believe, to the greater influence of the Arya Samaj reform movement in the Shanti Nagar region. Followers of Arya Samaj are hostile to the belief in and worship of ghosts and god-lings. Opler mentions eight women who sus-pected ghosts and sought the aid of a shaman because of menstrual pain, death of children, barrenness, miscarriage, and other ailments. Opler does not say whether these women merely suspected ghosts or whether they actually expe-rienced attacks of spirit possession before going to a shaman. In one case, a shaman induced a possession in order to identify and exorcise the ghost, but in the other cases, while the shaman confirmed the attribution of the difficulty to a ghost, it is not clear whether or not he induced a possession. In cases of this kind, where there is no attack of spirit possession or where posses-sion is induced by the activities of a shaman, the basic intrapsychic conditions associated with spirit possession may be minimal or lacking. Spirit possession of various kinds so permeates Indian culture that many people can become possessed, especially when aided by a skillful shaman or priest. Cases in which spontaneous attacks are lacking are probably best analyzed entirely from the point of view of precipitating events and secondary gains. Barren women, for example, can possibly convert the condemnation of relatives into sympathy by attributing their barrenness to ghosts.

## SUMMARY AND CONCLUSIONS

This paper has described and analyzed sev-eral cases of spirit possession which occurred in Shanti Nagar, a village in northern India near Delhi. These were all cases of spirit possession which were regarded as illness. Psychologically, spirit possession seems to fit contemporary de-scriptions of hysteria. Spirit possession is best analyzed as having two conditions: a basic con-dition due to the individual's intrapsychic ten-sion, and a precipitating condition due to an event or situation involving unusual stress or emotion. Precipitating conditions have two gen-eral characteristics: (1) the victim of spirit pos-

session is involved in difficulties with relatives of the nuclear or joint family, and (2) he is often in a situation where his expectations of mutual aid and support are low. The primary gain of an attack of spirit possession is to relieve the indi-vidual's intrapsychic tension; secondary gains include attention, sympathy, influencing rela-tives, and other manipulation of the individual's current situation. Sometimes spirit possession can develop into schizophrenia. Precipitating events may precede schizophrenia as well as hys-teria. Spirit possession appears to assume a basi-cally uniform pattern in northern India, although regional variation may occur in the behavior during an attack, whether nonrelatives as well as close relatives are involved in the tense situation preceding the attack, the frequency with which accusations of witchcraft occur, and the readiness of people to attribute a wide vari-ety of illness and misfortune to spirit posses-sion.

## NOTES

1. This paper is based on field work in the village of Shanti Nagar (a pseudonym) from November, 1957, to July, 1959. We thank the Social Science Research Council and the National Science Foundation for the postdoctoral fellowships which supported the fieldwork, and the Univer-sity of North Carolina for a faculty research grant to help with secretarial expenses. We also thank Margaret Mead and John J. Honigmann, who carefully read and criticized the manuscript. We thank Edward Harper who supplied us with a copy of his paper on spirit possession in southern India before it was readily available. We received it too late for inclusion in the body of our paper but have referred to it in footnotes. The names of individuals used in this paper are pseudonyms.

2. We did not take her temperature but doubt that she had a fever, for the villagers never regarded her ailment as a fever. However, Majumdar (1958: 236) reports spirit possession accompanied by a high fever.

3. Among the Havik Brahmins of southern India, spirit possession affects only women—with few

exceptions those who are married but do not have grown children. Harper (1963) suggests that this is due to the authority system of the Havik Brahmins.

4. One of the cases described by Harper (1963:168) is of a bride who suffered an attack of spirit possession a few minutes after entering the nuptial chamber.

5. One of the cases described by Harper (1963:167–168) resembles schizophrenia.

## BIBLIOGRAPHY

ABSE, D. W. 1959. Hysteria. American Handbook of Psychiatry, ed. S. Arieti 1:272–292. New York.

ARIETI, S. 1959. Schizophrenia: The Manifest Symptomatology, the Psychodynamic and Formal Mechanisms. American Handbook of Psychiatry, ed. S. Arieti 1: 445–484. New York.

CHODOFF, P., and H. LYONS. 1958. Hysteria, the Hysterical Personality and "Hysterical" Conversion. American Journal of Psychiatry 114: 734–740.

CROOKE, W. 1894. An Introduction to the Popular Religion and Folklore of Northern India. Allahabad.

FITZGERALD, O. W. S. 1948. Love Deprivation and the Hysterical Personality. Journal of Mental Science 94: 701–717.

FREED, S. A. 1963. Fictive Kinship in a North Indian Village. Ethnology 2: 86–103.

HARPER, E. B. 1963. Spirit Possession and Social Structure. Anthropology on the March, ed. B. Ratnam, pp. 165–177. Madras.

LEWIS, O. 1958. Village Life in Northern India. Urbana.

MAJUMDAR, D. N. 1958. Caste and Communication in a Indian Village. Bombay.

OPLER, M. E. 1958. Spirit Possession in a Rural Area of Northern India. Reader in Comparative Religion, ed. W. A. Lessa and E. Z. Vogt, pp. 553–566. Evanston.

PARKER, S. 1962. Eskimo Psychopathology in the Context of Eskimo Personality and Culture. American Anthropologist 64: 76–96.

TEMPLE, R. C., ed. 1884–1886. Panjab Notes and Queries, v. 2–3. London.

WARREN, H. C., ed. 1934. Dictionary of Psychology. Boston.

YAP, P. M. 1951. Mental Disease Peculiar to Certain Cultures: A Survey of Comparative Psychiatry. Journal of Mental Science 97: 313–327.

———. 1960. The Possession Syndrome: A Comparison of Hong Kong and French Findings. Journal of Mental Science 106: 114–137.

# 27

## DEMONIC POSSESSION IN ROMAN CATHOLIC SRI LANKA

### R. L. Stirrat

*Unlike Opler and the Freeds, R. L. Stirrat looks at the public demonic possession that occurs at a Catholic shrine in Sri Lanka (Ceylon). The people who come to the shrine for special rituals believe that evil spirits possess many individuals. Possession is at first marked only by unusual behavior or illness. To confirm the presence of an evil spirit, one can visit the shrine and participate in the ritual there. Faced by the power of God, evil spirits eventually must reveal themselves. The possessed go into a trance, the spirits talk, and measures are taken to drive them out. Stirrat sees this kind of demonic possession as a collective representation. As in a rite of passage, people are brought from an unnatural condition such as sickness to the normalcy of health. The incidence of possession is increased, argues Stirrat, by the belief that possession will occur in the presence of the shrine's holy power.*

My aim in this paper is to understand demonic possession as it exists amongst a section of the Roman Catholic population of Sri Lanka in terms of what the Annee Sociologique school once referred to as "collective representations." What I want to do is to approach the phenomenon which we call "demonic possession" in the context of a wider set of social constructions. In particular, I want to understand what makes demonic possession possible.[1] Second, I will try to show that an approach which starts off from this point of view and which accepts the social reality of possession can also throw some light on the actual incidence of demonic possession as a statistical phenomenon.

This desire to view demonic possession within such a framework derives from my dis-

satisfaction with other current approaches to the subject. In most cases they depend upon certain assumptions about the internal states of mind of those people who become possessed. They do this by inferring the unknown (the state of mind of the possessed) from the known (the incidence of possession; statements about possession) and then using the former to explain the latter. All the really interesting and significant processes are taking place in the mind of the possessed where the anthropologist cannot venture.

For instance, Obeyesekere (1970a; 1975b) sees possession as an "idiom" through which more "real" psychological problems are expressed.[2] These problems are "projected" into an unreal world of gods and demons which are "really" something else. Explanations of the incidence or form of demonic possession are to be sought in the individual psychologies of the actors concerned. Thus in a case Obeyesekere describes, "demonic possession . . . reflects serious 'pathology' and is an attempt to solve . . . intolerable psychological conflicts" (1970a:100).

Alternatively, we can consider the work of I. M. Lewis (1966; 1967; 1971). In terms of his theoretical framework, the data I shall be discussing here fall into what he calls, "peripheral possession cults." For him, possession by demons is a form of "insubordination;" of ritual rebellion against those who wield power and authority by the underprivileged. Thus malevolent possession is to be explained as "a means by which women, and sometimes other subject cat-

The fieldwork upon which this paper is based was carried out at various times during 1974 and 1975. I should like to thank the Social Science Research Council and the Carnegie Trust for the financial support they have given me. Anyone working in Sri Lanka must acknowledge their debt to Professor Gananath Obeyesekere and although I suspect he would disagree with much of my analysis here, I should like to thank him for his help, advice, and encouragement. Drs. M. C. Jedrej and B. Taylor; J. M. Hepworth and D. Winslow have read earlier drafts of this paper. Their help and advice have been invaluable. Finally, Paul Hershman read and commented on this paper before his tragic death.

[1]Here I should like to make a few points about definitions. By "possession" I mean a state that the actors themselves claim to be possession. Thus to be possessed does not necessarily mean being in a trance or in a fit. Admittedly, this begs the question of how we can be sure that "possession" is a competent translation of an ethnic category. Second, by "Catholic" I mean anyone who claims to be Roman Catholic, which covers a multitude of sins and again begs the question.

[2]I am aware here of the dangers of constructing straw men. But I choose Lewis, Obeyesekere, and Wilson as examples of common approaches to the subject. I have deliberately ignored writers such as Bourguignon (1965) for my interest is in "possession" rather than in altered states of consciousness.

egories, are enabled to protect their interests and prefer their claims and ambitions" (1966:322). Again, the argument rests upon the state of mind of those possessed. I would not deny that demonic possession can be used to express "insubordination," but so can a host of other actions. Such approaches do not tell us very much about the nature of possession.

Finally, we can consider Wilson's critique of Lewis (Wilson 1967a; 1967b). Rather than see possession as a means of protest, he proposes that demonic possession, or rather "peripheral possession cults," are the result of "status ambiguity." This generates tensions which are released through demonic possession. Again, the individual psychologies of the actors are crucial. Furthermore, as in the work of Lewis and Obeyesekere, there is the assumption that those who are possessed are in some sense "mentally unbalanced."

But what is interesting in Wilson's discussion of malevolent possession is his use of van Gennep's ideas concerning "rites of passage" (van Gennep 1960). Wilson argues that malevolent possession is a form of such rituals, and that it marks the transformation of individuals from one stage in their lives to other stages. I too am going to argue that demonic possession is a form of *rite de passage,* but not in quite the same way as Wilson.

Van Gennep, as is well known to every first year student of anthropology, discerned a recurring pattern in what he called *rites de passage:* in, "passages from one cosmic or social order to another." This constant ceremonial pattern, he argued, falls into three sections: rites of separation; rites of transition; and rites of incorporation or aggregation. Furthermore, different instances of *rites de passage* tend to emphasize certain of these stages rather than others, and each of these stages may in itself take the form of a *rite de passage.*

At one level, van Gennep was making some fairly banal comments. He likened society to a house of many rooms, the *rites de passage* marking and symbolizing a person's movement from one room to another. It is at this level that Gluckman was able to dismiss van Gennep's book as "boring" (Gluckman 1962:2,7), and at this level that Wilson appears to be basing his argument concerning demonic possession. Furthermore, Wilson appears to be arguing that rites of passage in general can be understood in terms of the psychologies of the actors.[3]

But there is a much more interesting aspect to van Gennep's argument. The rituals do not simply mark or symbolize changes in status because it is through these rituals that the person achieves his new status. The actual person is changed by these rituals. It is this aspect of his work which has been elaborated by various anthropologists and has been the basis for some of the more interesting developments in the study of ritual and symbolism.[4]

There are three points about these elaborations of van Gennep's original ideas which I think are worthy of note. First, his ideas are used not only to analyze the process of the subject from one state to another via a *rite de passage,* but they are also being used to deal with situations where the subject returns to his or her original state after the ritual. This is most clearly seen in Rigby's analysis of rites of reversal, Leach's of time, and Turner's of pilgrimages.

Second, *rites de passage* are concerned with discontinuities between normal states. The rites are, as it were, in the interstices of society.

Finally, *rites de passage* are closely concerned with the idea of "separation," either of the subject from a previous state, or of the subject from something we can call "dirt." Alternatively, *rites de passage* are concerned with investing the subject with something he or she lacks. It is as if the subject's *persona* were out of

---

[3]It is also possible to criticize Wilson along with Obeyesekere and Lewis in that they confuse "public" and "private" symbols. See Leach 1958.

[4]See Fortes 1962, 1968; Leach 1958; Rigby 1968; Turner 1969, 1974.

balance with the status which he or she is supposed to occupy.

In this paper I wish to show how concepts ultimately derived from van Gennep are useful in analyzing demonic possession as a collective representation. I will try to show that by using these concepts we can perceive an ultimate unity between life-cycle rituals, demonic possession, and physical illness in Roman Catholic Sri Lanka and perhaps elsewhere, and that this unity derives from a standard symbolic form of dealing with culturally defined abnormality. I will argue that an approach which begins with an appreciation of demonic possession as a part of social reality will lead to new questions being asked of the data. Instead of asking what people think, I shall be asking what people think with. Instead of asking who becomes possessed, I shall be asking who says they are possessed.

The data I am concerned with in this paper come from a shrine at a place called Kudagama. The village itself lies on the edge of the Kandyan hills about fifty miles from Colombo, and along with two or three other villages it forms a Roman Catholic enclave in an area otherwise staunchly Buddhist. Until the early 1970s, nothing of great interest ever seems to have happened in Kudagama, but in late 1971 or early 1972—the dates are all a bit vague—a priest called Father Camillus Jayamanne was appointed to the church of Our Lady of Lourdes at Kudagama. Very rapidly this church, the Way of the Cross leading up to the church, and the grotto behind the church became one of the most important shrines for Roman Catholics in Sri Lanka.

Father Jayamanne was a devotee of the Virgin Mary long before he came to Kudagama. Devotees of the shrine say that soon after his arrival, She appeared to him in a dream and told him that in a corner of the church he would find a thorn in a glass block, and that this thorn was from Christ's Crown of Thorns. Father Jayamanne found the Thorn and treated it with due reverence. In another dream he was informed

that it had supernatural powers and that it could heal both the physically and the spiritually sick. He used it to bless the sick from Kudagama village and so effected a number of miraculous cures. His fame spread and people began to come from farther and farther away to be blessed by Father Jayamanne and his miraculous Thorn.

Through further dreams, it is claimed that the priest learned that Kudagama had been chosen by the Virgin Mary as a holy place and, that in due time, She would appear at the shrine.[5] Father Jayamanne told the people of this message. Not only were the sick brought to be cured, but devotees of the Virgin Mary came to make vows, to deliver petitions, or simply to gain "blessings" (asiirvadaya). The crowds grew week by week.

Late in 1972 or early in 1973, a millennial movement began to develop, focussed on Kudagama. A hard core of devotees began to assert that the Virgin Mary would soon appear at Kudagama and that this would herald the imminent arrival of the end of the world and of the last battle between the forces of good and evil. The forces of good, led by the Virgin Mary, would be triumphant; the faithful would enjoy eternal salvation. The wicked and those who lacked faith would be condemned to eternal damnation.

Today, Father Jayamanne has gained a couple of more relics: two statues of the Virgin Mary. He himself has become something of a "relic" for he is infused with supernatural power and goodness. What is more, the shrine has become the major center for the conservative wing of the church. This development has faced the church as a whole with a major problem. For the moment they are leaving Kudagama well

---

[5]Father Jayamanne has a rather different version of what happened. For instance, he says that he did not find out about the Thorn through a dream, but from his predecessor in charge of the parish. Yet he does not deny that he has supernatural powers or that he has a special relationship with the Virgin Mary.

alone, hoping the shrine will disappear as quickly as it appeared.[6]

## II

Like the Buddhists of Sri Lanka, the Roman Catholics who patronize Kudagama possess a flourishing demonology. Compared with that of the Buddhists, the demonology of the Roman Catholics is rather eclectic, being a rag-bag drawing on the demons of the Christian tradition, the traditional evil creatures of Sinhalese Buddhism, and the gods of the Hindus and Buddhists.[7] Demons *(yakasha)* are spiritual creatures whose proper place is in hell *(apaaya)*. Although they are suffering in hell because of their evil deeds, they are still involved in a continual battle with the forces of good, the battlefield being mankind. But demons are unable to enter the world of man unless invited to do so by human beings. Demonic possession is one of the ways in which the demons attempt to subvert mankind.

Actual cases of possession can be caused in

---

[6]The rise of Kudagama and the increase in the frequency of demonic possession and possession by saints is all part of a much more widespread process of change occurring among the Roman Catholic population of Sri Lanka at the present time.

[7]The demons are thought to fall into a series of categories. First, there are the "fallen angels" such as Lucifer and Satan. Second, there are fallen men, a category which includes the Hindu and Buddhist gods such as Shiva, Kataragama, Kali, and Saman, plus the traditional evil creatures of the Sinhalese, including Maha Sohona, Mohini, and Kalu Kumaraya. Finally, there are the *peretayo* and the *malaperetayo,* ghosts of people whose souls are still "attached" to the things of this world. In some sense, the latter are related to Maha Sohona, but no one could elaborate this relationship. There is also a vague idea of hierarchy, with Satan at the top and the *peretayo* and *malaperetayo* at the bottom, but this hierarchy is not elaborated and demons do not have functional specialities. Finally, it would appear that this evil pantheon owes more to the low-country sinhalese than to the Kandyans.

two ways. Most frequently, possession is caused by sorcery *(huniyam).*[8] A client, almost always motivated by jealousy *(irishaava)* or unrequited love, employs a sorcerer *(kattaandiya)* who uses various spells and magical substances to attack a named victim. The demon who is sent by the sorcerer may find that the actual named victim is too "strong" to be possessed, in which case the demon will attack a "weaker" member of the chosen victim's household. Thus it is thought that an attack on any named victim is, in effect, an attack on the victim's whole household. Thus women and children, who are considered "weaker" than men, are more liable to demonic possession, even though the actual sorcery is frequently directed against the men of the house.

Not all cases of possession are caused by sorcery. Owing to the worship accorded demons by Buddhists and Hindus, demons are able to enter the world without being specifically invited to attack named victims. These demons are then able to enter people at will. Those who are particularly vulnerable are young women who are menstruating, particularly during their first menstruation.

Demons do not attack the soul *(aatmaya)* of their victims but rather the body *(kaya)* and the mind *(moleya,* lit. "brain"). Thus people who are charmed are physically or mentally ill, and indeed may eventually die as the result of the demon's attentions. But their souls are safe. Furthermore, only the good are possessed, not the bad or the evil. The latter are already doing the devil's work, so there is no point in possessing them.

The first signs of possession are varied. It may be a run of bad luck; it may be a series of illnesses, each in itself minor; it may be an illness which fails to respond to normal medical treatment; it may be a sudden change in behavior, such as a girl refusing to respect and honor her

---

[8]Sorcery does exist in Sri Lanka, as discussed by Obeyesekere (1975a). It would be interesting to know how the actual practice of sorcery ties up with what is going on at Kudagama, but as yet I have no idea.

parents in the normal way or a boy suddenly refusing to go to school or ceasing to do well in exams. Almost anything abnormal *can* be the first sign of possession.

Such events are not necessarily directly or consciously interpreted as demonic possession. Further evidence is required, and this usually takes the form of the subject entering a "trance" or a "fit" during which the demon names itself and "stops hiding." Almost always, a fit or a trance is brought on by the subject being exposed to "good sacred" objects, most commonly the rosary. Good Roman Catholics say the rosary every night, but a person who is possessed will try to avoid this ritual, for the demon is afraid of the power of the rosary. Only the strongest demons can withstand such power and remain "hidden" or "quiet" while the rosary is being said. Other occasions which may force the demon to show itself are when the subject enters a church, encounters a priest, a *suruvama* (holy statue), or a holy medallion or scapular.

Some of the most spectacular discoveries of possession take place at Kudagama itself. As I mentioned earlier, pilgrims come to the shrine out of faith or to make vows, as well as to be rid of demons. It is during such journeys that individuals may suddenly be discovered to be possessed; in some cases that they have been possessed for many years. This may happen as soon as the subject enters the sacred area of Kudagama, the subject collapsing in a fit, the demon screaming and wailing with fear. Others may survive this stage only to enter a fit during the Way of the Cross or the other rituals which take place every weekend.

The final test of whether or not a person is possessed is the Thorn blessing. Only the very strongest demons can remain hidden while the subject is receiving the Thorn blessing from Father Jayamanne. Thus, to take the blessing voluntarily is to assert that one is not possessed. To refuse or to avoid it is to tacitly admit that one is possessed or that one thinks one might be possessed. The situation is complicated by the fact that some people collapse even though they

are not possessed. The final diagnosis is made by Father Jayamanne who can "feel" whether or not a person is possessed. Thus some people who do not collapse are still possessed. In the last analysis, it is his word that decides whether or not a person is possessed.

In the context of possession, three "states of being" are recognized at Kudagama. First, there is the state of possession, usually referred to as *yaksha dosaya* or *aveesaya viima;* less frequently by *yaka vaeaehiila,* "covered by a demon." This implies that the subject is under supernatural attack and that the demon is in some sense within the subject, but normally the subject can still talk and act normally, is conscious of what is going on around him or her, and may well be unaware that he or she is possessed. The exposure of the subject to "good sacred" objects or situations forces the demon to show itself, and for the subject's personality to be subsumed by the personality of the demon. This state is known as *diistiya* or *mayam,* and the subject has no recollection afterwards of what happened during the trance. Finally, there is a state of being known as *aruda* or, more colloquially, as a *fit-eka,* a "fit." When in such a state, the demon in the body of the subject literally has a fit.[9]

During both trances and fits the subject assumes the *lakuna* (sign) of the demon which is possessing him or her.[10] Usually, this *lakuna*

---

[9]Linguistically, there seems to be a certain amount of confusion here. *Diistiya,* for instance, more normally means the "gaze" of a demon (Gombrich 1971:198). In Kudagama it is used to describe a trance and to distinguish it from a state of simply "being possessed."

[10]Thus subjects possessed by Kali display grasping hands; those possessed by Saman hold their hands parallel with their chests, palms facing outwards. As well as the actual *lakuna,* there is also a certain amount of difference in behavior between demons. The *peretayo* tend to roll on the ground eating dirt. Mohini usually acts in a very lascivious manner. When the subject is suffering from multiple possession, a trance involves a series of different displays depending upon which demon is involved at each moment.

involves the hands or the fingers being held in certain fixed positions modelled after those shown in pictures of Hindu and Buddhist gods. While the subject is in a trance, one can talk with the possessing demons. They are asked who sent them and why; when they are going to go; who the *kattaandiya* was who worked the spell, and so on. The demons also tell fortunes, foretell the future, and generally "know things which human beings cannot know." Some demons have a tendency to lie, but Kataragama who is said to have pretensions to godly status, always tells the truth.[11] While the demons are taken fairly seriously, people are not afraid of them. I was told, "You just have to be firm with them."

Trance states are also occasions for demons to throw abuse at the Virgin Mary, at Father Jayamanne, and at Catholicism in general. During the early stages of any service at Kudagama a number of demons will be engaged in sacriligeous behavior, often with sexual overtones.[12] Demons tend to gather together in the bodies of their victims, calling each other *machang* and joking and playing together.

As a general rule, trances precede fits, although sometimes subjects can enter fits directly. Fits are the result of exposure to particularly sacred phenomenon, notably the Thorn blessing and the Mass, but Holy Water and the touch of Father Jayamanne are also the occasions for violent fits. The demon in the body of the subject enters a fit because of the "power" of the religious objects. During the fit, the demon is suffering the fires of hell. Thus demons thrash around, screaming and yelling. They cry out that they are being burnt by the Holy Water,

and shout vile abuse at the Virgin Mary and Father Jayamanne. After a fit, the subject collapses and becomes unconscious.

Technically speaking, demons are not exorcised at Kudagama.[13] What Father Jayamanne does is to bless the sick. The process of driving out the demon is best described as a war of attrition; of making life so unpleasant for the demon that it eventually leaves the subject. Thus, the more frequently the subject enters a fit, the more quickly the demon is likely to go.

This process of attrition depends upon the continual exposure of the subject to "good sacred" objects and activities. Some subjects remain at the shrine for weeks on end, while others only come at weekends. As well as being taken to all the public rituals, they are also exposed to a whole series of private devotions and activities. The subjects are forced to drink Holy Water, literally by the gallon. Medallions and scapulars blessed by Father Jayamanne are draped around their necks. Their heads are rubbed with oil which has been blessed, and holy salt is rubbed into their bodies or given them to eat. Hymns are sung around them; prayers are said over them. The subject and the unfortunate demon are smothered in Roman Catholic ritual.

After each fit, the subject collapses. What happens to the demon at this point is not clear, the general opinion being that it is temporarily driven out of the subject by the force of the "good sacred" objects and rituals. Eventually, the demon will name a day on which it is going to leave the subject. Usually, demons do not lie about this. On the appointed day, the subject enters a fit in the Grotto of Our Lady of Lourdes. Then, sobbing and wailing, the subject rolls from the Grotto up the hill to the lifesize Crucifixion scene which marks the end of the Way of the Cross and which is referred to as "Calvary." All this time, the hands of the subject

---

[11]This fits in with Kataragama's rise in importance amongst the Buddhists of Sri Lanka. See Obeyesekere 1970b:58–60.

[12]Obviously what is happening here is an acting out of the opposition between Catholicism and Buddhism in Sri Lanka. Thus, although the demons revile and insult the Virgin Mary, in the end they acknowledge Her superior power. At the political level, this is nothing but wishful thinking.

---

[13]Father Jayamanne cannot exorcise demons as he has not received permission from the bishop. Also, the bishop has tried to stop him using the Thorn as it has not been certified by the Vatican as an approved relic.

are locked into the *lakuna* of the possessing demon. Once the foot of the Cross is reached, the subject, still in a fit, begins to climb the rocks to the Cross itself, all the time wailing *"mama yanavaa, mama yanavaa:"* "I am going, I am going." This whole process is said to be the demon's penance for possessing the subject. Once the subject is holding the Cross, the demon then begs forgiveness from the Virgin Mary and promises never to attack the victim again. Occasionally, the demon may even deliver a short homily on the stupidity of worshipping false gods and the evil that results from it. Finally, uttering a long wail, the demon leaves the subject who then collapses, unconscious.

Whilst holding the Cross, female subjects frequently masturbate against it, their legs around the shaft of the Cross whilst they move their bodies up and down. The point of orgasm appears to coincide with the point at which the demon leaves the subject. Obviously, male subjects would find this procedure rather difficult, and in their case there is no such masturbation.

Many subjects suffer from multiple possession. In such cases, a group of demons may all leave at the same time, but frequently the exit of one demon only allows another to enter, so the whole process may be repeated a number of times. In each case the demon must make penance to the Virgin Mary and must beg forgiveness. Otherwise the demon has not really left the subject.

The process is not complete at this point, however. The demon's reluctance to leave the subject is a result of the *kattaandiya's* sorcery, for the *kattaandiya* via his sorcery has "tied" *(baenda)* the demon, and the demon is "afraid" to leave the subject. So when the demon is expelled from the subject, it is likely to attack another member of the same household. Therefore, the sorcery must be "cut" (*huniyam kapanavaa,* "to cut the charm"). At Kudagama, it is claimed that Father Jayamanne can effectively "cut" the sorcery through his supernatural powers. In difficult cases, he asks for a floor plan of the subject's house. By inspecting the plan he can tell where the charm is hidden, and can thus

cleanse the house. Only in the most difficult cases, or where the subject's family is very important will Father Jayamanne visit the house himself and physically bless it.[14] Once the *huniyam* has been successfully cut, the demon then returns to attack the client of the *kattaandiya* who sent it. Many horrific tales are told of what happens to the perpetrators of sorcery.

This whole process of possession duplicates the "ceremonial form" outlined by van Gennep in *Les Rites de Passage.* The subject is first of all separated from his normal life by the introduction of the demon. The subject is "invested" with a demonic spirit. This makes the subject "abnormal:"[15] he or she is said to be "possessed" and during this state the subject is in a "marginal" state *vis a vis* the rest of society. During this marginal period, the subject is exposed to "good sacred" objects and situations which are designed to separate the subject and the cause of the subject's abnormality. This separation is achieved through the final eviction of the demon, and the subject can then be reintegrated into normal society. In sum, the subject is first separated from society; is then in a marginal state; and is finally reincorporated into society.

Furthermore, within this overall scheme, there are a number of internal processes which also display the same structure. The normal state for a possessed person is to be possessed. But upon exposure to abnormal "good sacred" objects, the subject enters a trance and then a fit before returning to a "normal" state of being possessed. Again, we have separation, transition, and reintegration.

Beside pointing out that formally possession

---

[14]The point is that once the charm has been located and neutralized by supernatural means, it disappears.

[15]The word "abnormal" is going to bear a rather heavy load in what follows. By "abnormal" I simply mean "out of the ordinary;" "exceptional." What is important is that, first, what is abnormal is defined as abnormal by the actors, and second, that abnormality is a relative state, so that what is normal in one situation is abnormal in another.

displays a structure similar to that of *rites de passage,* there are a number of other points worth making. First, the abnormal state of the subject is defined in terms of two categories, which should be kept separate, becoming confused: the spiritual beings of hell and the human beings of the world. It is this confusion which is crucial to the abnormal state of the subject, and the aim of the whole performance is to reassert the separate identity of these two categories.

This separation is achieved through the use of "good spiritual" matter which works to drive out the "bad spirit." And if the aim of the performance is to reassert the separate identity of the creatures of earth and the beings of hell, the "good spiritual" matter is itself a mixture of things of the earth and those of heaven. Kudagama itself is dedicated to the Virgin Mary. The church is in her name; so is the Grotto. Two of the miraculous objects in the church are statues of Her, and Father Jayamanne's power depends upon his special relationship with Her. The other supernatural being who recieves special attention at the shrine is Christ—in particular, Christ during His death. Thus, there is the Way of the Cross culminating in the massive Crucifixion scene, and one very important supernatural item: the Thorn from the crown Christ wore during His passion.

The Virgin Mary on the one hand, and the death of Christ on the other appear to me to be the ideal symbolic separators, for it was through the Virgin Mary that the spiritual entity of God and the human entity of the body were united into the abnormal "good sacred" entity Christ. And it was through Christ's death on the Cross that the categories of man and spirit were separated. Thus, the abnormal subjects (human plus demon) roll from the Grotto of the Virgin Mary to the Crucifix where the demon is separated from the subject. In the case of female subjects, this final act takes the form of a mystical sexual union of the flesh and the spirit. As the demon leaves, so Christ enters.

Furthermore, what is separated from the subject is dangerous, just as what is separated during *rites de passage* is dangerous, as Leach has pointed out. In this case, the demon is the dangerous entity which will either attack another member of the subject's family or will attack the perpetrator of the sorcery which first caused the possession. As in life-cycle rituals, so in demonic possession. A major theme is that of separation, and that which is separated is dangerous.

Finally, it is worth noting the strong belief at Kudagama that mankind is ultimately responsible for the existence of evil in the world. Demons can only enter the world and can only possess their victims with the active encouragement of man. Evil is the creation of man.

## III

So far, all that I have done is to illustrate how the schema which van Gennep discerned in his examination of *Rites de Passage* is also present in the process of demonic possession from the moment when the demon is said to enter the subject until the time at which the demon leaves the subject. I now want to suggest that this similarity is not simply a similarity of form but that there is also a much more significant, more abstract, and deeper identity between the processes of demonic possession, the process of life-cycle rituals, and the process of illness.

A possessed person at Kudagama and elsewhere is referred to as a *ledaa,* a word normally translated as "patient." A *ledaa* is said to be suffering from a *leda,* an "illness." At Kudagama, not only *ledaa* who are suffering from demonic possession come to be healed, but also people suffering from physical illnesses come in the hope of a miraculous cure. Furthermore, the first sign of demonic possession may be a physical illness, and the curing of the demonically possessed is achieved through "blessing the sick."

The course of physical illnesses takes much the form as that which I have claimed underlies the process of demonic possession. The subject first of all has to become "ill." This requires the subject to display certain symptoms which are defined as "illness," and in Sri Lanka as in Britain ritual specialists are usually required to endorse this definition. "Becoming ill" like "becoming possessed" makes the subject an abnormal person. Once the person is ill, the subject is treated as abnormal or extra-normal—what van Gennep would probably recognize as "sacred."[16] In extreme cases, this abnormal status is marked by the subject being spatially separated from normal life and placed in a hospital. In less extreme cases the separation is purely symbolic, such signifiers as towels over the subject's head being utilised to mark the abnormality. During the period of abnormality, the subject is liable to be treated with *behet* (medicine) designed to end the subject's abnormality. Finally, the patient is cured and allowed to return to normal life.

Both the overall form and many elements are duplicated in physical illness and in demonic possession. The symbolism of separation is crucial. The *behet* is designed to separate the subject from his illness, and the medicine in effect absorbs the anomalous substance which is causing the illness. Thus the *behet* and so on which have been used on the subject become dirty and dangerous and are thrown away.

There are also a number of interesting linguistic usages involved here, again involving the notion of separation. As I have already mentioned, for the demon to be thoroughly removed from the subject, Father Jayamanne must "cut" the sorcery: *huniyam kapanavaa*. In traditional forms of Catholic exorcism in Sri Lanka, limes were cut (*dehi kapanavaa*), and the cutting of limes is also important in Buddhist exorcisms and healing rituals and in a number of life cycle rituals. Finally, when a person is released from hospital, the colloquial expression which is used is *ticket kapanavaa,* "cutting the ticket." Actu-

ally, no ticket is cut, but the same symbolic process of separation is at work.

A second usage is that of *behet.* In the context of illness, I have glossed it as "medicine." But in the context of sorcery, the magical substances which form the charm are often referred to as *behet.* Thus *behet* is perhaps better described as the transforming substance; the "magical operator" which transforms the subject from sickness to health; from nonpossession to possession; from one state of being to another.

There is thus a congruence between physical illness and possession; between curing and exorcism. The forms of treatment are similar and similar symptoms can be construed as evidence of either possession or illness or both, a point which I shall return to later. But just as there is an overlap between physical illness and demonic possession, so there is an overlap between physical illness and life-cycle rituals.

In Sinhalese society as in our own, this overlap is most clearly seen in the case of childbirth. On the one hand, the birth of a child, especially a first child, is heavily ritualized for the mother. In the seventh month of pregnancy she returns to her mother's house and only eats certain types of food. After the birth, she should remain in her parent's house for a few months and then make a ceremonial return to her husband's house. Traditionally, a Roman Catholic mother could not attend church for a few months after birth. The birth of children other than the first child is less heavily ritualized but is still treated as an important ritual occasion. At the same time, childbirth is also considered a suitable case for hospital treatment and most births in Catholic areas take place in hospitals. The mother-to-be is referred to as a patient; she is treated with various "medicines" and the debris of childbirth is treated as a dangerous substance. As van Gennep wrote in 1908, ". . . nothing seems more natural than that she [i.e., the pregnant woman] should be treated as if she were ill" (van Gennep 1960:41).

Perhaps the best known example of a Sinhalese life-cycle ritual is that which takes place when a girl first menstruates, and which is much

---

[16]Here, I am thinking of Leach's comments in *Magical Hair:* "sacred = abnormal, special, otherworldly, royal, taboo, sick."

the same for both Roman Catholics and Buddhists. There is no need to describe it in detail, accounts being available in the writings of Leach (1970) and Yalman (1963). The only points I wish to make here are that, first, these sorts of ritual display most clearly the three stages delineated by van Gennep; second, that the major symbolic theme is that of separation, both of the subject from a previous state of childhood, and of "dirt" from the subject; and finally, that during the ritual the subject is treated with "ritually charged substances."[17] Also, limes are cut.

In summary then, illness, demonic possession, and life-cycle rituals display similar structural forms and share many common elements. We can recognize the existence of van Gennep's three stages in each process, the theme of separation, and the theme that what is separated from the subject is in some sense dangerous, whether it be the demon, the medicine which absorbed the illness, or the debris associated with a girl's first menstruation.

The problem now is to ascertain why there should be this similarity in "ceremonial form"; to identify what the processes of illness, of demonic possession, and of life-cycle rituals have in common. In a sense, the obvious answer is abnormality in the person of the subject, but it is worth saying much more about the nature of this abnormality.

Reading van Gennep, one is struck by the way in which his work is complementary to that of Durkheim and Mauss in *Primitive Classification*. Durkheim and Mauss were concerned with social categories; with collective representations such as clans, moieties, spatial regions, and so forth. Van Gennep is interested in what comes between these categories; with what happens in the anomalous zones outside the firm categories of the collective representations. Writers such as Leach (1964) and Douglas (1966) have made

great play with the interstices in systems of classification: with anomalies and ambiguities, and have seen in these areas various forms of the sacred, either "bad sacred," or dirt, which is dangerous and polluting, or "good sacred," which is still dangerous but also life-giving and holy. Similarly with van Gennep. He is dealing with the subject between social categories: with the subject in anomalous situations. And just as Leach and Douglas have pointed out how such anomalous situations can be sacred, so *rites de passage* involve the subject moving from the profane (normal) to the sacred (abnormal) and back to the profane (normal).[18]

The complementarity of van Gennep on the one hand and Durkheim and Mauss on the other is apparent on another level as well. The arguments developed by Durkheim and Mauss and their elaborators are primarily synchronic. They deal with timeless nonprocessual situations. Their focus is upon static society. Van Gennep is interested in a diachronic dimension: upon the subject passing through time (or space) from one category to another. *Rites de passage* are concerned with the process of the subject from childhood to adolescence; from life to death; from one country to another. Van Gennep is concerned with the progress of the individual through these anomalous zones between social categories.[19]

This processual or diachronic aspect of van Gennep's approach is most clearly seen in life-cycle rituals: in the ineluctable process of growing old. The subject passes inexorably from one category to another, transferred between these stages by *rites de passage*. But before the subject can be transferred, before the subject is a suitable case for treatment, the subject must in some sense fail to fit the criteria defining the category

---

[17]Unfortunately, Yalman does not tell us whether such "ritually charged substances" are known as *behet* or not. Obviously it would suit my argument if they were.

[18]See also Leach's treatment of time symbolism. (Leach 1961).

[19]In fact, a strong argument could be made that all processual situations are necessarily tripartite just as synchronic situations are bipartite.

presently occupied by the subject. The most obvious example here concerns girls who are "children"—but who suddenly start menstruating. While in one category, they exhibit criteria of another. They thus become out of balance with the category "child;" they become anomalous and therefore they are subjected to puberty rites. Thus the first step in the process is the identification of abnormality, and it is this which places the subject in a "transitional" or "marginal" state. The actual rite itself is only the final stage of a more inclusive process.

Similar sorts of things are happening with demonic possession and illness. In the first case, the subject is in an ambiguous state: in perhaps a sacred, but definitely an abnormal, state. Similarly with illness. Of course, I am not saying that life-cycle rituals are identical with the processes of illness or demonic possession. The former are very different in that ageing is a one-way process and life-cycle rituals are concerned with transferring the subject from one "normal" state to another "normal" but different state.[20] The processes of illness and demonic possession are concerned with shifting the subject back to the original "normal" state. But all are concerned with reasserting the "correct" and "proper" categories.

Abnormality in Sri Lanka (and I would suspect more generally) tends to be symbolized in a few forms: (a) the subject has something (x) which he shouldn't have. The treatment of the subject is concerned with removing this (x); or (b) the subject lacks something (y) which he should have. The treatment of the subject is concerned with investing the subject with (y); or (c) the subject has something he shouldn't have (x) and lacks something he should have (y). The treatment of the subject is concerned with removing (x) and investing the subject with (y).

It is easy enough to think up examples of all three types of abnormality, but in the present case, the first type is all that concerns us. Thus, in a girl's puberty rite the aim of the ritual, according to Leach's analysis, is to divest the girl of her "childness." Alternatively, the treatment of a physically ill patient is designed to divest the subject of his or her "illness."

Demonic possession is similarly of the first type. The subject is invested with a demon which should not be there, for the proper place for demons is in hell, and the proper condition for the subject is not to be possessed. The onset of possession thus marks a confusion of two categories which should be kept separate. The process of possession ends with the demon being expelled, thus removing the extraneous substance (x) which is causing the abnormality. By separating the demon from the subject, the separation of the subject from an abnormal state is achieved.[21] Furthermore, the "magical power" of what is separated derives from the fact that it is what caused the abnormality in the first place: it is the extraneous substance (x). What is separated is itself "anomalous" and so is classed as "dirt" (e.g. demons) or as "good sacred," and is thus the perfect separator.

In the present context we can also make similar connections at another level, or at least introduce more data which complement the existing schema.

As Douglas points out, in the transitional stages between categories there is "danger" (Douglas 1966:116). In Sri Lanka, menstruation, especially first menstruation, is a very dangerous state of being. During these times, the subject is peculiarly vulnerable to the attentions of demons, and the seclusion during puberty and menstruation is not simply to separate the abnormal from the normal, or to protect the nor-

---

[20]Yet old people are often thought of as becoming children once more and the identity of alternate generations in many societies is in a sense a machine for denying time in such a way.

[21]It could be argued that it is really of the third type. The masturbatory union between the girl and the Cross amounts to a replacement of the demon by the good spirit.

mal from the abnormal, but also to protect the abnormal female subject from dangerous supernatural agents. It is claimed that most cases of demonic possession affecting women begin during menstruation.[22]

Other life-cycle rituals mark similar vulnerable periods in a person's life. Childbirth and death are particularly dangerous but even an auspicious ceremony such as marriage can involve danger.[23] To be in any such abnormal state is to attract demons. Roman Catholics have particular problems for although they can use horoscopes to avoid especially dangerous times, horoscopes are themselves the work of the devil, and by using them one risks the attentions of demons. Even time is split into "safe" and "dangerous" periods. Thus midday and midnight, 6 A.M. (dawn) and 6 P.M. (dusk), are known as the *samayan velaava* or "devil time." During such in-between times, activities which might attract demons should be avoided. There seems little point in presenting the full catalog of such dangerous times.

The demons which can attack subjects during these dangerous periods are closely connected with illness. Even those Catholics who use western medicine and attend western doctors still believe that demonic forces are closely tied up with the incidence of disease, and that western medicine is often only able to cope with the symptoms and not the ultimate cause of disease. The ayurvedic tradition is much more explicit (see Obeyesekere n.d.). Through a complex series of concepts, demonic activity is thought to control the *dosa,* or humors of the body; the

dhattu, or components of the body; and the *bhutas,* or physical elements of the universe. One of the *bhutas* is fire. Through an increase in fire, the level of *pitta* (bile) in the body becomes excessive and this leads to "heaty" diseases such as the plague. Alternatively, too little bile causes "cooly" diseases such as chicken pox and measles. *Huniyam* (sorcery), which causes demonic possession, is also concerned with the manipulation of the seven *bhuta* and thus the sorcerer, through his sorcery, can cause physical as well as spiritual illness. Finally, demonology *(bhuta vidya)* is one of the eight specialities of ayurvedic medicine.

The demons both capitalize upon disorder and themselves create disorder. The anomalies and confusions which life-cycle rituals are concerned with are the incidents which place the subject at risk to the demons. The demons themselves cause the anomalies and confusions which are illness and possession. *Rites de passage* are concerned with passages through all these types of confusion.

Perhaps at this point it is worth trying to make my argument a bit clearer. I am claiming that abnormality depends upon the social recognition of abnormality. Life-cycle rituals are only one example of how to deal with one type of abnormality: with how to transfer the subject from an abnormal category to what is socially defined as one of normalcy. Possession and illness are similarly concerned with socially defined abnormality; thus it is not surprising that there are similar ways of dealing with them. But abnormality also implies danger, and thus the points of time at which life-cycle rituals take place are also those times when the subject is more vulnerable to the supernatural agents of disorder. What are generally recognized as *rites de passage* are only the final stages of more inclusive processes which begin when the subject enters the category of the abnormal. So exorcism, life-cycle rituals, and curing all take the form of moving the person from the abnormal to the normal. The total process thus involves the subject being shifted from

---

[22]If a girl for some reason misses her puberty rituals, then she is liable to all sorts of nasty experiences in later life. It is said that in Kandyan areas, boys occasionally go through very similar rites during puberty if they are being "problems" for their parents.

[23]It is almost as if danger were courted. At Catholic weddings as well as Buddhist ones, large quantities of food cooked in oil are prepared, and such food is particularly attractive to demons.

the normal to the abnormal and back to the normal.[24]

## IV

So far in this paper I have ignored the actual incidence of possession. Through developing some parallels and connections, I have argued that demonic possession as a collective representation forms part of a wider structure of collective representations. Demonic possession is concerned with abnormality as defined in terms of an ideology which stresses the spiritual aspect of the world. The means of dealing with either the abnormality expressed through demonic possession or the abnormality of life-cycle rituals are both expressed in terms of what van Gennep called "rites de passage." I now want to show how the approach I am trying to develop here can also illuminate to some extent the actual incidence of demonic possession.[25]

Producing satisfactory statistical data on possession at Kudagama is rather difficult for a number of reasons. In the first place, one is only seeing possession at Kudagama, and thus one can only talk about the social composition of the possessed themselves. It is therefore difficult to

view demonic possession within the wider framework of Roman Catholicism in Sri Lanka. Second, a pilgrimage site such as Kudagama is not the best of places to collect hard numerical data, for people are always disappearing into the crowd, moving around, and so forth. The numerical data is therefore somewhat impressionistic.[26]

One way of viewing the composition of the possessed is to count the number of people who are, or who become possessed, during the Thorn blessing. In all, I counted around 2,000 people receiving this blessing over a couple of weekends. Out of each thousand, 44 people became possessed. Thirty-five of these were young unmarried females; 4 were married females; 5 were young males. If one breaks down these figures further, around 7% of all females who receive the Thorn blessing become possessed. But if one looks only at the young unmarried women who supply the bulk of the possessed, then something approaching 25% of all females who receive the Thorn blessing and who are between the ages of puberty and marriage are possessed!

We can also look at the incidence of possession in other terms. Rather than look at the possessed as a percentage of those who receive the Thorn blessing, we can look at the social composition of those who are possessed. Not all of those who are possessed take the Thorn blessing every weekend. A rough breakdown of those who are possessed is as follows:

(a) Young women between the ages of 14 and 22, mainly from lower middle class urban backgrounds, form around 55% of all who are possessed.

(b) Middle aged women between 40 and 50,

---

[24]It is interesting to look at Turner's data in terms of this sort of framework. Turner makes a clear distinction between "rites of affliction" and "life-cycle rituals." Yet we find that "illness" among the Ndembu is known as *kubulakutooka:* "to lack whiteness or lack of purity" (Turner 1967:300) while an uncircumcised boy is known as *wunabulakutooka:* "one who lacks whiteness or purity," as is a menstruating woman (Turner 1967:153–54). I would suggest that his distinction between rites of affliction and life-cycle rituals is false; that they are all *rites de passage* as I have used the concept here.

[25]I should make it clear once more that I am not going to examine cases of possession in great detail for it is my aim to understand the collective representations rather than the individual experience of possession.

[26]One of the problems with my data is that they come from Kudagama and not from the possessed people's villages and towns. All my data come from informants equipped with hindsight who can construct the past to fit the present. Thus, what I have identified as the motive for possession, i.e. abnormality, may, it could be argued, be only a production of possession.

again mainly from urban backgrounds, but not as predominantly middle class as the first group, form around 25% of all cases of possession.

(c) Young men between 14 and 22, tending to come from more rural backgrounds than (a) or (b), and especially from richer peasant backgrounds, form around 15% of the total.

(d) A residual category consists mainly of the very young and the very old: the imbecilic and the senile, but also includes a very few adult men and women.

Overall, approximately 80% of all the possessed are women; and 70% of those are in their adolescence or early maturity.

These gross data can be interpreted in terms of the theoretical frameworks I mentioned in the introduction to this paper. Thus for I. M. Lewis, demonic possession is here the result of the relative powerlessness and low status of women. The only means available for them to express their opposition to this situation is through symbolic rebellion in the form of demonic possession. The fact that most cases are both young and from middle class backgrounds only reinforces this explanation, for it is the middle class which is most puritanical and which exercises most control over its daughters. A similar situation exists in the case of young men who are possessed. Great stress is placed by parents upon educational success on the part of their offspring. Yet objectively, education does not guarantee occupational or economic success, particularly for the youth in rural areas. Possession serves as a means by which sons can rebel against parental domination.

Alternatively, demonic possession could be interpreted in terms of Wilson's "status ambiguity," adolescent girls and boys and menopausal women being in ambiguous social situations and thus exposed to strains and tensions which are expressed through possession.

Finally, we could view possession in Obeyesekere's terms. I think he would argue that the incidence of female possession is related to women's "inability to handle aggression and sexual drives" owing to the cultural evaluation and definition of the female role. These problems are "projected" in possession and are thus expressed through a "culturally constituted fantasy" (1970a:107). Similarly, the young men are in a situation where they suffer from an internal conflict between the cultural (and familial) evaluation of success, and the pragmatic likelihood of failure. Possession allows these people to express and externalize their internal psychological problems.

I would reject all of these approaches for the reasons indicated earlier, and turn the focus away from the minds of those who are actually possessed towards the processes by which people come to be labeled as possessed. Here again, van Gennep's insights are useful.

The reason that I introduced life-cycle rituals and *rites de passage* into this discussion is not simply that the form of the rituals seems to parallel the form of possession, nor just that they are all dealing with abnormality, but that in life-cycle rituals we can see most clearly the socially constructed nature of abnormality. One of the points which van Gennep was continually making is that occasions such as physical puberty are not in themselves of significance. Rather, the actual physiological event may or may not be invested with significance by society. And of course, the actual *rite de passage* associated with puberty may in no way temporally coincide with the physical attainment of puberty. But what must happen is that the subject is defined as a suitable case for treatment before the ritual can take place. The subject must be declared abnormal. It is not the girl herself who declares, "I am abnormal:" it is other people who make this decision for her.

A similar situation exists in other contexts. Illness for instance does not simply exist: it has to be recognized as existing. On the one hand this involves a series of collective representations: an ideology of illness. On the other it involves a series of people who declare or define the subject as being ill. An individual finds it difficult to declare himself ill: illness depends upon others and it is these others who ultimately define the subject as ill or not ill.

Crime, too, is a similar sort of phenomenon. Crime and criminality can be approached in terms of how the individual becomes a criminal: what does criminal activity offer the individual; under what sorts of conditions does crime flourish, and so on. These are directly parallel to the questions Lewis is asking about possession.[27] But crime depends upon a series of rules which define certain actions as criminal, and so we can ask a whole series of alternative questions: why are certain actions defined as criminal? Who is making these definitions? How do concepts of crime fit into a wider series of collective representations? How are certain groups in society defined as criminal classes, and so on? And without laboring the comparison overmuch, the process of becoming mentally ill can similarly be understood not only in terms of how the individual becomes mentally ill, but how certain individuals are forced into a situation where they are defined as being mentally ill and, therefore, are mentally ill.[28]

Very similar processes are taking place at Kudagama. To be real, possession has to be defined as real not by the subject alone, but by others. If there is no such definition by others, then there is no possession. Furthermore, those subjects who become possessed are in a sense forced to be possessed. It is expected of them to be possessed. Talking to informants, both those who were possessed and those who were relations of possessed people, it becomes obvious that, at least with hindsight, the first signs of possession were some sort of abnormality. The subject began to act abnormally or "oddly," or unfortunate events began to happen to the family. At this point, subjects are under suspicion of

being possessed, and so are taken to various priests or to Kudagama. But the subjects, like their families, know what is going on: they share the same ideology and the pressure is on them to become possessed. If, as Lewis and Obeyesekere seem to suggest, possession is in some sense a "solution," it is not so much a solution for the subject but for the subject's family. For now the abnormality or the oddness is couched in a context in which it can be dealt with thanks to the help of the Virgin Mary. The key to possession is not to be found within the individual but in the ideology with which people think about the world.

This sort of process becomes quite clear at times. Admittedly, many subjects show definite signs of possession before they come to Kudagama: they enter trances at home or in their local churches. Others become possessed as soon as they arrive at Kudagama. But for all, the final arbiter of possession or nonpossession is Father Jayamanne. Once he has defined the subject as possessed, there is little the subject can do but be possessed. To refuse to be possessed is to deny the basic postulates of the ideology in which the subject believes, or alternatively, is a sign of such a serious case of possession that the possessing demon is strong enough to withstand the pressure to "show itself."

At times, people come to Kudagama to find out whether or not they are possessed. This is particularly true in cases where a child wishes to marry against his or her parents' wishes. The parents accuse the child of being possessed; the child denies it, and either comes to Kudagama to prove nonpossession, or is brought there to be proved possessed. What counts in the end is what Father Jayamanne says. If he says that the subject is possessed, then the subject is possessed. And at times, although it is very rare, Father Jayamanne will deny that someone who is screaming and wailing is possessed, and therefore such people are not possessed. They are frauds or they are mad.

The process of becoming possessed depends upon the subject being defined as possessed. But

---

[27]Alternatively, crime can be viewed as a type of "sickness;" as a disease. This would seem to parallel Obeyesekere's approach to possession.

[28]On the socially constructed nature of madness see for example Sasz 1971. On crime, Young (1971) and Cohen (1971) supply examples.

only certain people in certain social categories are liable to be defined as possessed.

If we look at the gross figures for demonic possession, it is obvious that young females are the most likely to be possessed and adult males the least likely to be possessed. This is exactly what one would expect given the ideology of possession. The young and the female are "weakest" and therefore more prone to the attentions of demons. Adult males are the "strongest" and thus least likely to be possessed. At the gross level then, the pattern of possession appears to be defined by the ideology of possession.

But we can also look at these figures in slightly more detail. Most of the possessed are female. Among females, the greatest number of cases are of young women between the ages of puberty and marriage, with a smaller concentration of cases around the early forties. I would suggest that these concentrations are again defined by the collective representations. Girls between puberty and marriage are in a "betwixt and between" stage. They are neither children nor fully adult women. They are sexually mature but still unmarried, and marriage is the correct state for sexually mature women. They are in a marginal state and therefore vulnerable to demonic attentions. On the other hand, the older women are passing from a state of fertility to nonfertility: from adulthood to old age. Again they are in a marginal state, neither fecund women nor fully asexual old women. Thus although women in general are more likely to be possessed than men, the frequency is greatest during these two ambiguous phases of the life-cycle.

Turning to males, they are in general less prone to demonic possession simply because they are male. Again, however, there is a concentration of cases around the age of adolescence: between the attainment of some sort of sexual maturity but before the final attainment of full maturity through marriage. Again they are in an anomalous state, neither children nor adults, and thus, like their female counterparts, they are more prone to possession than older or younger males.

In other words, my general contention is that the system of collective representations defines the incidence of possession. I am claiming that the ideological categories logically precede the actual incidence of possession rather than the ideology being generated by the incidence of possession.

But this is about as far as the methods employed in this paper will allow us to go in understanding the incidence of possession. Just as labeling theory in criminology will only allow us to specify the social categories of people from whom "criminals" are likely to come, so this approach to demonic possession will only allow the broad specification of categories of people likely or prone to be possessed. Unlike Lewis or Obeyesekere, I cannot claim to specify the exact situation in which an individual will or will not be or become possessed.

The reason for this is fairly obvious and can perhaps best be illustrated by a similar problem in kinship studies. If we look at so-called elementary kinship terminologies, we find that at the terminological level there is a prescription that individuals in certain social categories should marry. And, as various writers have shown, such a terminological sytem is often part of a much more general set of collective representations.

Yet when one examines the actual incidence of marriage, the picture is rather more complex. No matter what the terminology might imply, marriages between say "true and classificatory cross-cousins" are often rather infrequent. To understand the actual pattern of marriage, we have to use rather different methods from those used to understand the terminological system. What cannot be done is to reduce the one to the other, neither the marriage pattern to the terminology nor the terminology to the marriage pattern.

It seems to me that Lewis and Obeyesekere are attempting to make such a reduction. They are trying to reduce the collective representations of possession to the actual incidence of possession, and must necessarily fail in the endeavor. Similarly, it would be invalid to reduce the actual incidence (or incidents) of possession to the collective representations. The latter only set broad limits to the incidence: they define the possibilities of possession. But at a logical level, the collective representations precede the actual incidence or events of possession. Very simply, one can only become possessed if one has a category of possession. If not, it is rather difficult to persuade others of the reality of possession.

## BIBLIOGRAPHY

Bourguignon, E.
 1973 Religion, Altered States of Consciousness and Social Change. Columbus: Ohio State University Press.
Cohen, S., ed.
 1971 Images of Deviance. Harmondsworth: Penguin Books.
Douglas, M.
 1966 Purity and Danger. London: Routledge and Kegan Paul.
Durkheim, E. and M. Mauss
 1963 Primitive Classification. London: Cohen and West.
Fortes, M.
 1962 Ritual and Office in Tribal Society. Pp. 53–88 in Essays on the Ritual of Social Relations (ed. by M. Gluckman). Manchester: Manchester University Press.
 1968 Of Installation Ceremonies. Proceedings of the Royal Anthropological Institute for 1967:5–20.
Gluckman, M.
 1962 Essays on the Ritual of Social Relations. Manchester: Manchester University Press.
Gombrich, R.
 1971 Precept and Practice. Oxford: Oxford University Press.
Leach, E. R.
 1958 Magical Hair. Journal of the Royal Anthropological Institute (hereafter J.R.A.I.) 88:147–64.
 1961 Rethinking Anthropology. L. S. E. Monographs on Social Anthropology 22. London: Athlone Press.
 1964 Anthropological Aspects of Language: Animal Categories and Verbal Abuse. Pp. 23–63 in New Directions in the Study of Language (ed. by Eric H. Lenenberg). Boston: M.I.T. Press.
 1976 A Critique of Yalman's Interpretation of Sinhalese Girl's Puberty Ceremonial. Pp. 819–828 in Echanges et Communications (ed. by J. Pouillon and P. Maranda). The Hague: Mouton.
Lewis, I. M.
 1966 Spirit Possession and Deprivation Cults. Man N.S. 1:307–29.
 1967 Correspondence re Spirits and the Sex War. Man N.S. 2:626–28.
 1971 Ecstatic Religion. Harmondsworth: Penguin Books.
Obeyesekere, G.
 1970a The Idiom of Demonic Possession: A Case Study. Social Science and Medicine 4:97–109.
 1970b Religious Symbolism and Political Change in Ceylon. Modern Ceylon Studies 1:43–63.
 1975a Sorcery, Premeditated Murder and the Canalization of Aggression in Sri Lanka. Ethnology 14:1–24.
 1975b Psycho-Cultural Exegesis of a Case of Spirit Possession from Ceylon. In The Psychological Study of Theravada Societies (ed. by S. Piker). Contributions to Asian Studies 8. Leiden: Brill.
 n.d. The Impact of Ayurvedic Ideas on the Culture and the Individual in Ceylon. Forthcoming, in Towards a Comparative Study of Asian Medical Systems (ed. by C. Leslie). n.p.
Rigby, P.
 1968 Some Gogo Rituals of Purification: An Essay on Social and Moral Categories. Pp. 153–178 in Dialectic in Practical Religion (ed. by E. R. Leach) Cambridge Papers in Social Anthropology no. 5. London: Cambridge University Press.

SASZ, T. S.
   1971 The Manufacture of Madness. London: Routledge and Kegan Paul.

TURNER, V.
   1967 The Forest of Symbols. Ithaca: Cornell University Press.
   1969 The Ritual Process. London: Routledge and Kegan Paul.
   1974 Dramas, Fields and Metaphors. Ithaca: Cornell University Press.

VAN GENNEP, A.
   1960 The Rites of Passage. Chicago: University of Chicago Press.

WILSON, P. J.
   1967a Status Ambiguity and Spirit Possession. Man N.S. 2:366–78.
   1967b Correspondence re Spirits and the Sex War. Man N.S. 2:628–29.

YALMAN, NUR
   1963 On the Purity of Women in the Castes of Ceylon and Malabar. J.R.A.I. 93:25–58.
   1964 The Structure of Sinhalese Healing Rituals. Pp. 115–150 in Religion in South Asia (ed. by E. B. Harper). Seattle: Asian Society.

YOUNG, J.
   1971 The Drugtakers. London: MacGibbon and Kee.